Tuning and Sizing Windows® 2000 for Maximum Performance

ISBN 0-13-089105-3

90000

9 780130 891051

ADMINISTRATION

- Tuning and Sizing Windows 2000
  for Maximum Performance
  Aubley

- Windows 2000 Cluster Server Guidebook
  Libertone

- Windows 2000 Hardware and Disk Management
  Simmons

- Windows 2000 Server: Management and Control,
  Third Edition
  Spencer, Goncalves

- Creating Active Directory Infrastructures
  Simmons

- Windows 2000 Registry
  Sanna

- Configuring Windows 2000 Server
  Simmons

- Supporting Windows NT and 2000 Workstation
  and Server
  Mohr

- Zero Administration Kit for Windows
  McInerney

- Tuning and Sizing NT Server
  Aubley

- Windows NT 4.0 Server Security Guide
  Goncalves

- Windows NT Security
  McInerney

CERTIFICATION

- Core MCSE: Windows 2000 Edition
  Dell

- Core MCSE: Designing a Windows 2000 Directory
  Services Infrastructure
  Simmons

- MCSE: Implementing and Supporting Windows 98
  Dell

- Core MCSE
  Dell

- Core MCSE: Networking Essentials
  Keogh

- MCSE: Administering Microsoft SQL Server 7
  Byrne

- MCSE: Implementing and Supporting Microsoft
  Exchange Server 5.5
  Goncalves

- MCSE: Internetworking with Microsoft TCP/IP
  Ryvkin, Houde, Hoffman

- MCSE: Implementing and Supporting Microsoft Proxy
  Server 2.0
  Ryvkin, Hoffman

- MCSE: Implementing and Supporting Microsoft SNA
  Server 4.0
  Mariscal

- MCSE: Implementing and Supporting Microsoft Internet
  Information Server 4
  Dell

- MCSE: Implementing and Supporting Web Sites Using
  Microsoft Site Server 3
  Goncalves

- MCSE: Microsoft System Management Server 2
  Jewett

- MCSE: Implementing and Supporting Internet Explorer 5
  Dell

- Core MCSD: Designing and Implementing Desktop
  Applications with Microsoft Visual Basic 6
  Holzner

- MCSD: Planning and Implementing SQL Server 7
  Vacca

- MCSD: Designing and Implementing Web Sites with
  Microsoft FrontPage 98
  Karlins

PRENTICE HALL PTR MICROSOFT® TECHNOLOGIES SERIES

Tuning and Sizing Windows 2000 for Maximum Performance

Curt Aubley

Prentice Hall PTR, Upper Saddle River, NJ 07458
www.phptr.com

Library of Congress Cataloging-in-Publication Data

Aubley, Curt.
    Tuning and sizing Windows 2000 for maximum performance / Curt Aubley.
        p. cm. — (Prentice Hall PTR Microsoft technologies series)
    Includes index.
    ISBN 0-13-089105-3
        1. Microsoft Windows (Computer file) 2. Operating systems (Computers).
    I. Title.   II. Series.
    QA76.76.063 A87 2000
    005.4'4769—dc21

                                                                00-053763

Editorial/production supervision: *BooksCraft, Inc., Indianapolis, IN*
Acquisitions editor: *Mary Franz*
Editorial assistant: *Noreen Regina*
Marketing manager: *Dan De Pasquale*
Buyer: *Maura Zaldivar*
Cover design director: *Jerry Votta*
Cover designer: *Anthony Gemmellaro*
Project coordinator: *Anne Trowbridge*

© 2001 by Prentice Hall PTR
Prentice-Hall, Inc.
Upper Saddle River, NJ 07458

Prentice Hall books are widely used by corporations and government agencies for
training, marketing, and resale.

The publisher offers discounts on this book when ordered in bulk quantities.
For more information, contact:
Corporate Sales Department
Phone: 800-382-3419   Fax: 201-236-7141
E-mail: corpsales@prenhall.com

Or write:
Prentice Hall PTR
Corporate Sales Department
One Lake Street
Upper Saddle River, NJ 07458

Product and company names mentioned herein are the trademarks of their respective owners.

Printed in the United States of America

10 9 8 7 6 5 4 3 2 1

ISBN 0-13-089105-3

Prentice-Hall International (UK) Limited, *London*
Prentice-Hall of Australia Pty. Limited, *Sydney*
Prentice-Hall Canada Inc., *Toronto*
Prentice-Hall Hispanoamericana, S.A., *Mexico*
Prentice-Hall of India Private Limited, *New Delhi*
Prentice-Hall of Japan, Inc., *Tokyo*
Pearson Education Asia Pte. Ltd.
Editora Prentice-Hall do Brasil, Ltda., *Rio de Janeiro*

DEDICATION

This book is dedicated to my wife, Diane, and daughters, Aurora and Valerie

CONTENTS

Preface   xxvii

Acknowledgments   xxxi

About the Author   xxxiii

▼ One   Instant Rules of Thumb for Tuning and Sizing
Windows 2000   1

Gathering Performance Statistics: Start the Logs   3

Key Points to Remember When Using Sysmon   3

*Three Action Items to Complete So That All Relative Performance Counters Can
Be Collected   4*

Determining Which Applications (Processes) Are Running under Windows 2000   5

Windows 2000 Bottleneck Detection Strategy   6

General Windows 2000 System Observations   6

Key Performance Metrics to Observe in Detecting System Bottlenecks   7

Tools to Investigate Windows 2000 Subsystem Usage: A Quick
Reference Guide   7

Detecting Windows 2000 Bottlenecks   9

Detecting Windows 2000 Memory Bottlenecks   9

Detecting Windows 2000 Disk Bottlenecks   11

Detecting Windows 2000 Network Bottlenecks   12

Detecting Windows 2000 CPU Bottlenecks   13

Immediate Tuning Tips to Implement: The Tuning Process   15

Tuning Windows 2000 Resources   16

General System Hardware Tuning   16

Tuning Memory Resources   16

Tuning Disk Resources   20

Windows File-System-Level Tuning   23

Disk Subsystem SCSI Channel and Host Bus Adapter Tuning
Considerations   25

RAID Tuning Considerations   27

Additional Disk Subsystem Hardware—The Last Resort   29

Appropriate Use of RAID   29

Tuning Windows 2000 System's Network Subsystem   **32**

Lower the Overhead Associated with the Network Operations and Improve Efficiency   **32**

Remove Nonessential Network Protocols/Redirectors   32

Network Binding Search Order   33

Remove Unnecessary Windows 2000 Services   33

Special Network Tuning Note   33

Windows 2000 Administration-Level Tuning   **33**

Permanently Cache MAC (Media Access Control) Addresses   33

Controlling Network Users' Timeout Periods   34

Update to the Latest Software Revision Levels   34

Network Interface Card (NIC) Tuning   **34**

Basic NIC Tuning   34

IPSEC and TCP NIC-Based Off-Loading (Highly Recommended)   35

Avoid Automatic Network Interface Card Settings   35

Network Interface Card Changes—The Last Resort   35

Select a Different Networking Technology with Higher Bandwidth   36

Distributing Windows 2000 Network Load   **36**

Network Trunking   36

Network Segmentation   37

Tuning CPU Resources   **37**

Ensure Another System Resource Is Not Acting as a Bottleneck   37

Controlling Windows 2000's CPU Quantum Allotment   **38**

Windows 2000 Service Packs   **41**

Update Drivers for All Components and System BIOS   42

Upgrading the CPU(s)—The Last Resort   42

Adding More CPU(s)—The Last Resort, Part 2   42

Sizing Rules of Thumb for Windows 2000 Systems   **42**

Sizing Disk Subsystems   43
   Disk Subsystem Performance   43
   Disk Subsystem Storage Capacity   45
Disk Subsystem Availability   45
SCSI Bus Implementation   46
Determining the Number of Disk Drives per SCSI Bus   46
Sizing the CPU(s)   47
Sizing Network I/O Subsystems   48
Network Selection   48
The Number of Clients per Shared Network Segment   49
Server Network Interface Card Selections   49
Sizing Memory Requirements   50
Implementing Server Memory   51
Sizing and Tuning Specific Windows 2000–Based Implementations   52
Summary   52

▼ Two   Tuning Strategies and Measurement Gathering   53
Introduction   54
Setting Goals for Tuning Windows 2000–Based Systems   54
The Big Picture: Understanding the Entire Architecture   55
Tuning Strategy   58
Practical Guidelines   58
Tuning Methodology   59
Achieving a Nirvanic State   60
Focusing Your Tuning Efforts   62
The Tuning Process   63
   Conceptual Walkthrough of the Core Tuning Methodology   64
Performance Baselines   65
   Performance Baselines: Pre- and Postproduction
      Measurements   65

Developing Performance Baselines: Internal and Customer Perspective Baselines   66

Commercial Tools for Baseline Development through Stress Testing (Benchmarking)   67

Freely Available Tools for Baseline Development through Stress Testing (Benchmarking)   67

Performance Scripting Tools Provided in This Chapter   68

Internal Server Perspective Baseline Development through Pulse Testing   69

Customer Perspective Baseline Development through Pulse Testing   71

Scheduling Customer Perspective Scripts with Windows 2000   74

Enhancing Customer Perspective File Services Pulse Testing   76

Testing File Services Performance: CustomerPulseTest2.bat and CustomerBaseLineCheck2.pl   77

Advanced Customer Perspective Pulse Tests: Web Services   81

Tactical Steps Needed for Implementing Customer Perspective Web Service Pulse Test   82

Customizing the CPWMM Scripts   83

Performance Management   96

Statistics Gathering and Logging   96

Third-Party Performance Management Tools   96

Windows 2000 Performance Tools   97

Sysmon Operations   100

Sysmon Chart Mode   100

Key Sysmon Counters to Monitor   101

Sysmon Counter Log Mode   109

When to Collect Sysmon Data   110

Sysmon Alerts   112

Using Auditing to Zero in on Resource Usage   116

Windows Task Manager   117

Additional Performance-Related Tools from Windows 2000   120

Tlist.exe   121

Kill.exe   121

Windows 2000 Resource Kit Performance Management Tools   122

Ptree.exe   123

Sc.exe   123

CreateFil.exe   123

Ntimer.exe   123

WPerf.exe   123

Freeware Performance Management Tools   123

Filemon.exe   124

Regmon.exe   124

Handle.exe   125

Windows 2000 System Checkup   125

Windows 2000 Event Viewer(s)   126

Windows 2000 System Information   127

Putting It All Together: The Environment   128

Example Strategy and Tactics   128

Zeroing in on the Performance Problem   130

Summary   130

▼ Three Capacity Sizing   131

Introduction   131

Goals of Sizing   132

Reality of Sizing   132

Sizing Methodology   133

Exploring the Sizing Methodology in Detail   136

Step 1. Define Objective(s)   136

Step 2. Understand Business and Technical Requirements Needed
to Meet Your Objective(s)   137

Step 3. Determine Loading Characteristics   138

Step 4. Determine Performance Requirements   139

Step 5. Understand Future Business Requirements   140

Step 6. Understand Future System Architectures   140

Step 7. Configure the System   141

Step 8. Stress Test and Validate the Server Configuration   144

Step 9. Proactively Follow the Core Tuning Methodology during
Stress and Validation Testing   146

Step 10. Deploy the System into Production   146

Step 11. Proactively Follow the Tuning Methodology After the
    System Is Deployed   146

Benchmarks   147

Benchmarks Are Your Friends   147

What Are Industry Standard Benchmarks?   147

Where Do Benchmarks Fit in the Sizing Methodology?   148

Transaction Processing Council (TPC)   149

SPECweb99 (formerly SPECweb96)   155

NetBench   158

Historical Baselines   161

Where Do Historical Baselines Fit into the Sizing
    Methodology?   161

Using Historical Baselines   161

How Server Architecture Relationships Affect System Configurations   166

Properly Sizing Memory   169

Server I/O Relationships   169

Server CPUs Drive More than Applications Alone   171

Commercially Available Sizing Tools   171

Summary   172

▼ Four   CPU Performance   173

Introduction   173

Central Processing Unit   174

CPU System Architecture Review   175

Comparing CPU Architectures   175

Pentium III and Pentium III XEON CPUs   176

Helping Your System Scale   178

Planning around CPU and System Bus Bottlenecks   179

Choose Level 2 Cache Sizes Wisely   180

CPU Technology Is Always Changing (no surprise)   181

Comparing CPU Performance   182

Look at the Big Picture for CPU Selection   183

Should I Upgrade the CPU?   184

Windows 2000 and CPU Resource Usage   *186*

Processes, Threads, Jobs (New), and Context Switching   186

Windows 2000 and a Single CPU Environment   186

Windows 2000 and a Multiple CPU Environment—Symmetric Multiprocessing   187

Viewing Processes and Threads Running under Windows 2000   188

Determining Which Process Is Associated with Which Application   188

Windows 2000 Scheduler and Priority Levels   190

Affinity   191

Detecting CPU Bottlenecks   *193*

Quick Reference: Helpful Tools to Use When Tracking Down Windows 2000 Memory Details   193

Detecting Single CPU Server Bottlenecks   195

Detecting Multiple CPU Server Bottlenecks   196

Using the System: Processor Queue Length Counter Effectively   196

Artful CPU Bottleneck Detection and Tuning: %User and %Privileged Time   197

Applying Artful CPU Tuning: Privileged Mode and User Mode Processor Usage   198

Ideal Environment for Applying Privileged and User Mode Tuning: Artful CPU Bottleneck Detection and Tuning   201

Applying Artful Privileged and User Mode CPU Tuning Summary   202

Artful Tuning II: Adding Additional CPUs   202

Interrupt-Driven CPU Bottlenecks   203

Baselines Are Important for Bottleneck Detection   205

CPU Resource Usage Analysis with Sysmon   205

Sizing CPU Subsystems   *208*

Configure Enough RAM When Sizing the CPUs   209

Configure CPU Resources to Drive the Solution   209

CPU and Memory Sizing Relationships   *210*

Avoiding Resource Contention: Resource Partitioning and Server Consolidation CPU Example   211

Generic CPU Sizing Example   213

Tuning Strategies for Removing CPU Bottlenecks **214**

Hands-on Tactics for Tuning around CPU Bottlenecks 214

Thinking Outside of the Box **225**

Advanced Tuning: Helping Windows 2000 to Control Process
Priorities 225

Advanced Tuning: Helping Windows 2000 Control Application
(Process/Thread) Affinity 226

Use a Sound Affinity Tuning Methodology 227

Configuring Microsoft Interrupt-Affinity Filter Control Tool
(IntFiltr) 229

Summary **232**

▼ Five Windows 2000 and Memory Performance 233

Introduction **234**

Memory Hardware Technology Review **234**

SIMM and DIMM Server Memory 235

DRAM Future 236

Fast Page Mode (FPM) RAM 236

RAM Performance Considerations 238

RAM Interleaving 239

How Windows 2000 Uses Memory Resources **239**

Standard Physical Memory 240

Windows 2000 Memory Management 240

Windows 2000 Virtual Memory 241

Windows 2000 Pagefile 243

Pagefile Size Limits Virtual Memory Available to Process 244

Different Versions of Windows 2000 Equal Different
Memory Management Details 244

Beyond the 4GB RAM Limit: PAE and AWE 245

Windows 2000 File System Cache **246**

How the File System Cache Is Implemented 246

Application Level Control of Cache Manager Operations 247

File System Cache in a Read-Intensive Disk I/O
Environment 248

Sizing of the File System Cache   248

Investigating the File System Cache Behavior   249

The Effect of Adding More RAM for the File System Cache   252

Sysmon Counters Are Not Always What They Appear to Be   254

Thrashing: Extreme Paging at Its Worst   254

Windows 2000 Memory Strategies   256

Maximize Data Throughput for File Sharing   258

When Not to Use Maximize Throughput for File Sharing Memory
    Strategy   258

When to Use Maximize Data Throughput for Network
    Applications   259

Comparing Windows 2000 Memory Management Strategies   259

Understanding Your Environment Equals Performance   262

Sizing the Memory Subsystem   262

Use Historical Performance Information Whenever Possible   264

Memory Sizing Step by Step   264

Determining a Good Memory Size Starting Point   267

Memory Configuration Considerations   267

Benchmark Extrapolations and Server Guidelines   268

Sizing the Pagefile   269

Detecting Memory Bottlenecks   269

Quick Reference: Helpful Tools to Use When Tracking Down Windows 2000 Memory Details   270

What to Observe in Sysmon When Diagnosing a Memory Bottleneck   271

Memory Counter Relationships   271

Memory Pool Problems   273

Tuning Strategies for Removing Memory Bottlenecks   275

Hands-on Tactics for Tuning around Memory Bottlenecks   276

Ensure Another System Resource Is Not Acting as a
    Bottleneck   276

Controlling Windows 2000 Memory Management Strategy   276

Virtual Memory Optimization: Tuning the Pagefile   277

Configuring the Pagefile for Maximum Performance   278

Sizing the Pagefile   280

Configuring Multiple Pagefiles   281

Removal of Potential Memory Road Blocks   281

What to Avoid When Optimizing the Pagefile: Never Use RAID 5
for the Pagefile   281

What to Avoid When Optimizing the Pagefile 2: Never Use a
Second Partition on the Same Disk Drive for the Pagefile   281

Ensuring You Can Use All of Your Physical RAM   282

Maximum Registry Size Limit   282

Tuning Windows 2000 Kernel Paging Activities   283

Remove Unnecessary Workload from the System   283

Services Management   283

Blank Backgrounds and No Fancy Screen Savers Are Best   284

Identify and Remove Memory Leaks   286

Schedule Memory Intensive Jobs during Off-Peak Hours   286

Update Device Drivers, System BIOS, and Windows 2000   286

The Last Resort: Purchase More RAM   287

Avoid Paging and Keeping Applications Fed   287

Isolating the Guilty Memory Hog   287

Summary   288

▼ Six   Windows 2000 and Disk Subsystem Performance   289

Introduction   290

Disk Subsystem Technology: Following the Data   291

Disk Drive Technology   293

Basic Disk Drive Operation   293

Physical Disk Drive Performance   296

Disk Drive Selection   297

Performance Perspective: Physical Disk View vs. Windows 2000 View   299

Disk Subsystem Performance   300

Disk Subsystem Behavior Characteristics   300

Disk Subsystem Throughput   302

Disk Subsystem Workload   303

SCSI Technology   307

SCSI Bus Technology from a Practical Perspective   307

Implementing SCSI Technology   308

Determining SCSI Bus Throughput under Windows 2000   309

Fibre Channel Technology   *310*

Fibre Channel: Hubs vs. Switches   311

HBAs   *312*

System Interrupt Setting Strategy   313

HBA and CPU Power   313

HBA and Disk Drive Workload Sizing Example   314

I/O Bus Technology and Selection   *315*

PCI I/O Bus Architecture   316

Following the Data to Improve I/O Bus Scalability   318

Distributing CPU Power to the Peripherals to Improve I/O
Scalability   319

Next-Generation PCI I/O Bus   320

The System Bus   *320*

Next-Generation System Bus   321

Redundant Array of Inexpensive Disks (RAID)   *321*

RAID 0—Disk Striping   321

RAID 1—Disk Mirroring   *323*

RAID Levels 2, 3, 4, and Others   324

RAID 5—Disk Striping with Parity   *324*

RAID 10: Combining RAID 0 Stripes and Raid 1 Mirroring (1 +
0)   326

Just a Bunch of Disks (JBOD)   328

Implementing RAID with Windows 2000   328

Tuning Flexibility When Utilizing Hardware-Based RAID
Solutions   329

RAID Performance under Windows 2000   330

Sequential Disk Write Operations Throughput and Response
Time Analysis   332

Sequential Disk Read Operations Throughput and Response Time
Analysis   333

Random Disk Read Operations Throughput and Response Time
Analysis   335

Recommendations   335

Optimizing RAID Stripes   338

Stripe Size Optimization Shortcut   341

Scaling RAID Arrays   341

How Windows 2000 Uses the Disk Subsystem **345**

Caching Read Requests   345

Caching Write Requests   346

Windows 2000 Device Drivers **347**

Updated Windows 2000 Device Drivers Can Equal Better
  Performance   348

Sizing a Windows 2000 Disk I/O Subsystem **349**

Disk Subsystem Sizing Methodology: Step by Step   351

Use Historical Performance Information Whenever Possible   355

Disk Subsystem Sizing Example: Step by Step   356

Detecting Disk Subsystem Bottlenecks **361**

Quick Reference: Helpful Tools to Use When Tracking Down
  Windows 2000 Disk Subsystem Details   362

Detecting the Obvious Disk Subsystem Bottleneck   364

Determining the Disk Queue Length for RAID Devices   364

Calculating Disk Workload (I/Os per Second) for RAID
  Devices   364

Detecting the Not-So-Obvious Slow Disk   365

Tuning Strategies for Removing Disk Subsystem Bottlenecks **367**

Hands-on Tactics for Tuning around Disk Subsystem
  Bottlenecks   368

Windows File-System-Level Tuning   373

File System–Related Tuning **375**

File System Selection   375

Disabling Short-Name Generation   376

Disabling Last Access Updates   376

Defragmenting NTFS   376

Avoid Compression   377

Avoid Encryption   377

Tuning Disk Subsystem SCSI Channel and HBA **377**

Balance PCI Bus Usage   377

Group Similar Devices on the Same SCSI Channels   378

SCSI Command Queuing   378

Monolithic SCSI Drivers   379

Properly Configure the HBA   379

Update HBA Device Drivers and BIOS (Firmware)   380

RAID Tuning Considerations   *380*

   RAID Array Background Services   380

   Tuning RAID Controller Cache   380

   Setting RAID Stripe Sizes   381

   Single-Application Sequential Disk Behavior
     Dedication   381

   Hybrid Tuning: Grouping Similar Disk Activities
     Together   382

   Grouping Similar Physical Disk Drives into the Same Array for
     the Best Capacity and Performance   382

   Using More Than One RAID Level in Your Solution: Grouping
     Similar Disk Work Load Characteristics   382

   Data Placement and RAID Selection   384

   I/O Memory Lock Tuning   385

The Most Important Disk Tuning Concept   *385*

   Disk Capacity Storage and Disk Capacity Performance   385

Disk Storage Capacity Tuning   *386*

Additional Disk Subsystem Hardware—The Last Resort   *386*

Thinking Outside of the Box: Windows 2000 RAM Disk   *387*

   RAM Disk Technology   387

   Stress Test Environment and Results   388

Summary   *391*

▼ Seven Windows 2000 and Network Performance   393

Network Subsystem Technology: Following the Data   *395*

Network Interface Card   *397*

Relative Throughputs of Different Network Technologies   *397*

Realistic Network Throughput under Windows 2000   *398*

   Ethernet   399

Windows 2000 and GBE Performance   *402*

Applications Can Affect Network Performance   *403*

Windows 2000 Ethernet Performance Characteristics   *403*

Other Network Technologies   404

*Understanding the Network Architecture in Which Your Windows 2000 System
Operates   405*

When Is an Ethernet Switch Really Almost a Shared Ethernet
Hub   405

Windows 2000 Server Placement in the Network   405

How Windows 2000 Takes Advantage of the Network   409

Windows 2000 Networking Performance Considerations   409

New Windows 2000 TCP/IP Services That Affect
Performance   411

Windows 2000 TCP/IP Performance Enhancements   412

Windows 2000 Network Performance and the CPU   413

When to Use Multiple NICs   414

It Takes Two to Tango   414

Network Subsystem and Intelligent I/O (I2O) Technology   415

Sizing the Windows 2000 Network Subsystem   415

Key Facets of Network Subsystem Sizing   417

Network Subsystem Sizing Methodology: Step by Step   417

Use Historical Performance Information Whenever
Possible   420

Detecting Windows 2000 Network Bottlenecks   422

Quick Reference: Helpful Tools to Use When Tracking Down
Windows 2000 Network Subsystem Details   423

Always Consider the Big Picture   424

Tracking Down Network Bottlenecks with Sysmon
Objects and Counters   426

*Beyond Windows 2000 Systems: Tracking Down Internetwork Device
Performance Problems   429*

Tuning Strategies for Removing Network Subsystem Bottlenecks   431

Hands-on Tactics for Tuning around Network Subsystem
Bottlenecks   432

Advanced Tuning: Windows 2000 Interrupt Control
Manager   443

Summary   444

▼ Eight   Putting Theory into Practice: Sizing and Tuning Back Office
           Solution Scenarios   447

Introduction   448

Solution Scenario 1: Windows 2000 File Server Consolidation   450

   Introduction   450

   Application Description   450

   Application Performance Characterization   450

   Sysmon Objects and Counters: File Server Bottleneck Detection
      and Sizing   451

*Scenario 1 Step by Step: Sizing and Tuning a Mid-Range Windows 2000 File
Server   452*

   Sizing the Initial File Server Configuration   452

Windows 2000 File Server Sizing Configuration Chart Summary   462

Windows 2000 File Server Tuning Summary   463

   File Server-Specific Application Tuning   463

Solution Scenario 2: Windows 2000 Backup Servers   467

   Introduction   467

   Application Description   467

   Application Performance Characterization   467

   Real-World Backup Performance   472

   Sysmon Objects and Counters: Backup Server Bottleneck
      Detection and Sizing   474

Scenario 2 Step by Step: Mid-Range Windows 2000 Backup Server   475

   Sizing the Initial Backup Server Configuration   475

   Backup Zone Checking: Final Sanity Check for Backup Server
      Sizing   482

Backup Server Sizing Configuration Chart Summary   485

Windows 2000 Backup Server Tuning Summary   485

   Backup Server-Specific Application Tuning   485

Solution Scenario 3: Windows 2000 Exchange Servers   489

   Introduction   489

   Application Description   489

   Application Performance Characterization   489

   Sysmon Objects and Counters: Exchange Server Health,
      Bottleneck Detection, Tuning, and Sizing   491

Scenario 3 Step by Step: Mid-Range (3,000 User) Windows 2000 Exchange Server   *493*

Sizing the Initial Exchange Server Configuration   493

Exchange Server Sizing Configuration Chart Summary   *510*

Windows 2000 Exchange Server Tuning Summary   *511*

Exchange Server Specific Application Tuning   511

Solution Scenario 4: Database Server Implemented with Microsoft SQL 7.0   *516*

Introduction   516

Application Description   517

Application Performance Characterization   517

Sysmon Objects and Counters: Exchange Server Health, Bottleneck Detection, Tuning, and Sizing   518

Scenario 4 Step by Step: Sizing and Tuning Mid-Range Windows 2000 SQL Server   *521*

Sizing the Initial SQL Server Configuration   521

SQL Server Sizing Configuration Chart Summary   *533*

Windows 2000 SQL Server Tuning Summary   *533*

SQL Server–Specific Application Tuning   533

SQL Server CPU Tuning   534

SQL Server Disk Subsystem Tuning   538

Solution Scenario 5: World Wide Web Server Implemented with Microsoft IIS 5.0   *544*

Introduction   544

Application Description   544

Application Performance Characterization   544

Unleash Your Web Server's True Power!   546

Sysmon Objects and Counters: IIS 5.0 Server Health, Bottleneck Detection, Tuning, and Sizing   547

Scenario 5 Step by Step: Sizing and Tuning a Mid-Range Windows 2000 Web Server   *549*

Sizing the Initial Web Server Configuration   549

IIS 5.0 Web Server Sizing and Configuration Chart Summary   *560*

Windows 2000 IIS 5.0 Web Server Tuning   *561*

IIS 5.0 Web Server Specific Application Tuning   561

Strategy: Optimize the Windows 2000 Network Subsystem for Web-Based Workloads   562

Strategy: Tune the Web Server Software Engine to Use All Available Server Resources   566

Tune Your Web Application to Use Available CPU Resources   569

Tuning IIS 5 for Common Gateway Interface (CGI) Operations   572

ASP Caching   573

ASP CPU Optimization   574

Increasing Workload That IIS 5 Will Accept   574

Dropping Distracted Customers: Managing ASP Connections   574

Optimizing IIS for Web Publishing   575

In-Memory Document Cache (IIS 5 Metabase Value: CacheMaxDocMeta)   576

Include File Cache (IIS 5 Metabase Value: CacheMaxInclude)   577

Image File Cache (IIS 5 Metabase Value: CacheMaxImage)   577

Full-Text Search Index Size (IIS 5 Metabase Value: TextMemory)   578

Max Cached Document Size (IIS 5 Metabase Value: CacheMaxIncludeSize)   578

Thinking Outside of the Box: Xtune   579

Literally Thinking Outside of the Box: Network Load Balancing   580

Windows 2000 IIS 5 Web Server Tuning Summary   581

Web Server Solution Scenario Summary   586

Summary   586

Index   587

PREFACE

Someone asked me what this book is about, and my response was surprisingly simple, "It is all about making computers go faster, specifically Windows 2000 solutions go faster." When someone feels that their application is running slowly, it doesn't matter why. Is it a network problem? Is it a Windows 2000 Server issue, or perhaps a troublesome desktop? In this book, we focus on making Windows 2000 Server, workstations, and networks operate at their very best, so together they can provide the maximum performance possible. What are the common performance questions that surround Windows 2000 systems today? Can Windows 2000 actually be tuned? Where do I start when sizing a new Windows 2000 system? What size system is required? Will it scale as needed? Why does system performance appear sluggish? How do you determine if Windows 2000 has a bottleneck from a lack of resources? How can we help our solution to scale? Anyone developing Windows 2000 solutions commonly runs into these questions. Performance related issues arise in many enterprises; this book will help you to resolve these questions and more. The concepts and recommendations in this book are experience based, not just regurgitation of available reference material.

Feedback from my first book *Tuning and Sizing NT Server* (Prentice Hall, 1998) has been excellent. Some of these responses are posted on http://www.TuningAndSizingNT.com, while others have been incorporated into this book. Although many of the core performance concepts have stayed the same from Windows NT to Windows 2000, the approaches have been enhanced through continued research, testing, benchmarking, and developing new solutions from the workgroup to the enterprise level. A tremendous amount of new information and proven techniques is incorporated in this book. Approximately 50% of the material in this book is new. Key areas include: new Windows 2000 performance monitoring tools; new Windows 2000 tuning options; evaluation of the latest system technologies; insight into how Windows 2000 operates internally to take advantage of these technologies; and sizing and performance information on the latest disk, memory, and CPU subsystems.

This book takes a practical approach to tuning and sizing Windows 2000 systems so that you can immediately begin to maximize Windows 2000's overall performance. My approach is to discuss and characterize system-level hardware technologies and then explain how Windows 2000 takes advantage of them. Once this knowledge base is in place, the guesswork that revolves around tuning and sizing is eliminated. This in turn enables you to make more intelligent decisions regarding your Windows 2000 system's performance and optimization. Instead of providing lists of registry or other Windows 2000 variables that could possibly be changed (or found in the Windows 20000 documentation), specific rules of thumb are provided to help you get a jump start in the tuning and sizing of your Windows 2000 solution.

To help you integrate all of the information provided in this book, the final chapter incorporates in-depth sizing and tuning solution scenarios for File Servers and Server Consolidation, Backup Servers, Mail (Exchange) Servers, Database (Microsoft SQL 7) Servers, and Web (Microsoft IIS 5) Servers. These solution scenarios utilize the strategies; methodologies; rules of thumb; and bottleneck detection, tuning, and sizing techniques presented to size and then tune each solution. Specific application, Windows 2000, system and network component-level recommendations and performance test results are provided.

It is important to note that although numerous specific recommendations are provided, the concepts and principles discussed are applicable even as new Windows versions are released and server technology continues to improve. Of course the tools used to implement these concepts and principles will change. You can keep up with the new tools that can help your performance improvement efforts by periodically visiting http://www.TuningAndSizingNT.com. This web site also provides a location to share information surrounding the performance of Windows-based solutions.

Organization

Tuning and Sizing Windows 2000 follows the same approach as the *Tuning and Sizing NT Server* and jumps right in, with chapter 1 providing a series of quick tips and ideas that can be implemented immediately. These rules of thumb are ready to use as is, but are not thoroughly explained in the chapter. For those familiar with Windows 2000 and Windows NT, chapter 1 is a great place to start in the tuning process, while the beginner should consider the chapter a preview of what is to come and then move on to chapter 2. Continue reading the subsequent chapters to learn when to use the quick tips, what they do, and how to implement them and even more advanced techniques. A structured performance methodology is reviewed in chapter 2. In chapter 3, capacity planning of Windows 2000 is explored, providing a structured sizing methodology that discusses using native Windows 2000 tools, Windows 2000 support and resource kit tools, and freeware available for download from the Internet.

From there, the chapters follow a general information flow explaining the performance characteristics of system resources (CPU, memory, disk, and networks) from a system and component level; how Windows 2000 utilizes these system resources; and how to size the specific subsystems, detect bottlenecks, and explore specific tuning recommendations. Leading by example is something I consider important; who wants to end up like those humorous commercials that ask consultants to implement, and they don't know how! I use the techniques recommended in this book, and in chapter 8 I show you how.

Audience

Tuning and Sizing Windows 2000 is targeted for anyone who desires to learn where to start when sizing a new Windows 2000 solution (or migrating from a Windows NT–based system) or tuning a Windows 2000–based solution to operate faster than ever. To meet these goals, the following are investigated: hardware technology (workstation, server, and network), system design, Windows 2000 internals, system administration techniques, performance tool usage, and commercially available benchmarks. This book is not a basic system administration or troubleshooting book that also has some performance related information as an add-on. Here the focus is 100% on performance. Other facets of Windows 2000 solutions such as security, availability, system administration, and troubleshooting are mentioned as needed but only to enhance the performance or sizing of the overall Windows 2000 solution.

Everyone wants a high-performing system that is big enough to get the job done well, will efficiently use the resources that are available, and is not so overly configured that end users cannot use what they have purchased. With these thoughts in mind, performance should always be a consideration when developing a computer-based solution: system architects, system and network administrators, system engineers, software developers, and other IS professionals who develop or manage solutions based on Windows 2000 will find this book particularly helpful. This book helps those developing and managing Windows 2000 solutions to acquire a better understanding of the performance concepts involved with implementing specific solutions.

The book assumes a general knowledge of Windows 2000 or at least Windows NT planning, design, and administration. Because of this assumption, this book is targeted for medium to advanced levels. For some, much of this information will be new. Others may not feel comfortable with some of the advanced "Thinking Outside the Box" sections, while advanced Windows 2000 and Windows NT users may gravitate to these sections. Regardless of your experience level, you should review chapters 1, 2, 3, and 8 and then select the other material as it relates to your particular environment.

Which version of Windows 2000 is targeted? The entire family. The concepts are applicable to all versions of the Windows 2000 family of operating systems. Although the greatest focus is on Windows 2000 Server and Windows

2000 Advanced Server technology, wherever the other server technologies differ, they are brought to your attention.

Accompanying this book is a web site (http://www.TuningAndSizingNT.com) dedicated to the performance of Windows 2000 and NT that provides updates on Windows 2000 technology and book errata.

ACKNOWLEDGMENTS

First and foremost, thanks go to my wife, Diane, and daughters, Aurora and Valerie, who had incredible patience and provided support throughout the seven months needed to research, test, and produce this book.

Like many others, this book is not just the work of one person, but of many. A slightly different approach was taken for the technical review. Several experts in the field were summoned to review the entire book while subject matter experts in specific areas were contacted for individual section and chapter reviews. Special thanks go to my colleagues Dan Matlick and Troy Landry, Senior System Architects with OAO Corporation. Dan, Troy, and I spent many hours working together in the lab completing the associated tests, benchmarks, and specialized tools for this book. Special thanks also go to the outstanding and experienced technical team that reviewed the entire book: John Davenport, Senior Systems Engineer with Compaq; Ed Palmer, Senior Systems Engineer with Compaq; and Nick Cage, Windows 2000 Content Senior Technical Editor with Microsoft Corporation. Also, thanks go to the team who, among their various technical capabilities are also subject matter experts in numerous specific areas as well, provided reviews and feedback—occasionally in very short timeframes. This team included Arnie Shimo with MightyView.com; John Polen, who has spent many years supporting NASA; Janis Holloway, Jeff Lane, and Rick Patrick who support NASA and are with OAO Corporation; and Brian Gardner, Director of Strategic Technical Planning with Legato Corporation.

I would like to thank Compaq Corporation's Government Systems group for providing access to the large number of beefed-up Intel Servers, Neal Nelson and Associates for the use of their benchmarking software and insight into server technologies, Bluecurve Technologies for providing the enterprise version of their Dynameasure active measurement software, Post Point Software for providing their Xtune and Xcache software, and Sunbelt Software for providing various third-party software tools for performance enhancement testing.

Numerous people at Prentice Hall helped to keep this project on schedule; to all of them, I say thanks for the opportunity to publish another book.

And finally, I would like to extend a very special thanks to Mary Franz, my primary editor at Prentice Hall. Through conversations and her continuously supportive e-mails, she encouraged me to keep the high level of motivation that was required to make *Tuning and Sizing Windows 2000 for*

Maximum Performance a reality. Since this book is based on experience, Mary helped manage that fine line between quality work and market pressures and fended off the folks that wanted the book published earlier than personal and industry experience would dictate was acceptable.

Curt Aubley, Chief Information Officer and Chief Technology Office of OAO Corporation, has extensive experience in the IT arena—from developing solutions for multimillion dollar contracts to developing and rolling out internetworking and electronic mail solutions for more than 25,000 customers. This extensive experience encompasses managing, developing, leading, and implementing solutions in multiple areas of the IT arena. He received his Bachelor of Science degree in Electrical Engineering, with a Computer Engineering concentration from Northeastern University in Boston, completed Computer Engineering Graduate studies at the Air Force Institute of Technology in Dayton, OH, and is also a Microsoft Certified Systems Engineer (MCSE).

He has worked in the open systems environment for 14 years and specializes in operating systems (Windows 2000, Windows NT, UNIX, and Linux), Internetwork architectures, and performance. Mr. Aubley began evaluating, benchmarking, and developing solutions with Windows 2000's previous version, Windows NT, when it was first introduced as Windows NT Server version 3.1b. During his work in developing and managing mid- to large-scale enterprise open system solutions, he spent significant time on benchmarking, troubleshooting, testing, optimizing, sizing, and implementing a wide range of solutions.

Mr. Aubley includes among his accomplishments:

- Member of technical staff developing rocket guidance systems for Raytheon.
- Lead military performance engineer of enterprise performance project testing for the U.S. Army's Computer Engineering Center.
- Commander and chief engineer charged with developing and deploying the LAN/WAN and remote computer networks, electronic mail, and file server solutions that supported U.S. and international soldiers in Somalia, Africa.
- Senior system architect at AT&T Government Information Systems, responsible for the development and LTD testing of an open systems-based solution for a $100 million government contract solution that supported 3,000 WinTel client systems, 300 UNIX and NT Servers, and the LAN and WAN management system.
- Senior system architect at NCR's Government Division's High Availability and Electronic Commerce division, which developed various

intranet solutions, including supporting the UNIX and NT performance of a three-tier solution that culminated in the development of a single instance of a 4TB database.

- Chief architect for OAO Corporation's ODIN NASA contract for enterprise outsourcing that encompassed over 25,000 desktops, 300 UNIX and Windows 2000/NT Servers, and the associated internetwork that supported these and other customers. This solution also encompassed integrating an eCommerce solution based on Windows NT and Windows 2000 to support online transactions for any of the 25,000 customers and the end-to-end enterprise management system.
- CIO for OAO supporting enhanced secure RPN/VPN-based intranet, standardized desktop deployment, multilevel scalable antivirus solution, IT security enhancements, and Windows 2000 migration.

Mr. Aubley has published various papers and articles on UNIX, Linux, Networking, Windows NT, Windows 2000, and computer performance in *Windows NT Magazine*, *InfoWorld*, and *Windows 2000 Magazine*, among others, and he authored *Tuning and Sizing NT Server*, published by Prentice Hall in July 1998. He also teaches seminars at various conferences throughout the year.

As OAO's CTO and CIO, Mr. Aubley is responsible for establishing the overall technical direction for the company's customer solutions and internal IT systems. OAO Corporation is a 300+ million dollar corporation that focuses on system integration and engineering and enterprise outsourcing.

His OAO corporate press release is available at: http://www.OAO.com/praubley.htm and he also sponsors a supporting web site for Windows performance at: http://www.TuningAndSizingNT.com. His articles appear periodically in various trade press publications (*Windows 2000 [NT] Magazine*, etc.). You can reach him at CAubley@OAO.com.

Instant Rules of Thumb for Tuning and Sizing Windows 2000

CHAPTER OBJECTIVES

- Gathering Performance Statistics: Start the Logs........ *3*
- Three Action Items to Complete So That All Relative Performance Counters Can Be Collected........ *4*
- Determining Which Applications (Processes) Are Running under Windows 2000........ *5*
- Windows 2000 Bottleneck Detection Strategy........ *6*
- General Windows 2000 System Observations........ *6*
- Key Performance Metrics to Observe in Detecting System Bottlenecks........ *7*
- Detecting Windows 2000 Bottlenecks........ *9*
- Immediate Tuning Tips to Implement: The Tuning Process........ *15*
- Tuning Windows 2000 Resources........ *16*
- Tuning Windows 2000 System's Network Subsystem........ *32*
- Lower the Overhead Associated with the Network Operations and Improve Efficiency........ *32*
- Windows 2000 Administration-Level Tuning........ *33*
- Network Interface Card (NIC) Tuning........ *34*
- Distributing Windows 2000 Network Load........ *36*
- Tuning CPU Resources........ *37*
- Controlling Windows 2000's CPU Quantum Allotment........ *38*
- Windows 2000 Service Packs........ *41*

- Sizing Rules of Thumb for Windows 2000 Systems........ *42*
- Sizing Disk Subsystems........ *43*
- Disk Subsystem Availability........ *45*
- SCSI Bus Implementation........ *46*
- Determining the Number of Disk Drives per SCSI Bus........ *46*
- Sizing the CPU(s)........ *47*
- Sizing Network I/O Subsystems........ *48*
- Network Selection........ *48*
- The Number of Clients per Shared Network Segment........ *49*
- Server Network Interface Card Selections........ *49*
- Sizing Memory Requirements........ *50*
- Implementing Server Memory........ *51*
- Sizing and Tuning Specific Windows 2000–Based Implementations........ *52*

When reading technical material, do you hate weeding through countless pages of information before getting to the really good stuff? I do, and that is why I have decided to put some practical key points in the beginning of this book. This chapter provides little backup for the recommendations—just key points and rules of thumb you can immediately put to use. The chapters that follow explore these key points and rules in depth, along with more advanced techniques for tuning and sizing Windows 2000. We review each subsystem (CPU, memory, disk, network), investigating how the hardware technology works, how Windows 2000 takes advantage of the hardware from an internals perspective, and then onto how to detect bottlenecks and remove them through tuning and sizing. The last chapter takes all of this detailed information and incorporates it into various step-by-step sizing and tuning solution scenarios based on common back-office applications. Preview this chapter before looking at the other chapters to get a quick jumpstart into optimizing your Windows 2000 system. Then, as you read subsequent chapters, the rules of thumb and other tuning and sizing concepts discussed here will become more concrete in their usage. Later, you can use this chapter to refresh your memory.

Beware: knowing what each tuning technique does is more important than simply knowing which switch to flip! To fully comprehend the advantages and uses of these rules of thumb, read through the book's chapters. Being truly informed—not just knowing the tips but understanding the how and why they influence the behavior of Windows 2000—will help you make more intelligent decisions; it may also spark some alternate tuning ideas. Keep in mind that, although these tips can improve your tuning and sizing efforts, they may potentially have adverse effects if implemented incorrectly. The rules of thumb selected for presentation in this chapter were chosen based on the fact that they are relatively safe to implement and can immediately improve the performance of your Windows 2000 system. To say that you'll have an immediate improvement of the performance of your Windows 2000 system may be a strong statement, but it is a realistic one when you have an understanding of the workloads occurring in your Windows 2000 environment.

Be sure to make two good backups of the registry and your system, understand how to restore the system and registry, and test it to ensure that your process works before making any tuning changes. Actually, this concept holds true for any tuning; always understand and have a plan to reverse your efforts if needed. Then stress test or benchmark your new configuration to affirm that you have actually improved your Windows 2000 performance and that it is stable. Remember that the final true test of performance of an interactive application is always the end user's performance perception. Response time is king!

Gathering Performance Statistics: Start the Logs

Without some sort of baseline, either from internal or external metrics, you may never know how much you have improved the performance of your Windows 2000 system or how to detect current or potential bottlenecks. The information you collect using Windows 2000's System Monitor (Sysmon) is particularly important in tuning and capacity sizing. Sysmon should become one of your favorite tools. Chapter 2, "Tuning Strategies and Measurement Gathering," closely investigates how, when, and why to use the Sysmon-related actions in detail.

Key Points to Remember When Using Sysmon

STARTING SYSMON

Action: Start / Programs / Administrative Tools / Performance or run *perfmon.exe* from the command prompt.

CHART MODE • Good for looking at current activity or reviewing logs
    Action: Highlight System Monitor in left pane

ADDING COUNTERS TO ANY MODE • Sysmon contains a set number of objects. Each object contains subsequent specific counter metrics that can be collected.
    Action: Right-click Graphical Workspace (right pane of Sysmon) and select Add Counters (chart, log, etc.)

STARTING LOG MODE

To begin logging data with Sysmon, start Sysmon, expand Performance Logs & Alerts in the left pane, and highlight Counter Logs; then, in the right pane, right-click and select New Log Settings. At this point, provide a descriptive name for this log set, and then you will be presented with the Properties tabs of the log set you are creating. In the General tab, you must add those objects/counters combinations that you would like to log. It is important to note here that you can select All Counters per object and All Instances per object, but *not* for all objects/counters as was the case with Windows NT version 4. For example, if you select the object Processor, All Counters, All Instances, only the counters for the Processor object will be added to the log for monitoring. Thus, if you were to follow the methodology above for high-level basic monitoring, you would add all defined core instances for processor, network interface, memory, logical disk, server, system processor queue length, system, paging file, and the redirector. From here, select the Schedule tab and check the appropriate boxes to log performance data as you see fit.

Three Action Items to Complete So That All Relative Performance Counters Can Be Collected

To ensure that all relative performance counters can be collected, complete the following actions:

1. **Network Interface object counter activation.** To install the Network Interface object to Sysmon so that you can collect network interface card performance information, add the SNMP Agent service under Start / Settings / Control Panel / Add/Remove Programs / Add/Remove Windows Components / Windows Components Wizard / Management and Monitoring Tools and select Simple Network Management Protocol (SNMP). Adding this service installs the network interface segment object to Sysmon. *Security alert!* SNMP is a powerful management tool and is a must-have item, but it must be configured properly to ensure that it does not introduce a security risk into your Windows 2000 environment. At a minimum,

improve basic security of SNMP by selecting the SNMP service properties (Start / Administration Tools / Component Service / Services / SNMP Service); then highlight and select Properties, under the Trap and Security tabs, to ensure that a community name other than "public" is defined. For detailed hands-on, step-by-step information on Windows 2000 and Windows NT security, visit http://www.sans.org and http://www.nsa.gov.

2. **Network Segment object counter activation.** To install the Network Segment object to Sysmon and the real-time Network Monitor–based application, add the Network Tools and Agent under Start / Settings / Control Panel / Add/Remove Programs / Add/Remove Windows Components / Windows Components Wizard / Management and Monitoring Tools; then select Network Monitoring Tools. Network Segment is the only Sysmon object that may slightly detract from your system's networking performance. Collecting data using this object places the selected network interface card into promiscuous mode. Promiscuous mode forces the selected network interface card to read every packet that it observes on the network segment to which it is attached regardless of whether or not the network packet is destined for the server. This will add additional overhead to your server above and beyond the standard Sysmon application. Although this is a very helpful counter, use care when deciding when it is to be activated.

3. **Logical Disk object counter activation.** By default, Windows 2000 enables the physical disk counters. This is helpful if you have disks that are configured individually (no redundant array of inexpensive disks [RAID] sets or such). However, when you want to monitor logical disk drive performance, you must run diskperf –yv from the command line and reboot your system. Diskperf has several options that you can view by typing diskperf /? | more at the command line. This provides explanations for all of the diskperf options. The -y option suggested sets the system to start all disk performance counters when it is restarted (physical and logical). The -v option enables only the logical disk performance counters used for measuring performance of the logical drives created from combining drives into disk sets.

Determining Which Applications (Processes) Are Running under Windows 2000

When Sysmon is started in log mode, it will collect metrics only from processes that are currently running. If a job is started after the logging began, the job generating the load will not be able to be identified. An excellent technique to circumvent this Sysmon limitation is to generate an alert when resource usage levels increase above an acceptable threshold. This alert would then start a second copy of Sysmon so that the guilty process can be identified and dealt with accordingly.

Windows 2000 Bottleneck Detection Strategy

Wouldn't it be nice if you could observe just one or two metrics to determine what is going on in your Windows 2000 system? Unfortunately since the system's subsystems are all interrelated, so are the metrics that must be observed, even under Windows 2000. In chapter 2, "Tuning Strategies and Measurement Gathering," we investigate the importance of considering the entire server performance picture when trying to locate a Windows 2000 bottleneck. There can be more than one system resource area that is contributing to the throttling of Windows 2000's overall performance. Once all of the major system resource areas are evaluated, focus on improving the performance of the resource that is farthest to the left in the performance resource chart (Figure 1-1). This strategy will provide the greatest immediate gain to your Windows 2000 system's overall performance. Once one system resource is removed as the bottleneck, others may take its place, which will subsequently influence where you focus additional tuning efforts.

General Windows 2000 System Observations

The following are general observations we can make about Windows 2000 systems.

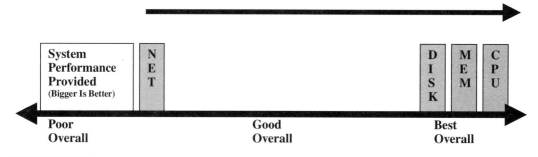

Tuning Goal: All System Resources Grouped to the Right

FIGURE 1-1   *Performance Resource Chart Indicating a Network Bottleneck*

1. Windows 2000 systems typically will run short of memory before any other system resources. Watch this resource closely.
2. Even when you are concerned about another potential resource bottleneck, ensure there is not a memory shortage.
3. Once memory shortages are ruled out, the disk and network subsystems are typically the next sources of contention.
4. You can achieve some of the greatest gains in Windows 2000 system performance tuning by properly tuning and sizing the memory subsystem, disk subsystem, and network subsystem, in that order.

Key Performance Metrics to Observe in Detecting System Bottlenecks

There are a dizzying number of Sysmon objects and counters to consider when sleuthing Windows 2000 system bottlenecks that are throttling back overall performance. In the next section a condensed version of the key metrics to observe when determining if a bottleneck is forming that will interfere with your server's overall performance. All of the metrics are available when using the default Windows 2000 system Sysmon tool. A common concern I hear is that some of these counters always display 0, which is misleading. Ensure that all of the Sysmon counters are turned on as outlined above in "Three Action Items to Complete So That All Relative Performance Counters Can Be Collected." If you do not activate the network and disk subsystem counters, you'll be trying to improve performance with only one-half of the picture!

These rules of thumb are generic and generally hold true. As you begin to collect measurements and develop a baseline on your particular Windows 2000 system(s), place particularly close attention to these objects and counters. Any drastic variation from the baseline you develop and/or trends observed over a given period of time—consecutive weeks for instance—can be cause for action. For example, if the Logical Disk: Transfers/sec on a particular disk drive have held steady at 50 transactions/sec for 4 weeks, then suddenly begin to increase at 5% each week, investigate and understand what is running on the system. Subsequently, develop an action plan to alleviate this ominous-looking condition that is developing before it becomes that bottleneck that slows down your entire system.

Tools to Investigate Windows 2000 Subsystem Usage: A Quick Reference Guide

Have you ever wondered which performance tools are available that you could use to dive into more detail than Sysmon, but did not want to hunt around for them? Some of the most popular tools for advanced subsystem analysis are listed in Table 1.1. Most of the tools functionally overlap each other in some fashion. If you do not find what you are looking for with one tool, try another! Do not be surprised if slightly different results are presented when querying for the same information.

TABLE 1.1 *Tools to Investigate Windows Subsystem Performance Characteristics*

Tool	Where Do You Find It? (Package)	Command Line Image	Key Times to Consider Using This Tool
Sysmon (System Monitor, Alerts, Logging)	Native to Windows 2000	Sysmon MMC (Perfmon)	Long-term trend analysis
Task Manager	Native to Windows 2000	Taskman.exe	Short-term analysis; track the I/O column counter to track I/O usage per process in real time
Filemon.exe	http:// sysinternals.com freeware	Filemon.exe	Details on which process is using which portions of the disk subsystem with details down to the file level
NTHandleEx	http:// sysinternals.com freeware	NTHandleEX.exe	Details on which files and DLLs the processes are using
Process Explode	Resource Kit	Pview.exe	Process details into how disk subsystem activities are run
Page Fault Monitor	Resource Kit	Pfmon.exe	Advanced debugging of specific applications
Process Viewer	Support tools on Windows 2000 media	Pviewer.exe	Detailed process and thread usage
Process Monitor	Support tools on Windows 2000 media	Pmon.exe	Command line tool needed to process usage
Process Status	Resource Kit	Pstat.exe	Provides a snapshot of processes and threads status from the command line; this has a long standard out display; consider running it by piping it into more (pstat | more)
Ping.exe	Native to Windows 2000	Ping.exe	Provides information on the response time of the network layer by sending generic **Internet Control Message Protocol** (ICMP) echoes; also immensely helpful in troubleshooting network connectivity problems

| | TABLE 1.1 | Tools to Investigate Windows Subsystem Performance Characteristics (Continued) | |

Tool	Where Do You Find It? (Package)	Command Line Image	Key Times to Consider Using This Tool
Pathping.exe	Native to Windows 2000	Pathping.exe	Provides the same information as ping.exe, tracert.exe, and more, such as detailed information on how each network device in the path is handling packets; if PathPing.exe shows network devices that are dropping packets, those network devices may be running low on CPU and memory resources and are not being able to keep up with demand
Netstat	Native to Windows 2000	Netstat.exe	Provides details on routing and which applications are using which ports on your system; helpful for TCP tuning, determining what is running on your system, and troubleshooting routing problems
Nbtstat	Native to Windows 2000	Nbtstat.exe	Advanced debugging of specific applications especially if using legacy WINS/NetBIOS connections; also helpful for tracking down which clients are using your system From a debugging perspective, the new –RR option enables the refreshing of the WINS database for the system it is run from.
Network Monitor	Native to Windows 2000 (must be installed though)	Netmon.exe	Network sniffer application that provides detailed information on the packets that are traversing your Windows 2000 system network connections; helpful in tracking down network problems and determining which clients are connecting to your system
Netdiag	Windows 2000 support Tools (found on Windows 2000 media)	Netdiag.exe	If your network connections are not healthy, they will not run fast; Netdiag provides a quick mechanism to check the health of the local systems network configuration

Detecting Windows 2000 Bottlenecks

Detecting Windows 2000 Memory Bottlenecks

Windows 2000 subsystems are all interrelated and subsequently so are the metrics to observe, even with Windows 2000. To determine whether your system has a memory bottleneck, use Sysmon to observe the relationship of the following metrics shown in Table 1.2.

| TABLE 1.2 | Core Perfmon Counters for Baselining and Memory Bottleneck Detection |

Object: Counter	Definition	Rule of Thumb for Bottleneck Detection
Memory: Available Bytes	Available Bytes is the amount of physical memory available to processes running on the system, in bytes.	Windows 2000 server will try to keep at least 4MB available as seen via this counter (unless using memory that has been tuned for file server operations, in which case it will be 1MB). If this value is near or under 4MB, pages/sec is high, and the disk drive where the pagefile is located is busy, there is a memory shortfall!
Memory: Pages/sec	Pages/sec is the number of pages read from the disk or written to the disk to resolve memory references that were not in memory at the time of reference.	This counter can be deceiving particularly on Enterprise class systems. High pages/sec activity is fine (>100) as this counter does measure grabbing data from disk. High values for this counter are not fine, if accompanied by a low Available Bytes indicator and sustained Disk Transfers/sec activity on the disk(s) where the paging file resides.
Memory: Pages Output/ sec	Pages Output/sec is the number of pages written to disk (pagefile) to free up space in physical memory. Pages are written back to disk only if they are changed in physical memory, so they are likely to hold data, not code.	A high rate of Pages Output/sec assists in the identification of a memory shortage. Specifically, if this value is high and the pages/sec value is high, you have low available memory, and the disk that holds your pagefile is busy, you are running short on RAM.
Logical Disk: Transfers/sec (for pagefile.sys disk drive(s))	Disk Transfers/sec is the rate of read and write operations on the disk.	If you observe any sustained disk activity on the disk drive on which the pagefile is located shown via the Disk Transfers/sec counter, the Available Bytes are hovering around 4MB, and Pages/sec is high, the Virtual Memory Manager is using the paging file significantly and the system is experiencing a memory bottleneck. Note the Disk Transfers/sec counter must point to disk drive(s) that contains paging system file(s), pagefile.sys.
Memory: Cache Bytes	Cache Bytes is the sum of the following counters: System Cache Resident Bytes, System Driver Resident Bytes, System Code Resident Bytes, and Pool Paged Resident Bytes.	This counter provides insight into how much of your physical RAM Windows 2000 is using for its dynamic disk cache, e.g., the file system cache and associated key system memory allocations. This is an important counter for troubleshooting if you have memory intensive applications.
Paging File: % Usage	The amount of the Paging File instance in use in percent.	If a large amount of the pagefile is used on a regular basis, consider adding (size of pagefile × % of pagefile in use) of RAM to your system.
Memory: Commit Limit	Commit Limit is the amount of virtual memory that can be committed without having to extend the paging file(s).	This counter provides insight if the pagefile is properly configured. If a pagefile is too small, it can limit the amount of physical RAM you can access.

TABLE 1.2	Core Perfmon Counters for Baselining and Memory Bottleneck Detection (Continued)

Object: Counter	Definition	Rule of Thumb for Bottleneck Detection
Server: Pool NonPaged Failures	The number of times allocations from NonPaged pool have failed.	If this value is >1 on a regular basis, there is not enough physical memory in the system.
Server: Pool Paged Failures	The number of times allocations from paged pool have failed.	If this value is >1 on a regular basis, there is not enough physical memory in the system or the paging file is too small.

Detecting Windows 2000 Disk Bottlenecks

Table 1.3 outlines the counters to observe when looking for disk bottlenecks.

TABLE 1.3	Core Sysmon Counters for Baselining and Disk Bottleneck Detection

Object: Counter	Definition	Rule of Thumb for Bottleneck Detection
Logical Disk: Average Disk Queue Length	Average Disk Queue Length is the average number of both read and write requests queued for the selected logical disk during the sample interval.	If this value is greater than 2–3 for a single disk drive and the Disk Transfers/sec is high (>100), the selected disk drive is becoming a bottleneck. This value is an average calculated during the Sysmon sample period. Use this counter to determine if there is a disk bottleneck, and use the Current Disk Queue Length counter to understand the actual workload distribution.
Logical Disk: Disk Transfers/sec	Displays the workload being experienced by the selected disk drive. Disk Transfers/sec is the rate of read and write operations (I/Os per second) on the selected disk.	If this value rises consistently above 100 for a single physical disk drive, observe if the Average Disk sec/Transfer counter is reporting values higher than your baseline or what you consider acceptable. If it is, then the disk drive is slowing down the overall system's performance.
Logical Disk: Average Disk sec/Transfer	Average disk sec/Transfer is the time in seconds of the average disk transfer.	When the Transfers/sec counter is consistently above 100 for a single disk drive, the Average Disk sec/Transfer should be observed to determine if it is rising above your baseline. As a rule of thumb, a value greater than 0.035 seconds indicates that the selected disk drive's response times are uncommonly slow.

| TABLE 1.3 | Core Sysmon Counters for Baselining and Disk Bottleneck Detection (Continued) |

Object: Counter	Definition	Rule of Thumb for Bottleneck Detection
Logical Disk: Disk Bytes/sec	Disk Bytes/sec is the rate bytes are transferred to or from the disk during write or read operations.	Sum this counter's value for each disk drive attached to the same SCSI/Fibre channel and compare it to 80% of the theoretical throughput for SCSI or Fibre channel technology in use. If the summation of Disk Bytes/sec is close to this 80% value, it is the SCSI/Fibre channel itself that is becoming the disk subsystem's bottleneck. Use this data and some basic math to review the complete disk subsystem data path.
Logical Disk: Split IO/sec	Split IO/sec reports the rate that I/Os to the disk were split into multiple I/Os.	A split I/O may result from requesting data in a size that is too large to fit into a single I/O or that the disk is fragmented. If you observe a higher rate than your normal baseline, run the Windows 2000 defragmenter to check if the disk subsystems are excessively fragmented.

Detecting Windows 2000 Network Bottlenecks

Table 1.4 outlines the counters to observe when sleuthing out network bottlenecks.

| TABLE 1.4 | Core Sysmon Counters for Baselining and Network Bottleneck Detection |

Object: Counter	Definition	Rule of Thumb for Bottleneck Detection
Network Interface: Output Queue Length	Output Queue Length is the length of the output packet queue (in packets).	If this value is longer than 3 for sustained periods of time (longer than 15 minutes), the selected network interface instance is becoming a network bottleneck. *Note: This is valid only for single-CPU systems.*
Network Segment: % Network Utilization	Percentage of network bandwidth in use on this network segment.	The network architecture in use determines the acceptable level of % Utilization. For Ethernet-based network segments, if this value is consistently above the 50–70% range, the network segment is becoming a bottleneck and is increasing the response times to everyone using the network.
Network Interface: Bytes Total/sec	Bytes Total/sec is the rate at which all bytes are sent and received on the selected network interface, including those bytes used as overhead (framing, etc.).	This value is directly related to the network architecture in use. If the value of Bytes Total/sec for the network instance is consistently close to the maximum transfer rates of your network and no other system resources are acting as a bottleneck, you have a network bottleneck on the specific network interface card (NIC) channel.

TABLE 1.4	Core Sysmon Counters for Baselining and Network Bottleneck Detection (Continued)	
Object: Counter	**Definition**	**Rule of Thumb for Bottleneck Detection**
Network Interface: Current Bandwidth	Current Bandwidth is an estimate of the interface's current bandwidth in bits per second.	For interfaces that do not vary in bandwidth or for those where no accurate estimation can be made, this value is the nominal bandwidth reported by Windows 2000. Use this information in conjunction with the Bytes Total/sec counter to determine the network utilization levels. Be careful! This counter states what Windows 2000 thinks the bandwidth is. Sometimes information provided by the NIC is incorrect.
Network Interface: Packets Outbound Errors and Received Errors	Packets Outbound Errors and Received Errors is the number of outbound packets that could not be transmitted/ received because of network errors.	If this value is >1, the selected network interface is experiencing network problems that are causing the network to slow (the system must spend resources handling the error and retransmit the data) and it will potentially become a bottleneck. This problem could be emanating from any NIC or network device connected to the network segment.
Redirector: Current Commands	Current Commands counts the number of requests to the Redirector that are currently queued for service.	If this number is much larger than the number of network adapter card channels being utilized in the system, then the network(s) and/or the server(s) being accessed are seriously bottlenecked.
Server: Work Item Shortage	The number of times STATUS_DATA_NOT_ ACCEPTED was returned at receive indication time.	This indicates that Windows 2000 has not allocated sufficient InitWorkItems or MaxWorkItems and this is causing network limitations. Consider tuning InitWorkItems or MaxWorkItems in the registry (under HKEY_LOCAL_MACHINE\SYSTEM\CurrentControlSet\ Services \LanmanServer).
Server: Pool NonPaged Failures	The number of times allocations from NonPaged pool have failed.	Windows 2000 network operations use paged pool and nonpaged pool memory. If this value is >1 on a regular basis, there is not enough physical memory in the server to support network operations.
Server: Pool Paged Failures	The number of times allocations from paged pool have failed.	Windows 2000 network operations use paged pool and nonpaged pool memory. If this value is >1 on a regular basis, there is not enough physical memory in the server to support network operations.

Detecting Windows 2000 CPU Bottlenecks

Table 1.5 outlines the counters to observe when looking for CPU bottlenecks.:

TABLE 1.5	Core Sysmon Counters for Baselining and CPU Bottleneck Detection

Object: Counter	Definition	Rule of Thumb for Bottleneck Detection
Processor: Processor Time–Total Instances	% Total Processor Time is expressed as a percentage of the elapsed time that a processor is busy executing a non-idle thread.	A high value for this counter is not a reason to be alarmed unless it is accompanied by a sustained System: Processor Queue Length greater than 2 or growing with an associated level of processor time greater than 90%; then the CPU is becoming a bottleneck. This rule holds true for single CPU Windows 2000 systems.
Processor: Processor Time–Total Instances	% Total Processor Time is expressed as a percentage of the elapsed time that a processor is busy executing a non-idle thread.	A high value for this counter is not a reason to be alarmed, unless it is accompanied with an aggregated System: Processor Queue Length sum greater than ($2 \times$ Number of CPUs) or growing with an associated level of total processor time greater than 90%; then the CPUs are becoming a bottleneck. This rule holds true for multi-CPU Windows 2000 systems.
System: Processor Queue Length	Processor Queue Length is the number of threads in the processor queue. There is a single queue for processor time even on computers with multiple processors. This counter counts ready threads only, not threads that are running.	If the sustained Queue Length is >2 or continuously growing with an associated level of Total Processor Time >90%, the CPU is becoming a bottleneck. This rule holds true for single CPU Windows 2000 systems.
Processor: % Interrupt Time	% Interrupt Time is expressed as a percentage of the elapsed time that the processor spent handling hardware interrupts.	This value in itself is not a true indicator of a processor bottleneck. The value of this counter is helping to determine where to focus your tuning efforts. If this counter is greater than 20% and rising compared to your baseline, consider completing diagnostics on the peripheral components to ensure they are operating within acceptable parameters.
Processor: % Privileged Time	% Privileged Time is expressed as a percentage of the elapsed time that the processor spent in privileged mode in non-idle threads.	If this value is greater than counter % User Time, then focus on tuning system resources and investigate how well the application is consuming the privileged time.
Processor: % User Time	% User Time is expressed as a percentage of the elapsed time that the processor spent the user mode in non-idle threads.	If this value is greater than counter % Privileged Time, then focusing on tuning of user/application processes and resources should yield a better return than focusing on server resource utilization.

TABLE 1.5	Core Sysmon Counters for Baselining and CPU Bottleneck Detection (Continued)	
Object: Counter	**Definition**	**Rule of Thumb for Bottleneck Detection**
Processor: Interrupts/sec	Interrupts/sec is the average number of hardware interrupts the processor is receiving and servicing in each second.	As hardware devices attached to the server (ex. network interface card) require attention, they interrupt the CPU to request service. Typical Intel CPUs run at 100 Interrupts/sec. If this value suddenly begins to rise when the workload has not increased, this can be an indication of a hardware problem (which robs valuable CPU cycles from processes that really need it!).
System: Context Switches/sec	Context Switches/sec is the combined rate at which all processors on the computer are switched from one thread to another. Context switches occur when a running thread voluntarily relinquishes the processor, is preempted by a higher priority ready thread, or switches between user mode and privileged (kernel) mode to use an Executive or subsystem service.	If excessive amounts of context switches are occurring, you may be able to improve CPU performance by binding the process experiencing the high context switch rates to a specific CPU by applying hard affinity with Task Manager.

Immediate Tuning Tips to Implement: The Tuning Process

Windows 2000 is instrumented in greater detail than Windows NT; thus there are far more counters available to choose from. Tables 1.2–1.5 provide a great quick reference to use when wading through the almost endless counters contained in Sysmon for identifying Windows 2000 system bottlenecks.

What approach should you take when tuning your Windows system? I've tried several and have found that the structured methodology in Table 1.6 assists in the tuning process and yields the best results with the least amount of effort time and time again. This is a helpful methodology to follow when tuning your Windows 2000 system–based solution. The concept of internal system resource usage and performance from the customer perspective is reviewed in detail in chapter 2. The executive summary is that you want to monitor resource usage inside of your system (e.g., % CPU usage) and also from the customer's perspective (e.g., how long does it take to deliver a server service such as downloading a web page at the customer's desktop).

Now that the key metrics to observe have been presented to help in locating those potential bottlenecks and we have a methodology to follow to assist in the tuning process, let's review general tuning tactics that we can implement to tune our way around Windows 2000 system bottlenecks.

TABLE 1.6	*Structured Approaches to the Tuning Process*

Step	Action
1	Always have a tested and validated backup of the system, files, applications, and registry before making any changes.
2	Monitor your Windows 2000 system and develop a baseline. *(Internal system resource usage and performance from the customer's perspective.)*
3	Proactively monitor your system. *(Internal system resource usage and performance from customer perspective.)*
4	Determine which resource is acting like or becoming a bottleneck. *(If none, look for factors outside your system that are relied on by following the data that your solution relies on.)*
5	Try a single change at a time when possible, and document all change(s) well.
6	Benchmark and test your system to determine if the change(s) is helpful and stable.
7	Return to step 3.

Tuning Windows 2000 Resources

General System Hardware Tuning

- Update the Basic Input/Output System (BIOS) and Windows 2000 drivers on all server hardware (includes motherboards and the associated adapters).
- Ensure BIOS is configured for maximum performance.
- Ensure BIOS performance settings match the hardware you have installed.
- Ensure you received the correct hardware.

Tuning Memory Resources

In this section, you will learn what you need to do to tune your Windows 2000 system's memory resources. First we'll come up with a memory management strategy, and then we'll work on putting that strategy into place.

SELECTING WINDOWS 2000 SYSTEM MEMORY MANAGEMENT STRATEGY

Windows 2000 incorporates the facilities needed to tune its primary memory management strategies. In chapter 5 we investigate the system's memory architecture and see how Windows 2000 system utilizes memory in much more detail.

First we'll talk about the most common technique used to control how Windows 2000 limited memory resources behave. Select Start / Settings / Network and Dial-Up Settings / Local Area Connection / Properties / File and Printer Sharing for Microsoft Networks. Then select the optimization level (memory management strategy). The selection you make here can have profound effects on how the server performs, so choose wisely.

OPTION 1: MAXIMIZE DATA THROUGHPUT FOR FILE SHARING • Select "Maximize Throughput for File Sharing" only if your Windows 2000 system acts as dedicated file server or if applications exhibit behaviors very similar to a file server that relies heavily on the file system cache. For those environments, this memory strategy provides the greatest level of performance. When this strategy is selected, the Windows 2000 Memory Manager gives priority for memory resources (working set size) to the file system cache over applications. Do not select this option if this system provides any other services besides that of a file server. If you are running any other applications on the Windows 2000 system such as Microsoft SQL Server or another memory-intensive application, the server might begin to *page* (swap information between RAM and the disk) excessively. If this occurs, it will lower the server's overall performance.

OPTION 2: MAXIMIZE DATA THROUGHPUT FOR NETWORK APPLICATIONS • Select this option for just about every type of server other than that of a file server. A Windows 2000 system allows less RAM for the dynamic file system cache so that running applications can have access to more RAM. With this option, its application tuning generally becomes more important. When you configure applications such as Oracle, Sybase, SQL Server, or Microsoft Exchange, you can tune them to use specified amounts of RAM for areas such as buffers for disk input/output (I/O) and general database caching. Knowing what is running on your system is particularly important here. If you allocate too much memory for each application in a multiapplication environment, excessive paging can turn into thrashing (extreme excessive paging), and you will have one slow system.

How large can the Windows 2000 file system cache grow? In general, up to 50% of available RAM. However, the amount of memory configured in the system influences how much RAM can be utilized for the file system cache. These details are provided in Table 1.7. If you are interested in more details on Table 1.7, head straight to chapter 5.

TABLE 1.7	Windows 2000 File System Cache Size Limits

Amount of Physical RAM in System	Minimum/Maximum File System Cache Size
2GB or greater	64–960MB
1GB	64–432MB
1GB with Application Terminal Services	64–448MB

OPTIMIZING VIRTUAL MEMORY

This is a good technique to implement because it can make your life a whole lot easier for a variety of tuning and sizing tasks. For maximum performance, design your systems with enough physical memory so the possibility of frequent paging is mitigated. However, if your system must page, tune the physical disk subsystem and the pagefile itself. The paging file system can be split up among 16 separate pagefile.sys file systems. More is better when it comes to paging files, unless you become excessive. A good rule of thumb is to split the paging file between two to four separate dedicated physical disk drives and, if possible, across different SCSI channels that do not also support slower small computer system interface (SCSI) devices such as tape units or DVD/CD RW/CD devices. This is an optimum virtual memory layout. Splitting the page files across more than 4 disk drives can add overhead to Windows 2000 and actually slow your system down in some instances.

The best tactic to use when implementing multiple pagefiles is to place them on their own identical dedicated disk drives with the pagefile configured the same size on each disk drive. Yes, this can add another ~$500 or so to your system cost, but, by isolating the pagefiles on their own disk drives, you obtain two advantages: improved performance and easier administration. First, pagefile access is sequential in nature. By providing the pagefile with its own disk, there are no other outside workloads being placed on the disk that might be contrary to the sequential nature of the pagefile workload. Grouping disk activities that are similar lowers the amount of physical disk head movement, thus producing improved response time from the disk subsystem. Second, when dedicated disks are used for the pagefile, it is much easier to distinguish between a very busy system and one that is experiencing memory problems. Sharing your pagefile disk with other applications makes it much more difficult to determine if paging activities are being caused by disk activity associated with the Virtual Memory Management (VMM) or by your applications. When all of the pagefiles are set to the same size, Windows 2000 will load balance the virtual memory usage among all of the pagefile instances. This improves performance if the system is experiencing paging activities and application startup.

The pagefile size and location is set by selecting Start / Settings / Control Panel / System / Performance / Virtual Memory / Settings.

You can set an initial and maximum size for the pagefile. To lower the possibility of virtual memory growing on an as-needed basis and adding even more overhead to an already overworked system, configure the initial and maximum size of the pagefile to twice the amount of physical memory found in the system, up to the 4GB RAM limit that many systems have.

To optimally set the pagefile, set the initial size parameter of the pagefile at % Usage peak value. As corollary to this rule of thumb, at a minimum, set the paging file initial size to twice the size of physical memory and, at a maximum, set it to two times physical RAM (to a maximum of 4GB). This will minimize spending any resource time extending the size of the pagefile and waiting for the pagefile extension to complete. Continue to observe your baseline. Constant use of the paging file is one of the major indications of a memory bottleneck.

REMOVE UNNECESSARY PROCESSES FROM THE SYSTEM

Every bit of RAM counts! Any processes that are not required to service your clients or manage your system should not be running on the system. Typically, areas to tune here are under Start / Programs / Administrative Tools / Component Services / Services. Why run the Fax service or File Replication if the system does not perform these functions? Any background processes that are started, even if not active, use RAM and potentially pagefile space.

SCHEDULE MEMORY-INTENSIVE JOBS DURING OFF-PEAK HOURS

This technique always seemed to be a bit of an easy-out strategy to alleviate memory problems, but it is effective and uses resources that may otherwise be idle. To schedule a job during an off-peak hour, use the at.exe command from the command prompt. If you do not care for the command line interface of the *at.exe* command that is native to Windows 2000 system, Windows 2000 includes a friendly scheduler located at: Start / Settings / Control Panel / Scheduled Tasks.

CONTROL WINDOWS 2000 KERNEL PAGING ACTIVITIES

Windows 2000 will page some portions of its own kernel to disk as Windows 2000 makes room in memory for other processes, such as placing the executive system drivers to disk when they have not recently been in use. This can be helpful for a system with a limited RAM supply. If your system has ample RAM (at least 128MB more RAM than is normally used by all of the process working sets on the system plus the RAM normally used by the file cache), then change the following registry entry: HKEY_LOCAL_MACHINE\SYSTEM\CurrentControlSet\Control\Session Manager\Memory Management\DisablePagingExecutive from the default value of 0 to 1. This change will force Windows keep the Windows 2000 executive (kernel) from paging any of its executive system drivers to disk and ensure that they are immediately available.

REMOVE UNNECESSARY PERSONAL ATTRIBUTES THAT USE MEMORY RESOURCES

The following memory tunables are common sense, but are shared here as a general reminder.

- Log off server. Staying logged on consumes resources that could be used for productive work by the system.
- If you decide not to log off but to lock the console, do not use a 3GL or other fancy screen savers because they consume resources.
- Do not use exotic wallpaper; it wastes memory resources.

PURCHASE MORE RAM—THE LAST RESORT

You'll find more tactics to tune around memory bottlenecks outlined in chapter 5, but when all strategies to tune the memory are exhausted and you have determined that the system is paging excessively, obtain additional RAM for the system. How much RAM to add is a function of current and future system load requirements and anticipated application requirements. To avoid paging, determine how much paging your system does and then add at least that amount. For example, if Paging file: % Usage Max is 20% and your paging file size is 1,000MB, consider adding at least 200MB. Also, when adding the memory to the system, select the RAM size so that it provides the highest density (for growth) while still providing the highest degree of memory interleaving (for performance).

Tuning Disk Resources

At first glance, it would appear that tuning a Windows 2000 system to remove a disk subsystem bottleneck is impossible and the only way to fix it is by adding additional disks. With all of the options and flexibility that are available with Windows 2000 systems, this cannot be farther from the truth. Now, purchasing more hardware is a valid technique, and we will discuss when it is appropriate to add disks. In chapter 6 we will discuss in much greater detail the server's disk subsystem architecture and how the Windows 2000 system utilizes the disk subsystem. For now, once the disk subsystem is determined to be a Windows 2000 system bottleneck, consider the tuning options in the sections below.

THE MOST IMPORTANT DISK TUNING CONCEPTS

DISK STORAGE CAPACITY *DOES NOT EQUAL* DISK CAPACITY PERFORMANCE ● This concept is reviewed in depth in chapter 6 because it is so important but commonly misunderstood. The basic concept to remember is that disk storage capacity does not equal disk performance! These are two different issues. It is fastest and easiest to explain this concept using an example.

Consider building a system that needed 18GB of usable storage that needs to be as fast as possible. Should you choose three 9GB disk drives in a RAID 5 array, which provides 18GB of usable storage to meet an 18GB disk requirement, or six 4GB disk drives in a RAID 5 array that provides 20GB of usable storage? Both solutions meet the storage requirement of 18GB of usable disk space, but the three 9GB solution provides a lower level of performance. Which to choose depends on the level of performance required and the economics of your situation.

If economics is a greater concern than disk performance scalability, the three 9GB disk drives meet the requirements. Alternatively, if performance is a more important factor, choose the six 4GB or twelve 2GB disk drive solution. Mileage may vary for every environment, but in general the addition of disk drives (spindles) can greatly improve your disk subsystem throughput performance and the quantity of I/Os supported per second. The three 9GB disk drive solution can support approximately 315 I/Os per second and a sustained physical drive sequential read throughput of 6MB/sec. The six 4GB disk drive solution supports 630 I/Os per second and a sustained physical drive sequential read throughput of 12MB/sec. This comparison is based on using the same family (SCSI connection, rpm level, etc.) of disk drives at different storage capacities.

DISK STORAGE CAPACITY TUNING • Is disk storage capacity related to tuning? Yes. In chapter 6 we investigate and determine that the seek time incurs the highest amount of overhead to the disk subsystem. As the space utilization of the disk drive exceeds 50%, any data required past the 50% mark causes the disk drive to seek at least halfway across the disk partition, which is time expensive. In a perfect world without budgets, always try to keep your disk drives less than 50% full. This is one of the reasons a new desktop always feels fast–the data is on the faster outside portion of the disk.

Keeping 50% of a disk drive free of data may not be realistic for all environments. However, target a maximum space usage capacity of 75%. This approach is a compromise for performance and also allows enough room for disk defragmentation tools to operate. If your disk space usage exceeds 75%, most defragmentation tools will not run effectively with only 25% of available space to operate in.

TUNE THE WINDOWS 2000 FILE SYSTEM CACHE USAGE—THE SECOND MOST IMPORTANT DISK TUNING • Memory tuning in the disk tuning section? Absolutely! Sufficient and properly tuned memory resources lower the workload on the disk subsystem and improve overall disk performance (refer to the section on selecting Windows 2000 system memory management strategy earlier in this chapter). Work to ensure that the Windows 2000 dynamic file system cache is configured to match your workload.

GENERAL DISK SUBSYSTEM TUNING

CONTROL ACCESS TO NETWORK-SHARED DISK SUBSYSTEM RESOURCES • It is common to find disk resources shared to the network under Windows 2000. If a specific popular network disk subsystem resource becomes a bottleneck, but it is not currently possible to tune around the bottleneck, what can you do? One technique is to control the number of concurrent users accessing the disk resource until the bottleneck can be removed. To control the concurrent user access for a specific shared resource, use the following command from the command prompt: c: > net share SharedDiskResource=F:\DirectoryShared / users:40 /remark: "For a limited time only 40 concurrent users can use this resource." Now that the shared resource access is limited, let's not allow people to tie up this popular shared resource. To control the amount of time a shared resource connection can sit idle before disconnecting the user, use the following command from the command prompt: c:>net config server /auto-disconnect:5. The net config server command sets the maximum number of minutes a user session can be inactive before it is disconnected. The default value for this command is 15 minutes. Also, this command is immediate and permanent. To change this value, you will need to rerun this command. For information on the status of a network share, perhaps to determine sessions timed out, run the following command from the command prompt: c:>net statistics server / more.

EVENLY DISTRIBUTE FILE SYSTEM ACTIVITY • Review the Sysmon logs regularly to ensure that you have evenly distributed the workload across the entire disk subsystem. If Logical Disk Average Disk Queues are greater than 2 requests per physical disk drive or Transfers/sec are greater than 100 transfers per second per physical disk drive, consider spreading the data of the affected logical drives to other physical devices that are less in demand. A common source of contention is having all applications loaded and running on the root Windows 2000 disk. The root disk is where WinNT (%SystemRoot%) resides, most commonly the C: partition. The root disk can quickly become a bottleneck from people accepting the default options during the installation of software.

To distribute the disk subsystem workload, you need to understand from where the workload is emanating. When you know this, you can work with the particular application generating the workload and tune it to place its data or logs in another location. Look at the documentation that is associated with the applications you are running. It is common that the documentation will provide insight into which files the application uses and where they reside by default.

A tool that is helpful in determining which processes are accessing which disk subsystems on your server is filemon.exe. This tool is freeware and is available at http://www.sysinternals.com.

LOW-LEVEL FORMAT DISK DRIVES BEFORE YOU FORMAT THEM UNDER WINDOWS 2000 • When using a SCSI disk drive on a different SCSI host bus adapter, always use the tools provided by the host bus adapters to low-level format the disk drive before attempting to create a file system on the drive with Windows 2000. The geometric translation combination in use varies between each host bus adapter and disk combination. When SCSI disk drives are placed onto a new host bus adapter, you want to ensure that the correct translation information is being used. Low-level formatting the disk drive with the tools provided by that host bus adapter vendor confirms that the translation in use is correct. This will ensure that the proper functionality, reported capacity, and performance are achieved when using the disk drive with Windows 2000.

Windows File-System-Level Tuning

ALLOCATE ONLY ONE WINDOWS 2000 LOGICAL PARTITION PER PHYSICAL DISK DRIVE

A technique that helps isolate disk performance problems and improves performance lowering the head movement rate over the disks is to format only one logical drive per physical drive. For example, if you have three disk drives, create only three logical drives C, D, and E.

MULTIPLE LOGICAL PARTITIONS FOR VERY LARGE RAID ARRAYS

Previously we recommended that you allocate only one partition per physical disk drive. For single disk drives and small RAID arrays, this is the recommended approach. However, with the advent of very-high-density disk drives and RAID technology, you should also consider multiple partitions in some circumstances. There are two reasons to consider multiple partitions. The first is availability. If you have ten 36GB disk drives in a RAID 5 array, there is 324GB of usable disk drive storage capacity. A single NTFS partition can be used, but if it becomes corrupt and the *chkdsk* command is needed to run against the partition, it can take an amazing amount of time to recover. The second reason to consider multiple partitions is also availability. One partition can be backed up while the other partitions are online. This slows down the backup process, but data is still available.

SELECT THE APPROPRIATE NTFS LOG FILE SIZE

The NTFS file system is a journaling file system; thus checkpoints are periodically written to the NTFS log located on each NTFS partition. For larger partitions, it is important that this log is large enough to support the file system activity and to ensure that the log file does not become fragmented. For larger NTFS volumes, increase the size of the NTFS log file size to 64MB by using the *chkdsk* command: *chkdsk drive-letter: /l:65536.*

SELECT THE APPROPRIATE ALLOCATION UNIT SIZE (ALU)

Match the file system ALU to the block size of the application you are using. If the SQL server is using an 8KB block size, when you format a file system on a new disk drive using the Logical Disk Manager, set the ALU to 8KB. Matching the file system block sizes can improve the efficiency of the disk transfers when you use the application. The Logical Disk Manager now supports a full range of ALU sizes. You can also use the format command from the command prompt in exchange for the Disk Administrator tool. An example of the *format* command used from the command line to set up an NTFS file system with a 64KB file system is: *format h: /FS: NTFS /A:64K.* For all of the format command options, type *format /?* at the command prompt.

DISABLE SHORT NAME GENERATION

Disabling short name generation on an NTFS partition can increase directory performance significantly if a high number on non-8.3 file names are in use (e.g., long file names). This is becoming increasingly common as legacy clients and applications are updated and retired. Windows 2000 must calculate the short 8.3-compliant file name every time a long Windows 2000 file name is used. This increases CPU overhead and causes additional writes to the disk subsystem. To disable short name generation, use REGEDIT32.exe to set the registry DWORD value of 1 in the following Registry location: HKEY_LOCAL_ MACHINE\SYSTEM\CurrentControlSet\Control\Filesystem\NtfsDisable8dot3n ameCreation. It is very important to remember that this will cause problems if legacy 16-bit MS-DOS and MS Windows–based applications are still in use on the Windows 2000 system you tune using this technique.

DISABLING LAST ACCESS UPDATES

Another registry tunable that can improve file system performance by lowering file system overhead is located in: HKEY_LOCAL_MACHINE\SYSTEM\ CurrentControlSet\Control\FileSystemNtfsDisableLastAccessUpdate. Changing the default REG_DWORD value of this key from 0 to 1 will stop Windows 2000 from updating the last access time/date stamp on directories as directory trees are traversed.

DEFRAGMENTING NTFS

Like any other file system, NTFS can become fragmented over time on heavily used disks. Windows 2000 does have a native defragmentation tool that is found at: Start / Programs / Accessories / System Tools / Disk Defragmenter. There are also commercial products available to defragment disk drives, which can improve performance of the file system. Current lists of defragment utilities are available at http://www.microsoft.com. Some of these disk fragmentation tools market that they not only defragment the file system, but also place files not touched for longer periods of time together on slower areas of the disk drive. Conversely marketed is that they group recently used files together on faster areas or on more commonly traveled areas of the disk. These techniques, if successful, will improve disk access time by lowering the time necessary for seek operations and will free up contiguous areas of the disk for Windows 2000's use. If these defragmentation tools are in use in your system, you may not want to utilize the tuning technique of disabling last access updates mentioned above. Using this tuning technique may cause a conflict with the defragmentation tool.

AVOID COMPRESSION

When file system compression is turned on, it taxes all of the system's resources. The CPU is needed to make the calculation, memory is required, and during this period the process is waiting for the disk I/O to complete. Unless absolutely necessary, do not use disk compression.

AVOID ENCRYPTION

When file system encryption is turned on, it taxes all of the system's resources. The CPU is needed to make the calculation, memory is required, and during this period the process is waiting for the disk I/O to complete. Unless absolutely necessary, do not use disk encryption. If encryption is needed, consider encrypting at the desktop level and then just saving the files to a server. Use only as needed.

Disk Subsystem SCSI Channel and Host Bus Adapter Tuning Considerations

BALANCE PERIPHERAL COMPONENT INTERFACE (PCI) BUS USAGE

Whenever possible, use the latest adapter technology. Currently, the latest adapter technology is a 64-bit PCI I20–enabled adapter. If using a system with a single PCI bus architecture, populate the PCI bus sights closest to the system bus first (Slot 0) with the adapter that is the most active. In some cases this will be the network interface card and in some cases this will be the SCSI host bus adapter—it depends on your environment. If your system supports two or more peer PCI buses, balance usage across the 64-bit PCI buses first. In general, place the SCSI/Fibre/RAID adapters on the separate bus rather than the network interface cards for optimum performance. Refer to chapter 3 for interrupt binding techniques that can aid in the performance of host bus adapters through binding CPU ownership to specific adapters.

GROUP SIMILAR DEVICES ON THE SAME SCSI CHANNELS

To maximize the performance and efficiency of your SCSI channels, group similar external devices on the same SCSI bus. By placing an active tape backup unit on the same SCSI bus as a 10-disk RAID 0 array, the tape backup device can effectively slow down access to the faster disk array. When SCSI commands are sent to request data from the tape backup unit, which is a slower device than a disk drive, the other devices on the SCSI bus must wait until the tape backup (or another slower) device transfer is complete before transferring the data associated with the other devices.

A good rule of thumb to follow is to place CD-ROMs on their own SCSI channels, place each tape unit on its own SCSI channel, and group disk drives with similar features (size, rpm) on their own SCSI channels. Also, avoid configuring SCSI devices using different levels of SCSI standards on the same SCSI channel because they will be limited to running at the speed of the slowest SCSI standard on the particular SCSI channel. For example, operating Fast and Wide SCSI (20 MB/sec) and Ultra Fast and Wide SCSI (40 MB/sec) on the same SCSI channel limits the SCSI channel to the slower Fast and Wide SCSI speed.

GROUP SIMILAR DISK CHARACTERISTICS

Either through reading those famous manuals (RTFM) that come with software products or by using Sysmon and filmon.exe (www.sysinternals.com), try to determine the characteristics of the disk I/O activities occurring on your server. Determine which applications exhibit sequential activities or random activities and which are read intensive or write intensive. Once you have determined the characteristics of your disk activities, group similar activities on the same disk drives or disk arrays. This is a corollary rule to evenly distributing file system activity. For example, place large log files on a disk drive that is separate from the general user database area.

Once the workload characteristics are understood and evenly distributed, group disk activities across the disk subsystems utilizing the various RAID levels based on the performance guidelines provided in the next section. For example, to improve the performance of sequential write-intensive log files, place them onto a RAID 0, 1, or 0+1 array and avoid RAID 5. For a predominantly random environment that is read intensive, RAID 0 and 5 are good selections. The more you understand your server's environment, the better tuned your Windows 2000 system solution will be.

SCSI COMMAND QUEUING

Some drivers for SCSI adapters have registry settings for SCSI command queuing. By increasing this value, you can improve the performance of the attached disk subsystem if it is large enough to support the additional load. When this value is increased, more SCSI commands can be in the disk device's queue. This technique is particularly helpful in disk array environments. Due to the multiple disk drive nature of disk arrays, they are capable of coalescing multiple SCSI requests in the most efficient manner to achieve higher levels of performance. Use this technique cautiously; test your performance before and after editing the registry values. For most large disk array environments (>10 disks), doubling the default value for the driver improves disk performance. Contact the disk adapter vendor for assistance in finding the SCSI command queuing entry in the registry. For example, for Symbios SCSI adapters whose default is 32, the SCSI command queue entry is located in the following location: HKey_Local_Machine\System\CurrentControlSet\Services\symc8xx\ Parameters\Device\NumberOfRequests (REG_DWORD 32).

RAID Tuning Considerations

RAID ARRAY BACKGROUND SERVICES

When Windows 2000 utilizes a disk array either through software or hardware implementation, the data consistency of the actual array is not checked. Parity or mirrored operations are completed, but the health of the disk array itself is not checked during regular disk I/O operations. Either through hardware implementation or Windows 2000 background services, vendors commonly implement routines to periodically check the disk array's health. This is an important activity that should occur on a regular basis.

TUNING RAID CONTROLLER CACHE

If there is a built-in cache on the RAID host bus adapter and a battery backup unit, the general rule of thumb is to configure it to ensure both the Read Ahead and the Write Back caching is turned on. The default setting for most adapter caches is Write Through. Having the Write Back cache enabled is particularly helpful in write-intensive environments implemented with RAID 5 disk arrays where there are pauses between periods of heavy disk activity. When your environment is characterized by heavy disk write activity followed by a lull, the Write Back cache takes advantage of this workload slowdown to write the cache data to disk.

SINGLE APPLICATION SEQUENTIAL DISK BEHAVIOR DEDICATION

Isolate sequentially accessed data on its own disk subsystem per application (thread) for maximum I/O performance. This maximizes the performance of the disk subsystem since it is supporting only one type of disk workload at a time. By dedicating the disk subsystem to a specific application, less contention is created, ensuring the disk characteristic you are planning for is occurring without outside interference. For example, if you have three applications that are sequential in nature but share the same portion of the disk subsystem, the sequential behavior will begin to have a more random behavior because the three applications might all be requesting the disk heads to move in different directions; this is what you can avoid by dedicating a single application to a disk subsystem portion. Common applications that sequentially access data include database log files and Windows 2000 pagefile.

HYBRID TUNING: GROUP SIMILAR DISK ACTIVITIES TOGETHER

It may not be possible to dedicate a specific application workload to a specific portion of the disk subsystem due to application or cost constraints. If this is the case, attempt to group workloads with similar characteristics together—for example, group all random disk activity on the same set of RAID arrays or group all sequential write behavior applications together.

GROUP SIMILAR PHYSICAL DISK DRIVES INTO THE SAME ARRAY FOR THE BEST CAPACITY AND PERFORMANCE

It is tempting to build a disk array from different makes and models of disk drives. Whatever is lying around the office will do, right? If you place a lower-capacity disk drive into an array with a higher-capacity disk drive, you lower the array's overall capacity. For example, placing a 2GB disk drive into a RAID 0 (stripe) array with four other 4GB disk drives limits the overall array capacity to $5 \times 2GB = 10GB$, not $4 \times 4GB + 2GB = 18GB$. This same concept is true for the performance of disk arrays. Grouping one older 5,400-rpm drive into the same array as 10,000-rpm disk drives lowers the overall performance of the array.

USE MORE THAN ONE RAID LEVEL IN YOUR SOLUTION: GROUP SIMILAR DISK WORKLOAD CHARACTERISTICS

You can group all of your disks into one large array and let the system's applications have at it. With fast enough hardware in large enough quantities, this tactic can actually provide acceptable performance. Unfortunately, implementing this tactic can become expensive and may not meet other requirements such as the required fault tolerance levels. To properly lay out the disk subsystem, you need to understand the technology you are implementing (hardware and software) and the server disk subsystem workload characteristics.

Once you have determined the characteristics of your disk workload activities, group similar activities on the same disk drives or arrays. This rule correlates with the rule to evenly distribute file system activity. For example, place large log files on a separate disk drive and file system instead of a general user database area. Once the workload characteristics are evenly distributed, group disk activities across the disk subsystems utilizing the various RAID levels based on the performance guidelines provided in the next section. For example, to improve the performance of sequentially write-intensive log files, place them onto RAID 0, 1, or 0+1 arrays and avoid RAID 5. For a predominantly random environment that is read intensive, RAID 0 and 5 are good selections. The more clearly you understand your environment, the better tuned your Windows 2000 system will be.

Additional Disk Subsystem Hardware—The Last Resort

Where a resource has become a bottleneck, you can choose to add more resources if all other efforts to improve performance do not meet your requirements or if you just need more disk storage capacity. Always select the fastest components that have a positive life cycle.

This could involve selecting the fastest available disk drives and disk adapter technology available for insertion into the fastest I/O bus available. For example, if there was a need to add three additional disk drives, selecting a PCI-based Ultra2 SCSI Disk Adapter and an Ultra2 SCSI Disk Drive rotating at 15,000 rpm would be a good place to start.

Appropriate Use of RAID

Adding RAID technology to your Windows 2000 system's disk subsystem is becoming a more common choice for enterprise servers to increase performance, disk management, and availability. RAID is a particularly excellent choice if multiple disk drives are available and it is not possible to break up the data files across separate disk drives to balance the use of the disk subsystem. A Windows 2000 system allows for the use of both software- and hardware-based RAID solutions. A good rule of thumb is to implement all RAID arrays, especially RAID 5, using a hardware-based solution. Hardware-based RAID solutions off-load the RAID calculations to a CPU on the RAID adapter.

The following outlines the performance and fault tolerance trade-offs of the various RAID levels.

RAID 0: DISK STRIPING

RAID level 0 stripes the disk activity across two or more disk drives. This logical layout provides the advantage of better performance for read, write, random, and sequential environments. Key points to remember when deciding whether or not to use RAID 0 technology:

- Use when there is not a concern or need for any fault tolerance.
- RAID 0 is not recommended for any critical files (operating system, pagefiles, logs, databases, etc.).
- Use when maximum performance is needed for all environments.
- Increasing the number of drives in the array improves the random I/O performance.
- This is helpful for temporary file placement for files that are not critical.
- There is a performance trade-off—if you lose one disk drive, you lose the entire array—and no fault tolerance.
- It provides great performance in a shared nothing cluster such as Windows 2000 Network Load Balancing services—if one server fails, others just pick up the slack, ensuring no loss of service.

RAID 1: DISK MIRRORING

RAID level 1 mirrors the disk activity across two disk drives. Key points to remember when deciding whether or not to use RAID 1 technology:

- Use when fault tolerance is needed and the storage capacity of a single disk drive is sufficient.
- RAID 1 provides complete data redundancy, even if you are using only two disks.
- It provides significant performance improvements over a single disk in a multiuser (workload) environment.
- It is well suited for write-intensive environments and great for single application log files. (For databases it improves fault tolerance if the log files are not on the same array as the database.)
- Use for the operating system to improve fault tolerance of the entire system.
- Use an intelligent hardware–based RAID controller for optimum performance and ease of maintenance.
- Performance trade-off: for this redundancy, the capacity of a RAID 1 mirror is lowered by 50%. For example, if you have two 9GB disk drives in a RAID 1 mirror, there is only 9GB of usable storage space.

RAID 2, 3, 4, AND OTHERS

These RAID levels are not commonly used in general computing environments, so they are not explored in this book. If you are interested in the other RAID level possibilities, search the Internet for RAID and a myriad of choices are presented.

RAID 5: DISK STRIPING WITH PARITY

RAID level 5 stripes the disk data with parity information across three or more disk drives. Key points to remember when deciding whether or not to use RAID 5 technology:

- RAID 5 is a good compromise between performance and cost to achieve fault tolerance for a disk subsystem.
- This RAID level provides fault tolerance through the use of parity information, allowing for the loss of one of the RAID 5 array's member disk drives without the loss of any data.
- It is outstanding for read-intensive environments (random or sequential).
- RAID 5 can be used for multiuser write-intensive environments, if latency is not a concern.
- It is not recommended for write-intensive environments where response time is considered important.

- Avoid using as location for single application/process log files or the Windows 2000 pagefile.
- RAID 5 is highly recommended to be implemented with hardware-based RAID controllers to off-load parity calculations from system CPUs and provide caching algorithms that help to minimize some of the performance degradation effects during write performance due to quadruple I/Os that are needed for each RAID 5 disk operation.
- Adding additional disk drives to a RAID 5 array does improve overall workload supported and subsequently increases performance.
- Performance trade-off #1: The capacity of a RAID 5 striping with parity is lowered by a factor of 1/(size of a disk drive member) due to parity generation (parity must be stored on every drive and takes up storage capacity). For example, a RAID 5 array composed of ten 36GB disk drives provides 324GB of usable disk storage space, not 360GB.
- Performance trade-off #2: The best RAID 5 implementation requires a hardware-based RAID adapter, which increases overall system cost.

RAID 10: DISK STRIPING OF DISK MIRRORS

RAID 10 stripes data (RAID 0) across two or more disk drives and then mirrors that set of RAID 0 disk drives with another set of RAID 0 disk drives to create a RAID 1–like configuration for fault tolerance. Chapter 6 has pictures to better illustrate this concept.

- RAID 10 is outstanding for all workloads (read/write/random/sequential).
- It provides high throughput and low latency for all environments.
- If cost is a concern, at least consider RAID 10 for all write-intensive environments (ones that cannot fit on the capacity of a single RAID 1 mirror).
- Use an intelligent hardware-based RAID controller for optimum performance and ease of maintenance.
- Performance trade-off #1: This is the most expensive RAID option and is thus normally used only if you have free flowing budget or business requirements that demand the absolute best performance and full fault tolerance.
- Performance trade-off #2: The trade-off for this performance improvement and high fault tolerance level is that the capacity of a RAID 10 mirror is lowered by 50%. For example, if you have two 9GB disk drives striped and mirrored with another two 9GB stripes, there is only 18GB of usable storage space.

The performance guide in Table 1.8 shows the relative performance ratings when comparing the various RAID options using a sector/stripe size of 128KB. Use this guide when selecting the appropriate performance level that matches your system's disk I/O characteristics.

TABLE 1.8	*Relative Performance of RAID Levels*			
Raid Level	**Random Read**	**Random Write**	**Sequential Read**	**Sequential Write**
Stripe (0)	1st	1st	1st	1st
Mirror (1)	4th	3rd	4th	3rd
Stripe w/Parity 12 Disk (5)	1st	4th	1st	4th
Mirrored Stripe Set 12 Disk (10)	1st	2nd	1st	2nd

Tuning Windows 2000 System's Network Subsystem

The network architecture that is in use directly influences the network performance relative to your Windows 2000 system. There are many facets of network architecture that can cause a network bottleneck. These facets include client configuration, application design, the physical network, network protocol, and network devices (routers, switches, etc.). Here we focus on improving the network performance from a Windows 2000 system's perspective. More advanced techniques for network subsystems such as advanced TCP/IP tuning are investigated in chapters 7 and 8.

Lower the Overhead Associated with the Network Operations and Improve Efficiency

Remove Nonessential Network Protocols/Redirectors

One technique that can help you optimize your Windows 2000's network subsystem performance is to bind only those protocols and redirectors (server components other than Windows 2000 server and workstation services) that your network is actually using to your network adapter. Binding is a technique Windows 2000 utilizes to establish a communications channel between the protocol driver (TCP/IP, IPX, etc.) and the NIC itself. These bindings are set under: Start / Settings / Network and Dial Up Connections / Local Area Connection Properties. Then check which protocols (TCP/IP, NetBEUI, etc.) are currently installed. Also check which redirectors (RIP for NwLink, RPC support for Banyan, etc.) are installed. Removing unnecessary protocols and redirectors lowers the amount of memory that Windows 2000 requires for network I/O (which can then be used for other tasks); ensures that your network is not generating any unnecessary traffic, such as unwanted broadcasts; and lowers the number of bindings that must be searched. For example, if you operate a TCP/IP-based network with Microsoft Clients, use only TCP/IP and Microsoft Client support.

Network Binding Search Order

If more than one network protocol or redirector is in use, tune the binding search order by placing the protocol/redirector most commonly used on the top of the bindings list. These bindings are set under: Start / Settings / Network and Dial Up Connections / Local Area Connection Properties. All network calls are routed to the protocol/redirector first on the list, and then Windows 2000 waits for a response before submitting to the next protocol/redirector.

Remove Unnecessary Windows 2000 Services

Similar to tuning the other Windows 2000 subsystems, you never want to run a service you do not need because it adds overhead to your system (potentially more network, memory, and CPU resource usage); furthermore, it may pose a security risk. For example, by default many folks will enable services such as simple TCP/IP services, but they are unaware of what these services provide. Few Windows 2000–based services or applications require these services, and having them enabled adds overhead to your system. Simple TCP/IP services also pose a potential security risk by providing services like character generation. Know what services and applications are running on your system and why they are running.

Special Network Tuning Note

Run the Windows 2000 Network Monitor tool on occasion (Start / Programs / Administrative Tools / Network Monitor) and watch what is running around on your network at the packet level. You might be surprised at what you see. You may have thought that you were standardized on one protocol or another, but then what are all of those other protocols running around taking up bandwidth on your network?

Windows 2000 Administration-Level Tuning

Permanently Cache MAC (Media Access Control) Addresses

A MAC address is a unique address that a manufacturer burns into a NIC, such as a 100BaseT Ethernet card. TCP/IP uses arp broadcasts over the network to associate an IP address with a physical layer MAC address. To lower the number of broadcasts and time required to obtain MAC addresses, you can permanently (until the next reboot unless a start-up script is used) place the associated MAC/IP address pair into memory. Use the following command sequence from the command prompt to implement: arp -s 137.111.141.101 01-01-01-12-s3-44. This feature is particularly helpful when accessing a commonly networked system that uses static IP addressing. This is not a suggested technique when the networked system uses dynamic IP addressing.

Controlling Network Users' Timeout Periods

There are only so many resources allocated for network connections, so, if a user strolled away from her desk to enjoy a sunny day, disconnect her. This frees up resources for active uses. The command net config server lists the Windows 2000 current settings. Running the command net config server /AUTODISCONNECT: 10 sets the automatic disconnect time (idle session time) to 10 minutes. This command is run from the Windows 2000 command line and is permanent until it is run again. The registry entry for this value is located at: HKEY_LOCAL_MACHINE\SYSTEM\CurentControlSet\ Services\lanmanServer\Parameters\Users.

Update to the Latest Software Revision Levels

As with other subsystems, always test and upgrade to the latest revisions of patches for Windows 2000 and associated device drivers for your NICs. Do not forget, especially for I20-enabled NICs, to update the BIOSs that reside on the NIC itself.

Network Interface Card (NIC) Tuning

Basic NIC Tuning

In some cases, it is possible to tune a NIC itself. Some NICs allow the maximum number of receive lists that the driver allocates for receive frames which can improve the NIC's performance. For example, the registry entry to add for a Compaq Netelligent 10/100TX NIC is MaxReceives. This key is a REG_DWORD and values are placed into it in hex. The Compaq web site, http://www.compaq.com, suggested increasing the MaxReceives counters for this NIC to 500 (a hex value of 0×1F4). Place this registry value into the following location:

```
HKEY_LOCAL_MACHINE\SYSTEM\CurrentControlSet\Services\
cpqnf3(#)\Parameters
```

Some of these tunables can also be set by selecting Start / Settings / Network and Dial Up Connections / Properties of LAN Adapter / Configure NIC / Advanced Tab. These settings can make a big difference. Since each NIC is a little different, specific recommendations are not included here. Back up your system before testing and watch memory usage. Some of these settings enable you to increase the buffers for the NIC itself, which is good, but that increased buffer memory must come from somewhere!

IPSEC and TCP NIC-Based Off-Loading (*Highly Recommended*)

For intense network environments, the combination of advanced Windows 2000 device drivers and advanced NIC technology enables many of the calculations associated with Windows 2000 networking to be off-loaded to the NIC itself; specifically Internet Protocol Security IPSEC and TCP operations. Two of the TCP operations that can be off-loaded onto NIC cards are checksums (receive and transmit) and segmentation calculations. For IPSEC-enabled NICs, the calculations required to encrypt the data are off-loaded onto the NIC card, which can result in substantially improved network performance and lowered CPU resource utilization! On tests I completed and in various other independently published tests, throughput improvements were commonly in the 10–25% range, with a subsequent reduction in CPU usage of 20–40%. This tuning technique is highly recommended for both Windows 2000–based servers and clients, but, as always, it is dependent on your specific environment.

Avoid Automatic Network Interface Card Settings

Setting the NIC properly is an area that is commonly taken for granted. Even though there are various standards defining the physical and logical specifications of network communications, some compatibility issues show up when you are not looking. Set your Windows 2000 system's NIC and any other network devices your system may communicate with to the best possible network speed setting available. For example, if full-duplex 100BaseTX is available and the other network devices support this setting, choose it. Only as a last resort select auto sensing. This does incur more work, but it can be well worth the effort as it guarantees the speed at which your network subsystem is operating.

Network Interface Card Changes—The Last Resort

When other network subsystem tuning options do not achieve your goals and all of the networking components in your Windows 2000–based solution are running at their optimum level, making a change at the hardware layer is the next logical step. The following are the key hardware level changes to consider:

● Selecting a different networking technology with higher bandwidth
● Distributing Windows 2000 network load

Select a Different Networking Technology with Higher Bandwidth

For your system select only stable PCI-based NICs that use the latest technology. Whenever possible, use 64-bit, 66-MHz, I20-enabled NIC cards that support off-loading network calculations. At a minimum, implement Fast Ethernet technology and consider Gigabit Ethernet technology in the future. There are other network technologies available, but none are as common. If you have a 10BaseTX-based network today, consider upgrading at least to 100BaseTX for your Windows 2000 system. Performance levels achieved always vary based on the workload, but, even with a fairly large deviation, which technology would you choose based on the test results in Table 1.9?

| **TABLE 1.9** | *Results of Using Higher Bandwidth* |

Network Technology **(Switched Full-Duplex Ethernet)**	**Real-World File Transfer** **Throughput (Mbits/sec)**
10BaseTX	7
100BaseTX Full Duplex	188
1000baseTX Full Duplex	680

Distributing Windows 2000 Network Load

If upgrading a single NIC's Ethernet channel does not meet your performance requirements, there are always more options. There are two primary techniques to increase the bandwidth to your Windows 2000 system when a single NIC upgrade is insufficient:

● Network trunking
● Network segmentation

Both are valid approaches, but network trunking is the preferred method for adding additional network channels to your Windows 2000 system because it scales better and has fewer infrastructure changes. Why increase your own workload if you don't have to?

Network Trunking

Network trunking takes multiple network segments or channels across the same or multiple NIC cards and has them work together to increase the overall bandwidth to your system. The most common four technologies supported by Windows 2000 are:

- Adaptive load balancing (ALB)
- Link aggregation
- Fast EtherChannel (FEC)
- Gigabit EtherChannel (GEC)

In summary, these bandwidth-enhancing technologies (investigated further in chapter 7) are implemented at the device driver and IP network layer. Implementing at this layer of the network stack enables these network performance enhancing technologies to work transparently to your applications; i.e., no application changes are needed to take advantage of the technology. This approach also lowers the overall hands-on administrative work that must be implemented because the Windows 2000 system still uses a single IP address for client connectivity; thus no client changes are required.

Network Segmentation

When a faster network technology and network trunking are not options, consider balancing your network load by distributing the more heavily used network segments between two or more NICs. Even though network segmentation can involve some new cabling (physical) and subneting (logical addressing) it is a proven technique that can optimize your Windows 2000 system's network I/O.

Tuning CPU Resources

Tuning CPU resources may initially conjure up opening your system and trying to determine what you can change, but this is not our goal in this section. A Windows 2000 system uses a priority-based round-robin scheduling algorithm to distribute process threads among the CPUs in the server. In chapter 4 we investigate issues surrounding the system's CPU performance and Windows 2000's use of scheduling algorithms, and we explore advanced techniques to tune these resources to your best advantage. Before getting to that level of tuning, we'll examine here numerous other techniques that can aid in tuning around CPU bottlenecks.

Ensure Another System Resource Is Not Acting as a Bottleneck

The most common occurrence I have encountered when tuning around CPU bottlenecks is the removal of other system bottlenecks, not CPU bottlenecks. If another system resource is acting as a bottleneck, it can appear that the

CPU is the actual bottleneck when it is not. Refer to chapter 2 to find out how to ensure that the other resources are not the bottleneck before spending your efforts tuning CPU resources. Some bottlenecks appear to be CPU related when they are not. For example, in extreme cases, memory bottlenecks disguise themselves as CPU problems. When Windows 2000 begins to run out of memory, it can exhibit a condition called *thrashing*. Thrashing is an excessive contention for physical memory. When this condition occurs, every request for memory results in paging activity to the pagefile on the disk drive(s). This results in an increased amount of CPU activity associated with moving memory pages around, not completing truly productive work. Why waste precious CPU cycles on this activity?

Avoid this condition by configuring a sufficient amount of RAM to avoid thrashing. The highest performing Windows 2000 systems I have encountered are sized and tuned with one basic strategy in mind: avoid paging. Many consider occasional paging to be acceptable, if it occurs infrequently. The more the system pages, the more CPU cycles are wasted on memory operations and the slower the final response times provided to your end users. To improve performance if the system must page, spread Windows 2000's pagefile across 2–4 dedicated disk drives sized identically (same size pagefile, same speed disk drives, same manufacturer, etc.). Refer to chapter 5 for the specifics on how to determine if your Windows 2000 server is paging and a step-by-step guide on spreading the pagefile across multiple disk drives.

Controlling Windows 2000's CPU Quantum Allotment

A quantum is the slice of time the thread is allowed to run on the CPU before the scheduler executes a context switch and moves it off of the CPU and moves the next ready-to-run thread onto the CPU.

For interactive workloads characterized by single-user workstations, Windows 2000 Professional assigns shorter, variable-length quanta to the running threads. Windows 2000 servers that support fewer applications require longer access to system resources. The Windows 2000 Server (and Advanced Server) assigns longer fixed-length quanta. Under Windows 2000, there is a point-and-click application available for influencing the quantum of foreground applications (those you interact with) and background applications. On the Performance tab of Start / Settings / Control Panel / System / Advanced / Performance Options, you can select Application Response Optimization for the Application (foreground) or for Background Services These options adjust the default quantum level of applications when you start them. For dedicated servers with larger applications running in the background, change this setting to Background Services. This will adjust the quantum of background services to 36 quanta. If you select the optimization for applications option, background processes are reduced to having 3 quanta of time while interactive processes have 9 quanta, and a priority scheduling boost of an additional two levels is applied as needed to keep Windows 2000 responsive to foreground interactive applications

OFF-LOAD WINDOWS 2000 CPU OVERHEAD

If the system is running out of CPU processing power, off-load Windows 2000 system activities that are not required or that can be implemented in other hardware. The areas normally associated with CPU overhead that can be removed or off-loaded are wasteful hardware components, disk compression, RAID operations, and security auditing.

REMOVE UNNECESSARY PROCESSES (APPLICATIONS, SERVICES, ETC.)

Run only applications and Windows 2000 services that are needed to perform the function that the system was designed to accomplish and that are used for managing the system. Any processes that are running consume CPU resources (and others); this is unneeded overhead that slows down your entire system. Another reason it is important to follow this approach is that many security-related problems occur because of the fact that a service or application that you do not need has been installed (if it was installed by default, you may not even have known it was installed) that creates a security breach that can be exploited.

Some commonly overlooked services and applications that can be shut down to lower overhead placed on your CPU resources are

- Remove exotic screen savers such as 3D pipes (or any 3GL screen savers) running on any servers. They consume precious system resources and look awful when the server begins to slow down. Consider locking the console or logging out and turning off the monitor.
- Stop license logging (these check to see if customer licenses for applications are current) if the system does not require this service.
- Stop the print spooler. Unless the system is used as a spooler, turn this off.
- Stop IIs and indexing services if they are not needed.
- Stop simple TCP/IP services (few applications use these services anymore, and they can easily be exploited for a denial-of-service attack).
- If you have installed a copy of Microsoft Office 97/2000, ensure that the FindFast.exe program is not configured to start by default.

SEARCH FOR WASTEFUL HARDWARE COMPONENTS

For enterprise servers, do not be surprised if Processor: % Interrupt Time is around 5–20% of the total CPU workload, particularly if the network and disk I/O are very heavy. There are, however, some components that behave better than others. Attempt to obtain NICs that truly support bus mastering and disk host bus adapters that support DMA transfers vs. PIO. Some disk and network adapters operate more efficiently than others, thus requiring fewer CPU cycles to operate. Trade magazines provide numerous comparisons of these products. One good source of information is the *Windows 2000 Magazine* web site located at: http:\\www.ntmag.com.

DO NOT IMPLEMENT COMPRESSION

Compression is nice for notebooks and some workstations, but it has little applicability for server class systems. Actively using compression on your system will increase your CPU overhead and slow your disk operations. If you must use compression, relegate its use to drives that are not accessed frequently and that are used for archiving only.

OFF-LOAD CPU-INTENSIVE OPERATIONS

RAID CALCULATIONS • Whenever possible, off-load CPU operations to secondary devices. Windows 2000 allows the native use of software-based RAID 5 implementations. RAID 5 requires constant parity computation every time data is written to a RAID 5 array. Off-load this by using a RAID controller with its own CPU for RAID calculations. This frees up CPU cycles for the application instead of wasting them on every disk write activity. Chapter 7 reviews RAID technologies and examines performance issues in depth.

TCP CHECKSUM OFF-LOADING TO THE NIC • As network packets arrive to a Windows 2000 system, a parity calculation is completed to ensure that the packet's contents have been correctly sent. If they have not been sent correctly—e.g., if they lost a bit or two on the way—a request is made for a retransmission. A combination of Windows 2000 advanced off-loading features in the new TCP/IP stack and new NICs with updated drivers now enables you to off-load this CPU intensive calculation to the NIC itself. This is normally set under Start / Settings / Network and Dial Up Connections / Local Area Connections / Configure / Advanced, and then enabling the NIC for checksum calculation off-load. Each NIC is slightly different, so the final wording may not be exact for these steps.

SECURITY AUDITING EQUALS CPU OVERHEAD

Security is important. When increased security levels are required, Windows 2000 auditing is activated (utilizing auditing for tuning is covered in chapter 2) and a certain level of overhead is introduced onto the system. The amount of overhead introduced is a function of the required level of auditing. The CPU is the system resource that shoulders most of the overhead associated with increased auditing. If auditing is required, do not turn it off. However, be aware that more CPU horsepower may be required to compensate for the increased security to provide the same level of performance experienced without auditing activated. This is a hidden cost to achieve improved security for a system.

ENCRYPTION EQUALS SIGNIFICANT CPU OVERHEAD

Security is important—many of my new customers are security conscious. Windows 2000 now has native file encryption available for use when increased security levels are required—an excellent feature if you have important data that must be kept confidential. However, it takes CPU resources to encrypt those files, memory resources to support the CPU, and slightly larger files to be stored in the disk subsystem. How much more CPU overhead is required? See chapter 4 for a detailed examination of these issues.

REMOVE FAULTY HARDWARE COMPONENTS

When a hardware device, such as a network interface card, interrupts the processor, the Windows 2000 system's Interrupt Handler will execute to handle the condition, usually by signaling I/O completion and possibly issuing another pending I/O request. Observe the Sysmon counter Processor: Interrupts/sec. If this number begins to grow compared to your baseline when under normal workload, there is a good possibility that a network device has become faulty. When a device becomes faulty, it may begin generating high numbers of interrupts, which inundate the CPU. This wastes precious CPU cycles. Removing the fault device will alleviate this situation.

SCHEDULE CPU-INTENSIVE JOBS DURING OFF-PEAK HOURS

This technique always seemed to be a bit of an easy-out strategy to alleviate CPU problems, but it is effective and uses resources that may have otherwise been idle. To schedule a job to run during off-peak hours, use the at command from the command prompt. To get directions on how to use the at command, type *at /? | more* at the command prompt. Also available is the at command's GUI counterpart, Scheduled Tasks, which is found at Start / Settings / Control Panel / Scheduled Tasks. The use of the Scheduled Task tool with screen shots can be found in chapter 2.

Windows 2000 Service Packs

Enterprise operating systems are becoming more feature rich and complicated by the minute, and thus they are prone to bugs. Microsoft publishes bug fixes or patches as Service Packs and Hotfixes. Stay abreast of these Service Packs because they commonly fix various functional problems and occasionally offer performance improvements. As with any new software, test it before it finds its way into a production environment. Don't become discouraged! This is a natural occurrence. I have never used an operating system that did *not* require periodic patches (UNIX Flavors, Linux, Microsoft).

Update Drivers for All Components and System BIOS

Using the latest drivers and system BIOS versions can yield much more efficient hardware systems. With improved efficiency, the CPU resource has less work to do, which yields more CPU cycles for productive work. Sometimes, with the new drivers, the devices are much faster too! Every hardware component in your system has a driver that should be updated on a regular basis after testing (plus drivers are normally free and can be obtained via the vendor's web site or support CD).

Upgrading the CPU(s)—The Last Resort

If the CPU is running at or near 100% for extended periods of time and none of the other system's resources are bottlenecks, then the system is running at its very best. You are getting an excellent return on investment (ROI)! If an even higher level of overall performance is required, it may be time to upgrade the CPU, the system components, or even the system itself.

Adding More CPU(s)—The Last Resort, Part 2

From a generic point of view, if Sysmon's System: Processor Queue Length in your environment is greater than two times the number of CPUs in your system for extended periods of time (5–10 minutes) or if you have multiple applications (processes) consuming high amounts of Processor: % User time, then your environment is a particularly good candidate for additional CPUs. The Windows 2000 family of operating systems currently supports up to 32 processors, although 1, 2, 4, and 8 CPU implementations are the most common Windows 2000 system implementations.

Sizing Rules of Thumb for Windows 2000 Systems

The following rules of thumb for sizing a Windows 2000 system, its associated subsystems, and subsequently key applications should be used before the total solution is configured. It is possible to provide a good sizing estimate by utilizing sound, logical sizing techniques. These are straightforward enough for any good information systems (IS) professional to apply them.

Follow this sound sizing methodology when developing a new Windows 2000 system:

1. Define objective(s).
2. Understand business and technical requirements needed to meet your objective.
3. Determine loading characteristics.
4. Determine performance requirements.
5. Understand future business requirements.
6. Understand future system architectures.
7. Configure the system.
8. Stress test to validate the system configuration.
9. Proactively follow the core tuning methodology during validations testing.
10. Deploy the system into production.
11. Proactively follow the core tuning methodology after the system is deployed.

Each of these steps influences both the type and amount of system hardware you will need to configure to meet your requirements for today and tomorrow. They are reviewed in detail in chapter 3 and used in chapter 8.

Historical information obtained from Windows 2000 or Windows NT systems running similar applications and experienced similar workloads is an excellent source of sizing information. In lieu of having historical information available, review the section on capacity sizing using industry standard benchmarks in chapter 3, which focuses on how to extrapolate from industry standard benchmarks when initially sizing your Windows 2000 system solution.

The following sections contain some specific Windows 2000 system sizing concerns that I commonly encounter.

Sizing Disk Subsystems

The primary areas to consider when sizing the disk subsystems are performance, capacity, and availability. Consider each of these factors jointly when configuring your I/O subsystem.

Disk Subsystem Performance

There are two facets to consider when sizing the disk subsystem. The first is how much data the disk subsystem can provide, which is dependent on how much throughput (MBytes/sec) it can support. The second is how fast the disk subsystem can respond to disk subsystem requests, which is based on how much workload the disk subsystem can support (Transfers/sec).

Disk drives from the same vendor's disk family, regardless of the disk capacity, provide similar levels of performance for both throughput and workload supported. For example, a single 9GB disk drive provides more disk capacity than a 4GB disk drive, but it does not provide significantly more throughput or workload performance.

Understanding the workload characteristics supported by your system greatly influences how to size the disk subsystem to meet your requirements. If we take the most common workload environment—a combination of random read and write operations in a multiuser environment—we can follow these basic rules of thumb when sizing the disk subsystem based on a single 10,000-rpm Ultra2 SCSI hard drive:

- Throughput: 1.11MB/sec per disk drive in a RAID 5 array
- Workload: 100 Transfers/sec per disk drive in a RAID 5 array

Sizing the throughput needed for a file server is relatively straightforward. If on average, you expect the number of concurrent users to be 60, with each person working with a 400KB file and a desired 2-second response time, you would use the following equation:

Throughput Needed = Number of concurrent users (60) × Size of average records (0.4MB) divided by Response Time (2 sec).

For this environment, a system that provides 12MB/sec (96Mbits/sec) is needed to meet the requirements. Since we know that a single disk drive in a RAID 5 array provides on average 1.11MB/sec in a random read-intensive environment, we would require:

Throughput required (12MB/sec) / Throughput per disk drive (1.11MB/sec/disk)

which works out to 10.8 disks, which you always round up to the next integer. Thus, to achieve 12MB/sec of continuous throughput, you need 11 disk drives. (This assumes physical disk performance only and does not include the file cache.)

Sizing the workload required is slightly more complicated because you must take into consideration the RAID technology in use. Details are provided on determining the workload for each major RAID level in chapter 6, but for now we will use RAID 5 since it is so common. For example, assume you needed to size a disk subsystem to support 300 physical disk subsystem database transactions/sec, where 60% of the transactions were read-intensive while the other 40% were write-intensive. Each disk in a RAID 5 array can support approximately 100 I/Os/sec in a random read/write environment; thus 3 disk drives could support the projected workload. However, remember that, for a RAID 5 array, you must calculate the write operation's overhead too. So the Transfers/sec that must really be supported are

(300 disk read Transfers/sec × 0.6) + [4 × (300 disk write Transfers/sec × 0.4))] × (1.25 utilization factor/100 Transfers/sec/disk)

which works out to approximately 8.2 disk drives, which you always round up to the next nearest integer to make 9. Here the utilization factor of 1.25, or 125%, is added to ensure that disk operations can be sustained at an 80% utilization rate. Each disk drive can support a random read/write workload of 100 transfers/sec, but the best response time is provided if they run at 80% of their maximum workload rate. For more detailed information on these disk concepts and equations, review chapter 6.

Disk Subsystem Storage Capacity

Now that you have determined the performance requirements to meet your needs, let's determine the size of the disk drives you'll need. Remember that the fastest portion of a disk drive is on the outer edge of the disk drive and that defragmentation tools require at least 20–25% free space to operate effectively. Taking this information into account along with the performance requirements we determined above, to determine the storage capacity of the disk drives, use the following formula:

(Storage Capacity needed × 1.33)/Number of Disk Drives needed to meet performance requirement

Why the factor of 1.33? This takes into account that we want to use only 75% of the available disk storage space. If, in our example, we needed to support at least 140GB of data, we would need [(140GB % 1.33)]/11 disk drives (from above example) which would need a 16.9GB disk drive, which is rounded up to an 18GB standard disk drive size.

Disk Subsystem Availability

If disk subsystem availability is important, consider only those RAID levels that provide redundancy—these are RAID 5, RAID 1, and RAID 10. Each RAID level incurs some level of storage overhead when implemented. For our example, if we used eleven 18GB drives in a single RAID 5 array, we would have 180GB (not 198GB) of usable storage, since the storage equivalent of one disk drive is lost to RAID 5 parity overhead. Remember our goal in the previous section on disk subsystem storage capacity was to ensure that no more than 75% of our disk storage was in use. Since we plan to require 140GB and have 180GB available, this works out to approximately 77% storage usage. This is a little more than what we had planned, but it is still acceptable. If we observe any performance slowdowns, we can easily add additional disks.

SCSI Bus Implementation

When considering how to configure your SCSI buses, review the various SCSI bus characteristics (see Table 1.10). Avoid configuring fast SCSI devices (disk drives) on the same SCSI bus as slow devices (tapes, CD-ROMs); this can potentially slow down access to your faster devices if all devices are active on the bus at the same time.

TABLE 1.10	*SCSI Bus Characteristics*	
Technology	**Theoretical Transfer Speed MB/sec**	**Realistic Transfer Speed (Estimated Real-World Performance) MB/sec**
Wide Ultra2 Fast SCSI	80	72
Ultra Wide Fast SCSI	40	32
Fast/Wide SCSI-2	20	16

Determining the Number of Disk Drives per SCSI Bus

The number of disk devices (disk drives or arrays) to configure per SCSI bus is a function of your environment. To determine the throughput of your disk devices, there are two primary options. First, you could use various third-party testing tools outlined in chapter 2. Second, you could use Sysmon. To use Sysmon when determining the throughput of each disk device, explore Sysmon's logical disk objects: bytes/sec. Then use the estimated SCSI real-world transfer speed given in Table 1.10 when configuring the number of disk drives per SCSI bus. For example, if you notice that each of your disk devices is providing 4MB/sec and you have four devices, your SCSI channel must support at least 16MB/sec. If these four disk devices are connected to a Fast/Wide SCSI-2 bus, which we can see from Table 1.10 will support 16MB/sec, configure any additional disk devices on a second SCSI bus.

If you do not have any historical data for your environment, when configuring the number of disk drives per SCSI bus a good rule of thumb is to estimate that each disk drive will provide 1–2MB/sec of data throughput. Remember that the throughput actually achieved is highly dependent on client load, effectiveness of the file system cache, application design, disk adapter model, and disk drive model.

Sizing the CPU(s)

The primary object when sizing the model and number of CPUs is directly related to the type of workload in the projected environment. The rule of thumb here is to configure the fastest CPU that is economically feasible and is supported by the application you wish to run. Business requirements and required resources to support Windows 2000–based applications are increasing constantly. Starting with the fastest possible CPU and a server architecture that can support multiple CPUs provides better long-term investment protection.

A Windows 2000 system is a multiprocess- and multithread-enabled operating system—without any real applications running under Windows 2000, there are multiple active processes and threads. Thus, additional CPUs are normally helpful to a degree. Consider your Windows 2000 system to be a candidate for a multiple CPU configuration if the following are relevant for your environment:

- More than one major application is running at a time.
- The application is multithreaded and was designed for a symmetric multiprocessing (SMP) environment.
- Utilizing the tuning methodology, you have determined that the server is CPU bound and the Server Work Queues: Queue Length is greater than two times the number of CPUs in the server.

Configure enough CPU resources to drive all of the server's applications and resources. With such a large Windows NT installed–based system available today, historical information is more abundant than it was just a few years ago. Using a combination of historical information and knowledge of what you plan to run on your server, construct a CPU sizing table similar to the one in Table 1.11 to assist in sizing the CPU subsystem. Table 1.11 shows an expected breakout of CPU usage based on the historical information available. In this example, we have determine the key applications running on the server and estimate overall CPU usage based on historical information. Now we have a starting point from which to build our system. For a reality check, remember that the physical server components rely on CPU resources to operate. If you upgrade from a 100BaseTX NIC to a 1000BaseTX NIC, expect to need more CPU resources to drive it! Always strive for a balanced system design.

Our reference here is a Pentium III 700MHz CPU. You may have a different reference. How do they relate? Refer to chapter 4's CPU discussion, or, for a quick reference, use Table 1.12 as a general reference.

TABLE 1.11	Initial CPU Sizing Example

Application	CPU Usage (Estimate) Based on Four Pentium III 700MHz CPUs w/2MB Level 2 Cache
Windows 2000 and SQL server, network operations	55% usage per CPU, CPU Queue of 2 (estimated)
Overhead for system management software running on server	1% (estimated)
Overhead for intrusion detection software	1% (estimated)
Overhead for replication software	10% (estimated)
Total estimated CPU usage	**62% per CPU**

TABLE 1.12	Relative CPU Performance (Server Consolidation Mapping) and Recommended RAM Requirements

CPU Class	Equivalent CPU Class	Minimum RAM (per CPU)
1 Pentium	2 80486s	16MB
1 Pentium II	2 Pentiums	32MB
1 Pentium Pro	2 Pentium IIs	128MB
1 Pentium III	2 Pentium Pros	256MB

Sizing Network I/O Subsystems

A Windows 2000 system requires good network performance because the network is the primary means used by clients to request services. This topic is reviewed in more depth in chapter 7.

Network Selection

A common misconception when configuring the network I/O subsystem is a misunderstanding of the actual throughput that the network can provide and the network characteristics needed to meet the requirements. Table 1.13 summarizes common network information.

Note that there are two key pieces of information presented in Table 1.13 to consider when configuring the server's network I/O. First, the theoretical throughputs of all of the various networks are typically referred to in bits/sec, *not* bytes/sec. Mixing up bits/sec and bytes/sec is surprisingly common.

TABLE 1.13	Relative Performance Provided Based on Network Technology in Use		
LAN Network Technology	**Throughput Megabits/sec**	**Throughput MB/sec**	**Topology-Media Access (Protocol Characteristics)**
Ethernet (10BaseT)	10	1.25	CSMA/CD
FDDI	100	12.5	Token passing
Ethernet (100BaseT)	100	12.5	CSMA/CD
Ethernet (100BaseT)	1000	125	CSMA/CD

When determining the aggregate network requirements of the clients the server is supporting, always keep this in mind.

Second, consider the topology-media access method of each network type. Each network type displays different response time characteristics under higher utilization levels. In a shared Ethernet environment, as the average network utilization increases above 20%, a Network General Expert Sniffer will generate an event that the network usage is becoming a potential bottleneck. The percentage utilization at which Ethernet performance degrades depends on your environment and the published reference you use. When Ethernet utilization rises above the 50–70% range, response times increase dramatically due to the associated network congestion. Higher utilization levels in the range of 60–80% are acceptable in switched-based Ethernet environments, but are highly dependent on the network architecture in place.

The Number of Clients per Shared Network Segment

A simplified rule of thumb for determining the number of clients to connect per network segment is: determine the worst-case acceptable throughput for each network client and then divide that amount into the selected network throughput. For example, if each client should have no less than 1.5Mbits/sec of available bandwidth and the network supports 100Mbits/sec, the segment could possibly support 66 clients. Unfortunately this simple calculation does not take into account the network media characteristics, but it does provide for a good starting point for the maximum amount of clients per network segment.

Server Network Interface Card Selections

The type and number of network cards is obviously dependent on the network architecture in which the server will be deployed. As before, there are two techniques we can use to obtain the information we need to determine the amount of network bandwidth required by the server.

First, if historical performance information is not available, survey your environment to determine required bandwidth and the subsequent number of NICs. If we know that the disk subsystem must be able to sustain 12MB/sec, then the network subsystem will also need to support this level of performance to get the data out to the clients (follow the data!); 12MB/sec translates to 96Mbits/sec of network subsystem performance. A full-duplex 100BaseTX environment should support this level of workload, but it will be close. To support this level of network subsystem performance, it would be time to consider upgrading to Gigabit Ethernet or trunking multiple 100BaseTX NICs together.

The second method for determining the bandwidth that the system must support is to review the Sysmon Network Interface: Bytes Total/sec for clients in their current environment. Summing the bytes/sec average values for the total number of clients you have can provide you with a network sizing reference point.

Sizing Memory Requirements

Vendors try their best to provide realistic information on memory requirements for systems that run their software applications. Unfortunately they are trying to sell a product as well; thus their estimates for system resources tend to be on the skinny side to say the least. But for a starting point, make sure that you take the following into consideration:

- All the applications running on the server
- Windows 2000 system's requirement
- Windows 2000 file system cache
- The number of concurrent users supported by the system
- The amount of system resources configured (CPU, disk, network, etc.)

To determine a good starting point for figuring memory size, use a combination of vendor information, historical information, and knowledge of what you plan to run on your system and construct a memory sizing table similar to Table 1.14 to assist in sizing the memory subsystem. In the example in Table 1.14, we are implementing a high-powered database server for 300 *concurrent* users.

Summing the metrics together suggests a starting memory size for the server of ~1.75GB.

For an alternative technique to size a system's memory, check out the Server Memory Assessment Engine online tool from Kingston Technology at http:\\www.kingston.com\servermap\. This online tool walks you through a questionnaire with a goal of making a memory sizing recommendation at the

TABLE 1.14 *Sizing the Memory Subsystem*	
Application	**Memory Usage (Working Set)**
Windows 2000 operating system requirement	128MB
Windows 2000 file system cache (maximum for configurations less than 1GB in size)	432MB
Overhead for system management software running on server	8MB
Overhead for intrusion detection software	12MB
Replication application	20MB
SQL server executables and cache	1,024MB
Each concurrent connection to SQL server (0.125MB × 300 customers)	38MB
Total estimated memory usage	**1.6GB**

end. It is a helpful tool for a second or third opinion, but keep in mind that Kingston is a company that specializes in selling RAM. Do not be surprised if the results are on the high side. Review chapter 3 and chapter 8's step-by-step solution scenarios for techniques to help you determine whether your system configuration will really meet your objectives.

At a minimum, regardless of the application environment, consider the CPU/memory ratios in Table 1.15 when configuring your server's memory. This will help to ensure that the CPUs are kept properly fed with data.

TABLE 1.15 *Recommended Memory-CPU Sizing Relationships*	
Number of Pentium III CPUs	**Minimum Amount of RAM (MB)**
1	256
2	512
4	1,024 (1GB)
8	2,048 (2GB)

Implementing Server Memory

When obtaining memory for your systems, make every effort to purchase the highest density, highest speed (megahertz [MHz]), and fastest memory (the lowest times are the best) available that still provide memory interleaving. Obtaining higher-density memory provides a better utilization of available memory slots for future memory expansion. Of course, if you think that the amount of RAM required by operating systems and software applications will actually decrease in the future, skip the previous rule of thumb.

Sizing and Tuning Specific Windows 2000—Based Implementations

The key to any sizing or tuning effort is understanding the types of workloads involved. Once you begin to understand the workloads involved and develop a system baseline, half the battle is already won. Never underestimate the power of an expert for a particular functional area. For example, to improve database server performance, contact or hire an expert for the database in use. Large performance gains are possible by tuning the database design, the actual queries, and the applications running on the database.

For a quick listing of the key performance tuning options for file servers, backup servers, database servers (SQL server), messaging servers (Exchange), and web servers (IIS 5), visit chapter 8. At the end of each section, there is a summary of tunables customized for that specific environment.

Summary

In this chapter, we reviewed tuning and sizing Windows 2000 systems from the perspective of immediate actions that can be completed to improve the overall performance of your Windows 2000–based system solution. While not all encompassing, this chapter provides a reference to the concepts and methodologies presented throughout the other chapters of this book. You may already be familiar with some of these tuning suggestions, while others may be new. The tuning tips and rules of thumb are explored in more depth in the subsequent chapters. This may lead you to reconsider some of the most common tuning tactics while introducing you to new tactics you may not have considered.

Tuning Strategies and Measurement Gathering

CHAPTER OBJECTIVES

- Introduction........ *54*
- Setting Goals for Tuning Windows 2000–Based Systems........ *54*
- The Big Picture: Understanding the Entire Architecture........ *55*
- Tuning Strategy........ *58*
- Practical Guidelines........ *58*
- Tuning Methodology........ *59*
- Achieving a Nirvanic State........ *60*
- Focusing Your Tuning Efforts........ *62*
- The Tuning Process........ *63*
- Performance Baselines........ *65*
- Customizing the CPWMM Scripts........ *83*
- Performance Management........ *96*
- Third-Party Performance Management Tools........ *96*
- Sysmon Operations........ *100*
- Using Auditing to Zero in on Resource Usage........ *116*
- Windows Task Manager........ *117*
- Additional Performance-Related Tools from Windows 2000........ *120*
- Windows 2000 Resource Kit Performance Management Tools........ *122*
- Freeware Performance Management Tools........ *123*
- Windows 2000 System Checkup........ *125*
- Putting It All Together: The Environment........ *128*

Introduction

In this chapter, we introduce and investigate the key tuning strategies that you can use to improve the performance of your Windows 2000–based solutions. In other words, we'll help you determine what is making your Windows 2000 system solution slow so you will know what, where, and how to make it faster! Once we have reviewed these strategies, we delve deeper into taking advantage of the numerous native measurement-gathering tools provided with Windows 2000. From the measurement tools perspective, we look closer at the tools included in Windows 2000, the Windows 2000 support tools, the Windows 2000 Resource Kit, and freeware available on the Internet, since these are what are commonly available to the professionals designing, implementing, and managing Windows 2000 solutions. Using a combination of these tools, there are several scripts provided to assist in monitoring, tracking, and diagnosing performance problems. We also list numerous commercial products that are available for performance management. At a minimum, you can use the commercial tools you select for a period of time before purchasing, so you can take them out for a test drive and see if they are applicable in your unique environment. The tuning strategies and measurement-gathering techniques reviewed in this chapter are not just theory based; they were developed and fine-tuned from real-world production environments and are also used throughout this book.

Setting Goals for Tuning Windows 2000—Based Systems

The Windows family of operating systems has moved quickly from providing workgroup class services to full-blown enterprise class services. The Windows 2000 operating system family was designed as a self-tuning, easily administered operating environment. From an operating-system-only perspective, this is commonly true. Although the operating system is the heart of any server solution, the key word here is *solution*. Windows 2000's ability to deliver is influenced by selection and sizing of the server hardware, drivers for the hardware, applications, and workload, as well as by how it is configured and administered and, of course, how well it is tuned! When you add all of these pieces together into an integrated server solution, the ability to apply experienced engineering comes into action.

Many of Windows 2000's system parameters are dynamically set, either while the system is running or during the boot process, based on the server resources available and the manner in which it is tuned. In achieving this dynamic configuration goal, Windows 2000 has succeeded in apparently removing many traditional administrative requirements, but it also obscures many tunables in the process. This is a tremendous benefit offered by Windows 2000 to novice- and intermediate-level technologists when compared to many other operating systems available today. With Windows 2000 technology, it is a little easier to implement a server solution. However, if you are reading this book, you do not want an out-of-the-box server solution! You want your integrated server solutions running at their very best!

There are numerous reasons why you may want to tune your Windows 2000–based solution. They include but are not limited to:

- Lowering the number of times you are called in to fix a slow system
- Improving the performance of services provided to your customers (improving their productivity!)
- Maximizing your return on investment (delaying the necessity of purchasing additional equipment)
- Getting more work done with less resources
- Efficiently using server hardware resources
- Managing system loads and resources
- Troubleshooting performance problems
- Obtaining capacity sizing and planning data for the future expansion of existing systems
- Removing bottlenecks that may limit the system's scalability
- Understanding how to develop future Windows 2000–based solution architectures

In short, the goal of tuning any Windows 2000 system is to understand the current environment well enough to plan for the future and to remove any current or potential system bottlenecks that may be throttling its overall performance!

By tuning and sizing your Windows 2000 systems, you ensure they are performing and scaling to the absolute highest levels possible. You might even have happier customers (although they will always want more) and spend less time providing support and more time learning, thereby enhancing your career.

The Big Picture: Understanding the Entire Architecture

There are two key concepts to keep in mind when considering the delivery of server services to a client: *client perception* of the delivery of server services and *following the data path through the architecture* used to deliver these server services. We will refer to both of these concepts throughout this book when developing solutions and tracking down performance problems. The concept of client perception—or how the end user perceives the performance of a server—is very important. End users do not care what is contributing to poor performance—they want to have as fast a response time as possible, to always be able to get to the application over the network, and to always have the computer work. Thus the performance of a server is ultimately dictated and judged by the clients' perceptions as they sit down at their workstations and try to complete their business requirements.

The second concept—to follow the data path through the architecture or to follow the data to deliver server services is very important when developing or troubleshooting your Windows 2000 solutions. I equate *follow the data* with *follow the money*—when you follow the money trail in business, you always find the decision maker or, in detective films, the crook who stole the money. When considering how your server services are being delivered to an end user, review the entire data path—from the client, over the network, and through the internal operations of the server providing the services as well as other servers that are being relied upon by the server providing services. Obviously investigating every facet of information systems architecture is beyond the scope of one nominally thick book, but we need, at a minimum, to point out key areas in the data path that can influence a client's perception. You would be amazed how many solutions are improved when you simply follow the data through your architecture. The key areas that can influence how well a server solution appears to be performing include:

- Client application performance
- Client workstation performance (specifically video performance and available RAM)
- Network connectivity to the workstation
- Type of network protocol in use
- Number of network devices between the client workstation and the server(s)
- Type of network devices between the client workstation and the server(s)
- Placement of Windows 2000 resources (catalog servers, domain controllers, DNS, etc.) and other resources the client and servers rely on
- Server application configuration
- Server operating system configuration
- Server hardware configuration
- Method of application communication between client application and server application (middleware/transaction monitor)
- Database design
- Database engine configuration
- Database query design

- Information technology security systems in place
- Overall server performance

So, what areas can you tune? There are a number of areas of a Windows 2000 system solution that you can tune. The benefits you obtain from your efforts depend greatly on what you decide to tune and when you decide to tune. When considering what to tune, remember to follow the data from your customer's perspective and track all dependencies that may influence the delivery of services. For example, a customer might start a workstation, log on to the network, and launch an application. That application may then call two different Windows 2000 systems over two different networks, which in turn may call other systems that they depend on. The following is a list of typical server areas you should consider tuning and the performance gains you might expect to obtain from your tuning efforts, followed by a performance improvement factor.

- Workstation hardware selection and configuration (20x)
- Workstation client application (10x)
- Overall server configuration (100x)
- Appropriate selection of server hardware for workload (100x)
- Server settings (30x)
- Server disk input/output (I/O) layout (50x)
- Server network subsystem (25x)
- Server application (30x)
- Windows 2000 kernel (registry) tuning (10x)
- Database configuration (50x)
- Database query tuning (50x)

These performance improvements represent the relative performance improvements compared to the other tunable areas; in some cases, overall performance may actually improve by the factor indicated. Do some of these factors appear high or low? They might. If your solution is already well designed and integrated, expect the factors to be high. However, if you inherited an intricate conglomeration that was built based on political or budgetary whims, expect these performance factors to be very low and expect even better gains. Of the tunable areas listed above, we will focus on overall server configuration, CPU, memory, network and disk subsystem layout, Windows 2000 server configuration and settings, network design, and Windows 2000 kernel (registry settings) tuning. Additionally, we will analyze some server applications (Microsoft IIs, Exchange, File Server, SQL Server, and Backup servers) and hardware technology in conjunction with the above-mentioned areas. We will investigate not just the *what* to tune, but the *how* and *why* so that you can make intelligent decisions. There will be particular emphasis on understanding how Windows 2000 internal operations, server hardware architectures, workloads, and network technology operate, as these are critical factors that influence the overall performance of your solution.

Tuning Strategy

There are two laws of tuning that always seem to pop up:

1. The law of trade-offs
2. The law of diminishing returns

For example, change the system settings for the Windows 2000 cache to favor the file system buffers, and application performance may suffer, and vice versa—there is always some type of trade-off. (The Windows 2000 server's file system cache is investigated in depth in chapter 5.) Consequently, there is only so much tuning that can be done until you reach a point where the additional performance gain is too time consuming and not worth additional effort. Typically, the start of the tuning process is where the greatest gains are achieved.

Tuning techniques can be viewed as *performance engineering*, which sounds very scientific. But tuning and sizing can be real challenges because they are not completely scientific; computer performance is part art and part science. Why? There are two primary aspects of computer performance that are in a constant state of flux: people and technology. People, or the clients your servers are supporting, can and do change the way they do business, especially when the demands placed on their business change. Technology is constantly changing as well. What you implement today may become outdated tomorrow. Thus, at some point you have to understand the future business needs and technology on the horizon and then implement your architecture taking these factors into consideration. Once you understand the concepts for tuning and sizing presented in this book, you can use them continuously even as business needs and technology change.

Even though the environment around the server may be constantly changing, you can still take a scientific approach. When developing a tuning strategy or methodology, think about why you might tune a system. Remember, your goal is to ensure that your server is performing at the highest performance level possible and that it is providing excellent services to your end user.

Practical Guidelines

Our focus here is on practical, real-world techniques. In a university environment, people develop elaborate methodologies that can take a fairly long time to implement; thus they spend vast quantities of time squeezing every last gram of performance out of each system resource. While this may be germane to a university environment, in the business world, we need to implement solutions intelligently (following all the processes for introducing solutions into a production environment) and quickly (do not move slowly; your competitor won't). This does not imply that long-term analysis is not helpful, but you must be realistic.

Hardware is relatively inexpensive when compared to the total cost of ownership items such as downtime that affects productivity and staffing costs. Therefore, keeping a server reasonably well tuned will provide excellent return on investment. The better the system runs, the less time it requires in the long term from the support teams. Since technology changes rapidly and client requirements and expectations often increase, the information gained from working with your current Windows 2000 and Windows NT systems is indispensable. We are fortunate that Windows NT–based solutions (upon which Windows 2000 is based) are more prevalent today than they were several years ago (Windows NT was the new kid on the block!). This offers us the opportunity to use current Windows-based systems to collect quantifiable information for tuning and sizing. This tuning and sizing information greatly aids in sizing additional server resources, configuring your next server solution, or even influencing the next overall information systems architecture that is put into place. It would be a crime not to use our lessons learned and historical and real-time data to your advantage!

Tuning Methodology

Spending your time making one resource of your Windows 2000 system fly is worthless if another resource of your system is causing the actual bottleneck(s). Never forget this! It's important enough to repeat: never forget this concept! A bottleneck is any system resource that limits the other system resources from running at their peak. System resources include processors (CPUs), disk subsystem (disk), memory (mem), network subsystem (net), the Windows 2000 operating system, and applications.

Having realistic expectations when tuning a system helps to keep you sane. Many resources can be sized and tuned, such as the disk I/O layout or file system cache strategies under Windows 2000. Other aspects may be out of your immediate control, such as the algorithm used for scheduling by the Windows 2000 operating system itself, applications for which you do not have access to the source code, or applications that do not allow internal resource configuration adjustments.

Focus your efforts in areas where you can make the greatest gain with the least amount of effort. Consider the performance resource chart (PRC) in Figure 2-1.

Tuning Goal: Ensure your system is performing and scaling to the absolute highest levels possible.

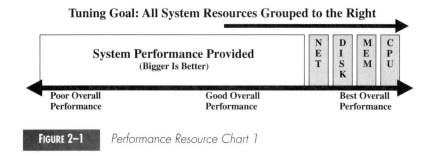

FIGURE 2-1 *Performance Resource Chart 1*

How to achieve this goal: Ensure that all system resources are grouped to the right as this enables the maximum amount of system performance to be provided.

As stated earlier, the ultimate goal when tuning a system to run at its absolute best is to have every system resource running at its optimal level such that it is not a significant limiting factor for any other resource. This means getting all of the system resources to the far right-hand side of PRC as shown in Figure 2-1 and having well-designed applications that can take advantage of your system resources. A perfectly tuned system would have each resource side by side, grouped at the right-hand side of the chart, indicating that each resource is running at its optimal level. This yields the best performance that the system can provide, as shown in the large gray area labeled "System Performance Provided." When this occurs and you require even more performance, it is time for additional resources or a new solution.

Achieving a Nirvanic State

How do you achieve this optimized state outlined above? It sounds wonderful from a strategy perspective, but, from an implementation perspective, what is the optimized state for each system resource? Optimally, when all resources are congregated at the right-hand side of Figure 2-1, you have achieved a well-tuned system, based on the resources available. Just as a reality check, you must have resources in your system if you wish to tune it. For example, a person once contacted me about tuning a system with 32MB of RAM and a Pentium 100 and was wondering why NT Workstation was running slowly. After looking at the system, I could see that it was running as well as it could; all resources were congregated to the right side of the PRC. There does come a time to upgrade.

In general, what state are you trying to achieve for each resource? General concepts and guidelines of what state to strive for when tuning each of the major system resources are listed in Table 2.1. Later in this chapter, we review how to measure each resource, and in subsequent chapters we will cover the hows and whys behind optimizing the system architecture and operating system for achieving the nirvanic state of each resource.

TABLE 2.1	*Conceptual Nirvanic State for Key Server Resources*
System Resource	**Nirvanic State to Achieve**
CPU Resource(s) Usage More details in chapter 4	There are no CPU queues (no one is waiting for CPU resources). The CPU is caching a lion's share of its operations in its Level 1, 2, or 3 high-speed cache or main memory. The CPU is not waiting for any other resource in order to complete its tasks. CPU cycles are focused on providing service to the application, not the server hardware. Applications can take advantage of the CPU resources available by using multiple threads, processes, etc. (example: 32 CPUs). The CPU is operating without errors.
Memory Resource Usage More details in chapter 5	Ensure there is sufficient main memory to hold the working sets of all applications and the Windows 2000 operating system; e.g., there are ample physical RAM resources to meet all memory requests. Sufficient memory is available to cache all disk and network requests, which helps keep the CPU(s) fed. Sufficient memory is available such that that Windows 2000 does not need to rely on virtual memory (paging) to the disk subsystem on a regular basis to fulfill resource requests. Applications that can take advantage of the memory resources available (example: if 512MB of RAM is available, the application can leverage/be configured and controlled by the administrator to take advantage of the amount of memory you desire). Memory (RAM) is operating without errors.
Disk Resource(s) Usage More details in chapter 6	There is sufficient memory that disk performance does not negatively influence end user response time. There are no disk queues (no other resources are waiting for disk operations to complete). When disk use is required: • There is sufficient disk capacity to store all required information. • There is sufficient disk performance that response time from disk requests is acceptable. • There is sufficient disk performance that disk queues do not form. The disk subsystem is efficient enough not to require a high amount of CPU cycles to operate. This disk subsystem is operating without errors.

TABLE 2.1	Conceptual Nirvanic State for Key Server Resources (Continued)
System Resource	**Nirvanic State to Achieve**
Network Resource Usage More details in chapter 7	There are no queues forming when using network resources.
	There is sufficient network bandwidth that bandwidth is not a limiting factor when passing data.
	The network subsystem is efficient enough not to require a high amount of CPU cycles to operate.
	There are no network-related errors from physical hardware or packet collisions on the network.
Application Resource Usage More details in chapter 8	The application is designed well to take advantage of Windows 2000 performance enhancement features such as Job objects, multiple CPUs, large memory, etc.
	The application is designed to take advantage of modern server and network architectures in place, such as simultaneously using multiple CPUs, grouping its I/O operations before requesting disk subsystem operations, etc.
	The application provides enablers such that system administrators can control system resource usage; for example, how much memory the application will use, how many CPUs the application will run on, where log files will reside, etc.
	The application provides specific performance counters so that its health and performance can be monitored.

Focusing Your Tuning Efforts

PRC 1 in Figure 2-1 depicts a balanced, well-sized and well-tuned server. PRC 2 in Figure 2-2 shows an unbalanced system, where the network subsystem is the factor that limits the system in providing services. Look at this performance chart with a simplistic view.

FIGURE 2-2   Performance Resource Chart 2

If I were on this performance line walking from left to right, the farther I could push (tune) all of the system's resources to the right, the better the performance I could provide for the entire integrated server solution (shown in gray). Although these figures show the four primary system resources, the same PRC concept applies when tuning other system resources such as applications.

The Tuning Process

What approach should you take when tuning your Windows system? I've tried several approaches and have found the methodology defined in Table 2.2 to be effective time and time again.

TABLE 2.2	*The Core Tuning Methodology*

Step	Action
1	Always have a tested and validated backup of the system, files, and registry before making any changes.
2	Monitor your system and develop a baseline. *(Internal system resource usage and from customer perspective)*
3	Proactively monitor your system. *(Internal system resource usage and from customer perspective)*
4	Determine which resource is acting like or becoming a bottleneck. (If none, by following the data, look for factors outside of your system that are relied on.)
5	Try a single change at a time, when possible, and document all change(s) well.
6	Benchmark and test your system to determine if the change(s) is helpful and stable.
7	Return to step 3.

Always ensure that you have the appropriate files backed up and understand how to restore your system back to its original state in the unlikely event that the tuning change you have made doesn't quite work out like you had planned. It is alarming how many people have told me that their system is completely backed up, but, when I inquire if they have ever actually tried to test restoring their systems—either data files or registry hives—they give a blank stare.

Being proactive about monitoring your system is monumental if you ever want to tune it well and be successful. As you monitor your system over time, you will begin to have a better understanding for what is normally running on the system as well as its performance characteristics. These last two points are helpful for performance tuning and eventual sizing of either expansions to your current system or deployment of a new system or overall architecture.

Conceptual Walkthrough of the Core Tuning Methodology

Deciding which resource is the bottleneck determines where to spend your cycles. Recite this one in your mind a few times and never forget it! For example, look at the PRC back in Figure 2-2. Notice that the network resource is at the undesirable far left position of the chart. This should be the obvious area on which to focus your efforts. Perhaps you change from a switched Ethernet 100BaseT (100 megabits/second) environment to a 1,000Mbit/sec switched GB Ethernet environment. This change may shift the PRC outlook by moving the network resource to the middle of the chart, halfway between the disk subsystem and memory resources as shown in PRC 3 in Figure 2-3. This results in removing the network subsystem as the primary bottleneck and an associated increase in the overall server performance service provided.

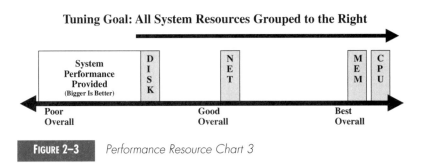

FIGURE 2–3   *Performance Resource Chart 3*

If, after continued proactive monitoring of the system, the system resources are still distributed roughly the same as shown in Figure 2-3, change the focus of your tuning efforts. Focusing any further effort on the network subsystem resource is not going yield any more gains! Do not waste your valuable time. Although it might be fun to play with that new trunked Gigabit Ethernet card system and associated switches, it will not improve the performance that the system is providing to your clients because the network is not the system resource throttling back your system's overall performance. As you improve one resource of your system, eventually another resource becomes the new bottleneck. Remember that all system resources are very closely interrelated.

If, after continued proactive monitoring of your system, you observe that the disk subsystem resource is now the cause of the new bottleneck, focus on removing it. Unfortunately, some people miss this. Do not fall into this trap of concentrating on improving the performance of the wrong system resource (even if it is fun to play with some new technology or work in an area you are familiar with). This warning is crucial to the tuning methodology and to sizing servers and getting servers to scale. Each of the major system resources is reviewed in depth in later chapters to help in identifying Windows 2000 system-related bottlenecks.

I have worked at locations where we determined that adding memory and tuning some applications would greatly improve the performance of the server, which it did. I returned a week later to find that even more RAM was added to speed things up since it worked before. However, it did not help this time. The customer was concerned that the system was not scaling. Was this true? No, because the memory resource was no longer the bottleneck! After following a solid tuning methodology, we discovered other bottlenecks and focused our attention on removing them. Other resources, which were not inhibiting overall system performance, were kept in check through proactive monitoring.

Performance Baselines

How do you determine how well a system is running? End users are typically not shy, to say the least, about expressing their opinions when their applications appear to be running slowly. Being flogged by an end user is something any information systems (IS) staff member would like to and can avoid. Following the core tuning methodology outlined in Table 2.2 can help you avoid having the end user as the primary mechanism for determining when performance problems are at hand.

If you know how your system is performing on a regular basis, you will know if the services it provides begin to suffer. If you do not know how your system performs under normal circumstances, how will you ever know if it is running poorly under a new or different load? Developing a performance baseline for your system is the first real step in assuring your system is running at its very best. A performance baseline provides quantifiable data that will tell you if your system is or is not providing services as intended. Once a solid performance baseline is developed, it becomes easier to determine if the end users are actually experiencing a system slowdown or if they are just having a bad day and have decided to share it with others. It also helps you to determine if your tuning techniques and efforts are effective.

Performance Baselines: Pre- and Postproduction Measurements

Develop your performance baseline *before* your system enters production and *after* it is in production. Why both? If you baseline your system before it enters production, you can determine if your solution will work under load and what the best possible performance can be in a controlled lab environment, not during production. Once you learn how well your system runs in the lab, this is the best it will operate unless you make a change to it. Now, once you enter production with your system, again baseline your system. By comparing the lab baseline with the production baseline, you can determine if there are other factors in your system that may be slowing down its delivery of services to your clients.

Developing Performance Baselines: Internal and Customer Perspective Baselines

When developing a performance baseline, you will want to baseline two areas:

- Internal resources and how well they are operating, such as what your system resource utilizations are.
- The performance of your system from your customer's perspective—customer perspective baselines determine how well your system is providing services to your clients.

In the section "Performance Statistics Gathering: Start the Logs" later in this chapter, we investigate using the tools native to Windows 2000 for monitoring and measuring the resource utilization of internal subsystems. For example, CPUs are running at 60% usage or disk usage is at 30%. However, your system must have a load placed on it for you to have something to measure or baseline.

How can you tell if that disk array you added is actually installed correctly and now improving your disk I/O performance? What about that new network interface card? It is easy to state that something is running much faster or slower, but it is more difficult to actually prove it by providing quantitative data. This can be an entertaining experience when someone who has run no baseline information or benchmarks makes bold statements on performance improvements! Just monitoring the internal subsystems' resource utilization does not provide the big-picture data to determine if a specific system has improved performance.

In an ideal world or in some larger environments, the common rule of thumb is to build an exact prototype that encompasses the applications, network architecture, clients, and servers; then test your solution before you place it into production by placing a controlled, repeatable workload against the solution—a benchmark. This technique ensures that the solution works and that it meets desired performance requirements.

Common tools to accomplish this level of testing are remote terminal emulators and remote workstation emulators. These tools can be set up to stress your prototype with increasing user loads, thus emulating the actual types of work that are indicative of your environment when your solution is placed into production. These tools help you to determine such information as response time for the end user and throughput of the system in use. I highly recommend that these types of tools be used for large rollouts. It is truly amazing what you will find and the experience you can gain prior to production. Once you test your configuration in a prototype or lab environment, you can determine how well your server and network architecture will perform before production. Thus, if in the production environment something seems slow, you can reuse these tools to determine if your solution is actually running slowly.

Commercial Tools for Baseline Development through Stress Testing (Benchmarking)

Some commercial software packages that are excellent for large-scale prototyping include the Neal Nelson Business Benchmark for NT/Windows 2000, available from Neal Nelson and Associates (312-755-1000, web address not available at this time); Dynameasure Enterprise, from Bluecurve (http://www.bluecurve.com); Load Runner, from Mercury Interactive (http://www.Mercury.com). The Neal Nelson and Bluecurve tools are used throughout this book for hands-on examples and case studies. These commercial testing tools can help you model your environment very closely to that which you plan to expect in production. Other general commercial benchmarks are explored in depth in chapter 3.

Freely Available Tools for Baseline Development through Stress Testing (Benchmarking)

Microsoft provides several free application-level stress testing tools that are available for download from their web site http://www.microsoft.com. These include LoadSim which stress tests messaging environments and WCAT which stress tests web server environments. Additional stress testing tools are available in the Windows 2000 server Resource Kit. The Windows 2000 server Resource Kit includes Media Load Simulator which generates clients' requests for streaming media and the Web Application Stress tool which simulates web-based workloads. Another friendly tool I find helpful for testing disk subsystems and network loads is Iometer from Intel (http://www.Intel.com). Iometer is used later in this book for several tests.

Not everyone has the time or budget to run elaborate tests using the commercial packages listed above to aid in developing a baseline. There are, however, more economical tests available to benchmark or check the pulse of your system to ensure it is performing the way it should. Even in a small environment, these economical baseline tests can be run. This example and subsequent examples throughout this book use tools from the Windows 2000 server and professional resource kits. These kits include invaluable information on the architecture of the Windows 2000 family of operating systems, troubleshooting hints, and helpful software tools. I strongly recommend anyone who actually performs any type of hands-on work with a Windows 2000 Server obtain these resource kits.

Performance Scripting Tools Provided in This Chapter

What if you wanted to complete some baseline or pulse testing, but had no budget for any new tools and what you needed was not available online? You are at the right place. Included in this chapter are several tools built with common scripting languages that you can use to baseline your Windows 2000 system and even measure the performance that file and web servers provide to your customers! The scripts presented in this chapter encompass

- **InternalDiskTest2.bat** This script measures the internal performance of moving files from one disk drive to another.
- **CustomerPerspectiveFileServicesModule.bat** This script creates a synthetic transaction (transferring a file across the network from one computer to another) and measures the performance of this transfer, similar to what a customer would experience if using a file server.
- **CustomerPulseTest2.bat and CustomerBaseLineCheck2.pl** These two scripts work in concert to automate the CustomerPerspective-FileServicesModule.bat script so that it can be automatically run over time to develop a baseline of file server throughput measurements.
- **CustomerWebMonitoringModuleScript.pl** This script is the base customer perspective monitor to determine how well a web site is responding to your customers. This script calls the poll.pl script to complete the actual http poll of the web site and calculates the response time. Based on this information, it logs the information into the Windows 2000 Event Log by calling Event.pl.
- **Poll.pl** This script is called by the CustomerWebMonitoringModuleScript.pl script and completes the actual work of generating a synthetic http transaction against the remote target web server to determine the response time needed to fetch the requested web page.
- **Event.pl** When called, this script writes event information into the Windows 2000 Event Log.
- **Optmod.pl** The optional module Optmod.pl is where the real proactive management occurs. If the time for the web page to be fetched exceeds your threshold, this script starts a tracert.exe to the remote web site to determine if there is a network-related problem at the TCP/IP layer and e-mails the administrator that there is a problem.

Internal Server Perspective Baseline Development through Pulse Testing

Before your system is placed into production, try the following simple test to determine how well your disk and memory subsystems are running. When creating this simple baseline, equate the running of these tests to that of a doctor taking your pulse while you are running on a treadmill. Thus, the running of stress tests or benchmarks is a form of *pulse testing*. The pulse test shown below is by no means a thorough benchmark to be used for system selection, but does provide a friendly framework of tests you can run to gain insight into how your internal subsystems are operating. The electronic copies of these scripts can be found via http://www.tuningandsizing.com. To prepare your systems to run this and subsequent scripts presented in this chapter, you must install two packages on your Windows 2000 system. First install the complete Windows 2000 server Resource Kit because several commands used in the scripts are not native to Windows 2000. Then install the Perl scripting language. The Windows 2000 server Resource Kit includes a copy of Perl that works, but I suggest downloading and installing the latest version from ActiveState at http://www.ActiveState.com. This is an easy package to install. If you take just the defaults, it will work like a champ! From here, the operation of the scripts below are self-explanatory. These are rapidly developed scripts. If after using them you improve them into eloquent works of art, send them to http://www.tuningandsizing.com where they will be tested and posted on the web for others to use.

Below is the InternalDiskTest.bat script. This script provides an easy mechanism to see how well Windows 2000 can create large files and how well the copy command can transfer files inside of your Windows 2000 system. When run, this simple script provides a measure of relative disk/memory subsystem performance of your system. When running this script, remember that the copy command is not a very efficient disk access application when compared to the Windows 2000 backup application or commercial backup applications that use their own version of the *copy* command.

EXAMPLE 2–1   *InternalDiskTest2.bat*

```
@echo off
REM # Turn off stdout echo
REM #####################################################
REM #
REM #   Copyright 2000, Curt Aubley
REM #
REM #   Script: InternalDiskTest2.bat
REM #           Simple file creation and file transfer script
REM #
REM #   Goal:   Take a system's pulse by creating and copying a file
REM #           between local disk drives
```

| **EXAMPLE 2-1** | *InternalDiskTest2.bat (continued)* |

```
REM #
REM #    Running Notes: Ensure that the creatfil.exe and timethis.exe commands
REM #    are in your path. If you wish to save your output to a file,
REM #    use the file creation Redirector ">" or file appending Redirector ">>"
REM #    Example: LocalDiskTest.bat > MyResults.txt
REM #    Script assumes c:\temp is on one disk drive and d:\temp is
REM #    on another disk drive
REM #
REM ############################################################

REM # Easy way to create a 50MB file (or any size you would like)
REM # creatfil.exe command from Windows 2000 Resource Kit
REM # Extra for experts: try the ntimer.exe command
REM # ntimer.exe provides some extra measurement options
REM # Clear screen to start
REM #

Cls

REM # Timing the actual file creation helps to test
REM # the write performance of the disk subsystem in use

echo Creating 50MB test file to test disk transfer time
echo on
timethis.exe "creatfil c:\temp\testfil2start.ded 50000"
@echo off

REM # Check size of File created
REM #
@Echo on
dir c:\temp\testfil2start.ded
@echo off

REM # copy file to locally connected disk
REM #
@echo on
timethis "copy c:\temp\testfil2start.ded d:\temp\testfil2end.ded"
@echo off

REM # Cleanup
REM #
del c:\temp\testfil2start.ded
del d:\temp\testfil2end.ded

REM ############
REM # End Script
REM ############
```

When run on a dual CPU Compaq DL-380, Pentium III 733MHz, 128MB, Ultra2 SCSI 10k rpm disk-based system, this test produced an elapsed time of 28.77 seconds to create a 50MB file (1.77Mbytes/sec) and a time of 36.1 seconds to copy a 50MB file between disks (1.38Mbytes/sec). When you think about these simple test results, they make sense. Creating a file is faster than if you read and then write a file (two operations). You can easily customize the basic parameters of size and number of iterations in Code Example 2-1 to make it more reflective of your environment. Note that small files will most likely be cached and will not measure physical disk performance. If you want a tougher test for your Windows 2000 system, edit the file creation section of the script in Code Example 2-1 that uses the *creathis.exe* command and set it to a value twice the size of your system's RAM. Just remember that this will drastically increase the time it takes to run your test.

Customer Perspective Baseline Development through Pulse Testing

Determining how well your system is providing services to your clients in a production environment is a difficult task since the mechanism to obtain these measurements is not native to Windows 2000 (or any other operating system, for that matter). The internal system baseline test in the preceding section provides insight into the performance of the memory/disk/read/write combination internal to your server. This is helpful information for developing an internal baseline before a system before it goes into production. It can also be run once in production to determine if all is still running as well as you had planned, especially after making any changes to the system such as updating device drivers. But what about your customers' perspective of the services you are providing? They are probably accessing servers over the network from their workstations. This concept of customer perspective is illustrated in Figure 2-4.

In today's world, everything can be virtual and exist anywhere on the network (Intranet/Internet). So it does not matter where a server physically resides, but in the case of customer perspective illustrated in Figure 2-4 it does. A key concept to understand when completing customer perspective baselining is the concept of following the data reviewed in the beginning of this chapter. In Figure 2-4 you see that a Windows 2000 system is placed in an area of the network (Zone A) that is indicative of where your end users are. Placement of this Windows 2000 system is important since it measures the same data paths that your customers use. Keep this design goal in mind when selecting a system location from which to run your customer perspective baseline tests.

Again, you can use a variety of commercial products to develop customer perspective baseline pulse tests that are indicative of your environment. These commercial tools were identified in the sections on commercial and freely available tools for baseline development earlier in this chapter.

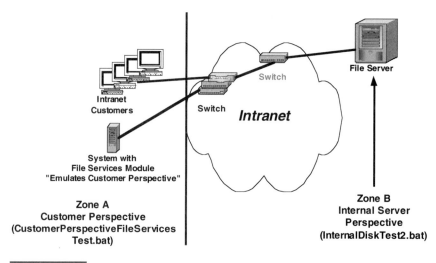

Intranet
Customers

Switch

Switch

File Server

Intranet

System with
File Services Module
"Emulates Customer Perspective"

Zone A
Customer Perspective
(CustomerPerspectiveFileServices
Test.bat)

Zone B
Internal Server
Perspective
(InternalDiskTest2.bat)

FIGURE 2–4   *Customer Perspective Conceptual Illustration*

Depending on the criticality of your business requirements and the size of your business, investing in these third-party tools may not be an option. However, you can place systems in your environment and run scripts that can provide basic emulation (synthetic transactions) of what your clients are experiencing.

There are several relatively easy techniques you can employ to understand the customer's perspective of the performance your Windows 2000 Server is providing. OK, it does take some effort. But once these techniques are integrated, you can automate taking baseline pulse tests so that you will be alerted when there is a problem, even while in production. To get you jump-started on developing your own customer perspective pulse tests, we have included two here (see Code Examples 2-2 and 2-3). One is for baselining file services and the other is for baselining web services.

CUSTOMER PERSPECTIVE PULSE TEST: FILE SERVICES

What is one of the most common server services provided today? File services. What typically does a customer do? She starts her desktop in the morning and, either through an automatic login script or manual means, she maps a network drive to a server so she can transfer files to and from the server as needed. It is surprisingly easy to provide basic emulation and to baseline your environment. Later we'll review how to automate this script so you can take pulse tests over time and compare them against your baseline to determine how well your servers are providing service. The CustomerPerspectiveFileServicesModule.bat script included here provides a mechanism to see how well the Windows 2000 *copy* command can transfer files over a network connection to your target

Windows 2000 server. A by-product of this script is that it also tests to see if your file server itself is available. When run repeatedly over time, it enables you to develop your baseline and monitor your server. This simple script provides a measure of relative file services performance from your customer's perspective.

EXAMPLE 2–2   *CustomerPerspectiveFileServicesModule.bat*

```
@echo off
REM # The above command turns off stdout echo
REM #######################################################
REM #
REM # Copyright 2000, Curt Aubley
REM #
REM # Script: CustomerPerspectiveFileServicesModule.bat
REM #         Simple network file transfer and time
REM #
REM # Goal:   Take a network file server's pulse by copying a file
REM #         to a remote server and then deleting it
REM #
REM # Running Notes: Ensure that the creatfil.exe and timethis.exe
REM #         commands are in your path. If you wish to save your
REM #         output to a file, use the Redirector ">" or ">>"
REM #         Example: DiskAndNetworkTest2.bat > MyNetResults.txt
REM #         Script assumes c:\temp is on local disk drive and
REM #         remote server UNC share is available on the target server
REM #
REM #
REM ########################################################

REM # Easy way to create a 10MB file
REM # creatfil.exe command from Windows 2000 Resource Kit
REM # Clear screen to start
REM #
cls
echo Creating 10MB test file to test disk transfer time
echo on
creatfil c:\temp\testfil2start.ded 10000
@echo off

REM # Check size of File created
REM #
@Echo on
dir c:\temp\testfil2start.ded
@echo off

REM #    Create Network Connection
REM #    Remember to put your server name and share in here!
net use k: \\megatron\c$
```

EXAMPLE 2–2	*CustomerPerspectiveFileServicesModule.bat (continued)*

```
REM # copy file to network connected disk/share
REM # timethis command located on Windows 2000 Resource Kit CD-ROM
REM #
@echo on
timethis "copy c:\temp\testfil2start.ded k:\temp\testfil2end.ded"
@echo off

REM # Cleanup
REM #
del c:\temp\testfil2start.ded
del k:\temp\testfil2end.ded
net use k: /delete

REM ############
REM # End Script
REM ############
```

When this script was run between a Pentium III, 256MB, Ultra 2 SCSI disk-based server and Pentium II desktop with 128MB, and a SCSI disk subsystem, on a dedicated 100BaseTX network, this test resulted in an elapsed time of 8 seconds, translating to a throughput measurement of 1.25MBytes/sec (10Mbits/sec). This test was completed on a dedicated network and a baseline network in an ideal environment.

We now know the best customer perspective performance we can achieve under ideal conditions for this baseline of a network file services environment. This becomes our ideal preproduction baseline. Although this baseline test was completed in an ideal environment, it still makes common sense to use the systems that depict your environment. Once the systems are placed into production, run the script again and compare the production results against the ideal environment results at various times throughout the day. This can be accomplished by having this script run periodically throughout the day using Windows 2000's Scheduler Service and redirecting the script output to a log file. Accomplish redirecting the script output by using the following Windows 2000 Scripting Series from the command prompt: CustomerPerspective-FileServicesModule.bat 1>> LocalDiskTest.log 2>> LocalDiskTest.log.error.

The >> operator appends the output of the Windows 2000 batch script to a file, so previous data is not lost. For this example, the standard out (1) information is sent to its own log file and standard error (2) is sent to its own error file for troubleshooting.

Scheduling Customer Perspective Scripts with Windows 2000

Windows 2000 has the *at.ex* command available via the command prompt to schedule tasks. A friendlier alternative to the command line *at* command is to use the built-in graphical interface for the Windows 2000 Task Scheduler. To start the Task Scheduler wizard, go to Start / Control Panel / Scheduled Tasks / Add a Scheduled Task. From here, it is relatively straightforward to follow the instructions and have your pulse script run on a regular basis. When you highlight your scheduled task and select properties, you have several options to customize how, when, and where your task runs. One of the nicest features of the Task Scheduler is being able to set for whom the scripts will run. In this manner, you do not have to run the script with administrator-level privileges, but as a user with the lowest privileges possible to run the test. Your local security team will particularly like this option as it lowers security risks associated with pulse testing since you do not have to run automated tasks with elevated privileges.

When should you run your script? I suggest running it during both off-hours and peak hours. In this manner, you get a better understanding of the workloads in your environment. If you feel running the pulse test is too much of a strain on your production networks and systems, consider running it with a smaller file transfer size and only every 30 minutes. The advanced properties of a scheduled task are shown in Figure 2-5.

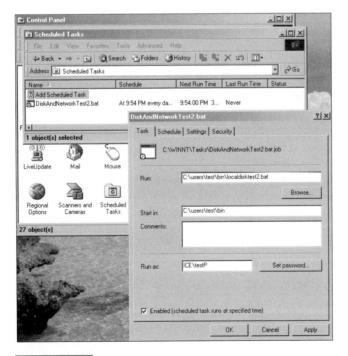

FIGURE 2–5   *The Windows 2000 Task Scheduler*

By analyzing the results of the server's pulse tests you have executed, you can decide what is acceptable and what is not. If, during pulse testing, the production results exceed your baseline such that it becomes unacceptable, you can take the appropriate actions, then rerun the pulse test to determine if your efforts to remove the bottleneck were successful. We look at locating disk subsystem bottlenecks and removing them in chapter 6. Network bottleneck resolution is reviewed in chapter 7.

Enhancing Customer Perspective File Services Pulse Testing

The simple example in Code Example 2-2 was chosen because it is easily implemented and because it is something that almost all servers need to do—transfer files to another computer. This simple script can be expanded using one of the more robust scripting languages available for Windows 2000 such as Perl for Windows 2000, VB scripting, or Windows Scripting Host. As Windows 2000 has moved into the enterprise, however, nice graphical user interfaces (GUIs) are getting new administrators up to speed on administrating a single server or small group of servers quickly. Anyone managing or testing a large Windows 2000 Server rollout appreciates the power of good scripting languages. For example, checking a registry entry on 300 servers via a GUI without making a mistake is a challenge and is time consuming without the aid of a good scripting language. In Windows 2000, almost all of the administrative tasks, which can be completed via the GUI, have command line equivalents. Perl for Windows 2000 provides Win32 modules to take advantage of these extensions so that you can automate helpful administrative tasks. I hack Perl scripts in NT/UNIX-Linux environments as needed and have found it helpful in Windows 2000 Server environments as well.

Using Perl32 and the Windows 2000 server Resource Kit, you can easily customize the Windows 2000 batch script CustomerPerspective-FileServicesModule.bat to calculate the throughput of the file server, log the data into a friendlier log file format, and send an alert to Windows 2000 server's Event Viewer (Start / Programs / Administrative Tools / Computer Management / Event Viewer / System) if your baseline threshold is crossed. Code Example 2-3 is an example Perl32 and Windows 2000 batch script combination customization of CustomerPerspectiveFileServicesModule.bat. The two scripts in Code Examples 2-3 and 2-4 work in concert to achieve our goals, with explanatory comments included in the scripts. These are rapidly developed scripts. If, after using them, you improve them into eloquent works of art, send them to TuningFeedback@TuningAndSizing.com where they will be tested and posted on the web for others to use.

Testing File Services Performance: CustomerPulseTest2.bat and CustomerBaseLineCheck2.pl

EXAMPLE 2-3   *CustomerPulseTest2.bat*

```
@echo off
REM # The above command turns off stdout echo
REM ##########################################################
REM #
REM #   Copyright 2000, Curt Aubley
REM #
REM #
REM #   Goal:    From a customer's perspective, take a file server's pulse by
REM #            mounting a remote server share and copying a file to the
REM #            remote server
REM #
REM #   Script: Simple file transfer and time Batch Scripts called by Perl
REM #            script CustomerBaselineCheck2.pl for data manipulation
REM #
REM #   Note:    Coordinate any changes between CustomerPulseTest2.bat
REM #            and CustomerBaselineCheck2.pl Perl script
REM #
REM #            -baseline value of acceptable transfer times
REM #             is influenced by size of file transferred
REM #            -Values are Set in BaseLineChecks.pl (self explained)
REM #
REM #            testfile2.ded - this is file to be transferred to the
REM #            network share remote host name
REM #
REM ##########################################################

REM # Easy way to create a 10MB file
REM # creatfil.exe command from Windows 2000 Resource Kit
REM #
creatfil c:\temp\testfil2.ded 10000

REM # Check size of File created and pass exact file to Perl script
REM #
dir c:\temp\testfil2.ded

REM # Set network share
REM # If this is changed, change remotehost name in BaseLineCheck.pl
REM #
net use k: \\megatron\c$

REM # copy file to network connected disk/share
REM # timethis command located on Windows 2000 Resource Kit CD-ROM
REM #
timethis "copy c:\temp\testfil2.ded k:\temp\testfil2.ded"
```

EXAMPLE 2–3   *CustomerPulseTest2.bat (continued)*

```
REM # Cleanup
REM #
del k:\temp\testfil2.ded
net use k: /delete

REM ############
REM # End Script
REM ############
```

EXAMPLE 2–4   *CustomerBaseLineCheck2.pl*

```
####################################################################
#
#   Curt Aubley, Copyright 2000
#
#   Perl Script: Rapid Prototype/Example for taking baseline
#                Measurements from outside your server e.g. your
#                Customers Perspective
#                Error checking for empty results, etc. left for
#                reader (I always wanted to say that)
#
#   What Script Does:
#                BaseLineCheck.pl is typically run from the Windows 2000
#                scheduler with the following output options
#                customerbaselinecheck.pl 1>>c:\temp\output.txt
#                2>>c:\temp\outputerrors.txt
#
#                This Perl script calls the Windows 2000 batch script
#                CustomerPulseTest2.bat which creates and times the
#                transfer of a 10MB file to a remote server
#                This script then compares the corresponding timing
#                results to the designated baseline and logs the
#                results in a log file and sends an alert to the
#                Windows 2000 event logs if the results are lower then the
#                baseline specified.
#
#   Key Notes:
#                 -Ensure this file (CustomerBaseLineCheck2.pl)
#                 and Windows 2000 batch script CustomerPulseTest2.bat are in the
#                 same directory
#                 -Only one file is not cleaned up, but it is over
#                 written
#                 c:\temp\output.txt. Use for debugging if needed
#
####################################################################
#
# Initialization
```

| **EXAMPLE 2–4** | *CustomerBaseLineCheck2.pl (continued)* |

```perl
#
#Path to .bat
$pulsetestlocation="c:/users/test/bin/CustomerPulseTest2.bat";
# Path to .bat
$remotehost="megatron";              # For log, indicate name of remote
# Server
$baseline=700000;                    # Minimum acceptable performance
# (Bytes/sec)                        # e.g. baseline value (bytes/sec)
$outputfile="c:/temp/output.txt";    # Where PulseTest.bat sends temporary
                                     # data temporary test results
$performanceunacceptable=0;          # Set performance test flag
                                     #  0 - indicates acceptable Performance
                                     #  1 - indicates unacceptable Performance
$baselinelogfile="c:/users/test/logs/baseline.log";  # Where to place
                                                     # results


# Call Windows 2000 Batch script to run PulseTest2.bat
#
system("$pulsetestlocation > $outputfile");

# Open temporary results file $outputfile from CustomerPulseTests.bat
#
open(IN, "$outputfile") ||
  die "cannot open $outputfile: $!";

# Get data from CustomerPulseTest2.bat
while (<IN>)
    {
    if (/Elapsed/)
        {
        chomp($_);         #Get time results
        $time=$_;
        }
    if (/Start/)          #Get date of tests
        {
        $temp_date=$_;
        }
     if (/File/)          #Get size of file sent
        {
        chomp($_);
        $size=$_;
        }
    }

# Close file
close(IN);

# Determine Transfer Time Values
```

EXAMPLE 2-4   *CustomerBaseLineCheck2.pl (continued)*

```perl
# Removing colons and normalize data
#
$hour=substr($time, 28, 2);
$min=substr($time, 31, 2);
$sec=substr($time, 34, 10);
$date=substr($temp_date, 28, 20);
$total_time= ($hour*3600) + ($min*60) + ($sec);

# Remove Commas and such to determine transfer file
#  Size for throughput calculation
#
$_=substr($size, 28, 20);
tr/0123456789//cd;
$filesize=$_;

# Finally, determine throughput
#
$throughput=$filesize/$total_time;

# Check to see how measured throughput compares to
#  minimum acceptable throughput
#
# If Transfer speed unacceptable, log the event
#  to Windows 2000 Server event log and baseline performance log

# Normalize data for comparison
#
$throughput1=sprintf("%.2f",$throughput);
$baseline1=sprintf("%.2f",$baseline);

if ($throughput1 lt $baseline1)
   {
    $performanceunacceptable=1;  # Set flag so that baseline log
   # updated w/error condition
     use Win32::Eventlog;        # Send error to NT Event log
   {
         my $number, $EventLog;
        # open the event log.
         Win32::EventLog::Open($EventLog , "Performance Baseline Perl App",
             '') || die $!;
                 # define the event to log.
       $Event =
       {
        'EventType' => EVENTLOG_INFORMATION_TYPE,
        'Category' => 0,
        'EventID' => 0x1003,
        'Data' => '',
```

EXAMPLE 2–4   *CustomerBaseLineCheck2.pl (continued)*

```
         'Strings' => "Unacceptable performance! Baseline: $baseline1 but
            measured throughput $throughput1 bytes/sec",
      };
        # report the event and check the error
          $EventLog->Report($Event) || die $!;
      }
#--
#-- Enter Code here to Start Sysmon Monitor Service Module
#--  if so desired
#--
   }


# Get This System's Information
#
use Win32;
$computername=Win32::NodeName;

# Print results to performance baseline log file (or database)
#
open(LOGFILE, ">> $baselinelogfile") ||
  die "cannot open $baselinelogfile: $!";

if ($performanceunacceptable eq 1)
    {
    printf LOGFILE "Error: Below Baseline($baseline1 bytes/sec)-";
    }

printf LOGFILE "$date, $computername Net Throughput to $remotehost:
            $throughput1 bytes/sec \n";

close(LOGFILE);

######################################################################
#
#    Script Ends Here
#
######################################################################
```

Advanced Customer Perspective Pulse Tests: Web Services

What about baselining other Windows 2000 environments from the customer's perspective? Across the industry, more and more applications are becoming web enabled. There is little reason for this trend to slow down anytime soon, so what about baselining the customer perspective of providing web services just like we did for file services earlier?

Again, it is important to follow the data to where your customers are and baseline the performance of the web services from their perspective. Figure 2-6 illustrates the different data paths that your customers may use.

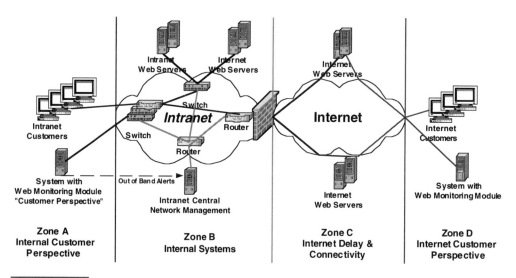

| **FIGURE 2-6** | *Customer Perspective Web Services Baseline* |

Tactical Steps Needed for Implementing Customer Perspective Web Service Pulse Test

We have our methodology to achieve our goals. Now, let's look at the steps needed to actually make this methodology a reality and have it work for you by walking through an example. We will go into more hands-on details on how to plan for and configure these scripts because these tactics are more advanced than what we used for customer perspective file services monitoring earlier in the chapter.

To get our planning started, we need the basic information on what you will manage. First, determine which web services you wish to monitor (specifically the web page's URLs). Then determine where your customers are located so you can select where to place your systems that will run the customer perspective web monitoring module scripts (CPWMM); decide how you would like to log the collected baseline information and who you wish to alert if there is a problem.

For this example, we will monitor http://insideweb1.mycompany.com, http://insideweb2.mycompany.com, http://www.NTmag.com, and http://www.OAO.com. All of these web sites will be monitored from our internal network (Zone A in Figure 2-6) at the network switch that My Company's

CEO is connected to. (Keeping the boss happy is half the battle!) Also, we will monitor our web services from a location to which the highest percentage of end users are connected (a different network switch in Zone A, Figure 2-6). If we detect a problem, we will have an e-mail alert sent to the pager of our SuperSA and an event sent to the CPWMM system's Windows 2000 Event Log; we will also write this data to a flat file. Embedded in this example is the option for storing this information in a Microsoft SQL 7 database via an ODBC call. Having a database to baseline web site performance over time provides a more robust mechanism for further analysis. Setting up the SQL database is left as an exercise for you, depending how you wish to keep your data.

To set up a CPWMM system to baseline your web sites, obtain a Windows 2000 system and ensure that the following is configured: TCP/IP, the Windows 2000 Resource Kit and the latest version of the Perl32 scripting language, and blat (a shareware command line e-mail client). Again note that we use Perl32 for our example, but you can use any scripting language you would like as long as you can make an http request without an actual browser—e.g., from the command line—and as long as you can call Windows 2000 command line tools. At this point, our CPWMM system infrastructure is in place. You will now need to install and customize the CustomerPerspectiveWebMonitoringModuleScript.pl and its associated modules for your environment.

The CPWMM scripts were not completed in a vacuum. I would like to give special thanks to my associate Troy Landry for working closely with me and leading scripting and testing of several of these modules which greatly aided in making these modules a reality in the timeframe needed to publish this book.

Customizing the CPWMM Scripts

To install the CPWMM Perl32 scripts (CustomerPerspectiveWebMonitoringModuleScript.pl, Poll.pl, Event.pl, Optmod.pl), download the CPWMM scripts from http://www.TuningAndSizing.com and place them all in the same directory on your Windows 2000 system. You could type them from the book examples, but you probably will want to skip that time-consuming activity and download them instead. In Code Examples 2-5–2-7, we have customized the scripts based on our example environment outlined above. The scripts are self-explanatory through the additional comments. Thus, as you read the script, it will become apparent what you will need to comment out and what you should keep by removing/adding, respectively, the # Perl comment symbol. We also have marked key areas of the script that state, "Customize me." As a reminder, the variables to review and update in the CustomerPerspectiveWebMonitoringModuleScript.pl are

- Baseline—denotes the maximum time in seconds that is acceptable for a web page request to complete
- Outputfile—defines the file in which results are kept
- Array variable—where you define which URLs you wish to monitor.

In the optmod.pl script, you will want to edit the Customize Me for E-Mail options to reflect those that you want paged via e-mail. I suggest running your scripts from the command line using the perl.exe –d option the first time you run them. The –d option enables you to step through the script line by line. This helps to ensure it is working well before you schedule its operation with the Window 2000 scheduler (Start / Settings / Control Panel / Scheduled Tasks / Add Scheduled Tasks).

The basic algorithm upon which these scripts operate is that it emulates a customer browsing a web site, by making a hypertext transfer protocol request (http) to the target web site(s) URLs and grabs the web pages one at a time. Looking for a GUI? One of the great things about Internet standards is that there is more than one way to implement a solution. You do not need a web browser to read a web page. Here we use a Win32 Perl API call (shown in the Poll.pl script Request[Get, $url]). Once the web page is fetched, we ensure that

- The web server responds within our performance time threshold
- The URL is available

This is shown in the CustomerPerspectiveWebMonitoringModuleScript.pl script section, # Once the baseline is crossed generate an error. The time taken to provide the web page is then logged. This ensures that the web server is responding as planned. If a web error is returned, does not respond within the proper performance level or is not responding at all, an e-mail alert is then sent to the pager of our SuperSA, an event is sent to the CPWMM system's Windows 2000 Event Log, and this data is also written to a flat file (this is completed in the event.pl and optmod.pl scripts). It is important to highlight that there are numerous actions that you can customize the script to complete. If you can run the action from the command line, you can have it started from within the CPWMM scripts.

Code Examples 2-5 through 2-8 comprise the CPWMM scripts.

EXAMPLE 2–5   *CustomerPerspectiveWebMonitoringModuleScript.pl*

```
###################################################################
#
#  Troy Landry, Curt Aubley,  V2.1 Copyright 2000
#
#  Version: CustomerWebMonitoringModuleScript.pl Version 2.1
#
#  Perl Script: Rapid Prototype/Example for taking baseline measurements from
#  outside your server from a customers point of view.
#
```

EXAMPLE 2–5   *CustomerPerspectiveWebMonitoringModuleScript.pl (continued)*

```
#   What module does:
#       CustomerWebMonitoringModuleScript.pl
#       is typically run from a scheduling program every 5-10 minutes.
# This module will call the specified URLs via HTP Gets and determine whether
# the site is responding or not.
# This script then compares the corresponding timing results to a designated
# baseline, logs the results in a log file and sends an alert to the NT event
# logs if the results are greater than the baseline specified.
#
#   Key Notes:
#   -Ensure this file and the polling program (Poll.pl) are in the same
#    directory
#   -Only one file is not cleaned up, but it is over written each time the
#    program is run and is called output.txt. Use for debugging if needed
#   -Windows 2000 Resource Kit needs to be installed for the Timethis command.
#
######################################################################

######################################################################
#
#    CUSTOMIZE ME!!!!
#
######################################################################

#   Initialization - Setting up of the Variables
#   $Baseline - Is the number of seconds which is deemed acceptable performance
#   $outputfile - The file where the results of the timethis command are placed

$baseline=5;
$outputfile="output.txt";

# Enter the web addresses you wish to monitor
# Ensure you place each site with Quotes around it and
# Separated by a comma e.g. ("www.yahoo.com","abc.com")

@array=("insideweb1.mycompany.com","insideweb2.mycompany.com","www.NTMag.com","
            www.oao.com");

######################################################################
#
#    End of Customization
#
######################################################################

# The counter for array.  The program will loop through once for each web
# address
$count=1;

while ($count <= @array){
```

EXAMPLE 2–5   *CustomerPerspectiveWebMonitoringModuleScript.pl (continued)*

```perl
# Run the program to time the URL connection.  This command
# ends up placing the timethis poll.pl (website address) >$outputfile
# command into a variable for the system command to run.
# The poll.pl program takes the website address as an argument and then
# does a get command to the webpage.  The time for the get to return
# is then placed in the $outputfile
@proglist=("Timethis ", join(" ","poll.pl",$array[$count-1])," >$outputfile");

system ("@proglist");

# Open temporary results file $outputfile and assigns IN as a file alias.
# If file is not able to be opened, the whole program stops

open(IN, "$outputfile") ||
  die "cannot open $outputfile: $!";

# In the output file the script looks for the keyword Elapsed.  Once found
# the chomp command removes the newline character and assigns the line
# that has elapsed in it to the $time variable.  Repeats the process to
# obtain the start time

  while (<IN>)
     {
     if (/Elapsed/)
         {
         chomp($_);            #Get time results
         $time=$_;
         }
     if (/Start/)              #Get date of tests
         {
         $temp_date=$_;
         }

     }

# Close file
close(IN);

# Determine Transfer Time Values
# Removing colons and normalize data

$hour=substr($time, 28, 2);
$min=substr($time, 31, 2);
$sec=substr($time, 34, 10);
$date1=join ("",substr($temp_date, 32, 6), ",",substr($temp_date, 48, 4));
$time=substr($temp_date, 39, 8);

# Pulls the date out
```

EXAMPLE 2–5   *CustomerPerspectiveWebMonitoringModuleScript.pl (continued)*

```perl
$date=join (" ", $date1, $time);

# Pulls the total time for retrieval
$total_time= ($hour*3600) + ($min*60) + ($sec);

# Setup Baseline numbers to check against
$total_time1=sprintf("%d",$total_time);
$baseline1=sprintf("%d",$baseline);

# Once the baseline is crossed generate an error. Here we write to the event
            log through another
# Program and call our optional module which performs a ping, tracert and send
            the log file
# to our SuperSA
if ($total_time1 > $baseline1)
    {
system("event.pl");
$prog1=join(" ","optmode.pl", $array[$count-1]);
system("$prog1");
    }

# Enter results into a file for future analysis.
#    Sets the log file up into the variable
$datatrend="webdata.txt";

# Opens the log file and if the log file does not open, the program dies
open (LOG, ">>webdata.txt")||
die "Cannot open $webdata: $!";

print LOG ($date);
print LOG (" $array[$count-1]");
print LOG (" $total_time \n");

close LOG;

#  If you wish to write to a SQL DB, uncomment to following lines

#########################################
#
#  Start SQL Section - Take One # symbol from each line
#
#########################################

## Setup ODBC to be able to write results to SQL DB
#use Win32::ODBC;
#
## Sends ODBC authorization and if fails writes out the error message
## Need to create an ODBC connection via control panel
```

EXAMPLE 2–5   *CustomerPerspectiveWebMonitoringModuleScript.pl (continued)*

```
#if (!($Data=new Win32::ODBC("DSN=[Your DSN NAME];UID=[User ID the DSN
            #requires];PWD=[Password for the DSN ID]"))) {
#  print "Error connecting to $DSN\n";
#  print "error: " . Win32::ODBC::Error();
#}
#$SqlStatement = "Insert INTO Baseline Values('$array[$count-
            1]','$total_time','$date')";
#
## Ensures that the DB will take the above statement
#if ($Data->Sql($SqlStatement))
#{
#  print ("SQL failed.\n");
#  print "Error: " . $Data->Error() . "\n";
#  $Data->Close();
#}

#######################################
#
#   End SQL Section
#
#######################################

# Allows the next website to be checked
$count++;
}

##########################################################################
#
#   Script Ends Here
#
##########################################################################
```

EXAMPLE 2–6   *Poll.pl*

```
##########################################################################
#
# Troy Landry, Copyright 2000
#
# Version:  Poll.pl Version 1.1
#
# Fetch a URL via http request and is used in conjunction with
# WebMonitoringModuleScript.pl to measure response time of websites
#
# The script performs an http get command and if the response is
# successful then the program continues, however if an error
# occurs then the program will wait 10 seconds before continuing
#
##########################################################################
```

EXAMPLE 2–6 *Poll.pl (continued)*

```
# Start the required Perl Modules
use URI::URL;
use LWP::UserAgent;
use Getopt::Long;

# Set the variable for the website to be
# monitored.  The @ARGV brings in the name
# of the website from the timer program

$target=join("","http://",@ARGV[0]);

#  Identifies the URL to be looked at
$url = new URI::URL $target;
$ua = new LWP::UserAgent;
$ua->agent("httpd-time/1.0 ". $ua->agent);

# Go out and request the URL
$req = new HTTP::Request(GET,$url);

# perform the http transaction
$get = $ua->request($req);

# If the page is retrieved successfully with no errors it does not do anything,
# however if there is an error, such as a 404 or 401, the program will delay
# 10 seconds to ensure the time goes over baseline requirements

if ($get->is_success)
{}
else
{
# Delay's the program for 10 seconds
   sleep (10);
}

#######################################################################
#
#    Script Ends Here
#
#######################################################################
```

EXAMPLE 2–7 *Event.pl*

```
#######################################################################
#
#  Troy Landry, Copyright  2000
#
#  Perl Script: Write an error to a NT Event Log
```

EXAMPLE 2–7   *Event.pl (continued)*

```
#
#   Version: Event.pl Version 1.1
#
#
############################################################################

#  Opens the Win32 Perl Module
use Win32::EventLog;
my $EventLog;

#  The actual data to be sent to the application log
my %event=( 'EventID',0xC0001003, 'EventType',EVENTLOG_ERROR_TYPE,
            'Category',3, 'Strings','Performance is unacceptable, check for
            bottlenecks');

# Opens the Eventlog with Web Performance used as the Source
$EventLog = new Win32::EventLog( 'Web Performance' ) || die $!;

# Writes the event to the event log
$EventLog->Report(\%event) || die $!;

############################################################################
#
#   Script Ends Here
#
############################################################################
```

EXAMPLE 2–8   *Optional Performance Diagnostic Module (optmod.pl)*

```
############################################################################
#
#  Troy Landry, Copyright  2000
#
#    Version: optmod.pl Version 1.1
#
#  This Module shows some examples of different notifications that you can
#  configure your Main Module to call and perform.  Below we have done a ping
#  and a tracert to the troubled servers.  The results are written to a log
#  file.  The module also sends an email to a user with the logfile as the
#  message body.
#
############################################################################

#  Sets up the Time Perl Module so that a time stamp can be inserted into the
#             log file
use Time::localtime;
```

EXAMPLE 2–8	*Optional Performance Diagnostic Module (optmod.pl) (continued)*

```perl
#    Sets the log file up into the variable
$tslogfile="tslogfile.txt";

# Opens the log file and if the log file does not open, the program dies
open (LOG, ">>tslogfile.txt")||
die "Cannot open $tslogfile: $!";

#  Generates the ping command with the variable passed from the main module
#   and outputs it to ouput.txt
$target = join(" ","ping",@ARGV[0],">output.txt");

#  Runs the ping command
system($target);

#  Opens the Output file for Ping in order to move the data into the log file
open(OUTPUT, "output.txt");

#  Selects the first line in the output file
$line=<OUTPUT>;

#  Places the timestamp into the log file
print LOG (ctime());

#  Goes through each line in the output file and copies it to the log file
while ($line ne"")
{
   print LOG ($line);
   $line=<OUTPUT>;
}

# Closes the output file
close (OUTPUT);

#  Generates the tracert command with the variable passed from the main module
#   and outputs it to ouput.txt
$target = join(" ","tracert",@ARGV[0],">output.txt");

#  Runs the tracert command
system ($target);

#  Opens the Output file for tracert  in order to move the data into the log
                file
open(OUTPUT, "output.txt");

#  Selects the first line in the output file
$line=<OUTPUT>;

#  Goes through each line in the output file and copies it to the log file
while ($line ne"")
```

EXAMPLE 2–8   *Optional Performance Diagnostic Module (optmod.pl) (continued)*

```perl
{
   print LOG ($line);
   $line=<OUTPUT>;
}
print LOG ("\n");

#  Closes the Output and the log file
close (OUTPUT);
close (LOG);

#  Sets up the command line to send an email using the blat program
#  Blat is shareware and can be downloaded via the Internet.
#  Blat needs to be installed and configured with an SMTP Server that is able
#  to receive email.

#####################################################################
#
#    CUSTOMIZE ME!!!!   For the Email options
#
#####################################################################

#  If you want more than one person to receive the email, separate each name
#                with a comma
#  Ensure there are no spaces after the comma
$emailto = "tlandry\@oaot.com, caubley\@oao.com";
$emailsender="tlandry\@oao.com"

$emailsubject = "Warning";

#The message body of the Email is in a file - In this case the logfile is being
#                sent
$emailMessage= "tslogfile.txt"

#####################################################################
#
#    End Email customization
#
#####################################################################

#  Generates the command line for blat and then runs the command
$email = join(" ","blat", $emailmessage, "-s", $emailsubject, "-t", $emailto
               ,"-f",$emailsender,"-q");
system($email);

#####################################################################
#
#    Script Ends Here
#
#####################################################################
```

Looking for a dedicated Windows 2000 system from which to run these scripts? It's not necessary. The system used to run the scripts can be shared with other applications, but it must be strategically located to represent the same data path your customers would take to access web services (I know I've repeated this statement several times, but it is so very important). From a system sizing perspective, when selecting a system on which to install the CPWMM, I have found that monitoring 20 servers with 10-minute intervals between these web pings generates a CPU load of less than 5% every 10 minutes on a dual Pentium III 450MHz CPU–based system.

PROACTIVE SYSTEM MANAGEMENT • Unlike the file services customer perspective scripts initially presented in this chapter, additional options are available in this CPWMM script. OK, these options can be added to the other scripts too, but doing so was left for the reader to copy, paste, and customize. What if the time for the web (http) request has now gone above our baseline? Be proactive! Do not wait for customers to complain or go to a competing web site! Take action. Have this script either track the problem or alert you in your favorite manner. In Code Example 2-5, we write a poorly performing web site event to the Windows 2000 Event Log. From here, there are many commercial management programs that can take over—they automatically scan the Windows 2000 Event Log for specific entries and alert you when these entries are made. Or you can use the Windows 2000 Event Viewer to review the event logs remotely as needed. Another option is to run a command line program that can call a variety of commands when an event occurs. For our example, we make a Perl32 system call that runs a script—optmod.pl—which in turn calls a freeware program called blat. Blat sends out an e-mail alert to our SuperSA's pager and to his home e-mail account. The CPWMM is very flexible and enables you to customize the script to accomplish whatever you need. All you need to be is creative! If you normally run certain commands from the command prompt to aid in your troubleshooting efforts, they can be added to run when you need them most: when the performance problem is detected! We all know that, when you visit a customer who is reporting a problem, the problem never occurs when you are looking over the customer's shoulder.

STEPS TO TEST CPWMM • Now that you have installed the CPWMM script code on your CPWMM system, you need to verify that it is working. In our scripts, I have set the baseline to 5 seconds. After 5 seconds, I expect the average customer to become irate. This value needs to be set to whatever you have established as an acceptable baseline for the web page retrieval. One of the best ways to determine an acceptable performance threshold is to sit at a workstation and try it yourself! Bring up some web pages you are interested in. How long is too long to fetch a web page for you? Another technique is to set the threshold very high and run the script for a while. This enables you to see what the average production response times are—you have found your baseline. Then go ahead and set the threshold commensurate with what you have observed. You may want to set it slightly higher than what you observe so that any small spike in traffic does not send you an alert. Review your performance logs on a regular basis. If you need to adjust the baseline in the future, it is as easy as changing one number! There are a couple of ways to test the alerts sent out from the script. The first is to enter a bogus address into the list of web addresses. You will then be ensured of at least one failure and corresponding event. With this situation, you will be able to test your notification system. The second is to lower the performance baseline to zero. This will ensure that *all* web pages will fail, and therefore set off your notification process.

CUSTOMER PERSPECTIVE SYSTEM PERFORMANCE AND TREND ANALYSIS • So far we have been notifying the SuperSA when individual problems arise. What about the situations where you would like to trend the baseline data? What happened last week? The CEO complained your web site was down, but was it really down? In order to detect trends, the data must be stored in some manner. In the CPWMM module in Code Example 2-5, we provide the code to write data to a SQL7.0 database. Although we use a SQL 7 database, the data can be kept in any ODBC-compliant database such as Access, Lotus Notes, or Oracle. In the database we store the web site being monitored, the time it took to retrieve the site, and a timestamp of when the page was retrieved. This data can then be mined for reporting purposes and analysis. The data can also be correlated and graphs can be generated through a number of products ranging from Microsoft Excel to Seagate's Crystal Reports. Figure 2-7 shows the availability of the web services being provided. This can be an important metric to share with your management. It might even help you get that raise! Wishful thinking, maybe, but it does look impressive and can actually be very beneficial. Figure 2-8 shows how the data can be correlated to show overall performance for the previous day. From a single screen, you can tell when the web server response time begins to lag. Once the data has been crunched and the graphs generated to meet your needs, you can post these on a web server for your information technology (IT) team, company president, or the general public to see how well everything is performing.

　　We have introduced this approach of baselining internal resource usage, customer perspective service delivery, and the associated tools used to accomplish these tasks to help you develop comparisons for your file and web server environment. Sending exceptions to the Windows 2000 Event Viewer and to you saves you the time it would take to constantly check the server pulse output baseline files. Once you begin to understand the characteristics of your environment, you will be far ahead in the game of performance management. In the next section we will outline how to automatically start the Windows 2000 Performance Monitor to aid in determining why the servers under test have exceeded your acceptable baseline.

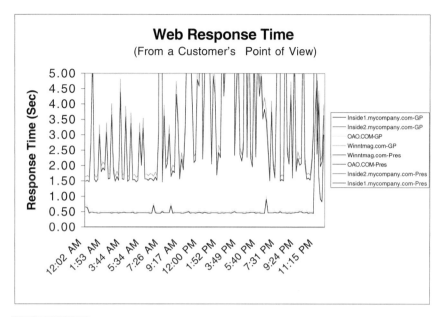

FIGURE 2-7   *Customer Perspective: Tracking Web Site Availability*

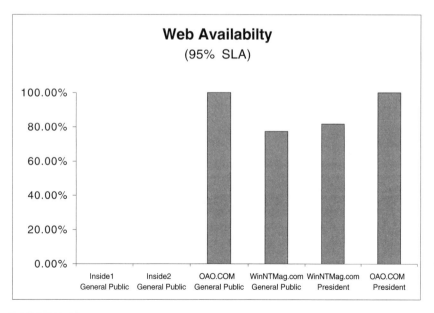

FIGURE 2-8   *Customer Perspective: Tracking Web Site Performance*

The most important concept to remember is to take the time to implement a suite of tests that measures the quantitative performance of your Windows 2000 server services and server subsystems. This empowers you to more accurately determine the health of your server and whether or not your tuning efforts are effective.

Performance Management

Statistics Gathering and Logging

Now that we have investigated how to measure the server services provided from the customer's perspective and how to emulate workloads to quantitatively measure internal subsystem performance (benchmarking), what about the resource utilization of the Windows 2000 system itself? The other primary and very important requirement for developing a baseline is a collection of resource usage statistics on the system(s). It is important to note that, in today's environments, few systems operate in a truly standalone mode. You will need to determine which systems are required to provide the particular service you wish and then monitor all of them as appropriate. Using these two approaches in concert (running pulse tests [both customer and internal] and collecting performance resource utilization data) helps you to determine when there is a problem or a potential problem while having the corresponding system resource information available to determine what is causing the bottleneck so you can remove it.

Third-Party Performance Management Tools

For larger environments, there are third-party tools that can be helpful in developing baselines and monitoring system performance but are not normally available to everyone working with Windows 2000 due to economics. Five such third-party technologies that I have found helpful are Hewlett Packard's OpenView ManageX (http://www.hp.com), BMC's Patrol (http://www.BMC.com), IBM's Tivoli (http://www.ibm.com), Concord NetHealth (http://www.Concord.com), CA's Unicenter (http://www.CA.com), and NetIQ's (http://www.NetIQ.com). I have used several of these tools in enterprise environments managing hundreds of servers. They can be very helpful, providing slick mechanisms that alert you, based on real-time, performance resource utilization problems; they also have extensive logging and report generation capabilities. If you do obtain and deploy these technologies, remember that they are not a point-and-click install! They require significant planning and customization because their built-in performance thresholds may not be indicative of your environment. Be careful as you begin to use these third-party tools—they become irreplaceable. There is real value added when you manage large numbers of systems with these tools. However, even though these tools assist you in identifying trends and performance problems, you will still find yourself using the native performance management tools in Windows 2000 for drilling into the real performance details.

Windows 2000 Performance Tools

The Windows 2000 Performance Monitor Console is the primary tool for collecting system resource usage data, developing a performance baseline, and determining the location of bottlenecks. For short-term performance investigations, Windows 2000's Task Manager is the tool of choice.

PERFORMANCE MONITOR VS. TASK MANAGER

Which tool is best for you? Most likely, you'll use both Performance Monitor and Task Manager depending on your mission. Performance Monitor is the tool of choice for obtaining detailed information, logging data for extended analysis, and collecting performance information based on performance events that occur within your system. Task Manager provides a quick look into what is occurring on your system but doesn't provide a mechanism for logging. However, Task Manager lets you manage applications (i.e., processes) to optimize the performance of your system or to stop rogue processes from adversely affecting your system.

PERFORMANCE MONITOR CONSOLE

The Performance Monitor Console actually contains two sets of tools—System Monitor and Performance Logs/Alerts—which are Microsoft Management Console (MMC) snap-ins. In some Windows 2000 literature, this performance tool is also generally referred to as System Monitor. Both use the same executable from the command line to start: perfmon.exe. In this book we will refer to this tool as Sysmon. Sysmon is the primary tool to utilize when tuning and sizing Windows 2000 systems. You would be wise to become intimately familiar with it. Locating a server bottleneck or sizing a system for increased workloads is not cut-and-dried. Monitoring only one server resource at a time can help you hone in on a bottleneck or a trend; however, to understand what is really happening, it is important to comprehend the relationships between the system resources. We will explore individual system resources in depth in later chapters, but, to gather the actual data needed to see these relationships, you should be familiar with what Sysmon can and cannot do for you.

Sysmon is a software tool that measures the usage of system resources either in real time or over a period time by logging resource utilization information into a file. Included with the standard Windows 2000 operating system are a series of objects that have subsequent counters associated with them. For example, one such object is the Processor object, which has numerous counters associated with it, such as %Processor Time and %User Time. Sysmon is extensible, which allows vendors to add additional functionality to the Sysmon tool through the addition of more objects and subsequent counters. When primary applications for Windows 2000 such as Internet Information Server (IIs) are installed, an entirely new set of objects are installed in addition to the default Performance Monitor objects to help analyze and tune that particular application.

We won't list every possible counter here since you can easily get this information from Sysmon itself or from the Microsoft Windows 2000 Resource Kits. We will cover the key Sysmon counters to monitor, the primary modes of operation when using Performance Monitor, and key pieces of information about using Performance Monitor that are not always apparent. Advanced individual counters found under Sysmon are reviewed in more detail in the later chapters that delve into the individual server resources.

UNDERSTANDING THE EFFECTS OF PERFORMANCE MONITORING

I commonly hear a question and a comment when discussing the subject of system monitoring. "How much overhead does starting these counters induce into my system?" and "I don't monitor the performance of my system because it might crash." It is true that, for whatever is being measured, you want to be careful not to add too much overhead to the system—you don't want what you are measuring to be heavily affected by the tool you are measuring it with. This was an issue in the days when systems were based on Intel 80386 and 80486 processors more than it is with more recent systems having Intel Pentium III, Intel Pentium III XEON, and Intel Itanium processors. The Windows 2000 Kernel is always collecting statistics on the objects that can be collected by Sysmon, regardless of whether Performance Monitor is running or not (except for a few cases that we will address). Thus, it does not matter if you are logging one or all of the objects available; the load placed on the server is not substantial unless the sampling period is set to less than 5 seconds between samples. However, when Performance Monitor is run in chart mode, it does use more CPU cycles than the other modes of operation due to updating the real-time graphical display. This assumes you are running one copy of Sysmon at a time. If you are running five or six copies of Sysmon on the same Windows 2000 system, your performance monitoring will begin to adversely affect your system. No laughing—I have seen this occurring in production environments!

Thus, the question of how much overhead is induced by starting these counters into a system is a good question to ask. The objects and counters outlined below (except where noted) would place a minimal additional load on any modern desktop or server.

The comment about not monitoring a system to avoid a crash is more alarming. Through benchmarking and real work practice, I have found that properly configured performance data collection incurs less than a 5% load on a system. It is always good to test any change in a lab/test environment prior to production, but, in general, running a copy of Sysmon will not place a noticeable load on your system. However, on the remote chance that Sysmon does add enough performance overhead to your system to cause it to stop operating, then you have bigger problems than performance management. This would indicate you have let performance management go unnoticed for too long and may now need to design a replacement system without any historical information on which to base your new design! Can you say *guesstimate*?

ACTIVATING ESSENTIAL PERFORMANCE MONITOR COUNTERS

My logical disk counters always display 0. Wow! Those disks are never bottlenecks! Not quite. There are some important objects and counters that are not started, or installed, by default. To ensure that all relative performance counters can be collected, complete the following actions:

1. **Network Interface object counter activation**. To install the Network Interface object to Sysmon so that you can collect network interface card performance information, add the SNMP Agent service: Start / Settings / Control Panel / Add/Remove Programs / Add/Remove Windows Components / Windows Components Wizard / Management and Monitoring Tools; then select Simple Network Management Protocol (SNMP). Adding this service installs the Network Interface object to Performance Monitor. Security Alert! SNMP is a powerful management tool and is a must-have item, but it must be configured properly to ensure that it does not introduce a security risk into your system. At a minimum, set the SNMP service properties (Start / Administration Tools / Component Service / Services / SNMP Service; then highlight and select Properties under the Trap and Security tabs and ensure that a community name other than "public" is defined. For detailed, hands-on, step-by-step information on Windows 2000/NT security, visit http://www.sans.org and http://www.nsa.gov.

2. **Network Segment object counter activation**. To install the Network Segment object to Performance Monitor and the real-time Network Monitor–based application, add the Network Tools and Agent under Start / Settings / Control Pane / Add/Remove Programs / Add/Remove Windows Components / Windows Components Wizard / Management and Monitoring Tools and select Network Monitoring Tools. Network Segment is the only System Monitor object that may slightly detract from your system's networking performance. Collecting data using this object places the selected network interface card into promiscuous mode. Promiscuous mode forces the selected network interface card to read every packet that it observes on the network segment it is attached to regardless of whether

or not the network packet is destined for the server. This will add additional overhead to your server above and beyond the standard Performance Monitor application. Although this is a very helpful counter, be careful when deciding when to activate it.

3. **Logical Disk object counter activation**. By default, Windows 2000 enables the physical disk counters. This is helpful if you have disks that are configured individually (no RAID sets or such). However, when you want to monitor logical disk drive performance, you must run diskperf – yv from the command line and reboot your system. Diskperf has several options which you can view by typing diskperf /? | more at the command line. This provides explanations for all of the diskperf options. The –y option suggested sets the system to start all disk performance counters when it is restarted (physical and logical). The -v option enables only the logical disk performance counters used for measuring performance of the logical drives created from combining drives into disk sets.

Sysmon Operations

Sysmon is an MMC snap-in. To invoke this tool, select Start / Programs / Administrative Tools / Performance. Alternatively, you can invoke Sysmon by selecting Start / Run, typing Perfmon in the open text box, and then pressing Enter. Sysmon provides the following features to monitor and analyze your system's performance.

- Sysmon allows real-time performance monitoring in chart, reporting, or histogram mode. To highlight the currently selected counter on your screen, press Ctrl+H. As you then scroll through the counters, Performance Monitor highlights the associated graph for each counter for easier viewing. (The backspace key doesn't provide this functionality as it did in NT 4.0.)
- Trace logs provide an advanced mechanism to analyze your system. Third-party or locally developed tools usually use this feature.
- Counter logs let you log performance data at a designated interval for local or remote Windows 2000 systems.
- Sysmon's alert feature enables you to start any action based on an event that you define (e.g., when your counters reach their maximum performance level thresholds).

Sysmon Chart Mode

Chart mode is a good mode to use when you want to determine what is currently happening on your system or to analyze a Sysmon log file. Using Chart mode's graphical output is helpful when viewing the different Windows 2000 resource relationships. I am often asked, "What counters should I observe when trying to understand what is going on with my system?" Although each system resource is investigated more closely in later chapters, I will say here that, if you add too many counters to the graphical workspace view, it is difficult to make heads or tails of what is going on, although it might look impressive to the common passerby or for executive presentations.

Key Sysmon Counters to Monitor

Another frequently asked question is, "What are the key performance counters I should monitor?" For detailed analysis, you may need to monitor a large number of Sysmon counters to isolate and resolve performance problems. Thus, as you log performance data over time (everyone does this, right?), consider collecting all of the counters available. However, as we will see later in this chapter, this long-term monitoring approach may consume so much disk space due to the high number of counters available with Windows 2000 that it may not be realistic. So consider this alternative approach to determine what you should monitor on a regular basis. When developing a performance baseline or tracking down performance problems, start from a high level with a few key or core counters to monitor; then, if something looks interesting enough to investigate, turn on all of the counters for a shorter period of time. A good analogy for this is what a medical doctor does when you come in with a complaint. Before a doctor sends you out to get an ultrasound, MRI, or some other advanced and detailed health exam, he looks at the basics: height, weight, pulse, temperature, etc.—you get the picture. If one of these core or key indicators is out of whack, then the flag goes up to investigate further. Take the same approach when baselining and isolating in your Windows 2000 systems. Conversely, when your pulse testing determines that the delivery of services is slow but the core Sysmon counters do not indicate a problem, you may need to log all of the counters to complete a more detailed analysis.

Sysmon allows you to save and provide a name for your Sysmon graphical workspace under Console / Save As. Once you save your workspace as an .msc file (MMC file), it is easy to set up a desktop shortcut (icon) to this view or to import it back into the Sysmon console. Thus, when the .msc icon is double-clicked, a copy of Performance Monitor with the saved workspace settings is launched (however, I have noticed that starting Sysmon in this manner appears slower than the methods outlined earlier). To set up a shortcut to a specific .msc file, right-click on an open area of the Windows 2000 console, select New / Shortcut, browse the file system to locate the .msc file that was saved, and then name your shortcut. Using this technique, I created .msc files for each of the primary server resources so that it is easy to observe key server relationships with a few clicks of the mouse. OK, so you can actually view all of these consoles in one Sysmon view, but that makes viewing the charts difficult. The .msc files for baselining and monitoring your system are: core-cpu-resources.msc, core-memory-resources.msc, core-disk-resources.msc, and core-network-resources.msc. Pictures and words are nice, but I'd rather have the code. These core system resource Sysmon workspaces can be downloaded from http://www.TuningAndSizing.com.

Table 2.3 contains the recommended core counters to monitor at a minimum to baseline your Windows 2000 system and obtain a basic indication of how your system is performing. Tables 2.3 through 2.6 are for quick reference only. We go into these objects and counters in more detail in subsequent chapters.

After each table that outlines core objects and subsequent counters to monitor at a minimum, screen shots illustrate their use in Sysmon.

| **TABLE 2.3** | Core CPU Sysmon Counters to Monitor, Definitions and Bottleneck Detection |

Object: Counter	Definition	Rule of Thumb for Bottleneck Detection
Processor: Processor Time–Total Instances	% Total Processor Time is expressed as a percentage of the elapsed time that a processor is busy executing a non-idle thread.	A high value for this counter is not a reason to be alarmed unless it is accompanied by a sustained System: Processor Queue Length greater than 2 or growing with an associated level of processor time greater than 90%; then the CPU is becoming a bottleneck. This rule holds true for single CPU Windows 2000 systems.
Processor: Processor Time–Total Instances	% Total Processor Time is expressed as a percentage of the elapsed time that a processor is busy executing a non-idle thread.	A high value for this counter is not a reason to be alarmed, unless it is accompanied with an aggregated System: Processor Queue Length sum greater than ($2 \times$ Number of CPUs) or growing with an associated level of total processor time greater than 90%; then the CPUs are becoming a bottleneck. This rule holds true for multi-CPU Windows 2000 systems.
System: Processor Queue Length	Processor Queue Length is the number of threads in the processor queue. There is a single queue for processor time even on computers with multiple processors. This counter counts ready threads only, not threads that are running.	If the sustained Queue Length is >2 or continuously growing with an associated level of Total Processor Time >90%, the CPU is becoming a bottleneck. This rule holds true for single CPU Windows 2000 systems.

| TABLE 2.3 | Core CPU Sysmon Counters to Monitor. Definitions and Bottleneck Detection (Continued) |

Object: Counter	Definition	Rule of Thumb for Bottleneck Detection
Processor: % Interrupt Time	% Interrupt Time is expressed as a percentage of the elapsed time that the processor spent handling hardware interrupts.	This value in itself is not a true indicator of a processor bottleneck. The value of this counter is helping to determine where to focus your tuning efforts. If this counter is greater than 20% and rising compared to your baseline, consider completing diagnostics on the peripheral components to ensure they are operating within acceptable parameters.
Processor: % Privileged Time	% Privileged Time is expressed as a percentage of the elapsed time that the processor spent in privileged mode in non-idle threads.	If this value is greater than counter % User Time, then focus on tuning system resources and investigate how well the application is consuming the privileged time.
Processor: % User Time	% User Time is expressed as a percentage of the elapsed time that the processor spent the user mode in non-idle threads.	If this value is greater than counter % Privileged Time, then focusing on tuning of user/application processes and resources should yield a better return than focusing on server resource utilization.
Processor: Interrupts/sec	Interrupts/sec is the average number of hardware interrupts the processor is receiving and servicing in each second.	As hardware devices attached to the server (ex. network interface card) require attention, they interrupt the CPU to request service. Typical Intel CPUs run at 100 Interrupts/sec. If this value suddenly begins to rise when the workload has not increased, this can be an indication of a hardware problem (which robs valuable CPU cycles from processes that really need it!).
System: Context Switches/sec	Context Switches/sec is the combined rate at which all processors on the computer are switched from one thread to another. Context switches occur when a running thread voluntarily relinquishes the processor, is preempted by a higher priority ready thread, or switches between user mode and privileged (kernel) mode to use an Executive or subsystem service.	If excessive amounts of context switches are occurring, you may be able to improve CPU performance by binding the process experiencing the high context switch rates to a specific CPU by applying hard affinity with Task Manager.

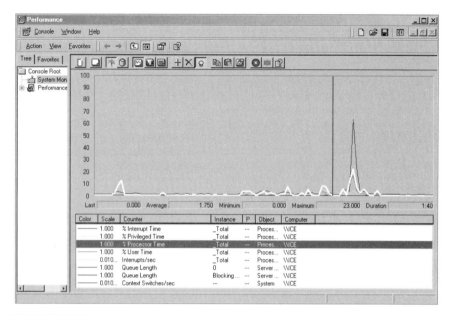

FIGURE 2–9 *Core-CPU-Resource-Usage.msc*

TABLE 2.4 *Core Disk Subsystem Sysmon Counters to Monitor: Definitions and Bottleneck Detection*

Object: Counter	Definition	Rule of Thumb for Bottleneck Detection
Logical Disk: Average Disk Queue Length	Average Disk Queue Length is the average number of both read and write requests that were queued for the selected logical disk during the sample interval.	If this value is greater than 2 for a single disk drive and the disk transfers/sec are high (>100), the selected disk drive is becoming a bottleneck. This value is an average calculated during the Sysmon sample period. Use this counter to determine if there is a disk bottleneck and the Current Disk Queue Length counter to understand the actual workload distribution.
Logical Disk: Disk Transfers/sec	Disk Transfers/sec is the rate of read and write operations on the selected disk.	If this value rises consistently above 80 for a single physical disk drive, observe if the Average Disk sec/Transfer counter is reporting values higher than your baseline or what you consider acceptable. If it is, then the disk drive is slowing down the overall system's performance.

TABLE 2.4	Core Disk Subsystem Sysmon Counters to Monitor: Definitions and Bottleneck Detection (Continued)

Object: Counter	Definition	Rule of Thumb for Bottleneck Detection
Logical Disk: Average Disk sec/Transfer	Average Disk sec/Transfer is the time in seconds of the average disk transfer.	When the Transfers/sec counter is consistently above 80 for a single disk drive, the Average Disk sec/Transfer should be observed to determine if it is rising above your baseline. A value greater than 0.09 seconds indicates that the selected disk drive's response time is uncommonly slow.
Logical Disk: Disk Bytes/sec	Disk Bytes/sec is the rate bytes are transferred to or from the disk during write or read operations.	Sum this counter's value for each disk drive attached to the same SCSI/fibre channel and compare it to 80% of the theoretical throughput for SCSI or fibre channel technology in use. If the summation of Disk Bytes/sec is close to this 80% value, it is the SCSI or financial bus itself that is becoming the disk subsystem's bottleneck. Use this data and some math to review the complete disk subsystem data path.
Logical Disk: Split IO/Sec	Split IO/sec reports the rate that I/Os to the disk were split into multiple I/Os.	A split I/O may result from requesting data in a size that is too large to fit into a single I/O or it may mean that the disk is fragmented. If you observe a higher rate than your normal baseline, run the Windows 2000 defragmenter to check if the disk subsystems are excessively fragmented.

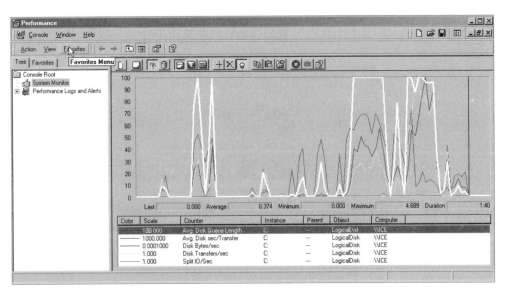

FIGURE 2–10	Core Disk Subsystem Sysmon Counters to Monitor: Core-Disk-Resource-Usage.pmw

TABLE 2.5	Core Memory Subsystem Sysmon Counters to Monitor: Definitions and Bottleneck Detection

Object:Counter	Definition	Rule of Thumb for Bottleneck Detection
Memory:Available Bytes	Available Bytes is the amount of physical memory available to processes running on the system, in bytes.	Windows 2000 Server will try to keep at least 4MB available as seen via this counter (unless using memory has been tuned for file server operations, in which case it will be 1MB). If this value is near or under 4MB and Pages/sec is high, and the disk drive where the page file is located is busy, there is a memory shortfall.
Memory: Pages/sec	Pages/sec is the number of pages read from the disk or written to the disk to resolve memory references that were not in memory at the time of reference.	This counter can be deceiving particularly on Enterprise class systems. High Pages/sec activity is fine (>100 as this counter does measure grabbing data from disk). High values for this counter are not fine if accompanied by a low Available Bytes indicator and sustained Disk Transfers/sec activity on the disk(s) where the paging file resides.
Memory: Pages Output/sec	Pages Output/sec is the number of pages written to disk (page file) to free up space in physical memory. Pages are written back to disk only if they are changed in physical memory, so they are likely to hold data, not code.	A high rate of Pages Output/sec assists in the identification of a memory shortage. Specifically, if this value is high and the Pages/sec value is high, you have low available memory, and the disk that holds your pagefile is busy, you are running short on RAM.
Logical Disk: Transfers/sec (For page file.sys disk drive[s])	Disk Transfers/sec is the rate of read and write operations on the disk.	If you observe any sustained disk activity on the disk drive in which the page file is located shown via the Disk Transfers/sec counter, the Available Bytes are hovering around 4MB, and Pages/sec is high, the Virtual Memory Manager is using the paging file significantly and the server is experiencing a memory bottleneck. Note the Disk Transfers/sec counter must point to disk drive(s) that contains paging system file(s), pagefile.sys.
Memory: Cache Bytes	Cache Bytes is the sum of the System Cache Resident Bytes, System Driver Resident Bytes, System Code Resident Bytes, and Pool Paged Resident Bytes counters.	This counter provides insight into how much of your physical RAM Windows 2000 is using for its dynamic disk cache, e.g., the file system cache and associated key system memory allocations. This is an important counter for troubleshooting if you have memory-intensive applications.
Paging File: % Usage	The amount of the Paging File instance in use in percent.	If a large amount of the pagefile is used on a regular basis, consider adding (Size of pagefile × % of pagefile in use) of RAM to your system.

TABLE 2.5   *Core Memory Subsystem Sysmon Counters to Monitor: Definitions and Bottleneck Detection (Continued)*

Object:Counter	Definition	Rule of Thumb for Bottleneck Detection
Memory: Commit Limit	Commit Limit is the amount of virtual memory that can be committed without having to extend the paging file(s).	This counter provides insight into whether the page file is properly configured. If a pagefile is too small, it can limit the amount of physical RAM you can access.
Server: Pool Nonpaged Failures	The number of times allocations from Nonpaged pool have failed.	If this value is >1 on a regular basis, there is not enough physical memory in the server.
Server: Pool Paged Failures	The number of times allocations from paged pool have failed.	If this value is >1 on a regular basis, there is not enough physical memory in the server or the paging file is too small.

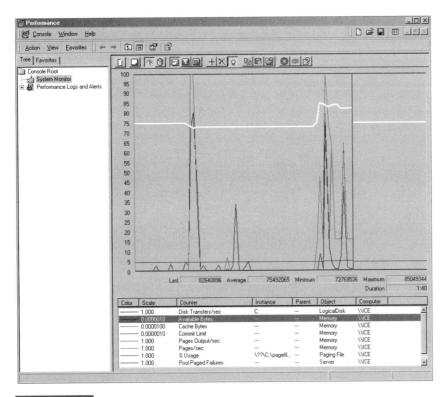

FIGURE 2–11   *Core Sysmon Memory Counters to Monitor: Core-Memory-Resource-Usage.pmw*

| TABLE 2.6 | *Core Network Subsystem Sysmon Counters to Monitor: Definitions and Bottleneck Detection* |

Object/Counter	Definition	Rule of Thumb for Bottleneck Detection
Network Interface: Output Queue Length	Output Queue Length is the length of the output packet queue (in packets).	If this value is longer than 3 for sustained periods of time (longer than 15 minutes), the selected network interface instance is becoming a network bottleneck. (This is valid only for single-CPU Windows 2000 systems.)
Network Interface: Bytes Total/sec	Bytes Total/sec is the rate that all bytes are sent and received on the selected network interface, including those bytes used as overhead (framing, etc.).	This value is directly related to the network architecture in use. If the value of Bytes Total/sec for the network instance is close to the maximum transfer rates of your network, and the Output Queue Length is >3, you have a network bottleneck.
Network Interface: Current Bandwidth	Current Bandwidth is an estimate of the interface's current bandwidth in bits per second.	For interfaces that do not vary in bandwidth or for those where no accurate estimation can be made, this value is the nominal bandwidth reported by Windows 2000. Use this information in conjunction with the Bytes Total/sec counter to determine the network utilization levels. Be careful! This counter states what Windows 2000 thinks the bandwidth is. Sometimes information provided by the NIC is incorrect.
Network Interface: Packets Outbound and Received Errors	Packets Outbound Errors/Received is the number of outbound packets that could not be transmitted/processed because of network errors.	If this value is >1, the selected network interface is experiencing network problems that are causing the network to slow and potentially become a bottleneck. This problem could be emanating from any NIC or network device connected to the network segment.
Redirector: Current Commands	Current Commands counts the number of requests to the Redirector that are currently queued for service.	If this number is much larger than the number of network adapter cards installed in the computer, then the network(s) and/or the server(s) being accessed are seriously bottlenecked.
Server: Work Item Shortage	The number of times STATUS_DATA_NOT_ACCEPTED was returned at receive indication time.	This indicates that Windows 2000 has not allocated sufficient InitWorkItems or MaxWorkItems, which is causing network limitations. Consider tuning the InitWorkItems or MaxWorkItems parameters to remove this bottleneck.

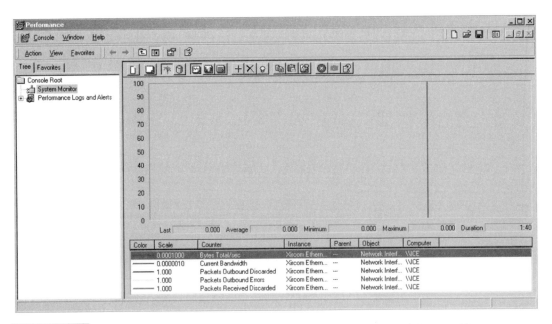

FIGURE 2–12   *Core Network Subsystem Sysmon Counters to Monitor: Network-Resource-Usage.pmw*

Note that you may need to customize which counters you use in addition to the core counters recommended depending on your specific environment. Additional counters are reviewed in chapters dedicated to specific subsystems. If your physical system environment differs (number of instances) from the figures illustrated in Figures 2-9–2-12 and Tables 2.3–2.6 in areas such as network or disk subsystems, you may need to change the number of instances (the actual physical device instances) in Sysmon. Even though these are good counters to observe when gaining an immediate understanding of system resource usage, you should experiment with others as well. There are numerous other objects and counters available under Sysmon that provide additional detailed insight into the performance of your system for your particular environment. We investigate numerous advanced counters in later chapters.

Sysmon Counter Log Mode

Sysmon's log mode allows for the long-term collection of Windows 2000 performance data. Collection of long-term data facilitates the detection of bottlenecks and helps you to determine system trends for troubleshooting, capacity sizing data, and baseline comparison analysis. Performance logging in Windows 2000 is now a service! This enables increased performance collection functionality compared to Windows NT 4. Note that, with this architectural change, there is no reason to add the monitor service from the Windows NT 4 Resource Kit, as was needed for this functionality in NT 4. Having the logging function running as a service provides numerous benefits such as: no need to log in to ensure logging is occurring, more options of when it starts/ stops, ability to use Windows 2000 Resource Kit tools such as *sc.exe* to remotely start and stop the system, and an increased number of log file formats that are supported..

To begin logging data with Sysmon, start Sysmon, expand Performance Logs & Alerts in the left pane, highlight Counter Logs, and then in the right pane right click and select New Log Settings. At this point, provide a descriptive name for this log set, and you will be presented with the properties tabs of the log set you are creating. In the general tab, you must add those objects/ counters combinations that you would like to log. It is important to note here that you can select All Counters per object and All Instances per object, but NOT for all objects/counters as was the case with Windows NT 4. For example, if you select the Processor object, all counters, all instances, only the counters for the Processor object will be added to the log for monitoring. Thus, if you were to follow the methodology above for high-level basic monitoring, you would add all defined core instances for Processor, Network Interface, Memory, Logical Disk, Server, System Processor Queue Length, System, Paging File, and the Redirector. From here, select the schedule tab and check the appropriate boxes to log performance data as you see fit.

When to Collect Sysmon Data

When should performance data be collected? The ideal answer is all of the time, since you may need the data for future sizing requirements or to troubleshoot a problem. The major stumbling block when running Sysmon logs all of the time is disk space. When you log data, you need to place it somewhere. Table 2.7 outlines the amount of data that is logged when all objects are selected for measurement compared to the core counter sets outlined in Tables 2.3–2.6. Use Table 2.7 for general planning purposes only. The number of processes that are currently running, the number of instances of hardware, and the addition of Performance Monitor objects (that may have been added via additional application installations) influence the amount of data logged.

The frequency of the sampling period depends on your environment and what you want to accomplish. Obviously, the shorter the sampling period, the better the chance that you will discover any temporary workload surges on the system. Conversely, the amount of disk space used can become prohibitive. Sysmon provides several options that can help put you in more of a commanding position when it comes to controlling the amount of disk space taken for performance logging. Two of the most helpful options are Binary Circular Logging and Sysmon's Logging Scheduler. When

TABLE 2.7	Performance Monitor Log Rate

Performance Monitor Log Growth Rate

Goal	Sampling Period	Sampling Strategy	Log File Size in 1 Hour
Detailed troubleshooting	Once every second	All counters	720KB × 3,600 = **2.59GB/hour**
		Core counters	8KB × 3,600 = **28.8MB/hour**
Short-term analysis	Once every 5 seconds	All counters	720KB/sec × 12 x 60 = **518MB/hour**
		Core counters	8KB/sec × 12 x 60 = **5.7MB/hour**
Long-term analysis	Once every 10 minutes	All counters	720KB/sec × 6= **4.3MB/hour**
		Core counters	8KB/sec × 12 x 60 = **0.48MB/hour**

circular logging is enabled, Sysmon is set to use only a predefined log file size and then it will begin rewriting the file. Why would you want this? Perhaps you are interested in keeping only 7 days of performance information on your Windows 2000 system. You can then set your log file size appropriately to hold 7 days of core data (~84MB of core counter collection). Once the log file reaches the maximum size you have defined, Sysmon logging will rewrite over the same space. In this manner, you will always have at least a one-week baseline available. To access circular logging, select the properties page of the Sysmon log set you are interested in and select the Log File tab to access the circular logging option.

What if you want to keep logs weekly, but would like to store these logs on a central file server for safekeeping so as to not tie up disk space on the local system? To implement this strategy, select properties for the Sysmon log set in question and choose the Schedule tab. Under the Schedule tab (shown in Figure 2-13), you can have the scheduler stop logging after 7 days, then run a batch script to move your logs to the central file server, and delete the local file. Once Sysmon runs the batch file, it will then restart the logs and increment the name of the new log.

If you were developing a prototype, a more frequent sampling rate would provide the increased granularity required to understand the detailed workload characteristics and for analysis. For general system health, 9 out of 10 engineers surveyed recommend between 10 and 20 minutes between samples. After reviewing the 10- to 20-minute sampling period data, there may be times that you need to start a copy of Sysmon with a higher sampling period and an associated higher number of objects/counters to assist in isolating problem areas. But of course you really want detailed data when an actual performance problem occurs. This is when Sysmon's alerting function can become a useful ally.

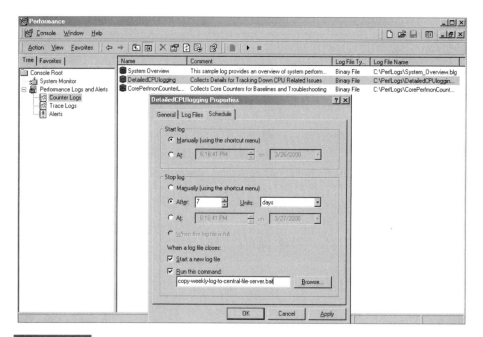

FIGURE 2–13 *Scheduling Sysmon Log Sets*

Sysmon Alerts

Have customers complained about poor system performance, but when you investigated everything looked fine (the magical look-over-the-shoulder resolution)? Are they running Sysmon in a high-level mode to avoid logging tons of data, but need detailed data for sporadic problems? Performance Monitor's alert feature comes to the rescue in these types of situations. OK, not quite to the rescue, but it can be very useful. Under Sysmon's alert mode, you can easily set thresholds for various system resource parameters that in turn trigger other events. This is helpful in reducing the amount of time required to review the performance logs. This tool can become even more powerful when coupled with the Sysmon logging service. Use these two tools in concert. You can start a second copy of Sysmon to log current data at a higher sampling rate for a given amount of time to assist in sleuthing out the real performance problem.

SETTING UP SYSMON ALERTS

To take advantage of Sysmon, first determine what to alert on. As a starting point on what to alert on and associated thresholds to use, Sysmon counters are presented in Table 2.8.

TABLE 2.8	*When to Alert—Sysmon Counters Thresholds*

Object: Counter on which to Alert	Threshold	Why
Logical Disk: Average Disk Queue Length (all instances)	2	You should investigate if you must wait in line for system resources on a regular basis.
Server Work Queue	2	You should investigate if you must wait in line for system resources on a regular basis.
Memory: Available Bytes	4.5MB	If the amount of physical memory (RAM) is consistently low, you should investigate this condition—it can cause the system to run very slowly.
Network Interface: Bytes/sec	80% of network medium in use	If the network usage is consistently running at this level, this could affect this and other systems and should be investigated.

For example, let's set an alert to start a copy of the Performance Monitor counter logs to track down detailed processor and CPU information when CPU usage exceeds 98%. (Occasional peaks in CPU usage might trigger this alert even when a problem doesn't exist. You can use third-party tools to start additional performance collection based on more advanced logical sequences—i.e., when CPU usage exceeds 90% for 5 minutes *and* the System Processor Queue Length is greater than 1, start additional performance data collection.) To configure this alert, start System Monitor, then in the left pane expand Performance Logs & Alerts and highlight Alerts. Right-click in the right pane and select New, Create New Alert Settings, and a name. Add the counters you want to monitor and their thresholds for triggering an action; select the Action tab, the Start Performance Log option, a counter log to start, and the Schedule tab; fill in the times you want the monitor to run. For this example we are targeting CPU-related issues. For Figure 2-14, I previously configured a Sysmon log set with all instances selected for the following objects: Processor, Process, Server, System Processor Queue Length, System, Threads, and Object.

With this configuration, Sysmon will alert you when your system has a performance problem, and the software will provide you with quantifiable and empirical data that illustrates which process is causing the problem.

Performance Monitor's alert feature is flexible. You can tell the alert function to start any script or application. For example, you can have the system send you an e-mail message or start a batch file that pings (i.e., *ping.exe*), then trace routes (i.e., *tracert.exe*), or run the new *pathping.exe* command to troubleshoot the network path to a distant system with which you want to interact. In this manner, you can measure the network response time to determine whether your network has problems in other locations besides the server.

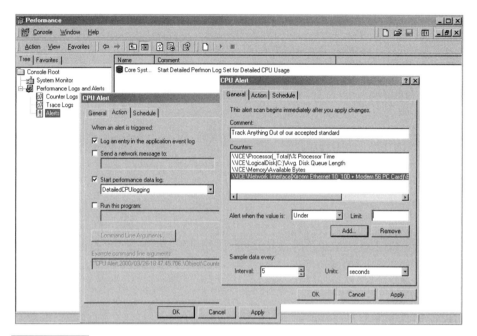

FIGURE 2–14   *Configuring Sysmon Alerts*

CASE STUDY: USING WINDOWS 2000 PERFORMANCE TOOLS AND CUSTOMER PER-SPECTIVE TO ISOLATE WEB PERFORMANCE PROBLEMS • When something is running poorly, you immediately need the appropriate data to track down and determine a resolution. For this high-level example, we will focus on tracking down web services delivery problems by using the tools presented thus far in this chapter. In the CustomerPerspectiveWebMonitoringModuleScript.pl script (CPWMM) (see Code Example 2-5), we sent an alert to the SuperSA when there was a problem. What about sending some diagnostic information too? From the CPWMM, we can add several key actions to help isolate problems related to providing web services.

When the web server does not respond appropriately, we can add these key troubleshooting actions: ping.exe and tracert.exe. This is accomplished in the CPWMM script—right after the comment "# Once the baseline is crossed generate an error" we can generate the actions we want by calling another Perl32 module named optmod.pl (shown above in Code Example 2-8). We can then log these results by writing them to a log file and have them sent to our SuperSA. Why ping the web site? If the server is not responding to a web request adequately, we can determine general network latency by using the *ping* command included with Windows 2000. Ping provides the generic round-trip packet response time to the problematic web server in question. This provides insight into whether the server or network is completely down or whether the overall network latency is slowing down the delivery of web pages. If there is a network problem, which network device is unavailable or running slow? To isolate these types of problems, we can use the *tracert.exe* (or *pathping.exe*) command that is also included in Windows 2000. Tracert checks the generic data packet response time from the perspective of every network route or hop. An example tracert.exe output is included in Figure 2-15. With this information, you can determine where the slowest path is between your CPWMM system (your customers) and your web site or which network link has failed.

Tracing route to www.yahoo.com [204.71.200.68] over a maximum of 30 hops:

```
 1 <10 ms   <10 ms   <10 ms   212.119.249.199
 2 140 ms    78 ms    47 ms   dca1-cpe7-s6.atlas.digex.net [206.181.92.65]
 3  78 ms    63 ms    94 ms   dca1-core11-g2-0.atlas.digex.net [165.117.17.20]
 4 109 ms   141 ms   125 ms   dca1-core12-pos6-0.atlas.digex.net [165.117.59.98]
 5 109 ms    78 ms   109 ms   s2-0-0.br2.iad.gblx.net [209.143.255.49]
 6  62 ms    63 ms    94 ms   pos9-0-155m.cr1.iad3.gblx.net [208.178.254.117]
 7 219 ms   218 ms   204 ms   pos6-0-622m.cr2.snv.gblx.net [206.132.151.14]
 8  79 ms    78 ms    62 ms   pos1-0-2488m.hr8.snv.gblx.net [206.132.254.41]
 9 125 ms    78 ms    93 ms   bas1r-ge3-0-hr8.snv.yahoo.com [208.178.103.62]
10  93 ms    94 ms    94 ms   www3.yahoo.com [204.71.200.68]
Trace complete.
```

FIGURE 2–15   *Isolating Network Problems with Tracert.exe*

New for Windows 2000, but not included in the optmod.pl script is the pathping.exe command. This command gives you finer grain control over the number of hops when trying to locate your web site, time to wait before attempts, the number of tries per network hop, and the ability to determine the functionality available on the network in such areas as layer 2 priority and RSVP support. Type pathping.exe \? from the command line to learn about this new network troubleshooting tool.

What about the server itself? Most likely you have the Windows 2000 performance collection monitor Sysmon enabled and running on your web server as we have outlined above. You can then match the timeframe when your CPWMM system (customers) experienced web server problems to the associated Sysmon data, which you can review to isolate server-side problems. Yes, we will go into more in-depth bottleneck investigations in later chapters, but I thought it was important to illustrate the *big picture* now so that you can see the value and the interrelation of the measurement tools presented thus far. The combination of customer perspective data from CPWMM, network performance diagnostic information, and Sysmon data from the server provides you with a formidable arsenal to track, troubleshoot, and resolve web services performance issues before they become problems.

Using Auditing to Zero in on Resource Usage

What two words come to mind when server auditing is mentioned? *Overhead* and *slow!* These are the most typical responses. Auditing does add a certain amount of overhead to any system. The amount of overhead incurred is a function of the level of auditing that is turned on and the amount of load placed on the system. This is a direct proportional relationship. The more auditing options selected and the more the server is used, the higher account-ing overhead percentage there is. Auditing is typically associated with secu-rity, but here we use auditing to our advantage to zero in on who is running processes that are placing load on the system. By being selective when choos-ing the system auditing metrics to collect, we can make system auditing be helpful while not introducing a significant overhead onto the server.

What are the typical areas that are audited? You can use file tracking to determine where and which files are being used and who is using them. Pro-cess/object tracking can help determine who is running which background processes. This information is important when trying to load balance your system either by controlling which server the application is run on or deter-mining the best time to run a particular application.

How do you set auditing for file use? The approach is similar regardless of whether you are auditing a local computer or one that is part of an active directory domain. First, auditing must be enabled. To enable auditing on your local system, start up a Microsoft Management Console (MMC) from the com-mand line using the /a option, *mmc /a* and then add the Group Policy object by selecting Add from the MMC menu. Now that you have the console ready, traverse the following path in the left pane: Windows Settings / Security Set-tings / Local Policies / Audit Policies / Audit / System Events. Once the Group Policy object is activated, use Explorer to locate folders or files you would like track access to. Once found, highlight and right-click the folder/file, Properties, Security, Advanced, Auditing, Add a user (commonly everyone); then select what auditable events you would like to track. To track object use, follow these same steps except do not use Explorer to select folders/files to audit. Instead, select Audit Object Access and Process Tracking. The results from auditing these events are found in the Windows 2000 Security Event Viewer located at Start / Programs / Administration Tools / Component Services / Event Viewer / Security. *Be careful when using auditing for performance/sys-tem monitoring or even security monitoring.* On a very busy system, auditing too many areas places a significant load on your system. Always test any changes in a lab environment under load before heading off into production!

Windows Task Manager

Task Manager was the best software performance monitoring and management tool addition to NT 4 from Windows 2000 3.51. It has been enhanced for Windows 2000. The new information provided by Task Manager was previously only available by using a combination of Resource Kit and third-party tools, but they were neither as friendly nor installed by default. There are several options to launch Task Manager: right-click the Windows 2000 tool bar and select Task Manager, type in *taskmgr.exe* from the command prompt, or select Task Manager after pressing ctrl-alt-delete at the same time. Task Manager is a tool that provides a current look at what is running on your system from three different perspectives: applications, processes, and performance. Task Manager provides an almost instantaneous view of how your system is running as shown in Figure 2-16.

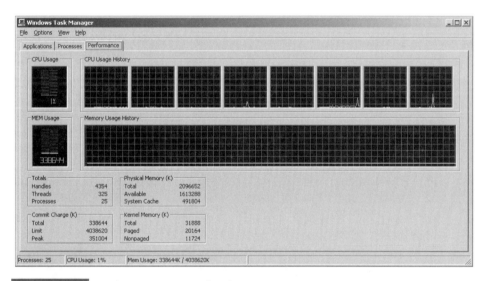

FIGURE 2-16   *Task Manager Overall Performance View*

Since Task Manager does not have a file-logging mode, this tool is not helpful for long-term or baseline logging, but it is very helpful in isolating and managing active performance problems. In later chapters, we go into the details of these management options. As a preview, with Task Manager you can kill a rogue process and all processes spawned by that process, change the priority of specific processes, and even apply affinity to specific processor and process combinations. All of these functions are accessed by selecting the process in the Task Manager process view, right-clicking the process, then selecting the desired action (see Figure 2-17).

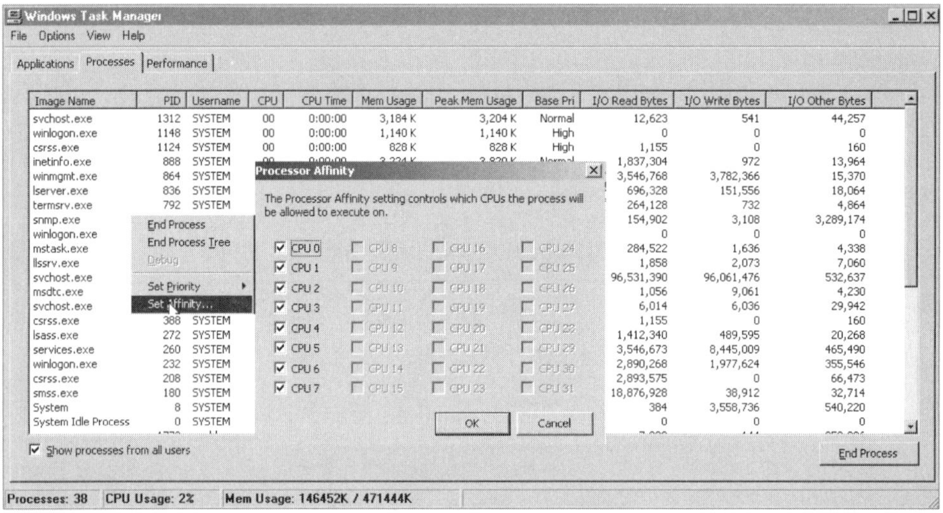

FIGURE 2-17 *Managing Windows 2000 Processes with Task Manager*

For example, suppose the system has suddenly become CPU bound; at about the same time an end user mentions that some of his applications have gone astray and are not responding. Using Task Manager's Process view, you can quickly determine which processes are running amok and analyze their system usage. You can also quickly determine if the processes in question are continually using more RAM, how much CPU time they are accumulating, and how much disk activity the process is consuming; then you can kill them off if needed by right-clicking on the process and selecting End Process. Or, you may just want to lower the priority of the process in question again by right clicking on the process and selecting a lower priority level. These are advanced system administration and performance management approaches, so take care. Do not kill anything if you do not know exactly what it is or you could cause more harm than good. Task Manager is very similar to the UNIX tool top in depicting which processes are running and which resources they are consuming.

Understanding what processes are normally being executed on your system is helpful with troubleshooting performance problems. Task Manager is a great tool for instantly observing what processes are running on your server. Figure 2-17 provides an illustration of the extensive information that Task Manager can quickly provide. The following fields are shown:

- **Image Name**–depicts the processes that are in memory and can be run on the CPU
- **PID**–Process ID (assigned by Windows 2000 upon creation)

- **Username**–which user is running the application (particularly useful when running Terminal Services
- **CPU**–current CPU usage
- **CPU Time**–accumulated CPU time since the process was started
- **Memory Usage**–the amount of physical RAM the process is currently occupying
- **Peak Memory Usage**–the maximum amount of RAM the process has requested
- **Base Priority**–at what priority level a process is running
- **I/O Read Bytes**–how much disk/network read activity the process has completed (NEW)
- **I/O Write Bytes**–how much disk/network write activity the process has completed (NEW)
- **I/O Other Bytes**–how much activity the process has completed that does not fall into the fields above, such as sending output to the console (NEW)

Performance Monitor can provide similar information, although it is not as easy to use as Task Manager, but its data can be logged. When looking at these process outputs, some of the processes that are presented may seem obvious—their image name is descriptive—and some will seem alien. The following is a listing and definition of the common processes that run in the background after a Windows 2000 server installation, before additional applications and services are installed or running.

services–Service Controller (also known as Service Control Manager) starts all the services. A number of Win32 services developed for Windows 2000 have been written to share the Service Controller's process in order to conserve system resources. Some of these services in the Service Control Manager include PlugPlay, ProtectedStorage, seclogon, Trk-Wks, Wmi, Alerter, Browser, Dhcp, dmserver, Dnscache, Eventlog, lanmanserver, lanmanworkstation, LmHosts, and Messenger.

idle process–Contains one thread for each CPU in the system to account for idle time.

svhost–shared service area that can include EventSystem, RasMan, etc.

csrss–Client Server Runtime Subsystem provides text window support, shutdown, and hard error handling to Windows 2000 environment subsystems (user mode portion of the Win32 subsystem).

explorer—a segment of the user interface that lets users open documents and applications from a hierarchical display.

llssrv—License Logging Service, the service that logs the licensing data for license manager in Windows 2000.

mstask—Windows 2000 Task Scheduler.

lsass—Local Security Administration Subsystem runs the local security authority component of NT security subsystem. This process handles aspects of security administration on the local computer, including access and permissions. The Net Logon Service shares this process.

ntvdm—Windows 2000 virtual DOS Machine, which simulates a 16-bit environment for MS-DOS and 16-bit Windows applications.

mmc—This process image can be running a variety of applications such as Windows 2000 admin tools or Performance Monitor.

smss—Session Manage Subsystem, which creates the user mode environment that provides the visible interface to Windows 2000.

spoolss—spooler subsystem, which controls despooling of printer data from disk to printer.

system—contains system (memory manager, cache manager, virtual memory manager, threads that handle lazy writing by file system, virtual memory modified page writing, working set trimming, and similar system functions).

taskmgr—Task Manager executable.

winlogon—Logon process executable manages log on/off and remote Performance Monitor data requests.

When you use Task Manager, have you found that there are additional processes running on your system that you are not aware of? Multiple copies even? Of course you must know what is running on your system to optimize and troubleshoot it. In the next section are several tools that I have found to be very helpful for tracking down what is running on your system but are not available when you install the base Windows 2000 operating system.

Additional Performance-Related Tools from Windows 2000

The following tools were included in previous Windows resource kits, but are now part of the Windows 2000 support tools, located on the Windows 2000 operating system CD-ROM in the \support directory. The support Tools must be installed separately from the Windows 2000 operating system. While there are numerous helpful tools available from the Support Tools section, reviewed here are only the tools I have found helpful in advanced administration of Windows 2000 systems for performance-related issues.

Tlist.exe

This tool is awesome! This is a command line tool that enables you to delve much deeper into the processes running on your system so that you can find out what is really running on your Windows 2000 system. When you run *tlist.exe | more* from the command line, you are provided with a listing of the process ID (PID), the process image name, and some basic image information if available. For example, Windows 2000 services share many image names but since each may be running a different task, it becomes difficult to determine which process is running what. In the Task Manager process list, you may have noticed that there are several copies of mmc.exe running, each with its own PID. To determine which process is running what, use Tlist! Figure 2-18 exhibits how you can quickly isolate this information via various tlist command line options. The first command run is *tlist | find "mmc"* which selects only the output lines from the tlist that contain the mmc string. With this information, you can determine which mmc is running what and the associated PID. Why is this important? If you have ever had an mmc hang on you and needed to kill it off, how would you know which mmc image to kill? The next line in Figure 2-18 is tlist –s | more. The -s option helps to determine which services (i.e., the name given to the service in the registry) are associated with each image (program/binary). Again, besides entertainment value, why would you want this information? I have run into some services that were not configured correctly that began to extract excessive resources from Windows 2000 systems. With tlist and Sysmon, I was able to narrow down the service that was causing the problem and resolve the situation. There are many more helpful options that tlist provides such as listing all the Dynamic Linked Libraries (DLLs) that a process has loaded. I strongly suggest giving tlist a test drive. It is read-only, so you really cannot do much damage with it. For all of the tlist options, run tlist /? from the command line.

Kill.exe

Kill is another Windows 2000 support tool addition. With this command line tool, you must be *very careful* because it is very powerful. In a nutshell, Kill enables you to kill just about every process available. Yes, even processes that will immediately bring Windows 2000 to a screeching halt! (I do not suggest testing that one unless you are on a lab system that you do not mind trashing your system.) Why such a tool? There are some poorly written applications that run amok, and Task Manager will not let you kill them with its GUI. Although Windows 2000 keeps the application from crashing your system, what if it must be removed to enable other applications to work properly? Kill to the rescue. Run Kill from the command line with the PID of the image you wish to stop. Running Kill in this manner "requests" that the application stop running. When run with the /f option, the application is forced to die. I have

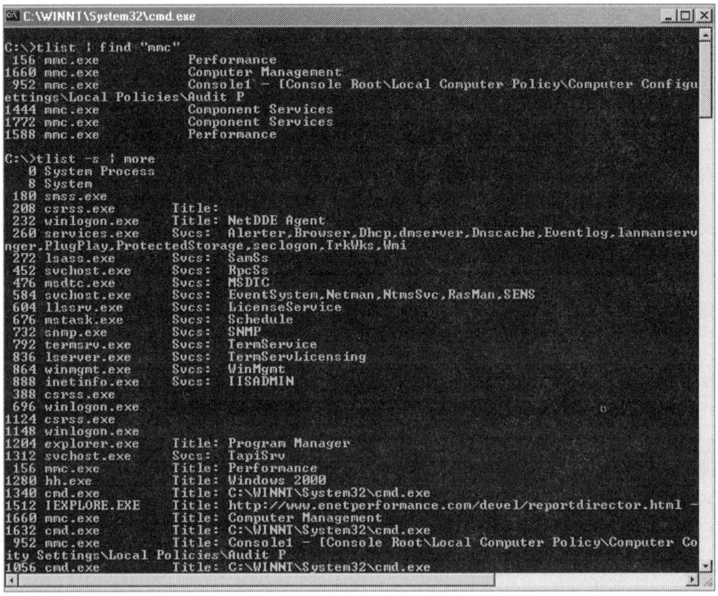

FIGURE 2–18   *Tlist Image Tracking*

found this tool very helpful in production environments where the vendor support team requests that the system be rebooted—very undesirable at the time—to fix the problem. However, in reality no reboot is necessary. What is really needed is the removal of a component of their application, which can be accomplished with the Kill command. Wrkill.exe, a network-aware and GUI version of Kill, is available with the Windows 2000 Resource Kit and performs functions similar to the command line version. As with any powerful set of tools, watch the security settings closely.

Windows 2000 Resource Kit Performance Management Tools

There are many helpful tools outlined in the Windows 2000 Resource Kit for administering, monitoring, and stress testing your Windows 2000 system's environment. I strongly urge you to review the tools it provides. The Windows 2000 Resource Kit does a nice job explaining how to use a variety of its tools. The following sections briefly describe several that I have found helpful.

Ptree.exe

Ptree.exe is another option for advanced removal of processes running locally and remotely and their associated subprocesses and threads. The concepts are similar to those reviewed above for the *kill.exe* command. However, the installation does take a few more steps and a reboot. These directions are available in the Windows 2000 Resource Kit.

Sc.exe

The service controller tool provides a powerful instrument to monitor and manage local and remote services operating on Windows 2000 systems. This tool used in conjunction with Tlist provides the mechanism to investigate and troubleshoot service problems in depth and to learn what is truly running on your system.

CreateFil.exe

Enables the creation of any size files. This is very helpful when running performance tests.

Ntimer.exe

Ntimer is a command line tool that measures how long a program runs. It shows elapsed time (ETime), time in user mode (UTime), and time in privileged mode (KTime). These are expressed in hours:minutes:seconds:milliseconds.

WPerf.exe

WPerf provides real-time information on the performance of your system and a multipanel display that looks great. It provides a friendly insight on how your internal system resource usage is moving along.

Freeware Performance Management Tools

The combination of Windows 2000 and the Windows 2000 Resource Kit provides an excellent arsenal of performance management tools. However, there are many creative people in the world, and many of them share their expertise over the Internet. The following are several freeware tools you should add to your performance management arsenal that will help provide insight into the hows and whys that native Windows 2000 tools do not cover.

Filemon.exe

Sometimes you may not know which files to track, or even which files are being accessed on a particular volume, which becomes important when trying to load balance your disk I/O subsystem. For this task, try the freeware tool Filmon.exe from the http://www.systinternals.com. This is an excellent tool used to investigate which files are being accessed and which processes are responsible for this access. Figure 2-19 shows an example output from the Filmon.exe tool.

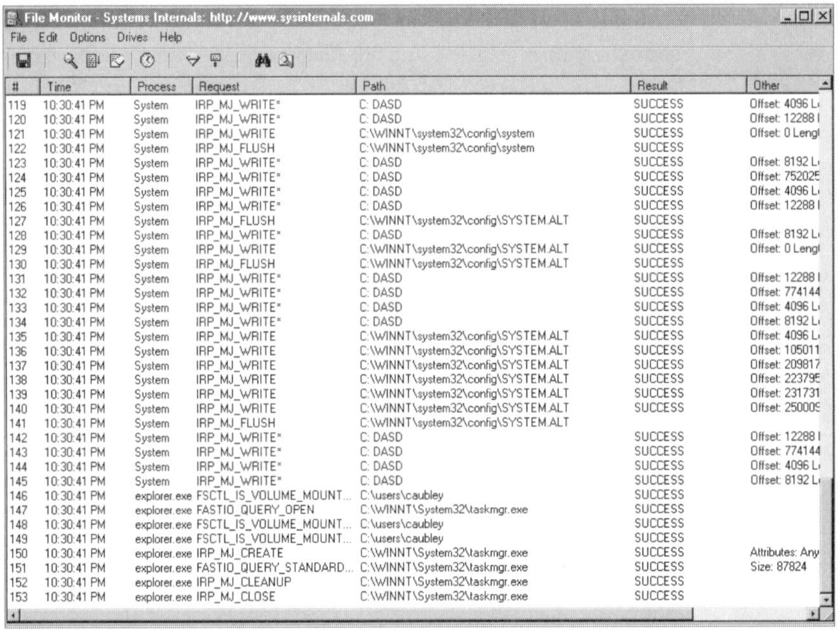

FIGURE 2–19   *Using Filmon.exe to Track All File Accesses (Where and by Whom)*

Regmon.exe

The behavior of many applications is dictated by how their setup files and registry are configured. Sometimes it can be difficult to determine what the application relies on if it is not well documented. To determine this information, use Filemon.exe (above) and try the freeware tool Regmon.exe from the http://www.systinternals.com. This is an excellent tool used to investigate which registry entries are being accessed and which processes are responsible for this access. Figure 2-20 shows a sample output from the Regmon.exe tool.

#	Time	Process	Request	Path	Result	Other
66	42.08272979	mmc.exe	CloseKey	HKLM\System\CurrentControlSet\Control\ContentIndex	SUCCESS	Key: 0xE27BE270
67	47.08916894	mmc.exe	OpenKey	HKLM\System\CurrentControlSet\Control\ContentIndex	SUCCESS	Key: 0xE27BE270
68	47.08993936	mmc.exe	CloseKey	HKLM\System\CurrentControlSet\Control\ContentIndex	SUCCESS	Key: 0xE27BE270
69	51.44145331	snagit32.exe	OpenKey	HKLM\Software\Microsoft\DirectDraw	SUCCESS	Key: 0xE13009F0
70	51.44149522	snagit32.exe	QueryValue	HKLM\Software\Microsoft\DirectDraw\EnumerateAttachedSecondaries	NOTFOUND	
71	51.44157232	snagit32.exe	CloseKey	HKLM\Software\Microsoft\DirectDraw	SUCCESS	Key: 0xE13009F0
72	51.56000274	snagit32.exe	OpenKey	HKLM\Hardware\DeviceMap\VIDEO	SUCCESS	Key: 0xE2552390
73	51.56004939	snagit32.exe	QueryValue	HKLM\Hardware\DeviceMap\VIDEO\MaxObjectNumber	SUCCESS	0x2
74	51.56014549	snagit32.exe	CloseKey	HKLM\Hardware\DeviceMap\VIDEO	SUCCESS	Key: 0xE2552390
75	51.56027456	snagit32.exe	OpenKey	HKLM\SYSTEM\CURRENTCONTROLSET\ENUM	SUCCESS	Key: 0xE1493B10
76	51.56038212	snagit32.exe	OpenKey	HKLM\SYSTEM\CURRENTCONTROLSET\ENUM\PCI\VEN_1002&DEV_4C4D&...	SUCCESS	Key: 0xE28688B0
77	51.56042374	snagit32.exe	CloseKey	HKLM\SYSTEM\CURRENTCONTROLSET\ENUM	SUCCESS	Key: 0xE1493B10
78	51.56046956	snagit32.exe	QueryValue	HKLM\SYSTEM\CURRENTCONTROLSET\ENUM\PCI\VEN_1002&DEV_4C4D&...	BUFTOOS...	
79	51.56051984	snagit32.exe	QueryValue	HKLM\SYSTEM\CURRENTCONTROLSET\ENUM\PCI\VEN_1002&DEV_4C4D&...	SUCCESS	"PCI\VEN_1002&DEV_4C4...
80	51.56057208	snagit32.exe	CloseKey	HKLM\SYSTEM\CURRENTCONTROLSET\ENUM\PCI\VEN_1002&DEV_4C4D&...	SUCCESS	Key: 0xE28688B0
81	51.56065198	snagit32.exe	OpenKey	HKLM\SYSTEM\CURRENTCONTROLSET\ENUM	SUCCESS	Key: 0xE2871FD0
82	51.56072154	snagit32.exe	OpenKey	HKLM\SYSTEM\CURRENTCONTROLSET\ENUM\PCI\VEN_1002&DEV_4C4D&...	SUCCESS	Key: 0xE13AE510
83	51.56077714	snagit32.exe	CloseKey	HKLM\SYSTEM\CURRENTCONTROLSET\ENUM	SUCCESS	Key: 0xE2871FD0
84	51.56081737	snagit32.exe	QueryValue	HKLM\SYSTEM\CURRENTCONTROLSET\ENUM\PCI\VEN_1002&DEV_4C4D&...	BUFTOOS...	
85	51.56086179	snagit32.exe	QueryValue	HKLM\SYSTEM\CURRENTCONTROLSET\ENUM\PCI\VEN_1002&DEV_4C4D&...	SUCCESS	"PCI\VEN_1002&DEV_4C4...
86	51.56090509	snagit32.exe	CloseKey	HKLM\SYSTEM\CURRENTCONTROLSET\ENUM\PCI\VEN_1002&DEV_4C4D&...	SUCCESS	Key: 0xE13AE510
87	51.56097800	snagit32.exe	OpenKey	HKLM\Hardware\DeviceMap\Video	SUCCESS	Key: 0xE13AE510
88	51.56102186	snagit32.exe	OpenKey	HKLM\Hardware\DeviceMap\Video\\Device\Video0	SUCCESS	"\REGISTRY\Machine\Syst...
89	51.56107746	snagit32.exe	CloseKey	HKLM\Hardware\DeviceMap\Video	SUCCESS	Key: 0xE13AE510
90	51.56116965	snagit32.exe	OpenKey	HKLM\Hardware\DeviceMap\VIDEO	SUCCESS	Key: 0xE13AE510
91	51.56120596	snagit32.exe	QueryValue	HKLM\Hardware\DeviceMap\VIDEO\MaxObjectNumber	SUCCESS	0x2
92	51.56124563	snagit32.exe	CloseKey	HKLM\Hardware\DeviceMap\VIDEO	SUCCESS	Key: 0xE13AE510
93	51.56132693	snagit32.exe	OpenKey	HKLM\Hardware\DeviceMap\Video	SUCCESS	Key: 0xE13AE510
94	51.56137442	snagit32.exe	OpenKey	HKLM\Hardware\DeviceMap\Video\\Device\Video2	SUCCESS	"\REGISTRY\Machine\Syst...
95	51.56142973	snagit32.exe	CloseKey	HKLM\Hardware\DeviceMap\Video	SUCCESS	Key: 0xE13AE510
96	51.56151550	snagit32.exe	OpenKey	HKLM\Hardware\DeviceMap\VIDEO	SUCCESS	Key: 0xE13AE510
97	51.56155182	snagit32.exe	QueryValue	HKLM\Hardware\DeviceMap\VIDEO\MaxObjectNumber	SUCCESS	0x2
98	51.56159121	snagit32.exe	CloseKey	HKLM\Hardware\DeviceMap\VIDEO	SUCCESS	Key: 0xE13AE510

FIGURE 2–20   *Regmon.exe Display*

Handle.exe

Handle.exe enables you to dig deeper into the applications that are running on your system and to find out what dependencies they have such as which handles and DLLs the processes have opened or loaded. This tool is available as freeware from http://www.systinternals.com. Its display consists of two windows (see Figure 2-21), where the top window always shows a list of the currently active processes. The bottom window displays in handle mode—you'll see the handles that the process selected in the top window has opened; if it is in DLL mode, you'll see the DLLs that the process has loaded. Handle.exe also has a powerful search capability that will quickly show you which processes have particular handles opened or DLLs loaded. The unique capabilities of Handle.exe make it useful for tracking down DLL version problems or for handling leaks, as well as providing insight into the way NT and applications work.

Windows 2000 System Checkup

If your server's hardware and software components are not all working properly, they will never be able to perform well. Analogous to a car with an 8-cylinder engine, if only 5 of the 8 cylinders are running correctly, the biggest

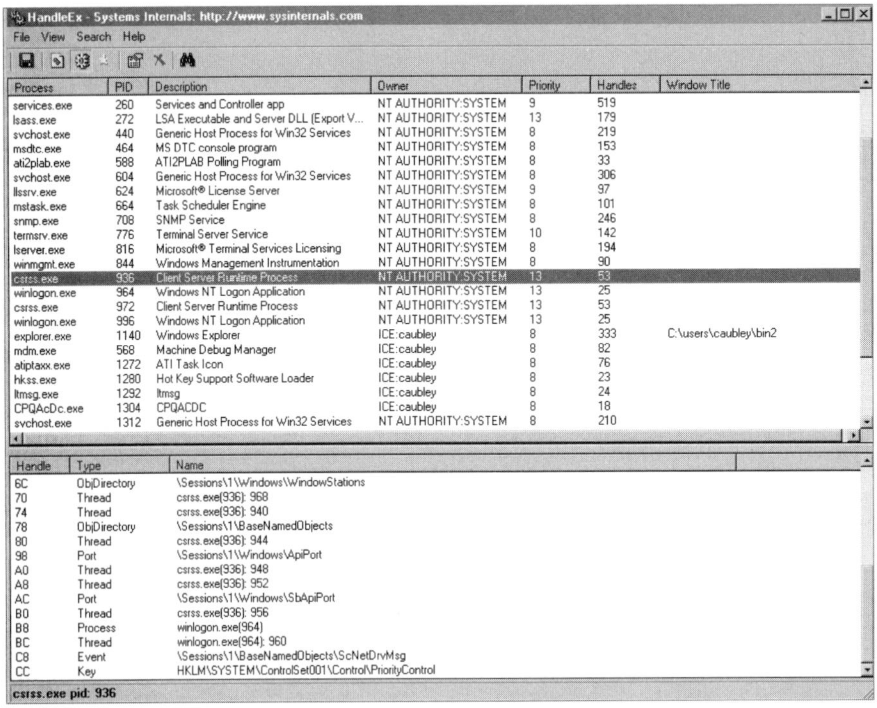

HandleEx - Systems Internals: http://www.sysinternals.com

File View Search Help

Process	PID	Description	Owner	Priority	Handles	Window Title
services.exe	260	Services and Controller app	NT AUTHORITY:SYSTEM	9	519	
lsass.exe	272	LSA Executable and Server DLL (Export V...	NT AUTHORITY:SYSTEM	13	179	
svchost.exe	440	Generic Host Process for Win32 Services	NT AUTHORITY:SYSTEM	8	219	
msdtc.exe	464	MS DTC console program	NT AUTHORITY:SYSTEM	8	153	
ati2plab.exe	588	ATI2PLAB Polling Program	NT AUTHORITY:SYSTEM	8	33	
svchost.exe	604	Generic Host Process for Win32 Services	NT AUTHORITY:SYSTEM	8	306	
llssrv.exe	624	Microsoft® License Server	NT AUTHORITY:SYSTEM	9	97	
mstask.exe	664	Task Scheduler Engine	NT AUTHORITY:SYSTEM	8	101	
snmp.exe	708	SNMP Service	NT AUTHORITY:SYSTEM	8	246	
termsrv.exe	776	Terminal Server Service	NT AUTHORITY:SYSTEM	10	142	
lserver.exe	816	Microsoft® Terminal Services Licensing	NT AUTHORITY:SYSTEM	8	194	
winmgmt.exe	844	Windows Management Instrumentation	NT AUTHORITY:SYSTEM	8	90	
csrss.exe	936	Client Server Runtime Process	NT AUTHORITY:SYSTEM	13	53	
winlogon.exe	964	Windows NT Logon Application	NT AUTHORITY:SYSTEM	13	25	
csrss.exe	972	Client Server Runtime Process	NT AUTHORITY:SYSTEM	13	53	
winlogon.exe	996	Windows NT Logon Application	NT AUTHORITY:SYSTEM	13	25	
explorer.exe	1140	Windows Explorer	ICE:caubley	8	333	C:\users\caubley\bin2
mdm.exe	568	Machine Debug Manager	ICE:caubley	8	82	
atiptaxx.exe	1272	ATI Task Icon	ICE:caubley	8	76	
hkss.exe	1280	Hot Key Support Software Loader	ICE:caubley	8	23	
ltmsg.exe	1292	ltmsg	ICE:caubley	8	24	
CPQAcDc.exe	1304	CPQACDC	ICE:caubley	8	18	
svchost.exe	1312	Generic Host Process for Win32 Services	NT AUTHORITY:SYSTEM	8	210	

Handle	Type	Name
6C	ObjDirectory	\Sessions\1\Windows\WindowStations
70	Thread	csrss.exe(936): 968
74	Thread	csrss.exe(936): 940
78	ObjDirectory	\Sessions\1\BaseNamedObjects
80	Thread	csrss.exe(936): 944
98	Port	\Sessions\1\Windows\ApiPort
A0	Thread	csrss.exe(936): 948
A8	Thread	csrss.exe(936): 952
AC	Port	\Sessions\1\Windows\SbApiPort
B0	Thread	csrss.exe(936): 956
B8	Process	winlogon.exe(964)
BC	Thread	winlogon.exe(964): 960
C8	Event	\Sessions\1\BaseNamedObjects\ScNetDrvMsg
CC	Key	HKLM\SYSTEM\ControlSet001\Control\PriorityControl

csrss.exe pid: 936

FIGURE 2–21 *Handle.exe*

concern is not the top speed you will be able to obtain in the race, but if you can race at all. Below are some of the tools I've found useful in assuring that your Windows 2000 system is running on all cylinders.

Windows 2000 Event Viewer(s)

Windows 2000's Event Viewer, found under Start / Programs / Administrative Tools / Computer Management / System Tools / Event Viewer allows for a quick check to see if all applications, services, drivers, etc., have started correctly. The Event Viewer provides a centralized logging point for most of Windows 2000 server's functions. The Event Viewer is broken down into three primary areas: System, Security, and Application. Additional areas are added depending on how your system is configured. For example, if you are running DNS services, expect to find a Domain Name Server (DNS) server log file under the Event Viewer. Make it a point to review these on a regular basis. Before a server is ready to enter production, I always reboot a few times and ensure that the Event Viewer logs are clear of any errors. Start with a system that is operating correctly.

Windows 2000 System Information

Have you ever had a hard time trying to determine how the hardware components in your Windows 2000 Server were configured? Interrupt levels? Memory configuration? System Information is found under Start / Programs / Administrative Tools / Computer Management / System Information. You can also start System Information by typing winmsd.exe at the command prompt. This is one of the easiest methods to determine operating system version, service packs installed, resource usage, and memory use.

The System Information tool contains a plethora of information on the way Windows 2000 perceives your hardware interaction. Some key folders to review under System Information include (under Hardware Resources) the Conflicts/Sharing folder and (under Components) the Problem Devices folder (see Figure 2-22). To remove issues you find here, you will most likely need to refer back to the BIOS configuration of your hardware supplier.

Detailed hardware usage information can be found for such areas as interrupts, I/O ports, Direct Memory Access (DMA), and memory resources. Under the System Information tool, you can quickly see how these resources are used. Even with plug-and-play PCI-enabled BIOSs, most servers today have server tools that must be executed before Windows 2000 is booted. These tools are usually executed from a bootable CD-ROM, DOS diskette, or special partition to ensure that the hardware resources are set up correctly. These tools take a hardware perspective of the server. Although Windows 2000 does do a much better job than previous Windows versions in the area of plug and play, it is always smart to doublecheck. Using the Windows 2000 System Information tool, you get Windows 2000's software perspective of what is in the server and how Windows 2000 is using the resources. Sometimes the server hardware and operating system tools do not quite match; thus it is important to check both when putting your Windows 2000 solution into place for performance and troubleshooting.

From a configuration management perspective, the information provided with this tool is excellent. Windows 2000 includes the *winrep.exe* tool which is targeted for support personnel. Run this tool and you can collect information with its wizard format such as customer contact information and problems that are occurring, and then the tool collects all of the same information provided when you run System Information. When complete, winrep.exe creates an output file that you can save as a configuration control document. On a security side note, remember that this tool may collect information that you might not want to share with a support team, so be careful where you store this information and whom you share it with.

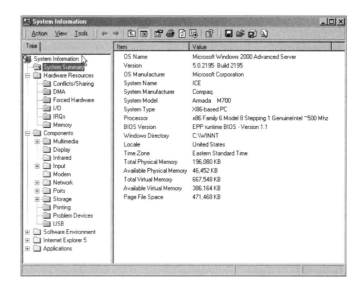

FIGURE 2–22   *Windows 2000 System Information Tool* (winmsd.ex)

Putting It All Together: The Environment

Now that we have the strategies, methodologies, and even some code to help in the development of your baselines and the monitoring of your system's performance, let's walk through an example. Let's say that Aurora has developed a Windows 2000 solution that encompasses 25 Windows 2000 servers connected through a local area network (LAN) servicing 5,000 clients. Due to time constraints, she decides to develop an ideal baseline using two key file servers before they are placed into production. She runs the CustomerPulseTest2.bat and CustomerBaseLineCheck2.pl test combination (shown in Code Examples 2-3 and 2-4) and finds that her throughput measures 920,000 bytes/sec, which she feels is acceptable for her ideal environment.

Example Strategy and Tactics

The Windows 2000 solution is placed into production, and Aurora runs the CustomerPulseTest2.bat and CustomerBaseLineCheck2.pl scripts at various times throughout the work week using the Windows 2000 server scheduler. Since Aurora does not know what is normal for her production environment, she sets the minimum acceptable baseline value ($baseline) equal to a low value of 100 bytes/sec in the BaseLineCheck.pl script so that no alerts are generated. After 7 days of collecting data, her baseline.log file looks like Figure 2-23.

```
Mon Nov 03 14:00:00, PRIME Net Throughput to megatron: 834012.05 bytes/sec
Tue Nov 04 14:00:00, PRIME Net Throughput to megatron: 851417.64 bytes/sec
Wed Nov 05 14:00:00, PRIME Net Throughput to megatron: 834759.93 bytes/sec
Thu Nov 06 14:00:00, PRIME Net Throughput to megatron: 851346.86 bytes/sec
Fri Nov 07 14:00:00, PRIME Net Throughput to megatron: 852764.82 bytes/sec
Mon Nov 10 14:00:00, PRIME Net Throughput to megatron: 809550.16 bytes/sec
Tue Nov 11 14:00:00, PRIME Net Throughput to megatron: 771665.41 bytes/sec
```

FIGURE 2–23   *Baseline.log After 7 Days*

After reviewing the performance monitor logs for the selected servers and not noticing anything out of the ordinary, she takes the average of the baseline.log results. Since Aurora is overloaded with other projects to complete and does not want to be alerted every time there is a slight change in the workloads, she factors in an 18-% surge rate to determine an approximate value of 700,000 bytes/sec as an acceptable performance baseline. She then starts the scripts, allowing them to run without intervention and without constant monitoring. Several weeks pass by and she gets an e-mail that states Error: Below Baseline(700000.00 bytes/sec)-Wed Nov 12 14:00:00, PRIME Net Throughput to megatron: 587998.85 bytes/sec.

Aurora then reviews the baseline.log files for PRIME and MEGATRON for any time/date patterns associated with the unacceptable performance levels shown in the e-mail she received.

```
Error: Below Baseline(700000.00 bytes/sec)-Wed Nov 12 14:00:00, PRIME Net
         Throughput to megatron: 587998.85 bytes/sec
Error: Below Baseline(700000.00 bytes/sec)-Thu Nov 13 14:00:00, PRIME Net
         Throughput to megatron: 582977.51 bytes/sec
Error: Below Baseline(700000.00 bytes/sec)-Fri Nov 14 14:00:00, PRIME Net
         Throughput to megatron: 569331.70 bytes/sec
Mon Nov 17 14:00:00, PRIME Net Throughput to megatron: 735632.18 bytes/sec
Tue Nov 18 14:00:00, PRIME Net Throughput to megatron: 709092.17 bytes/sec
Error: Below Baseline(700000.00 bytes/sec)-Wed Nov 19 14:00:00, PRIME Net
         Throughput to megatron: 587998.85 bytes/sec
Error: Below Baseline(700000.00 bytes/sec)-Thu Nov 20 14:00:00, PRIME Net
         Throughput to megatron: 582977.51 bytes/sec
Error: Below Baseline(700000.00 bytes/sec)-Fri Nov 21 14:00:00, PRIME Net
         Throughput to megatron: 569331.70 bytes/sec
```

FIGURE 2–24   *Automated File Server Performance Baseline*

Zeroing in on the Performance Problem

Aurora decides to work late Friday, hoping to fix this impending performance problem before end users begin to complain. After reviewing the Sysmon logs and the Perl script's output logs, she finds that the CPU on the system is pegged at 100% and the System Processor Queue Length is backing up during the same time periods as the baseline test. Reviewing the Process object under Sysmon, she notices that the scheduler is very CPU intensive and is starting a stored procedure database program. The program being run is for data not required until the following day. Cleverly, Aurora changes the scheduled run time for this program to off-peak business hours. This small change now allows the system to be more responsive, exhibiting characteristics that are now back to the normal baseline she observed earlier. Case closed, Aurora saves the day and is able to enjoy a nice weekend away from the office.

Summary

This chapter covered the strategies and methodologies for tuning Windows 2000. Once this foundation was in place, we then reviewed key tools that help in implementing these performance strategies. We then gave examples using the strategies and technology provided in the chapter. This chapter showed that it is crucial to have an understanding of what is occurring in your Windows 2000 system and surrounding environment. It is important to understand that, as either hardware or software technology changes, you can apply the strategies outlined in this chapter.

Capacity Sizing

CHAPTER OBJECTIVES

- Introduction........ *131*
- Goals of Sizing........ *132*
- Reality of Sizing........ *132*
- Sizing Methodology........ *133*
- Exploring the Sizing Methodology in Detail........ *136*
- Benchmarks........ *147*
- Historical Baselines........ *161*
- How Server Architecture Relationships Affect System Configurations........ *166*
- Properly Sizing Memory........ *169*
- Server I/O Relationships........ *169*
- Server CPUs Drive More than Applications Alone........ *171*
- Commercially Available Sizing Tools........ *171*

Introduction

In this chapter, we introduce and investigate the key strategies and tactics you can use to size your Windows 2000-based solutions. Or, in other words, this chapter will give you the tools to determine how much system hardware you will need to implement your solution so that it meets your performance goals while maximizing your return on investment. Once these sizing strategies are reviewed, we delve deeply into taking advantage of the numerous industry benchmarks, historical information, and current trends in system technology to implement an appropriately sized Windows 2000 solution to meet your needs.

The sizing strategies and tactics reviewed in this chapter are not just theory based; they have been developed and fine-tuned from real-world production environments and are used throughout this book. So you can see them in action.

Goals of Sizing

If you want to determine the configuration of a new Windows 2000–based solution to meet your needs for today and tomorrow, where do you start? If a vendor's sales literature states that only 32MB of RAM is required to run the application, will that really be enough? This is only the beginning of the questions that will be addressed in this chapter. Sizing encompasses several areas:

1. Developing a Windows 2000 solution that meets your business requirements
2. Developing a specific system configuration to meet the Windows 2000 technical requirements
3. Adding additional capacity to an existing Windows 2000 configuration
4. Staying one step ahead of the demand for your Windows 2000 system services

If money were not an object, everyone would purchase the largest and latest system technology without blinking an eye. Unfortunately, when developing a solution that might encompass 300 servers, spending an extra $5,000 per server results in an additional cost of $1.5 million. Even if the environment is smaller, few people want to spend their budgets on solutions that do not meet their requirements or on hardware that sits around being about as productive as a large paperweight.

Reality of Sizing

Similar to tuning, capacity sizing and planning is part art and part science. Sizing a Windows 2000 system to provide a solution can be a challenge if you don't follow a sound approach. When discussions begin on sizing a system for a new environment, the first volleys tend to go something like this:

System Engineer:	So, what business problem are you trying to solve?
Customer:	We want a new database server for our business. How many users can a Windows 2000 system support?
System Engineer:	I would like to learn more about your environment. What type of users will use the system and what is the concurrency rate?
Customer:	We do not know yet. So how many users can the server support?
System Engineer:	We will need to complete some investigations into your environment before determining the number of users that the system might support.
Customer:	OK, so how many users will it support?

Interesting paradox, isn't it? The system engineer could simply choose an arbitrary number based on his own experience or extrapolate from a commercial benchmark, but how would he know if this selection would pertain to the customer's environment at all? He wouldn't and you won't either. Until you understand the environment that the system will support, it is difficult to provide a realistic answer to the "how many" question, nor is it advisable to suggest an initial Windows 2000 configuration or solution architecture.

Sizing Methodology

As we prepare to size a Windows 2000 system solution, we will gather a significant amount of information and make various assumptions. We will avoid conversations like the one above by learning as much as possible about the requirements. Why make any assumptions? How many and the type of assumptions you make depend upon your environment, time line, and economics. Even if you study a problem and model it long enough with the most sophisticated mathematical algorithms, you still will not size a Windows 2000 system perfectly. You will get close, but not perfect. Why? Similar to tuning, there is a primary aspect of sizing that is in a constant state of flux: people. People, or the clients your servers are supporting, can and do change the way they do business, especially when the demands placed on their businesses change.

Perhaps you planned on having 100 order-entry personnel working concurrently 70% of the time. Suddenly, their "talking mouse" product takes off.

Overnight, the company adds another 100 order-entry contractors working concurrently 90% of the time. This would drastically influence the server's workload and your sizing estimates. Business requirements and end users' habits perennially change as their environments change. This will subsequently influence your system load, which will change your sizing characteristics. The human factor is why sizing and tuning are based in both art and science.

Fortunately, it is possible to provide a good sizing estimate by utilizing sound, logical sizing techniques that any good IS professional can apply. Follow this core sizing methodology when developing a new Windows 2000 system-based solution:

Step	Action
TABLE 3.1	*Core Sizing Methodology*
1.	Define objective(s).
2.	Understand business and technical requirements needed to meet your objective(s).
3.	Determine loading characteristics.
4.	Determine performance requirements.
5.	Understand future business requirements.
6.	Understand future server architectures.
7.	Configure the system.
8.	Stress test to validate the system configuration.
9.	Proactively follow the core tuning methodology during validations testing.
10.	Deploy the system into production.
11.	Proactively follow the core tuning methodology after the system is deployed.

Each of these steps influences both the type and amount of system hardware required to meet your objectives. Figure 3-1 illustrates the core sizing methodology.

You can also consider a higher level of abstraction when thinking of the core sizing methodology. Consider this approach as a complete life cycle. The core sizing methodology can be broken down into several general components, which we'll call steps. Steps 1–6 cover planning, step 7 (parts 7.1–7.7) covers design, steps 8–10 cover implementation, and step 11 encompasses proactive management. Thus all these steps together provide a planning, design, implementation, and management methodology approach, which is illustrated in Figure 3-2.

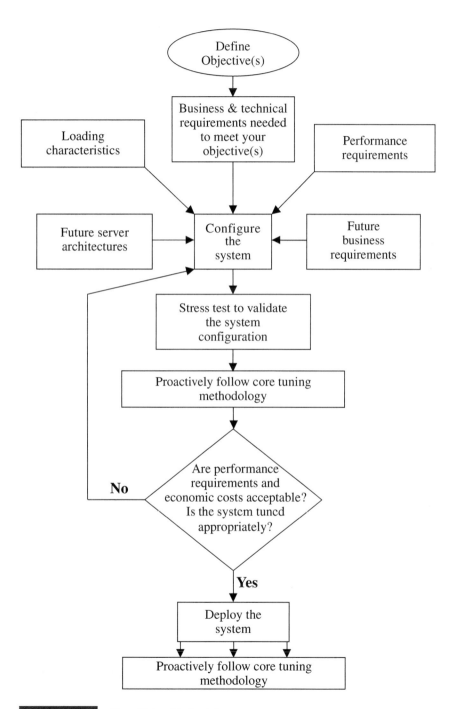

FIGURE 3–1   *Core Sizing Methodology*

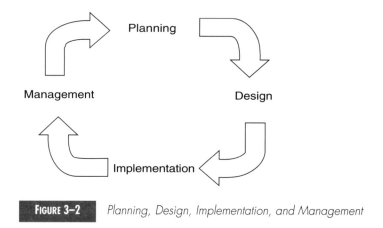

FIGURE 3-2   *Planning, Design, Implementation, and Management*

We will explore each step of the sizing methodology in more detail. Even as we look at the methodology in more detail, *keep in mind that every environment is different.* So, if we do not address an area that concerns you in our explanation of one of these steps, feel free to expand it! There is no substitute for experience. Use this methodology as a framework that will help you develop your solution, not as gospel.

In chapter 7, we will apply this methodology to several sizing case studies.

Exploring the Sizing Methodology in Detail

Step 1. Define Objective(s)

Defining the system objective is straightforward. Why do you require this system? What part of the solution will the system perform? This list can get long quickly, but some of the possibilities include: domain controller (PDC), catalog server (CS), domain name server (DNS), file server, web server, mail server, database server, and on and on. Defining your objective helps to determine where, in your overall system architecture, it makes sense to locate it. For example, placing a site's file server on-site close to the actual users can help lower network latency (WAN vs. LAN) when accessing the server and can help control network traffic patterns. (Latency is defined as the time spent waiting for a result. Typically, it is the end user waiting for a result.) The trade-off for this example is that there is an increased system management complexity associated with managing distributed server architectures.

Once the objective is defined, it becomes easier to characterize the type of workloads the server will experience. The workload characterization directly affects tuning Windows 2000 systems. Understanding the load characterization also is the key to the initial system configuration that is illustrated step-by-step in chapter 7. Although Windows 2000 lends itself to distributed application architectures, it is becoming more common to see numerous server functions being combined into fewer, but larger Windows 2000 Super Servers (2–32 CPU-based systems). This makes the need for understanding the various types of load characterizations even more important.

Step 2. Understand Business and Technical Requirements Needed to Meet Your Objective(s)

The primary questions to answer in this step are

- Which application(s) will meet your functional objective(s)?
- What are the availability requirements?
- What are the ramifications if your system is down?
- What are the disk subsystem storage capacity requirements?
- What are the disk subsystem performance requirements?

If you were developing a database application, you would need to decide which database to use, such as SQL Server, SQL Server Enterprise Edition, NCR Teradata, Oracle, or one of the many others. There is a plethora of questions that surround the determination of which application to use. Some of the most common questions are scalability of the product, opinions of other customers using the product in similar environments, development environments, future plans for the product, and such. The application that you choose to meet your objective will affect which types of system resources are needed to support running the application.

Just as Windows 2000 has a minimum recommended server configuration—set somewhere around an Intel Pentium CPU 133MHz with at least 64MB of RAM (which I'm sure everyone thinks is realistic)—so will other applications that you are considering. Remember that, when a vendor mentions the minimum configuration needed to run the application, they typically really *mean* the *minimum* needed just to make it run. This minimum-hardware recommendation is sometimes referred to as the "vendor dream sheet." Add 100 concurrent users and the suggested minimum server resource requirements are tossed out the window. I guess you just need to read the fine print and understand the vendor's target market.

Three things typically drive the availability requirements—how important is the objective you are fulfilling, how big is your budget, and what is the payback required if the system fails (service level agreements [SLAs]). If the system is a local file and print server, the system configuration will most likely require a lower factor of availability. At the other end of the spectrum, if the solution is a web server that processes transactions for your retail outlet on the Internet and is your primary eCommerce presence, a clustered solution may be advisable to ensure a very high availability rate. A system is typically defined as critical in your architecture if the business would lose revenue or have dramatically lowered productivity if the system were to fail.

Storage requirements are not as self-defining as they might appear. We will investigate the availability, capacity, and performance requirements of the disk subsystems that will greatly influence the final system configuration later on in chapter 6 as well as in chapter 8's case studies.

Step 3. Determine Loading Characteristics

Determining loading characteristics of the server can take time and occasionally be laborious, but it is extremely important. The loading characteristics typically drive the bulk of the system resources needed to provide a solution that runs in a manner acceptable to both the customers and the business. Key information you want to obtain when trying to determine the loading characteristics includes:

- Number of total users
- Number of concurrent users (users that are actually requesting something from the server at the same time)
- Transaction rates
- Read or write environment characteristics
- Size of records
- Physical location of users (influences communications such as WAN, LAN, Dial Up, and Terminal Services)
- Type of work the user will complete (order entry, mailing out electronic advertisements, home accounts usage, research, etc.)

There are two ways to collect workload information: collecting historical workload information on existing systems and estimating workload without having existing systems to learn from. As you might guess, it is preferable to collect historical information from systems currently running applications similar to your own planned environments. This is where the concepts from chapter 2 come into play.

If you have already been collecting system statistics, you can determine how current systems are performing and extrapolate possible future loading requirements. If you haven't been following the methodologies outlined in chapter 2, it is not too late to start. Occasionally it is possible to meet with people in other businesses who have implemented a similar solution and to subsequently obtain their performance metrics to determine loading characteristics for your own system.

If you do not have any historical data to use, you can survey the current and/or potential customers to estimate what future workloads will be encountered. You can accomplish this through a variety of methods such as e-mailing them questionnaires to determine work habits or enlisting the support of several good interns to question the end users and complete the surveys you have developed.

In either case, a reasonable estimate is possible, which will help provide you with an initial starting point.

Step 4. Determine Performance Requirements

The two most common measurements of performance are *response time* and *throughput*. Response time is what the end user experiences. How long does it take for the system to respond to my request? Always remember that, between the system and the customer, there are several layers of system architecture (other than the server) that may influence the customer's perceived response time. Throughput is the amount of work that the system can complete in a defined period of time. These two concepts are somewhat opposing in nature. If a system is very busy completing a large amount of work, the throughput is good. Unfortunately, if the server is busy completing a large amount of work, a customer's request will not be serviced as fast. Conversely, if the system is not busy completing a high level of work—its throughput level is lower at the moment—the system will be able to service that customer's request in a timely fashion, thus providing good response time.

For any interactive application that is ultimately used daily by an end user, there is only one true measure of performance: response time. It does not matter what type of scientific or engineering mumbo jumbo is used to explain what is happening on the desktop, server, or the network; if the customer requires a 5-second-or-less response time, then that is the standard they will expect. Setting customer expectations is very important. Working with your clients to determine acceptable response times can both drive the system configurations and establish a metric of your job performance.

Working with the client to set realistic performance expectations is important. If you and the client decide subsecond response time is the ultimate performance metric, then be sure you quantify when this is realistic. If you are setting up a database to support a web-based order-entry environment, quantify your performance metric for both response time and user concurrency rate. *Concurrency rate* is the amount of time concurrent users are actively working with the system. You may support 2,000 users with your system, but only 200 of them access the server at any given time. This is a 10% concurrency rate. For example, you may agree that subsecond response time will be provided for local users (LAN connected) when less than 200 users are accessing the server concurrently. Many Windows 2000 environments are deployed in a client-server fashion, which allows a single Windows 2000 system to support more users than if they were logged directly into the server, as is the case in some UNIX and Windows 2000 Terminal Services/Citrix multiuser environments.

Throughput metrics for server environments are a more applicable measure of performance when the supporting application is not interactive or when most of the work is completed offline in a batch mode. Some example throughput metrics for a server are quantified by the number of mail messages the server can process per hour or the number of accounting queries that can be completed per 8-hour evening time window so that they are available the next business day.

Step 5. Understand Future Business Requirements

Whenever someone mentions futures, I think of psychics or palm readers. Although some people believe in this, I prefer to look at more scientific futures. When thinking about business requirement futures, revisit steps 1 through 4 and ask yourself, "Will my business objectives be the same?" "How much growth do I anticipate?" For business futures, the two areas of concern are deciding if the system will need to support additional applications and whether the workload will increase. Both of these areas will affect your system architecture. If your future looks stable, perhaps a 1–2 CPU Windows 2000 system will suffice. If the business is rapidly growing, perhaps a 2–8 CPU Windows 2000 system should be considered. By spending time understanding future business requirements before sizing the server, future server growth can easily be proactively planned for instead of reacted to.

Step 6. Understand Future System Architectures

As technology rapidly advances, vendors look to deploy newer technology in an effort to garner market share. In completing this mission, individual vendors or vendor consortiums develop new technologies, hoping they will evolve into standards either through lobbying efforts aimed at the various standards groups (IEEE, The Open Group, etc.) or by sheer market share. Why be concerned about this when configuring your system? If the technology you've chosen quickly becomes discontinued or never develops a growing market presence, you can find yourself locked into a single vendor, which can result in drastically higher prices for parts and upgrades. Or you may not be able to purchase parts. You may recall some years ago when two new I/O bus standards were emerging: PCI and Micro Channel. At that time, you could have purchased a PCI-based SCSI host adapter or a Micro Channel–based SCSI host adapter. If you had chosen the Micro Channel–based SCSI adapter, today you would have a difficult time locating additional, competitively priced Micro Channel–based SCSI controllers.

The moral of this story: consider all of the technology your system will need to support today and tomorrow to meet your requirements. Deciding which technology will win or lose in the long run is a formidable task. If you adhere to technologies that follow both industry group standards and have a promising market share forecast, you will most likely be safe. Key factors to consider when choosing a system technology to implement are given in Table 3.2.

TABLE 3.2	Key Factors When Choosing a System Technology
Key System Factor	**Definition**
Service and support	Warranty options, technical support for software, technical support for hardware, etc. Many times the cost of the maintenance is more than the initial system purchase. Negotiate both initial system price and long-term maintenance options for the best possible price during the initial vendor selection. (Vendors are much more flexible during the initial sale vs. later upgrades. They are also more flexible at the end of their sales quarter so they can make quota.)
CPU scalability	Number, speed, and future caches that are planned to be supported.
Memory scalability	Maximum amount and types of memory supported.
I/O scalability	Number of peer I/O (PCI today) buses the server can scale to and available I/O slots.
Internal disk capacity	Number of internal disk drives the system can support.
External disk array support	Number of external disk drives the server will support.
Redundant array of inexpensive disks (RAID) support	Both internal and external RAID devices. Does the RAID system support hot swappable drives and dynamic online expansion of the file system? Must you boot into DOS to configure the array?
Communication adapter support	LAN and WAN connectivity.
Fault tolerance features	Hot pluggable power supplies, redundant fans, etc.
System management features	Adherence to system management standards such as Wired For Management (WFM), Web Enabled Management (WEBM), Windows Management Interface (WMI), Desktop Management Interface (DMI), Simple Network Management Protocol (SNMP), etc.

Step 7. Configure the System

Finally, to the good stuff! At this point, you can configure the system. Choose the system resources required to meet your objectives, with consideration for steps 1 through 6, and obtain the system. As you configure the system, look at each individual resource to make sure it meets the overall system configuration. Software and hardware vendors are good sources of information for suggested configurations from which to begin your configuration efforts. Reviewing relevant industry benchmarks (explored in depth later in this chapter) also can help to provide insight into the initial configuration. Substeps 7.1 through 7.7 will guide you through the actual system configuration process.

Case studies in chapter 9 provide examples that will help to solidify the configuration process.

Having some sort of idea on how each system resource works and how it relates to the overall system performance is helpful when configuring your system. Chapters 4 through 7 review in depth each system resource. Then in chapter 8's case studies, this methodology is thrust into action as each facet of several system scenarios are sized, configured, tuned, and stress tested.

7.1 APPLICATION CHARACTERISTICS REVIEW

Complete some research on how the application typically behaves. For example, Microsoft Exchange environments are characterized by the following resource usage activity: disk: active; memory: active; processor: medium; network: medium. Even closer review of the application in use may dictate the network or disk subsystem design. Also determine if the application can support a redundant array of inexpensive servers (RAIS). Can the application live or run on multiple systems or does its architecture take advantage of only one system at a time?

7.2 REVIEW EACH SYSTEM RESOURCE

DISK I/O REQUIREMENTS • When sizing disk I/O subsystems, consider availability, capacity (available disk storage), and performance requirements. Understanding the disk I/O subsystem characteristics (read/write usage and workload of the disk I/O subsystem) is helpful for initial layout and future tuning of the disk I/O subsystem. Remember when sizing disk subsystems, disk capacity does *not* equal disk performance. For example, four 9GB disk drives provide roughly twice the throughput for your applications as two 18GB disk drives.

CPU REQUIREMENTS • When sizing the level of CPU power required, keep in mind the application requirements and processing power that are required to drive supporting disk and network subsystems. Sizing CPUs is an additive process. For example, if a CPU equates to 100% and two CPUs equate to 200%, and you have three applications each needing 40% CPU usage, you would require two CPUs.

(You can run stress tests or obtain historical information to determine how much in the way of system resources an application will need.)

MEMORY REQUIREMENTS • When sizing the amount of memory to place into the system, consider all the application and operating system requirements. Sizing the memory subsystem is an additive process of all applications and/or workloads you desire to run concurrently. Some memory resources are shared between processes running under Windows 2000, but on the safer, more conservative side of sizing, still consider sizing the memory subsystem as an additive process. Take into consideration operating system requirements, Windows 2000 file system cache needs (dynamic disk buffer cache), and application needs. Application memory requirements are more than just the memory space needed to run the application. Application memory also encompasses memory needed to support its data sets and users. For example, a database engine may have a per-user memory requirement of 0.250MB per user. If the database will support 500 users, an additional 125MB of memory would be needed on top of any other memory requirements.

NETWORK I/O REQUIREMENTS • The amount of data that the server provides and the characteristics of the applications in use dictate the type and number of network interface cards. Access patterns of the server influence the type of protocol to use. Token passing protocols such as FDDI exhibit better degradation characteristics than shared bus protocols such as Ethernet. Also select a network adapter that provides the best performance for the network architecture in use. If the environment is Ethernet, obtain a network adapter that supports bus mastering and an onboard CPU for off-loading network calculations from the main CPUs. Also, if multiple network segments will be needed, select a network adapter that contains more than one Ethernet channel. This conserves system adapter expansion slots in the server which can later be used for other functions.

7.3 INITIAL HARDWARE CONFIGURATION AND TUNING

In this step, the initial configuration of the server hardware begins to take shape based on substeps 7.1 and 7.2.

7.4 INITIAL SOFTWARE CONFIGURATION AND TUNING

In this step, the initial software configuration of the server begins to take shape based on substeps 7.1 and 7.2.

7.5 INITIAL OVERALL TUNING

Reviewing the load characteristics and completing research on the application in use is helpful when tuning the hardware and software. Review chapter 1 as a reference and guide for tuning the server before stress testing or deploying the Windows 2000 system.

7.6 SYSTEM ARCHITECTURE RELATIONSHIP CHECK

This is a final commonsense check of a server. Review chapter 1 as a reference before stress testing or deploying the final Windows 2000 configuration. Look for configuration options that are strange, such as a server with 4GB of RAM, 1 disk drive, and 1 CPU. Strive to develop a balanced system design by trying to avoid starting with a system bottleneck. Completing some basic arithmetic of the I/O subsystem for a worst-case scenario can help to disqualify poor disk I/O designs.

7.7 FUTURE BUSINESS AND SYSTEM ARCHITECTURES CHECK REVIEW

Will the system have room to grow if needed? Steps 5 and 6 of the core sizing methodology (Table 3.1) points out that it is important to obtain this information. This step is the actual contingency planning. If the system will need to support an increased role in the future, how will you actually accomplish meeting those goals? For example, if the server needs 1GB of RAM today, but will need to support 2GB in the future, pay close attention to the density of the RAM initially purchased. If your RAM is so dense that all available memory slots are filled, you will not be able to increase memory size in the future without throwing away or redeploying the current investment. A better strategy is to obtain higher density SIMMs/DIMMs today. Then, as memory is needed in the future, you can simply add it to the current configuration instead of removing the old RAM.

Step 8. Stress Test and Validate the Server Configuration

This is a crucial step that must be done before actually deploying the system. How can you be sure that the system will meet your performance requirements and run correctly with various applications running simultaneously under load without crashing? In the tuning methodology outlined in chapter 2, we reviewed taking a baseline of your system before deploying it to determine what performance level would be possible in a nonproduction environment. This information was then used when taking the server's pulse in the production environment for comparison and to aid in determining if tuning was necessary.

We use this same concept for sizing, but when initial sizing is your goal, do not just take the server's pulse. To determine if the server will withstand the types of stress and workloads that you expect it to support in production, stress the server in the most realistic manner possible. This preproduction load testing becomes your validation baseline. If the validation baseline proves to be unacceptable, do not deploy the system. Revisit the requirements and configuration, and then use the core tuning methodology (Table 3.1, step 9) to tune your system before it enters production. Continue this iterative process until you can meet the desired performance levels. There are various products you can use to stress test your system before production; some of them are outlined in chapter 2.

Now that you have developed your validation baseline, which includes measurements such as response time, throughput, and system resource usage, you can feel comfortable that your solution will meet your current requirements. You also have a baseline reference for future tuning efforts. But why stop there? Is meeting the performance requirements under the current workload really good enough? What if there is a landslide of increased system loads? Will the system seize up faster than a truck transmission without transmission fluid? Or will the server support the additional load gracefully until it begins an honorable death?

To determine if the system will support additional workloads, it is important to take into consideration future business requirements and then stress your system accordingly. By stressing the system past its breaking point, you gain an enormous insight into future capacity planning and tuning. Figure 3-3 illustrates a system's breaking point. The "knee" in the curve in Figure 3-3 is a classic illustration of the beginning of the end for any system, indicating that a resource (or resources) on the system became a bottleneck as the load increased past 120 users.

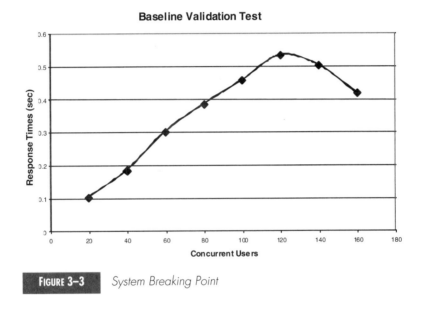

Baseline Validation Test

FIGURE 3-3 *System Breaking Point*

Obviously, a curve depicting a slowly decreasing degradation slope is desirable. What defines acceptable and unacceptable performance are the business requirements. Knowing where the degradation occurs and the rate of degradation is helpful for planning—these two factors indicate how well the system can weather a load storm.

If your business requirements are to support 100 concurrent users today and 200 in 3 months, it would be wise to have a validated baseline that shows not only if the system will support 100 users today, but if it will support the 200 users of tomorrow. Through iterative testing and using the core tuning methodology in conjunction with a system-loading tool, you can identify system bottlenecks, tune around them, and obtain the highest level of performance from the current configuration. In chapter 8's case studies, we explore these concepts with real examples. Once this iterative testing no longer yields significant gains, review the data to determine which system resources will require additional hardware or software changes to meet the projected workloads. If the system architecture has met its realistic scalability limit, consider adding additional resources to the system or distributing the increasing workload to additional systems as appropriate. With the advent of small servers (1–2 CPUs) that are particularly powerful and the improved distributed system management tools included in Windows 2000, you can employ multiple less-expensive systems to meet your goals. This concept of using high-speed, but smaller and less-expensive systems is referred to as *redundant array of inexpensive servers* or RAIS. RAIS systems can provide powerful solutions but are very application dependent. Using this approach, even if your system solution meets only today's needs, you can budget and plan for the upgrade to support the projected workload increases of tomorrow.

Step 9. Proactively Follow the Core Tuning Methodology during Stress and Validation Testing

Tuning and sizing techniques work best when they are utilized in concert. Use the core tuning methodology when load testing your system solution prior to deployment. Typically, it is much easier to tune around system bottlenecks before a system is running a mission-critical application because these tuning efforts must be properly planned and reviewed by your own configuration control management team before any changes can be made on production systems. Another benefit of this technique is the development of the system's pulse baselines, which are used for future comparisons of system resource usage. Even if it is not possible to load test your system prior to deployment, review chapter 1 for general tuning recommendations before deploying the system into production.

Step 10. Deploy the System into Production

Why state the obvious? This step defines itself. I wanted to show a clear distinction between baseline validation and tuning of the preproduction system and the deployed system. It is much easier to tune and validate a system before it enters production.

Step 11. Proactively Follow the Tuning Methodology After the System Is Deployed

Environments do change. The information gathered following the core tuning methodology is helpful for staying one step in front of user demand by identifying current load demands and potential system bottlenecks. Also, use this information when developing and sizing future system solutions and when adding additional capacity to your current system(s). If you have not quantifiably determined where and how to add additional capacity to your system, you are at great risk of wasting your initial investment.

Benchmarks

Benchmarks Are Your Friends

Historical data and user surveys are great techniques for obtaining information that will influence the sizing and configuration of your systems. But where can you obtain information about sizing and performance of new technologies that you do not have historical data for? Industry standard benchmarks! Industry benchmarks help to cause marketing chaos, both for vendors as they compete for marketing dominance and for the decision makers as they are blitzed with marketing advertisements, but they also can come to the rescue of that same decision maker. If you understand what the industry benchmark results represent and how to use them to your advantage, they are an outstanding addition to your sizing arsenal. Always remember that, while no single benchmark can fully characterize overall system performance perfectly, the results of a variety of realistic benchmarks provide valuable insight into expected real performance for sizing and tuning efforts.

What Are Industry Standard Benchmarks?

In basic terms, a benchmark is any measurable reproducible test—sounds simple, because the concept is simple. What is not simple is developing benchmarks that measure what you want them to measure and agreeing upon how that measurement is to be taken. Various vendors from time to time do agree on, or at least support, various benchmarks. If there is enough support for a particular benchmark, they can become industry standard benchmarks. Now, in theory, if one vendor runs standard benchmark A and another vendor runs standard benchmark A, you should be able to examine the results in an apples-to-apples comparison. Since industry benchmarks carry, in a manner of speaking, bragging rights with them for those vendors who do well in them, these benchmarks are powerful marketing tools. Vendors will always try to one-up their competition, which results in continuous benchmarking of the latest system hardware and software technologies, thus creating the leapfrog effect. This is an advantage to you! In a way, you have teams of the best engineers from every vendor trying to make their server solutions run faster and faster.

There are several standard industry benchmarks that are released publicly and are beneficial to any tuning and sizing effort. We will review several of the most common industry benchmarks for the Windows 2000 system environment, explaining what they are and how they might be helpful. Industry consortiums such as the Transaction Processing Council (TPC) and the Standard Performance Evaluation Corporation (SPEC) produce some industry standard benchmarks. Some companies develop and sell their own benchmarks. This class of benchmarks become industry standards through their marketing efforts and market share. Two commercial benchmark vendors include AIM and Neal Nelson & Associates. Other benchmarks are available free of charge from groups like Ziff-Davis and various universities.

The baseline validation test that we described earlier in the sizing methodology is also a benchmark, a very specific benchmark that depicts a particular environment—yours. Benchmarking a system in your specific environment is the best way to determine if the system will meet your requirements. The number of benchmarks available today is ever increasing as new technologies are introduced. As technology evolves, so must the benchmarks used to measure new emerging technologies so that this new technology can be fully utilized (similar to developers updating their applications from using 32 bits to 64 to 128 bits of a CPU). If benchmarks were not updated over time, their results would become less meaningful and consequently less valuable.

Where Do Benchmarks Fit in the Sizing Methodology?

You can gain valuable insight into system sizing configurations and software tuning techniques from the many industry standard benchmarks available, the results of which are updated frequently. Once you obtain the pertinent information, apply it to the various steps outlined in the core sizing methodology. Industry standard benchmark information is most applicable to step 7, configuring the system. If the loading characteristics (step 3) and performance requirements (step 4) are similar to that of the benchmark environment, the benchmark provides an immediate basis to extrapolate from for the initial system configuration created in step 7. Even if the industry standard benchmark most similar to your environment does not match exactly, system sizing information and software tuning information can still be extrapolated from these benchmarks and applied to the sizing environment in Steps 7 and 9. This approach provides you with an excellent jump-start in sizing your system. Always ensure you select the appropriate industry benchmark—the one that most closely emulates your environment. To accomplish this, you must understand what some of the key industry benchmarks represent and how you can use them, which we'll talk about in the next section.

Transaction Processing Council (TPC)

TPC produces various server benchmarks that are run by the major server vendors. There are numerous TPC benchmarks: TPC-A, TPC-B, TPC-C, TPC-D, TPC-H, and TPC-W. As benchmarks improve, so does the system technology that is under test. Thus, if the system technology has improved but improvements are not made to the benchmark technology, the validity of the benchmark results becomes suspect. Currently the TPC-A, TPC-B, and TPC-D benchmarks fall into this category of benchmarks and are no longer actively supported by the vendor community. For this discussion, these benchmarks are omitted since results for these platforms are no longer published. Information on the definitions and results of the TPC benchmarks is available on the Internet at http://www.tpc.org. TPC-C, TPC-H, and TPC-W can be applicable to the Windows 2000 server database and web server environments if you understand what the benchmark is intended for and what it measures. Although these benchmarks are audited, I do not recommend making purchase decisions solely on the results of industry standard benchmarks such as the TPC-based benchmarks.

TPC-C EXPLANATION

The TPC-C benchmark focuses on a transaction-based database server environment. The TPC-C benchmark defines that five different transactions are active on the system. The benchmark defines throughput as how many New-Order transactions per minute a server can support while keeping the response times for these transactions at less than 5 seconds. Thus the primary measurement of the TPC-C benchmark is a measure of maximum sustained system performance. Therefore, to achieve a 1,000 transaction-C actions per minute (tpmC) rating, a server must be generating 1,000 new-order transactions per minute while fulfilling the rest of the TPC-C transaction mix workload requirements.

Most Windows 2000 Server–based TPC-C benchmark solutions are designed for a clieWindows 2000 environment. In this environment, the clients support the major portion of the front-end application processing requirements and the server supports the database from which the application requests information. If you extrapolate information from the TPC-C benchmark test results, remember how the solution architecture is defined and the type of transaction the server is supporting. Consider yourself lucky if your environment matches directly up to the TPC-C environment, because it then becomes a little easier to use the TPC-C to your advantage when sizing your server. If you have a Windows 2000 Server database environment, but your transaction model does not line up exactly with the TPC-C model, TPC-C benchmark results can still be helpful to a degree.

EXAMPLE TPC-C RESULTS

Figure 3-4 is a TPC-C executive summary downloaded from the publicly available TPC web site.

Compaq Computer	ProLiant 8500-700-192P	TPC-C Rev. 3.5
Corporation	Client/Server	Report Date: Oct 6,2000

Total System Cost	TPC-C Throughput	Price/Performance	Availability Date
$10,445,169	**505,302.77**	**$20.68**	**Nov 30, 2000**

Processors	Database	Operating System	Other Software	Number Users
192 Pentium III Xeon 700 MHz	Microsoft SQL Server 2000 Enterprise Edition	Windows 2000 Advanced Server	Microsoft Visual C++ Microsoft COM+	**432,000**

		Server		Clients	
System Components	Quantity	Description	Quantity	Description
Processor	192	700MHz Pentium III Xeon w/ 2MB Cache	96	Pentium III 800Mhz/256K
Memory	384	512MB	192	128MB
Disk Controllers	120	Compaq SMART Array Controller 5304	48	Integrated SCSI RAID Controller
	24	Integrated SCSI RAID Controller		
Disk Drives	72	9.1GB 10K Ultra2 Universal SCSI Drives	48	9.1GB 10K Ultra2 SCSI Drives
	2496	18GB 15K Ultra3 Universal SCSI Drives		
Total Storage		42.37 TeraBytes		436.8 GB
Tape Drives	1	4/8 GB SLR Tape Drive		

FIGURE 3–4   *A TPC-C Executive Summary (Courtesy of Compaq Computer Corporation*

Compaq Computer Corporation		ProLiant 8500-700-192P Client/Server				TPC-C Rev. 3.5	
						Report Date:	6-Oct-00
Description	Part Number	Third Party Brand	Unit Price	Qty	Extended Price	5 yr. Maint. Price	

Description	Part Number	Third Party Brand	Pricing	Unit Price	Qty	Extended Price	5 yr. Maint. Price
Server Hardware							
ProLiant 8500R X700-2M 8P - 4 GB SD RAM - 8 Pentium III Xeon/700MHz 2MB Cache - Dual 10/100 NIC - Intg. Smart Array Controller	168758-001		1	78,400	24	1,881,600	
1GB Memory Kit SDRAM	328806-B21		1	4,301	96	412,877	
Compaq SMART Array Controller 5304 - 4 SCSI Chan.	158939-B21		1	2,463	120	295,646	
StorageWorks Enclosure Model 4214R	103381-001		1	2,912	216	628,992	
Dual I/O Module for StorageWorks 4214R	119829-B21		1	560	24	13,440	
Compaq V500 Color Monitor	325900-001		1	172	24	4,140	
4/8-GB SLR Tape Drive - Internal	295480-B22		1	448	1	448	
Compaq Rack Model 7142	165753-001		1	1,680	24	40,320	
Compaq Rack Coupling Kit	165064-001		1	152	23	3,503	
Compaq Rack Sidewall Kit	165852-001		1	208	1	208	
R3000 UPS	242705-001		1	1,786	24	42,874	
ServerNet II PCI Adapter	422869-001		1	890	24	21,370	
ServerNet II 12 Port Switch	452219-001		1	4,984	6	29,904	
LinkSys 24 Port 10/100 Switch DSS224	DEH4067	Linksys	3	580	3	1,740	See Note 1
9.1 GB Hot-Plug Wide U2 10K 1"	328939-B22		1	469	72	33,788	
18.2 GB Hot-Plug Wide U3 15K 1"	188122-B22		1	939	2496	2,342,646	
ProLiant Enterprise Server - Parts Exchange - 1 Year	PES-PE-1Y-SU		1	597	48		28,656
ProLiant Storage System - Parts Exchange - 1 Year	PSS-PE-1YEAR		1	255	48		12,240
Onsite 5x8 4 Hr Service Upgrade from Compaq Std Svc	OS-8X5X4-SU	Amherst	1				460,272
					Subtotal	5,753,395	501,168
Server Software							
Microsoft SQL Server 2000 Enterprise	810-00946	Microsoft	2	15,802	192	3,033,984	251,400
Microsoft Visual C++ 6.0	048-00317	Microsoft	2	549	1	549	Incl Above
Microsoft Windows 2000 Advance Server	C10-00475	Microsoft	2	2,399	24	57,576	Incl Above
					Subtotal	3,092,109	251,400
Client Hardware							
ProLiant DL360R P800/133 128MB M1	161080-001		1	4,816	48	231,168	
PIII 800/133-256 Processor kit	161084-B21		1	1,063	48	51,018	
128 MB 133 DIMM	128277-B21		1	311	144	44,836	
Compaq Rack Model 7142	165753-001		1	1,680	2	3,360	
Compaq Rack Coupling Kit	165664-001		1	152	2	305	
Compaq V500 Color Monitor	325900-001		1	172	48	8,279	
9.1GB Wide U2 10K	328939-B22		1	469	48	22,525	
ProLiant Workgroup Server - Parts Exchange - 1 Year	FM-LOPRT-12		1	259	96		24,864
Onsite 5x8 4 Hr Service Upgrade from Compaq Std Svc	OS-8X5X4-SU	Amherst	1				28,919
					Subtotal	361,491	53,783
Client Software							
Microsoft Windows 2000 Server	C11-00821	Microsoft	2	738	48	35,424	Incl. Above
					Subtotal	35,424	0
User Connectivity							
LinkSys 16 Port 10/100 Switch EF2S16	DEH5117	LinkSys	3	330	53	17,489	See Note 1
NetCruiser Tech 17-port 10Mbps Ethernet hub	HB-1017DX/P	NetCruiser	4	36.00	29938	1,077,768	See Note 1
					Subtotal	1,095,257	0
Large Purchase and Cash discount	9.0%	Amherst	1			($648,913)	($89,946)
					Total	$9,688,763	$756,405

Prices used in TPC benchmarks reflect the actual prices a customer would pay for a one-time purchase of the stated components. Individually negotiated discounts are not permitted. Special prices based on assumptions about past or future purchases are not permitted. All discounts reflect standard pricing policies for the listed components. For complete details, see the pricing sections of the TPC benchmark pricing specifications. If you find that the stated prices are not available according to these terms, please inform the TPC at pricing@tpc.org. Thank you.

Five-Year Cost of Ownership: **$10,445,169**

tpmC Rating: **505,302.77**

$ / tpmC: **$20.68**

Pricing: 1=Amherst Computer Products 2=Microsoft 3=MicroWAREHOUSE 4=NetCruiser Technologies

Note 1 = 5 Year warranty with 10% Spares -

Note:The benchmark results and test methodology were audited by Lorna LMnghtree of Performance Metrics, Inc.

FIGURE 3–4 *A TPC-C Executive Summary (Courtesy of Compaq Computer Corporation (continued)*

EXTRAPOLATING TPC-C RESULTS

TPC-C executive summaries are available for a myriad of server platforms. Occasionally check the web site (http://www.tpc.org) for the latest information. Vendors add and withdraw benchmark results over time. Using the TPC-C executive summary available as of 11/9/2000 in Figure 3.4, let's review some of the notable pieces of information and point out facts that you might find applicable for any environment:

- Total Number of Windows 2000 Servers used: 24.
- Single-node server configuration information is outlined below for: CPU, RAM, DISK, network resources.
- 8 CPUs needed for calculations and to drive large external disk arrays.
- 8 GB of RAM. Large amounts of RAM required for operating system and database application. This large amount of RAM improves overall performance by allowing the database to cache in RAM actions that may have needed disk access.
- 2496 external disk drives. Increased number of disk drives is used to support the high transaction rate. Note that these drives were 18GB 15,000rpm Ultra3 disk drives. A lower number of disk drives could have been used if the disk capacity of each drive was doubled to 36GB per disk drive. However, if this increased capacity approach was used, e.g., with one-half of the available disk drives removed, disk subsystem performance would have lowered by approximately one-half.
- 120 available external Ultra2 SCSI-based RAID adapters (5 adapters per server with 4 Ultra3 SCSI channels each). Reviewing the executive summary, 12 disk drives were configured per Ultra3 SCSI channel.
- One dual-channel 100BaseT network interface card. Even supporting a high number of concurrent users, this client-server-based benchmark's workload does not require a high network bandwidth environment.
- Maximum number of concurrent users supported: 432,000 (or 18,000 per node).
- Version of operating system: Windows 2000 Advanced Server. Windows 2000 Advanced Server enables the application to access 7GB of RAM with 1GB of RAM reserved for the operating system.
- TPC-C throughput: 505,302 tpmC.
- Price/performance: $20.68/transaction.
- Database: Microsoft SQL Server 2000 Enterprise Edition.

From this information it is possible to extrapolate key pieces of information such as the disk I/O configuration. Here, 104 external drives are needed per node, not due as much to capacity requirements as to transaction rate requirements. Regardless of the size of the disk drives, individual disk drives can support only so many input/output transactions per second, thus the need for an increased number of disk drives. Keep this in mind when configuring a database or a transaction-based environment, or even when planning how long it will take to complete a backup of your system. In general, the more disks you have in your system, the faster the disk subsystem will operate and consequently the faster your backups will be completed. More specific disk I/O rules-of-thumb examples are pointed out in chapters 1, 6, and 8.

TPC-C SIZING PITFALLS

There are some downsides to using TPC-C information to help size your configuration. TPC-C benchmarks are expensive for vendors to run, thus limiting the number of available TPC-C configurations you can reference to aid in sizing your system. This particular solution architecture uses 24 servers in an independent, shared nothing cluster to achieve enterprise class scalability. You may not need a Windows 2000 solution this powerful, but it is nice to know there is room to grow! Do not assume that if you broke this configuration apart you would achieve only ~21,000tpmC of TPC-C throughput per system. TPC-C solutions optimized for a single server (8 CPUs) have achieved ratings of over 40,000tpmC. The pitfall here is that, even in a share-nothing cluster, you do not achieve perfect scaling, but even that is always improving.

The low numbers of real clients driving this benchmark has a somewhat negative effect when using TPC-C results to help size your server's active connections. Most TPC-C benchmarks utilize some type of transaction processing (TP) monitor—in this case the one included with SQL Server 2000 Enterprise. Using a transaction monitor greatly aids in managing your systems. One way a transaction monitor accomplishes this is by multiplexing the connections into the database, in essence lowering the number of active connections into the database. If you are not using a transaction monitor, the subsequent increase in active connections into the database server increases the load on the server and lowers the number of concurrent users that can be supported. How much of the load is increased on the server is application dependent, but I typically lower the number of concurrent users supports by at least 25% just to be safe.

FURTHER INFORMATION ON TPC-C

TPC-C is best used to approximate server solutions of similar environments. Even if your environment is not a perfect fit with the TPC-C environment, look between the lines to gain configuration and sizing insights. For more in-depth information on TPC-C benchmark results, full disclosure reports are available but are quite thick; thus I resisted the impulse of including one here. Full disclosure reports provide specific information on any tuning completed above and beyond the default installation of the software used for the benchmark. It is a good exercise to review these reports because they provide insight into which areas you should investigate when tuning Windows 2000 systems and the various database engines they support.

TPC-D

TPC-D was a popular benchmark for simulating data warehouse environments but has since been retired and replaced by TPC-H.

TPC-H

The TPC-H benchmark represents large decision-support database or data warehouse environments that, through a random mix of complex, decision-support and simple ad hoc or unanticipated queries, are processed against a large database designed to be resistant to performance tuning. These ad hoc queries are in contrast to the Online Transaction Processing (OLTP)-based queries represented by the TPC-C benchmarks above. The TPC-H benchmark suite is considered a tougher benchmark due to its ad hoc nature. The targeted customer environments are those environments that do not run canned (i.e., store procedure) database queries; rather they are the environments where the customer might ask, "How well did sales of new Corvettes go when they were sold on rainy Saturdays during April and May by someone named Valerie for the last 50 years with discounts no greater than 2% and when Mars lined up with Saturn?" OK, perhaps this is not the most applicable query, but you get the point about the complexity.

The size of the databases used in the benchmark can vary from 100GB to terabytes (TB). So, if you are looking to see how a certain hardware/software combination will perform, ensure that you choose a database size representative of your environment. It's important to remember that some database engines do much better than others when the amount of data becomes very large. Just because a specific TPC-H benchmark test may be targeted at 100GB of raw data, the actual size of the database may grow to a size three times that when factors such as space for indexes and the typical extra space for temporary data are figured in. For example, when I reviewed some recent TPC-H test results for 100GB of raw data, the actual size of the database was 340GB.

TPC-W

The TPC-W benchmark is targeted to represent eCommerce web-based business environments such as retail outlets, software distribution, airline reservations, and electronic stock trades over the Internet or Intranet. This benchmark has been released, but at the time of this book's writing, there were no published reports about it for us to analyze. eCommerce will continue to grow in quantum leaps in the coming years, so expect either this or other benchmarks targeted at simulating eCommerce environments to become more popular with customers and subsequently with the vendors providing eCommerce solutions. Sizing an eCommerce solution is critical because, if you do not size, tune, and implement your solution well, your livelihood is directly impacted. If customers or business partners cannot reliably depend on your services, you lose out on revenue and probably your position in the market place.

eCommerce environments are more than just the web-enabled front ends. They are composed of and depend on many of the electronic environments such as database and e-mail systems that are investigated throughout this book.

SPECweb99 (formerly SPECweb96)

Standard Performance Evaluation Corporation (SPEC) is a nonprofit corporation that publishes a variety of benchmarks intended to help evaluate different areas of computer performance. The SPECweb99 benchmark suite is particularly relevant for the Windows 2000 web server services environment. Information and results for SPEC benchmarks are available from http://www.spec.org.

SPECweb99 recently replaced SPECweb96 as SPEC's standardized benchmark designed to measure a server's ability to act as a World Wide Web server. The workload for this benchmark simulates the accesses to a web service provider, where the server supports the home page for a number of different organizations. This benchmark reports the throughput that a World Wide Web server can support. Where SPECweb96 defined throughput as the sustained number of hypertext transfer protocol (http) operations per second, SPECweb99 defines throughput as the measurement of simultaneous web connections that the web server can support.

To understand what this throughput result is really providing, let's review the characteristics of this benchmark and investigate what is being measured a little more closely. The SPECweb99 workload simulates the accesses to a web server, where the server supports the home page for a number of different organizations. Each home page is a collection of files ranging in size from small icons to large documents or images. As in the real world, certain files within the home page are more popular than others. The dynamic GETs simulate the common practice of rotating advertisements on a web page and using cookie table lookups. The POSTs simulate the entry of user data into a log file on the server, such as might happen during a user registration sequence. SPECweb99 also uses dynamic GETs, static GETs, POST operations, Keepalives (HTTP 1.0) persistent connections (HTTP 1.1), and interclient communication using sockets.

Dynamic content—consisting of 16% POSTs, 41.5% GETs, 42% GETs with cookies, and 0.5% Common Gateway Interface (CGI) GETs—comprises 30% of the overall workload. SPEC determined the access patterns to the files from the analysis of the actual web server logs. SPECweb99 directs 35% of its activity to the smallest class, 50% to the 1-to-10KB class, 14% percent to the 10-to-100KB class, and 1% to the largest files. Within each class there are non-linear distributions of accesses, reflecting the fact that certain files are more popular than others.

Once the SPECweb99 benchmark is run, a SPECweb99 rating is provided that corresponds to the number of simultaneous users that the web server can support while under the SPECweb99 workload outlined above. This rating is determined by requesting a predefined benchmark workload that a web server is able to support while still meeting specific throughput and error rate requirements. The benchmark uses a client/server test environment where external clients emulate web users that drive HTTP-based requests against the web server under test. The maximum simultaneous throughput rating that the server can support is defined as when the transfer rate back to the clients falls below 320,000 bits per second (40,000 bytes/sec).

Each HTTP request takes a certain amount of elapsed time to complete depending on the file size. SPECweb99 forces the client to read responses in chunks of 1,460 bytes or less. Theoretically, a 1,460-byte chunk of data over a 400,000-bits/sec line would arrive every 0.03 seconds. Since the implementation does not actually restrict the line speed of the connection, arrival time calculations are used to determine how long the operation should take at 400,000 bits/sec. This calculated sleeping at the end of the operation enforces operation duration. Thus this determines the "think time" that each emulated web user must wait before making another request.

As with the TPC-C benchmark, vendors disclose executive summary reports of their SPECweb99 results. Figure 3-5 contains a sample report.

APPLYING SPECWEB99 RESULTS

So, how can this information be helpful in sizing and configuring your Windows 2000 systems as web servers? This benchmark (and benchmarks similar in nature) can help significantly if you keep in mind what is actually tested. The obvious information provided is that, if you are looking to support 732 simultaneous users, each sustaining a varied distribution of web-based operations, then you have your basic server configuration. Specific Windows 2000 server configuration information to take note of here is the significant network I/O sizing required to support this level of simultaneous throughput. The amount of performance that can be provided by such a small Windows 2000 server configuration may be surprising to many.

SPECWEB99 CONCERNS

When using this benchmark for a sizing reference, take note that, due to the very short think time each user has, it really is a simultaneous workload. Few sites have this many customers accessing the web server at the exact same time. Look closer at the amount of data that the web server is capable of delivering. For the example above, the amount of data delivered when 732 customers are all pulling data at the benchmark minimum allowable throughput level of 320,000 bits/sec translates into 234Mbits/sec. If you were serving this data over the Internet, you would require six T3 (45Mbits/sec each) lines to the Internet! If you keep in mind the big picture or end result, it really is not that difficult to be able to use SPECweb99 results to your sizing advantage or for comparison of web server software and hardware.

SPECweb99 Result
>   Dell Computer Corporation: PowerEdge 2400/667
>   Microsoft: Internet Information Server 5.0
>   SPECweb99 = 732
>   Test Date: Mar-2000
>   Tested By:
>   Dell Computer Corp.
>   Hardware Avail: Feb-2000 OS Avail: Feb-2000 HTTP Software Avail: Feb-2000
>   Sup. Software Avail: -- SPEC license #: 55

Hardware
>   Vendor: Dell Computer Corporation
>   Model: PowerEdge 2400/667
>   Processor: 667MHz Pentium III
>   # Processors: 1
>   Primary Cache: 16KBI+16KBD on chip
>   Secondary Cache: 256KB(I+D) on chip
>   Other Cache: None
>   Memory: 2GB
>   Disk Subsystem: 5 9GB 10KRPM drives
>   Disk Controllers: Onboard PERC2/Si RAID
>   Other Hardware: 1 Alteon ACEswitch 180

Software
>   Operating System: Windows 2000 Advanced Server
>   File System: NTFS
>   Other Software: None

HTTP Software
>   Vendor: Microsoft
>   HTTP Software: Internet Information Server 5.0
>   API: ISAPI
>   Server Cache: None
>   Log Mode: W3C Extended Log File Format

Test Sponsor
>   Test Date: Mar-2000
>   Tested By: Dell Computer Corp.
>   SPEC License: 55

Network
>   # of Controllers: 1
>   Network Controllers: Alteon AceNIC PCI
>   # of Nets: 1
>   Type of Nets: Gigabit Ethernet
>   Network Speed: 1Gb/s
>   MSL (sec): 30 (Non RFC1122)
>   Time-Wait (sec): 60 (Non RFC1122)
>   MTU: 1500

Clients
>   # of Clients: 5
>   Model: Dell Precision 410
>   Processor: 450MHz Pentium II
>   # of Processors: 2
>   Memory: 128MB
>   Network Controller: Alteon AceNIC PCI
>   Operating System: Windows 2000 Professional
>   Compiler: Microsoft Visual C++ 6.0

FIGURE 3–5   *Sample Report—SPECweb99 Result*

SPECWEB99 FUTURE WEB SIZING EXAMPLE

SPECweb99 information is also helpful for future sizing. Perhaps you are planning for an increase in simultaneous users at your web site, beyond your current configuration. Will additional resources allow your software/hardware solution to support additional users? Review the http://www.spec.org web pages and look for a configuration that might be similar to what you are interested in. Again, running benchmarks is expensive, so the available list of varied configurations to choose from may be limited. On the positive side, there *is* a list. Even if the benchmark results of the exact server configuration you are seeking is not yet available, a similar architecture may be. For example, if you have an Intel-based system (which you probably do if you are running Windows 2000), look at the results of other hardware vendors that provide Intel based solutions (see Table 3.3). Each vendor has its own unique value added, but the core system architecture is Intel so the overall results are comparable enough to provide a good general estimate.

TABLE 3.3   *Compaq and Dell SPECweb99 Results*

	Compaq	**Dell**	**Primary Difference**
CPU	Two 993MHz Pentium III XEON w/256KB L2 Cache	Four 700MHz Pentium III XEON w/2MB L2 Cache	2 CPUs and increase of L2 cache from 512KB to 2MB
Disk	Similar	Similar	N/A
Network	Similar	Similar	N/A
Memory	4GB	8GB	Addition of 4GB
Software Configuration	Similar	Similar	N/A
SpecWeb99 Results (simultaneous connections)	1098	1598	Improved performance of 500 simultaneous connections.

NetBench

The Ziff-Davis Benchmark Operation produces a series of benchmarks encompassing a variety of areas; they can be downloaded from: http://www1.zdnet.com/zdbop/zdbop.html. Of these benchmarks, NetBench is a particularly helpful benchmark to use when testing Windows 2000 systems as file servers. NetBench exercises network file I/O requests in a file server environment, producing a bytes/sec server I/O throughput score and associated response time information. The NetBench benchmark program measures how well a file server handles typical office productivity application file I/O request workloads by stressing the file server with various client types. The clients exercise the Windows 2000 system with requests for network file operations. Each client tallies how many bytes of data are moved to and from the server and how long the process takes. The client then uses this information to calculate its throughput for that test mix.

The primary benefit of this benchmark is that several trade magazines run this test suite against numerous vendors' servers and configurations; thus a fair amount of data is available. I doubt there is any coincidence that most of the magazines using the Ziff-Davis benchmarks fall under the Ziff-Davis ownership umbrella. These published results are beneficial for determining initial sizing configurations of Windows 2000 systems by providing information such as how much network throughput a specific server configuration can support and determining the associated number of office-environment clients the Windows 2000 file server can handle. The results in Figure 3-6 are from the January 2000 issue of *PC Magazine* on its public Web site: http://www.zdnet.com/products/stories/reviews/0,4161,2426083,00.html.

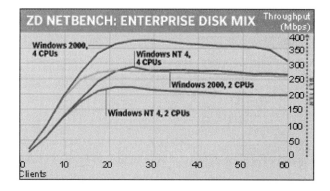

FIGURE 3–6   *Windows 2000 Server NetBench Results: Enterprise Disk Mix*

ANALYZING NETBENCH RESULTS

NetBench places particular stress on the network, disk, memory, and CPU subsystems—in that order. This is indicative of what you find in a file server environment. This type of testing is highly susceptible to the choice of the network and disk components along with the server configurations. So what sizing information can be gleaned from Figure 3-6? It depends on your environment. For the benchmark results displayed in Figure 3-6, four server configurations were used. Here we will focus on analyzing the two Windows 2000–based results, although it is interesting to see how much better Windows 2000 did than its Windows 2000 4 predecessor. In later chapters, we'll show you how improvements in the Windows 2000 operating system improved its capabilities regarding overall performance.

All of the tests in Figure 3-6 were run on a Compaq ProLiant 7000 server, equipped with four Intel 450MHz XEON processors with 1MB of L2 cache and 1GB of RAM. The RAID array was composed of 14 disks and was configured at RAID level 5, write-through with a 32KB cluster size. The server had two Alteon AceNIC Gigabit Ethernet (10/100/1000Base-T) network adapters set for gigabit connections (1,000Mbits/sec). The network that connected the server to the clients was a full-duplex-switched network that enabled 60 desktops to drive the benchmark. To run the two CPU test configuration benchmarks, the system was configured to use only two CPUs by editing the boot.ini file and adding the switch "\MAXCPU:2" and rebooting the system. All other aspects of the configuration stayed the same for the two CPU configuration benchmark runs.

If your requirements indicate the need to support 60 concurrent clients while sustaining 225Megabits/sec of network throughput, then the basic two-CPU server configuration tested in Figure 3-6 will meet that requirement. If, however, your requirements dictate supporting 60 concurrent clients while sustaining a throughput requirement of 375Megabits/sec, than you would have to increase your server configuration by two CPUs. Both of these results reflect a very busy client base. However, if historical information you researched characterizes your environment as such, these results can have very important initial sizing ramifications. For example, what if your current customer base needs only the performance provided by the two-CPU configuration, but in 6 months you expect twice the workload? With this information, you may opt for a server capable of supporting four CPUs, even though you need only two for the next 6 months. Upgrading two CPUs is much less time consuming than bringing up a completely new Windows 2000 system. Another example might be your restore-to-service goals—e.g., backing up and restoring your system from a tape backup unit on the network. You might determine that, to meet your server backup requirements, a higher level of performance is needed (assuming you are backing up the server across the network) than the two-CPU system provides. Again, with this information, you may decide to initially obtain a server with four CPUs instead of two to meet your goals.

NETBENCH LIMITATIONS

There are two limiting factors for this benchmark: the workload mix and client loads. As with other benchmarks, if your environment is not indicative of general office productivity applications, the results provided by this benchmark are less helpful. Generating a significant amount of load is costly (time and money) in a NetBench environment due to the large number of client PCs required to generate workload levels high enough to properly stress higher-end servers (in this example, 60 desktops were brought on line to drive the benchmark). Higher-end Windows 2000 servers can be equated with workhorses, not racehorses. If workload levels are not high enough on larger Windows 2000 server configurations, the server's real capabilities will not be fully tested.

Historical Baselines

Where Do Historical Baselines Fit into the Sizing Methodology?

Have you ever met a technical team that was designing a new solution or in the middle of rolling out a new system and asked, "Why did you configure your Windows 2000 system like that?" I bet you received a blank stare in response. The blank stare means they guessed. Some hardware vendors love these people since they are so easy to take advantage of. Why take advantage of them? Because, without any quantifiable information to size their systems, most people tend to want to be on the safe side and order more hardware than they need, thus making the hardware vendor's sales team quite happy because it is that much closer to meeting its sales quota. The better hardware vendors will work with you or at least provide some guidance as to why a certain configuration meets the goals of certain environments. So, why guess? With so many systems based on Windows NT 4 (which is what Windows 2000 is based on) in the enterprise, historical information is available to help you in sizing your systems!

   Historical baselines are particularly useful when applied to steps 3 and 7 of the sizing methodology (see Table 3.1). In step 3 (determining loading characteristics), having historical information to base the loading analysis on is quite helpful and is illustrated below. Once you understand the characteristics and can quantify the workloads that will need to be supported by the system, configuring a Windows 2000 system to meet your requirements becomes more realistic since you can leap directly into placing an optimum configuration (and perhaps save some money). Oh yeah, and no one will snicker at you when they ask you to justify or quantify your solution.

Using Historical Baselines

In several locations throughout this chapter, we alluded to using current performance logs from Sysmon to help you understand and characterize your environment so you could determine if any of the industry benchmarks investigated might meet your performance information needs. In chapter 2 we talked about the use of Sysmon-generated performance logs. How can you use these Sysmon logs to your advantage for longer-term capacity sizing and planning? When reviewing Sysmon log data in chart mode, Sysmon allows performance data to be exported into a variety of formats by right-clicking in the right-hand side of the Sysmon chart area. Available export formats include tabular delimited fields (.tsv) and web format (HTML). The .tsv export format can be imported into a database of your choice for more advanced and long-term analyses to determine future trends. A slightly less complex but helpful method is to export this information into a spreadsheet. Once the data is inside of the spreadsheet, you can then exploit some of the spreadsheet's basic trend analysis capabilities.

To generate a disk I/O analysis graph similar to the graph in Figure 3-7, follow these steps.

1. Launch Sysmon by selecting Start / Administrative Tools / Performance Monitor.
2. In the right-hand side of the Sysmon chart, select the View Log Data radio button, and select the Sysmon log file you wish to analyze. (Note: You must already have created a log file for this step. Refer to chapter 2 for the steps associated with creating a log file using Sysmon.)
3. Under Logical Disk Object, select %Disk Time.
4. Under File / Export Chart, save your data in the .tsv file format.
5. Launch your spreadsheet; this example is based on Microsoft Excel.
6. Open the .tsv file you exported and follow Excel's Data Import Wizard.
7. Highlight the performance data %Disk Time and Time/Date Stamp.
8. Select Chart Wizard and follow the Wizard's steps to create the graph.
9. Once the graph is created, right-click on the %Disk Time data series.
10. While the data series is selected, right-click the data series and choose Add Trend Line.
11. For this example, I used a linear trend line.
12. Right clicking the newly created trend line allows access to trend line Format / Options.
13. Under Options, enter the number of units for future forecast.
14. Congratulations! You now have a basic capacity sizing projection chart!

Following these steps on generating a disk I/O analysis graph, I generated the disk I/O trend analysis for use in capacity planning shown in Figure 3-7. This graph depicts one disk drive's %Disk Time historical usage (the jagged line) and a 30-day projected %Disk Time usage (the straight line). The disk usage for this drive is steadily increasing, with a current %Disk Time hovering in the 50% range. A 50% utilization is acceptable, but, as the % disk utilization increases past the 80% utilization range, disk response time begins to dramatically increase. If disk response increases, so will the associated activity that requires that disk request. Thus, the final response time the user experiences will also increase, which is what we want to avoid happening on a regular basis.

So what do you do with this data? Head back to chapter 2 and use the tuning methodology in conjunction with chapter 7 to determine possible solutions to this pending disk bottleneck. Some of the solutions can encompass techniques ranging from changing this configuration from a single disk device to a RAID device, tuning the allocation unit size (ALU), changing the RAID level in use, or redistributing some of the disk workload to other disk devices in the system. If the solution involves the purchase of additional hardware resources, use this trend analysis to help justify the decision.

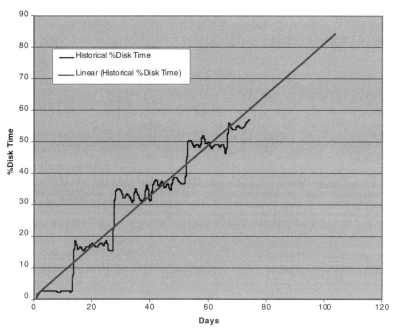

FIGURE 3–7 *Disk Usage Capacity Planning*

There is, however, an assumption made here that this disk usage pattern would continue into the future. This is where the art of sizing comes into play, since you will have to take into consideration factors such as future business requirements and continued use of this application by customers as the company grows. For example, if you found that during the holiday rush in December, your workloads drove your system to consistent 80% disk usage, and December is your busiest season, what should you do? Determine if your company plans on a bigger holiday season next year. If this is the case, you have a few months to plan any changes, but you will be ready for that next, and hopefully bigger, holiday rush.

This same capacity planning technique can be used to project the future capacity usage and potential bottlenecks for all of the major server resources. What should you analyze and graph? Chapter 1 has several tables that outline detection of system bottlenecks. Use these tables as a guide when deciding which Sysmon objects to use for sizing trend analysis. The same Sysmon objects that are helpful for detecting system bottlenecks are also helpful for sizing systems too. In particular, look closely at the Process object's counters. They enable you to obtain sizing information for specific applications. This process/application information is very helpful when considering server consolidations or when you are just upgrading your server because you can determine CPU, memory, and disk usage of multiple applications and then extrapolate what would be needed if all of the applications ran on the same server. For convenience, some of the key Sysmon objects and counters to consider for capacity planning and trend analysis are listed in Tables 3.4 and 3.5.

| **TABLE 3.4** | *Key Sysmon Processor Objects and Counters and Their Relevance to Sizing a System* |

Process Counters Object: Counter	**Definition**	**Relevance to Sizing a System**
Process: Processor Time	%Processor Time is the percentage of elapsed time that all of the threads of this process used the processor to execute instructions.	This counter displays how much total CPU usage this process (application) uses. Consider the type of processor the process is running on for server consolidations.
Process: I/O Read bytes/sec & I/O Write bytes/sec	The rate the process is reading bytes from I/O operations. This counter counts all I/O activity generated by the process to include file, network, and device I/Os.	These two counters provide insight into both the characteristics and performance of the disk I/O subsystem usage by the process. Use this information to determine type of RAID subsystem to use and the number of disk drives to use.
Process: Working Set	Working Set peak is the maximum number of bytes in the Working Set of this process at any point in time. The Working Set is the set of memory pages touched recently by the threads in the process	This counter provides insight into how much physical memory the process typically uses. With this information, you can determine how much RAM is needed to keep the process in physical memory vs. relying on virtual memory via the pagefile(s) located on the disk drive(s).

| **TABLE 3.5** | *Key Sysmon Memory and Disk Objects and Counters to Consider for Capacity Planning and Trend Analysis* |

	Definition	**Rule of Thumb for Bottleneck Detection and for Sizing**
Memory Counters Object: Counter		
Memory: Available Bytes	Available Bytes is the amount of physical memory available to processes running on the system, in bytes.	Windows 2000 server will try to keep at least 4MB available as seen via this counter. If this value is close to or under 4MB, pages/sec is high, and the disk drive where the pagefile is located is busy, there is a memory shortfall.

TABLE 3.5	*Key Sysmon Memory and Disk Objects and Counters to Consider for Capacity Planning and Trend Analysis (Continued)*

	Definition	Rule of Thumb for Bottleneck Detection and for Sizing
Memory: Pages Output/sec	Pages Output/sec is the number of pages written to disk (pagefile) to free up space in physical memory. Pages are written back to disk only if they are changed in physical memory, so they are likely to hold data, not code.	A high rate of Pages Output/sec assists in the identification of a memory shortage. Specifically, if this value is high and the pages/sec value is high, you have low available memory, and the disk that holds your pagefile is busy, you are running short on RAM.
Paging File: % Usage	The amount of the pagefile instance in use in percent.	If a large amount of pagefile is used on a regular basis, consider adding (Size of pageFile × % of pagefile in use) of RAM to your system.
Disk Counters Object: Counter		
Logical Disk: Average Disk Queue Length	Average Disk Queue Length is the average number of both read and write requests that was queued for the selected logical disk during the sample interval.	If this value is greater than 2 for a single disk drive and the Disk Transfers/sec is high (>50), the selected disk drive is becoming a bottleneck. This value is an average calculated during the Sysmon sample period. Use this counter to determine if there is a disk bottleneck, and use the Current Disk Queue Length counter to understand the actual workload distribution.
Logical Disk: Average Disk sec/Transfer	Average disk sec/Transfer is the time in seconds of the average disk transfer.	When the Transfers/sec counter is consistently above 80 for a single disk drive, the Average Disk sec/Transfer should be observed to determine if it is rising above your baseline. A value greater than 0.09 seconds indicates that the selected disk drive's response times are uncommonly slow.
Network Counters Object: Counter		
Network Interface: Bytes Total/sec	Bytes total per second is the rate that all bytes are sent and received on the selected network interface, including those bytes used as overhead (framing, etc.).	This value is directly related to the network architecture in use. If the value of Bytes Total/sec for the network instance is close to the maximum transfer rates of your network, and the Output Queue Length is >3, you have a network bottleneck.

| **TABLE 3.5** | *Key Sysmon Memory and Disk Objects and Counters to Consider for Capacity Planning and Trend Analysis (Continued)* |

	Definition	**Rule of Thumb for Bottleneck Detection and for Sizing**
CPU Counters **Object: Counter**		
Processor: % Total Processor Time	% Total Processor Time is expressed as a percentage of the elapsed time that a processor is busy executing a non-idle thread.	A high value for this counter is not a reason to be alarmed unless it is accompanied by a Server Work Queue Length greater than 2 or growing with an associated level of processor time greater then 90%; then the CPU is becoming a bottleneck. This rule holds true for single CPU Windows 2000 systems.
Server: Server Work Queues Queue Length	Queue Length is the current length of the server work queue for this CPU instance.	If the Queue Length is >2 or continuously growing with an associated level of Total Processor Time >90%, the CPU is becoming a bottleneck. This rule holds true for single CPU Windows 2000 systems.

Of course, this capacity sizing technique is helpful only if you proactively monitor and keep accurate records on the systems that are managed. So why not track performance logs of at least your most crucial servers? Keeping good records is the key to staying one step ahead in the capacity planning game!

How Server Architecture Relationships Affect System Configurations

Throughout this chapter, the focus has been on determining the requirements needed to develop our solution and subsequently each system component. From a configuration standpoint, system architecture is reviewed more closely for each system resource (CPU, memory, disk, and network) in later chapters with specific recommendations. For now, let's take a step back and look at the entire system architecture as it relates to the final configuration.

When configuring your system, it is important to understand the relationships of the various system components and how data is moved throughout a system. Once you begin to understand these relationships, it is possible to size balanced Windows 2000 system configurations that do not introduce bottlenecks before you even begin. Standard high-volume (SHV) server boards produced by Intel are what many of today's hardware manufacturers use for the basis of for their 2-, 4-, and 8-CPU Windows 2000 Server implementations. This enables hardware manufacturers to capitalize on the economies of scale associated with the high volume of SHV server motherboards produced by Intel, while they focus on their value-add differentiations. This approach lowers the overall cost of producing a system because this enables the research and design costs to spread across millions of units sold. Figure 3-8 is a logical illustration of a Pentium III XEON-based SHV design.

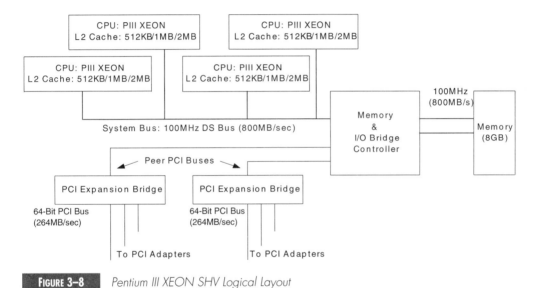

FIGURE 3–8   *Pentium III XEON SHV Logical Layout*

The server's primary system bus operates at 100MHz and provides 800MB/sec of throughput. Attached to the system bus are up to four Pentium III XEON CPUs operating up to 833Mhz, up to 8GB of RAM (currently rated at 50 nanoseconds [ns]), and two peer PCI I/O buses each operating at 266 MB/sec. Understanding the speeds and feeds of the system is less important at the moment than understanding the relationships between them. Let's look at these speeds and feeds from two perspectives:

1. The time it takes to get data to the CPU
2. How the data gets from the I/O subsystem to the CPU

The time it takes to get data to the CPU drastically affects the server's overall performance (see Table 3.5). A nanosecond is a small quantity of time that is difficult to put into perspective. Look at the graphical depiction (Figure 3-9) of access times to the various server resources outlined in Table 3.6.

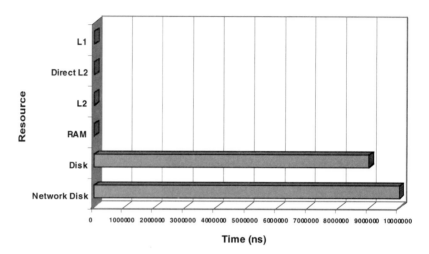

FIGURE 3-9   *Getting to the Data—Relative Access Speeds of System Components*

TABLE 3.6   *Time Needed to Obtain Data from Server Resources*

Resource	Time (ns)
CPU to L1 cache	2
CPU to directly connected L2 cache	2
CPU to indirectly connected L2 cache	4
CPU to main memory/RAM	50–70
CPU to disk drives	9,000,000–35,000,000
CPU to network-connected disk resource	10,000,000–250,000,000

To help put this into perspective, let's associate these nanoseconds with seconds. Now, if you needed a piece of information to complete your job and go home and the information was in level 2 cache, it would take all of 2 seconds to gather the data, and then shortly thereafter, you would go home. If the information you required were on the disk drives, you would have to wait 9,000,000 seconds or 2,500 hours. Which would you prefer? The primary objective of the simplified graph in Figure 3-9 is to drive home the importance of the long wait times required to get data from other than local cache or main memory.

Amazing, isn't it? While the CPU waits for data from the disk, it could be sitting around idle. Keeping a CPU properly presented with or fed data allows the CPU to be more efficient. The reference to "efficient" here is in the context that the CPU is running a productive action vs. sitting and waiting for the data it needs.

Properly Sizing Memory

It becomes even more important to size your system's memory properly now that enterprise Windows 2000–based servers are becoming common as it affects overall budgets and performance. Determining the appropriate amount of RAM to configure will greatly affect your server performance. To keep a Pentium III XEON CPU-class-based Windows 2000 server properly fed, 256MB of RAM per CPU is required at a minimum. With 256MB of RAM, Windows 2000's entire working set (~60 MB) can fit into memory, there is some application space available, and there is still some RAM available for Windows 2000's dynamic file system caching. Of course, permanently saved data on disk drives will need to be accessed at some point, but it would be prudent to avoid accessing the disk drives unless absolutely necessary. Having enough memory available gives Windows 2000's dynamic file system cache the ability to lower the number of disk transactions by caching many of these disk transactions into RAM. For example, every time the system must access the disk, the CPU waits the equivalent of driving several times from New York to LA before it can continue processing that process's (thread's) request. Having enough RAM available to avoid constantly traveling to the disk for data drastically improves the server's performance. Yes, the CPU may be processing other application requests while it waits for the data to be fetched by the I/O subsystem, but do you really care if the application you are interacting with that is waiting on that data from/to the disk(s)?

Server I/O Relationships

Now let's look how data gets from the I/O subsystem to the CPU. Different Windows 2000 architectures are capable of providing certain levels of theoretical I/O performance. The advanced SHV architecture shown in Figure 3-8 can support a very large amount of external disk arrays. In theory, one SHV-based server can support in excess of 7 Terabytes of external disk storage. Now, whether all of this data is actually active and usable is another story. To be using this amount of storage, a very well-thought-out design is needed (see chapter 7). The Compaq TPC-C executive summary report (see Figure 3-4) illustrated one particularly large configuration, which supported 180 disk drives for 1.8 Terabytes of disk space per node for a total of 21.6 Terabytes. The Compaq 8500 8-CPU superserver is based on the Intel Profusion SHV server technology in conjunction with Compaq technology.

The General Intel SHV I/O subsystem uses two 64-bit peer PCI buses (528MB/sec) aggregate, which, in essence, feed a single, faster XEON system bus (800MB/sec) via the advanced memory and I/O controller. You cannot influence these access speeds, but you should be aware that you can easily influence how the I/O system is configured and subsequently used. When considering the I/O layout, think of plumbing (we'll skip the various I/O overheads for now). Consider Figures 3-10 and 3-11. Obviously you would want to avoid Figure 3-11. This is the same concept when configuring the I/O subsystem. Following the sizing methodology and chapter 6 along with some experience, you can determine how many I/O devices will be active at any one time. For a worst-case scenario, you can consider all I/O devices active at the same time. If your server will support six PCI I/O cards and the configuration calls for three Gigabit Ethernet network cards (250MB/sec) and two Quad Ultra Fast and Wide SCSI cards (~480MB/sec), there is a problem. The aggregate I/O throughput of these devices—730MB/sec—will greatly overflow the 532MB/sec available from the two peer PCI buses in an SHV-based server. The moral of the story: *even if the server specifications state that the server can be configured in a certain manner, it is not always wise to do so.*

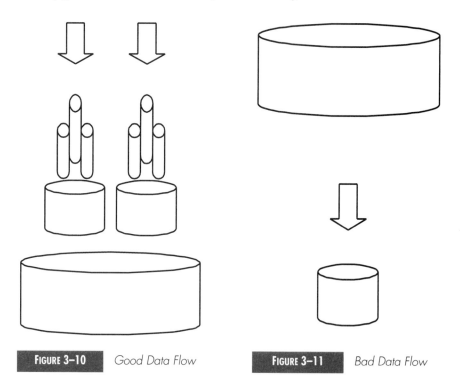

FIGURE 3-10   *Good Data Flow*   **FIGURE 3-11**   *Bad Data Flow*

Server CPUs Drive More than Applications Alone

Now that we have considered the sizing relationship of the main memory and I/O subsystem, never forget the CPU processing power required to drive the entire system. Driving high levels of I/O requires a significant amount of processing power. The amount of CPU power required to accomplish this should decrease once I20 technology becomes more common and processing I/O subsystem requests become more distributed internally to the system. More detailed information on these two topics is provided in chapters 5 and 7.

Until then, keep in mind that you must share the direct processing power needed for application calculations with the processing power required to drive the I/O subsystem.

This concept of ensuring that there is enough CPU processing power becomes relevant when, after following the sizing methodology, you determine the need for a Windows 2000 system to provide very high levels of I/O throughput. Perhaps the requirements call for a communications application driving multiple Gigabit Ethernet lines in conjunction with another application that has high processing requirements. At that point, sizing requirements may have outgrown the SHV architecture, and you should consider a more scalable system design that supports higher numbers of CPUs, PCI buses, and memory. With the introduction of commodity-priced 8-CPU-based servers, choosing a more scalable server platform is much more realistic than in years past. Another option, commonly used before the advent of higher-scaling commodity Intel CPU-based servers for the Windows 2000 environment, is distributing the application(s) among multiple servers as needed to meet the requirements. This approach requires more time and effort to manage, since you have many distributed servers, which subsequently increases your overall total cost of ownership (TCO). Although you must keep availability requirements in mind, fully distributing every possible function is no longer needed since 2-CPU systems of today (Pentium III XEON) are faster than quad-CPU systems of the past (Pentium Pro) and provide sufficient computing power to avoid extremely large tiny tot distributed server farms.

Commercially Available Sizing Tools

With this wealth of information presented thus far, hasn't someone tried to develop an automated tool for sizing systems? The answer is yes. There are several software tools you can download from the Internet that provide some good general sizing assistance/guidance. Why guidance? These tools are based on many of the benchmarks shown in this chapter, as well as the vendors' experience with their own products. I recommend trying these sizing tools if they are applicable to your environment. In addition to these tools, use the core sizing methodology, because the methodology will actually help you to answer the questions that the tools request so that they can generate system configuration recommendations. Intel provides a link on its web site http://www.intel.com/eBusiness/server/resources/performance/sizing.htm that provides pointers to the server sizing tools available from a variety of vendors such as Compaq, Dell, and Oracle. Sizing tools are most commonly available for database and exchange environments. Also helpful is the fact that each manufacturer's sizing tool includes assistance in determining all of the parts required to build the recommended system. Surprising that, after they help you to size your Windows 2000 system, they provide you with a parts sheet to hand to their sales team!

Summary

In this chapter, we explored a sizing methodology that you can use when sizing any Windows 2000–based system solution regardless of the current technology level in use. We covered Windows 2000 system sizing aids such as industry standard benchmarks and historical data trend usage (baselines) to help you gain a more realistic start in your sizing efforts. In addition, we investigated system architecture relationships, which provide insight into the relationships of system resources, while using the extensive capabilities and limitations of modern SHV servers as a reference example. Understanding your business and technical goals, workload environment, and the system architectures available today, along with knowing how and why Windows 2000 operates as it does, leads to well-sized and -configured Windows 2000 systems that provide outstanding building blocks for your solutions.

CPU Performance

CHAPTER OBJECTIVES

- Introduction........ *173*
- Central Processing Unit........ *174*
- Pentium III and Pentium III XEON CPUs........ *176*
- Windows 2000 and CPU Resource Usage........ *186*
- Detecting CPU Bottlenecks........ *193*
- Sizing CPU Subsystems........ *208*
- CPU and Memory Sizing Relationships........ *210*
- Tuning Strategies for Removing CPU Bottlenecks........ *214*
- Thinking Outside of the Box........ *225*

Introduction

To tune or size a Windows 2000 system, it is important to understand how and why the system hardware, operating system, and applications actually work as they do. It is tempting at first to just jump in and start adding this or tuning that. However, when you understand how each component works with the others, you'll be able to tune and size system resources for maximum performance without a lot of trial and error. In this and the following chapters, descriptions, explanations, and examples are provided to help you understand how the system components interact.

Armed with this information, you can remove some of the "black magic" of tuning and sizing and employ more effective tactics. Knowing which "knob to turn" to tune a Windows 2000 system is good; understanding when to "turn a tuning knob" and why it will help is better.

This chapter focuses on Windows 2000 and the CPU subsystem. CPU performance is investigated from several perspectives. First, we review general CPU architecture to determine the relative performance of several available CPU models and what, from a system architecture perspective, influences CPU performance. Second, we look at how Windows 2000 takes advantage of CPU resources. Once our foundation of CPU knowledge is established, we determine when CPU bottlenecks occur while running Windows 2000. From there we move into sizing CPU subsystems. Then, with an understanding of how to identify CPU bottlenecks and how to size CPU subsystems, we build upon this foundation and examine how to tune around CPU bottlenecks. The bottleneck detection techniques and sizing and tuning strategies reviewed in this chapter are not just based on theory; they were developed and fine tuned in real-world production environments and are crucial to understanding the rest of this book.

Central Processing Unit

The Central Processing Unit (CPU) is the glamour queen of any system. It is the single most important resource in the system because it processes various requests from applications and subsequent end users. It is important to keep the CPU(s) fed with the information it needs to complete its requested actions. When other system resources wait on the CPU, the CPU is the bottleneck. When the CPU waits on other resources in the system, the bottleneck is elsewhere.

It is common for businesses to assume that if they add another CPU, the overall performance of their system will improve. Unfortunately, adding another CPU does not always improve performance. This fact is reinforced by each of the case studies in chapter 7. The case studies demonstrate that to improve the performance additional or faster CPUs are not always required. This fundamental fact is restated a million times throughout this book (okay, a million may be a slight exaggeration), but it is worth repeating. Too often I have read published documents that mention, "...we added a CPU, but it did not improve the performance. This software/hardware/application does not scale...". Although this is occasionally true, it is my experience that, more often than not, the CPU is not the limiting factor. I hope you remember to take this into consideration before deciding to increase the speed or number of CPUs in your server. There is nothing more disappointing than adding a $1,000 CPU only to find out nothing has improved!

CPU System Architecture Review

This section covers some of the key system architecture factors that influence CPU effectiveness, relative performance of CPUs available today, and guidelines on the selection of a CPU. This section is not a complex review of CPU and system architectures and does not require a doctorate in computer engineering to understand. If you are curious about lower level details of computer architectures, John Hennessy and David Patterson authored an excellent book on the topic titled *Computer Architecture: A Quantitative Approach.*

Microsoft and Intel focus on high volume to generate their revenue. This results in systems with generally lower price points that provide outstanding price/performance results when compared to their UNIX and mainframe competitors. Intel developed a series of Standard High Volume (SHV) system motherboards, which are the basis of many of the 1, 1–2, 1–4, and 1–8 CPU-based desktops and servers on the market today. Even the high-end Intel-based 32-CPU systems from Compaq and Unisys use the SHV-based systems as building blocks of their systems. Intel's Pentium III XEON-based SHV design is referenced here to explain various factors influencing CPU performance. This is not an endorsement of Intel-only server solutions; however, it is a popular architecture that provides a good reference to illustrate server architecture principles. Figure 4-1 is a logical illustration of an SHV motherboard.

Current Intel CPU offerings supported in the 1–8 based CPU server class operate at *internal* clock speeds over 900MHz. The system bus on the SHV motherboard operates at 100MHz. The system bus provides the data path between the CPU, memory, and the I/O subsystem. Obviously, there is a bit of a discrepancy between the speed at which the system bus operates and the speed at which the CPU(s) operate. For a CPU to be effective, both data and instructions must be moved into the CPU so that it can be kept productive performing the requested tasks. When data that the CPU requires are not available, it waits. This is commonly referred to as a CPU wait state. Under Windows 2000, while a CPU waits for data or is not busy operating on another task, Windows 2000's System Idle Process occupies the CPU. You can see the System Idle Process under Task Manager, process view.

Comparing CPU Architectures

The CPU can be in a waiting mode for a variety of reasons, such as waiting for a disk operation, network operation, memory operation, etc. A key goal of a

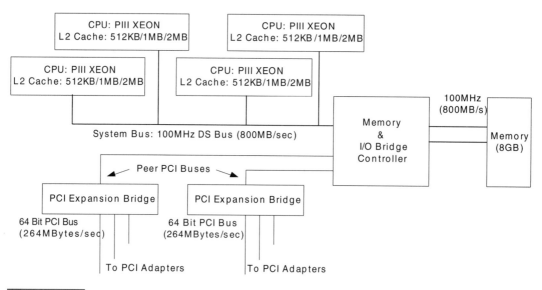

FIGURE 4–1   *Pentium III XEON Intel Standard High Volume (SHV) Logical System Layout*

high-performance system is to keep the CPU processing efficiently—data and instructions must constantly flow into the CPU as requested—in essence keeping the CPU fed. To accomplish this task, a memory hierarchy is created. The most common memory hierarchies are constructed of a Level 1 cache, a Level 2 cache, and the main memory (RAM). On some systems, a third level, or Level 3 cache, is also introduced, but this approach is becoming less popular. The type, size, levels, and speed of each level of the memory hierarchy are dictated by a combination of the CPU and system architecture. Economics are reflected in the memory hierarchy, as each faster level of cache (where Level 1 is faster than main memory RAM) is more expensive then the next to implement. Table 4.1 shows the relative speeds and sizes of various levels of memory access for the popular Pentium III and Pentium III XEON line of CPUs.

Pentium III and Pentium III XEON CPUs

The Pentium III and Pentium III XEON CPUs access Level 1 and Level 2 caches that are actually built on the same physical chip as the CPU itself. This approach is referred to as a Dual Independent Bus (DIB) architecture that enables the CPU to access its Level 2 cache without traversing the system bus. An illustration of the DIB architecture is shown in Figure 4-2, which depicts the Pentium III CPU and Dual Independent Bus architecture. These CPUs

TABLE 4.1	*Relative Speed and Sizes of Various Level of Memory Access*			
	Pentium III	**Pentium III XEON**	**Pentium III (600E and above)**	**Pentium III XEON**
CPU Speed (frequency)	1GHz	833MHz		
			Speed at which memory is accessed	
L1 Cache	16KB data, 16KB instructions	16KB data, 16KB instructions	L1 accessed at CPU speed	L1 accessed at CPU speed
L2 Cache (Advanced Transfer Cache)	256K, 512K (Denoted with "E" notation)	512KB, 1MB, 2MB	L2 accessed at CPU speed	L2 accessed at CPU speed
System Bus Speed Supported	133MHz (Denoted with "B" notation)	100MHz	N/A	N/A
Main Memory (RAM) Support	4GB	*16GB	Memory accessed at 133MHz	Memory accessed at 100MHz
Multiprocessor CPU Bus Support	2	8	N/A	N/A

* **Physical Address Extension** (PAE X86) is a feature of only Windows 2000 Advanced Server and Data Center. See chapter 5 for more information on this feature.

Note: The data specifications for all Intel Processors can be obtained from the Intel Corporation's public web site: http://www.intel.com.

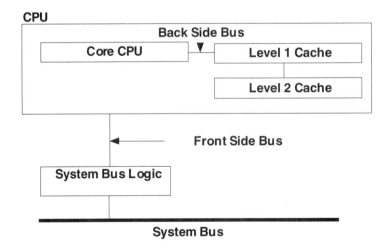

| **FIGURE 4–2** | *Logical Architecture of Pentium III Dual Independent Bus (DIB)* |

implement the DIB architecture such that they access the Level 2 cached data at the same frequency (speed) as the process core (i.e., the speed that the CPU itself is running). Intel refers to this high-speed Level 2 cache design as Advanced Transfer Cache (ATC). The more data and instructions that can be fetched from the Level 1 or Level 2 cache, the less data and instructions must traverse the slower system bus. This improves the system's overall ability to scale and helps it ultimately to run faster.

The major difference between the Pentium III and Pentium III XEON CPUs is their respective scalability. The Pentium III provides slightly higher performance in single and dual CPU configuration because it supports higher CPU frequencies than the Pentium III XEON; it supports a higher system bus and frequency; and it has an associated higher performance memory sub-system. The Pentium III achieves this at a slightly lower cost than the Pentium III XEON, thus it is more common to see Pentium III-based workstations and low-end servers (1–2 CPUs). The advantages of the Pentium III XEON-class CPUs come into play in the higher end server environments where your goal is to support increased workloads. The Pentium III XEON-based servers have the associated logic built into the CPU to support up to eight CPUs and 16GB of RAM. Note that to access this 16GB of RAM, Intel enhanced the Pentium III XEON to support Physical Address Extension (PAE X86). To access this additional memory space, you must be running Windows 2000 Advanced Server and have an application that is coded to take advantage of the PAE extensions through the Windows 2000 APIs. See chapter 5, Windows 2000 and Memory Performance, for more information on PAE.

There is also a speed differential in frequency of the system bus that is supported by the Pentium III and Pentium III XEON. This occurs due to the electrical characteristics of the system bus itself. As you make a system bus faster—that is, run at a higher frequency—the physical length of the system bus naturally becomes shorter. With this shorter bus, you support less electrical loads (CPUs). Now, you can overcome this known fact of physics and electrical engineering, but it is difficult. Thus, you will typically observe faster system buses released that support one and 1–2 CPU configurations far sooner than having that same, faster system bus support 4 CPU systems. Not to worry. There are always some outstanding engineers who are changing what the physicist said could or could not be done. The Pentium III XEON-based servers overcome some of the limitations of a slower system bus by supporting much larger, full-speed Level 2 cache sizes which lowers the system bus overhead.

Helping Your System Scale

With CPU speeds doubling in performance every 18 months (Moore's Law) or faster, CPUs are capable of completing more and more work at a faster pace. A problem occurs when the system bus speed and CPU speed become so unequal that the system bus becomes the limiting factor for system performance, not the CPU. When this occurs, system manufacturers tend to do one of two things: increase the size of the caches on the CPU and/or replace the system bus. Cache size is an important consideration when selecting a CPU. Increased cache sizes keep the CPU fed at a higher rate so the CPU can complete more work in a more efficient manner. Also very important is the fact that larger CPU caches result in less data traversing the system bus, in essence lowering the system bus's congestion levels. This results in improved overall performance and scalability. However, when a new system bus is desired you will also need a forklift (a completely new system) upgrade for improved performance from your server (assuming that the CPU/System Bus is the bottleneck).

Planning around CPU and System Bus Bottlenecks

Based on the above concepts, the choices you make when purchasing a system influence your return on investment or length of time the system can meet your needs before throwing parts away. If, when using the Core Sizing methodology from chapter 3, you discover that only one or two CPUs are required, a smaller cache is recommended ($\leq$512KB). Why? In 1–2 CPU environments, a larger cache is not normally that beneficial from a price/performance point of view. The server's system bus typically is not saturated in smaller servers because of the fact there are not enough I/O buses available to saturate it. It is common for the latest generation of CPU technology to be introduced in workstations and smaller servers first. Then, as the motherboard designs catch up, they become capable of supporting the latest CPUs in greater than two CPU configurations.

Applications that rely on a larger Level 2 cache may perform better with the larger and faster Level 2 caches provided by the Pentium III XEON CPU. Such applications include many of the database engines available today, such as SQL Server and Oracle, and web servers such as IIS. The Pentium III CPU is available only in servers supporting 1–2 CPUs. If your processing requirements are greater than what two Pentium III CPUs can provide, then the Pentium III XEON is a better choice. Systems running Windows 2000 currently can support up to 32 Pentium III XEON-based CPUs. The TPC-C results demonstrate the increase in performance provided by the Pentium III XEON. Shared-nothing SQL Server clusters using 8-CPU Pentium III XEON-based servers currently provide the highest TPC-C results of all of the published TPC reports, which includes various flavors of UNIX and the IBM AS/400. This is an astounding feat as it was completed for a much lower price than its UNIX and AS/400 competitors.

Choose Level 2 Cache Sizes Wisely

If, when using the Core Sizing Methodology (chapter 3), you determine that you need to start with two CPUs, or four CPUs, and definitely plan to increase the number of CPUs in the future, opt for the fastest CPU with the largest cache size possible. Don't be misled here—you want the fastest CPU that the system can support in a greater-than-two CPU arrangement. But after selecting your CPU, if you have a choice between 512K, 1MB, and 2MB Level 2 cache sizes, and it is economically feasible, select the larger cache version of the fastest CPU. Using this strategy, better long-term performance will be available as more and more CPUs are placed into the server's system bus.

For example, many 4-CPU capable servers are initially configured with two CPUs and the smaller 512KB Level 2 caches. This works well in the 1–2 CPU environment. In fact, it provides much better price/performance than their 1MB or 2MB cache counterparts. Unfortunately, when the server was completely configured with four CPUs—all using 512KB-sized Level 2 caches—performance scalability was severely limited compared to similarly configured 4-CPU servers with the 2MB cache. The CPUs were not the limiting factor; the small cache and stressed system bus were the bottleneck culprits! To illustrate this concept of Level 2 cache performance influence, consider the Ziff Davis Server Bench performance results that compare the difference of 1MB and 2MB Pentium III XEON 550MHz CPU configurations in a HP LX 6000 Class server. The results of this benchmark are shown in Figure 4-3.

Should you buy that larger second level cache? Is it worth it? Of course, you should follow methodologies outlined in chapter 3 and run tests that are indicative of your environment. However, this Ziff Davis benchmark shows the possible gains that larger second level caches have in multiprocessor environments. In the single CPU environment, the performance gains attained when the second 1MB of Level 2 cache was added proved helpful by adding an extra 15 to 75 transactions per second. Is this meager gain worth an extra $1,000 (this was the cost of adding an extra 1MB of Level 2 cache to one CPU the last time I checked the web)? For the 6-CPU multiprocessor environments, the additional 1MB of Level 2 cache per CPU was much more influential, adding from 50 to 550 transactions per second that the system could support. Is this worth it? There is a different answer for every environment. If you have an application that only supports taking advantage of one server at a time, then the extra cache is probably worth the investment for you. The extra 1MB of Level 2 cache really can make a difference, in the right environments (e.g., database, web, intense file servers).

As CPU technology advances and SMP-based system bus technology does not, do not be surprised as newer CPUs introduced for the current Windows 2000 technology are introduced with larger and larger caches. Vendors

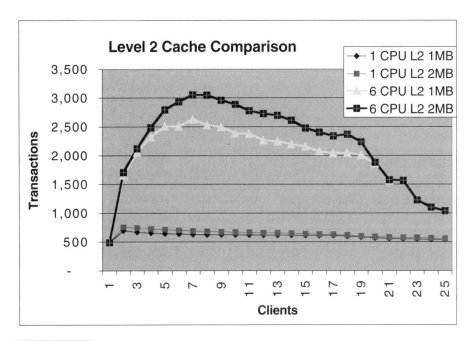

FIGURE 4-3 *Level 2 Cache Comparison of the HP LX 6000 using the Ziff Davis Lab's Server Bench Benchmark*

are just trying to stretch the life cycles of their products. I use Intel CPUs for the examples in this chapter, but this is a general computer industry observation of numerous vendors; thus this is not an Intel-specific observation. When caches get particularly large, the vendor is compensating for lower system bus speeds that are getting closer to saturation. As long as you obtain the performance level you require, the CPU system bus relationship is a trivial matter. However, it is entirely possible that a new overall server architecture is right around the corner, which can influence the system you ultimately purchase.

CPU Technology Is Always Changing (no surprise)

I have encountered various vendors' propaganda stating that the next generation Intel CPU, the Itanium (IA-64 Merced) will provide significantly higher levels of CPU performance than the current Pentium III CPU family (IA-32). This should hold true as the new architecture provides a full 64-bit CPU computing architecture and a multitude of new technologies emerge to improve overall CPU performance. Windows 2000 will take advantage of this new 64-

bit CPU with updated versions that are based on a 64-bit architecture, not 32-bit. From an overall system architecture perspective, taking advantage of this higher level of CPU performance requires a significantly faster system bus. The next generation of Intel SHV board that will support the Intel's Itanium CPU is based on improved system bus and higher bandwidth I/O buses. Until this next generation of SHV-based servers arrives, if you require higher levels of processing power, consider servers based on increased numbers of CPUs. There are several vendors now shipping creatively designed 4-CPU through 32-CPU Pentium III XEON-based servers that are based on hybrid designs of Intel's current SHV.

Comparing CPU Performance

Factors such as the internal CPU instruction set, internal design, cache design, number of instructions the CPU completes per clock cycle, etc., all influence the performance of a CPU. The speed (MHz) of a specific CPU does not directly translate into guaranteed higher levels of CPU performance unless you compare CPUs in the same family generation. Table 4.2 shows a relative comparison of CPU performance. Note the performance difference between the Pentium III 600E series (2110) and Pentium III 600MHz (1930). This occurred since the "E" series employed the full speed 256KB Level 2 Advanced Transfer Cache compared to the larger standard, but half speed, 512KB Level 2 cache found on the Pentium III 600MHz and below CPUs.

TABLE 4.2	*Relative CPU Performance Levels—Pentium III CPUs*
CPU	**iCOMP index 3.0**
Pentium III 1000B MHz	3280
Pentium III 866MHz	2890
Pentium III 800MHz	2690
Pentium III 750MHz	2540
Pentium III 700MHz	2420
Pentium III 650MHz	2270
Pentium III 600E MHz	
(L2 256k ATC Full Speed)	2110
Pentium III 600MHz (L2 512k)	1930
Pentium III 550MHz	1780
Pentium III 500MHz	1850

The above list illustrates the relative performance of different Intel CPUs from the perspective of the Intel iCOMP Index 3.0 suite. The iCOMP index provides a relative measure of microprocessor performance. It is not a traditional benchmark, but a collection of benchmarks used to calculate an index of relative processor performance and is published by the Intel Corporation on the web site http://www.intel.com. iCOMP Index is a weighted average of six industry standard benchmarks that measures 32-bit processor performance:

1. Wintune* 98 Advanced CPU Integer test = 20%
2. CPUmark* 99 = 20%.
3. 3D WinBench* 99—3D Lighting and Transformation test = 20%. This benchmark was designed to measure the performance of the 3D geometry and lighting calculations used in 3D games.
4. WinBench* 99—FPU WinMark = 5% Floating point performance is important for 3D games, as well as high-end productivity applications such as engineering and finance programs.
5. MultimediaMark* 99 = 25%. Multimedia benchmarks measure performance of audio, video, imaging, educational, creativity, and numerous Internet applications.
6. Jmark* 2.0 processor test = 10%. This benchmark measures Java which is increasingly becoming a widely accepted technology in the Internet.

These types of synthetic benchmarks, such as the ones that are encompassed in iCOMP, are helpful to use when comparing CPUs because they exercise both CPU and associated memory subsystems extensively. What they do not measure is overall system performance. Because of this, it is not possible to obtain a direct extrapolation between the CPU synthetic benchmark result and the amount of performance that you can expect your system to provide. If your environment is very computationally intensive or CPU bound, you can make a partial extrapolation from CPU synthetic benchmarks. The CPU(s) are, however, one major factor which affects the system's overall performance.

Look at the Big Picture for CPU Selection

Let's step back and look at the big picture. To get the longest life possible out of your system, the basic rule of thumb is to obtain the fastest, highest density components and use them to populate a system that will support the increased workloads and performance levels you define at a price you can afford. There is always a trade-off somewhere. For CPUs, the economic trade-off is timeliness of the technology. As new CPUs are introduced to the market, they are initially priced much higher than current technology. Also in conjunction with the introduction of a new CPU, the older CPU technology price will erode and become more attractive. Now a decision is required: choose the newer technology at a premium price or wait until the next generation?

If you are deploying a brand-new server and the highest levels of performance are required, newer technology will normally provide a good long-term return on investment, while immediately meeting your performance needs. If you are considering upgrading the type and/or number of CPUs in your current system, first ensure that the CPU(s) are the bottleneck (stay tuned, we look at this later in this chapter). Then, consider waiting a release or two before upgrading CPUs. When the new CPU release provides a 10% or better relative performance gain, the upgrade is more realistically justified. Of course, there is also the traditional bragging right associated with having the latest and greatest technology that must always be considered.

Should I Upgrade the CPU?

The overall performance a new CPU(s) provides for your environment is the real determining factor when selecting the CPU to meet your requirements. Just because one CPU is faster than another CPU in a benchmark that only tests the CPU and memory performance is not a good indication that your server will benefit from such an upgrade. Running the stress and validation tests developed for your environment (outlined in the Core Sizing Methodology section of chapter 3) with the new CPU technology installed is the best way to benchmark your system. In this way, you can determine exactly how much improvement can be expected in your environment when you upgrade CPUs. Once you have this information, you can make a decision on whether the cost of the new CPU(s) justifies the associated performance the upgrade delivers.

When you do not have your own stress test or benchmarks to use, consider extrapolating from Industry Standard Benchmarks that are outlined in chapter 3. For example, if your environment is representative of a large client-server transaction-based database, and you determine that the CPU subsystem is the bottleneck in your system's overall performance, review a benchmark relevant to your environment such as the TPC-C database benchmark. This comparison will determine if a faster CPU or the addition of another CPU might help the performance of your system. Table 4.3 shows various TPC-C results.

From these TPC-C results, you can deduce that upgrading from Configuration 1 using one 600MHz/512KB Pentium III CPU to Configuration 2 using two 600MHz/512KB Pentium III CPUs yields over a 59% improvement in the number of transactions supported. What is particularly nice about comparing results of Configuration 1 and Configuration 2 is that the CPU and memory configurations between both tests are very, very similar. There are more disk drives in Configuration 2, but this is to be expected since, with additional CPU processing power, additional disk drives can be supported

| TABLE 4.3 | *Comparing Overall Server Performance with the TPC-C Benchmark* |

Base Configuration (Type of CPUs)	Performance Level (tpmC)	Amount of Memory	Number of Disks	NT/Windows 2000 Server Release Level	Database Release
Configuration 1 Compaq 3000 1 - Pentium III 600MHz/512KB cache	8,049	3GB	64	NT 4EE SP4	SQL Server 7
Configuration 2 Compaq 3000 Two Pentium III 600MHz/ 512KB cache	13,598	3GB	114	NT 4EE SP4	SQL Server 7
Configuration 3 Dell 6100 4 – Pentium Pro 200MHz/1MB cache	10,984	4GB	133	NT 4EE SP4	SQL Server 6.5
Configuration 4 Compaq 6400R 4 - Pentium III XEON 550MHz/2MB cache	25,633	4GB	240	NT 4EE SP4	SQL Server 7
Configuration 5 Compaq 8000 8 - Pentium III XEON 550MHz/ 2MB cache	40,168	4GB	397	NT 4EE SP4	SQL Server 7
Configuration 6 Compaq ML-530 2 - Pentium III XEON 800 MHz/256KB cache	16,133	4GB	140	Windows 2000 Advanced Server	SQL 2000

and are needed to provide a balanced system. Thus, because the CPUs are the key difference between the configurations, it is a good estimation that the second CPU is what provided the additional level of performance provided it was fed with the addition of more disk drives. What if you need even more performance in the future? Would two more CPUs help? From the information provided by Configurations 4 and 5, additional CPUs would help improve the transaction rate, as long as the corresponding disk drives were added too!

Be careful when reviewing benchmark results published by vendors. Many times, it is not only one facet of the system that has changed, but also a version of database software, or a major hardware change such as an additional 1GB of memory, or a combination thereof. Adding additional CPUs, or changing CPUs, can be helpful, but you need to look at the big picture, too. When comparing systems using Industry Standard Benchmarks, select the benchmark that is as close to your own environment as possible. Then take into consideration differences in the configuration so that you are not comparing apples to oranges.

Windows 2000 and CPU Resource Usage

Now that we have established a general understanding of relative CPU performance and a few system factors that influence CPU performance, let's investigate how Windows 2000 takes advantage of the processing power of the
system hardware. With an understanding of both the hardware's system architecture and the operating system, it becomes much easier to detect, then tune
around CPU bottlenecks.them. Windows 2000 is a time-sharing, symmetric
multiprocessing operating system that is fully reentrant, employs preemptive
multitasking, virtual memory, and soft affinity. Before we look at the details
on how Windows 2000 accomplishes this long and bold statement, let's
quickly review a few key operating system concepts.

Processes, Threads, Jobs (New), and Context Switching

In Windows 2000, a process represents an instance of an executing program
(application). Each process must have at least one thread of execution, since it
is each thread object that executes program code for the process. Also, it is
important to note that the schedulable entity by the Windows 2000 kernel is the
thread object, not the processor object. Windows 2000 introduces a new object
called the "job object." A job object's function is to enable groups of processes
(and their threads) to be managed as a single unit. This enables much better
auditing and accounting for processes that are started and terminated on the
system as part of the job. Prior to Windows 2000, these processes could have
stopped and started without closely tracked audit controls. Jobs also enable
stopping (killing) complete process trees (you can see this under Task Manager
by right-clicking a process and observing the "End Process Tree" option).

A context switch is the action that takes place when the processor
switches from one process's executable thread to another executable thread.
From a CPU perspective, context switches are necessary as one thread
replaces another on the CPU, but are costly due to the housekeeping (virtual
address space tracking, thread state management, CPU registry contents, kernel pointers, etc.) required for each context switch. However, context switches
that occur between threads from the same process are less costly (lower overhead), since threads from the same process share the same address space of
the process. Although these explanations are dry, they solidify our common
foundation of operating system knowledge for future discussions.

Windows 2000 and a Single CPU Environment

So how does a single CPU Windows 2000 multitask? Actually, it doesn't if you
consider multitasking as the completion of several threads concurrently. The

CPU actually switches between threads so fast that it just appears that the threads are running concurrently. Some processes are monolithic, which means that the process does not spawn multiple threads of execution, just one—itself. Multithreaded processes or applications are composed of many threads of execution, some of which can run concurrently. When a context switch occurs under Windows 2000, it is expensive from the CPU's point of view because of the associated housekeeping (virtual address space tracking, thread state management, etc.) required to change from running one thread to another. Switching between threads in the same process is less CPU expensive than switching a completely new single-threaded process, since a thread from a specific process operates within the memory address space of the process it was spawned from. Windows 2000 can still multitask on a single CPU system when there are monolithic and multithreaded applications running concurrently.

Windows 2000 and a Multiple CPU Environment—Symmetric Multiprocessing

When a system contains greater than one CPU in a Symmetric Multiprocessor system (SMP)—i.e., a multiprocessor environment—Windows 2000 automatically takes advantage of these additional CPUs by concurrently executing threads across the multiple CPUs on whichever CPU is available. An SMP designed system is one in which all system resources are shared and each CPU is equal in its control of the system, so there is not a master CPU that the other CPUs must report to. In multiple CPU system environments, true multitasking is accomplished. That is, two or more threads can be running at the same time. Windows 2000 is capable of supporting 32 processors in an SMP configuration and could theoretically be extended to even more. What most people purchase is Windows 2000 Professional (1–2 CPUs) or Windows 2000 Server version that can support 1–4 CPUs. One to eight CPU servers are becoming more common. Table 4.4 outlines how many CPUs are supported in each version of the Windows 2000 Family.

In years past, vendors would obtain special licenses for the system hardware when supporting greater than four CPUs. Vendors such as NCR and Sequent have produced high-end servers that ran Windows 2000 in the 1–16 CPU range for several years. These vendors' server operations were gobbled up in server vendor consolidations. Now, vendors such as Compaq, IBM, Dell, HP, and Unisys provide 8 CPU-based servers and Unisys and Compaq provide servers supporting up to 32 CPUs. It is only recently that the volume and marketplace for enterprise servers have reached a point to catch Microsoft's interest, thus the mass market commercial availability of Windows 2000 Advanced Server and Data Center.

| TABLE 4.4 | Windows 2000 Family CPU Support | | | |

Edition	Number of Processors Supported	Physical Memory Supported	General Notes
Windows 2000 Professional	2	4GB	Desktop Operating System
Windows 2000 Server	4	4GB	Windows 2000 Server supports being a domain controller, Domain Controller [NTLM (Legacy Win9x/NT desktops) and Kerbeous (Windows 2000 Pro Desktops), Active Directory server), software-based RAID, DHCP, DNS, WINS, DFS, Certificate Server, Remote Installation Services, and Terminal Server
Windows 2000 Advanced Server	8	8GB	All of the features of Windows 2000 Server, support for Terminal Server Applications, and support for 2-node clusters (shared-nothing and shared disk-based clusters)
Windows 2000 Data Center Server*	32	64GB	All of the features of Windows 2000 Server and 4-node clusters advanced management tools such as the Process Control Manager tool

*Note: Data Center is not sold as stand-alone software, but as bundled packages of tested hardware and software.

Viewing Processes and Threads Running under Windows 2000

There are multiple processes, containing one or more threads, running under Windows 2000 at all times. Take a look for yourself by starting Task Manager. Start Task Manager by pressing ctrl+alt+delete at the same time and then choose Task Manager. Select processes / tab / view, select columns, then select threads. You can now view the processes running under Windows 2000 and the associated number of threads each process is running. Figure 4-4 shows a Task Manager view of a relatively idle Windows 2000 Advanced Server system.

Notice in Figure 4-4 how the core Windows 2000 *System* process contains 44 threads while even the Microsoft Word 2000 process (WINWORD.EXE) contains 5 threads.

Determining Which Process Is Associated with Which Application

When you start Task Manager or Sysmon in the process view, you can view which processes are running under Windows 2000. In chapter 2, a list is provided of the common processes that run under Windows 2000. Some

Image Name	PID	Session ID	CPU	CPU Time	Mem Usage	Base Pri	Handles	Threads
System Idle Process	0	0	98	5:19:49	16 K	N/A	0	1
WINWORD.EXE	1360	0	00	0:00:59	940 K	Normal	205	5
System	8	0	00	0:00:22	212 K	Normal	143	44
csrss.exe	208	0	01	0:00:19	2,428 K	High	358	11
IEXPLORE.EXE	1328	0	00	0:00:10	960 K	Normal	383	14
explorer.exe	1132	0	01	0:00:10	2,668 K	Normal	330	18
winmgmt.exe	844	0	00	0:00:09	168 K	Normal	91	3
winlogon.exe	232	0	00	0:00:05	2,656 K	High	389	17
services.exe	260	0	00	0:00:02	5,008 K	Normal	520	30
OUTLOOK.EXE	1404	0	00	0:00:01	3,916 K	Normal	216	6
svchost.exe	588	0	00	0:00:01	5,108 K	Normal	315	18
smss.exe	180	0	00	0:00:00	344 K	Normal	50	6
lsass.exe	272	0	00	0:00:00	3,748 K	High	190	12
taskmgr.exe	660	0	00	0:00:00	1,344 K	High	48	3
snagit32.exe	1180	0	00	0:00:00	4,020 K	Normal	76	2
svchost.exe	452	0	00	0:00:00	2,564 K	Normal	233	8
mdm.exe	1104	0	00	0:00:00	2,100 K	Normal	83	3
lserver.exe	816	0	00	0:00:00	4,420 K	Normal	191	14
snmp.exe	724	0	00	0:00:00	3,324 K	Normal	246	6
svchost.exe	1252	0	00	0:00:00	3,188 K	Normal	208	12
sndvol32.exe	912	0	00	0:00:00	184 K	Normal	51	2
msdtc.exe	476	0	00	0:00:00	3,152 K	Normal	154	20
termsrv.exe	780	0	00	0:00:00	2,892 K	Normal	145	17
mstask.exe	680	0	00	0:00:00	2,924 K	Normal	101	7
MAPISP32.EXE	1264	0	00	0:00:00	3,492 K	Normal	139	5
OSA.EXE	1244	0	00	0:00:00	2,024 K	Normal	46	2
llssrv.exe	608	0	00	0:00:00	1,752 K	Normal	97	9
csrss.exe	972	2	00	0:00:00	828 K	High	53	6
winlogon.exe	996	2	00	0:00:00	1,140 K	High	25	1

☑ Show processes from all users   End Process

Processes: 31   CPU Usage: 2%   Mem Usage: 108476K / 471444K

FIGURE 4–4   *Viewing Processes Running under Windows 2000 with the Task Manager*

processes are easy to associate with their application. For example, when Task Manager is started, the process taskmgr.exe shows up in the Task Manager process view. Sometimes it is difficult to determine or distinguish which process is associated with a particular application. If the process is not well known, ensure all new applications are stopped. Start Task Manager and take note of the currently running processes. Now, start your application. Review Task Manager again and the new process will be added to the process list. Understanding what processes are running on your system and what application they are associated with becomes important later in this chapter when trying to isolate CPU usage patterns for tuning and sizing. In the Windows 2000 Resource Kit and support tools CD, there are tools such as "*tlist*.exe" and "*sc*.exe" that aid in tracking down what is running on your system. Also, in chapter 2 is a list of common processes that run under Windows 2000.

Windows 2000 Scheduler and Priority Levels

Now that we have all of these processes and threads running around, how does Windows 2000 coordinate which thread or threads get to use the CPU(s)? The Windows 2000 kernel includes the scheduler. The Windows 2000 kernel schedules ready threads for processor time based upon their dynamic priority, a number from 0 to 31 that represents the relative importance of the task. Windows 2000 uses a priority-based round robin scheduling algorithm to distribute threads among the CPUs in the system. The higher the priority number, the higher the thread's priority level (don't laugh, some operating systems use a reverse numeric number to priority level schema). The base priority of a thread varies only within +/−2 from the base priority of its process. The highest priority thread always runs on the processor, even if this requires that a lower priority thread be preempted. This allows Windows 2000 processes to complete background tasks that are needed to keep the system running. Threads will run on the CPU until they reach the end of their quantum (slice of time the thread is allowed to run on the CPU), become I/O bound, or are preempted by a higher priority thread. Most applications started by users run at the normal priority level. The easiest way to see the current priority of a process (application) that is running is to use Task Manager. The base priority information of processes can be viewed in Figure 4-4. Sysmon also has an option under Process: Priority Base. Table 4.5 shows Windows 2000's priority levels.

Windows 2000's scheduler tries to be fair about who gets access to CPU resources in an effort to ensure that all threads do get access to the resource. On a CPU bound server it is possible, however unlikely, that some threads become starved for CPU attention. Refer back to the Task Manager in Figure 4-4 and you can see the relative priority levels for the various processes. Notice how some processes are running at high priority levels (11–15) such as the lsass.exe process (Local Security Administration Subsystem). Chapter 2 has a listing of common processes and what they are responsible for. If you are interested in an even more detailed process view that shows the priority level for each thread, run pviewer.exe from the Windows 2000 Support Tools. The thread priorities of the explorer.exe process are illustrated in Figure 4-5.

Consider the scheduler as a traffic cop standing in the front of a single file line to see a teller. The customers in the line are ready-to-run threads, and the teller is the CPU. When you get into the line is important, but the traffic cop can move anyone to the front of the line at his discretion based on how important he feels the customer is (priority). This is annoying, but necessary. If a person gets to the teller and makes a request that is completed by another division of the bank, such as loans (disk drives), that person is sent back to the line and other customers are serviced while the first waits on the other division. If the teller is fast enough, perhaps working at 100% of his

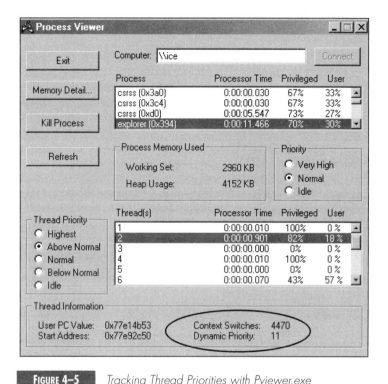

FIGURE 4-5   *Tracking Thread Priorities with Pviewer.exe*

capacity, he will be able to service everyone without a long line forming. The bank owners are psyched; they are getting a great return on their teller investment. Conversely, when the teller cannot keep up with the service requests, the line grows. The bank owners (not to mention the customers in line) are, to say the least, frustrated.

Under Windows 2000, if the ready queue is consistently greater than two to four times the number of CPUs in the system, then the CPU is becoming a bottleneck. Conversely, a CPU running near 100% of its capacity is not a bottleneck if the queue is not greater then two to four threads and not growing. In this environment, you are getting the most out of your CPU investment. I prefer to have the CPUs completing productive work as often as possible!

Affinity

In the CPU Performance section above, we mentioned that the CPU provides the best possible performance if the data it requires can be found in the Level 1 or Level 2 cache. This concept of keeping data consistently in cache

TABLE 4.5	*Windows 2000 Priority Levels*

Thread Priorities in Windows 2000		
Base	**Priority class**	**Thread priority**
31	Real-time	Time critical
26	Real-time	Highest
25	Real-time	Above normal
24	Real-time	Normal
23	Real-time	Below normal
22	Real-time	Lowest
16	Real-time	Idle
15	Idle, Normal, or High	Time critical
15	High	Highest
14	High	Above normal
13	High	Normal
12	High	Below normal
11	High	Lowest
10	Normal	Highest
9	Normal	Above normal
8	**Normal (default)**	**Normal (default)**
7	Normal	Below normal
6	Normal	Lowest
6	Idle	Highest
5	Idle	Above Normal
4	Idle	Normal
3	Idle	Below normal
2	Idle	Lowest
1	Idle, Normal, or High	Idle
0	Reserved for Operating System	N/A

is referred to as cache coherency and is largely affected by the workload and how well the application is coded. When the data are not available in the cache, the system bus is traversed to obtain the data from either the memory or I/O subsystem. This slows down the CPU from completing the thread's request. If this is an SMP-based server with more than one CPU, the extra data on the system bus can slow down the other CPUs since only one request can traverse the system bus at a time. This directly influences the overall scalability of the system.

To increase the chances of a cache hit, Windows 2000 employs soft affinity when assigning threads to processors. If all other factors are equal, Windows 2000 tries to run the thread on the CPU it last executed on. If the CPU the thread last executed on is not available, the Windows 2000 scheduler dispatches the thread to the next available CPU. This concept is soft affinity, which is implemented inside of the Windows 2000 kernel. Using this approach enables Windows 2000 to scale quite well. Conversely, hard affinity binds a particular thread or process permanently to a specific CPU. The more successful Windows 2000's scheduler is in applying the soft affinity strategy, the more efficient and better performing the entire system becomes. Providing good system performance is not entirely on Windows 2000's shoulders. How well the application is designed, including effective use of cache, and how well the system's hardware is designed also influence the system's overall performance just as much as, if not more than, Windows 2000 itself.

Detecting CPU Bottlenecks

Recall from chapter 2 that it is important to consider the entire system performance picture when trying to locate a Windows 2000 bottleneck. There can be more than one system resource area throttling the system's overall performance. Once all of the major system resource areas are evaluated, focus in on the resource that is farthest to the left in the Performance Resource Chart introduced in chapter 2 and repeated here in Figure 4-6 for reference. This strategy will provide the greatest immediate gain to the system's overall performance. For the discussions in this chapter, all of the other system resources have already been investigated and determined not to be a bottleneck in the system's overall performance. Remember to revisit the Performance Resource Chart after tuning around a CPU bottleneck. Once one system resource is removed as the bottleneck, others may take its place and will subsequently influence where you focus additional tuning efforts.

Quick Reference: Helpful Tools to Use When Tracking Down Windows 2000 Memory Details

Throughout this section on bottleneck detection, several different tools are used to track down memory details. Having a tool to complete this mission is nice; having specific examples of how to use specific tools is even better. In

Tuning Goal: All System Resources Grouped to the Right

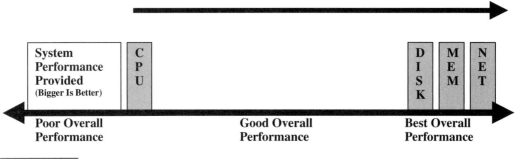

| FIGURE 4–6 | *Performance Resource Chart Indicating a CPU Bottleneck* |

this chapter, some specific examples are provided. I used to fumble through books looking for that helpful tool I read about but did not take notes on. Thus, Table 4.6 is a quick reference guide to the tools used to investigate memory use in Windows 2000. If you do not find what you are looking for with one tool, try another! Even if you find what you are looking for, try look-

TABLE 4.6	*Tools to Investigate Memory Usage*		
Tool	**Where do you find it? (Package) /**	**Command Line Image**	**Key times to consider using this tool**
Sysmon	Native to Windows 2000	Perfmon	Long-term trend analysis
Task Manager	Native to Windows 2000	Taskman.exe	Short-term analysis
Process Viewer	Support Tools on Windows 2000 media	Pviewer.exe	Detailed process and thread usage
Process Monitor	Support Tools on Windows 2000 media	Pmon.exe	Command line tool to track process usage
Process Explode	Resource Kit	Pview.exe	Very detailed memory usage statistics
Page Fault Monitor	Resource Kit	Pfmon.exe	Advanced debugging of specific applications
Process Status	Resource Kit	Pstat.exe	Provides a snapshot of processes and threads status from the command line. This has a long standard out display. Considering running it by piping it into more (*pstat | more*).

ing for that information with a different tool. Using different tools to investigate the same problem may present the information so that it helps generate that idea you were looking for. Note, most tools obtain and present information in slightly different ways. Don't be surprised if different results are presented when querying for the same information.

Detecting Single CPU Server Bottlenecks

Now that you are properly armed with information regarding system CPU performance and how Windows 2000 takes advantage of your system's iron, let's focus on detecting CPU bottlenecks while running Windows 2000. As you will see, the two tools described in chapter 2 are your best friends when trying to locate a CPU bottleneck: Task Manager and Sysmon.

From the information provided throughout this chapter on how Windows 2000 uses the CPU, it should be apparent that a system whose CPUs are running at or near 100% is not always bottlenecked by the CPU. So when is the CPU the system bottleneck? When the CPU is not keeping up with the workload being requested of it, the CPU has become the bottleneck in the overall system's performance. To determine if this is happening on a *single* CPU server, review the relationship of the following counters under Sysmon: Processor: %Processor Time and System: Processor Queue Length. Sysmon defines %Processor Time as "a percentage of the elapsed time that a processor is busy executing a non-Idle thread. It can be viewed as the fraction of time spent doing useful work. Each processor is assigned an idle thread in the Idle process which consumes those unproductive processor cycles not used by any other threads. Sysmon defines Processor Queue Length as the number of threads in the processor queue. There is a single queue for processor time even on computers with multiple processors. Unlike the disk counters, this counter counts ready threads only, not threads that are running. A sustained processor queue of greater than two threads generally indicates processor congestion. This counter displays the last observed value only; it is not an average."

Basically, if the CPU is busy completing productive work and is running at a high capacity level greater than 80–90% and the System: Processor Queue Length is consistently greater than two and growing, then the CPU is the unquestionable bottleneck throttling back the system's performance. If this occurs only during occasional load storms, it can be tolerated. However, if this condition continues for long periods of time—such as over 5–10 minutes during normal business hours—end users' response times will increase; that is, it will take longer for requested tasks to complete. When the CPU becomes a bottleneck, even a simple task such as responding to a network request from an end user takes longer to complete since the network requests must wait in line to get service from the CPU.

Detecting Multiple CPU Server Bottlenecks

This same CPU bottleneck detection concept applies when looking for CPU bottlenecks in a multiple (SMP) CPU system configuration, with the addition of some third-grade math (or, with today's focus on education, perhaps first-grade math). When using Sysmon: Processor: %Processor Time in a multiple CPU system, there is a counter instance for each CPU in the system. Looking at each instance is helpful for tuning (locating applications that are using only one CPU in a multiuser system), but for bottleneck detection it is easier to use Processor: %Processor Time and selecting the _Total instance. Sysmon sums all of the CPU(s) time and provides a cumulative view of overall processor usage in the _Total instance. For the System: Processor Queue Length, there is no summing to complete since Windows 2000 has only one queue for obtaining queue length. You have a CPU bottleneck if the Processor: %Processor Time Total Instance is greater than 80—90% and the sustained processor queue length is greater than two times the number of CPUs in the system. Yes, some book definitions would extrapolate out to four times the number of CPUs in the system, but it is my experience that for multiple CPU environments, a 2 times recommendation is a more realistic indication of a CPU bottleneck. For example, in a 4-CPU server, if the %Total Processor Time is greater than 80–90%, and the processor queue length is greater than eight, then the CPUs are the bottleneck in the system.

Another, less obvious SMP system bottleneck can occur when there are too many CPUs in a system. Although not as common as it was in the past, some applications just do not efficiently take advantage of all of the CPUs in the system. This has little to do with Windows 2000, but is pertinent to the application(s) you run. How do you detect this? Monitor the Processor: %Processor Time for each CPU instance in the system at the same time. In this manner, you can observe how well the application's processing load is being distributed across all of the CPUs in the system. If you observe two CPUs running at 85% and two CPUs running at 2%, there is a problem. The application is not taking advantage of the CPUs, and the CPUs that are not being leveraged actually place an overhead load on the system, which is not desirable. You have paid for the CPUs not in use! In the tuning section we will review approaches of tuning around this problem.

Using the System: Processor Queue Length Counter Effectively

Trade-offs are everywhere. I don't know if you noticed a small fact in the Sysmon System: Process Queue Length definition that states "This counter displays the last observed value only; it is not an average." To use this counter effectively, you must run Sysmon in both a granular fashion and for extended periods of time. Being an instant counter, this counter only reports on what is happening at one point in time. Thus, if your sampling period is too broad, you may be missing the times when the run queue is longer than you might want and you are catching it only when it is short. This concept is referred to as the Nyquist effect.

To avoid this, Sysmon must be run at higher sampling rate. How high of a sampling rate you run Sysmon depends upon your environment, but when isolating system work queue problems, run Sysmon at 5-second intervals. Any lower than 5-second intervals, Sysmon may begin to influence system performance beyond acceptable levels on systems using older (prior to Intel Pentium class CPUs). This is something that is observable and actually is an overexaggerated example of the Heisenberg principle, which states that you cannot measure something without affecting it (the system that you are monitoring) in some manner. On multiple CPU systems using at least Intel Pentium III class CPUs, you can run Sysmon in a very granular 1 sec/sample-logging mode for key counters without adversely affecting the system being monitored. (Watch your log size growth rates though!)

Here, we try to minimize the extent to which we affect the system. Running Sysmon at a sampling rate of 1 or even 5 seconds all of the time is unrealistic since it would create some enormous Sysmon log files. Typically, you want to sample at a 5-second rate when the CPU usage is greater than 60%. Refer to chapter 2 for an example of using Sysmon's alert mode. Running a second copy of Sysmon for a dedicated amount of time at a finer grain sampling interval helps to zero in on CPU bottlenecks.

Artful CPU Bottleneck Detection and Tuning: %User and %Privileged Time

Okay, you think it can't be that easy to detect a CPU bottleneck, but it really is. Of course, computer performance is part art. (I have to try and say that at least once a chapter as a reality check.) There are times when knowing your system environment is more important than just following the rules of thumb in the Detecting Single CPU System Bottlenecks or Detecting Multiple CPU Bottlenecks sections. Reviewing detailed factors associated with CPU performance—such as CPU resource usage, types of applications running on your system, and workload distribution—you can determine when upgrading to a faster CPU or additional CPUs may be prudent.

Based upon the above information, if you understand where Windows 2000 is spending its processor time, it enables you to focus where and how you design and tune your Windows 2000 system. You can determine where Windows 2000 is focusing its processing time by watching the Sysmon object/counter: Processor: %Privileged Time and Processor: %User Time. By observing these two counters, you can determine how often the CPU is running in user or privileged mode.

Windows 2000 has two basic modes of operation: user mode and kernel (privileged) mode. The primary difference between these modes is that if a process needs access to something controlled by Windows 2000, such as access to a disk drive, the process that is running in user mode must make a system call to the Windows 2000 kernel. This call typically occurs through the Kernel Mode Win32 API and is a privileged mode of operations where the code has direct access to all memory, user mode processes, and hardware (from Nagar, *Windows 2000/Windows 2000 File Systems Internals: A Developers Guide*, O'Reilly). When the Windows 2000 kernel is processing the user mode process's request, it is doing so in privileged mode. For Intel-based CPU architectures, this means that privileged mode is running in ring mode 0, which allows it access to lower level functions. (This factoid was even on the old Microsoft NT 4 Server exam.)

Sysmon defines Processor: %Privileged Time as " . . . the percentage of non-idle processor time spent in privileged mode. (Privileged mode is a processing mode designed for operating system components and hardware-manipulating drivers. It allows direct access to hardware and all memory. The alternative, user mode, is a restricted processing mode designed for applications, environment subsystems, and integral subsystems. The operating system switches application threads to privileged mode to access operating system services.) %Privileged Time includes time servicing interrupts and DPCs. A high rate of privileged time might be attributable to a large number of interrupts generated by a failing device. This counter displays the average busy time as a percentage of the sample time."

Sysmon defines Processor: %User Time as: " . . . the percentage of non-idle processor time spent in user mode. (User mode is a restricted processing mode designed for applications, environment subsystems, and integral subsystems. The alternative, privileged mode, is designed for operating system components and allows direct access to hardware and all memory. The operating system switches application threads to privileged mode to access operating system services.) This counter displays the average busy time as a percentage of the sample time."

Applying Artful CPU Tuning: Privileged Mode and User Mode Processor Usage

So how does one use this knowledge? Look at the two Sysmon charts displayed in Figure 4-7 and Figure 4-8.

Figure 4-7 shows that most of the processing on this server is being completed in privileged mode. When each process running on this system was looked at closely, it was the System process that was guilty of hogging most of the server's CPU resources. The System process contains system threads that handle lazy writing by file system, virtual memory modified page writing, working set trimming, and similar Windows 2000 system functions. This particular server was working as a large-scale file server. As such, most of its processing is dedicated to providing file services, which are a privileged mode of operation. This now makes sense of why the System process was so busy; it was busy providing services required to serve files for 200+ users.

The CPU usage depicted above is quite heavy. To determine if faster CPUs would improve the server's performance to the end users, we ran this exact test a second time with faster CPUs. Even with the faster CPUs, the server did not provide any tangible overall performance improvements to the end users. The tests that we ran provide two key pieces of information:

- A faster CPU can provide support for more disk drives and networks, but it does not make disk drives or networks run any faster (which is where the bottleneck was occurring).
- If a majority of the processing time is spent in privileged mode, follow the rule of thumb stated above to determine if the CPUs are the bottleneck.

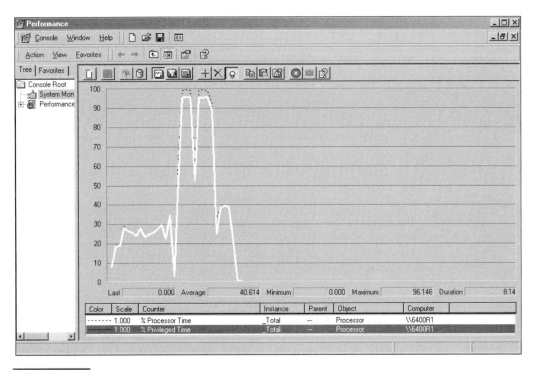

FIGURE 4-7   *Sysmon Chart Showing Privileged Mode Hogging the CPU*

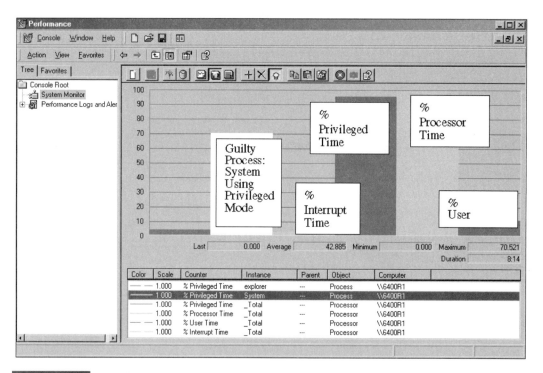

FIGURE 4–8 *Sysmon Chart Showing the Guilty Process Hogging Privileged Mode CPU Operation*

If, however, the %User Time is high (>60%) and the %Privileged Time is low (<40%), determine what type of application is running on the server. If you have a server application that completes a high number of calculation requests of the CPU and the Sysmon statistics gathered do not quite meet the rule of thumb criteria for a CPU bottleneck, a faster CPU will help your performance.

Why is this? Let's try to explain this concept with a little more detail. Normally, when a CPU is running at greater than 80% of its capacity and no threads are waiting in the System: Processor Queue, you are getting a good return on your investment. When none of the other server resources are bottlenecks and the CPU is running as fast as it can, the CPU is the bottleneck. This may sound strange. The CPU is not a bottleneck in the traditional sense that is defined above; the CPU is keeping up with the requested workload. What has happened is that the CPU cannot help the server complete its workload any faster. Thus, the server is just running as fast as it can. When this occurs, one way to help your user mode application complete its computations faster is to provide it with a faster CPU. Of course when you do this, closely watch the other server resources to ensure that the bottleneck has not shifted and they have become the bottleneck. You can always make your application code more efficient, too, if you have access to the source code.

Ideal Environment for Applying Privileged and User Mode Tuning: Artful CPU Bottleneck Detection and Tuning

In Figure 4-9, there are multiple applications running and the CPU is running at a high rate, close to 90%, the System: Processor Queue Length is zero, and the process activity is occurring in user mode.

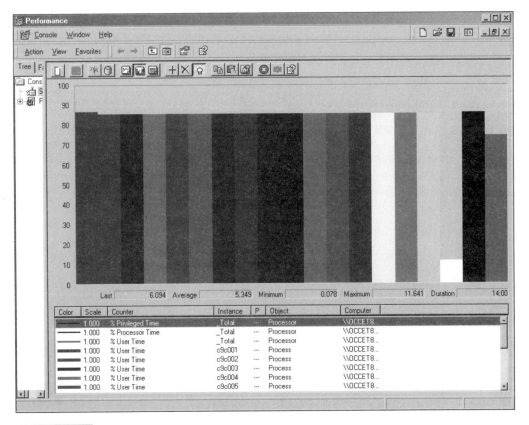

FIGURE 4–9   *Sysmon Screenshot of a Server That Is a Candidate for Artful Tuning*

Figure 4-9 is a perfect example of when artful tuning can be applied. The CPU is not the bottleneck in this example. All processes are running in user mode and consuming close to 90% of available resources. All of the other (non-CPU) server resources were checked to ensure that they were not the cause of any bottlenecks. This server is just flat out running as fast as it can. To improve the performance of this server workload, faster CPUs were implemented. This provided faster response times for this Windows 2000 server environment.

Since this workload was occurring in user mode, another option to improve performance would have been to work with the developer of this application to produce a more efficient application. This is a good option if you can arrange access to the source code. If you cannot arrange for access to the source code, and a higher level of performance is required, follow the artful tuning technique to determine when server is a candidate for a faster CPU to help overall performance.

Applying Artful Privileged and User Mode CPU Tuning Summary

If your application is running predominately in user mode, faster CPUs will most likely improve your application's performance. If your application is predominately running in privileged mode, faster CPUs will most likely not be helpful, as the application is waiting on system resources. In this environment, look for other possible bottleneck areas and work with the application so that when it does request privileged mode resources, it does so more efficiently. Also, if you do not find any bottlenecks in a system that has an application optimized as well as it can be and still spends a majority of its time in privileged mode, seek out more efficient system hardware and peripherals (network cards, disk adapters, controllers, etc.).

Artful Tuning II: Adding Additional CPUs

Throughout this chapter, system scaling is discussed. For now, when might a system be a candidate for multiple CPUs to improve its scalability? When an application is designed to support multiple processes and/or threads at the same time, or when there are multiple applications running on the system concurrently. If either of these cases pertains to your environment and the current CPU is a bottleneck (greater than 80–90% overall CPU utilization and a System: Processor Queue Length greater than two times the number of CPUs in the system), the system is an excellent candidate for additional CPUs to improve its scalability. If after the addition of a second CPU performance improves but there is a still a CPU bottleneck occurring, consider the addition of even more CPUs. Be careful when adding additional CPUs that the other Windows 2000 resources are up to the task of supporting the increased processing power. In particular, watch the memory and disk subsystem closely for possible bottlenecks, as they must be capable of feeding the CPUs at a high rate to keep them productive.

This Artful Tuning II technique was applied in the server environment depicted in Figure 4-9, which shows a system that is a candidate for Artful Tuning. Why? This Compaq 8000 server is running as fast as it can. No bottlenecks, two CPUs (capable of eight), multiprocess application, and no access to the source code. Since more than 20 separate processes are running in this environment, if we can provide more CPU time to each process, the overall response time should improve. The addition of a second, third, fourth, and up to eighth CPU consecutively improved the overall response time for the application. Additional memory and disk subsystem resources were added to ensure that the CPUs were kept fed and that no new bottlenecks were created with the addition of more CPU resources.

Remember that when you tune your system without understanding what your system is doing and how it is behaving, you are guessing! Avoid guessing whenever possible, since it lengthens the time it takes to get your system running at its peak and incurs costs in both time and money. Without knowing your environment, it is close to impossible to know if implementing this nontraditional CPU bottleneck removal technique will be effective or not.

Interrupt-Driven CPU Bottlenecks

In general, when a device in a system such as a network interface card needs servicing, it generates an interrupt that must be processed by a CPU. I refer to "servicing" as any generic hardware function (mouse, network interface card, etc.) that requires CPU attention, such as passing network data into memory. Using Sysmon, you can observe both the number of interrupts that are being generated by using the counter Processor: Interrupts/sec and determine the percentage of the CPU that is being used to service the interrupts by observing Processor: %Interrupt Time. Sysmon defines Interrupts/sec as " . . . the average number of hardware interrupts the processor is receiving and servicing in each second. It does not include DPCs, which are counted separately. This value is an indirect indicator of the activity of devices that generate interrupts, such as the system clock, the mouse, disk drivers, data communication lines, network interface cards, and other peripheral devices. These devices normally interrupt the processor when they have completed a task or require attention. Normal thread execution is suspended during interrupts. Most system clocks interrupt the processor every 10 milliseconds, creating a background of interrupt activity. This counter displays the difference between the values observed in the last two samples, divided by the duration of the sample interval."

Sysmon defines %Interrupt Time as " . . . the percentage of time the processor spent receiving and servicing hardware interrupts during the sample interval. This value is an indirect indicator of the activity of devices that generate interrupts, such as the system clock, the mouse, disk drivers, data communication lines, network interface cards, and other peripheral devices. These devices normally interrupt the processor when they have completed a task or require attention. Normal thread execution is suspended during interrupts. Most system clocks interrupt the processor every 10 milliseconds, creating a background of interrupt activity. This counter displays the average busy time as a percentage of the sample time."

On an Intel CPU-based system operating without any workloads, it is normal to observe at least 100 interrupts per second. This is caused by the Intel CPU processor clock interrupts. On a heavily loaded server supporting 400 users, the interrupts/sec can easily reach much higher levels. High interrupt levels are shown in Figure 4-10.

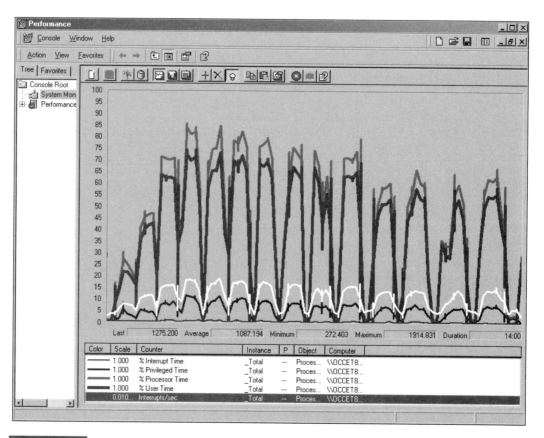

FIGURE 4–10 *Acceptable High Interrupt/sec Rates When Supporting 400 Concurrent Users*

This Sysmon graph is from a Compaq 8000 server configured with 2 - 100BaseT NICs, 1GB of RAM, 4 Pentium III 550MHz/1MB cache CPUs, and 20 9GB disk drives under a maximum load of 400 concurrent users implementing a generic transaction-processing workload. The Interrupts/sec are actually off of the Sysmon scale, noted by the 0.010 scale factor. Under the heaviest load, the Total Interrupts/sec was over 1900 interrupts/sec. This test was run repeatedly to verify the results. On every test run under the full 400-user load, the Interrupts/sec levels were roughly the same. Thus, for this workload, 1900 interrupts per second consumed 1.5% of all the CPU resources for immediate action requests (shown by the %Total Interrupt Time) and 2% of the CPU for deferred requests (shown by %Total DPC Time). This is the baseline for this server.

Baselines Are Important for Bottleneck Detection

If the Interrupts/sec in this example ever increased significantly over the baseline 1900 interrupts/sec for the same workload, it would be a flag that there is a problem with a hardware device. When a hardware device begins to generate high rates of unjustified interrupts, it consumes precious CPU cycles. To the extreme, the hardware device can actually be the cause of an interrupt-driven CPU bottleneck. To tune around this problem, you must troubleshoot your server hardware and remove the component that is malfunctioning. This in itself can be difficult. The system's Power On Self Test (POST) or network driver loop back test normally found under Start / Settings / Control Panel / Networks / Local Area Networks Properties / Configure Adapter is helpful in tracking down hardware problems. If Windows 2000 detects the problem, check Windows 2000's event log for errors that might lead you to the troublesome critter.

There is no steadfast rule of thumb stating if the number of interrupts per second is over X amount, you have a hardware problem or a interrupt-driven bottleneck. Just as in this example, whether you have a problem or not is based on your environment and the baseline you develop. Whenever the Interrupts/sec start to increase and the workload is the same as usual, it is time to investigate and troubleshoot your system's hardware devices.

CPU Resource Usage Analysis with Sysmon

In chapter 2 we covered the core Sysmon objects and counters to observe when quickly trying to assess if your system is bottlenecked by lack of CPU resources. Here, key Sysmon counters are reviewed a little closer so that you can analyze CPU resource usage and develop your baseline. This information is helpful for detecting where bottlenecks are occurring, and determining where, from a CPU tuning perspective, it would be beneficial to tune!

TABLE 4.7	*Key Sysmon Counters to Observe When Analyzing and Detecting a CPU(s) Bottleneck*	

Object/Counter	Definition	Rule of Thumb for Bottleneck Detection
Processor: Processor Time _Total Instance	% Total Processor Time is expressed as a percentage of the elapsed time that a processor is busy executing a non-idle thread.	A high value for this counter is not a reason to be alarmed, unless it is accompanied by an aggregated System: Processor Queue Length sum greater than (2 × Number of CPUs) or growing with an associated level of total processor time greater than 80-90%; then the CPUs are becoming a bottleneck. This rule holds true for multi-CPU Windows 2000 Systems.
System: Processor Queue Length	Processor Queue Length is the number of threads in the processor queue. There is a single queue for processor time even on computers with multiple processors. This counter counts ready threads only, not threads that are running.	Single CPU Systems If the sustained Queue Length is >2 for extended periods of time (5-10 minutes) or continuously growing with an associated level of Total Processor time >80-90%, the CPU is becoming a bottleneck as it cannot keep up with the requested workload. This rule holds true for single CPU Windows 2000 systems. Multiple CPU Systems If the sustained Queue Length is > 2 × the number of CPUs in the system for extended periods of time (5-10 minutes) or continuously growing with an associated level of Total Processor time >80-90%, the CPU is becoming a bottleneck as it cannot keep up with the requested workload. This rule holds true for multiple CPU Windows 2000 systems.
Processor: %Interrupt Time	%Interrupt Time is expressed as a percentage of the elapsed time that the processor spent handling hardware interrupts.	This value in itself is not a true indicator of a processor bottleneck. The value of this counter is helping to determine where to focus your tuning efforts. If this counter is greater than 20% and rising (without accompanying workload increases) compared to your baseline, consider completing diagnostics on the peripheral components to ensure they are operating within acceptable parameters.
Processor: Interrupts/sec	Interrupts/sec is the average number of hardware interrupts the processor is receiving and servicing in each second.	As hardware devices attached to the server (Example: a network interface card) require attention, they interrupt the CPU to request service. Typical Intel CPUs run at 100 interrupts/sec. If this value suddenly begins to rise when the workload has not increased, this can be an indication of a hardware problem (which robs valuable CPU cycles from processes that really need it!)

TABLE 4.7	Key Sysmon Counters to Observe When Analyzing and Detecting a CPU(s) Bottleneck (Continued)

Object/Counter	Definition	Rule of Thumb for Bottleneck Detection
Processor: %Privileged Time	%Privileged Time is expressed as a percentage of the elapsed time that the processor spent in privileged mode in non-idle threads.	If this value is greater than the counter %User Time, then focus on investigating how to improve kernel-related operations such as how well Windows 2000 and the hardware platform are working together (obtain more efficient hardware, tune Windows 2000) and how well the application is requesting kernel services.
Processor: %User Time	%User Time is expressed as a percentage of the elapsed time that the processor spent in user mode in non-idle threads.	If this value is greater than counter %Privileged Time, then focusing on tuning of application efficiency and resources should yield a better return than focusing on kernel-related improvements such as system resource utilization.
Process: %Processor Time	Processor Time is the percentage of elapsed time that all of the threads of this process used the processor to execute instructions. Note: On multiprocessor machines the maximum value of the counter is $100\% \times$ the number of processors.	Select all processes that are currently running and display them in Sysmon's histogram mode. This technique can quickly show which processes are consuming the highest level of CPU time and thus who might be the culprit for the CPU bottleneck.
System: Context Switches/sec	Context Switches/sec is the combined rate at which all processors on the computer are switched from one thread to another. Context switches occur when a running thread voluntarily relinquishes the processor, is preempted by a higher priority ready thread, or switches between user mode and privileged (kernel) mode to use an Executive or subsystem service.	Context switches are necessary but expensive from the perspective that they require system resources every time they occur. If excessive amounts of context switches are occurring (greater than your baseline without a corresponding workload increase), you may be able to improve CPU performance by binding the process experiencing the high context switch rates to a specific CPU by applying hard affinity with Task Manager. If application source code is available, you may investigate making it more efficient.

Sizing CPU Subsystems

Sizing the type and number of CPUs required is directly related to the type of workload in the current and projected environment. The typical rule of thumb here when configuring your system is to select the fastest CPU and largest L2 cache that is economically feasible and is supported by the application you wish to run.

Sizing the CPU subsystem is an additive process. Take into account each major activity that is occurring on the system. To help in determining the amount of processing power you need, follow the Core Sizing Methodology from chapter 3. Use of historical data, stress testing your solution, extrapolating from industry benchmarks or CPU configuration based on what your system will support are all good techniques to use when sizing the CPU subsystem. These techniques are used in the case studies in chapter 8. When using these techniques, you remove the guesswork in CPU selection and sizing and can quantifiably rationalize why your systems are configured as they are.

Business requirements and required resources to support Windows 2000–based applications are increasing constantly; thus it is important to understand the performance characteristics and architecture of the application(s) that you deploy. If the application does not support operating across multiple systems to improve overall performance and is limited to running on a single system, start with the fastest possible CPU, largest Level 2 cache, and a system architecture that can support multiple CPUs (within your budget, of course). This approach provides better long-term investment protection because you can increase the system's capacity by adding additional system resources such as CPUs, memory, etc., as needed to meet your goals. This single-system, in-the-box approach to sizing and scaling is referred to as vertical scaling. However, if your application does support increasing capacity by adding additional systems, then consider starting with a smaller 1–2 CPU system. With this approach, as more capacity is needed, just add another complete system. This approach is referred to as horizontal scaling, or Redundant Array of Inexpensive Servers (RAIS). An example application that works in this manner is Windows Network Load Balancing (WNLB). WNLB enables web-based workloads to be load balanced across up to 32 physically separate web servers.

Even without any specific additional applications running under Windows 2000, there are multiple active processes and threads running at all times. Thus, additional CPUs normally are helpful to a degree. Consider your

Windows 2000 a candidate for a multiple CPU configuration if the following criteria apply to your environment:

- More than one major application (process) is running at a time.
- The application is multithreaded and was designed for a Symmetric Multi Processing (SMP) environment.
- Using the tuning methodology, you have determined that the server is CPU bound and the System: Processor Queue Length is greater than two times the number of CPUs in the server.

Configure Enough RAM When Sizing the CPUs

New operating systems and applications always want more and more memory. But this is the CPU chapter? The importance of configuring enough memory should be apparent from the discussion of CPU architectures and performance at the beginning of this chapter. In short, if enough memory is not configured, you do not keep the CPU fed. If the CPU must wait for data, it is not productive. Configuring a 1000MHz Pentium III–based system with 16MB of RAM will never keep the CPU fed. If you were to do this, you might as well not waste money on the 1GHz Pentium III, and purchase a less expensive 100MHz Pentium I CPU. Why? By not having enough memory available to keep the 1GHz Pentium III fed, you slow it down significantly. Does the performance level really lower to that of a 100MHz Pentium? Well, not exactly, but the performance level does drop drastically. I hope that this point is clear. For a single CPU Pentium III class CPU or above, configure at least 256MB per CPU as a minimum.

Configure CPU Resources to Drive the Solution

Configure enough CPU resources to drive all of the system's resources. One area that is overlooked when sizing the amount of CPU power required for a solution is the amount of CPU power required for driving the disk and networking I/O subsystems. From our discussions above, each hardware device added to a system required some amount of CPU resources to operate, as each device will eventually interrupt the system for servicing. In Table 4.3, one of the reasons Configuration 6 needed additional CPU resources was that it supported 26 more disk drives and more networking overhead which required the CPUs to support a higher level of hardware interrupts. Stress tests and historical data are the two best sources of information to determine how much CPU power is required.

CPU and Memory Sizing Relationships

Throughout this book, industry benchmarks, case studies, and general stress tests are completed and referenced. Does this mean that, even for a generic system, great lengths must be taken every time just to obtain a basic system configuration? Not all the time, but it is the most proactive approach. In chapter 8, we review specific system configurations for a variety of applications. Here we review key system architecture guidelines and rules of thumb to take into account when developing your solutions from a CPU resource perspective. In Table 4.8, you will find CPU sizing rules of thumb that were obtained from industry benchmarks, work outlined in this book, and personal experience.

| TABLE 4.8 | Relative CPU Performance (Server Consolidation Mapping) and Recommended RAM Requirements |

CPU Class	Equivalent CPU Class	Minimum RAM (per CPU)
1 - Pentium	2 - 80486	16MB
1 - Pentium II	2 - Pentium	32MB
1 - Pentium Pro	2 - Pentium II	128MB
1 - Pentium III	2 - Pentium Pro	256MB

Table 4.8 can be used as a starting point for initial system configurations, server consolidations, and a general reality check while following the Core Sizing and Tuning Methodologies discussed in chapter 3. For example, if you have four servers, each of which is configured with two 133MHz Pentium class CPUs operating at 80% utilization per CPU, you would need CPU-based computing power that is equivalent to (or better than) eight Pentium class CPUs (assuming 20% room for workload surges). Eight Pentium class CPUs are roughly equivalent to four Pentium II CPUs, or two Pentium Pro CPUs, or one Pentium III class CPU. Eight Pentium class CPUs are equivalent to one Pentium III CPU? Yes! This CPU-based server consolidation mapping is correct from a CPU-only performance perspective. However, there are many other technical and business factors to consider, and these are outlined in The Core Sizing Methodology in chapter 3. Examples of other factors are application architecture, availability, network requirements, etc.

Earlier in this chapter, we closely reviewed CPU cache performance and the effects it has on overall scalability of your solution. Today, there are a number of systems that support almost every combination of CPU configuration. In Table 4.9, the general rules of thumb for Level 2 cache configuration are presented with respect to the total number of CPUs in the system. These rules of thumb greatly influence the throughput and scaling that your system can achieve as well as your planning for the future. If you plan to grow vertically (adding CPUs inside the system), then always go with the size of Level 2 cache recommended in Table 4.9 for the maximum number of CPUs that you plan to expand to. For example, if you plan to expand your system to six CPUs, but will start with only two CPUs, obtain CPUs with 2MB of cache. Why? If you do not, you will need to reallocate the CPUs to another system when it is time to upgrade, since you cannot update the Level 2 cache size alone (it is built into the chip).

TABLE 4.9	*SMP CPU and Level 2 Configuration Rules of Thumb*
Number of Pentium III E/ XEON Class CPU(s)	**L2 Cache (ATC – Full Speed)**
1	256KB
2	256/512KB
3	1MB
4	1MB
6	2MB
8	2MB

Avoiding Resource Contention: Resource Partitioning and Server Consolidation CPU Example

Another CPU sizing area that is important to consider is keeping the CPUs properly fed with data from the system's other resources without creating any resource contentions. Resource contentions lead to bottlenecks that limit the system's overall performance. To help illustrate the concept of resource partitioning to avoid contention, consider running two major applications on the same Windows 2000 server (perhaps due to a server consolidation, poor maintenance history, cost concerns, etc.). When configuring the system resources to support these two applications, you must configure CPU, Memory (RAM), Disk, and Network resources. It is possible to size and configure the system's resources in a manner that lowers contention and ensures the CPUs are fed as well as possible. Figure 4-11 shows an example of how to partition resources to mitigate resource contention.

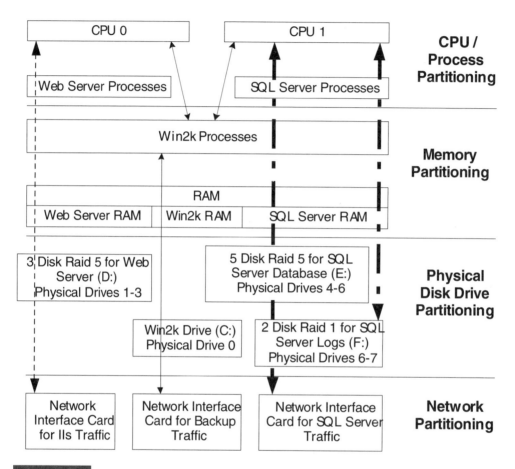

FIGURE 4-11   *Resource Partitioning and Avoiding Resource Contention to Keeping the CPU Resources Fed*

It is possible to support a web server (IIs) and database (SQL 7) on a single CPU system, but for this example, we will make the assumption that while following the Core Sizing Methodology from chapter 3, you determined two CPUs were needed. With two applications active at the same time on the system, resources for both must be accounted for and configured. For CPU resource usage, you can allow Windows 2000, IIs, and SQL 7 all to be handled by the Windows 2000 scheduler. You could also bind SQL 7 to one CPU (using settings in the application itself), or use Task Manager to bind each application to its own CPU by setting its affinity accordingly. Implementing affinity (binding) is investigated later in this chapter.

Although RAM resources are shared to a certain degree among the applications and the operating system, sizing RAM resources is an additive process. You must, however, allot enough RAM for each application and the Windows 2000 operating system itself to efficiently operate in (no paging!). Both IIs and SQL 7 are robust and enable the administrator to control how much RAM each application can use; thus you have great control of overall RAM usage on the system. This ensures one application does not starve or constrain another.

Disk resources are the most common location where constraints are introduced. If we have three applications running simultaneously, do you really want them all to attempt accessing the same physical disk drive (regardless of disk partitioning (C:, D:, E:, etc.) at the same time? In Figure 4-11, each application has its own disk resources assigned. In this manner, there are fewer possibilities that one application's request for disk resources will adversely affect another application's request. This approach of dedicating disk resources to a specific application eases administration, as it is easier to tune the disk resources for the application's specific workload characteristics, bring one application down for maintenance (not the entire system), determine where to add disk capacity and when additional disk drives are needed to improve performance. Why is it easier to manage performance? Since you know which application is using which drives, you can correlate the disk activity of the disk subsystem directly to a specific application. This in turn enables the tuning of that specific disk subsystem to the specific needs of that application. In Figure 4-11, for example, if you observe that the logical disk drive F: (Physical Drives 6 and 7) above is running slow and building a queue, you know without a shadow of a doubt that the SQL server logs need attention. Understanding that only log data is placed on the drive set, which is sequential and write intensive in manner, you may consider implementing a RAID 10 set (chapter 7) to alleviate the bottleneck. This is a different approach than what would have been used when removing a SQL 7 database bottleneck occurring on logical drive E: (Physical Disks 4, 5, and 6).

Finally, do not forget about your network resources! With VLAN technology becoming more common in today's networks, using multiple network interface cards (NICs) in a single system is becoming much more popular. In this example, the web server is configured to support a specific IP address/NIC, the SQL Server application uses another IP address/NIC, and all backup operations are run on a completely separate IP address/NIC to avoid any contention with the services you are planning to deliver. Using a separate dedicated network for system backups is a form of server area network (SAN).

Generic CPU Sizing Example

If you wanted to develop a server solution that supported 200 total concurrent end users with file services you could extrapolate part of the CPU sizing information from the chapter 8 file server case study.

In the file server case study, we find that when supporting 50 concurrent users, 48% of the capacity of a single 550MHz Pentium III CPU was used. The final file server configuration included a 10-disk external disk array, 256MB of RAM, and a single 100BaseTX NIC. Extrapolating from this, to support 200 users (four times as many) would require: two Pentium III CPUs running at 96% of capacity, 512MB of RAM, 40 disk drives, and four 100BaseT NICs.

How well do sizing extrapolations work? Generally they provide a good starting point; then through a combination of stress testing and proactive system performance management, you can tune your system to meet your needs. For this specific extrapolation, it was very close to what was actually needed when I worked with a large file server supporting 200 concurrent users. The only item that was slightly higher than expected was that 3.2 CPUs are actually required instead of 2. This was due in part to the fact that one other application was running concurrently on the system and a Gigabit Ethernet Adapter was needed. Fortunately, we learned about these increased processing requirements by stress testing the server before deployment. Being somewhat conservative (and having a decent budget), we actually configured four CPUs to support possible workload storms.

Tuning Strategies for Removing CPU Bottlenecks

At first glance, it would appear that tuning a Windows 2000 system to remove a CPU bottleneck is difficult and the only possibility is upgrading to faster or additional CPUs. This is a normal response. Now, purchasing more hardware is a valid technique and we will later discuss when it is appropriate to upgrade or add CPUs. But let's review some options we can complete without spending more money on new hardware. The solution scenarios presented in chapter 8 move step-by-step through the strategies and tactics involved with tuning various areas of Windows 2000 and from some scenarios clearly show what levels of performance improvements are associated with the tuning steps implemented.

Hands-on Tactics for Tuning around CPU Bottlenecks

In this section, we review the strategies surrounding CPU tuning and then get into the specifics. I cannot stress enough the importance of how critical it is to not just know which "operating system knob to tweak," but also to understand why something can or may need to be changed. The following are the primary strategies to consider when tuning around a CPU bottleneck:

- Ensure another server resource is not acting as a bottleneck
- Remove unnecessary workloads (applications, services, etc.)
- Off-load system CPU overhead
- Upgrade to faster CPUs
- Add additional CPUs
- Control when application jobs are run
- Tune Windows 2000 Quantum
- Update device drivers, system BIOS, and Windows 2000
- Advanced Tuning—Think Outside of the Box
  - Tune Windows 2000 to control process priorities
  - Tune Windows 2000 control process affinity
  - Tune Windows 2000 control interrupt affinity (new Windows 2000 tool!)

ENSURE ANOTHER SYSTEM RESOURCE IS NOT ACTING AS A BOTTLENECK

The most common problem I encounter when tuning around CPU bottlenecks is the removal of other system bottlenecks, not CPU bottlenecks. If another system resource is acting as a bottleneck, it can appear that the CPU is the actual bottleneck when it is not. Refer to chapter 2's The Core Tuning Methodology to ensure that the other resources are not the bottleneck before spending effort tuning CPU resources. Some bottlenecks appear to be CPU related when they are not. For example, memory bottlenecks in extreme cases disguise themselves as CPU problems. When Windows 2000 begins to run out of memory, it can exhibit a condition called thrashing. Thrashing is an excessive contention for physical memory. When this condition occurs, every request for memory results in paging activity to the pagefile on the disk drive(s). This results in an increased amount of CPU activity associated with moving memory pages around, not completing truly productive work. Why waste precious CPU cycles on this activity? Refer to chapter 3's The Core Tuning Methodology to ensure that other resources are not the bottleneck before spending effort tuning CPU resources.

Avoid this condition by configuring a sufficient amount of RAM to avoid thrashing. The highest performing Windows 2000 systems I encounter are sized and tuned with one basic strategy in mind: avoid paging. Many consider infrequent paging acceptable. The more the system pages, the more CPU cycles are wasted on memory operations and the slower the final response times provided to your end users. To improve performance if the system must page, spread Windows 2000's pagefile across two to four dedicated disk drives sized identically (same size pagefile, same speed disk drives, same manufacturer, etc.). Refer to chapter 6 for the specifics on how to determine if you Windows 2000 Server is paging and a step-by-step guide on spreading the pagefile across multiple disk drives.

OFF-LOAD CPU OVERHEAD

If the system is running out of CPU processing power, off-load Windows 2000 activities that are not required or can be implemented on another system. The areas normally associated with CPU overhead that can be removed or off-loaded are listed below.

REMOVE UNNECESSARY PROCESSES (APPLICATIONS, SERVICES, ETC.)

Run only applications and Windows 2000 services that are needed to perform the function that the system was designed to accomplish and that are used for managing the system. Any processes that are running consume CPU resources (and others); this is unneeded overhead that slows down your entire system. Another reason it is important to follow this approach is that many security-related problems occur because a service or application you did not need was installed (you may not even have known; it was installed by default) which creates a security breach that can be exploited. For example, it was common practice at one time to load Microsoft IIs's examples as default. These examples, although helpful to developers and those learning IIs, ended up becoming portals into any system in which they were installed, becoming a *big* security risk. They were an unneeded risk, too, if you never intended to use them anyway!

Use Sysmon, Process: %Processor Time, and search for applications that are consuming CPU time. Ensure that these applications are really required for desired system operation. Alternatively, start Task Manager and click on the CPU column. Task Manager will list the processes that are using the highest level of CPU performance at the top of the chart. Also, use Task Manager to look for runaway applications. If an application is not responding and appears to be continuously hogging resources, kill the process using Task Manager or one of the other tools outlined in chapter 2. Note: always know what you are killing and try it first on an identical system in the lab before actually removing the application in a production environment.

More applications are taking advantage of Windows 2000's services as a mechanism to start background processes and operate. There are many more services available by default in Windows 2000. Look under Start / Programs / Administration Tools / Computer Management / Services and Applications / Services. It is an amazing list, isn't it? Based on how you installed Windows 2000, you probably have many more services than you were aware of. Check every one! You would be surprised what might be running on your system.

Windows 2000 can actually run with only the following services started: workstation and server. All other services are not required for basic Windows

2000 operations. Keeping the EventLog service active is a good idea for monitoring the health of your system and applications. Any services not required for the operation of your system should be disabled. Following are some commonly overlooked services and applications that can be shut down to reduce the burden on your CPU resources.

- Remove exotic screen savers such as 3D pipes (or any 3GL screen savers) running on any servers. They consume precious server resources and look awful when the server begins to slow down. Consider locking the console or logging out and turning off the monitor.
- Stop license logging, which checks to see if customer licenses for applications are current, if the system does not require this service.
- Stop the print spooler. Unless the system is used as a spooler, turn this off.
- Stop IIs and the indexing services if they are not used.
- Stop Simple TCP/IP services (few applications use these services anymore and they can easily be exploited for a denial-of-service attack).
- If you have installed a copy of Microsoft Office 97/2000, ensure that the FindFast.exe program is not configured to start by default.

These tactics are implemented in chapter 8's File Server Solution Scenario. Several nonessential background processes and services are removed. Using this tactic not only removes stress on the CPU, but it also frees up the memory these processes and services were using. Keeping a baseline of what processes are running on your system helps to identify unwanted and unknown processes improving both performance and security of the system.

SEARCH FOR INEFFICIENT/WASTEFUL HARDWARE COMPONENTS

For enterprise servers, do not be surprised if Processor: %Interrupt Time is around 5–20% of the total CPU workload, particularly if the network and disk I/O is very heavy. There are, however, some components that behave better than others. Attempt to obtain network interface cards that truly support bus mastering and disk adapters that support DMA transfers versus PIO. Some disk and network adapters operate more efficiently than others by having their own CPUs interact directly with the memory subsystem, grouping requests for CPU resources instead of sending them individually; thus, they require fewer CPU cycles to operate. Trade magazines provide numerous comparisons of these products. One good source of information is the Windows 2000 Magazine web site located at: http:\\www.ntmag.com. You can run your own tests, too. Run a stress test against your system and watch Sysmon's Processor: %Processor Time, Processor: %Interrupt Time, and Processor: Interrupts/sec. Remove the old component and install the component that you think is more efficient, remembering to update any drivers and configuration settings to take advantage of the new hardware. Rerun your stress test and watch the same counters. If your performance measurements from your stress tests are the same or better and the %Interrupt Time and Interrupts/sec are lower, you have found a more efficient solution. This frees CPU cycles for more productive activities.

DO NOT IMPLEMENT COMPRESSION

Compression is nice for notebooks and some workstations, but it has little applicability for server class systems. Actively using compression on your system will increase your CPU overhead and slow your disk operations. If you must use compression, relegate its use to drives that are not frequently accessed and are used for archiving only.

OFF-LOAD CPU-INTENSIVE OPERATIONS: RAID CALCULATIONS

Whenever possible, off-load CPU operations to secondary devices. Windows 2000 allows the native use of software-based RAID 5 implementations. RAID 5 requires constant parity computation every time data is written to a RAID 5 array. Off-load this by using a RAID controller with its own CPU for RAID calculations. This frees up CPU cycles for the application, instead of wasting them on every disk write activity. Chapter 6, Windows 2000 and Disk Performance, reviews RAID technologies and examines performance issues in depth.

OFF-LOAD CPU-INTENSIVE OPERATIONS: TCP CHECKSUM OFF-LOADING TO THE NIC

As network packets arrive at a Windows 2000 system, a parity calculation is completed to ensure the packet's contents have been correctly sent. If they have not been correctly sent—that is, if they lost a bit or two on the way—a request is made for a retransmission. A combination of Windows 2000 advanced off-loading features in the new TCP/IP stack and new NIC cards with updated drivers now enable you to off-load this CPU-intensive calculation to the NIC itself. This is normally set under Start / Settings / Network and Dialup Connections / Local Area Connections / Configure / Advanced and then enabling the NIC for check sum calculation off-load. Each NIC is slightly different, so the final wording may not be exact for these steps.

OFF-LOAD CPU-INTENSIVE OPERATIONS: SECURITY (IPSEC) CALCULATIONS

Security is becoming more important daily. An excellent functionality addition to Windows 2000 is the ability to natively support Virtual Private Network (VPN) connections as either a server or a client. This technology is reviewed in chapter 7, but as a quick teaser, VPN technology enables an encrypted tunnel to be created from a client to the server over a TCP/IP-based network. Once created, all data between the client and server are encrypted. Layer 2 Tunneling Protocol (L2TP) is the standard used to create the tunnel, and the

IP-based encryption technology is an Internet standard referred to as Internet Protocol Security (IPSec). Who does all of this encryption in a client to server IPSEC connection? The main CPUs! Can this be a significant amount of overhead? Yes! If you are considering improving the security of your solutions, plan to obtain NICs that support IPSec off-loading. In the file server tests run in later chapters, and my own experience, using a NIC that supports IPSec off-loading can lower CPU overhead on the main CPUs by 10–20%. Under light loads on systems with the latest CPU technology, you will see lower gains. On systems that support a high amount of IPSec traffic, or systems with older CPUs, you will see enormous gains in the overall performance of your system and amount of overhead that is removed and relegated to the NIC(s).

SECURITY AUDITING EQUALS CPU OVERHEAD

Security is important. When increased security levels are required, Windows 2000 auditing is activated (using auditing for tuning investigations was covered in chapter 2) and a certain level of overhead is introduced onto the system. The amount of overhead introduced is a function of the required level of auditing. The CPU is the system resource that shoulders most of the overhead associated with increased auditing. If auditing is required, do not turn it off. However, be aware that more CPU horsepower may be required to compensate for the increased security to provide the same level of performance experienced without auditing activated. This is a hidden cost to achieve improved security for a system.

ENCRYPTION EQUALS SIGNIFICANT CPU OVERHEAD

Security is important. Can you tell many of my new customers are security conscious? When increased security levels are required, Windows 2000 now has native file encryption available. If you have important data that must be kept confidential, it is excellent that Windows 2000 now includes this feature. However, it takes CPU resources to encrypt those files, memory resources to support the CPU, and slightly larger files to be stored in the disk subsystem. How much more CPU overhead is required? To find out, I ran the Neal Nelson Business Benchmark multiuser sequential read/write test suite (Tests 18/19) test on a Compaq 6400R with two Pentium III 550MHz CPUs, 512MB of RAM, and a nine-disk RAID 5 array that was configured to use the encrypted file system. The results? Under heavy load (about 200 medium users), CPU usage jumped, on average, an additional 10% when file encryption was turned on. That additional 10% was privileged mode overhead that resulted from the encryption calculations. Security will become more and more important as more businesses move to the Internet. Be sure to calculate this security overhead when sizing your systems. More CPU resources will be required!

REMOVE FAULTY HARDWARE COMPONENTS

When a hardware device such as a network interface card interrupts the processor, Windows 2000's Interrupt Handler will execute to handle the condition, usually by signaling I/O completion and possibly issuing another pending I/O request. Observe the Sysmon counter Processor: Interrupts/sec. If this number begins to grow compared to your baseline when under normal workload, there is a good possibility that a network device has become faulty. When a device becomes faulty, it may begin generating high numbers of interrupts, which inundate the CPU and waste precious CPU cycles. Remove the faulty device and your problem will be resolved.

UPGRADING TO FASTER CPUS

If the CPU is running at or near 100% for extended periods of time and all of the other system resources are not bottlenecks, then the system is running at its very best. You are getting an excellent return on investment (ROI)! If an even higher level of overall performance is required, however, it may be time to upgrade the CPU, the system components, or even the system itself.

The obvious way to alleviate processor bottlenecks is to move to a faster CPU. If your application is known to be computation-intensive and your Processor: %User Time dominates your server's processing environment, you are a prime candidate to reap the benefits of a faster CPU. Once the CPU is upgraded, do not forget to check the server resources to ensure that the bottleneck has not shifted with the addition of a faster CPU. Talk about disappointment! Have you ever seen someone upgrade to a faster CPU yet nothing improves—or it gets worse—because there is now a memory or other resource bottleneck? It is not a pretty sight.

If you have a multiuser system using multithreaded applications or multiple single threaded applications, you can preserve your investment (i.e., not throw out the older CPU when the new one arrives) by adding additional processors. A discussion on this topic is next.

ADDING MORE CPUS

The effectiveness of adding CPUs for Windows 2000, or any other operating system for that matter, can spark serious debates. In a perfect world, if the system were CPU-bound, adding an additional CPU would improve performance 100%. This is considered linear scaling. Figure 4-12 illustrates perfect and not-so-perfect scaling.

My view of scaling is that if your performance increases enough to justify the cost of the additional CPUs, the system scales. Perhaps a simple view, but I have worked with many people who prefer to add a little more power to their current system versus purchasing a completely new system due to the hardware and management costs associated with a new system. How well

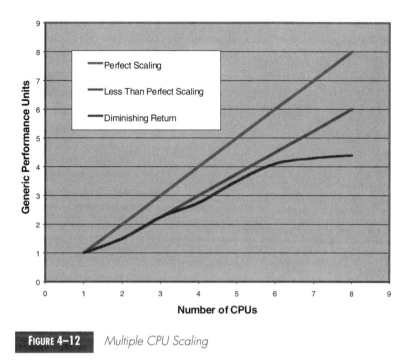

FIGURE 4-12   *Multiple CPU Scaling*

your systems scale is closely tied to your environment. Factors such as the application design, system hardware, communications, client application, and Windows 2000 itself directly influence how well your system will scale. From a generic point of view, if the System: Processor Queue Length in your environment is greater than two times the number of CPUs in your system for extended periods of time (5–10 minutes) or you have multiple applications (processes) consuming high amounts of Processor: %User Time, then your environment is a candidate for additional CPUs.

Adding more CPUs does not directly dictate that your system will run faster. Why add more CPUs if the system is not running faster? Because the system can complete more work before the performance service level degrades. I once heard a general statement that summed this concept up well: "Servers are more like workhorses than racehorses while workstations are racehorses." Although the response time may or may not improve for the end user when multiple CPUs are used, servers will provide the same level of good response times to more users than before the addition of multiple CPUs. If your goal is faster response times to an increased number of end users, consider both faster and additional CPUs.

DETERMINING IF MULTIPLE CPUS ARE HELPING

To test how well an application under Windows 2000 scales, disable all CPUs except for one and start Sysmon in logging mode with all key counters activated. On a multiprocessor system, this can be accomplished by editing the c:\boot.ini (assuming c: is where you installed Windows 2000) and adding the following switch: /NUMPROC=1 to the end of the startup boot entry as in this example:

```
Multi(0)disk(0)rdisk(0)partition(1)\WINNT="Microsoft Windows 2000
Advanced Server Single CPU Option Using NUMPROC" /fastdetect /
NUMPROC=1
```

Run the application and measure the performance of the application. Collect all of the Sysmon data and measure performance results of the application. Ensure that there are no system bottlenecks besides possibly the CPU. Add another CPU or, if multiple CPUs are already in your system, set /NUMPROC=2 and rerun the same test. Review your data. In this manner, you can determine how well additional CPUs are affecting the application's performance. After continued iterative testing, you will come to a point where additional CPUs are added but performance is not improved, or you will hit the limit of the number of CPUs your system can physically support. This is the point to which the single application scales. This same technique can be applied when operating multiple applications on one server. Tools to complete these types of tests are outlined in chapter 2 and implemented in chapter 8.

NOTHING IS BETTER THAN PROOF: MULTIPLE PROCESSOR TEST RESULTS

If you have followed the above rules of thumb when deciding to add more CPUs, you have a better-than-average chance that your overall performance will improve. In fact, if you follow the proactive management approach outlined in chapter 2, you will be able to quantify your improvements or lack thereof! However, there is nothing like a good stress test that emulates your environment to determine what level of performance is achieved when adding CPUs. If your own stress test is not in your future, typical applications that take advantage of four or more CPUs are the many database engines available for Windows 2000.

To emulate a transaction-based environment, a Compaq 8000 server was configured with 1.5GB of RAM, seven 10K rpm UltraFast SCSI disk drives, and eight Pentium III 550MHz/1MB cache CPUs. The Neal Nelson Business Benchmark for Windows 2000 was configured to emulate 400 mid-level users in a transactional database workload and was run against 4-CPU and 8-CPU configurations. The results are provided in Table 4.10.

TABLE 4.10	*Average Response Time Between 4-CPU and 8-CPU Configurations as Measured by the Neal Nelson Business Benchmark for Windows 2000*

Configuration	Compaq 8000 Configuration 1	Compaq 8000 Configuration 2
Number of Pentium III 55MHz/1MB cache CPUs	4	8
Amount of Memory (RAM)	1.5GB	1.5GB
Disk Drives	6 (1 for Windows 2000, 5 for Database)	6 (1 for Windows 2000, for 5 Database)
Operating System	Windows 2000 Advanced Server	Windows 2000 Advanced Server
Average Response Time (lower is better)	*55 seconds*	*30 seconds (25 seconds better!)*

There is more to these results than just book propaganda here. First, it demonstrates that—if in an appropriate environment—very good scalability is obtainable. In fact, these results are near perfect. Second, it is important to note that enough RAM was configured such that disk usage was minimal. There is no doubt that if the four additional CPUs were added, but the other system resources were not properly configured, contention for resources would have occurred, creating bottlenecks in the system that would have inhibited overall performance and scaling of Windows 2000.

In real-world environments, I have observed many situations where adding CPUs to a CPU-bound system resulted in significant performance improvements.

SCHEDULE CPU INTENSIVE JOBS DURING OFF-PEAK HOURS

This technique always seemed to be a bit of an easy-out strategy to alleviate CPU problems, but it is effective and uses resources that may have otherwise been idle. To schedule a job to run during off-peak hours, use the *at* command from the command prompt. To get directions on how to use the *at* command, type *at* /? | more at the command prompt. Also available is the *at* command's GUI counterpart Scheduled Tasks, which is found at Start / Settings / Control Panel / Scheduled Tasks. The use of the Scheduled Task tool with screen shots can be found in chapter 2.

WINDOWS 2000 SERVICE PACKS

Enterprise operating systems are becoming more feature rich and complicated by the minute thus they are prone to bugs. Microsoft publishes bug fixes or patches as Service Packs and hotfixes. Stay abreast of these Service Packs as they commonly fix various functional problems and occasionally offer performance improvements. As with any new software, test it before putting it in a production environment. Don't become discouraged! I have never used an operating system that did not require periodic patches (UNIX Flavors, Linux, Microsoft).

UPDATE DRIVERS FOR ALL COMPONENTS AND SYSTEM BIOS

Using the latest drivers and system BIOS versions can yield much more efficient hardware systems. With improved efficiency, the amount of work the CPU resource must complete is less, which yields more CPU cycles for productive work. Sometimes, with the new drivers, the devices are much faster too! Every hardware component in your system has drivers that should be updated on a regular basis after testing (plus they are normally free and obtained via the vendor's web site or support CD).

Some of the more advanced components, those that encompass some type of embedded CPU technology such as RAID Adapters and the System Motherboard, require their on-board BIOS to be updated too. How much of an improvement can you expect? I have observed results that range from nothing, to improved stability, to 60% improvement in efficiency (less CPU workloads) and improvements in overall performance. Work with your vendor and ask the tough questions, such as "When did you update the driver?", "What did it fix?", and "Do you have any tests results?" Even after these questions are appropriately responded to, test out any changes in the lab before entering production with them!

CONTROLLING WINDOWS 2000'S CPU QUANTUM ALLOTMENT

A quantum is the slice of time the thread is allowed to run on the CPU before the scheduler executes a context switch and moves it off of the CPU so that the next thread is ready to run. A thread can also be preempted from using its allotted quantum if a higher priority thread comes along. There are three quantum values (as of the initial Windows 2000 release). The Hardware Abstract Layer (HAL) from the manufacturer of the system defines the quantum periods. In general, for a single CPU system, three quantums are equal to 10 milliseconds; for multi-CPU Pentium-based systems, a quantum is equal to 15 milliseconds.

For interactive workloads characterized by single user workstations, Windows 2000 Professional assigns shorter variable length quantums to the running threads. Windows 2000 servers that support fewer applications require longer access to system resources. Windows 2000 Server (and Advanced Server) assigns longer fixed-length quantums. Under Windows 2000, there is a point-and-click application available for influencing the quantum of foreground (those you interact with) and background applications. On the Performance tab of Start / Settings / Control Panel / System / Advanced / Performance Options, you can select Application Response Optimization for the application (foreground) or for background services. These options adjust the default quantum level of applications when you start them. For dedicated servers with larger applications running in the background, change this setting to background services. This will adjust the quantum of background services to 36 quantums. If you select the optimization for applications option, background processes are reduced to having three quantums of time while interactive processes receive nine quantums and a priority boost of an additional two levels, which is applied as needed to keep Windows 2000 responsive to foreground interactive applications.

In Windows 2000 Beta 1, more options were presented for controlling quantums. These options were not included in the production release of Windows 2000. Perhaps in the future third-party tools will provide this tuning flexibility.

Thinking Outside of the Box

If you are not feeling bold and adventurous, skip to the next chapter now. This section is definitely for those who want to really tune their Windows 2000 CPU subsystem to improve their system's overall performance. Those of you who are still here will learn some advanced tuning techniques.

Advanced Tuning: Helping Windows 2000 to Control Process Priorities

Windows 2000 does a very good job of controlling process priorities. But every environment is different, and a good system engineer and/or administrator will understand his or her own environment best. You can tune CPU performance by using Task Manager to identify the process that is consuming most of the CPU time or not obtaining enough CPU time, then adjust priority levels accordingly. We reviewed Windows 2000's 31 distinct priority levels. A process starts with a base priority level and its threads can vary two levels higher or lower than its base. If you have a particularly busy CPU and you wish to influence which processes have access to more CPU resources than others to meet your needs, consider tuning a process's priority level by starting Task Manager, selecting the process's priority you wish to tune, then selecting Real-time, High, Normal, or Low priority. Be careful when you set the processor's priority to real time—the process can become selfish and never release the CPU. If the process won't release the CPU, your system might become unstable; a selfish process is particularly dangerous on a single CPU system. If you are planning to test tuning processes in real time, I strongly suggest trying this only on systems with two or more CPUs. Typically staying with the non-real-time options is safer and can provide good results depending on your environment.

To implement priority changes on a more permanent basis (priority level changes using Task Manager results are only in place until the next time a system reboots or the process is stopped) use the *start* command. The *start* command can be placed in shell scripts that are run at system startup or directly from a command prompt. To review the start command's options, enter *start /? | more*. If you script this functionality so it can be automatically run at startup when an icon is launched, run the start command from inside the command prompt executable. For example, if you wanted to start application super.exe at a higher priority level, you would run the following command sequence: *"cmd.exe /C start.exe /high super.exe"*. Using this approach, the Windows 2000 command interpreter will start the application and then close the command prompt process. For more cmd.ex options, run "cmd.exe /?" from the command prompt.

Advanced Tuning: Helping Windows 2000 Control Application (Process/Thread) Affinity

Windows 2000's scheduler (built into the Windows 2000 kernel) provides very good general management of thread allocations to the various CPUs in single CPU and SMP-based system environments. On multiprocessor computers, the Windows 2000 scheduler distributes thread-processing requests over all processors based on thread priority. Often, even though Windows 2000 uses soft affinity (reviewed earlier in this chapter), threads still end up running across more than one processor. For some environments that rely heavily on Level 2 cache performance, Windows 2000 and the applications running on your system can use some tuning assistance to take full advantage of your system's resources.

In the beginning of this chapter, the importance of cache hits and keeping unneeded data off of the system bus was discussed. To help Windows 2000 do a better job accomplishing this, hard affinity can be applied to permanently bind a process or threads to a specific CPU or set of CPUs. When hard affinity is set, the designated process and associated threads are forced to always return to the same processor. This dramatically improves the overall Level 2 cache hit rates and subsequently improves performance.

This tuning technique is not for all environments. A good rule of thumb is that applying affinity is applicable when there are multiple applications running on the system or when multiple instances of a database are in use on the same server. For example, while I was working in one particular customer environment, they used four instances of Oracle running concurrently on the same server. The performance provided by the 4-CPU system was okay, but nothing to write home about. In an attempt to improve the system's performance, each Oracle instance was bound to its own CPU. All other processes and threads were under normal Windows 2000 control. So what was the result? A significant increase in overall performance was achieved. How could we be sure that applying hard affinity to the Oracle was what actually improved the server performance? The stress test workload remained the same and no other tuning attempts or other changes were made.

Use a Sound Affinity Tuning Methodology

Regardless of which tool is used to apply hard affinity (Task Manager or settings in the application itself such as those included SQL Server), it is important to follow a methodical approach when implementing this CPU tuning tactic. Run your application(s) and develop a performance baseline. Then apply hard affinity to one application at a time. Once the hard affinity is applied, test the performance of your application. If the performance improves, move onto the next application. As you continue your testing, log what is working and what is not. Eventually you will have a matrix such as the one shown in Table 4.11. Determining the correct mix takes time and is definitely for those people who want the highest level of performance from their system.

TABLE 4.11   *Affinity Application Distribution*

	Microsoft IIs Web Server	SQL Server Instance 1	SQL Server Instance 2	Custom Application 1
CPU 1	X			
CPU 2	X			
CPU 3		X		
CPU 4		X		
CPU 5			X	
CPU 6				X

HOW TO IMPLEMENT APPLICATION (PROCESS) LEVEL HARD AFFINITY

Windows 2000 provides the ability to assign hard affinity at the process level using Task Manager. To set affinity on a specific application (process), start Task Manager by pressing ctrl+alt+delete and selecting Task Manager. At this point, select the process(es) that you wish to apply affinity to by left-clicking the target process(es) to highlight it, then right-click it and select Processor Affinity. You can then set which CPUs you would like to bind the process(es) to. Figure 4-13 shows how a process's affinity is set on eight CPUs.

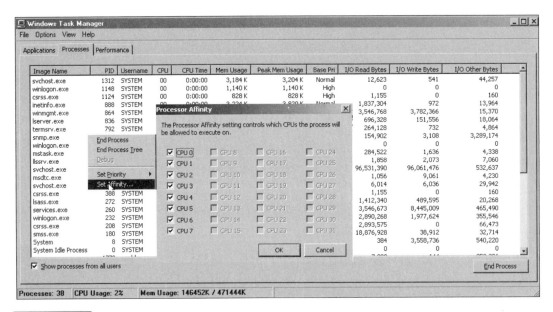

FIGURE 4-13 *Using Windows 2000's Task Manager to Apply Hard Affinity*

It is convenient to have this functionality built into Task Manager, but it requires manual intervention. There is currently no mechanism under Task Manager to automatically reapply the hard affinity settings you configured if the server reboots. Thus, if the system reboots, you must manually reallocate the hard affinity settings to the CPUs as needed.

ADVANCED TUNING TECHNIQUE: MICROSOFT INTERRUPT-AFFINITY FILTER CONTROL TOOL

Hardware devices want their fair share of CPU resources, too! The Windows 2000 Resource Kit now provides a tool that enables you to control—that is, tune—which hardware interrupts are serviced by which CPUs. Why would you consider doing this? To improve performance! There are several specific scenarios when you would consider applying interrupt-based affinity.

- **An Interrupt-Driven Unbalanced System**

    How do you know if this is occurring? Review the CPU usage distribution of the Processor: %Interrupt Time and Processor Interrupts/sec counters. Are some CPUs bearing more of the interrupt workload than other CPUs? This can adversely affect overall system performance.

- **Improve Response Time to Hardware Devices**

  Binding specific interrupts to a specific CPU or CPUs can improve response time to the hardware device and lower system bus congestion. How does this help? In multiprocessor systems, if a hardware device requests services, the CPU can defer responding to the hardware device to another CPU. This is called Deferred Procedure Call (DPC). By mapping a specific interrupt to a specific CPU, the amount of DPC traffic between CPUs is lowered.

- **High DPC Rate from the Processor: DPC Rate Counter**

  This is another indication that the Interrupt-Affinity Filer Control Tool might help balance DPC processing. By mapping a specific interrupt to a specific CPU, you can force improved distribution of interrupt processing.

In general, a typical system configuration that is conducive to tuning interrupt affinity is a multi-CPU system that contains multiple, interrupt-driven hardware devices. To find out if a hardware device even has interrupts to manage, run use the System Information MMC snap in via Start / Administrative Tools / Computer Management / System Tools / System Information or type in the command *winmsd.exe* from the Windows 2000 command prompt. Once the System Information tool is running, look at Hardware Resources / IRQs for a listing of interrupts and hardware device association. A physical example configuration that is a target for interrupts tuning would be a large file server with four CPUs and four network interface cards. For this example, you would bind the interrupt from each NIC to a specific CPU, in essence ensuring interrupt distribution across all CPUs.

Configuring Microsoft Interrupt-Affinity Filter Control Tool (IntFiltr)

To install IntFiltr, locate the IntFiltr folder on the Windows 2000 Resource Kit and then complete the following steps:

1. As with any technology you introduce into your environment, test this tool on a nonproduction system to ensure it behaves as you envision. Also, back up your system and registry.

2. Copy the IntFiltr folder to a folder on your system, and then copy intfiltr.sys to your %SYSTEMROOT%\system32\drivers directory (this is typically c:\system32\drivers).

3. Update your registry to include the changes listed in intfiltr.reg. To make these changes, you can just run 'regedit intfiltr.reg' and it will automatically update your registry.

Once installed, start IntFiltr by running intfiltr.exe from the command line. Once started, you are presented with the GUI presented here in Figure 4-14.

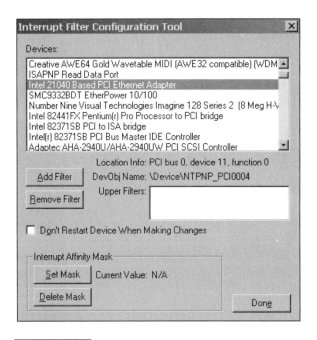

FIGURE 4–14 *Configuring the IntFiltr Interrupt Affinity Tool*

The GUI provides a listing of all the devices in the system. Highlight the device whose interrupts you wish to tune and then select add filter to turn interrupt filtering on for that device. Now that the filter is activated, select the Set Mask radio button and select the CPU or CPUs to bind the target device's interrupts to. Once the mask is set, the current value will change with the current CPU mask information. This configuration series is depicted in Figure 4-15.

From here, you can restart the device on line or reboot the system to activate the filter. To update the filter settings in the future, start *IntFiltr.exe* and scroll down to the target device. At this point, you will see the current filter/mask settings that can be adjusted as needed, based on your proactive performance management process!

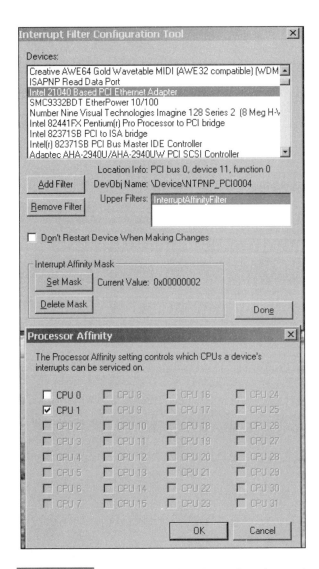

Setting the IntFiltr's Filter and Mask to Bind a Device's Interrupt Traffic to a Single CPU

Summary

In this chapter, Windows 2000 CPU performance was investigated from both a hardware and a software perspective. If you take anything away from this chapter, remember at least these points. First, it is important to understand not only what to change when tuning Windows 2000 CPU resources, but why it should be changed and how the change will affect the system. This enables you to more effectively tune your Windows 2000 system. Second, by understanding what is happening in your environment, it is possible to tune Windows 2000's overall CPU performance to its maximum!

Windows 2000 and Memory Performance

CHAPTER OBJECTIVES

- Introduction........ *234*
- Memory Hardware Technology Review........ *234*
- How Windows 2000 Uses Memory Resources........ *239*
- Windows 2000 File System Cache........ *246*
- Sizing the Memory Subsystem........ *262*
- Detecting Memory Bottlenecks........ *269*
- Quick Reference: Helpful Tools to Use When Tracking Down
  Windows 2000 Memory Details........ *270*
- What to Observe in Sysmon When Diagnosing a Memory
  Bottleneck........ *271*
- Tuning Strategies for Removing Memory Bottlenecks........ *275*
- Hands-on Tactics for Tuning around Memory Bottlenecks........ *276*
- Removal of Potential Memory Road Blocks........ *281*
- Remove Unnecessary Workload from the System........ *283*
- The Last Resort: Purchase More RAM........ *287*

Introduction

To tune or size a Windows 2000 system, it is important to understand how and why the system hardware, operating system, and applications work as they do. It is tempting at first to just jump in and add this or tune that. But when you understand how each component works with the others, you can tune and size system resources for maximum performance without much trial and error. In this and in chapters 6–8, descriptions, explanations, and examples are provided to help you understand how the system components interact. Armed with this information, you can disregard some of the "black magic" of tuning and sizing and employ more effective tactics. Knowing which "knob to turn" to tune a Windows 2000 system is good; understanding when to "turn a tuning knob" and why it will help is better.

This chapter we focus on Windows 2000 and the memory subsystem. Memory performance is investigated from several perspectives. First, general hardware-based memory architecture is reviewed to determine the relative performance of several available memory technologies and what, from a system architecture perspective, influences memory performance so that you get the most out of a system's memory subsystem. Second, we'll look at how Windows 2000 takes advantage of and uses the memory subsystem. Once our foundation of memory knowledge is established, we can determine when memory bottlenecks are occurring while running Windows 2000. We then move into sizing memory subsystems. We conclude by examining hands-on tactics for tuning around memory bottlenecks. Windows 2000's memory subsystem allows for an amazing amount of tuning flexibility. The bottleneck detection techniques, sizing, and tuning strategies and tactics reviewed in this chapter are not just theory based, they were developed from real-world production environments and are used throughout the rest of this book.

Memory Hardware Technology Review

Random Access Memory (RAM) is the gateway to maximum Windows 2000 performance. In chapter 4, Windows 2000 and CPU Performance, the importance of properly sized and utilized CPU Level 1 and Level 2 caches was stressed. When the data that the CPU requires are not found in its local cache, it looks to main memory—that is, RAM. RAM is accessed over the front side system bus. Accessing required data from RAM is tremendously faster than touching a physical device such as a disk drive. Data found in memory are accessed at an average speed of 50 nanoseconds (ns). If the data required are located on a physical disk drive, then the average access time takes an enormous leap to 8–11msec! Think of this as the difference between walking to the TV to change the channel versus running a 26-mile marathon to change the channel! This is not an exaggeration. So, which option would you prefer?

Obviously, at some point, data must be brought in from the disk subsystem. We'll look at disk subsystems in depth in chapter 6. For now, once the data are in memory, you want to access the data at the highest speed possible. When implementing workstation technology, there are more RAM options available than in the server space. Why? Single user versus multiple user support. If a workstation hiccups, one person is annoyed. If a server hiccups, many users are affected. It is almost a guarantee that one of the customers serviced by the hiccuping server is someone who controls your raise or bonus at the end of the year. Over time, many of the new technologies introduced in workstations mature and make their way into servers—server motherboard designs improve and error control techniques are matched up with the newer RAM technology. This lag time of adding technology upgrades and RAM error control slows the introduction of new RAM technologies into servers compared to new RAM technologies introduced into workstations. As CPU power has increased, vendors have recognized the need to develop faster access to the memory subsystem if this increased CPU power is to be unleashed.

SIMM and DIMM Server Memory

How can errors occur in RAM? RAM is actually composed of Dynamic Random Access Components that must keep electrically charged or data are lost. To compensate for the possibility that a RAM component might lose a charge, a variety of error-checking technologies are available for system memory subsystems. For servers, the most common error checking is Error Checking and Correcting (ECC) based RAM. Using ECC based memory subsystem, if a single bit error is detected it is corrected before any real harm is done. Today, ECC memory is available in either Single Inline Memory Modules (SIMM) or Dual Inline Memory Modules (DIMM). The primary difference between SIMM and DIMM memory is that DIMM has a wider data path density and higher memory capacity. This higher memory capacity lets the system motherboard support twice the RAM possible with SIMM technology. DIMM memory uses 132-pin connectors, while SIMM memory uses 72-pin technology. To support higher DIMM memory modules, the system motherboard must be able to accommodate the different DIMM pin outs. Those systems that accommodate either memory technology configure memory through the use of a daughter card attachment directly into the memory bus connector that attaches into the motherboard (not a PCI slot). Intel's Standard High Volume (SHV) motherboard design—used as a reference in several chapters—is an example of a server motherboard that supports either DIMM or SIMM memory modules through the use of a daughter card.

DIMM PERFORMANCE ALERT

Be careful when using the newer, high density DIMMs in servers that previously were using SIMM memory modules. To effectively use the DIMM technology and provide performance levels similar to those of their SIMM counterparts, the BIOS level on the server may require updating. Check with the hardware vendor. Typically, although not always, new BIOS versions are downloadable from the vendor's web site.

DRAM Future

DRAM is implemented using several different technology types. At their core, all of these different memory types are similar. They differ mostly in the way that they are organized and how the memory is accessed. The oldest or conventional DRAM DIMM uses the standard memory addressing method, where the first row's address is sent to memory and then the column address. At least six members of the current and upcoming DRAMs are included in the field of next-generation memory: Fast Page Mode, EDO, SDRAM, SDRAM II (DDR), Direct Rambus, and SLDRAM. The following is a list of various RAM technologies you should be aware of as they slowly work their way into the server technology arena.

Fast Page Mode (FPM) RAM

Fast page mode memory is slightly faster than conventional DRAM. While standard DRAM requires that a row and column be sent for each access, FPM RAM works by sending the row address just once for many accesses to memory in locations near each other, improving access time. This is the most common DIMM implementation.

EDO

EDO (Extended Data Out) DRAM technology shortens the read cycle between memory and the CPU. On computer systems designed to support it, EDO memory allows a CPU to access memory 10–20% faster than comparable fast-page mode chips.

SYNCHRONOUS DRAM (SDRAM)

With asynchronous DRAMs such as EDO or FPM, it is common to add extra wait states to the access timing for the memory to compensate for memory that was too slow. Synchronous DRAM uses a clock to synchronize signal input and output on a memory chip. The clock is coordinated with the front side bus of the CPU so the timing of the memory chips and the timing of the CPU are "in synch." SDRAM is tied to the front side system bus clock and it is designed to be able to read or write from memory in burst mode at one clock cycle per access (no wait states) at memory bus speeds to match the front side system bus (currently 66MHz, 100MHz, 133MHz). SDRAM saves time in executing commands and transmitting data, thereby increasing the overall performance of the computer. In pure memory speed tests, SDRAM is about 50% faster than EDO memory, with estimated server memory performance gains of around 25%.

DOUBLE-DATA RATE (DDR)

Double-data rate SDRAM is a faster version of SDRAM that is able to read data on both the rising and the falling edge of the front side system bus clock, thus doubling the data rate of the memory chip. Think of the system clock as a pendulum of a cuckoo clock. In SDRAM, when the pendulum swings left, data is transferred. In DDR SDRAM, data is transferred when the pendulum swings to the left and to the right. For example, if your system bus operates at 133MHz, DDR SDRAM data can be accessed at 266MHz. Note: As was mentioned in chapter 4, the system bus speed (MHz) is different than the CPU speed (MHz). DDR SDRAM is implemented in DIMM configurations and is not backward compatible with SDRAM. DDR is available in ECC and parity checking mode options, so it will appeal to both desktop and server solution vendors. This may help keep its volume up and costs down. This is not the most advanced memory technology, but it dramatically improves on standard SDRAM while keeping costs down.

RAMBUS DRAM (RDRAM)

RDRAM is a design developed by a company called Rambus, Inc. RDRAM is extremely fast and uses a narrow, high-bandwidth channel to transmit data at speeds about ten times faster than standard DRAM. Two other flavors of RDRAM are also under research: Concurrent and Direct RDRAM. Concurrent is based on the fundamental design of the standard RDRAM, yet is enhanced to increase speed and performance. Direct is also based on RDRAM, yet through additional enhancements will be even faster than concurrent RDRAM. RDRAM is somewhat controversial as Rambus has the patent on this technology and vendors creating RAM using this technology must pay a royalty fee. Also, Rambus has not hit high volume, so this memory technology typically costs more that the other RAM technology options listed above. For this higher performance memory option, there is a leap in pricing that accompanies it.

SYNCLINK DRAM (SLDRAM)

SLDRAM is a "joint effort" DRAM that may be the closest speed competitor with Rambus. Development is coordinated through a consortium of 12 DRAM manufacturers and system companies. SLDRAM is an enhanced line extension of SDRAM architecture that extends the current four-bank design to 16 banks. SLDRAM is currently in the development stage.

Table 5.1 illustrates the various relative performance levels of the RAM technologies reviewed.

TABLE 5.1   *Memory Technologies*

	FPM	EDO	SDRAM	DDR SDRAM	SLDRAM	RDRAM
Peak Bandwidth (Up to)	66MB/sec (60–80ns access)	66MB/sec (50–60ns access)	800MB/sec (7–15ns access)	1600MB/sec	400MB/sec	2.6 GB/sec
MHz	66MHz	66MHz	100/133MHz	200/266MHz	400MHz	800MHz
Standard Body	JEDEC	JEDEC	JEDEC	JEDEC	SLDRAM Consortium	Rambus

It is important to understand that even though the relative performance between the RAM technologies affects overall system performance, there is never a guarantee that your system's performance will improve by the amount shown between the various technologies. It is safe to state that some performance improvements will be achieved when implementing the newer technologies. Always run a stress test that is indicative of your environment to ensure what additional performance you will obtain before making an investment in that latest technology!

RAM Performance Considerations

The primary consideration when obtaining RAM is that you want it to be as fast as possible—no surprise here. The most obvious RAM characteristic to take notice of is the speed at which the RAM operates. Pay close attention when selecting RAM for your system; be sure that you are obtaining the fastest ECC supported memory possible for your system's chipset and bus. A nanosecond is only a billionth of a second. So, what's a nanosecond between friends? Quite a bit if you consider that the memory subsystem is accessed millions of times a second; each access adds up. Consider paying close attention to your configuration and ensure that 50ns RAM was delivered versus 80ns RAM. If you do, you have now improved every potential RAM access by 60%. In reality, due to the various timing considerations between the CPU and the memory subsystem, the effect that this selection has on overall server performance is less than this calculated comparison. Regardless of the exact performance, it is worth the effort to obtain the fastest memory possible, as it will provide system performance improvements of varying magnitudes depending on your environment. Although a rarity, do not mix and match different RAM modules within the same system. If the system does function, it will be throttled by the speed and access technique of the slowest memory module.

RAM Interleaving

Interleaving is a memory technique that can improve your system performance. In general, the purpose of interleaving is to take advantage of the potential memory bandwidth of the entire available RAM subsystem. [Hennessey and Patterson, *Computer Architecture a Quantitative Approach*, Morgan Kaufman, 1996, p. 431] Memory chips can be organized into banks to read or write multiple words of data at a time rather than one word of data at a time. By providing more data per memory access, the effective memory access speed is improved and potentially fewer memory accesses are required over the system bus. Less data having to traverse the server's system bus is always a good thing.

Windows 2000 normally supports one-, two-, and four-way interleaving. Avoid one-way interleaving. Four-way interleaving provides the highest level of performance. In achieving the various interleaving levels there are some trade-offs. SIMM memory must be configured in even memory bank sets (two banks provide a full 64 bits of access to the CPU data bus). To achieve higher interleaving levels when the amount of RAM is relatively small in the server, lower density memory modules must be used. When you use lower density memory modules, the maximum amount of RAM that can be configured in the server is limited due to the available memory slots being filled.

To avoid this, apply the Core Sizing Methodology from chapter 3 and pay close attention to future business requirements. If the future business requirements will require supporting higher amounts of RAM, use the highest density RAM possible that meets your current requirements. Using this strategy yields a memory subsystem that can be interleaved and will allow for projected growth without trading out lower density memory modules in the future. For this concept to be effective, you may need to slightly overconfigure the memory subsystem initially and let your workload catch up. In the short term this is more expensive. In the long term it is more cost effective.

How Windows 2000 Uses Memory Resources

Windows 2000 implements the same memory management approach regardless of the version of the Windows 2000 family you are implementing. However, depending on the version of Windows 2000 that you operate, the amount of physical memory you have in your system and how you tune Windows 2000 will influence the behavior of Windows 2000's memory management of processes—specifically, how much memory processes can access and how memory is allotted. Here, we will first explore the key components of the Windows 2000 memory management that are common to the entire Windows 2000 family. Later in this chapter, we examine key memory management behavior differences between members of the Windows 2000 family.

Standard Physical Memory

Windows 2000 is based on 32-bit code; this provides 2^{32} possible memory addresses or 4,294,967,296 bytes (4GB) of usable memory space for each process. As of the writing of this book, Microsoft announced that work has already begun to move Windows 2000 to a full 64-bit operating system. Why? Ever growing business and technical requirements will demand that more computing resources are provided. To meet this demand, moving Windows 2000 to a full 64-bit implementation makes sense. This will enable Windows 2000 to dramatically improve its scalability as it will support 64-bit operations and 2^{64} possible memory addresses or 18,446,744,073,709,551,616 bytes of usable memory in a flat memory model which is easier for developers to work with. Of course, there needs to be some system hardware to support this expanded computing space. Intel is working with several other vendors to bring its full 64-bit Itanium (Merced) next generation CPU to market. The Intel Itanium CPU will provide support for very large memory (VLM) architectures (the exact size is still open) and a new processing design—which Intel has dubbed Explicitly Parallel Instruction Computing (EPIC)—which enables more actions to occur per CPU cycle. As for memory, 2^{64} is a lot of memory, at least compared to today's systems. (Some day we might say, "Oh, you only have five terabytes . . . What is that, a desktop? How can you run anything?" but not yet.) Expect a little more time for vendors to provide systems that can support that amount of physical memory.

Windows 2000 Memory Management

The Windows 2000 memory management functions are implemented in the Windows 2000 kernel. The Virtual Memory Manager (VMM) in conjunction with the Cache Manager (CM) are the primary Windows 2000 system components that cooperate with the memory manager for overall Windows 2000 memory management. When a program is started, which we will refer to as a process, hard page faults are generated to bring the data from the disk subsystem into the memory subsystem. A soft page fault occurs if the process's request for data or instructions can be resolved by the VMM in physical memory, without traveling to the disk subsystem. As each process is brought into memory, the physical memory that the process occupies is referred to as its working set. At the same time that the process is brought into physical memory, the process's virtual memory is allotted. That is, how much memory the process initially thinks that it may need. It becomes important to understand these activities on your system when you wish to tune or size your system (how much RAM should be used, pagefile sizes, placement of applications on disk drives, etc.). To gather an understanding of what is occurring on your system, you can use Sysmon to observe these activities as outlined in Table 5.2.

TABLE 5.2	Monitoring Windows 2000 Memory Management Operations	
Memory Activity	**Performance Monitor Object: Counter (instance)**	**Counter Definition**
Hard Page Faults	Memory: Pages Input/sec	Pages Input/sec is the number of pages read from disk to resolve hard page faults. Hard page faults occur when a process requires code or data that are not in its working set or elsewhere in physical memory, and must be retrieved from disk.
Soft Page Faults	There is no counter that tracks soft page faults. But, if you subtract Pages Input/sec from Page Faults/sec, you can get a good estimate of the soft page fault rates.	Page Faults/sec is the overall rate faulted pages are handled by the processor. It is measured in numbers of pages faulted per second. A page fault occurs when a process requires code or data that is not in its working set (its space in physical memory). This counter includes both hard faults (those that require disk access) and soft faults (where the faulted page is found elsewhere in physical memory). Most processors can handle large numbers of soft faults without consequence. However, hard faults can cause significant delays.
Process Working Set Size	Process: Working Set (select process instance of interest)	Working Set is the current number of bytes that reside in physical memory for the selected process. This is part of the overall virtual address space for the selected process. The Working Set is the set of memory pages touched recently by the threads in the process. If free memory in the computer is above a threshold, pages are left in the Working Set of a process even if they are not in use. When free memory falls below a threshold, pages are trimmed from Working Sets. If they are needed they will then be soft-faulted back into the Working Set before they leave main memory.
Process Virtual Address Space	Process: Virtual Bytes	Virtual Bytes is the current size in bytes of the virtual address space the process is using. Use of virtual address space does not necessarily imply corresponding use of either disk or main memory pages. Virtual space is finite, and by using too much, the process can limit its ability to load libraries.

Windows 2000 Virtual Memory

What happens on systems that do not have a full 4GB of physical memory? This is where Windows 2000's memory management system implements virtual memory. Virtual memory is a strategy that provides the illusion that a full 4GB of physical memory is available, even if it is not. From a process's perspective, it does not know how much memory is physically in the system. The VMM handles mapping physically available memory (RAM) into a virtual address space. When there is not enough physical memory to go around, the VMM leverages additional virtual memory space located on the Windows 2000 system pagefile(s).

It is not efficient to bring every bit of a process's actual code and data into physical memory, since many pieces of the process's code are not required for the process to complete its immediate task. The VMM brings in pages of memory required by the process on an as-needed basis. The size of a page of memory varies by operating system and CPU architecture. For Windows 2000 running on an Intel-based CPU, pages are 4KB in size. By using this paging strategy, Windows 2000 conserves physical memory and allows multiple processes to simultaneously use the memory subsystem. As a process requests either data or program code from the disk, the VMM generates additional hard page faults (and soft page faults), as additional pages of memory are needed. In this manner, the working set of each process can grow as needed, up to a point (covered next).

HOW MUCH MEMORY DOES EACH PROCESS GET?

Does Windows 2000 really provide each process a full 4GB of RAM? Not exactly. Windows 2000 sets aside memory space for operating system specific tasks, which also must reside in this same 4GB of usable space. To achieve this, Windows 2000 VMM divides the 4GB range of addresses allocated to each process into two halves. A 2GB range is dedicated to user-mode virtual addresses, called user space, and another 2GB range contains kernel-mode virtual addresses, called kernel space, which is shared among all processes. The 2GB of user-mode virtual addresses are not accessible by other processes in the server (unless you are employing interprocess communication) while the kernel-mode addresses are dedicated to operating system activities, which are shared among all processes running on the system. These operating system activities include kernel mode actions requested by the processes.

Why is this important? Unless you always have 4GB of RAM in the system, Windows 2000 must map this 4GB data space into a nonexistent physical RAM space that is referred to as virtual memory. The process thinks it has access to a full 2GB of physical memory even when that much RAM may not be physically available. When physical memory is no longer available, the VMM uses Windows 2000's pagefile. If the pagefile is too small or is not configured to grow as needed, then the process is not able to proceed.

What happens if you have an application that would run better if it had a 3GB/1GB split? This is possible by tuning Windows 2000. Edit the boot.ini file and add the /3GB parameter to the startup line switch to take advantage of this alternate memory management strategy. An example boot.ini file would read: [boot loader] timeout=30 default=multi(0)disk(0)rdisk(0)partition(1)\WINNT Multi(0)disk(0)rdisk(0)partition(1)\WINNT="Microsoft Windows 2000 Advanced Server" /fastdetect /3GB.

With this option enabled, 3GB of memory is reserved for applications and up to 1GB for Windows 2000 operating system functions. This enables applications to capitalize on the merits of using more RAM to avoid disk activities, which allows Windows 2000 to reach higher performance levels.

Of course, the application must first be "3GB/1GB Aware" so that it is capable of taking advantage of the additional memory space. Once properly tuned (this is completed in the application source code), the extra memory spaces that the application takes advantage of can result in much higher levels of performance. There are always trade-offs. For this increased performance level, you incur the risk of losing more data if the system were to crash for any number of reasons. Today's system technology has numerous high availability features and clustering technologies, so this risk can be minimized by using a sound architecture. In effect, this potential data loss trade-off is offset by another trade-off—cost. In a clustered environment, a minimum of two servers are required; thus, you can have high performance and high availability. Of course, there are other trade-offs always lurking out there somewhere.

Windows 2000 Pagefile

The pagefile is an area on the disk subsystem where memory pages are placed when there is not enough available physical memory (RAM). You can see the actual pagefile area on the disk drive by enabling the Windows 2000 Explorer application (Start / Programs / Accessories / Explorer) to view hidden files under Tools / folder options and then select the show all files option. The actual pagefile shown under Explorer is named: pagefile.sys. The pagefile.sys is sometimes referred to as the physical (non-RAM) portion of virtual memory. The VMM begins paging data to the pagefile when a process requests more physical memory than is currently available on the system; that is, all of the physical memory is already allocated to other processes. To make room in physical memory, the VMM cuts down or trims the working set of other processes whose pages have not recently been referenced. When a process's working set is trimmed, VMM pages the trimmed process's memory information onto the pagefile. (Actually it is moved to a free list and, if it is needed and the page state requires to be saved, it is moved to the pagefile. For our purposes it is more important to understand the general concept.) Thus, in the future, if the process that was trimmed needs its data back, the VMM can page the copy of the process's data back into physical memory from the pagefile.

Windows 2000 configures the pagefile when you initially install the operating system and is capable of supporting 16 different pagefiles. The default size of the pagefile is physical memory + 12MB. The pagefile is then placed on the root disk drive (the drive where %SystemRoot% lives); typically the C: drive. For smaller systems that do not page often and do not have particularly heavy loads placed on them with respect to their capacity, this strategy is adequate. What happens if a process needs more virtual memory than the pagefile is configured for, or if the pagefile is heavily used? Depending on the pagefile configuration, it will grow or increase the size of the pagefile as needed to meet the system's demands. We review tuning memory resources later in this chapter, which will reveal why growing the pagefile as needed is not a good virtual memory management strategy and should be avoided.

Pagefile Size Limits Virtual Memory Available to Process

When a process requests code or data, it is paged into physical memory from the disk subsystem. At that time, the VMM reserves space for that page in the pagefile residing on a physical disk drive(s) just in case the page of data needs to be paged out of memory. This does not mean that the pagefile is used; an area of it is just reserved for its possible future use. Physical memory under Windows 2000 needs to be backed by the pagefile; thus, the size of the pagefile limits the amount of data that can be stored in memory. *This is important to remember!*

Even though the dedicated, theoretical virtual memory space available to a process by default is 2GB, in reality the virtual memory available to the process is limited to the maximum size of pagefile that is configured. This is true for the other sharable 2GB of virtual memory reserved for the Windows 2000 operating system operations also. When a process requests memory that is beyond what the VMM can actually map to the pagefile, a virtual memory conflict occurs. This results in an error code being returned to the application. If you wish to use that 2GB of physical memory you purchased for your system, ensure that a pagefile is created that is, at a minimum, the same size as physical RAM. Smaller pagefile configurations will cause you to lose out on your investment—you won't be able to use that RAM! By default, I strongly recommend creating a pagefile twice the size of physical memory, at a minimum.

You can observe the current memory limit on your Windows 2000 system by looking at Sysmon's memory object commit limit counter. Sysmon defines the commit limit as "the amount of virtual memory that can be committed without having to extend the paging file(s). It is measured in bytes. (Committed memory is physical memory for which space has been reserved on the disk paging files. There can be one paging file on each logical drive.) If the paging file(s) are be expanded, this limit increases accordingly."

Different Versions of Windows 2000 Equal Different Memory Management Details

In general, the manner in which Windows 2000 manages the memory subsystem is the same across its different versions. However, each version of

Windows 2000 supports different amounts of physical memory, and each version's default optimizations are slightly different based on its target operational function. The most obvious differences in memory resource management between the different versions of Windows 2000 are outlined in Table 5.3.

TABLE 5.3	Windows 2000 Family Memory Options		
Edition	**Default Memory Usage Strategy (Properties | LAN Adapter | Properties | File and Print Sharing)**	**Physical Memory Supported**	**Target Environment & *Quantum Allotment* (Control Panel | Advanced | Application Response Time Optimized For....)**
Windows 2000 Professional	Maximum Throughput for File Sharing	4GB	Desktop Operating System *Application Response Time optimized for: Applications*
Windows 2000 Server	Maximum Throughput for File Sharing	4GB	Server Operating System *Application Response Time optimized for: Background Services*
Windows 2000 Advanced Server (Application Terminal Services Activated)	Maximum Throughput for Network Applications	8GB	Server and Application Terminal Services Operating System *Application Response Time optimized for: Applications*
Windows 2000 Data Center Server	Maximum Throughput for Network Applications (Estimated)	64GB	Server and Application Terminal Services Operating System *Application Response Time optimized for: Applications*

Beyond the 4GB RAM Limit: PAE and AWE

How is it possible that different versions of Windows 2000 support different amounts of physical memory? In the beginning of this chapter, it was stated that Windows 2000 is a 32-bit operating system, which limits the amount of addressable RAM to 2^{32}. We need some more bits somewhere. It would have been nice if a 64-bit chip was available that Windows 2000 was commercially available to run on, but with the support for the 64-bit Compaq (DEC) Alpha dropped, there is no immediately available 64-bit CPU. The Intel Itanium is estimated to be available later in 2000 or early 2001. To improve scalability, Intel provided the Physical Address Extension (PAE) to its 32-bit CPU line since introducing the Pentium Pro architecture. PAE increases the memory support to 36 bits of memory address access. Thirty-six bits provides 68,719,476,736 (68GB) of addressable space. Room to grow—for a while at least!

Windows 2000 takes advantage of the PAE extensions itself (as can be seen in Table 5.3) and provides a mechanism for applications to take advantage of the PAE extensions through its own set of application programming interfaces (APIs) associated with its Advanced Windowing Extensions (AWE). Using these APIs, developers can make their applications PAE aware and improve their scalability by using more RAM. Primarily, the AWE provides a window mapping into the physical memory addresses above 4GB. The real challenge is finding applications that take advantage of this PAE and AWE combination. I envision that few, very high-end applications will take advantage of this new technology, because 64-bit editions of Windows 2000 and support system architectures are not that far away and demand for Very Large Memory (VLM) has not yet reached a high volume status (yet). Thus many are focusing on the 64-bit environment, which supports a traditional flat memory model and provides a stronger long-term strategy for applications developers.

Windows 2000 File System Cache

Windows 2000 uses file system caching to improve I/O subsystem performance. So why include this information in the chapter on memory performance? The file system cache uses the same physical memory that applications would like to use. Understanding how the file system cache operates and why will enable you to improve the overall scalability of your system, tune the file system to optimize your system, and provide additional insight into sizing Windows 2000 solutions.

What is the file system cache? Windows 2000 dynamically allocates an area of physical memory to cache data written and read from the I/O subsystem. The area in the virtual memory hierarchy where the VMM places the file system cache used by the cache manager (CM) is in the upper 2GB or kernel accessed memory area that is shared among all processes. In this manner, all processes have access to the file system cache. The goal of the file system cache is to lower the number of times that the physical devices attached to the server's I/O subsystem must be accessed. By lowering the number of times that the physical subsystem must be accessed, less time is required to obtain the requested data and overall system performance is greatly improved.

How the File System Cache Is Implemented

When a process requests data from the disk subsystem, the I/O Manager works in conjunction with the CM to obtain the requested data. The file system cache is beneficial for both read- and write-intensive environments. When the I/O manager requests that data files are to be written to (or read from) the disk subsystem, the CM steps in. Once the CM has control of the data, it informs the process that the disk request is complete, even though it is in cache, not the disk, but eventually will get written to the disk subsystem via the lazy write mechanism. This approach to caching data is referred to as "write-back cache." The CM groups the modified data in its cache before actually writing it to the disk subsystem at a later time. This second cache strategy is referred to as a "lazy write." The combination of write-back cache and lazy-write processes provides improved responsiveness to the application and subsequently to the end users, since they do not have to wait for the data to be physically written to disk, which is a very slow physical process when compared to RAM access. This lazy write activity varies slightly with the configuration and version of Windows 2000 you are using, but in general occurs once per minute, flushing 1/8 of its cache contents that require disk submission. You can monitor the lazy writer in action by viewing Sysmon Cache: Lazy Write Flushes/sec. Grouping disk writes in cache means that when the CM does write the data to the disk subsystem via the lazy write mechanism, it is written in larger chunks. In this manner, the disk I/O is more efficient and there is a better chance that the data will be written to disk in a contiguous fashion. This technique of grouping data into larger chunks before writing it to disk is sometimes referred to as "spatial locality."

The manner that Windows 2000 manages the file system cache is one of the reasons that you do not want to just power off a Windows 2000–based system instead of using the shutdown command. When you use the shutdown command, all cache data is flushed to the disk subsystem. As an administrator you can force the cache contents to flush by using the *sync.exe* freeware application from http://www.sysinternals.com. This is very similar to the sync command found in UNIX and Linux.

Application Level Control of Cache Manager Operations

For some environments, applications manage caching of their own data and prefer that the file system cache does not get involved. This occurs in applications such as Oracle Databases, Microsoft's SQL Server, and Microsoft Exchange to name a few. There are several methods application developers use to avoid file system cache intervention. One method is to use mapped files and another is to specify the FILE_FLAG_NO_BUFFERING parameter. This is not a flag set in the registry, but a flag that the application sets when requesting I/O operations of Windows 2000 Server's I/O Manager. More information on the application developer options is available at the Microsoft web site (http://www.Microsoft.com) in their Software Developer Kits, Driver Development Kits, and Installable File System Kit.

The important point to note here is that you should be aware of which applications do and do not use Windows 2000's dynamic file system cache, as it will influence how you tune your system. For example, SQL Server 7/ SQL Server 2000 enables administrators to directly control how much memory it uses. This is an important fact to know if you are looking to optimize your solution! For example, perhaps you are running a custom application and SQL 7 and you have only 768MB of RAM. Since both applications will want their own memory space and the customer application will use the file system cache, you could configure SQL 7 to use only 256MB of RAM leaving the remaining RAM to the custom application, file system cache, and other operating system functions.

File System Cache in a Read-Intensive Disk I/O Environment

When the CM's predictive algorithm detects sequential reading characteristics occurring, it employs the same read-ahead cache strategy that the VMM employs when working with the pagefile. When a process requests data from the disk subsystem, additional data is then obtained above and beyond what was originally requested by the process. The next few bytes are read from the disk subsystem and placed into the file system cache. When this strategy is effective, it provides significant performance advantages to the system, since processes' data requests are filed in memory (soft page fault) versus the disk subsystem (hard page fault). If other processes are not making memory requests, the file system cache's working set can grow to use a large amount of memory; this is outlined in the next section, Sizing of the File System Cache. A disk subsystem that is defragmented on a regular basis (i.e., groups data contiguously on the disk subsystem) also helps to improve file system cache effectiveness.

Sizing of the File System Cache

How big can the file system cache grow? Understanding how large the file system cache can grow greatly influences how you size your memory subsystem. The size that the file system cache can grow is directly related to the amount of physical memory in the system and how the system is tuned. Table 5.4 shows the minimum and maximum file system cache sizes. (The information in Table 5.4 is adapted from *Windows 2000 Internals.*)

TABLE 5.4   *File System Cache Size Limits*

Amount of Physical RAM in System	Minimum/Maximum File System Cache Size
2GB or greater	64-960MB
1GB	64-432MB
1GB with Application Terminal Services	64-448MB

Table 5.4 takes into account only file system cache memory requirements. Consider a scenario where you have 20 disk-intensive applications, each application (process) requires 50MB of physical RAM to run well (its

working set) and relies on the file system cache (default application behavior), and you want the maximum performance possible for your system. To size the memory resources for such a system, you would allocate memory for:

- 1000MB: Applications (50MB/Application * 20 Applications)
- 960MB: Maximum Size of File System Cache (from chart above)
- 128MB: Windows 2000 Server (this value will vary based on services running in background)
- 5MB: Server Management Agent
- 5MB: Security Management Agent (Intrusion Detection)
- 2162MB: Total

Note that in an actual system, the system motherboard would dictate the specific memory configuration supported, typically in 256MB or 512MB chunks, so this total would need to be rounded up.

Investigating the File System Cache Behavior

This sizing information looks interesting, but is this actually realistic? To investigate the file system cache behavior in a variety of environments, we used the Nelson Business Benchmark Suite for Windows 2000. Neal Nelson and Associates commercially produce this benchmark suite. Unfortunately, the company's web site is not available to the general public; however, the company is based in Chicago and can be reached at 312-755-1000. The Business Benchmark provides a suite of 30 tests for exercising either Windows 2000 or UNIX servers. Each test measures a different area of Windows 2000 performance ranging from a simulated database environment to specific, disk subsystem stress tests. Each test is run under increased workload levels to a published maximum of 50. To specifically illustrate the merits and pitfalls of Windows 2000's file system cache we selected "Test 18: 1024-byte Sequential Reads from Windows 2000 Files" to exercise the server up to a load level of 20 copies. This 20-copy load level equates to approximately 400 light users.

The first stress test was run on a Compaq 6400R configured with Windows 2000 Server, two Pentium III XEON 550MHz CPUs, three Ultra-Fast/Wide SCSI-2 10,000rpm Disk Drives in a RAID 5 array (Windows 2000 and pagefile were on two other separate disks), and 256MB of RAM. The second stress test was run with 2GB of RAM in the system. As each workload level test is run from 1 to 20, as reported by the benchmark, larger and larger working set files are used by the benchmark. Figure 5-1 shows the throughput levels achieved.

First, let's review the benchmark results with 256MB of RAM configured. When under light loads, throughput levels to this three-disk RAID 5 subsystem ramped up to 120MB/sec! This is fantastic! A three-disk RAID 5 configuration that provides this level of performance is very impressive. Not quite! To help understand what is happening during this test, review Figure 5-2, which is the Sysmon chart generated from the Sysmon logs collected during this test.

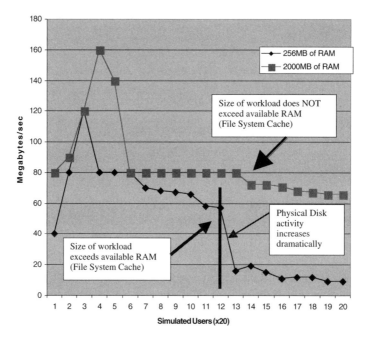

FIGURE 5-1 *Windows 2000 File System Cache Benchmark Results*

In this 256MB RAM test (Figure 5-1), performance is fantastic up until load factor 12. The disk subsystem is getting 60–120MB/sec of throughput! At load factor 12, the benchmark began to use a work file with a size greater than the server allowed the file system cache to grow to (117MB of 256MB in this configuration). At load level 11, the work file size is 130MB and continues to increase; thus the file system cache becomes less and less effective in caching the requested data. By the time the benchmark reaches load level 13, which uses a work file size of 250MB, Windows 2000's file system cache is well defeated since the work file is much bigger than the file system cache can grow (it stopped growing in this test at 117MB of cache) while physical reads from the actual disk drives have increased to support the workload.

The physical disk activity shown in Figure 5-2 is via the Transfers/sec counter. Under the heaviest loads, performance suddenly drops to 9MB/sec of throughput, which is about 3MB/sec per drive in the array. Achieving 3MB/sec per disk drive in a RAID 5 array while under a read intensive, multiuser workload is actually quite good (more on this in chapter 6). Note that even with the disk subsystem running well, as the workload increased the response time from the disk drives themselves dramatically increased as shown with the Avg. Sec/Transfer counter.

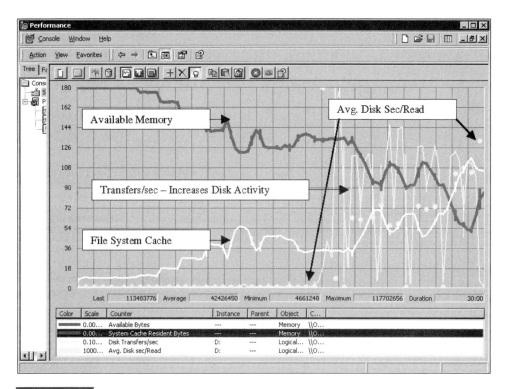

FIGURE 5-2   *More Data Than File System Cache*

Looking at the Sysmon results in Figure 5-2, the following two key memory counters from the Memory object are shown to characterize the memory subsystem—Available Bytes and Cache Bytes. Windows 2000's Sysmon defines the Cache Bytes counter as "the sum of the System Cache Resident Bytes, System Driver Resident Bytes, System Code Resident Bytes, and Pool Paged Resident Bytes counters. This counter displays the last observed value only; it is not an average." Available bytes is defined as " . . . the amount of physical memory available to processes running on the computer, in bytes. It is calculated by summing space on the Zeroed, Free, and Stand by memory lists. Free memory is ready for use; Zeroed memory is pages of memory filled with zeros to prevent later processes from seeing data used by a previous process. Standby memory is memory removed from a process' working set (its physical memory) on route to disk, but is still available to be recalled. This counter displays the last observed value only; it is not an average."

When reviewing Figure 5-2, it is important to observe that Windows 2000 committed a significant amount of memory to the file system cache. You can observe how the file system cache (Cache Bytes) dynamically grows as the load generated by the benchmark increases. Do not get discouraged; this

252 Chapter 5 ● **Windows 2000 and Memory Performance**

is what the file system cache is supposed to do! The file system cache grows so that it can cache more and more of the disk I/O activity. Also, not shown as obviously in Figure 5-2 but reflected in the benchmark results, the server's performance degraded as the load increased because the server ran out of file system cache to use, so more physical disk activity was required to meet the workload demands. Even with this overwhelming workload (by design), Windows 2000 did not force itself into paging, based on file system cache demands. This is important to note. Windows 2000 has improved its memory management over what it was in Windows NT. This is the biggest difference I found during testing, that Windows 2000 did not overcommit itself based on file system cache requirements, regardless of the memory management strategy that Windows 2000 is tuned to.

Under the lighter loads—less than load level 12—the file system cache directly contributed to great disk subsystem performance as it dynamically increased its size to meet requested tasks and it ramped up very quickly to meet the workload demands. But, as the workload increased, the file system cache became less and less effective. This illustrates the positive and negative influence that the file system cache can have. *Properly sized and tuned, the file system cache is a great ally.* On the negative side, if other applications are placed on a file server experiencing heavy workloads, their performance will suffer. To understand how to control the file system cache's behavior for your advantage, read on to this chapter's Windows 2000 Memory Strategies section.

The Effect of Adding More RAM for the File System Cache

What occurs when you introduce even more RAM into a disk-intensive environment like those reviewed above? From the tests it would appear that if the Windows 2000 system had additional physical memory, system performance could be greatly improved. Would Windows 2000 take advantage of more RAM and, if so, how much memory would help? During the above stress test, each of the 20 processes ran with a working set of 5MB and was accessing a read-intensive file that was more than 700MB in size at peak workload. To determine how much memory would actually be allotted to the file system cache if more memory were added, another test was run on a Compaq 8000 configured in the same manner but with 2GB of RAM. Figure 5-3 shows the Sysmon results of running the same benchmark but with 2GB of physical RAM configured.

So what is happening here? As this workload gradually increased, the available memory lowered (top line in graph) as the file system cache size increased (lower line in graph). Here, our file system cache was increased to 512MB, a significant amount of caching in this read-intensive test. Overall performance was dramatic. Under the heaviest workload, throughput was kept above 60MB/sec. Looking at these results from another perspective, it took 77 seconds (per user, based on a 400-user load) to complete the benchmark when using 256MB of RAM (117MB file system cache) while with 2GB, the

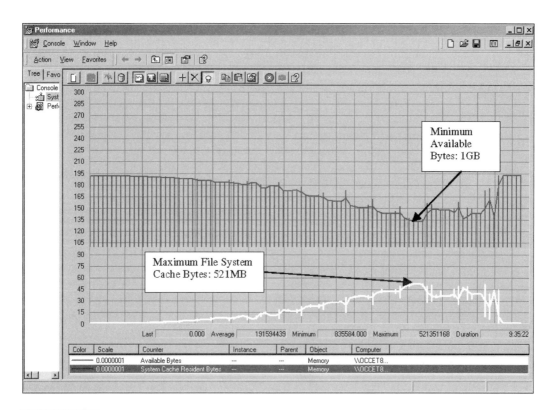

FIGURE 5-3   *Sizing the File System Cache Usage with a Disk-Intensive Workload*

benchmark completed in 11 sec (per user, based on a 400-user load)! Was it worth the investment in additional RAM? Always run tests that are indicative of your environment to answer these types of questions, but if your environment has a significant amount of read-intensive I/O to complete, the additional RAM would most likely be justified. Note, if a system was to be developed and the workload it would experience was indicative of these stress tests, we would have only added 1GB of RAM, not 2 for this particular workload. Of course, selecting only 1GB of RAM would limit our file system cache growth to 432MB (see Table 5.4 above) based on Windows 2000's design.

This is very important! If you purchased another 512MB of RAM for this system environment with the intent of improving file system cache (and overall file system performance), it would not help!

Remember, from Table 5.4 above, you need 2GB of physical RAM in the system to enable the file system cache to grow past 432MB to the full 960MB.

Now, do not think this information is for all Windows 2000 environments. To the contrary, this observation is only for this file-intensive environment (similar to that of a file server). If you had other memory-intensive tasks running on your system, the addition of 512MB RAM would be used by Windows 2000 for these other applications if they requested it.

Why wasn't more memory allotted to the file system cache in our 2GB test? Two reasons. The Windows 2000 memory management was tuned to favor the applications running (more below on this) and the characteristics of the workload itself. Note, a 4GB pagefile was used in this test.

This amount of additional RAM was added just to prove the point that configuring sufficient resources for Windows 2000 to take advantage of does result in significant overall performance improvements.

Question for experts: If another 1GB of RAM was added (for a total of 3GB) to the system, would the system run faster? (The answer is below in the memory sizing section of this chapter.)

Sysmon Counters Are Not Always What They Appear to Be

Sysmon counters are not always what they appear to be, so look closely at the definitions as you use them. When reviewing the Sysmon results above, you may notice that the Sysmon Memory: System Cache Resident Bytes counters were used. Why not the Memory: Cache bytes? Both are helpful counters if you understand what they are measuring. The System Cache Resident Bytes counter measures how much physical memory the file system cache is using. The Cache counter measures the same information as the System Cache Resident Bytes and more. The Memory: Cache counter also collects information on the System Driver Resident Bytes, System Code Resident Bytes, and Pool Paged Resident Bytes. This is important information, but more information than we were looking for. How much difference is there between these two counters? This difference is illustrated in Figure 5-4, which was extracted from another file system cache test.

Thrashing: Extreme Paging at Its Worst

What happens if application requirements, file system cache, and operating system requirements for memory overwhelm the available physical memory? The system will begin to page to fulfill memory requirements. What is wrong with paging? Nothing actually; it is part of normal Windows 2000 operations. The degree of paging is important, however, if you have any interest in performance. Paging can occur at increased levels on busy systems. If a process requests a page of data, and there is no physical memory for that page to be placed, the VMM will trim the working set of other processes to make room in physical memory for the new page of data. When this occurs, the least recently used data from processes' working sets is stolen (removed) from physical memory and sent (paged) to the pagefile. Later, if the process whose memory was stolen requires the data that is resident back on the pagefile, the VMM will page this data back into physical memory (this is one form of hard page fault).

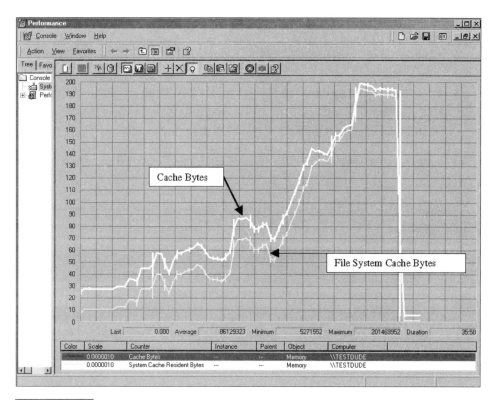

FIGURE 5–4   *File System Cache Size Reality Check: Cache Bytes vs. System Cache Resident Bytes*

A problem occurs when the VMM must move data back into physical memory for processes, and to accomplish this it must trim the working set of another process that will *soon* need that data again. Now when the other process turns around and requires its data back, which is in the pagefile again, the VMM must now trim the working set of another process to get the requested page back into physical memory. Having the VMM write data to the pagefile often is not that serious a condition. What is serious, though, is when the VMM must frequently read and write to and from the pagefile (hard page faults) to fulfill the requests of multiple processes or process threads, all clamoring for physical memory; then there is contention for physical memory.

When contention for physical memory occurs in the vicious circle described above, the VMM is trimming the working set of one process at a very high rate just to fulfill another process's memory requests. As this occurs, all of the system resources are placed under increased stress just to complete memory operations. More CPU cycles are needed to move the data into and out of memory (both physical and virtual), versus being used for productive work. The disk where the pagefile resides becomes active at ever higher rates.

This undesirable condition of memory contention is referred to as thrashing. This thrashing condition commonly clouds the detection of the real system bottleneck. Under the worst circumstances on a heavily loaded system, thrashing can make it appear that there is a disk or CPU bottleneck when in reality there is a memory bottleneck.

Windows 2000 Memory Strategies

How Windows 2000's file system cache interacts with other processes becomes very important when tuning your system. Windows 2000 enables you to influence how the memory subsystem is used. By wisely selecting Windows 2000's memory management strategy, you influence how much memory Windows 2000 uses for various processes' working sets in memory. Properly setting Windows 2000's memory strategy is the first step in avoiding

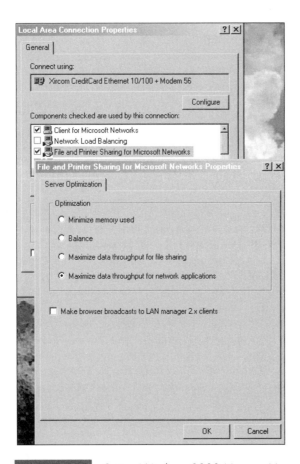

FIGURE 5–5   *Setting Windows 2000 Memory Management Options*

thrashing. For most multiuser enterprise environments, two options for tuning Windows 2000's memory strategy are of particular interest: (1) Maximize Data Throughput for File Sharing and (2) Maximize Data Throughput for Network Applications. (See Figure 5-5 and Table 5.5.) These options are chosen by selecting Start / Settings / Network and Dial-Up Settings / Local Area Connection / Properties / File and Printer Sharing for Microsoft Networks, then selecting the optimization level (memory management strategy). When you make your selection, the system will not request that a reboot is needed. This is not true. After several tests, it was determined that if the system's power was not cycled, the new memory management strategy does not go into full effect. What a fancy way to state, "reboot the computer."

When you make these memory management changes in the GUI interface, what actually occurs is that the registry is tuned. The following is the registry variable that is altered and what the associated possible values are:

```
HKEY_LOCAL_MACHINE/System/CurrentControlSet/Control/Session
Manager/Memory Management/LargeSystemCache
REG_DWORD
```

Table 5.5	*Windows 2000 Memory Management Tuning Options*
Value	**Definition**
0	Establishes a standard size file system cache of approximately 8MB. The system allows changed pages to remain in physical memory until the number of available pages drops to approximately 1,000 pages (4MB). This setting is recommended for servers running applications that do their own memory caching, such as Microsoft SQL Server, and for applications that perform best with ample memory, such as Internet Information Services. [GUI: Maximize Data Throughput for Network Applications] [The working sets of processes have higher priority for memory than the working set of the file system cache]
1	Establishes a large system cache working set that can expand to physical memory, minus 4 MB, if needed (depends on the amount of memory in the system). The system allows changed pages to remain in physical memory until the number of available pages drops to approximately 250 pages (1Mbyte). This setting is recommended for file servers running Windows 2000 Server. [GUI: Maximize Data Throughput for File Sharing option] [File system cache working set has a higher priority vs. other process' working sets]

We have covered quite a bit of ground on memory management. Table 5.6 shows the various effects of memory management tuning and how each version of the Windows 2000 family is configured by default (out of the box).

TABLE 5.6 *How Selecting the Memory Management Strategy Affects Different Versions of Windows 2000*

Windows 2000 Version	Default Memory Management	Effect on Working Set	Effect on File System Cache
Professional	Maximize data throughput for network applications	Favors processes over file system cache	Lazy Writer flushes file system cache more often to disk.
Server	Maximize data throughput for file sharing	Favors file system cache over processes	Enables file system cache to grow to its maximum (based on system resources)
Advanced Server	Maximize data throughput for network applications	Favors processes over file system cache	File system cache size is limited in growth if processes require more of the available RAM
Advanced Server with Terminal Services Activated	Maximize data throughput for file sharing	Favors file system cache over processes	Enables file system cache to grow to its maximum (based on system resources)

Maximize Data Throughput for File Sharing

When you select Maximize Data Throughput for File Sharing, Windows 2000 favors the working set of the file system cache over the other processes' working sets running on your system. This gives priority for space in memory to the file system cache. With this setting, if the VMM needs to trim a process's working set, it will select other processes before the file system cache process. Yes, the file system cache is similar to other processes in the fact it has a working set that can be controlled.

When using Maximize Throughput for File Sharing, Windows 2000 uses all available memory for the file system cache (dynamic disk buffer allocation). This option is good when you use your Windows 2000 system only as a file server or other application that exhibits file-server-like characteristics. Allocating a majority of memory for the file system cache generally enhances disk and network I/O performance. It is good to use Windows 2000's default Maximize Throughput for File Sharing setting when the server is a dedicated file server or has more than 2GB of physical RAM and its application does not use more than 1.2GB of RAM or when an application exhibits file-server-like characteristics and relies on the file system cache.

When Not to Use Maximize Throughput for File Sharing Memory Strategy

It is not advisable to select this option when you are running multiple memory intensive applications under Windows 2000. When you start a client/server application such as Microsoft SQL Server or another memory-intensive application, the server might begin to thrash. Remember that when Maximize Throughput for File Sharing memory strategy is in use, the VMM favors the file system cache over the other processes running on the system. Thus, if you are running processes that are demanding memory or which you have allocated memory to and the file system cache is demanding memory, somebody loses. This loss will be in your applications performance.

If the system you are fielding is under constant heavy loads and the memory subsystem is paging or thrashing, use one of the techniques outlined in this chapter's Tuning around Memory Bottlenecks section to remove the memory bottleneck. If you are unable to tune around the memory bottleneck, consider changing the memory strategy. When a high load on the system is characterized by heavy I/O subsystem use, the file system cache growing to use a majority of the system memory actually becomes a hindrance. When all of the memory in the system is used, the system will potentially begin to heavily page. When this occurs, the paging activity loads outweigh the benefits of the file system cache. To avoid allowing the file system cache to use all of the system's memory in this environment, it is better to use the Maximize Data Throughput for Network Applications memory strategy.

When to Use Maximize Data Throughput for Network Applications

The second primary option for tuning Windows 2000's memory strategy is Maximize Data Throughput for Network Applications. When you select this option, Windows 2000 allocates less RAM for the file system cache so that running applications can have access to more RAM. Windows 2000 thus favors the working set of all processes over that of file system cache process. When this memory strategy option is selected, application memory tuning becomes much more important. When you configure applications such as SQL Server or Microsoft Exchange, you can tune them to use specified amounts of RAM for areas such as buffers for disk operations and database caches.

Comparing Windows 2000 Memory Management Strategies

One way to illustrate the importance of selecting the correct Windows 2000 memory strategy is to run a specific workload on a server using the Maximize Data Throughput for Network Applications. Then, run that same workload on the exact server configuration, but change the memory strategy to Maximize Throughput for File Sharing. This illustration was accomplished by using Neal Nelson and Associate's Business Benchmark (NNBBM) Simulated Database Test. This stress test was run to a workload level (copy level) of 20. As the test is run, each workload level places an increasing amount of stress onto the server. At load level 1, 10 users are simulated; at load level 2, 20 users are simulated; and so on up to a selected maximum of 20 copies or 400 users. At each workload level, the average amount of time required to complete the database task by all users is recorded in seconds. Since this is a timed test, the lower the reported results, the better. The stress test results are shown in Figure 5-6.

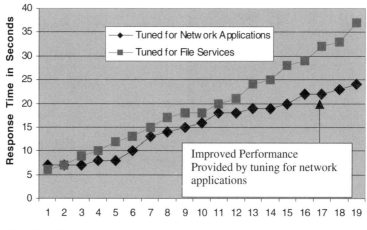

FIGURE 5-6   *Windows 2000 Memory Strategy Comparison (Note: Lower values on this NNBBM Database Windows 2000 Memory Strategy Comparison indicate better performance.)*

In Figure 5-6 we observe that under lighter loads (less than workload level 13), there is not a great performance difference between the two memory management strategies. But as the workload increases past workload level 14, the performance difference becomes greater and greater. In fact, starting at workload level 14, the difference in the server's response times between the server's memory management strategy tests increases from 120% to over 150%! By choosing the incorrect memory strategy, you may not notice a problem at first. But, when the server is under heavier loads, the difference will become apparent and the end users will think that the server has died and should be sent to the junkyard of poor performing servers.

The primary reason for the poor performance results of the Maximize Data Throughput for File Sharing memory strategy under this database-intensive heavy load was the fact that the file system cache consumed so much of the server's memory that the database users were subsequently starved for memory (not quite starved, but definitely underfed). This imbalance of memory did not result in thrashing, but with the VMM favoring the file system cache, it was the database users' work sets that were targeted for paging to disk.

QUANTIFYING THE ACTUAL MEMORY DIFFERENCES IN MEMORY MANAGEMENT OPTIONS

In the above test, we quantified the difference in memory performance management strategies by performance results achieved running a synthetic benchmark. But what was the underlying difference in memory management between the two tests? Figures 5-7 and 5-8 show how the two strategies fared.

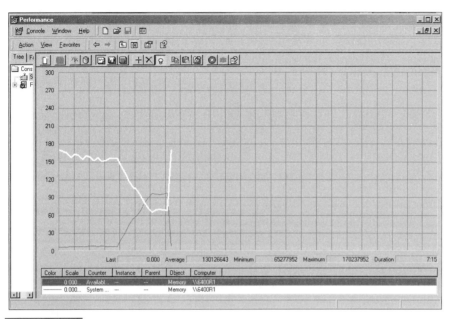

FIGURE 5–7   *Optimizing Windows 2000 Memory Management for File-Based Applications [Same Workload]*

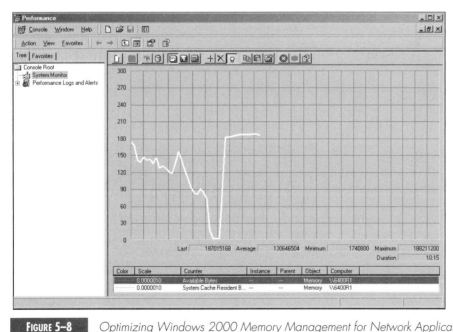

FIGURE 5–8   *Optimizing Windows 2000 Memory Management for Network Applications [Same Workload]*

Both tests were run with the same workload. When using the Maximize Data Throughput for Network Applications, the server favored the database processes running on the server and allotted additional memory for them as needed. This resulted in improved overall performance and leveraging of the system's resources.

Understanding Your Environment Equals Performance

You no doubt are picking up on one of this book's themes that will be repeated several more times. Knowing what is running on your system is particularly important when tuning applications' memory settings. If you allocate too much memory for each application in a multiapplication environment, there will be contention for physical memory. When this happens, the system will thrash and you will end up with one slow system!

To properly tune an application's memory usage requires a good understanding of the application in use. Never underestimate the power of an expert or hesitate to develop a relationship with a consultant who dedicates him- or herself to a specific environment. Consultants who specialize in improving the performance of specific application/database can easily earn their keep during a short-term engagement designed to improve the performance of your Windows 2000 application-specific solution. Whenever using outside consultants, use the opportunity to work with them to learn how they are tuning the system. They may improve performance by making better use of the system's memory, optimizing database design, optimizing the queries, or other factors that can improve the overall system's performance for the particular application environment you are working in.

Sizing the Memory Subsystem

Over time it is inevitable that Windows 2000 and applications need more and more memory. When is the last time you heard a vendor mention that the new software product uses half of the RAM that the previous version did? The good news is that the price of RAM has continually fallen over the last several years. (Sure, there have been a few bumps along the way, but in general the price per megabyte has fallen over the years.) With this in mind and the performance degradation that occurs when there is an insufficient amount of RAM in the system, why not just stock every server to the max? Well, memory is not that cheap yet.

Sizing the amount of memory required is directly related to the type of workload in the current and projected environments. Memory resources are a shared resource. A shared resource is one that cannot be physically separated (unless using multiple systems), such as providing one disk drive for one application and a physically different second drive for another application. For example, if you have 10 processes running on your Windows 2000 system, all of these processes share the same physical memory. This concept of shared memory resources is illustrated in the memory resource section of Figure 5-9.

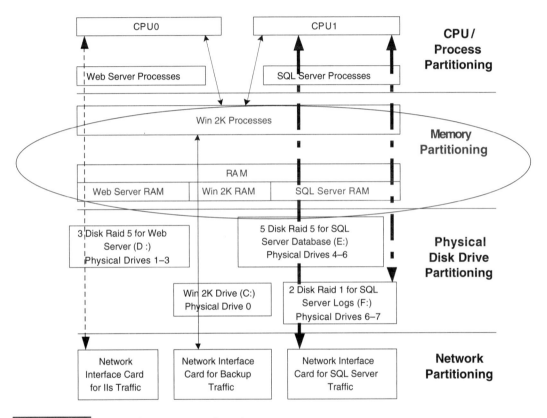

FIGURE 5-9   *Physical Memory—A Shared Resource*

Some of the more advanced applications (such as SQL, IIs, Oracle, etc.) enable you to control how much of the shared memory resources they have access to through their own configuration, which greatly aids in both sizing and tuning. Current versions of Windows 2000 do not enable you to control how much memory each application or process running on your system has access to, although its memory management algorithms are well optimized. Perhaps Windows 2000 Data Center or a third party will provide an administrator level tool that enables process/application level memory control.

When sizing the memory subsystem, follow the Core Sizing Methodology from chapter 3 so that key facets surrounding your solution are taken into consideration. The size of the memory subsystem directly relates to the performance levels that you wish to achieve.

The best performing Windows 2000 solutions I have encountered are configured to avoid *any* paging during regular workload periods and cache as much data as possible!

By avoiding paging as much as possible the system provides the maximum level of performance. It keeps the CPUs fed and avoids unnecessary disk activity by caching as much data as possible. Also remember to follow the Core Tuning Methodology after fielding your solution. Then, if the workload in your environment changes, you can tune around any system bottlenecks to avoid paging before there are any real performance problems. When sizing the memory subsystem, you want to achieve the following:

- Maximum performance
- Cache as much data as possible
- Avoid paging on a regular basis
- Minimum RAM required to meet performance goals
- Highest density RAM modules that enable system growth options (this avoids throwing RAM away when memory requirements increase)

Use Historical Performance Information Whenever Possible

Historical information is the best place to start when sizing the memory subsystem. If you are going to deploy a system in your department to support 200 users running a 50GB SQL database, find out if another department has implemented a similar solution. If they have, observe how their systems work with their applications to determine if response times are adequate for your environment. Also, ask to review their performance logs to determine how much memory is normally being used and how much, if any, paging is occurring. Use the information you obtain to size your memory subsystem.

Windows 2000's Sysmon tool provides insight into how each process is behaving on your system, which is crucial information when trying to determine how much memory is required for your new system. By understanding the memory characteristics and behavior of processes running under load, you can extrapolate from this information for your own system. Table 5.7 outlines the key Sysmon counters you should review for that similar system when sizing your memory subsystem.

Memory Sizing Step by Step

Vendors try their best to provide realistic information on memory requirements for systems that run their software applications. Keep in mind that they are trying to sell their product as well; thus their estimates for server resources tend to be on the skinny side to say the least—no need to scare off a potential

TABLE 5.7   *Key Sysmon Counters to Track When Sizing Windows 2000's Memory Subsystem*

Object/Counter	Definition	Use for Sizing the Memory Subsystem
Memory: Available Bytes	Available Bytes is the amount of physical memory available to processes running on the system, in bytes.	The amount of memory used by the current system is your starting point. From here, you can determine if you need more or less based on your projected workload and the data you obtain during the sizing process. When available memory runs low (<4MB), the system may page, which is something you want to avoid as much as possible. Depending on your needs and budget, try to keep at least 64MB (or 5%) of your memory subsystem in reserve for workload surges. Note: for eCommerce systems you want to plan for the worst-case scenario of memory usage and then add an extra 5%.
Memory: Cache Bytes	Cache Bytes is the sum of the System Cache Resident Bytes, System Driver Resident Bytes, System Code Resident Bytes, and Pool Paged Resident Bytes counters.	This counter provides insight into how much of your physical RAM Windows 2000 is using for its dynamic disk cache and pooled memory areas. This value will be used in your memory sizing calculations
Paging File: %Usage	The amount of the pagefile instance in use in percent.	Some applications require large amounts of virtual memory to be mapped even though it is not used. Track pagefile usage so that it is set large enough to accommodate your applications.
Memory: Commit Limit	Commit Limit is the amount of virtual memory that can be committed without having to extend the paging file(s).	This counter provides insight into whether the pagefile is properly configured. If a pagefile is too small, it can limit the amount of physical RAM you can access.
Process: Track all process instances you plan to place on your new system	Pagefile Bytes Peak	Tracking how much of the pagefile is in use can help determine overall pagefile requirements. Pagefile Bytes Peak is the maximum number of bytes this process has used in the paging file(s). Paging files are used to store pages of memory used by the process that are not contained in other files. Paging files are shared by all processes, and lack of space in paging files can prevent other processes from allocating memory.
	Virtual Bytes Peak	Track how much virtual bytes are in use so you can help determine overall memory requirements. Virtual Bytes Peak is the maximum number of bytes of virtual address space the process has used at any one time. Use of virtual address space does not necessarily imply corresponding use of either disk or main memory pages. Virtual space is however finite, and by using too much, the process might limit its ability to load libraries.

TABLE 5.7	*Key Sysmon Counters to Track When Sizing Windows 2000's Memory Subsystem (Continued)*	
Object/Counter	**Definition**	**Use for Sizing the Memory Subsystem**
	Working Set Peak	The working set counter is very important to track. It shows you how much physical memory the process has needed at any one time. As a minimum, configure your memory to ensure that this much physical memory is available for this process. Working Set Peak is the maximum number of bytes in the working set of this process at any point in time. The working set is the set of memory pages touched recently by the threads in the process. If free memory in the computer is above a threshold, pages are left in the working set of a process even if they are not in use. When free memory falls below a threshold, pages are trimmed from working sets. If they are needed they will then be soft-faulted back into the working set before they leave main memory.

customer. They also do not know your environment as well as you do, so mileage will vary. For a good starting point when sizing the memory resources for any solution, ensure you take into consideration the following:

- All applications that the system is running (obtain this information based on Table 5.7)
- Windows 2000's requirement (obtain this information based on Table 5.7)
- Wink's file system cache usage (obtain this information based on Table 5.7)
- The number of concurrent users the system is supporting (business requirements driven)
- The amount of server resources configured (CPU, disk, network, etc.)

As stated earlier, sizing memory subsystems is an additive process (okay, so there are some shared structures and libraries, but let's not get too picky here; sizing and tuning is part art). If you are running two database instances, and each instance requires 64MB of RAM, then configure for 128MB of RAM to avoid any memory contention. Understanding what is going to run on your system is always important. Add up the maximum requirements for each application and then add in the memory needed for Windows 2000's file system cache. If the application will be part of an interactive clieWindows 2000 solution, add the amount of memory that is estimated to be required for each user.

For example, for many database environments it is typical to configure 0.250MB of RAM per concurrent user connection. Thus, for 100 concurrent users, add an additional 25MB of RAM to the system configuration. If you are conservative and want better performance, consider 0.5MB per user. If you think the disk I/O subsystem will provide a high enough performance level for your solution, configure 0.125MB per concurrent user. Although 0.250MB is a good rule of thumb, always contact the vendor that is supplying the database for recommendations. Vendors will be vendors—they want the sale—so beware of anyone who claims a particularly low per-user RAM recommendation. You may want to consider speaking to some of their current customers and see what configuration they are using for their solution. Again, refer back to historical baselines and information

Determining a Good Memory Size Starting Point

To get a good initial memory configuration, sum the vendor recommendations for all of the areas outlined above. For example, if you were implementing a server to support both a database and web server application for 60 *concurrent* database users (this implies there may be more web users connected, but of those connected web users, 60 are accessing the data too via the web server):

- All applications that the server is running
  Database Application—256MB
  Web Server—128MB
- Windows 2000 Server Requirement
  128MB
- Wink's file system cache usage
  128MB
  Note: The database is tuned to limit its memory use to 256MB and the web server is tuned to grow its memory use to 128MB and use the file system cache.
- The number of concurrent users the server is supporting
  60 × 0.250KB of RAM for each connection

Summing these metrics together suggests a starting memory size for the server of 655MB—not quite a power of two, so it is time to make a decision. Most hardware vendors will support 512MB, 768MB, or 1GB increments. If you have the budget, 768MB is the safest and most cost effective for this solution. From here—either through stress testing or proactive management of the solution in a real-world environment—you will determine how much additional tuning or resources your solution will need.

Memory Configuration Considerations

If you wish to consider an alternate view of sizing a server's memory, check out the Server Memory Assessment Engine. This is an online tool from Kingston Technology located at http:\\www.kingston.com\servermap\. This online tool walks you through a questionnaire with a goal of making a memory sizing recommendation at the end. It is a helpful tool for a second or third opinion, but as before, keep in mind that Kingston is a company that specializes in selling RAM. Do not be surprised by the results. Review chapter 3, Capacity Sizing, for techniques to determine if your system configuration will really meet your objectives.

At a minimum, regardless of the application environment, consider Table 5.8's CPU/Memory ratios when configuring your server's memory for Pentium III class CPUs and above.

TABLE 5.8	*CPU to RAM Minimum Ratios*

Number of CPUs	Minimum Amount of RAM (MB)
1	256
2	512
4	1024 (1GB)
6	1536 (1.5GB)
8	2048 (2GB)

Following the values shown in Table 5.8 will help ensure that the CPUs are kept properly fed. This information is based on personal experience and industry observations.

Benchmark Extrapolations and Server Guidelines

Extrapolating benchmarks from systems similar to yours is also a good technique for initially sizing your memory subsystem. This technique was used in the Web Server Case Study example in chapter 8. The memory subsystems for most systems have some sort of memory guidelines. So do not be too concerned with getting the number of megabytes down to a perfect science. If you determine that 120.5MB are required, the server configuration guidelines will require a 128MB minimum configuration.

I do not want to trivialize sizing the memory subsystem. It is always better to have a little more memory than needed, within reason. By properly sizing the memory subsystem, you avoid placing more memory in the server than required, which is wasteful and costly. Saving just 128MB of RAM per server in a large Windows 2000 rollout could result in a significant overall savings. Stress testing your final solution, outlined in Step 9 of the Core Sizing Methodology, is the best way to ensure that you have developed a solid solution that will meet your goals.

Sizing the Pagefile

Sizing the pagefile is an important consideration in the design of your overall solution. This important topic is discussed in depth in the Virtual Memory Optimization and Sizing the pagefile sections later in this chapter.

Detecting Memory Bottlenecks

Recall from chapter 2 that it is important to consider the entire system performance picture when trying to locate a Windows 2000 system bottleneck. There can be more than one system resource area contributing to the throttling of the system's overall performance. Once all of the major system resource areas are evaluated, focus in on the resource that is farthest to the left in the Performance Resource Chart introduced in chapter 2 and repeated here as Figure 5-10 for reference. This strategy will provide the greatest immediate gain to the system's overall performance. For this discussion, all other (besides memory) system resources have already been investigated and determined not to be a bottleneck. Remember to revisit the Performance Resource Chart after tuning around a memory bottleneck. Once one system resource is removed as the bottleneck, others may take its place, which will subsequently influence where you focus additional tuning efforts.

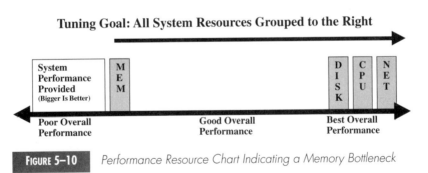

Tuning Goal: All System Resources Grouped to the Right

System Performance Provided (Bigger Is Better)	MEM

Poor Overall Performance   Good Overall Performance   Best Overall Performance

FIGURE 5–10 *Performance Resource Chart Indicating a Memory Bottleneck*

Unless you jumped right to this section of the book, it should be apparent to you when Windows 2000 is experiencing a memory bottleneck. In general, if all the physical memory resources are in use, as shown under Sysmon's memory object's available bytes counters and the system has begun paging the trimmed working set of processes to the pagefile, then Windows 2000 is becoming short on memory resources. How low must memory resources be for Windows 2000 to begin paging? It is based on how you have tuned the memory management strategy. If you have employed "Maximum Data Throughput for Network Applications," the low memory threshold is

4MB. If you have employed "Maximum Data Throughput for File Services," the low memory threshold is 1MB. Internally, Windows 2000 uses two kernel variables, MmAvailablePages and MmMinimumFreePages, to determine the threshold when memory is getting low enough to page (MmAvailablePages is less than MmMinimumFreePages) which is similar to the SVR4.x UNIX and its variants minfree/lotsfree memory thresholds. As long as MmAvailablePages is greater than MmMinimumFreePages, life is good.

By enabling Windows 2000 to efficiently use all the memory it can, you will be getting a return on your investment. Unfortunately, if the system begins to page excessively, to the point of thrashing, you have a serious memory bottleneck that can cause response time to be slow and the system will appear to have crashed. Anytime the system pages, the response time to the application or the customer is affected in some negative manner. In essence, a queue is formed as processes must wait longer than desired for physical memory resources.

Quick Reference: Helpful Tools to Use When Tracking Down Windows 2000 Memory Details

Throughout this section on bottleneck detection, several different tools are used to track down memory details. Having a tool to complete this mission is nice; having specific examples of how to use each tool is even better. In this and other chapters, some specific examples are provided. I used to fumble through books looking for that helpful tool I read about but did not take notes on, so Table 5.9 lists tools that will help investigate memory use in Windows 2000. Most of the tools functionally overlap each other in some fashion. If you do not find what you are looking for with one tool, try another! Regardless of overlaps or not, sometimes just being able to investigate and interrogate the memory resources in slightly different ways can help to spark that idea that helps you to find what you are looking for. Note, most tools obtain and present information slightly differently. Do not be surprised if slightly different results are presented when querying for the same information.

TABLE 5.9   *Tools to Investigate Memory Usage*

Tool	Where do you find it? (Package) /	Command Line Image	Key times to consider using this tool
Sysmon (System Monitor, Alerts, Logging)	Native to Windows 2000	Perfmon.exe	Long-term trend analysis.
Task Manager	Native to Windows 2000	Taskman.exe	Short-term analysis

	TABLE 5.9	*Tools to Investigate Memory Usage (Continued)*		
Tool	**Where do you find it? (Package) /**	**Command Line Image**	**Key times to consider using this tool**	

Tool	**Where do you find it? (Package) /**	**Command Line Image**	**Key times to consider using this tool**
Process Viewer	Support Tools on Windows 2000 media	Pviewer.exe	Detailed process and thread usage
Process Monitor	Support Tools on Windows 2000 media	Pmon.exe	Command line tool needed to process usage.
Process Explode	Resource Kit	Pview.exe	Very detailed memory usage statistics
Page Fault Monitor	Resource Kit	Pfmon.exe	Advanced debugging of specific applications
Process Status	Resource Kit	Pstat.exe	Provides a snapshot of processes and threads status from the command line. This has a long standard out display. Considering running it by piping it into more (*pstat | more*).

What to Observe in Sysmon When Diagnosing a Memory Bottleneck

A system's subsystems are all interrelated and, subsequently, so are the metrics to observe, even with Windows 2000. To determine whether your system has a memory bottleneck, use Sysmon to observe the relationship of the metrics shown in Table 5.10.

Memory Counter Relationships

When memory bottlenecks form, there is a rolling snowball effect. When Windows 2000's available bytes counter lowers to the 4MB level, the system is using all available physical memory except for the bare minimum that it needs for core operating system functions to keep the system stable. To compensate for the lack of physical memory, the VMM begins to trim the working sets of processes, paging portions of them to the disk to make physical memory available. As other processes need the paged data back in physical memory, the VMM pages the data from the pagefile back into memory and makes room for these pages by paging other processes' data to disk. Pages/ sec is the number of pages read from the disk or written to the disk to resolve memory references to pages that were not in memory at the time of the reference. As the VMM increases its disk activity associated with using the pagefile, the Pages/sec counter increases. The Memory object counter, Pages

TABLE 5.10	*Core Sysmon Counters for Baselining and Memory Bottleneck Detection*	
Object/Counter	**Definition**	**Rule of Thumb for Bottleneck Detection**
Memory: Available Bytes	Available Bytes is the amount of physical memory available to processes running on the system, in bytes.	Windows 2000 Server will try to keep at least 4MB available as seen via this counter (unless memory has been tuned for File Server operations, in which case it will be 1MB). If this value is near or under 4MB and Pages/sec is high, and the disk drive where the pagefile is located is busy, there is a memory shortfall.
Memory: Pages/sec	Pages/sec is the number of pages read from the disk or written to the disk to resolve memory references that were not in memory at the time of reference.	This counter can be deceiving particularly on Enterprise class systems. High Pages/sec activity is fine (>100) as this counter does measure grabbing data from disk. High values for this counter are not fine, however, if they are accompanied by a low Available Bytes indicator and sustained Disk Transfers/sec activity on the disk(s) where the paging file resides.
Memory: Pages Output/sec	Pages Output/sec is the number of pages written to disk (pagefile) to free up space in physical memory. Pages are written back to disk only if they are changed in physical memory, so they are likely to hold data, not code.	A high rate of Pages Output/sec assists in the identification of a memory shortage. Specifically, if this value is high and the Pages/sec value is high, you have low available memory, and the disk that holds your pagefile is busy; you are running short on RAM.
Logical Disk: Transfers/sec (For pagefile.sys disk drive(s))	Disk Transfers/sec is the rate of read and write operations on the disk.	If you observe any sustained disk activity on the disk drive where the pagefile is located shown via the Disk Transfers/sec counter, the Available Bytes are hovering around 4MB, and Pages/sec is high, the Virtual Memory Manager is using the paging file significantly and the system is experiencing a memory bottleneck. Note the Disk Transfers/sec counter must point to disk drive(s) that contains paging system file(s), pagefile.sys.
Memory: Cache Bytes	Cache Bytes is the sum of the System Cache Resident Bytes, System Driver Resident Bytes, System Code Resident Bytes, and Pool Paged Resident Bytes counters.	This counter provides insight into how much of your physical RAM Windows 2000 is using for its dynamic disk cache; i.e., the file system cache and associated key system memory allocations. This is an important counter for troubleshooting if you have memory intensive applications.
Paging File: %Usage	The amount of the pagefile instance in use in percent.	If a large amount of pagefile is used on a regular basis, consider adding (Size of pagefile × % of pagefile in use) of RAM to your system.

TABLE 5.10	Core Sysmon Counters for Baselining and Memory Bottleneck Detection (Continued)	
Object/Counter	**Definition**	**Rule of Thumb for Bottleneck Detection**
Memory: Commit Limit	Commit Limit is the amount of virtual memory that can be committed without having to extend the paging file(s).	This counter provides insight into if the pagefile is properly configured. If a pagefile is too small, it can limit the amount of physical RAM you can access.
Server: Pool NonPaged Failures	The number of times allocations from NonPaged pool have failed.	If this value is >1 on a regular basis, there is not enough physical memory in the system.
Server: Pool Paged Failures	The number of times allocations from paged pool have failed.	If this value is >1 on a regular basis, there is not enough physical memory in the system or the paging file is too small.

Output/sec, is effective to track and determine the number of pages written to disk (pagefile) to free up space in physical memory.

The real challenge here is to ensure that the Pages/sec and Pages Output/sec counters represent the disk activity associated with the VMM working with the pagefile. The Pages/sec counter displays hard page faults that are not only related to the pagefile, but to other disk operations too. Thus, to determine if the increase in Pages/sec is associated with the memory shortfall—noted by a low available bytes and increased Pages/sec—we must determine if hard page faults being generated are associated with the disk drive on which the pagefile is located. If the disk that houses the pagefile displays a %Disk Time over 10% (single disk configuration) of the time or Transfers/sec is greater than 10 (single disk configuration), you are starting to have a problem. This assumes a dedicated disk is used for housing the pagefile, or else this disk increase could be attributed to another application. Chapter 6 reviews techniques to track who is using the disk subsystem with a freeware tool Filemon.exe.

As the memory shortfall continues to get worse, the pagefile disk is used more and more. The % Disk Time and the Transfers/sec increase as pages are written and read to the pagefile disk. In a worst-case scenario, the process is not only waiting due to a lack of memory, but also on overworked disk drive(s). This is exemplified when the Logical Disk objects counter Average Disk Queue Length increases beyond two on the disk drive that houses the pagefile. When this occurs, processes begin to wait even longer to have their memory requests fulfilled since they are now waiting in line to use the pagefile.

Memory Pool Problems

Windows 2000 allocates pools of memory where the operating system and its components obtain data storage, some of which are for critical operations. To access these pools of memory, processes must enter privileged, or Kernel, mode. These Kernel mode pooled resources are divided into two "pools": Paged Pool and NonPaged Pool. Data residing in the Paged Pool can be swapped out to the pagefile by the VMM. Data residing in the NonPaged Pool is not allowed to be paged to the pagefile, as this information is deemed critical for the operation of Windows 2000. These are important resources. Thus, if Windows 2000 reports it is having a problem allocating memory for these memory pools, there is a critical memory shortage. These memory pool problems are detected by checking under Sysmon's server object: Pool NonPaged Failures and Pool Paged Failures counters. If these counters are ever greater than one, there is a serious memory shortage that could affect Windows 2000 operation.

The amount of pooled memory is configured by Windows 2000 dynamically upon boot. The maximum size of pooled memory by default is shown in Table 5.11.

TABLE 5.11   *Maximum Size for Pooled Memory*

Memory Pool Type	Default Maximum Size (Physical RAM)
Paged	491MB
NonPaged	256MB Note: If using the boot.ini /3GB switch, this value lowers to 128MB

This becomes important because there are some applications that are not as well behaved as others and may request more pooled memory than is available by default. I have also observed unique workloads that strain pooled memory resources, but not others. If this occurs, it is possible to tune around the initial pooled memory sizes and control facets of pooled resource quotas by editing the registry entries shown in Table 5.12 (found under HKEY_LOCAL_MACHINE\System\CurrentControlSet\Control\Session Manager\Memory Management\).

TABLE 5.12   *Tuning Pooled Memory Resources*

Registry Entry	Default/ Range	Range	Definition
NonPagedPoolSize	0x0 bytes	See Table 5.11	An area of system memory reserved for objects that must remain in physical memory as long as they are active.
PagedPoolSize	0x0 bytes	See Table 5.11	An area of system memory that stores objects that can be transferred to the paging files on disk when they are not being used. This frees up physical memory for objects that are recently or frequently accessed.

TABLE 5.12	Tuning Pooled Memory Resources (Continued)			
Registry Entry	**Default/ Range**	**Range**	**Definition**
NonPagedPoolQuota	0MB	1–128MB	Establishes the maximum space in the NonPaged pool that can be allocated by any process.
PagedPoolQuota	0MB	1–128MB	Establishes the maximum space in the Paged pool that can be allocated by any process.

As always, ensure you have a recent, tested backup plus restore, and test any changes in a lab environment before trying them in production. There are no rules of thumb for tuning these options as the default is typically acceptable and any tuning is based on your specific environment. When working with memory tunables, watch your available bytes closely so that you do not tune yourself into a low memory condition.

Tuning Strategies for Removing Memory Bottlenecks

Insufficient memory leads to one of the most common bottlenecks you find when using Windows 2000. Purchasing more hardware is a valid technique and we will discuss when it is appropriate to add memory. The case studies presented in chapter 8 move step-by-step through the strategies and tactics involved with tuning various areas of Windows 2000 and several back-office applications.

In this section, we will review the strategies surrounding memory tuning and then get into the actual hands-on tactics. Now that we have configured and sized the fastest memory subsystem, we understand how Windows 2000 uses the memory subsystem, and we know how to detect when memory bottlenecks are forming, let's use this information to our advantage. However, I cannot stress enough how critical it is to know more than which "operating system knob to tweak." We must also understand why something can or may need to be changed. Following are the primary strategies to consider when tuning around a memory bottleneck:

- Ensure another system resource is not acting as a bottleneck
- Select the appropriate memory management strategy
- Tune and optimize Virtual Memory (pagefile)
- Remove potential memory roadblocks
- Remove unnecessary workload from the system (applications, services, etc.)
- Control when application jobs are run
- Update device drivers, system BIOS, and Windows 2000

- Add additional RAM
- Advanced tuning—thinking outside of the box
- SuperCache

At this point, we will review a variety of practical, hands-on tactics that we can use to implement these strategies.

Hands-on Tactics for Tuning around Memory Bottlenecks

Ensure Another System Resource Is Not Acting as a Bottleneck

A common occurrence I have encountered when tuning around memory bottle-necks is that I must remove other system bottlenecks. If another system resource is acting as a bottleneck, adding more RAM will not significantly improve overall performance (although you will make your hardware vendor happy). Refer to chapter 2's Tuning Methodology section to ensure that the other resources are not the bottleneck before spending effort tuning memory resources. Some bottlenecks appear to be memory related when they are not. For example, disk bottlenecks in extreme cases disguise themselves as memory problems. Most people understand that it is important to size their system with plenty of RAM. However, it is common to find the disk subsystem very under-configured. When the disk subsystem is not properly configured for maximum performance, it can appear that the file system cache is not effective, or when paging is needed, that the pagefile is operating on an overworked disk drive! Yes, many a poor pagefile is sitting on a disk that also houses heavily used data files! If and when the system must page memory to disk, having it page to a fast, dedicated disk drive will lessen its effects on overall system performance!

Avoid this condition by configuring the disk subsystem from both a per-formance perspective and a capacity perspective. Refer to chapter 6 on con-figuring disk subsystems.

Controlling Windows 2000 Memory Management Strategy

RAM is a limited resource, and Windows lets you tune how it uses its mem-ory subsystem. For most multiuser enterprise environments, two options for tuning Windows 2000 memory strategy are of particular interest: Maximize Data Throughput for File Sharing and Maximize Data Throughput for Net-work Applications. These options are chosen by selecting Start / Settings / Network and Dial Up Settings / Local Area Connection / Properties / File and Printer Sharing for Microsoft Networks, then selecting the optimization level (memory management strategy). This dialog box offers the five options. The selection made here can have profound effects on how the server performs, so choose wisely. The details of how these memory strategies influence Windows 2000's memory management are reviewed in Table 5.13, a Windows 2000 memory management chart to use as a guideline when choosing memory strategies.

| **TABLE 5.13** | *Guidelines for Choosing Windows 2000 Memory Strategies* |

Windows 2000 Environment	Windows 2000 Memory Management Strategy	
	Maximize Data Throughput for File Sharing	**Maximize Data Throughput for Network Applications**
Databases (Oracle, Informix, SQL Server, etc)		X
Electronic Mail Servers (Exchange, Lotus)		X
Web Servers (IIs, Site Server, iPlanet/ Netscape, Apache)		X
Web Servers and Database on the same server		X
Dedicated File Server	X	
DHCP, WINS, or NetWare Services		X
Domain Controllers and DNS Servers		X
Terminal Services		X
Any environment that is unable to avoid thrashing including file servers (You can revert to the other memory strategy once the memory bottleneck is rcsolved)		X

If your specific application acts like a dedicated file server, you should consider selecting the Maximize Data Throughput for File Sharing. But, as shown in Table 5.13, in all other cases select the alternate tuning strategy option. Note an exception (however rare) to these rules occurs when greater than 2GB of RAM are configured in your system and you want the file system cache to grow to a full 960MB. For those specific cases where you have plenty of memory, select Maximize Data Throughput for File Sharing.

Virtual Memory Optimization: Tuning the Pagefile

For maximum performance, design your systems with enough physical memory so the possibility of frequent paging is mitigated. However, if your system must page, tune the physical disk subsystem and the pagefile itself. This is a good approach to implement that can make your life a whole lot easier for a variety of tuning and sizing tasks. The paging file system can be split up among 16 separate pagefile.sys file systems. More is better when it comes to paging files, unless you become excessive. A good rule of thumb is to split the paging file among two to four separate dedicated physical disk drives and, if possible, across different SCSI channels that do not also support slower SCSI devices such as tape units or DVD/CD RW/CD devices. This is an optimum virtual memory layout. Splitting the pagefiles across more than four disk drives can add overhead to Windows 2000 and actually slow your system down in some instances.

The best tactic to use when implementing multiple pagefiles is to place them on their own identical, dedicated disk drives with the pagefile configured the same size on each disk drive. Yes, this can add another $800 U.S. or so to your system cost, but by isolating the pagefiles on their own disk drives, you gain two advantages—improved performance and easier administration. First, pagefile access is sequential in nature. By providing the pagefile its own disk, there are no other outside workloads being placed on the disk that might be contrary to the sequential nature of the pagefile workload. Grouping disk activities that are similar lowers the amount of physical disk head movement, thus producing improved response time from the disk subsystem. Second, when dedicated disks are used for the pagefile, it is much easier to distinguish between a very busy system and one that is experiencing memory problems. Sharing your pagefile disk with other applications makes it much more difficult to determine if paging activities are being caused by disk activity associated with the VMM or by your applications. When all of the pagefiles are set to the same size, Windows 2000 will balance the virtual memory usage among all of the pagefile instances. This improves performance if the system is experiencing paging activities and application startup.

Configuring the Pagefile for Maximum Performance

Under Start / Settings / Control Panel / System / Performance / Virtual Memory / Settings are the configuration settings for the pagefile (Figure 5-11).

You can set an initial and maximum size for the pagefile. To lower the possibility of virtual memory growing on an as-needed basis and adding even more overhead to an already overworked system, configure the initial and maximum size of the pagefile to twice the amount of physical memory found in the system, up to the 4GB RAM limit.

Why configure a pagefile so large? Two important reasons—performance and functionality. From a functionality perspective, you do not want an important application to suddenly feel boxed in and stop running because of a virtual memory limitation. This statement is based on concepts presented in the pagefile Size Limits Virtual Memory Available section. Systems with

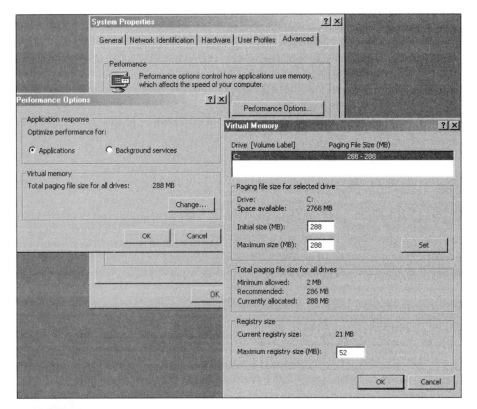

FIGURE 5-11   *Configuring The Pagefile*

larger memory configurations should be configured with pagefiles that are twice that of physical memory, up to a 4GB limit. Microsoft Knowledge base article Q171793 (http:\\www.microsoftt.com\kb) alludes to the fact that in larger server memory configurations, having a pagefile smaller than actual physical memory will "affect the total memory commit size for applications." Personal experience has shown this to be true.

From a performance perspective, defining a large pagefile is a strategic decision. Windows 2000 can dynamically increase the size of the pagefile on the fly, up to the pagefile's maximum size setting, which is great! This is how Windows 2000 helps to avoid virtual memory conflicts. Unfortunately, when Windows 2000 grows past the initial pagefile setting, it requires resources to grow the pagefile. If the system requires the pagefile to be resized, it is a good bet that memory resources are already becoming scarce. When Windows 2000 dynamically resizes the pagefile, this causes the system to use even more resources during a system's time of need that adds even more performance problems to the already besieged server.

The VMM writes pages of data to the pagefile in a sequential fashion. The VMM employs a read-ahead caching strategy when working with the pagefile to move potential memory pages back into physical memory. The VMM hopes that the next page requested from the pagefile is already back in memory, thus only incurring a less costly soft page fault. For this strategy to be most effective, the pagefile located on the disk drive must be contiguous. Contiguous data implies that the data is grouped together on the same area of the disk drive such that less physical disk movement is required to obtain the data. When Windows 2000 dynamically adds more space to the pagefile, there is no guarantee that the additional pagefile space will be placed onto the disk drive in a contiguous fashion in respect to where the current pagefile.sys is located. When this happens, the pagefile becomes fragmented on the disk subsystem it resides on. Now, when memory pages are written to or read from the new dynamically grown pagefile, additional performance will be lost as the physical disk drive must wander around the disk subsystem to access the pagefile.

Windows 2000 now includes a disk Defragmentation tool which is located at Start / Programs / Accessories / System Tools / Disk Defragmenter. Optimally, you would want to place your pagefile(s) on new, freshly formatted NTFS simple disks. This would ensure no disk fragmentation. If this is not an option, run the disk Defragmentation tool immediately after installation or when any changes in the pagefiles are made.

Sizing the Pagefile

When you create the pagefile(s), you are asked to set the initial and maximum size of the paging file. Under Sysmon, observe the Paging File: %Usage Peak parameter. To optimally set the pagefile, set the initial and maximum size parameter to that %Usage Peak value. This limits the size of the pagefile to exactly what is needed and can improve the time required by the VMM to locate data in the pagefile. Although this is an optimum layout, it can limit virtual memory expansion. This approach is typically optimal when running applications that will not need more memory than is available in physical RAM and is normally relegated to desktops/workstations and small-dedicated servers.

As a corollary to this rule of thumb for small systems, at a minimum and by default (your process, not Windows 2000's), set the paging file initial size to twice the size of physical memory and the maximum size for the pagefile to twice the size physical memory (to a maximum of 4GB). This will minimize spending any resource time extending the size of the Paging file and waiting for the Paging file extension to complete. Dynamic expansion of the pagefile can also cause fragmentation of the pagefile on the disk drive, which lowers overall pagefile performance. By setting the pagefile size initially to twice the RAM configured, the amount of virtual memory that your processes can map their data to increases.

Configuring Multiple Pagefiles

To implement multiple pagefiles, first select the disk drives that are to be dedicated to containing the pagefile and nothing else. Select Start / Settings / Control Panel / System / Performance / Virtual Memory / Settings. Then, select Virtual Memory and create the new paging files, one for each dedicated disk. After the new paging file systems are in place, remove the default pagefile.sys on the root disk. Remove the root disk pagefile by selecting the root drive and then setting the minimum and maximum pagefile size to zero. This will improve your virtual memory (paging) performance. The system will be required to reboot before the new pagefile design is activated.

Removal of Potential Memory Road Blocks

What to Avoid When Optimizing the Pagefile: Never Use RAID 5 for the Pagefile

Another technique used when implementing multidisk pagefile configurations is to place pagefiles on disk arrays. (Disk array RAID technology is reviewed closely in chapter 6). Always avoid this! You could place your pagefile across a RAID 5 array stripe set with parity, which can survive a single disk failure. NEVER, EVER, EVER do this. The pagefile disk workload is write intensive. Even with write-back cache enabled, RAID 5 arrays provide lower levels of write performance than their single disk counterparts. Using a RAID 5 array for a pagefile home is like a racing car with its parking brake on. It will still work, but wow, will it be slow. If this does not make sense, you may not be aware of the performance characteristics and details on how RAID 5 operates. As a refresher, review RAID 5 concepts in chapter 6.

Placing the pagefile on a RAID 0 array stripe set will improve the pagefile's performance, similar to the example above, when the pagefile is individually placed on two or more separate disk drives. This technique is not recommended. If you lose one disk drive in a RAID 0 array, the entire pagefile is lost as a RAID 0 array cannot sustain a single disk drive failure. If a very high availability configuration is required, consider a RAID 1 or RAID 10 configuration for the pagefile.

What to Avoid When Optimizing the Pagefile 2: Never Use a Second Partition on the Same Disk Drive for the Pagefile

With the advent of larger capacity disk drives, many root disk drives in Windows 2000 configurations are split into C: and D: partitions. Do not place the pagefile on the second partition! Why? This will cause increased latency. The disk heads will need to move halfway across the disk drive (assuming you partitioned the disk drive in half) every time it must be accessed. Thus, if Windows 2000 is installed on C: and the pagefile on D:, the disk heads will be running back and forth all of the time where disk latency is greatest. Also, the first partition is placed on the outside edge of the disk drive platter, which is the fastest, and the second partition is placed closer to the center of the platter, which is slower. If you must partition a large drive in half, place the pagefile on the first partition created. In this example, that would be the C: partition. Place files that are rarely accessed on the second partition, D:. Detailed information on disk latency is presented in chapter 6.

Ensuring You Can Use All of Your Physical RAM

The size of the pagefile can limit the amount of physical RAM you can use in your system. To avoid this, ensure that the size of the pagefile is at least equal to the amount of RAM or follow the recommended paging file size of twice that of RAM. How can you determine how much memory Windows 2000 can commit? Determine how much memory your applications can access by using Sysmon to observe the memory object's Commit Limit counter. The commit limit is defined under Sysmon as "the amount of virtual memory that can be committed without having to extend the paging file(s). It is measured in bytes. (Committed memory is physical memory for which space has been reserved on the disk paging files. There can be one paging file on each logical drive.) If the paging file(s) are to be expanded, this limit increases accordingly. This counter displays the last observed value only; it is not an average."

By starting with a pagefile two times the size of the RAM, you allow processes access to that much virtual memory immediately, even if it is not needed. Under a heavy workload surge, it is good to provide your applications room to grow so that they can accommodate the surge. Smaller pagefiles are more efficient than larger pagefiles, but limit your memory scalability. The performance hit incurred by Windows 2000 dynamically sizing the pagefile outweighs the benefits that a smaller pagefile provides.

Maximum Registry Size Limit

This value is set under Start / Settings / Control Panel / System / Performance / Virtual Memory / Settings. Although this tunable does not improve performance, it can limit it. Typically, double the default value of this variable. Even though this will increase registry key size, it will not cause the system's initial request for memory to increase. It will also allow the registry more room to grow if needed, which can aid in avoiding resource limitations under Windows 2000. Note that the Registry Size Limit memory needs are allocated from the paged pool memory allocation that is limited to 491MB under Windows 2000. You can force Windows 2000 to recalculate its internal tuning settings such as this one by running net config server \srvcomment"<text>" from the command prompt and rebooting the server. This is a good command to run if you want the Maximum Registry Size Limit to be calculated by Windows 2000 again or whenever new hardware is configured into the system.

It is important to note when the "net config" commands are used, it forces system configuration updates and causes Windows 2000 not to dynamically adjust its configurations if new hardware is introduced into the system. To return to dynamic configuration mode, you must edit the registry

```
HKEY_LOCAL_MACHINE\\SYSTEM\CurrentControlSet\Services\LanmanServe
r\Parameters
```

and remove all entries except the following: EnableSharedNetDrives, Lmannounce, NullSessionPipes,NullSessionShares Size. For more information on this feature, head over to http://support.microsoft.com/support/kb/articles/ Q128/1/67.asp?vote=1& and review Article ID: Q128167.

Tuning Windows 2000 Kernel Paging Activities

Windows 2000 will page some portions of its own kernel to disk, such as the Windows 2000 executive system drivers when they have not recently been in use, to make room in memory for other processes. This is helpful for a system with a limited RAM supply. If your system has ample RAM—that is, at least 128MB more RAM than is normally found under Sysmon's memory object Available Bytes—change the following registry entry:

```
HKEY_LOCAL_MACHINE\SYSTEM\CurrentControlSet\Control\Session
Manager\Memory Management\DisablePagingExecutive
```

from the default value of 0 to1. This change will force Windows 2000 to keep the Windows 2000 executive (kernel) from paging any of its executive system drivers to disk and ensure that they are immediately available if needed. Always back up and understand how to restore Windows 2000's registry before making any changes to it.

Remove Unnecessary Workload from the System

Services Management

Every byte of RAM is sacred (or at least costs money). Use memory resources wisely. Any processes that are not required to service your clients, manage your system, or secure it should not be running on the system. You should know this information for security as well as performance reasons. If a Trojan horse application is slipped onto your system without your knowledge, your system might run slower and could be compromised or be used to compromise another system.

Beyond knowing which processes are currently running, you need to know what the processes do. Why run a service or application in the background if you don't need it? For example, why have Remote Access Service (RAS) turned on if your Windows 2000 system does not require RAS? By turning off unnecessary background processes, you free memory resources for applications and portions of Windows 2000 that really need the resources. Windows 2000 introduces a plethora of additional services and services options that were not native in Windows 2000. Review every single one! Knowing your system and understanding the functions you want Windows 2000 to perform will help you tune the system. Under Task Manager / Processes Tab, you can terminate a process by right-clicking on the process and then selecting End Process (similar to the UNIX kill command). The Windows 2000 Resource Kit provides a command line interface kill command version also. (Multiple process kill options were reviewed in chapter 2.)

Unfortunately, ending an unneeded process is only a temporary fix. If you started the process as a background service, the process will start again when you cycle power on the system. To avoid this situation, control how processes are started and stopped on the system. Figure 5-12 shows that from Start / Settings / Administration Tools / Computer Management / Services and Applications / Services, you can control whether background processes start automatically, start manually, or are disabled when you boot the server. Be careful which processes you kill or decide not to start, because some processes (server and workstation) are essential for basic Windows 2000 operation.

Keep a close watch on your system using the Services MMC snap in after installing new applications. More and more applications are slipping additional background services into this area. Here are common services that can be set to manually start up: Alerter, ClipBook, Server, Computer Browser, Messenger, Remote Access, AutoDial Manager, Server, TCP/IP simple services, and Telephony. Windows can actually run with only the following two services started: Workstation and Server. Which services you run is a function of your environment.

Blank Backgrounds and No Fancy Screen Savers Are Best

Remove any backgrounds and any fancy screen savers that may be in place on your system's console. This may seem trivial, but a few megabytes of RAM can help keep a busy server in the safe zone of available memory and avoid the paging performance penalty. Servers tend to sit in the designated com-

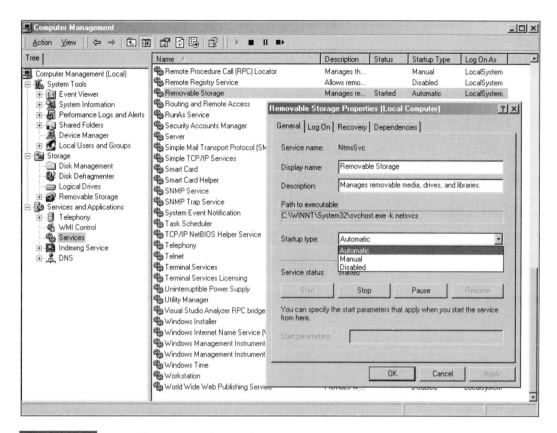

Controlling Startup of a Windows 2000 Service

puter room by themselves anyway. For desktops, the fancy wallpaper can
steal more than 1MB of RAM. If you have only 64 or 128MB of RAM, you need
that 1MB!

If you really love that background wallpaper or that 3GL screen saver, at
least find out how much memory you are donating for a pretty backdrop and
idle time pictures. Run Task Manager and look at the available bytes counter
and wait a few moments for the system to settle. Once it does, write down the
value, and then change the background wallpaper. Again, wait a few
moments for Task Manager's available memory to settle, and note the difference. Is it worth it? You be the judge. You can also use Sysmon's memory
object available bytes to complete the same exercise over the network to
monitor how much memory (and other resources) that critical screen saver is
demanding. A blank, console locking screen saver is not exciting but gets the
job done.

Identify and Remove Memory Leaks

A memory leak can occur when a process allocates memory and either never returns it or continues to increase its memory usage when the server is idle. It is possible to determine if there is a memory leak occurring on the system, but it is a challenge. Using either Task Manager or Sysmon, you can detect memory leaks. What you are in search of is an application that that is continually increasing its working set even when the server is idle. Under Sysmon, review Processor: %Processor Time, and Process: Working Set. When you add the Process: Working Set counter under Sysmon's add function, select Process, Working Set, click on the first process, then press the shift key and the end key concurrently. This will select all of the current processes running on the server, then select add. Also add Process: Virtual Bytes for all processes. At this point, it is wait and see. Look for %Processor time to be quiescent and the other two selected memory counters to grow for specific processes. If you observe a process using more memory without additional workload, you have isolated the memory-leaking process. To make this task easier, use Sysmon's logging mode and allow Sysmon to run overnight or any other time the system is under its lowest workloads.

If you have the source code, you can use source code debuggers to troubleshoot the leak. If it is a commercial application that appears leaky, look for application patches on the software vendor's web site or contact the vendor directly.

Schedule Memory Intensive Jobs during Off-Peak Hours

This technique always seemed to be a bit of an easy-out strategy to alleviate memory problems, but it is effective and uses resources that may have otherwise been idle. To schedule a job during an off-peak hour, use the "at" command from the command prompt or the Windows 2000 task schedule available under the control panel (review in chapter 2). To review the currently scheduled background processes, run at.exe at the command prompt. For a listing of the "at" command options, run at /? at the command prompt. Using either command, you can connect to and schedule background processes on local or remote Windows 2000 systems.

Most commercial packages that schedule batch (noninteractive application) jobs do so on the hour or half hour. If you have the option, track which jobs are running when to avoid conflicts. Also, if you schedule your own customer jobs (such as a backup), schedule them an off time such as 12:38 A.M.

Update Device Drivers, System BIOS, and Windows 2000

The system's BIOS levels, device drivers, and Windows 2000 itself must be updated and maintained. Why? Over time, even the most tested code will need some type of maintenance. Obtain, test, and deploy the latest software updates on a regular basis. Many times they provide basic fixes, additional functionality, and occasionally a few new bugs.

The Last Resort: Purchase More RAM

Avoid Paging and Keeping Applications Fed

The highest performing Windows 2000 systems I have encountered are sized and tuned with one basic strategy in mind: Avoid excessive disk access from activities such as paging and application disk access. Many consider occasional paging acceptable, if it occurs infrequently. The more the system pages, the more CPU cycles are wasted on memory operations and the slower the final response times provided to your customers. Applications leverage either the file system cache or you can designate the application's own memory space for caching its activities. Adding additional memory can remove memory bottlenecks and improve the overall performance of the system as long as you can take advantage of the additional RAM.

Isolating the Guilty Memory Hog

If the system begins to page to an unacceptable degree, use Sysmon and Task Manager to isolate the applications or processes that are draining excessive memory and tune down the memory allocated to them (if possible). If the application source code is available, you can work with the developers to improve overall memory performance. If all of the applications operating on the system are required, adding more RAM to a server whose performance is limited by RAM resources will result in improved overall server performance.

DETERMINING HOW MUCH MEMORY TO ADD

When all strategies to tune the memory are exhausted and you have determined that the system is paging excessively, obtain additional RAM. How much RAM to add is a function of current and future system load requirements and anticipated application requirements. To avoid paging, determine how much paging your system does, then add at least that amount. For example, if the pagefile object's % Usage Max counter is 20% and your paging file size is 1000MB, consider adding at least 200MB. When adding memory to the system, select the RAM sizes such that they provide the highest density while still providing the highest degree of memory interleaving for growth and performance, respectively.

Summary

This chapter gave a building block approach to Windows 2000 and memory performance. Once an understanding of the base memory hardware technology that is used in a modern system was completed, we investigated how Windows 20000 uses the memory resources provided to it. Once these two pieces of the puzzle were covered, we reviewed how to size the memory subsystem, how to detect memory bottlenecks, and how to tune around them. By understanding what is happening in your environment and how and why Windows 2000 provides memory management, you can maximize your tuning and sizing efforts when implementing Windows 2000 solutions. This will ensure that Windows 2000 provides the maximum performance for your specific environment.

Windows 2000 and Disk Subsystem Performance

CHAPTER OBJECTIVES

- Introduction........ *290*
- Disk Subsystem Technology: Following the Data........ *291*
- Disk Drive Technology........ *293*
- Disk Drive Selection........ *297*
- Performance Perspective: Physical Disk View vs. Windows 2000 View........ *299*
- Disk Subsystem Performance........ *300*
- SCSI Technology........ *307*
- Fibre Channel Technology........ *310*
- HBAs........ *312*
- I/O Bus Technology and Selection........ *315*
- The System Bus........ *320*
- Redundant Array of Inexpensive Disks (RAID)........ *321*
- RAID 1–Disk Mirroring........ *323*
- RAID 5–Disk Striping with Parity........ *324*
- How Windows 2000 Uses the Disk Subsystem........ *345*
- Windows 2000 Device Drivers........ *347*
- Sizing a Windows 2000 Disk I/O Subsystem........ *349*
- Detecting Disk Subsystem Bottlenecks........ *361*
- Tuning Strategies for Removing Disk Subsystem Bottlenecks........ *367*
- File System–Related Tuning........ *375*
- Tuning Disk Subsystem SCSI Channel and HBA........ *377*

● RAID Tuning Considerations........ *380*
● The Most Important Disk Tuning Concept........ *385*
● Disk Storage Capacity Tuning........ *386*
● Additional Disk Subsystem Hardware–The Last Resort........ *386*
● Thinking Outside of the Box: Windows 2000 RAM Disk........ *387*

> *"Tuning your systems for maximum performance enhances the service provided to customers and extends the longevity of your system. This results in improved return on investment." —Anonymous performance engineer*

Introduction

If you want to tune or size a Windows 2000 system, it is important to have an understanding of how the system hardware, operating system, and applications actually work. When you understand how and why these various components of an overall solution are trying to complete their respective tasks, you will be much better equipped to help them complete their tasks by tuning and sizing the system resources for maximum performance. This is exactly what we will show you how to do in this and each of the other subsystem chapters. We'll provide descriptions, explanations, and examples to help you understand how the system components interact. Armed with this information, some of the black magic of tuning and sizing will disappear, and you can begin to use more effective tuning and sizing tactics. It is tempting to just jump in and start adding this or tuning that. Knowing which "knob to turn" to tune a Windows 2000 system is good; understanding when to "turn a tuning knob" and why it will help is better.

In this chapter, we focus on the disk subsystem portion of a Windows 2000 solution, where you will find the greatest amount of flexibility that you can directly influence. The disk subsystem is an area in which having an understanding from strictly a Windows 2000 perspective is not enough. The old adage of understanding either software or hardware blurs dramatically when it comes to the disk subsystem—the variety of configurations available for the disk subsystem is broad.

We investigate overall disk performance from several perspectives. To get a handle on this important topic, we follow the data flow from the disk drive through the system to the CPU(s). Using this data path as a guide, we review each of the critical system components from a performance perspective, illustrating some of the technology's strengths and weaknesses. This knowledge enables you to get the most out of a system's disk subsystem. If you understand the flow of data through the system, then how the disk subsystem operates becomes much more apparent. Once the disk subsystem technology is explored, we then investigate how Windows 2000 takes advantage of it.

When we have established a foundation of disk subsystem knowledge, we determine when disk subsystem bottlenecks are occurring while running Windows 2000. Then we move into sizing disk subsystems. From there, we build on bottleneck detection and disk subsystem sizing information by examining strategies and hands-on tactics on how to tune around disk subsystem bottlenecks. Windows 2000 support for disk subsystems allows for an amazing amount of tuning flexibility, more than any other subsystem. The bottleneck detection techniques and the sizing and tuning strategies and tactics reviewed in this chapter are not just based on theory; they were developed and fine-tuned from real-world production environments and are also used throughout the rest of this book.

Disk Subsystem Technology: Following the Data

The quantity of data needed for an enterprise-level system cannot be kept in RAM, even with Windows 2000 Advanced Server or Data Center family members. A fast disk subsystem lends itself to providing significant transaction rates and good overall system performance. The standard high volume (SHV) server logical diagram that was used in earlier chapters is utilized here as our reference system architecture. Adding the primary components required in accessing the disk subsystem, we arrive at the following logical data flow diagram shown in Figure 6-1.

It is important to understand the different transfer rates of each component of the system and the system's disk subsystem. This information helps you to size your systems properly and identify potential bottlenecks that can throttle your system's overall performance. In Figure 6-1, data travels in the following manner: from the actual disk drive to the embedded disk controller located on the disk drive unit (<20MB/sec real-world load), up the Ultra2 Fast and Wide SCSI channel at 80MB/sec, through PCI (stands for peripheral component interconnect) slot 1 on PCI Bus 1 at 264MB/sec to the memory subsystem (800MB/sec), and then transferred to the CPU at a Pentium III front-side system bus speed of 800MB/sec.

Review each link in the data path. It is the weakest link that throttles the overall disk subsystem performance.

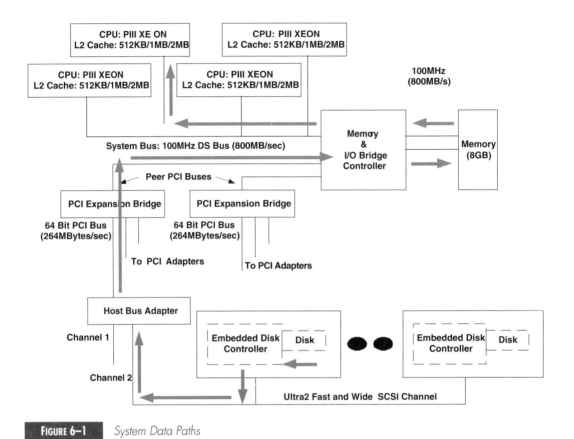

FIGURE 6-1 *System Data Paths*

If one component is trying to send more data than the next component can handle (accept), there is a bottleneck. A good analogy involves plumbing: if the primary water pipe carrying water away from your basement is 5 inches in diameter and you have ten 2-inch pipes placing water into the 5-inch pipe, water will be spilling out, your basement will be flooding, and no one will be happy.

By completing a little mathematical word problem, you can avoid bottlenecks even before they begin. For example, placing two 3-channel Ultra2 SCSI adapters (theoretical aggregate maximum throughput of 2 × [3 × 80MB/sec = 480MB/sec]) into a single PCI bus can overwhelm a single PCI bus data link if all of the SCSI channels are active. A single 64-bit 33MHz PCI bus can support a theoretical maximum of only 264MB/sec. Jamming 480MB/sec of data into it just does not work very well. If you had actually implemented this configuration, you would have created a bottleneck from the start. Placing each one of the 3-channel Ultra2 Fast and Wide SCSI cards onto their own respective peer PCI bus will spread the disk I/O activities across 528MB of total aggregate PCI bus throughput.

Disk Drive Technology

The disk drive itself is the slowest link of the data path. A disk drive is a series of stacked platters with very small heads that read and write the data to the various platters. These platters rotate or spin at very high speeds, currently up to 15,000rpm. As disk requests come from Windows 2000, the heads move accordingly over the platters to obtain the requested data. When characterizing the physical performance of disk drives, we must understand the following key factors at a minimum:

- **Rotational latency.** The time required for the disk platter to spin one complete revolution.
- **Seek time.** The time required for the motion of the disk head as it moves to/from a particular track on the disk platter. This is the most expensive portion of overall latency (wait time) when disk movement is needed.
- **Access time.** The average length of time it takes the disk to seek to the required track plus the amount of time it takes for the disk to spin the data under the head (average seek time + average latency).

Figure 6-2 is an illustration of a disk drive as if you were looking at it from the top (a bird's-eye view), and Figure 6-3 is a disk drive from the side.

There are a variety of terms to describe the different disk operations. From a disk vendor's perspective, one of the goals is to lower the amount of time required when retrieving data from a disk drive. Table 6.1 defines the most common terms.

Basic Disk Drive Operation

Each disk drive is a stack of disk platters (Figure 6-3) that is broken into cylinders, tracks, sectors, and clusters. When the disk drive is low-level formatted, logical tracks (logical concentric circles on the disk platters used for locating data on the disk itself) are established and the disk geometry of the disk drive is determined. Do not confuse low-level formatting using the HBA (Host Bus Adapter, sometimes referred to as a disk controller) with formatting the disk drive with a file system (FAT, NTFS, FAT32) using Windows 2000. Low-level formatting is not normally a function available directly from Windows 2000 but is provided by the HBA vendor. For example, the low-level format tool for Adaptec SCSI HBAs is available when a system starts by pressing ctrl+a during

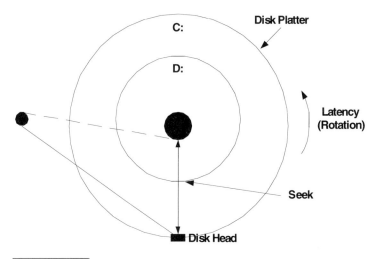

FIGURE 6–2   *Top View of a Disk Drive*

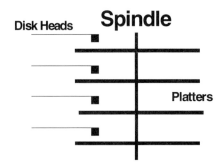

FIGURE 6–3   *Side View of a Disk Drive*

TABLE 6.1   *Disk Drive Technology Definitions*

Common Term Used to Describe Disk Drive Operations	Definitions
Track	A logically defined band of data on the disk platter. Envision tracks as concentric circles on the disk platter (Figure 6-4).
Sector	The smaller sections of data into which a logical track is divided.
Latency—rotational	The time required for the disk platter to spin one complete revolution.
Average latency	The time that the disk head waits for a sector to arrive as the disk platter rotates (like a spinning CD-ROM). On average you will have to wait for approximately one-half the rotational time of the drive platter for the sector to arrive.

TABLE 6.1	*Disk Drive Technology Definitions (Continued)*
Common Term Used to Describe Disk Drive Operations	**Definitions**
Seek time	The time required for the motion of the disk head as it moves to/from a particular track on the disk platter. This is the most expensive portion of overall latency (wait time) when disk movement is needed.
Average seek time	The time required for disk head to move to/from a particular track half on the disk drive platter. On average, this will be the time it takes the disk head to travel halfway across the disk platter.
Access time (average)	The average length of time it takes the disk to seek to the required track plus the amount of time it takes for the disk to spin the data under the head (average seek time + average latency).
Transfer rate	The speed at which the data bits are being transferred to/from the internal disk drive buffer.
Windows 2000 transfer rate	The speed at which the data bits are being transferred externally from the disk drive through the SCSI data path to the system such that Windows 2000 processes can use the data.
Disk platter rotation (rpm)	The measurement of the rotational speed of a disk drive platter on a per-minute basis; how fast the disk platters spin.

the system's power-on self-test (POST) as the Adaptec SCSI adapter is detected by the server. This type of HBA tool is started either during the POST of the server or by booting the system into MS-DOS using a boot floppy, or by a Windows 2000 native application provided by the vendor who manufactured the disk adapter. Track numbers start at 0, where track 0 is the outermost track of the disk. These outermost tracks of the disk are actually the fastest portion of the disk drive. Since the outer tracks are faster than the inner tracks, this is one of the reasons disk drive manufacturers generally provide throughput in ranges (5–40MB/sec) when describing their products.

> *It is important to note that when Windows 2000 creates a logical partition, the partition is created from the outside of the disk toward the inside of the disk. Thus, if you create two partitions—C: and D:—the C: partition is faster due to more tracks being available per cylinder and less distances to travel for disk seeks.*

Performance is not really affected until available disk drive space is less than 40%, assuming one Windows 2000 partition covers the entire disk drive. When 60% of the disk drive is used, the remaining free space is located closer to the disk's spindle at the center of the disk drive, which operates at a lower performance level.

Each track is broken down into sectors, normally 512KB in size. Part of the process is completed when you format a disk drive under Windows 2000 using the *format.exe* command or Logical Disk Manager (an MMC snap-in commonly found under Start / Programs / Administration Tools / Computer Management / Storage / Disk Management). When the disk drive is formatted, the sectors get grouped into clusters. Clusters are referenced under Windows 2000 as the allocation unit (ALU) size for the file system. The vertical stacking of tracks form cylinders. Figure 6-4 depicts tracks, sectors, and clusters.

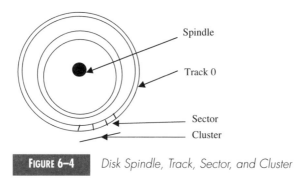

FIGURE 6–4   *Disk Spindle, Track, Sector, and Cluster*

Physical Disk Drive Performance

Great information. Now, how do these disk drive definitions relate to overall performance of a disk drive? When the data requested by a Windows 2000 process is identified on the disk drive, the disk head (which is a small transducer that reads magnetic media) seeks to the appropriate track by moving either toward the center or toward the edge of the disk drive (*seek time*). The head then waits for the platter to spin until the proper sector of data is under the disk head (*rotational latency*). Once the data is under the head, the data is read. The combination of the seek time and rotational time associated with obtaining the data is the *access time*. The data collected from the disk platters is then transferred to the embedded disk controller that is physically located on the disk drive unit. The embedded controller is the equivalent of a miniaturized computer—it contains a small CPU and its own memory to obtain and transfer data from the physical disk drive. From here, the data is moved to the SCSI bus and on through the I/O subsystem.

> *The two most costly portions of accessing data from a disk drive process are the seek time (the time it takes for the head to move to the correct track) and the rotational latency (the rotation time of the disk platters).*

Cost here is referenced in time. The longer it takes for the physical activity to be completed, the longer the process under Windows 2000 must wait for its data. To get an understanding of what contributes to the relative time required to get data from the disk subsystem to the PCI bus, look at the pie chart in Figure 6-5.

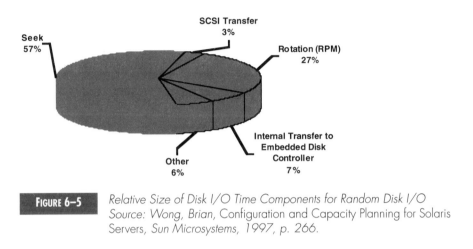

| FIGURE 6–5 | *Relative Size of Disk I/O Time Components for Random Disk I/O* |

Source: Wong, Brian, Configuration and Capacity Planning for Solaris Servers, Sun Microsystems, 1997, p. 266.

Disk Drive Selection

Now that we have reviewed some of the key underlying technologies used to implement disk technology, how do you take advantage of it? Later in this chapter, we will be using this information when explaining RAID technology and Windows 2000 disk subsystem tuning techniques. For now, use this knowledge when selecting the disk drive technology for your system. Unless you're a vendor, you will not actually be changing the internal disk characteristics. What you *can* do, though, is select the fastest disk drives possible that fit into your budget. Table 6.2 lists some of the current disk drive technologies found in a quick check of the Internet.

Pay attention to the details when ordering and receiving your products! Vendors do their best, but check the disk drives very closely when they arrive. We received a large shipment of disks that were supposed to be 10,000rpm drives with 1MB internal caches, but they were 7,200rpm drives with 512KB caches. In general, a 15,000rpm drive provides roughly 30% more performance than a 10,000rpm drive, while a 10,000rpm drive provides approximately 30% more performance than a 7,200rpm drive. So watch those orders closely.

In this book, the focus is on SCSI and fibre channel disk drive technology. Why not IDE/ATA (this stands for integrated drive electronics/AT attachment) or EIDE/PATA (enhanced IDE/performance ATA)? If you are very concerned about budget, EIDE/PATA-based disk drives are a sound choice

| **TABLE 6.2** | *SCSI Disk Drive Technology Specifications* |

Brand	Capacity (GB)	Embedded Disk Controller Buffer Size	RPM	Seek Time (milliseconds [ms])	SCSI Type
IBM UltraStar 5400	4.3	512KB	5,400	8.0	Ultra SCSI
Seagate Barracuda7200	4.5	512KB	7,200	8.0	Ultra SCSI
IBM UltraStar 18LZX	18.2	2–8MB	7,200	4.9	Ultra160 SCSI
Seagate Barracuda	4.5	512KB	10,000	7.5	Ultra SCSI
IBM UltraStar 9ZX	9.1	1MB	10,000	6.3	Ultra2 SCSI
Seagate Cheetah 18XL	18.4	1–8MB	10,000	5.2	Ultra160 SCSI
Seagate Cheetah73	73	1–8MB	10,000	6.0	Ultra2 SCSI
Seagate Cheetah X15	18.2	1–16MB	15,000	3.9	Ultra160SCSI

and are very good for single-user desktops and CD-ROM units on systems. However, when your goal is high performance, redundancy, and scalability, EIDE does not cut it. EIDE does not support key items such as plug and play, parallel operations to support multiuser environments, command queuing, or adding a higher (>3) number of drives to its bus. I strongly recommend that EIDE drives never be used in servers or high-end workstations.

Table 6.3 provides insight into the theoretical performance of common disk drive technologies.

| **TABLE 6.3** | *IDE/EIDE/SCSI Disk Drive Technology Comparison* |

IDE/ATA	EIDE/Performance ATA	Below Ultra3 SCSI Standards	Ultra3 SCSI
Disk data transfer rate describes how fast data can actually be read or written to the physical platters inside the drive (commonly referred to as *internal* transfer rate).			
10–19MB/sec	19–25MB/sec	25–33MB/sec	33–40MB/sec
Disk cache memory is the physical computer memory chips on a disk drive where data is stored temporarily on the drive until the HBA requests the data. Cache acts as a buffer between the data on the disk platters and the HBA.			
128–256KB	512 KB	512KB–1MB	4–16MB
Average disk access time describes how fast the drive can locate data on the disk platters and is especially important in a file server or similar random-access environment.			
9.5–10.5ms	8.5–9.0ms	6.8–8.0ms	5.2–5.7ms
Disk rotational speed indicates the maximum speed at which the platters can spin to place a particular data storage point under the read/write heads. Rotational speed as a measurement is determined by the maximum number of revolutions the platters can make in 1minute (rpm). Generally, a higher rpm produces a better internal data transfer rate, a lower access time, and better overall drive performance.			
5,400rpm	7,200rpm	7,200–10,000rpm	15,000rpm

Performance Perspective: Physical Disk View vs. Windows 2000 View

It is all a matter of perspective when measuring performance. Performance information provided by vendors on their disk drives can be impressive. For some of the drives listed in Table 6.3, the vendor's list sustained data rates of up to 33MB/sec. Unfortunately, this performance information is not measured for actual Windows 2000 application environments, so mileage will vary, dramatically. When disk drive vendors provide throughput measurements for specific disk drives, it is from their perspective. They quote the burst speed from the embedded disk controller cache to the SCSI bus. This does not take into consideration the most costly portion of the disk activity—the actual physical activities (seek and rotation) associated with an application obtaining data. Vendors are in business to sell disks, so this recording practice is accepted and common. Sometimes more relevant data is available. When choosing a disk drive unit or comparing them, look closely at the fine print so that you can determine what vendors are really reporting. Understand the value of these measurements, but do not allow them to skew your expectation of what to expect in a real-world deployment.

To determine a general rule of thumb about the performance that is actually provided for your environment, you can create a complete system-level stress test, develop your baseline, then change a single component (disk drive or disk array), and determine what effect it has. You can also test components in your Windows 2000 system on a per-component basis in a controlled environment. There are various publicly available component testing tools, such as Intel's Galileo disk testing tool. You can get more information about Galileo by visiting the web site at http://developer.intel.com/design/servers/devtools/iometer. The Windows 2000 Resource Kit also contains a disk testing tool called Response Probe, with a thorough explanation of its use. Also, some trade magazines like *Windows 2000 Magazine* provide condensed instructions on using its Response Probe.

Many of the disk testing tools that exercise disk I/O do so by setting the appropriate application code flags to bypass the Windows 2000 file system cache and test the physical disk drive directly. Although this technique is useful in pure performance testing environments, I prefer to use tools that test system components in ways that represent actual or closer-to-real-life Windows 2000 environments. This is our perspective here: to measure performance from the view of the average application. In most environments, the Windows 2000 file system cache is used. There are times, however, when either the file system cache is not effective because the environment is truly random in nature, or it is defeated due to the sheer size of the files being moved to and from the disk drives. In either case, the file system cache influences the overall throughput achieved. Even applications that do bypass the file system cache implement their own file caching strategies, which results in similar results.

Disk Subsystem Performance

When looking at disk subsystem performance, there are several aspects to understand to maximize overall performance:

- Disk subsystem behavior characteristics
- Disk subsystem throughput
- Disk subsystem workload

Understanding these three facets of disk subsystem performance and tuning and sizing accordingly can dramatically influence the overall performance of your Windows 2000 solution.

Disk Subsystem Behavior Characteristics

Due to the physical characteristics of disk drives, how the disk drive is used influences the overall performance provided. There are three primary disk workload characteristics to understand: sequential reads and writes, random reads and writes, and random hybrids.

SEQUENTIAL READ/WRITE ENVIRONMENTS

Sequential read-disk workloads read data from the disk drive in a sequential fashion. When this occurs, data is available in the same track or in tracks located close to each other. Due to this proximity, overall seek activities are lower due to the fact that sequential seek activities incur less track-to-track movements to obtain the data. Most disk drive manufacturers provide performance data on access times for the various disk drive activities. After visiting one vendor's site, I obtained information on a relatively mainstream 10,000rpm Ultra2 SCSI disk drive. The average track-to-track seek time was 0.6ms for read activities and 0.9ms for write activities. The average latency due to disk rotation was 2.98ms. Thus, it takes 3.58ms to read data and 3.88ms to write sequential data. If an Ultra160 15,000rpm disk drive were to be used for the sequential read access, transaction time would improve to 2.5ms (0.5 + 2), while random write performance would improve to 2.7ms.

The primary differences between read and write access for sequential disk access transactions are based on memory and RAID configuration considerations. Windows 2000's file system cache and I/O Cache Manager (CM) have a very positive influence on sequential read access. The combination of caching the data in the file system cache and the Windows 2000 read-ahead algorithm, which reads more data than is requested, improves overall read performance. From a write perspective, the file system cache and the I/O manager's lazy writer functionality (reviewed in chapter 5) improve write performance by caching write operations, but not as substantially as read operations. Some RAID configurations behave better for write-intensive tasks than others and will be reviewed later in this chapter. By dedicating a portion of the disk subsystem to an application that is write or read sequential in nature, excellent throughput can be achieved. This is particularly important for file and video servers that provide large files.

RANDOM READ/WRITE ENVIRONMENTS

Random disk activities incur many more seek activities than sequentially accessed data. This results in much higher access times to get to the data and subsequently lowers the overall throughput that can be provided. Using the same disk drive vendor-provided statistics, an average random disk transaction takes approximately 5.2ms (read)/6ms (write) to seek the proper track but still has the same average disk rotation latency of 2.98ms. These combine for a grand total of 8.18ms for random read access and 8.98ms for random write activities. Consequently, random disk behavior is approximately 40% slower (commonly more) than sequentially accessed data. What a case for organizing your data in a sequential manner if possible! If an Ultra160 15,000rpm disk drive was used for a sequential based read workload, sequential read access improves to 5.9ms (3.9ms + 2ms) while random read performance improves to 7.0ms (4.5ms + 2.5ms).

HYBRID ENVIRONMENTS (WELL TUNED THROUGH GROUPING SIMILAR DISK BEHAVIORS)

The previous two disk behavior environments assumed a single-user, single-application environment. What happens when you have multiple applications or users all accessing the same disk subsystem where sequential data resides? A random hybrid behavior develops. For example, 10 database applications may all have sequentially write-intensive logging tasks on a dedicated RAID 1 disk subsystem. You might think that the performance characteristics would reflect that of a write-intensive environment. However, since multiple applications are accessing the dedicated RAID 1 disk subsystem, the workload behavior becomes somewhat random in nature, but not fully. You do gain benefits from grouping similar disk activities together on the same disk subsystem, but they do not realize the same gains you might expect from an exclusive disk subsystem ownership arrangement. To avoid disk hybrids, you can invest in more, perhaps smaller, physical disk drives and dedicate them based not only on their disk behavior, but on specific applications to lower the negative randomization effects incurred by multiworkload environments.

Disk Subsystem Throughput

DISK SUBSYSTEM THROUGHPUT FROM AN APPLICATION PERSPECTIVE

To determine the throughput that a single disk drive can achieve, we employed two sets of tests. To emulate a single-user—e.g., workstation—environment, we developed an application that moved data as fast as possible from/to the disk subsystem to memory. The goal for this test was to characterize single-user desktop environments. For multiuser, server-like environments, we used the Neal Nelson Business Benchmark suite for Windows 2000. This test suite is a commercial product, so it is not free. If you are interested in this product, you can contact the company directly at 312-755-1000 (sorry, no external web site URL available).

Using this suite of tests, various disk loads were placed on a Compaq 8000 server with 256MB of RAM, two Pentium III 550Mhz CPUs, and three Ultra2 SCSI 10,000rpm disk drives. The disk drives were configured with Windows 2000 on one separate disk drive, the pagefile on another, and the workload target on the third. The test suite was run up to a 16-copy workload, which corresponds to 320 users and a disk work file size of 400MB. At this heavy load, the file system cache on a server with 256MB is still used, but in reality it was defeated, and the actual performance of the physical disk drive was obtained in both a single-user and simulated multiuser environment. Table 6.4 lists the results for various disk characteristic environments.

TABLE 6.4	*Physical Disk Drive Performance: Single Disk*
Test Characteristics Using 400MB Work File (Note: 256MB of system RAM forces physical disk usage)	***Single* 10,000rpm Ultra2 SCSI Disk Drive Configuration (Throughput achieved as reported by the application) (MB/sec)**
Single Thread (1 user) Test	
Sequential Reads 400MB File	13.8
Sequential Writes of 400MB File	6.8
Multithread (~400 simultaneous user) Test	
Sequential Reads of 1,024-byte Records	11.3
Sequential Writes of 1,024-byte Records	5.7
PseudoRandom Reads of 4,096-byte Records	3.32

The disk vendor rated this particular disk drive used in the performance tests at 25–40MB/sec for disk to internal disk controller cache throughput. The results obtained by measuring the performance of the single disk drive are substantially less than what was recorded from the vendor-provided disk specifications, but remember that this test measured the disk performance from the perspective of an application under an intensive workload, not a pure hardware perspective. Now, vendors are not really trying to deceive you; they are just playing the benchmark marketing game and must measure their performance from a pure hardware perspective, not from an application perspective. For example, to achieve the 25–40MB/sec, the vendor utilized a sector size of 2MB and measured performance much lower in the data path. In contrast to the vendor's specific test configuration and approach, most commercial SCSI HBAs default (which people surprisingly and typically accept at face value) to a sector size of 512KB—a big difference.

The throughput levels obtained when completing disk activities are based on, among other things, your user's access patterns and application environment. The amount of throughput possible is directly influenced by how efficient the application is with its disk I/O usage and how it implements block and buffer sizes. If an application utilizes very large block and buffer sizes, much higher throughput levels can be achieved. Since fewer disk commands are used to obtain/send the data, overall overhead is lower and performance is higher. Table 6.5 provides key information on the Windows 2000 disk subsystem characterizations that we will utilize later in this chapter when detecting bottlenecks, tuning, and sizing the Windows 2000 disk subsystem.

Disk Subsystem Workload

DISK TRANSACTION WORKLOAD: I/O OPERATIONS PER SECOND

Throughput (MB/sec) is only one measure of disk drive performance. Also important are the number of disk I/O operations (transaction workload) that a disk drive can support and the response time (latency) from each transaction. There are several methods to define and measure what an actual disk I/O transaction is. Here, we define a disk I/O request as a general term that refers to a read or write request, and we measure it with reference to Sysmon's Logical Disk objects Transfers/sec counter.

As the disk workload increases (as the number of I/Os per second increases), the disk drive provides higher and higher throughput until a queue begins to form. Once the queue becomes greater than 2–3 outstanding disk requests (this varies by disk drive manufacturer), the disk drive's response time performance can begin to degrade beyond acceptable levels. Degradation experienced is the amount of time a Windows 2000 process must wait for the disk operation to complete. This response time slowdown occurs because the disk drive cannot support any more workload (I/Os per second); thus a performance plateau occurs (maximum throughput occurs and is sustained) and disk requests begin to queue as they wait exponentially longer for service.

Thus, the important point to understand is that the disk drive itself can support only a certain level of disk activity as defined by the number of I/O operations per second. The amount of disk utilization increases based on increased I/O operations per second, as does the throughput. This sounds great. Your throughput is increasing, and more data is being retrieved/sent from the disk drive. Unfortunately, it takes longer to service those disk I/O requests as the disk utilization increases. More work is completed (throughput), but, as the disk drive's queues pass 2–3 outstanding requests per drive, the response time back to the requested process falls off. The vendor you choose, your environment, and your acceptable disk response time determine the accepted level of utilization (disk I/Os per second) that a specific disk drive can support before unacceptable disk queues begin and response time becomes unacceptable.

Here we define the response time for the worst-case acceptable disk response to be 0.035 seconds or 3.5ms and a sustained disk queue of 2. This typically works out to an 80% utilization level when using a single 10,000rpm Ultra3 SCSI disk drive. With this baseline, testing, real-world system monitoring, and vendor information are all combined to produce the rules of thumb shown in Table 6.5 for the maximum number of I/Os per second that a single disk drive can support, segregated based on disk workload characteristics.

| **TABLE 6.5** | *Rule of Thumb for Maximum Recommended Disk I/O Workload Chart (conservative)* |

Disk Behavior Characteristics 9GB Ultra2 SCSI 10,000rpm Disk Drive	**Maximum Recommended I/Os per Second before Excessive Degradation (~80% of theoretical averaged against testing and the real world)**	**Theoretical Workload Latency (Time it takes to retrieve I/O)**
Physical Sequential Reads (Typified by video servers)	240	279
Physical Sequential Writes (Typified by log files)	200	258
Physical Random Reads (Typified by multiuser databases)	105	122
Physical Random Writes (Typified by multiuser databases)	90	111
Hybrid (Well tuned via grouping similar disk behaviors)	150	**N/A**

You can determine that the I/Os per second are occurring on a Windows 2000 system by using Sysmon's Logical Disk counter: Transfers/sec (reads/sec + writes/sec). To determine how long the I/O operations are taking to complete, review Average Disk sec/read, Average Disk sec/write and Average Disk sec/transfer.

Take note that the amount of work that a single disk drive can support does not noticeably increase as disk capacity increases!

Or, in other words, higher capacity disk drives do not equal faster disk drives!

Faster rotating disk drives, larger disk caches, improved integration, and higher-density disk technology improve performance!

The graph in Figure 6-6 was obtained from a server when the user load was increased in blocks of 20 users against the same disk I/O subsystem that consisted of 10 Ultra Fast and Wide 9GB disk drives in a RAID 5 configuration. Measurements were taken of the various disk utilization levels as the user loads increased. Note the amount of time a process's disk request must stay in the disk queue before receiving service.

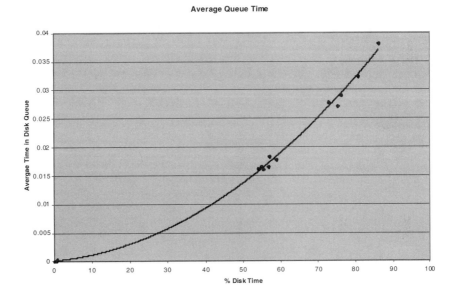

FIGURE 6–6   *Disk Subsystem Average Queue Time*

The graph in Figure 6-6 illustrates that, when the disk is under increased workload levels noted by the %Disk Time, the time disk requests must wait in the disk queue increases at 60% and drastically increases at 80%. What was interesting in this specific environment was that the throughput provided increased along with the Average Time in Queue for the disk requests. So there is a trade-off—response time in essence degrades, but the throughput increases. What is best? It depends on your environment. A video server that has its data buffered before viewing at the distant end can accept more latency while capitalizing on the increased throughput. An interactive database that is used by a customer is very sensitive to latency and can accept lower overall throughput.

The %Disk Time counter under Sysmon can be deceiving and is not a very good indicator of an overloaded disk drive, particularly in multidisk configurations. A high %Disk Time alone is not a true qualifier of an overworked disk drive in a Windows 2000 environment. Table 6.5 helps to provide insight into determining when a disk drive is overworked. But what if you are not familiar with the disk drive technology you are using? Track the Sysmon Logical Average Disk Queue and Sysmon Logical Average Disk sec/Read counters. From another environment, the Sysmon data was collected and graphed (see Figure 6-7).

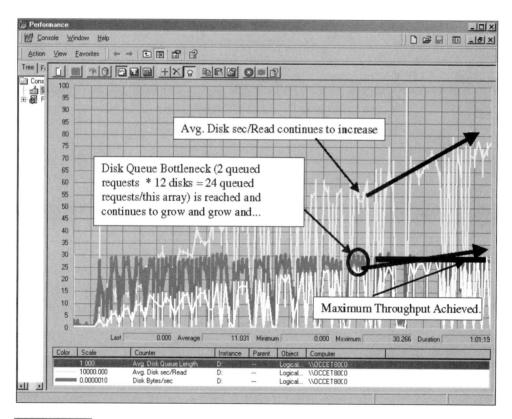

FIGURE 6–7   *Analyzing Disk Workload's Effect on Performance*

Grasping how long a millisecond is does not come easy for everyone (including me), so the Average Disk second/Transfer is scaled for this graph by a factor of 10,000. The Disk Queue counter reached its saturation point at 2 × the number of spindles (disks) in the disk array. Once this occurred and the workload continued, the disk queues continued to grow. The disk drive at this point began to get overloaded. However, the throughput provided by the disk array eventually reached a plateau and did not provide any additional throughput (thus the growing disk queue). The Average Disk sec/Read began to increase from 0.005 to 0.0075. A 66% slowdown! Imagine a process having to wait 75 normalized seconds for a disk request to be returned. That is an eternity from the CPU's perspective.

SCSI Technology

SCSI Bus Technology from a Practical Perspective

SCSI (pronounced "scuzzy") stands for small computer system interface peripheral bus and is the most common and predominant technology used to connect disk devices to servers in use today. Other technologies that were once on the horizon are now beginning to show themselves in the marketplace, but none are as prevalent as SCSI. This is due to the fact that SCSI is cost effective and the technology continues to improve. Later in this chapter we will discuss fibre channel technology because it has made significant inroads into the disk subsystem arena, especially for very large environments (greater than 50 disk drives) and for server area network (SAN) implementations.

SCSI buses are available in a variety of technology standards, each backward compatible with the last, except where the width of the bus in bits makes this unrealistic. One of the advantages of SCSI is that the intelligence of the bus is actually spread across the peripheral devices. Each SCSI device normally has an embedded controller built into it, such as a SCSI disk drive. SCSI has various electrical standards associated with it as well as a standard protocol, which allows an HBA to communicate with the devices on the bus. Intelligent SCSI devices receive SCSI commands and can disconnect from the SCSI bus while completing the requested action, such as obtaining a block of data from a disk array. In this interrupt-driven approach, other devices are *not* waiting to access the bus while other devices are making the necessary calculations to complete the request. Modern SCSI bus technology (SCSI-2 and beyond) allows these SCSI commands to be queued so that the embedded controller can decide which commands to execute first for optimum performance.

As with any protocol implementation, the protocol adds some overhead to the bus for each transaction. When smaller allocation unit (ALU) sizes are in use by Windows 2000 or specific applications make numerous small block disk requests, more of the available SCSI bandwidth is used for SCSI protocol overhead to track and manage all of these small-size requests. Conversely, when larger ALU sizes are implemented under Windows 2000 by more efficient applications, less SCSI bandwidth is sacrificed to SCSI command overhead; thus more bandwidth is available for actual data. The larger the block size used for data transfer, the higher the overall throughput that can be achieved (less data used for managing the data transfer). Due to this SCSI command protocol overhead, as a general rule of thumb, do not expect more than 80–90% of the theoretical SCSI I/O channel bandwidth to actually be available for data. Table 6.6 charts the history of SCSI and fibre channel bus technologies over the past several years through the present.

TABLE 6.6 SCSI and Fibre Channel Technology History

SCSI Interface	Theoretical Maximum Bandwidth (MB/sec)	Practical Bandwidth (MB/sec)	Bus Width (bits)	Maximum Number of SCSI Devices (or fibre channel)	Maximum Bus Length (meters)	
					Single Ended	Differential
SCSI-1	5	4	8	8	6	25
Fast Narrow SCSI-2	10	8	8	8	6	25
Fast Wide SCSI-2	20	16	16	16	6	25
Ultra SCSI-2	20	16	8	8	1.5	25
	20	16	8	4	3	NA
Ultra Wide SCSI-2	40	32	16	16	NA	25
	40	32	16	8	1.5	NA
	40	32	16	4	3	NA
Ultra2 SCSI Fast 40	40	32	16	2	NA	25
	40	32	16	8	NA	12
Wide Ultra2 SCSI Fast 40	80	64	16	16	NA	12
Fibre Channel Arbitrated Loop (FC-AL)	100	90	N/A	126	30 for Copper	Up to 10,000
Ultra160 SCSI (Ultra3)	160	144	16	16	NA	12
2GB Fibre Channel	200	190	N/A	126	NA	Up to 10,000
Ultra320 SCSI Future	320	Future	Future	Future	Future	Future

Implementing SCSI Technology

So which SCSI technology is best for you? Fortunately, SCSI technology auto-negotiates the protocol and therefore the subsequent speed for devices on the SCSI bus. This is good and bad. The autonegotiation lowers the number of problems encountered when migrating or updating your disk technology. Unfortunately, you can't have it all in the SCSI world. If the SCSI bus you are implementing has a combination of Fast and Wide SCSI-2 devices and Ultra Wide SCSI-3 devices, you are limited to running the SCSI bus at the lowest common speed, which, in this case, would be the Fast and Wide SCSI-2 device. If you try to run a SCSI channel at ultra-SCSI speeds (normally set with the HBA configuration software, not via Windows 2000) with a staggered set of disk technologies, SCSI timeouts will occur due to the variances in the impedances of the ultra-SCSI and non-ultra-SCSI devices. These SCSI timeouts are routed either to Windows 2000 event log or to the HBA-specific monitoring software under Windows 2000 or both.

Is there that much overall performance detectable between various SCSI bus technologies such as Ultra Wide SCSI-2 operating at 40MB/sec vs. Ultra160 operating at 160MB/sec? The primary difference is the number of disk drives that each SCSI bus can support before becoming saturated. If you place a single disk drive on either bus in a typical Windows 2000 environment, you would not notice a significant performance difference. Why? As observed in Figure 6-5, most of the time associated with getting data from the disk drive is due to the disk seek movements and latency times incurred from platter rotation. Initial tests show that transfers using Ultra160 are between 0.01ms and 0.03ms faster than Ultra Wide SCSI-3. This is not quite enough of an improvement to rip out your current Ultra Wide SCSI-3 investment and replace it with Ultra160. However, the price of Ultra160 is now quite competitive with other bus technologies, so if you are planning a new disk subsystem, the slightly faster Ultra160 solution is easily justified.

What Ultra160 does bring is the capability of supporting more disk drives on a single SCSI bus than was previously possible. If you expect 5MB/sec of throughput from each disk drive, with Ultra160 you can configure 30 disk drives per SCSI bus channel vs. a previous maximum of 10. These disk-drive-to-SCSI-bus ratios are based on the initial best-case throughput estimate of 5MB/sec per disk drive. OK, someone will take notice that you cannot place 30 disk drives on a single Ultra160 bus, which can address only 16 devices at a time. To support 30 disk drives on a bus that can support only 16 drives, you must implement smart external RAID units that manage your external disks and then present them as a single unit to your Ultra160 HBA.

Determining SCSI Bus Throughput under Windows 2000

How can you tell how many disk drives to configure per SCSI bus? First, understand your system environment. Windows 2000 does not instinctively throw up a red flag and alert you to the fact that your SCSI channel is saturated. A good rule of thumb (also found in Table 6.4): estimate 8MB/sec of throughput for general sequential environments and 3MB/sec of throughput for random-disk-I/O-based environments for each 10,000rpm Ultra2 or above class disk drive. For example, if you are implementing a single Ultra2 SCSI channel that will support a random disk I/O environment, you can configure up to 26 disk drives per Ultra2 SCSI channel. This provides an initial maximum Windows 2000 disk subsystem configuration sizing estimate for a single-channel environment.

How can you be sure that you have not overconfigured or underconfigured the SCSI channel? Proactively monitor your system's performance during regular business operations (expecting another answer?). One technique to determine the throughput of the SCSI bus under Windows 2000 is to use Sysmon's Logical Disk object's Disk Bytes/sec counter. This counter reports the data rate in bytes that are transferred to or from the disk during write or read operations. Using Sysmon, select Logical Disk: Disk Bytes/sec and then select all of the disk drives connected to the same physical SCSI channel that you are investigating (you must understand the system's physical-to-logical mapping configuration to correlate which disk drives/partitions are on which SCSI bus). Then, sum the average, minimum, and maximum values report under Disk Bytes/sec for each of the disk drives on a particular SCSI channel by hand or export the chart to a spreadsheet file, and then sum up the results. Just selecting the _Total instance under the Disk Bytes/sec counter will not provide valid information unless all disks are on the same physical bus. Once you get the final result, compare this value to the theoretical and practical SCSI throughput values shown in Table 6.6. If the value of the summed Disk Bytes/sec is within 20% of the practical maximum throughput of the bus, consider adding another SCSI channel. If the summation values are much less than the practical SCSI throughput shown in Table 6.6, you have room to add more disk drives to the current SCSI channel.

Fibre Channel Technology

Fibre channel technology is poised to eventually replace SCSI technology as the disk subsystem interconnect of choice in the coming years and has already made significant inroads into high-end Windows 2000 system configurations for servers. Fibre channel is based on ANSI standards similar to SCSI and is the next step in the disk I/O connectivity evolution. Parallel SCSI will eventually reach its electrical limitations, hence slowing its continued performance enhancements. Of course, every time you hear this, someone at a place like Bell Labs comes up with a creative solution, thus overcoming accepted electrical characteristics. For example, Adaptec successfully introduced the Ultra160 technology, which brought SCSI technology back as a competitive overall throughput alternative to fibre channel. In lieu of these pure performance leapfrog gains, fibre channel also brings more options to the disk subsystem realm. Fibre channel's primary strength lies in the fact that it can be implemented over fiber optics and is serial in nature, as opposed to the parallel nature of SCSI. With the use of fiber optics, fibre channel provides:

- Increased throughput
- Less distance limitations, i.e., more options
- More topology implementation options than traditional SCSI technologies
- Easier cabling (The simplicity of fibre channel cabling makes management easier, with fewer impedance issues and associated data integrity problems.)
- Higher numbers of disk drives supported
- Improved security
- Less susceptibility to environmental factors

Currently, throughput for a fibre channel bus ranges up to 200MB/sec. When implementing fibre channel, various topologies can be used, including arbitrated loop (most common), point-to-point, and switched implementations. Where differential SCSI is limited to 25 meters from the server to the disk drive, the fiber optic implementation of fibre channel allows for distances of up to 10,000 meters (10 kilometers or 6.25 miles). This increased distance option allows for more flexibility in planning for disasters and overall system architectures. Even at a relatively high throughput of 200MB/sec, if you place your disk drives 10 kilometers away from your Windows 2000 server, the laws of physics do kick in. Since the speed of light has not changed recently, implementing wide-area topologies does introduce latency into the solution, which slows overall performance—a factor to consider when developing your fibre channel–based solutions.

Even with the new features and possibilities that fibre channel brings, the same concepts apply that we used when reviewing SCSI technologies. The primary performance hindrance of a disk drive attached to a fibre channel bus is still the physical disk drive limitations of the disk drive itself. With fibre channel, more disk drives per fibre channel bus channel can be supported due to the higher available throughput.

Fibre channel is initially being offered as an HBA to attach external disk drives with little intelligence in the HBA. Fibre channel HBAs are typically paired with an intelligent external disk array device. In this configuration, the intelligent external disk array device provides the hardware RAID implementation and the fibre channel HBA provides the connectivity back into the server.

Fibre Channel: Hubs vs. Switches

When implementing a fibre channel–based solution, you have two choices at the basic topology level: hub-based and switch-based implementations. In the hub approach, all devices connected to the fibre channel system are done in a shared contiguous bus configuration. An analogy to this is the old shared Ethernet hub-based network solutions. Even with the most recent 200MB/sec specification for fibre channel, this bandwidth is shared with all devices connected to the hub. Obviously fibre channel has a much improved access protocol than shared Ethernet, but it is still a shared medium. For example, if 10 devices are attached to a 200MB/sec fibre channel hub, in a worst-case scenario, each device has only 20MB/sec of bandwidth to use.

In a switch-based fibre channel implementation, bandwidth is dedicated to each device, which removes sharing of bandwidth (unless two devices wish to communicate with a third device at the same time). Prices for fibre channel hubs and switches are just now starting to become comparable. If you have the budget, opt for a switched implementation because it provides more overall performance, and some third-party software packages provide the ability to use the higher bandwidth this approach provides. For example, some packages provide the ability to back up separate disk drive arrays to separate backup systems. In a switched environment, two devices can communicate with two other devices at the same time without sharing the same bandwidth.

HBAs

The next step in the data path, after the disk drive controller places data onto the SCSI or fibre channel bus, is to get the requested data onto the PCI bus. The HBA performs this operation and is also referred to as a disk controller or RAID controller. HBAs provide a range of functions from basic SCSI connectivity to complex RAID support. There are three primary distinguishable features that separate the various HBAs available today: the number and type of SCSI channels supported, amount of system CPU overhead introduced, the RAID support level, and the I/O workload supported.

The channel density that a SCSI HBA supports impacts the amount of disk devices that Windows 2000 can support and how they are configured in the server. Today, one HBA can support from one to four onboard SCSI channels. This allows for the conservation of those precious PCI slots available on the system. Utilizing these higher-density HBAs, an SHV-based server can support up to five HBAs for a total of 20 SCSI channels. Whether or not configuring that many SCSI channels in a single SHV-based Windows 2000 system is a good idea depends upon your environment. If you do implement high numbers of HBAs in a single Intel-based SHV server, you will most likely run into a shortage of interrupts. Each server vendor implements the setup of interrupts in a slightly different manner, so I will refer you to your vendor's server documentation for the steps to follow for interrupt control. If your solution demands that a high number of external disk drives be configured, I strongly encourage you to consider fibre channel technology instead of SCSI for its ease of implementation.

System Interrupt Setting Strategy

Regardless of how you set the interrupts, if you must share interrupts between devices configured in your server, try to share the interrupts between those devices that use the same Windows 2000 driver. This helps to improve overall performance. The concept of plug-and-play PCI takes a backseat when configuring high-end Windows 2000 servers that require sharable PCI interrupts to support a higher number of peripheral devices. Windows 2000 does provide a diagnostics tool—Windows 2000 system information, reviewed in chapter 2 (winmsd.exe)—that helps to determine which interrupts are associated with which devices. There is a wealth of low-level Windows 2000 information provided by this tool. If you have not already investigated this tool, I urge you to take a moment to see what it has to offer. This tool can also be run from the command line on local or remote Windows 2000 systems and can be used easily to get a quick inventory of a Windows 2000 system.

HBA and CPU Power

Each HBA interrupts Windows 2000 when an operation requires system CPU intervention. The amount of CPU cycles required varies among HBAs. The CPU time required to service an HBA is considered to be the overhead the HBA places onto the system. This overhead is actually good in one sense because it is used to get data from the disk drives to the CPU so that productive work can be completed. Other I/O devices such as network interface cards (NICs) also introduce this CPU interrupt overhead as well. It is important to be aware that CPU cycles are required to drive the I/O subsystem. For smaller systems that are configured with small disk subsystems, the CPU overhead introduced by the disk arrays is not significant enough to worry about. As Windows 2000–based solutions continue to get larger and larger, the amount of CPU cycles required to drive the disk subsystem becomes more of an influencing factor. If the system application requires a great deal of computational power and there is a large amount of disk I/O activity, CPU power must be planned to support both.

Various vendor specification sheets for 4-, 8-, and even 32-CPU Pentium III servers state that multiple terabytes of disk can be connected to one server. One vendor stated support for 7TB. From a connectivity perspective, this is possible, but to have a Windows 2000 system actually drive a disk subsystem of this size (assuming that all of the disks and applications are active) takes some planning! If you examine the TPC-C benchmark closely, for example, you will notice that, for the larger (4–8 CPUs) Windows 2000 benchmarks, 1.1–1.8TB of disk drive space is configured on average. In these benchmark environments, vendors wish to get the highest performance rating at the lowest cost. For this reason, disks are normally not configured into the solution unless they are actually in use. If you compare the server hardware you have obtained with a benchmark configuration similar to your environment—such as TPC-C—you can gather some insight into how many active disk drives can realistically be supported by your server architecture as well as the CPU power needed to take advantage of it.

These test results are subject to many factors—e.g., Windows 2000 version, tuning and configuration, database version, and number of clients—but they still provide a rough estimate of the relative sizing between CPUs, SCSI channels, and disk drives in a client-server or eCommerce database supporting environment. Table 6.7 provides some insight into the CPU power and disk subsystem configuration used for recent TPC-C benchmarks.

| **TABLE 6.7** | *Utilizing TPC-C Results to Determine Relative Disk Subsystem Requirements* |

Number & Type of CPUs	Memory	Number of HBAs	Number/Type of Disk Drives	Amount of Disk Space Configured (approximate)	Disk Drives per SCSI Channel
1 Pentium III 600MHz/256KB	3GB	3-2 channels	64/9.1GB	576GB	12
2 Pentium III 600MHz/256KB	1GB	4-3 channels	114/9.1GB	1TB	12
8 Pentium III 550MHz/2MB	4GB	7-2 channels	172/9.1GB	1.5TB	12

HBA and Disk Drive Workload Sizing Example

We had to consider more than throughput when reviewing a disk drive's performance, and we also have to consider more than the number of SCSI channels that an HBA can support. When sizing the number of HBAs required, consider the theoretical I/Os per second that the HBAs can support as well. For example, if you are configuring 10 disk drives for a sequentially intensive disk subsystem environment, do the associated math. Each 10,000rpm Ultra160SCSI disk drive in a sequential environment should be able to support up to 240 disk I/O operations per second and 8MB/sec of throughput. An implementation with 10 disk drives would therefore require an HBA or HBAs that can support 2,400 I/Os per second and 80MB/sec of aggregate throughput. To fulfill this outlined requirement, a 2-channel Ultra2 Compaq RAID HBA could be used. A Compaq RAID HBA meets the throughput requirement (80MB/sec per channel) and allows room for growth by providing a second usable SCSI channel, and it has a workload rating of 3,400 I/Os per second, which also provides room for growth. You can obtain this type of performance data from the server or HBA vendor's web site or by contacting them directly.

I/O Bus Technology and Selection

From the peripheral adapter (HBA, NIC, etc.), data is passed to the I/O bus on its way to the system bus. From a legacy perspective, Intel-based systems have supported numerous system bus and I/O bus technologies throughout the years. The trend is to remove support for these older I/O bus technologies since this approach results in lowering configuration options which in turn lowers overall cost of ownership for customers. It also removes research and development (R&D) investments needed to support legacy technology while removing some of the limiting factors introduced by having to support legacy technology. Some environments still require the use of legacy peripheral adapters such as those based on industry standard architecture (ISA, 8MB/sec), extended industry standard architecture (EISA, 33MB/sec), and microchannel architecture (MCA, 80MB/sec) I/O buses. EISA and ISA bus support is still designed into many PCI-based systems today, but that number is dwindling fast.

The older SHV-based server provides a bridge to an EISA I/O bus, thus providing several slots for EISA/ISA-based I/O cards. Microchannel-based servers are rarely produced with the most recent Intel CPU architectures.

Avoid using any legacy bus-based I/O cards. Unless you have no other choice for your environments, legacy-based I/O cards (ISA, EISA, and MCA) should never be used in your enterprise class Windows 2000 systems. These older I/O cards do not provide nearly the level of performance of modern 32- and 64-bit PCI cards which support bus mastering and direct DMA support and PCI burst speed support. In fact, using this older technology in a newer system can actually slow down the modern technology in that same system!

Current-generation PCI I/O subsystem technology arrives in several flavors. The current PCI technologies available are listed in Table 6.8.

TABLE 6.8	Current PCI I/O Bus Technology Speed	
Bus Width (bits)	**Speed (MHz)**	**Transfer Rate (MB/sec)**
32	33	132
32	66	264
64	33	264
64	66	528

Driver development and peripheral components are extremely important when maximizing the performance of your Windows 2000 solutions. Industry R&D investment is now focused on 64-bit PCI technology, which will result in the best drivers and devices. Again, like CPU technology, obtaining the leading-edge technology that is garnering the greatest amount of investment will yield the highest performing, longer-term solution and will provide a stronger return on investment. The recommended current I/O technology of choice is 64-bit PCI I/O technology.

PCI I/O Bus Architecture

There are numerous approaches to implementing PCI-based I/O subsystems. At the core of all of the approaches, there is a PCI chip set that connects the PCI bus or buses to the memory subsystem and main (front-side) system bus. Two approaches are bridged and peer-based PCI technology implementations.

BRIDGED PCI APPROACH

Bridged PCI technology is typically implemented in workstations and low-end servers. Electrically, a PCI bus can support only so many electrical loads (PCI devices). To extend the number of devices that a PCI bus can support (which adds the slots that you can plug those PCI devices into), a second PCI bus is added to the first via an electrical connector. This electrical connector is commonly referred to as a *PCI bridge*. A logical architecture of a bridged-based PCI I/O bus is shown in Figure 6-8.

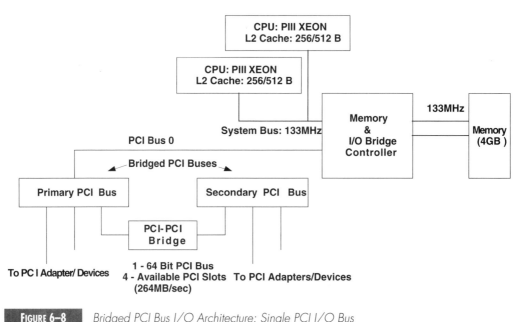

FIGURE 6-8   *Bridged PCI Bus I/O Architecture: Single PCI I/O Bus*

Using PCI bridge technology does not increase the available bandwidth; it just enables additional devices to be added. This is very important because some people think that having additional PCI slots available equals more available bandwidth. When adding PCI devices to a system with a single bus bridged PCI architecture, place the devices needing the highest speed in the first slot (slot 1), which is physically closest to the system bus. There is usually a diagram inside the system case with the PCI bus information on it. PCI bus priority is based on which slot the device actually resides in in the PCI bus. The lower the slot number, the higher the priority. Or, in other words, if you have a low PCI slot number, you get service first and are scanned first during power up. Populate the PCI bus from the lowest slot number to the highest. Any devices that are on the bridged or extended portion of the PCI bus will incur latency due to the bridge. This latency has lowered over the years as the industry has developed improved PCI bridges and device drivers, but it is still a delay you can avoid.

Key items to remember when populating an I/O system with a single PCI bus or bridged PCI bus:

- *Populate the lowest slot number in the PCI bus.*
- *Populate all slots in the primary PCI bus before populating the secondary PCI bus.*
- *Do not attempt to load balance the primary and secondary PCI buses.*
- *Place devices that require high amounts of interrupts (those without their own onboard CPU) in the first slot.*

PEER PCI BUS APPROACH

So, what is a manufacturer to do if more I/O bandwidth is needed? Add additional, physically separate PCI buses. When more than one physically separate PCI bus is added to the system design, the system is referred to as having peer PCI bus architecture. If the first bus operated at 33Mhz and is 64 bits wide, it provides 264MB/sec of throughput and typically supports at least four electrical loads for PCI devices. When a peer PCI bus is added, which can be any of the technologies that were outlined in Table 6.8, it adds additional bandwidth and corresponding electrical load support. For our example, if the added PCI bus is identical to the first, now the system will support 528MB/sec of throughput and 8 total PCI device slots. Figure 6-9 is an example of a peer PCI-based system. As an example, the Compaq 6400R, has two peer 64-bit 33MHz PCI I/O buses.

When configuring a system that is designed with peer PCI buses, use them to your advantage. The most obvious technique when using peer PCI buses is to ensure you do not put more PCI devices into a single bus than it can support. A key theme of this chapter is to follow the data and avoid system-level bottlenecks. From a PCI priority perspective, PCI bus 0 is scanned

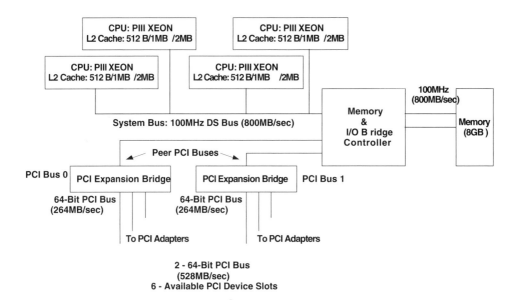

FIGURE 6–9   *Peer PCI Bus I/O Architecture (Standard High-Volume Server Approach)*

first, then PCI bus 1, during the system boot process. Since each individual PCI bus has its own electrical negotiations that occur, you can also improve performance by balancing your PCI devices across each peer bus, regardless of whether throughput is a concern. For example, if you have a dual SCSI HBA, place it in PCI bus 0, slot 1. If you also have a Gigabit Ethernet adapter, place it into PCI bus 1, slot 1. Now, the throughput workload is balanced between the two buses, and each adapter has first priority on all bus negotiations on its perspective PCI bus.

Key items to remember when populating Peer PCI Bus I/O system:

- *Populate the lowest slot number in the PCI bus.*
- *Load balance PCI devices across all PCI buses.*
- *Separate devices that require high amounts of interrupts (those without their own onboard CPU) between the buses.*
- *Track overall throughput of devices to ensure PCI bus is not overwhelmed.*
- *If possible, choose two NICs and place them across the PCI buses vs. having one NIC with two channels.*

Following the Data to Improve I/O Bus Scalability

Continuing our journey of following the data flowing from the disk drive through the peripheral adapter (HBA, NIC, etc.), data is passed to the PCI-based I/O bus on its way to the system bus. The importance of the I/O bus comes into effect when sizing and tuning the system. You do not want to overwhelm the theoretical bandwidth of the I/O subsystem, or you will create a bottleneck before you even apply stress to the systems.

For example, placing two fibre channel controllers in the same PCI bus does not make sense. Why? Follow the data. If we assume that both channels are fully active, when we follow the data path, this 400MB/sec of throughput feeds a 264MB/sec I/O bus, thus resulting in an I/O bottleneck. A better approach would be to each fibre channel controller into its own separate PCI bus. Taking this approach, a 200MB/sec fibre channel controller feeds a 264MB/sec PCI bus.

Although CPUs are normally the center of attention, it is the increased I/O throughput that provides the real advantage for databases and other I/O-intense server applications. The larger Windows 2000 family members such as Advanced Server and Data Center, which support larger-scale hardware platforms, also support much higher I/O throughputs.

Distributing CPU Power to the Peripherals to Improve I/O Scalability

There are two primary limiting factors when working with I/O operations besides the physical disk drive itself. Software is actually the first area that slows down I/O operations. There are many operating system layers and device drive layers that slow down I/O operations before they ever reach the actual hardware. Second, even with bus mastering technology that allows PCI devices to detach from the bus to perform operations, peripheral devices still rely on a high number of CPU interrupts to complete the requested I/O tasks. This software and hardware combination lowers the overall scalability of a server.

To overcome these system limitations, an Intelligent I/O Initiative (I2O) special interest group was formed. Many vendors are now endorsing it. I2O technology attempts to improve overall I/O performance. The first major change is in the operating system software architecture. In I2O software architecture, the driver is split. The operating system module portion of the driver handles I/O interaction with the operating system, thereby controlling I/O subsystem access to the CPU. The hardware device module is the other part of the I2O subsystem which manages how hardware controllers interact with I2O-compatible I/O devices to gain access to I/O services. The goal of this new design is to lower the overhead associated with I/O operations traversing the operating system hierarchy to the device and to standardize device driver development and management.

Another benefit of I2O technology is the advent of truly intelligent peripherals. These I2O-based peripheral devices are able to operate without constantly interrupting the CPU for their operations. Many of these devices will include their own CPU and memory subsystems; this off-loads the actual device activities from the system's CPU and greatly improves the performance of the peripheral card, lowers the traffic on the system and I/O buses, and lowers the amount of CPU power required for I/O operations. It allows the system's CPU to focus its attention on more productive application and user-related tasks and improves overall server throughput by lowering system bus contention. I2O disk I/O devices will still need to interrupt the CPU, not for their internal operations, but when the requested data is available for transfer up the data path.

When selecting system hardware, especially servers, seek I2O-enabled systems and peripherals.

Next-Generation PCI I/O Bus

The current PCI bus employs a combination of standards, with 64-bit 33MHz (264MB/sec) producing the highest throughput today for a PCI-based I/O subsystem. Current PCI bus technology also supports the ability to hot swap PCI adapter cards; this technology is most common in new systems. While 64-bit 66MHz (528MB/sec)-based PCI technology is available, it is only beginning to trickle into the mainstream.

The next-generation PCI bus is based on a PCI-X. PCI-X is planned to be backward compatible and will provide a 133MHz bus and 64 bits of bandwidth, enabling up to 1GB/sec throughput. To accommodate this next generation of I/O bus, both Windows 2000 and the system hardware must be capable of taking advantage of the new I/O design. Windows 2000 will support the next-generation I/O bus and will most likely provide a service pack update to support it. From a system hardware perspective, current Windows 2000 systems that support 32- or 64-bit/66MHz PCI I/O buses will require a motherboard swap-out or an incredibly creative solution (or kludgey, depending how you look at it) to support the forthcoming PCI-X I/O bus.

The System Bus

The system bus is the final data highway that leads to both the memory and CPU subsystems. The SHV-based reference server's system bus is 128 bits wide and supports a bandwidth of 800MB/sec. The system bus was reviewed in detail in chapter 5. It should be very clear that the system bus is the backbone of any Windows 2000 solution. It is startling when the system bus or front-side system bus is referred to as the PCI bus—it makes you wonder what they are referring to.

Next-Generation System Bus

The next generation of SHV server bus is currently being touted as operating at 400MHz, which would support having two PCI-X I/O buses feeding it. This technology utilized in conjunction with a new generation of CPUs and memory technology will improve overall Windows 2000 technology performance. A new system bus for the server's motherboard is not a trivial plug-in upgrade. For a server to be upgraded to the new system bus, the server's motherboard would have to be completely replaced and the power and cooling system would need to be capable of accommodating the new electrical loads. By the time the motherboard is replaced, it might be less expensive to purchase a new server with the latest technology and just redeploy the older technology as a complete system to a lab or less critical activity.

Redundant Array of Inexpensive Disks (RAID)

It should be obvious by following the data path through our SHV-based reference system that a single disk drive cannot provide enough performance capacity to meet the performance requirements of an enterprise Windows 2000 solution, nor can it even begin to tax the server's I/O subsystem. RAID allows for the grouping of multiple smaller (i.e., inexpensive) disk drives into larger logical disk devices. Adding RAID technology to your system's disk I/O subsystem is becoming a more common choice to increase performance capacity, increase disk space capacity, ease disk management, and improve availability for all classes of systems.

RAID is a particularly excellent choice if multiple disk drives are available and it is not possible to break up the data files across separate disk drives to balance the use of the disk subsystem. Implementing a RAID array, you can place data files onto a single logical drive under Windows 2000 that takes advantage of the multiple drives composing the actual RAID array. Windows 2000 allows for the use of both software- and hardware-based RAID solutions.

The following sections outline descriptions, basic performance, and fault tolerance trade-offs of the various RAID levels.

RAID 0—Disk Striping

RAID level 0 evenly stripes the disk activity across two or more disk drives. This logical layout provides the advantage of better performance for read, write, random, and sequential environments. RAID 0 also provides direct disk capacity improvement. When two disk drives are configured in a RAID 0 array, the total available disk space is the sum of the capacity of each individual disk drive in the array. If three 9GB disk drives are configured as a RAID 0 array, there is 27GB of user-available data space.

When a RAID 0 array is implemented, the average seek time required to access the data is lowered when compared to that of a single disk drive. This is one of the ways in which a RAID 0 or any of the RAID levels improves performance. The trade-off for using RAID 0 is it provides no fault tolerance. If you lose one drive in your RAID 0 disk array, you will lose the data for the entire array. In a RAID 0 environment, increasing the number of drives in the array improves the overall I/O performance.

To determine the workload (I/Os per second, i.e., the number of transfers per second) of each disk in a RAID 0 array, use the following equation:

(disk reads/sec + disk writes/sec)/(number of disks in the RAID array)

If your Sysmon Logical Disk counter: Avg. Disk Queue Length divided by the number of disks in the array exceeds 2, you have a serious bottleneck in a RAID 0 striped array. Adding additional drives in the array increases the workload that the array can support and improves the overall performance provided.

MEAN TIME BETWEEN FAILURES (MTBF)

RAID 0 does not provide any fault tolerance. Thus a question you should consider is: How often could I lose a disk drive? The MTBF of a modern disk drive runs as high as 1 million hours and is improving all the time. But this is the mean value—some fail early (commonly within the first week), some later. Predictive failure technology is now commonplace and incorporated in most disk drives at even the desktop level. The drive itself tracks internal errors and, if you install the management software that comes with your system, commonly it will track this information and inform you of a pending disk failure. The only time I have observed this technology not working was when it was not installed. Read those docs that arrive with your system!

The more disk drives you have in an array, the higher the chance one will fail. How is this possible? Statistics. The formula to determine the MTBF of a system is:

$$\text{MTBF} = 1 \: / \: (1/N1 + 1/N2 + \ldots 1/NX)$$

where N is the MTBF of each component and X is the number components. For example, using a MTBF of 500,000 hours for a disk drive (I just grabbed an MTBF for a disk drive from a vendor's web site), if you have two disk drives, the MTBF = 1 / (1/500,000 + 1/500,000), which works out to 454,545 hours. If three drives are in use in the array, the MTBF for the disk array lowers to 238,095 hours! I have had the opportunity to design, benchmark, and work with a team to bring into production multi-TB systems. At one site that continued to grow (over 4TB with 4GB and 9GB disk drives), they actually had a shopping cart full of tested new disk drives that they would use when alerted of a disk drive failure. They would then walk around with their cart changing out failed disk drives on a regular basis. For this environment, they used RAID 1, 10, and 5—no RAID 0 due to their business requirements.

If you are going to use RAID 0, make sure you plan accordingly. If the data residing on the array is valuable, do not use RAID 0. If the improved disk subsystem performance is needed but availability has been planned around using clustering technology or another technique, RAID 0 can become a valuable technique for improving disk subsystem performance.

RAID 1—Disk Mirroring

RAID level 1 mirrors (duplicates) the disk activity across two disk drives, thus providing full redundancy. This logical layout provides for better read performance, especially in multiuser environments, but slightly lower performance in write-intensive environments. When data is read from a RAID 1 mirror, it does not matter which disk drive in the array provides the data—each individual drive can perform simultaneous read operations; thus the read operations are typically dispatched across the different drives in the array. This is referred to as a *split seek*—two seeks can occur simultaneously, which improves read performance. Once the data is provided by either disk drive in the array, the HBA considers it valid and continues on.

Writing to the RAID 1 array works slightly differently. Each write must be sent to each drive in the RAID 1 mirror so that all data is kept identical. Since each disk drive operates independently, one drive may run slower than the other. Because of this, the HBA/controller must wait until both drives in the array acknowledge a successful write before moving on (or caching it). These algorithms for write activity contribute to generally slightly lower write performance when compared to a single disk drive configuration.

To determine the workload (I/Os per second) of each disk in a RAID 1 array (i.e., the number of transfers per second), use the following equation:

[disk reads/sec + (2 × disk writes/sec)] / (number of disks in the RAID array)

Today's RAID 1 mirrors use a two-disk configuration. Historically, RAID 1 arrays support a slightly lower workload in a write-intensive environment than systems with one hard disk. However, if you use modern, I2O-enabled, hardware-cache-based RAID controllers, RAID 1 write performance can be comparable to if not better than a single disk drive. You can determine the disk queues of a RAID 1 array by dividing the Avg. Disk Queue Length by the number of disks in the array. If this value consistently exceeds 2–3, you have a serious bottleneck in a RAID 1 mirror.

RAID 1 provides complete data redundancy, even if you are using only two disks. The trade-off for this high level of fault tolerance is that the capacity of a RAID 1 two-disk mirror is lowered by 50%. For example, if you have two 9GB disk drives in a RAID 1 mirror, there is only 9GB of storage space available to Windows 2000.

RAID Levels 2, 3, 4, and Others

These RAID levels are not commonly used in general computing environments, so they are not addressed here. If you are curious, seek a more in-depth understanding of RAID technology, or if are just looking for some trivia facts, search the web for "RAID technology." You can also visit the web pages of one of the many hardware-based RAID manufacturers such as Adaptec, AMI, DPT, or Mylex (just to name a few) for a complete definition of all of these RAID levels. The RAID Advisory Board also keeps a web site located at http://www.raid-advisory.com/. As you peruse these different web sites you may find it interesting how each site interprets RAID technology just a little differently, each adding its own spin.

RAID 5—Disk Striping with Parity

RAID 5 provides fault tolerance and improved performance for most environments. It stripes the disk activity data and calculated parity data across three or more disk drives in a rotating fashion. When data is written to a RAID 5 array, the data is broken up and written to all of the disk drives in the array, except for the logical parity drive. For each write transaction, the parity information must be generated and updated. In this manner, RAID 5 provides fault tolerance for your array.

In RAID 5, the logical parity disk is rotated among all of the disk drives in the array. For example, if there are three drives in logical RAID 5 array—composed of disk 1, disk 2, and disk 3—as the first set of data is written to the array, it is placed onto disk 1 and disk 2, while the parity information is written to disk 3. Subsequently, when the second set of data is written to the RAID 5 array, data is written to disk 1 and disk 3 and the parity information is written to disk 2 and so on in the rotating order. In this manner, parity information is spread across all of the disk drives in the RAID 5 array. To lower the confusion level with this concept, review the illustration of data placement in a RAID 5 array in Figure 6-10. If one drive were to fail, there is enough parity information available on the surviving disk drives in the RAID 5 array to continue disk operations and to rebuild the failed disk drive's data when the failed drive is replaced with a working disk drive.

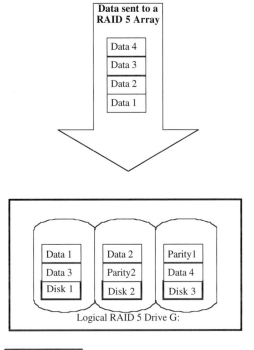

FIGURE 6–10   Writing Data to a RAID 5 Array

If the system experiences its regular workload during reconstruction of a failed drive, from the parity located on the other disk drives in the array, the performance provided by the RAID 5 array to the system will be greatly degraded.

Disk write operations take longer to complete in a RAID 5 array than any other RAID configuration. Under normal RAID 5 operations, for every write operation, parity must be calculated. When you initially low-level format a RAID 5 array, with the HBA-provided software tools (i.e., this is not the same as formatting a drive using Windows 2000) the HBA/controller clears the data on the RAID 5 array and resets the parity across the array. Now, when a disk write operation occurs in a RAID 5 array, the following actions occur:

- Data is *written* (1) to the disk array.
- The data is then *read* (2) and the parity information is *read* (3) from the disk array.
- An exclusive or (XOR) operation is completed on the read data and the read parity information to determine the new parity information.
- The new parity information is then *written* (4) to disk.

Thus, for every RAID 5 write operation, four physical disk operations are required (read data, read parity, compute parity [CPU action, not disk], write data, write parity). It is these write characteristics of RAID 5 that cause the slower write performance. Also, RAID 5 operations do incur higher CPU overhead due to these parity calculations. The main CPUs can be used for these operations; however, to improve scalability, most RAID solutions are implemented with hardware-based RAID controllers that have their own CPUs. This off-loads CPU activity associated with parity generation from the main CPUs to the RAID controller.

On the bright side, the RAID 5 disk stripe with parity environment is similar to a RAID 0 stripe set for read-intensive environments. Data is spread across the drives in the RAID 5 array, so you glean the advantage of having multiple disks servicing your requests at the same time. A RAID 5 array with five disks supports almost five times as much workload and up to five times as many outstanding disk requests as a one-disk system before becoming a bottleneck. To calculate how many disk requests a single drive in a RAID 5 array is supporting, use the following formula:

[disk reads/sec + (4 × disk writes/sec)] / (number of disks in the RAID array)

To determine the upper limit for the disk queues in a RAID 5 environment, multiply the numbers of disk drives in the array by 2.

RAID level 5 provides data redundancy, allowing for the loss of one of the array's member disk drives without the loss of any data. If one drive fails, once it is replaced with a new drive, the RAID 5 array will recreate the lost drive by using the parity information on the existing drives. If two drives in the same RAID 5 array fail, all data in that array is lost. Of course, that is what good backup strategies are for. The trade-off for this redundancy is that the capacity of a RAID 5 stripe with parity is lowered by a factor of 1/(size of one disk drive member). For example, if you have three 9GB disk drives in a RAID 5 array, there is 18GB of usable storage space. If there were ten 9GB disk drives in a RAID 5 array, there would be 81GB of usable disk space—a capacity loss of only 1/10. In RAID 5 environments, increasing the number of drives in the array improves the random read I/O performance as well as the write performance.

RAID 10: Combining RAID 0 Stripes and Raid 1 Mirroring (1 + 0)

RAID 10 stripes data across two or more drives (RAID 0) and then mirrors that logical drive set with another stripe set for fault tolerance (RAID 1). Consider RAID 10 a marriage of RAID 0 and RAID 1. This logical combination layout provides better overall performance than a direct implementation of RAID 1, the performance enhancements of RAID 0, and the fault tolerance features of RAID 1. Figure 6-11 illustrates a RAID 10 array.

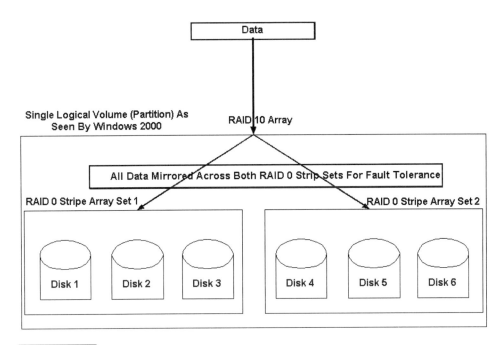

RAID 10 Array

From a performance perspective, RAID 1 offers dramatic performance improvements for write operations. When a write is performed, it must be written to each of the underlying RAID 0 array stripe sets. Since each underlying RAID array is actually a RAID 0 array, no write penalty is incurred as in RAID 5; thus the overall performance is improved even though the transaction is not considered complete until both of the underlying RAID 0 stripe sets acknowledge a successful write. For example, a 12-disk RAID 10 array provides a 25% improvement in write operations throughput.

Read operations also are improved as reads are submitted to both RAID 0 stripe sets in a split-seek fashion which enables parallel independent searches by each array. For read-intensive operations, a RAID 10 appears as one large RAID 4 array and provides similar performance to that of a RAID 5 array. For example, from a read performance perspective, a 12-disk RAID 10 array provides roughly the same level of read performance as a 12-disk RAID 5 array.

To calculate how many disk requests a single disk in a RAID 10 array can support, use the following formula:

[disk reads/sec + (2 × disk writes/sec)] / (number of disks in the RAID array)

To determine the upper limit for the disk queues in a RAID 10 environment, multiply the number of disk drives in the array by 2.

The trade-off for these performance improvements and high level of fault tolerance is that the capacity of a RAID 10 mirror is lowered by 50%, just as it is for a direct RAID 1 mirror implementation. For example, if you have six 9GB disk drives in a RAID 0 stripe that is mirrored to another quantity of six 9GB disk drives in a RAID 0 stripe, there is only 56GB of usable storage space. This RAID configuration provides for excellent performance in all disk environments and complete fault tolerance. It is, however, the most costly RAID implementation per usable MB.

Just a Bunch of Disks (JBOD)

JBOD borders on a trivia fact, but is referenced in some RAID literature so I will mention it here. Depending on the vendor, JBOD is referred to in many different contexts. Someone must have become tired of referring to a single disk drive operating on its own without the influence of any RAID level, thus the phrase just a bunch of disks, or JBOD. In any case, now you can sound extra technical when referring to any single stand-alone disk drive not associated with RAID levels.

> *For optimum performance and efficient capacity usage, for all RAID levels, it is important to remember that the disk drives used in the array should always have the same performance characteristics and capacity. Ideally they should be from the same disk drive manufacturer.*

Implementing RAID with Windows 2000

You can use Windows 2000 to implement RAID level 0 or 1 without worrying about a significant performance overhead penalty. Windows 2000 refers to RAID 0 as a stripe set, RAID 1 as a mirror set, and RAID 5 as RAID-5. Do not use Windows 2000 to implement a software-based RAID 5 solution unless there is a significant amount of server CPU capacity available that can be allotted for calculating the parity calculations required for RAID 5. To implement RAID 0, 1, or 5 under Windows 2000, use the Logical Disk Manager which is found under Start / Programs / Administrative Tools / Computer Manager / Storage / Disk Management. We have omitted the steps to configure one of the supported Windows 2000 software-based RAID levels since Windows 2000 actually provides good step-by-step instructions under the Logical Disk Manager Help menu option.

HARDWARE-BASED RAID

A good rule of thumb is to implement all RAID arrays—especially RAID 5—using hardware-based RAID solutions. Hardware-based RAID solutions offload the RAID calculations from the system CPU to a CPU on the RAID HBA and do not occupy any precious RAM on the server the way software RAID implementations do. Hardware-based RAID solutions also shield Windows 2000 from problems in the underlying array disk drives. However, Windows 2000 does provide a solid and cost-effective solution for smaller Windows 2000 environments.

OTHER BENEFITS OF HARDWARE-BASED RAID

When a RAID 1 mirror is implemented under Windows 2000 and the primary disk drive fails, what happens when the system reboots? It doesn't. First, the failed drive must be replaced with the new disk drive. Then you must utilize a Windows 2000 boot diskette so that you can tell Windows 2000 to boot from the second disk drive in the RAID 1 mirror. Hopefully, you created this diskette and tested its functionality before there was a problem. Once the Windows 2000 system is back on its feet, you can use Windows 2000 LDM to recreate the mirrors on the new disk drive.

Use of a hardware-based RAID controller avoids this problem. The hardware-based RAID controller shields Windows 2000 from disk problems that are covered by the various RAID levels. In generic terms, when a disk drive fails in hardware-based RAID implementation, the following occurs:

- One disk drive fails if the RAID 1 mirror fails.
- The fault indicator light above the drive is displayed.
- A hardware RAID-controller-provided service running under Windows 2000 detects the disk problem and sends the alert to the event log and console (if not another alternate mechanism as well).
- At this point, someone hopefully notices the problem.
- The old disk drive is removed.
- If the drive is hot pluggable, the hardware RAID controller shields Windows 2000 from the fact that one of its drives was just removed; thus a system reboot is not required.
- A new drive is inserted to replace the failed drive.
- Either the drive begins an automatic rebuild or the hardware RAID vendor supplies a tool to initiate the rebuilding of the new drive from the mirrored information of the old drive.

Is a hardware-based RAID HBA the best option for you? It depends on the performance level required and budget available. With many of the components of low-end Windows 2000s commoditized, a hardware-based RAID solution is a sound investment. I prefer to use hardware RAID controllers on all server-class Windows 2000 solutions for higher availability and lower administration.

Tuning Flexibility When Utilizing Hardware-Based RAID Solutions

The primary advantage when using a hardware-based RAID solution is the increased overall performance that it can provide, particularly on servers that are CPU bound. Besides off-loading server CPU and memory resources to the RAID HBA, read and write performance of the array can be improved through the use of another level of cache (fast RAM) on the RAID HBA itself. The advantages of an extra layer of cache vary for each Windows 2000 environment. The advantage of having a RAID HBA-level cache is that it allows the algorithms in the hardware-based RAID more flexibility when working with the arrays it is controlling. Some hardware-based RAID solutions provide a tunable read-ahead caching algorithm that can complement the Windows 2000 file system cache.

Hardware-based RAID caches exhibit higher levels of added value when they are used in conjunction with RAID 5 implementations. Caches on RAID HBAs are normally set to a write-through mode by default, which allows data to pass directly through the cache. This does not provide any significant performance improvements. The default setting in place by most vendors is to have the cache selected for write-through operations—this ensures data integrity in the face of a power outage. If the RAID HBA does not included a battery backup for the cache and power is lost to the server, there is a potential for data loss. If the cache is supported by a battery backup system on the RAID HBA, you can set the cache for write-back functionality with confidence. Even if the RAID HBA cache is supported by a battery backup, some enterprise-level RAID HBAs employ write-back cache mirroring for an even higher level of cache fault tolerance. Write-back cache mirroring copies the write-back data to another memory area on another RAID HBA. The level of performance and protection you should use depends on your requirements.

The write-back cache setting is configured on a Windows 2000 system by tools provided by the RAID HBA manufacturer. The write-back cache signals to the requesting process that the data is committed to the disk drive once it is resident in the hardware-based RAID HBA cache before the data is physically committed to the disk drive. When this occurs, the Windows 2000 process reaps the benefit of writing data to a faster cache holding area. The RAID HBA can then calculate the required parity and commit the data to the RAID 5 array as needed. As long as the write-back cache is activated, the caching RAID controller helps compensate for the inherent disk write overhead associated with implementing a RAID 5 solution.

RAID Performance under Windows 2000

How do you decide which RAID level provides the highest performance levels for you? It depends on your environment, your budget, and the level of fault tolerance required. Running RAID 5 can make what gains? RAID 10? To determine the performance of each RAID level under various workloads in a Windows 2000 environment, a series of stress tests was run.

This test series was run on a Compaq 8000 with two Pentium III XEON 550MHz/2MB cache CPUs, 256MB of RAM, and Windows 2000 server. The disk subsystem used the Compaq Smart Array RAID Controller 4250Es with 64MB of onboard battery-backed cache. Ultra2 SCSI 10,000rpm disk drives were used for all tests, with the number of target disk drives varying from 1 to 12 disk drives, depending on the test. Windows 2000 was installed on its own separate disk drive, and a separate disk drive was used for the pagefile. All disks were configured with an NTFS file system and an ALU of 4KB.

All tests were run using the Neal Nelson Business Benchmark for Windows 2000. This benchmark has over 30 tests to characterize your Windows 2000 system performance. The following benchmark tests were selected to characterize the disk subsystem of Windows 2000:

- Test 19: Sequential Disk Write Operations (see Figures 6-12 and 6-13)
- Test 18: Sequential Disk Read Operations (see Figures 6-14 and 6-15)
- Test 26: Random Disk Read Operations (see Figures 6-16 and 6-17)

All tests were run with an increasing multiuser workload from 10 to 40 copies (20 to 800 users). At each workload level, a larger and larger work file was used starting at 98MB to 6GB. This ensured not only that the Windows 2000 files' disk cache was active but also that it was overwhelmed (by design) so that we could determine the physical performance characteristics of the disk subsystems. Each graph was truncated to show the physical disk performance. If the graphs were not truncated, you would have observed outstanding performance throughput of over 260MB/sec, which was achieved before the work file size overshadowed the file system cache.

This is a worst-case scenario that is very helpful for tuning, sizing, and overall system design. These results show the best physical disk subsystem performance that an application running under Windows 2000 should expect; both the throughput that can be achieved and the disk subsystem response time (latency) is investigated. Some applications such as backups rely on throughput, while a database application is typically concerned more with latency (response time). If it is a very well-written application, an efficient application itself may improve performance over the benchmark used here.

With appropriate tuning of Windows 2000 and the addition of more RAM, the amount of workload each disk subsystem test could support would increase due to the Windows 2000 dynamic file system cache, since it would increase the number of disk I/O operations that can be completed (logical disk I/O operations that are completed in cache) thus improving throughput and lowering latency. In chapter 5, similar stress tests were completed to characterize the Windows 2000 memory subsystem and the benefits of the file system cache. Do not use these tests as a benchmark to select a vendor, but as a general guide to Windows 2000 and disk subsystem performance characteristics.

Sequential Disk Write Operations Throughput and Response Time Analysis

SEQUENTIAL WRITE ANALYSIS AND OBSERVATIONS

This test is more of a hybrid of sequential disk access and random disk accesses, since it is a multiuser workload. Multiuser workloads are more indicative of server environments. Many simulated users were all trying to complete sequential tasks; thus disk accesses are somewhat random in nature, but the test still takes advantage of sequentially oriented operations. These tests confirm the performance descriptions for the RAID levels above, but show an interesting twist on how well each RAID level scales—in other words, if we add more disks, how much throughput is added and how well does the system perform?

Look closely at the performance and response time information on the graphs in Figures 6-12 and 6-13. Even though some of the plotted curves in the graphs look closer in performance when there are more disk drives in use, the differences are significant. For example, at the highest workload level of 800 users and a 6GB workload, the 12-disk RAID 10 configuration provides 3MB/sec better throughput than the 12-disk RAID 5 array. The 12-disk RAID 10 configuration also enables the workloads to be completed 84 seconds faster than its 12-disk RAID 5 counterpart. Remember that this is a multiuser test. What does this mean? It means that each one of the 800 users was able to complete his individual tasks 84 seconds faster using the 12-disk RAID 10 configuration! This is almost 3 minutes faster. Would your customers be happy

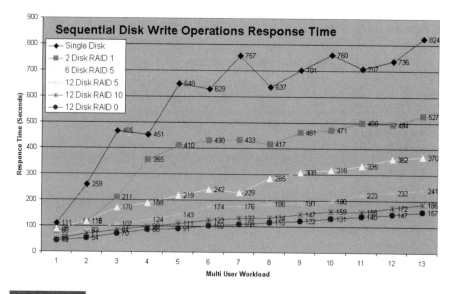

| FIGURE 6–12 | *Sequential Disk Write Operations Response Time [Note: LOWER is better]* |

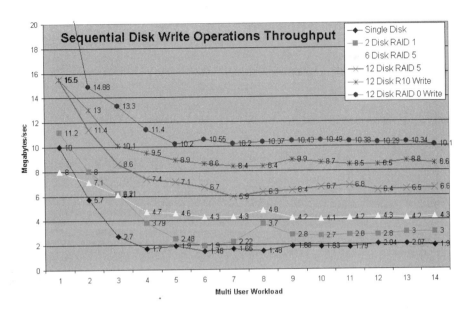

FIGURE 6–13   *Sequential Disk Write Operations Throughput [Note: HIGHER is better}*

running a write-intensive application almost 3 minutes faster? Knowing your environment and selecting, through tuning and sizing, the appropriate RAID subsystem can make a world of difference.

One item here may look strange. The 6-disk RAID 5 array provided more improved performance than the 2-disk RAID 1 array. But what about that overhead due to the extra disk operations needed when write operations are completed on a RAID 5 array? They are still there, but, due to the multiuser nature of the sequentially write-intensive test, the RAID 5 array's four additional disks provided the needed performance boost. If this workload were not multiuser in nature, completely generated by a single thread or application such as the Windows 2000 pagefile or a log file for a specific database, then the RAID 1 array would have produced better performance than the RAID 5 array. For maximum performance RAID 0 was head and shoulders above all of the different combinations.

Sequential Disk Read Operations Throughput and Response Time Analysis

SEQUENTIAL READ OBSERVATIONS AND ANALYSIS

Again, this test, represented in Figures 6-14 and 6-15, is more of a hybrid of sequential disk access and random disk accesses, since it is a multiuser workload. Multiuser workloads are more indicative of server environments. Many

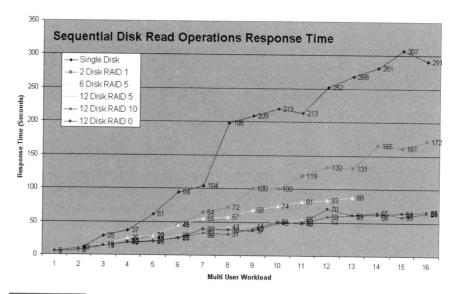

FIGURE 6-14   *Sequential Disk Read Operations Response Time [Note: LOWER is better]*

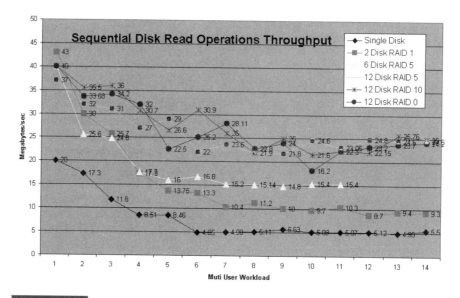

FIGURE 6-15   *Sequential Disk Read Operations Throughput [Note: HIGHER is better}*

simulated users were all trying to complete sequential tasks; thus disk accesses are somewhat random in nature, but the test still takes advantage of sequentially oriented operations. These tests confirm the performance descriptions for the RAID levels above. In other words, if we add more disks, how much throughput is added and how well does the system perform?

You can observe a significant performance improvement as we move from a single disk to two disks in a RAID 1 configuration, to a 6-disk RAID 5. The 2-disk RAID 1 configuration almost doubles the performance of a single disk. This type of performance is directly related to having an intelligent RAID controller that optimizes split read operations and uses both disks well. However, notice how close the 12-disk RAID 0, RAID 10, and RAID 5 results are. What is causing this? In a sequential (slightly random) read-based workload, all of these RAID options exhibit similar throughput performance characteristics. All three RAID environments engage all 12 of their spindles (disks) fully for read operations. This is contrary to the write environment we reviewed earlier, where performance differences between these RAID levels were much more significant.

Random Disk Read Operations Throughput and Response Time Analysis

RANDOM READ ANALYSIS & OBSERVATIONS

Multiuser read and write random access workloads are the most difficult for any I/O subsystem to handle and are the most common. Multiuser workloads are more indicative of server environments. The performance provided in the sequential environment is dramatically better than a random environment as it provides over 25MB/sec of throughput compared to the random environment's throughput of just over 8MB/sec under the heaviest loads. However, we found performance characteristics (not performance levels) here similar to those we found in the sequential read-intensive environment. This is from the perspective that the 12-disk RAID 10, 12-disk RAID 5, and 12-disk RAID 0 environments all used all of their spindles (disk drives) when providing random read access to the multiuser environment, thus providing a similar performance.

Recommendations

OK, we have covered an extensive number of performance tests for RAID subsystems. What are some recommendations from this performance stress test and from real-world practical experience?

RAID 0 RECOMMENDATIONS

- Use when there is not concern or need for any fault tolerance.
- Not recommended for any critical files (operating system, pagefiles, logs, databases, etc.).
- Use when maximum performance is needed for all workload environments.

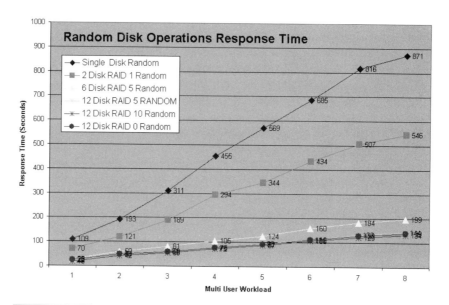

FIGURE 6–16 *Random Disk Read Operations Response Time [Note: LOWER is better}*

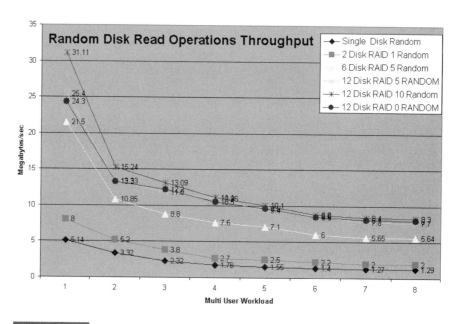

FIGURE 6–17 *Random Disk Read Operations Throughput [Note: HIGHER is better}*

- Increasing the number of drives in the array improves the random I/O performance.
- Helpful for temporary file placement for files that are not critical.
- Performance trade-off: If you lose one disk drive, you lose the entire array; no fault tolerance.
- Provides great performance in a shared-nothing cluster such as Windows 2000 network load balancing services; if one server fails, others just pick up the slack ensuring no loss of service.

RAID 1 RECOMMENDATIONS

- Use when fault tolerance is needed and the storage capacity of a single disk drive is sufficient.
- Provides complete data redundancy, even if you are using only two disks.
- Provides significant performance improvements over a single disk in a multiuser (workload) environment.
- Well suited for write-intensive environments; great for single-application log files. (For databases, it improves fault tolerance if the log files are not on the same array as the database.)
- Use for the operating system to improve fault tolerance of the entire system.
- Use an intelligent hardware-based RAID controller for optimum performance and ease of maintenance.
- Performance trade-off: For this redundancy, the capacity of a RAID 1 mirror is lowered by 50%. For example, if you have two 9GB disk drives in a RAID 1 mirror, there is only 9GB of usable storage space.

RAID 5 RECOMMENDATIONS

- A good compromise between performance and cost to achieve fault tolerance for disk subsystem.
- This RAID level provides fault tolerance through the use of parity information, allowing for the loss of one of the RAID 5 array's member disk drives without the loss of any data.
- Outstanding for read-intensive environments (random or sequential).
- Can be used for multiuser write-intensive environments if latency is not a concern.
- Not recommended for write-intensive environments where response time is considered important.
- Avoid using as location for single-application/process log files or the Windows 2000 pagefile.
- Highly recommended to be implemented with hardware-based RAID controllers to off-load parity calculations from system CPUs and provide caching algorithms that help to minimize some of the perfor-

mance degradation effects during write performance due to quadruple I/Os that are needed.

- Adding additional disk drives to a RAID 5 array does improve overall workload supported and subsequently increases performance provided.
- Performance trade-off: First, the storage capacity of one disk (from a logical perspective) is lost due to parity generation (parity must be stored on every drive and takes up storage capacity). For example, a RAID 5 array composed of ten 36GB disk drives provides 324GB of usable disk storage space, not 360GB. Second, the best RAID 5 implementation requires a hardware-based RAID adapter, which increases overall system cost.

RAID 10 RECOMMENDATIONS

- Outstanding for all workloads (read/write/random/sequential).
- Provides high throughput and low latency for all environments.
- If cost is a concern, at least consider RAID 10 for all write-intensive environments (those that cannot fit on the capacity of a single RAID 1 mirror).
- Use an intelligent hardware-based RAID controller for optimum performance and ease of maintenance.
- Performance trade-off #1: Most expensive RAID option, thus normally used only if you have a free-flowing budget or business requirements that demand the absolute best performance and full fault tolerance.
- Performance trade-off #2: The trade-off for this performance improvement and high fault-tolerance level is that the capacity of a RAID 10 mirror is lowered by 50%. For example, if you have two 9GB disk drives striped and mirrored with another two 9GB stripes, there is only 18GB of usable storage space.

The executive results of the exhaustive tests are shown in Table 6.9. Note that this is an executive summary and that the detailed information is in the RAID performance graphs in Figures 6-12–6-17. The upper portion of Table 6.9 depicts a single disk drive that is faster than a single disk drive from various RAID arrays. All of the RAID performance numbers were normalized to their single disk elements. However, the RAID numbers are scalable; thus, as additional disks are added, increased workloads are supported, which enables lower latency and higher throughput. When you look at the lower portion of Table 6.9, you can see the scalability of RAID technology.

Optimizing RAID Stripes

When data is written to a RAID array—for example, a RAID 0 array composed of four disk drives—the data is broken into chunks, and these chunks of data

TABLE 6.9	*Executive Summary of RAID Performance*

Test Characteristics using 400MB Work File Baseline (256MB of system RAM—forces physical disk usage) Multiuser Test (~400 simultaneous users)	10,000rpm Ultra2 SCSI RAID Disk Drive Configuration Average Per-drive Throughput Achieved as Reported by the Application (MB/sec)				
Workload Characteristics	**No RAID (single disk)**	**RAID 1**	**RAID 0**	**RAID 5**	**RAID 10**
Sequential Reads of 1,024 Byte Records	17.3	15	2.8	2.67	2.95
Sequential Writes of 1,024 Byte Records	5.7	4	1.2	0.95	1.08
Pseudorandom Reads of 4,096 Byte Records	3.32	2.6	1.1	1.11	1.27

	Multidrive Results Where Applicable				
Workload Characteristics	**No RAID (single disk)**	**2-Disk RAID 1**	**12-Disk RAID 0**	**12-Disk RAID 5**	**12-Disk RAID 10**
Sequential Reads of 1,024 Byte Records	17.3	30	33.6	32	35.5
Sequential Writes of 1,024 Byte Records	5.7	8	14.8	11.4	13
Pseudorandom Reads of 4,096 Byte Records	3.32	5.2	13.3	13.2	15.24

are placed onto each drive in the array. The size of this logically continuous chunk of data placed onto each drive in the array is referred to as the *stripe size*. The *stripe width* is the number of disk drives in the array. There will be no test on this later, but try to keep stripe size (chunk) and stripe width straight in your mind. In a RAID 5 array, the stripe width is one less than the number of drives in the array, since logically one drive is used for parity and only parity information is written to it, no data.

Even though hardware-based RAID technology can provide the highest level of performance through the efficient use of writes, reads, and advanced algorithms, if the data is much larger than the optimum stripe size, more writes are required. If the data is smaller than the optimum stripe size, then the reads are less efficient due to the fact that the unused portion of the strip size is wasted. You can determine the size of the I/O operations and how often they occur in your system by separating disk activities across as many individual disk devices as needed to isolate the different disk activities that are occurring. Next, use Sysmon to monitor the Logical Disk object's counters Average Disk Bytes/Write, Avg. Bytes/Read, and Avg. Bytes/Transfer to determine the workload characteristics of your disk subsystem. These counters will show the average number of bytes transferred to the disk during write/read and overall disk operations.

The optimum stripe size (chunk) is a function of the application in use. Ideally, we want the typical I/O size to be the same as the stripe width times the stripe size (chunk). So, to determine the optimum stripe size (chunk), divide the typical I/O size by the stripe width.

For example, if Sysmon's Logical Disk object's Avg. Disk Bytes/Write were 64KB and you had a 4-disk RAID 0 array, the optimum stripe size would be 64KB/4, which is 16KB.

When optimum stripe size (chunk) is found, use this data when low-level formatting your hardware-based RAID solution with the tools provided by the RAID vendor. For our example, you could then use these tools to initially low-level format (initialize) your RAID array with a 16KB chunk size for your 4-disk RAID 0 array. An example RAID initialization and management tool is the Compaq Array Configuration Utility shown in Figure 6-18.

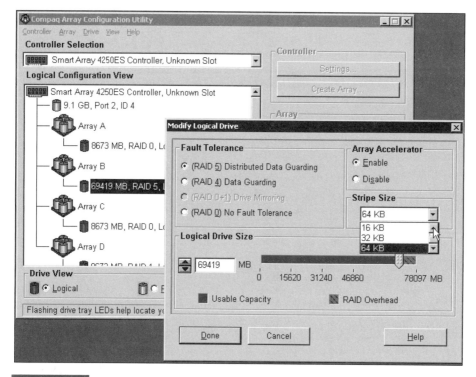

FIGURE 6–18   *Using Compaq's RAID Array Configuration Utility*

Setting the low-level stripe size is not an option when using Windows 2000's built-in software RAID. However, under Windows 2000 you can take the chunk size optimization up one level to the operating system and format that freshly created RAID array partition with an NTFS file system with a cluster size of 16KB. Matching the cluster size of NTFS and the RAID array chunk size does improve disk subsystem performance. This is completed by selecting the ALU size when using the Logical Volume Manager GUI (right next to where you select the file system type) or from the command line using the *format.exe* command (format F: /fs:ntfs /a:16k). More information is provided on ALU sizing and tactics later in this chapter.

Stripe Size Optimization Shortcut

I know determining the optimum stripe size (chunk) is time consuming, but it can be worth the effort. Looking at the relative RAID performance charts in Table 6.9, in separate tests when the stripe size is set from 64 sectors/stripe to 128 sectors/stripe to match the application workload, there is a significant performance increase across most of the different RAID configurations and disk loads. At the point where the stripe size (chunk) closely matches the application's I/O characteristics, the best performance is achieved. If you are not interested in this level of tuning, try at least to determine if the general disk characteristics are either sequential or random in nature. In general, larger stripe sizes provide better performance for large sequential data transfers, while smaller random data transfers benefit from smaller stripe sizes (less chunk space to read).

Table 6.9 is a technical executive summary, and even this can be a challenge to decipher, so we compiled a condensed reference chart (see Table 6.10). This performance guide shows the relative performance ratings when comparing the various RAID options using a sector/stripe size of 128KB. Use this guide when selecting the appropriate performance level that matches your system's disk I/O characteristics and overall disk subsystem goals.

TABLE 6.10 *Condensed Version of the Relative RAID Performance Chart*

Raid Level	Random Read	Random Write	Sequential Read	Sequential Write
Stripe (0)	1st	1st	1st	1st
Mirror (1)	4th	3rd	4th	3rd
Stripe w/Parity 12 Disk	1st	4th	1st	4th
Mirrored Stripe Set 12 Disk	1st	2nd	1st	3rd

Scaling RAID Arrays

Now that we have covered the respective performance levels of the various RAID levels, let's discuss how well Windows 2000 takes advantage of RAID arrays when comparing them from the perspective of increasing the number of disk drives in an array. To find out how well RAID arrays scale, we ran a series of tests on the most common RAID implementation, RAID 5 (see Figures 6-19 and 6-20 and Table 6.11). These results are for a random read operations environment. Windows 2000 will in fact take advantage of additional drives in RAID arrays as illustrated in Table 6.11. There are performance

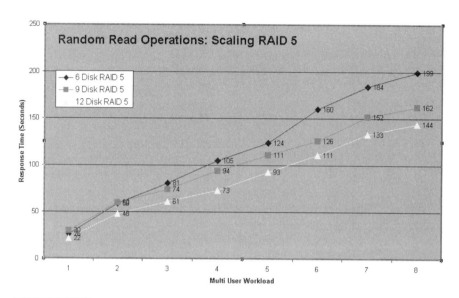

FIGURE 6–19   *Sequential Disk Read Operations Response Time [Note: LOWER is better}*

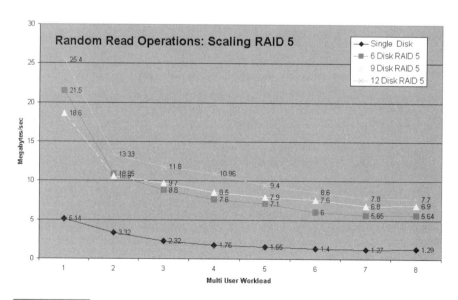

FIGURE 6–20   *Random Disk Read Operations: Scaling a RAID 5 Array Throughput [Note: HIGHER is better}*

improvements across the board. The performance increase is not a perfect one-to-one ratio, but the improvements are significant as additional disks are added. The RAID controller used in this test was the 64-bit, Ultra2 Compaq 4250ES with 64MB of onboard cache.

TABLE 6.11	Scaling RAID 5 Results			
Pseudorandom Reads of 4,096-byte Records	**Throughput (MB/sec)**	**Percent (%) Improvement**	**Response Time (sec)**	**Percent (%) Improvement**
Single Disk	1.29	Baseline	871	Baseline
6-Disk RAID 5	7.6	589%	199	437%
9-Disk RAID 5	9.7	751%	162	185%
12-Disk RAID 5	11.8	914%	144	165%

All RAID controllers are not created equal; thus do not take the RAID scaling results shown in Table 6.11 for granted. One year before this test was completed, a similar stress test was completed on another vendor's RAID controller and the results were not as stellar (see Figure 6-21). This vendor's RAID controller subsystem provided good response time scaling up to and including when six disk drives were used. Beyond six disk drives, very little performance increase was observed. If all you needed was more disk storage capacity, this solution would still be acceptable. But if you wanted both disk storage and disk performance increases when adding additional disk drives to this RAID 5 array, it would be time to find a better RAID controller.

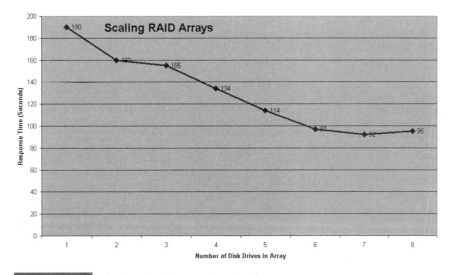

FIGURE 6–21   Scaling RAID Array—Poor Results

This is not earth-shattering information, but it is very useful when sizing a Windows 2000 disk I/O subsystem. With this information in hand, you can now have a good general idea of what you might experience when implementing larger disk arrays.

USING SYSMON TO INVESTIGATE THE DISK ARRAY SCALING

In the 12-disk RAID 5 array from our test (see Table 6.11), from a Windows 2000 perspective, the highest throughput measured once the disk cache was defeated was 13.5MB/sec, as measured by Sysmon Logical Disk object's Disk Bytes/sec counter. This is very close to what the test suite application reported for the random reads of 4,096-byte records test. From an I/O workload perspective, Sysmon reported that the maximum Transfers/sec was 1,600. For RAID 5 arrays, the Transfers/sec counter reported is not directly representative of the actual workload that the disk array is experiencing. To determine RAID 5 stripe-with-parity I/Os per second for each disk drive in the array, use the formula:

[Disk Reads/sec + (4 × Disk Writes/sec)] / (number of drives in this RAID 5 array)

For this random read environment, the I/Os per second for each disk drive in the array works out to [1,500 + (4 × 105)] / 12 = 160 I/Os per second. From a pure physical disk drive perspective, the number of disk I/O operations that a 10,000rpm Ultra1 disk drive should support is 105. Where did the extra 55 I/O operations come from? Remember, we ran all tests from the perspective of a Windows 2000 application. Thus the Windows 2000 application's file system cache and the 64MB of cache on the RAID controller both contribute to supporting a higher workload, even when working with large workloads that in essence defeat the file system cache. If you are curious, Table 6.5 only slightly considers memory caching for the basic workload rules of thumb, which is just a little conservative. With this conservative approach to workload support estimation, your system has a better chance of supporting your planned design.

The RAID 5 array in our test was composed of 12 disk drives in a single logical unit (LUN) configuration. From a Windows 2000 perspective, the RAID array appears only as a single physical device (you can have several Win2000 partitions on the RAID array) that is now capable of supporting a higher number of concurrent I/O requests because of the multiple drive configurations. There were no other devices connected to this SCSI channel. From provided information and from an understanding of the configuration, you can conclude that the 80MB/sec SCSI bus was not near saturation and that the disk array could support a slightly increased workload. Each disk in the disk array can support approximately 160 I/O operations on its own (in this random read-intensive workload environment).

How Windows 2000 Uses the Disk Subsystem

Windows 2000 implements several techniques to improve overall I/O performance when working with the disk subsystem: file system caching, disk read ahead, lazy writes, and lazy commits. Windows 2000's I/O Manager manages all requests of the disk subsystem. The process that Windows 2000 actually utilizes when interacting with the physical device is quite complex; in fact, entire books are dedicated to the topic. For an in-depth look at the I/O Manager, review *Inside Windows 2000*, 3rd Edition, published by Microsoft Press and authored by Mark Rusinovich and David Solmon (September 2000). Another good book on this topic is *Windows 2000 File System Internals* published by O'Reilly and authored by Rajeev Nagar. For this discussion, I will focus on some of the performance aspects of the Windows 2000 I/O process.

Caching Read Requests

Unless a process specifically requests that the file system cache not be used to obtain data from the disk subsystem, the I/O Manager passes the request for data to the Cache Manager (CM). When the CM obtains the request, it first checks the file system cache that resides in physical memory (RAM) to see if the requested data is available there (the file system cache was investigated in depth in chapter 6). If the data is found in the file system cache, it is returned to the requesting process. This is the best way to implement disk I/O. Avoid physical disk activity completely. By avoiding actual physical disk drive activity, the data is presented to the requesting process faster and overall server performance increases. In testing where the file system cache is effective, applications can achieve over 200MB/sec of throughput. Having an application that takes advantage of a properly tuned Windows 2000 system results in a night-and-day difference in overall performance.

If the data is not found in the file system cache, it is read from the physical disk drive itself. To increase the chances that the next request for data from the process is found in the file system cache, the CM employs an *intelligent disk read-ahead caching algorithm*. Statistically, there is a good chance that the next piece of data requested by the process will be close to the last, a concept referred to as *locality of reference*. To capitalize on this, the CM reads ahead on the disk drive and obtains slightly more data than required in the hope that the next data requested will already be in the file system cache. In Windows 2000, the CM also looks for disk request patterns and adjusts how much data is obtained and where on the disk it is obtained. If the CM detects randomly accessed data, it actually keeps a small history on the disk access characteristics and tries to estimate where the next request will occur and read ahead and fetch that page. If the CM detects sequential disk access activities, it increases the size and optimizes the location of where read-ahead data is brought into the file system cache. Depending on the data access patterns of the process, the read-ahead functionality can operate in the forward or reverse direction of the file data.

Having your disk drive properly defragmented helps the CM in this process since you in essence pregroup data together on the disk drive (defragmented) vs. having the data fragmented around the disk drive.

Caching Write Requests

When data is written to the disk subsystem, the I/O Manager again invokes the Cache Manager unless otherwise requested not to do so. The CM will place the data into the file system cache and report back to the process that the data write is complete. This is a write-back cache approach. The Windows 2000 CM then calls the Memory Manager to flush the cached data to disk. By somewhat falsely reporting back to the process that the data is committed to disk, the process can trot off on its merry way faster than if it had to wait on the actual physical disk I/O.

Referencing Table 6.9, the throughput recorded when completing an actual sequential write to the disk drive was 5.7MB/sec compared to over 200MB/sec when the data could be cached (not shown in the table, but recorded during the same test suite). There is a trade-off for this performance enhancement. If the system suddenly loses power, data can be lost. The NTFS file system does utilize techniques to compensate for potential data inconsistencies that could occur due to a power loss. Data that has not actually been committed to the disk drives still resides in the file system cache; this is one of the reasons Windows wants you to use the shutdown command to turn off Windows 2000 as opposed to simply shutting down the power via the power switch.

At some point the data destined for the disk subsystem must be moved to the actual physical disk drives. This process is a *lazy write* (data written to disk when Windows 2000 feels it does not affect performance as much). Typically, one-eighth to one-quarter of the file system cache is written to disk once per second. This rate varies based on the workload placed on the system and can be observed with Sysmon's Cache object counter Lazy Write Flushes/sec, defined by the Sysmon tool as "the rate at which the Lazy Writer thread has written to disk. Lazy Writing is the process of updating the disk after the page has been changed in memory, so that the application that changed the file does not have to wait for the disk write to be complete before proceeding. More than one page can be transferred by each write operation."

The lazy commit write process improves the disk subsystem's efficiency by grouping the data before writing it to disk; once it does group the data, it then writes the data in a more contiguous fashion onto the physical disk which improves overall performance (writes now, read later!).

The Linux/UNIX sync command forces a flush of the disk buffers to disk. Mark Russinovish developed a similar tool under Windows 2000 named Sync.exe to accomplish this same task. When you run Sync from the command line, the file system cache is immediately flushed. This freeware tool is available from http://www.Ntinternals.com. There is no reason why you have to use this tool because Windows 2000's file system cache flushing algorithm works well. If, however, you are working with some very important data and you want to make sure the data is committed to the actual physical disk when you want it to be, such as making sure a few hundred pages of a book you are working on are committed to physical disk, it is a helpful tool.

Windows 2000 Device Drivers

A device driver, such as a SCSI HBA driver, is a specialized piece of code that enables Windows 2000 and specific hardware devices to communicate. HBA device drivers are pieces of software that are commonly overlooked but have a great impact on the performance obtained by external devices attached to the system.

For example, there are several steps that the SCSI driver code must traverse when data is read or written to a SCSI-based device. Each one of these code path steps adds a certain amount of overhead to the I/O data path. Why is this important? The more steps that the code path must take, the slower the access is to an external device. As Windows 2000 continues to mature at a rapid rate, so do the crucial device drivers that drive the disk subsystems.

Windows 2000 has a very defined structure for device driver developers to follow. For people not writing the device driver codes, but just implementing solutions with them, it is imperative to keep abreast of the latest driver technologies. Available operating systems such as Linux publicly distribute their source code in the hope that, if something looks inefficient, someone will take the time to improve it. For Linux, this process works surprisingly well. Information on Linux is available on a variety of web sites throughout the Internet. A good place to start if you are interested in obtaining information on this operating system is http://www.linux.org.

In the Windows 2000 realm, we are dependent on the independent vendor for device driver updates and improvements. From a performance perspective, vendors are always working to make their device drivers more efficient and faster. *More efficient* refers to the amount of overhead added to the server's CPUs to drive the external device. The more efficient the device driver is, the more work it can complete with the least amount of direct CPU cycles. From a speed perspective, when the number of code paths traversed is lowered, improved efficiency is achieved which leads to obtaining the data from the external device in less time. Microsoft has implemented a certified device driver program that should aid in both performance and stability of device drivers used with Windows 2000.

It does not matter how fast the external device is; if the device driver is not written well and is not stable, access to the external device will be limited. One way to guarantee that your device driver runs as fast as possible is to ensure that the device driver in use is the latest and greatest from the vendor's device manufacturers. Some smart devices such as hardware RAID HBAs also have their own BIOS, or firmware. If a peripheral device has its own firmware, then it may also require periodic updates. There is nothing wrong with the device drivers provided on the Windows 2000 CD-ROM distribution, but if the manufacture date of the CD-ROM is 6 months ago, the device drivers it contains may have undergone two new iterations in that time span.

Updated Windows 2000 Device Drivers Can Equal Better Performance

Once Windows 2000 is installed, we usually forget the device drivers. If the system runs reliably, who cares? If you want the best-performing system, you *should* care. With a multitude of vendors producing devices for systems, it may be time consuming to check all of the vendors' web sites on a regular basis to download new device driver releases. To help mitigate this challenge, many sites are now setting standard system configurations to ensure that the same solution is used across their enterprises to lower integration and operational issues such as device driver updates. Using this standard-based approach, once you have tested a new device driver and determined that it is stable and that it improves performance, you can use it across 50 systems, vs. running 50 separate tests and tracking 50 separate device driver versions. We recently upgraded systems from Windows NT 4 to Windows 2000 and compared the performance between using the legacy device drivers left over from NT 4 and new Windows 2000 device drivers from the vendor's web site. The new drivers were much faster! You always want to choose the fastest and most reliable devices for your system. We ran our own evaluation, but some online magazines run tests periodically that help provide insight on the performance improvements that a new device driver can make to your system. Table 6.12 is a chart of our results.

TABLE 6.12	*Windows 2000 Device Driver Comparison*

SCSI HBA	**Device Driver Version**	**% Improvement**
Compaq RAID Controller (internal)	Latest driver from vendor	+7.33%
Compaq RAID Controller (external)	Latest driver from vendor	+13.09%

As you can see from these results, updating your device driver influences the performance that you can achieve. These performance improvements have an even bigger impact on your system's overall performance as the Windows 2000 solutions get larger and larger. Some vendors develop specialized drivers for their benchmark tests, which they subsequently allow public access to. In particular, some vendors have developed what is referred to as *monolithic SCSI drivers*. These monolithic drivers can provide higher levels of SCSI performance, yet they utilize lower amounts of the system's CPU. To obtain these monolithic SCSI drivers, contact your server or SCSI HBA manufacturer or server manufacturer for availability.

As with any new technology, always test the new device driver in a nonproduction environment to ensure there aren't any problems with the revision of the device you have deployed before fielding the new drivers. I personally have experienced huge performance improvements in the disk I/O subsystems when updating the device's onboard firmware and the associated Windows 2000 device driver.

Sizing a Windows 2000 Disk I/O Subsystem

Over time it is inevitable that Windows 2000 and applications need more and more disk capacity for storage and performance. The good news is that the price of disk drive storage capacity has continually fallen over the last several years. The challenge is that, although you can now obtain a disk drive that supports 72GB or more of storage, that disk drive is not 36 times faster than a 2GB disk drive! This is one of the key challenges faced when sizing a disk subsystem for Windows 2000. Fortunately for you, the designer of a disk subsystem solution, the combination of a flexible Windows 2000 architecture and advances in disk subsystem technology makes the disk subsystem the most flexible portion of your system!

Sizing the disk subsystem is directly related to your business needs and the type of workload in the current and projected environment. Disk subsystem resources can be both a shared resource and dedicated resource. A *shared resource* is one that cannot be physically separated (unless using multiple systems) such as a shared file server data area for multiple users. A *dedicated resource* is one that is used for a single process/thread and those process/thread activities only. These concepts of shared and dedicated disk resources are illustrated in the physical disk drive partitioning section of Figure 6-22.

Vendors provide very basic information on disk subsystem requirements, usually relegated to storage capacity and not referencing performance capacity needed to run their software applications. Keep in mind that they are trying to sell their products—their estimates for system resources tend to be on the skinny side, to say the least; no need to scare off a potential customer. Throughout this chapter, references to sizing the I/O subsystem for a Windows 2000 solution are intertwined in the various sections presented. In this sizing section, the focus is on the most common areas of concern that I have encountered when sizing the disk I/O subsystem.

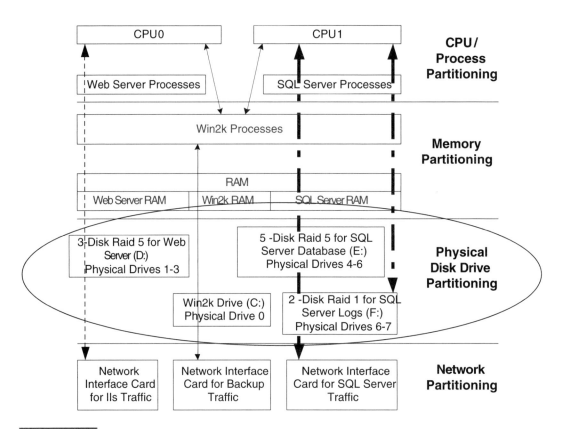

FIGURE 6–22   *Partitioning Disk Resources*

Here we focus on sizing the disk subsystem, but do not forget the rest of the system! Even when sizing the disk subsystem, follow the core sizing methodology from chapter 3 so that key facets surrounding your solution are taken into consideration.

The best performing Windows 2000 disk subsystem solutions I have encountered are configured, keeping the following in mind:

- *To cache as much of the disk operations in memory as possible (logical disk I/O operations)*
- *So that when disk operations are needed, the disk subsystem is always operating at less than 80% of its performance capacity (I/Os per second)*
- *To never let disk storage exceed 60% of available storage capacity*
- *So that sustained disk queues are never higher than 2–3 service requests per disk drive during regular workload periods (peak workload periods if a critical system)*

Disk Subsystem Sizing Methodology: Step by Step

Disk storage capacity vs. disk performance capacity—there is an important distinction between providing enough disk storage capacity to meet your requirements and providing enough disk performance capacity to meet those same requirements. We will focus on this topic, but, when sizing the disk subsystem, also consider the following selection factors at a minimum:

1. Cost
2. Fault tolerance level required (availability)
3. Performance capacity needed (throughput, latency, I/Os per second)
4. Backup speed
5. The amount of system resources configured such as CPU, memory, disks, and network
6. Windows 2000's requirements (operating system, pagefile)
7. Storage capacity needed (amount of usable disk space required)
8. Data path sanity check

While these are not the only factors you must consider when sizing and selecting your disk subsystem, they do cover the major areas of concern. As with all methodologies presented in this book, use them as a guide, not gospel. If you have more criteria you want to add, go for it and have fun!

Let's look at each of these storage selection factors a little closer.

COST

If the initial hardware cost is the only factor, then the highest-density disk drives will provide the most effective cost solution. A few years ago this would not have been the case, but today, with the commoditization of low-end Windows 2000 servers, one 9GB disk drive can be less expensive than two 4GB disk drives. Making the decision totally on cost is sometimes the only option. However, if you want a good, long-term solution that meets your performance and management objectives, choosing the minimum number of disk drives based on cost alone rarely will meet your needs.

FAULT TOLERANCE LEVEL REQUIRED (AVAILABILITY)

Choose the appropriate RAID that will provide the level of data protection you require. It is easier to configure and manage a Windows 2000 system that has one large, single RAID 5 disk array than a system with some combination of RAID levels. This premise aligns with obtaining the highest-density drives and placing them into a RAID 5 array. If, however, some of your data is truly critical and the workload disk characteristics are varied, having additional disk drives provides not only more fault tolerance options, but more tuning options as well. If seven 4GB disk drives were selected (let's leave the usable disk space requirement out of this for a moment) and you had a requirement to house a particularly important database that could survive a dual disk drive crash, you have options. With the seven 4GB disk drives, you could implement a RAID 1 mirror consisting of two disk drives for the logs and a RAID 5 array with the other five disk drives for the database. This would improve your mean time between failures because each disk array is considered a separate system. MTBF calculations were covered earlier in this chapter. Using a combination of RAID levels to implement the fault tolerance required can help improve the overall performance and availability and lower overall disk subsystem costs by enabling you to group noncritical with critical data and split data groups based on performance needs.

PERFORMANCE CAPACITY NEEDED (THROUGHPUT, LATENCY, I/OS PER SECOND)

The next factor to consider is performance. Always note that the workload level in I/Os per second and throughput that the disk subsystem will be required to support is separate from storage capacity. Yes, we must say that a lot in this chapter so that you never forget. The performance requirements of your application will typically drive the number of disk drives needed in your overall Windows 2000 solution. Do not hesitate to use multiple RAID sets, each using different RAID levels to meet your performance requirements. Before you can plan for your performance capacity needs, there are several pieces of information that are needed:

- Business requirements: These are covered in the core sizing methodology section in chapter 3, but are mentioned here just as a reminder of why the system is being built and the mission it needs to complete.
- Disk characteristics of all applications that the system is running (sequential, random, read, write): From the extensive discussions above, it should be obvious why this information is very important—it directly influences the type of disk subsystem put into place. Use the recommended Sysmon counters below with historical information in Table 6.13 to determine disk usage characteristics.
- Where the applications are placing stress on your disk subsystem: Even with RAID technology, it is important to understand where the disk subsystem is under the greatest stress and which applications (processes) are causing it. This enables you to spread the workload across multiple disk arrays or add drives to an array. If you do not know which application is generating the load, it becomes difficult to tune the application workload (i.e., where it writes/reads its data).
- Windows 2000 file system cache usage: With a well-designed system, many of the physical disk I/O operations can be turned into logical disk I/O operations by servicing them with the file system cache or the cache of the application you are working with. With Windows 2000's dynamically sized file system cache, the addition of physical memory to the server can improve your disk subsystem performance.

When more disk operations are cached, the disk I/Os per sec that actually make it to the disk subsystem are lowered. If this occurs, fewer disk drives are required to meet the workload (I/Os per second) requirement since there are fewer I/Os per second to support. Higher throughputs are also achieved when disk requests are fulfilled in cache.

There is no steadfast rule of thumb on disk storage to memory ratios that always works. For this decision, your environment really dictates what is best. As a starting point, configure your system with the amount of memory outlined in chapter 5. Then observe the Logical Disk: Transfers/sec and Memory: Cache Bytes counters to determine if adding more memory is helping. If the Logical Disk: Transfers/sec goes down while the Memory: Cache Bytes goes up without a memory bottleneck forming when more memory is added to the system, the additional RAM is beneficial in relieving some of the disk I/O workload. Of course this is only a valid observation if the workload placed onto the system is similar before and after the additional RAM is added. Cache memory placed onto hardware-based RAID solutions can also increase the amount of work a disk subsystem can withstand.

- Response time (latency) and throughput and workload (I/Os per second): These requirements are business requirements driven. The greater the performance needed to meet your business requirements, the better the response time and throughput needed. Slow disk subsystems directly affect response time. There are examples of this in the next section where we identify disk subsystem bottlenecks. Remember when designing your disk subsystem to design it such that it does not need to utilize a rate greater than 80% or the system will begin to slow down exponentially.

- The number of disk drives per SCSI/fibre channel: This factor is commonly overlooked—do not overload the channels that are used to connect your disk subsystem (SCSI/fibre channel) to your overall I/O subsystem (PCI buses). Plain and simple, the more disks and SCSI buses that are implemented, the more disk subsystem performance. This is a true statement up to the point when either the aggregate throughput of the I/O buses is overwhelmed or there is not enough CPU horsepower to drive the extensive disk arrays and the application at the same time.

BACKUP SPEED

Depending on the environment, some people will move this up to the top of the sizing list. If you have a business requirement of a 4-hour return to service, and you have an 8-hour backup window, your disk subsystem performance requirements may rise drastically. Since, during backups, the physical disk drives must be read, you can use the disk subsystem performance graphs in Figures 6-12 through 6-17 to plan your performance needs backing up your system (read) and restoring back into service (write) as an initial baseline. Backup applications are typically optimized for disk operations, but it is wise to test both backup and restore speeds and compare them against performance characteristics presented in this chapter to see how well they are doing.

THE AMOUNT OF SYSTEM RESOURCES CONFIGURED, SUCH AS CPU, MEMORY, DISKS, AND NETWORK

Don't forget about the rest of the system. You will need CPU cycles to drive the disk subsystem and the other components you require. For example, during one test when a 12-disk RAID 5 array was supporting 700 Transfers/sec, over 20% of two Pentium III 550MHz CPUs were needed. The same is true for memory resources (covered earlier) and for network support, which must be large enough to feed the bytes coming from the disk subsystem onto the network.

WINDOWS 2000'S REQUIREMENTS

Windows 2000 and any applications that are configured will need both storage and performance capacity. Typically, Windows 2000 is configured onto RAID 1 arrays for speeding the time needed to restore the system to service and for overall availability. It is recommended that pagefiles be placed on their own physical disk drive(s) to improve performance, or at least that they be placed onto a disk subsystem that gets the least use in the system (never on a RAID 5 array).

STORAGE CAPACITY NEEDED (AMOUNT OF USABLE DISK SPACE REQUIRED)

Perhaps cost is not your driving factor. If this is the case, let's look at the other disk storage selection factors, e.g., the amount of usable disk space required. This becomes a factor for two reasons. First, if you have only five disk bays available in your system and require more, an external array solution is required which adds to your cost considerations. Second, the higher the disk drives' density, the more data is lost to fault-tolerance RAID features. If you have a RAID 5 array and implement it with four 9GB disk drives, you will lose 9GB of disk space due to parity storage vs. only 4GB of storage space lost if you implement with seven 4GB disks. When working with RAID devices, remember to complete the math equation for the RAID levels chosen to ensure that you end up with the amount of usable disk space you desire.

When determining the *storage* capacity requirement, the number of disks needed is the minimum needed; *performance* capacity requirements may demand additional drives. When planning for storage, plan to use only 60% of the usable disk space to ensure maximum performance from the physical disk drives themselves and to allow for enough room to run disk defragmentation tools.

DATA PATH SANITY CHECK

It is not desirable to configure huge data paths that overwhelm the SCSI channel, HBA, or I/O channel. After developing the disk drive or array solution, follow the data path. Utilize the performance charts in this chapter to aid in making an initial sanity check to ensure that none of the data paths are overloaded before you field the solution.

Use Historical Performance Information Whenever Possible

Historical information is the best place to start when sizing the disk subsystem. If you are going to deploy a system in your department to support 200 users running a 50GB SQL database, find out if another department has implemented a similar solution. If you find a similar situation, observe the end users working with their applications to determine if the response times you observe are adequate for your environment. Also, ask to review the performance logs to determine how the disk subsystem is being stressed; how much memory is normally being used; how much, if any, paging is occurring; the CPU utilization rates; and how much network bandwidth is needed. Use the information you obtain to size your disk subsystem.

Windows 2000's Sysmon tool provides much better insight into how each process is behaving on your system, which is crucial information when trying to determine how much memory is required for your new system. By understanding the disk subsystem characteristics and the behavior of running processes under load, you can extrapolate information you can use for your own system. If historical information is not available, consider industry standard benchmarks that might be similar to your environment. You will be seeking the information outlined in Table 6.13 when reviewing historical information.

Table 6.13 outlines the key Sysmon counters to review from a similar system when sizing your disk subsystem.

TABLE 6.13	*Counters Helpful for Sizing the Disk Subsystem*

Object: Counter	**Definition**	**Why Use for Sizing the Disk Subsystem**
Logical Disk: Average Disk Queue Length	Average Disk Queue Length is the average number of both read and write requests queued for the selected logical disk during the sample interval.	If this value is greater than 2 for a single disk drive and the Disk Transfers/sec are high (>100), the selected disk drive (or array) is becoming a bottleneck. This value is an average calculated during the Sysmon sample period. Use this counter to determine if there is a disk bottleneck and the Current Disk Queue Length counter to understand the actual workload distribution. This information is helpful to determine if the current disk subsystem can support its workload.

TABLE 6.13	Counters Helpful for Sizing the Disk Subsystem (Continued)	
Object: Counter	**Definition**	**Why Use for Sizing the Disk Subsystem**
Logical Disk: Disk Transfers/sec	Average Disk Transfers/sec is the rate of read and write operations on the disk.	Transfers/sec are synonymous with I/Os per second referred to throughout this chapter. By understanding the amount of workload the disk subsystem is supporting and the corresponding number of customers, you can estimate the number of customers/ workload rate and then size your disk subsystem accordingly.
Logical Disk: Disk Bytes/sec	Disk Bytes/sec is the rate bytes are transferred to or from the disk during write or read operations.	Sum this counter's value for each disk drive attached to the same SCSI/fibre channel and compare it to 80% of the theoretical throughput for SCSI or fibre channel technology in use. If the summation of Disk Bytes/sec is close to this 80% value, it is the SCSI or financial bus itself that is becoming the disk subsystem's bottleneck. Use this data and some math to review the complete disk subsystem data path. And determine the number of SCSI or fibre channels that may be needed.
Logical Disk: %Disk Read Time	%Disk Read Time is the percentage of elapsed time that the selected disk drive is busy servicing read requests.	Use this data to determine which RAID level is best for your environment.
Logical Disk: %Disk Write Time	%Disk Write Time is the percentage of elapsed time that the selected disk drive is busy servicing write requests.	Use this data to determine which RAID level is best for your environment.

Disk Subsystem Sizing Example: Step by Step

To illustrate the difference between storage and performance capacity when sizing a disk subsystem, let's walk through an example and then use the disk storage selection factors from the Disk Subsystem Sizing Methodology section to help make the selection. For this example, we have determined—from both historical information and extrapolation from industry standard benchmarks that are similar to our environment—that

- This is a critical SQL server database supporting an online eCommerce solution.
- Database size is 100GB.
- Log file size is 6GB with a transaction rate of 300 transactions/sec.
- Overall anticipated transactions/sec is 6,000 transactions/sec.
- Return to service is 4 hours.
- Backup window is 8 hours.

Let's now use the disk subsystem sizing methodology outlined earlier to develop a disk.

COST

Cost is a consideration, but it is more important to provide a solution that works well for the customer, as it is critical to the success of the business.

FAULT TOLERANCE LEVEL REQUIRED (AVAILABILITY)

Fault tolerance is a requirement for this system because it is critical to business operations. Also, this is not a clustered system, and all files are deemed important; thus, RAID 0 is not an option for this solution.

PERFORMANCE CAPACITY NEEDED (THROUGHPUT, LATENCY, I/OS PER SECOND)

- **Business requirements.** This is a very important system for this company; it must be responsive enough to meet customer response time requirements of less than 3 seconds.
- **Disk characteristics of all applications that the system is running (sequential, random, read, write).** From Sysmon we have determined the following:
  - SQL server: primary database—random workload; typical transfer is 8KB, mix of 50% reads and 50% writes
  - SQL server: log files—sequential workload, typical transfer is 8KB, 100% write intensive
  - Windows 2000 core operating system—random workload, read intensive
  - Windows 2000 pagefile—sequential workload, mix between read and write activities
- **Where the applications are placing stress onto your disk subsystem.** All of the applications identified below can be tuned so that they store (place) their files on the disk subsystem where you want them.
- **Windows 2000 file system cache usage.** The goal is to cache between 90% and 100% of all SQL transactions. SQL has its own cache so Windows 2000's file system cache will be used, but not as the primary caching mechanism for the application. Based on historical information, 1GB of RAM under a similar project workload resulted in caching 92% of database activities. Our goal is always to keep everything in memory, but how well the cache performs is dependent on key factors such as the workload, database design, and application design. .
- **Throughput and workload (I/Os per second).** The database must be able to support 6,000 transactions/sec. If 90% of the transactions were cached, this would leave 600 transactions/sec to be supported

by the disk subsystem supporting the database. To meet this performance requirement and the need for fault tolerance requirement, a RAID 5 array will be used. Remember that, for a RAID 5 array, you must calculate the write operation's overhead. Since each disk in a RAID array can support approximately 150 I/Os per second, a RAID 0 array would require (600 I/Os × 1.25 utilization factor) / 150 I/Os which works out to five disk drives (which you round up to the nearest integer if needed). However, since we need some fault tolerance, we have decided to use a RAID 5 array. Thus the actual I/Os per second that must be supported equals

{[(300 disk reads/sec) + (4 × 300 disk writes/sec)] × 1.25 utilization factor} / 150

which works out to 13 disk drives. Here the utilization factor of 1.25, or 120%, is added to ensure that disk operations can be sustained at an 80% utilization factor.

The log file transaction rate was measured to be 300 transactions/ sec with a 70% cache hit ratio, which results in 90 I/Os per second that will be needed to support the log file workload (30% of the transactions make it directly to disk). Since fault tolerance is required, we will not place the log file on the same array as the database for two reasons: performance and fault tolerance. Having two separate arrays improves the mean time between failures for each array. Thus, if we lost two drives—one in the array housing the database and the other in the array housing the logs, we are still operational. If we lose a third drive, perhaps in the database array, all is not lost. The database can be restored from our backup medium, and then the transaction logs (on another array) can be used to restore anything that was lost with the database array failure.

To support the log files, a RAID 1 array would be desirable due to cost considerations. Because of this, the actual number of I/Os that must be supported equals

{[0 disk reads/sec + (2 × 90 disk writes/sec)] × 1.25 utilization factor} / 150

This works out to 1.5 disks, which we round up to the next integer. Thus a 2-disk RAID 1 array will meet our projected needs. If this workload begins to increase, we will consider a RAID 10 array in the future.

For our Windows 2000 operating system workload, we have observed less than 90 I/Os per second. Thus the operating system and database application will reside on their own 2-disk RAID 1 array. We do not anticipate heavy paging, but just in case a single disk drive is dedicated to supporting the pagefile.

- **The number of disk drives per SCSI/fibre channel.** Two Ultra2 SCSI channels will be utilized. The first channel is for internal disks that comprise the two RAID 1 arrays and 1 JBOD disk. A second channel will be used to connect our external 13-disk RAID 5 disk array, which can potentially generate the greatest throughput during backups—31MB/sec (estimated). This is not sufficient to compromise an Ultra2 SCSI channel rated at 80MB/sec.

BACKUP SPEED

Our backup requirements are that the system be completely backed up in an 8-hour period and restored within 4 hours. To improve overall performance, we have dedicated disk resources to each application. This enables us to determine backup and restore performance based on the sequential read and write performance throughput tests earlier in this chapter. This is a good estimate of the backup performance our system should be able to achieve. Dedicated backup software should actually do better. Note: we are looking at the performance of only the disk subsystem in this example. In chapter 8, we take a closer look at all facets of high-performance backup solutions.

- Backing up the database based on a 100GB database across the 13-disk RAID 5 array (sequential read) will occur at approximately 34.71MB/ sec (based on Table 6.9: 13 disk drives × 2.67MB/sec = 34.71MB/sec), or 124GB/hour. Thus, our backups will take less than 1 hour to back up. Note that this is the speed with which we can get data *off* of the disk array; getting it *to* your backup medium is another story.
- Restoring the database, assuming no rollbacks are needed from the logs, is a sequential write process that occurs at approximately 12.35MB/sec (based again on Table 6.9: 13 disk drives × 0.95MB/sec = 12.35MB/sec) or 44.4GB/hour. Thus it will take approximately 2.25 hours to restore the database.
- Some folks back up the log files and some folks don't. For the sake of this example, we will. Based on a 6GB log file across the 2-disk RAID 1 array, sequential read backups will occur at approximately 30MB/ sec, or 108GB/hour. Thus there are no problems meeting our backup window.
- Restoring the log files, if you are inclined to do so, is a sequential write process that occurs at approximately 8MB/sec or 32GB/hour. Again, there is no problem meeting our restore-to-service level agreement.

THE AMOUNT OF SYSTEM RESOURCES CONFIGURED, SUCH AS CPU, MEMORY, DISKS, AND NETWORK

Remember not to forget about the rest of the system. CPU usage is an additive process. Therefore, to drive the 12-disk RAID 5 array at maximum throughput levels, approximately 20% of two Pentium III 550Mhz/2MB CPUs are required. From historical information, we find that a database half this size requires 80% of a Pentium III 550Mhz/2MB CPU, assuming at least 10% of the CPU is needed for network activity and another 10% for intrusion detection/management agents running on the server. This works out to 1.1 CPUs. Rounding up to the next integer, we find that we will need at least two Pentium III 550Mhz/2MB CPUs to meet our requirements.

Network usage is minimum for this solution, as this system is the back end for a web-based eCommerce site. The front-end web servers handle a bulk of the network traffic. However, to meet the backup requirements, a 12.5MB/sec (100BaseTX[100Mbit/sec]) network connection is not sufficient. To meet the backup requirements, a 1000BaseTX—e.g., Gigabit Ethernet—network interface card is used.

Memory is very important since we are counting on it to cache the bulk of the database I/O activities. Sizing memory is an additive process. For this solution, the simple equation for memory needs is

operating system (128MB) + file system cache (128MB) + database application (32MB) + database caches (726MB) + intrusion detection /management agents (10MB) = 1GB of RAM

For more details on configuring memory subsystems, refer to Chapter 8's solution scenarios.

WINDOWS 2000'S REQUIREMENTS

Windows 2000 will be configured on its own RAID 1 array to improve fault tolerance, and the pagefile will be placed on its own dedicated disk.

STORAGE CAPACITY NEEDED (AMOUNT OF USABLE DISK SPACE REQUIRED)

Using the 60% rule of thumb for disk storage and the other factors covered earlier, we determine the disk storage requirements as shown in Table 6.14. Something looks strange in the table, doesn't it? Why use a 9GB disk drive when a 2GB or 4GB disk drive will do for the operating system? Manufacturing! It has become difficult to obtain smaller-sized disk drives in quantity in a timely fashion from disk manufacturers. In fact, due to the laws of supply and demand, we have found that a 4GB disk drive costs approximately the same as a 9GB drive! So, why not use the larger drive? Someday you'll probably need it.

TABLE 6.14 *Storage Capacity Example*

Application	Required Storage	Partition/RAID Array	Disk Size	Total Storage
Windows 2000	600MB	C: 2-disk RAID 1	9GB	9GB
Database Application	250MB	C: 2-disk RAID 1	9GB	9GB
Pagefile	2GB (twice the size of RAM)	P: 2-disk RAID 1	9GB	9GB

Application	Required Storage	Partition/RAID Array	Disk Size	Total Storage
TABLE 6.14		*Storage Capacity Example (Continued)*		
Database	100GB	D: 13-disk RAID 5	18GB	216GB of usable disk space (13 drives × 18GB/drive – 1 drive for RAID 5 overhead) × 0.6 storage utilization rate. Target maximum available storage: 129GB
Log Files	6GB	L: 2-disk RAID 1	9GB	9GB

DATA PATH SANITY CHECK

Based on this solution, two Pentium III CPUs, 1GB of RAM, 2 SCSI channels, and 18 disk drives—nothing appears out of the ordinary.

Detecting Disk Subsystem Bottlenecks

Recall from chapter 2 that it is important to consider the entire system performance picture when trying to locate a Windows 2000 system bottleneck. There can be more than one system resource area that is contributing to the throttling of the system's overall performance. Once you have evaluated all of the major system resource areas, focus on the resource that is farthest to the left in the performance resource chart in Figure 6-23 (this chart was originally introduced as Figure 2-1 and is repeated here for your convenience). This strategy will provide the greatest immediate gain to the system's overall performance. For this discussion, all other system resources (except for the disk subsystem) have already been investigated and determined not to be the bottleneck interfering with the system's performance. Remember to revisit the performance resource chart after tuning around a memory bottleneck. Once

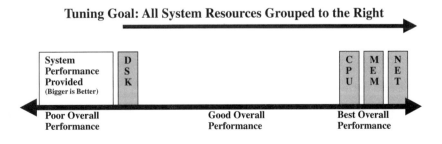

FIGURE 6-23   *Performance Resource Chart Depicting a Disk Resource Bottleneck*

one system resource is removed as the bottleneck, others may take its place, which will subsequently influence where you focus additional tuning efforts.

Quick Reference: Helpful Tools to Use When Tracking Down Windows 2000 Disk Subsystem Details

Throughout this section on bottleneck detection, several different tools will be used to track down disk subsystem details. Having a tool to complete this mission is nice; having specific examples showing how to use specific tools is even better. In this and the other chapters, we will provide some specific examples. It used to bug me when I had to fumble through books trying to find that helpful tool I read about but did not take notes on, so Table 6.15 is a list of tools used for investigating memory use in Windows 2000 for your quick reference. Most tools functionally overlap each other in some fashion. If you do not find what you are looking for with one tool, try another! Regardless of overlaps, sometimes just being able to investigate and interrogate the memory resources in a slightly different manner can spark that idea that helps you find what you are looking for. Note that most tools obtain and present information slightly differently. Do not be surprised if you get slightly different results when querying for the same information.

When a disk drive is unable to keep pace with the requested workload (I/Os per second) it becomes overworked and the response time that the disk

TABLE 6.15 *Tools to Use for Investigating Disk Subsystem Usage*

Tool	Where Do You Find It? (Package)	Command Line Image	When to Consider Using Each Tool
Sysmon (System Monitor, Alerts, Logging)	Native to Windows 2000	Sysmon MMC (Sysmon)	Long-term trend analysis.
Task Manager	Native to Windows 2000	Taskman.exe	Short-term analysis. Track the I/O column counter to track I/O usage per process in real time.
Filemon.exe	http://sysinternals.com freeware	Filemon.exe	Details on which process is using which portions of the disk subsystem with details down to the file level.
HandleEx	http://sysinternals.com freeware	Handle.exe	Details on which files and DLLs processes are using.
Process Explode	Resource Kit	Pview.exe	Process details into how disk subsystem activities are run.
Page Fault Monitor	Resource Kit	Pfmon.exe	Advanced debugging of specific applications.

drive provides begins to degrade. If the requested workload increases even more, the disk I/O requests begin to back up. When this occurs, disk queues form. When disk queues form, the Windows 2000 or application process requesting a disk I/O operation must wait in line for service from the disk subsystem. This worst-case disk I/O queuing is easier to detect than the slowing disk response time. Both are forms of disk bottlenecks. Table 6.16 outlines the counters to observe when sleuthing out disk bottlenecks.

TABLE 6.16 *Core Sysmon Counters for Baselining and Disk Bottleneck Detection*

Object: Counter	Definition	Rule of Thumb for Bottleneck Detection
Logical Disk: Average Disk Queue Length	Average Disk Queue Length is the average number of both read and write requests queued for the selected logical disk during the sample interval.	If this value is greater than 2–3 for a single disk drive and the Disk Transfers/sec are high (>100), the selected disk drive is becoming a bottleneck. This value is an average calculated during the Sysmon sample period. Use this counter to determine if there is a disk bottleneck, and use the Current Disk Queue Length counter to understand the actual workload distribution.
Logical Disk: Disk Transfers/sec	Displays the workload being experienced by the selected disk drive. Disk Transfers/sec is the rate of read and write operations (I/Os per second) on the selected disk.	If this value rises consistently above 100 for a single physical disk drive, observe if the Average Disk sec/Transfer counter is reporting values higher than your baseline or what you consider acceptable. If it is, then the disk drive is slowing down the overall system's performance.
Logical Disk: Average Disk sec/Transfer	Average disk sec/Transfer is the time in seconds of the average disk transfer.	When the Transfers/sec counter is consistently above 100 for a single disk drive, the Average Disk sec/Transfer should be observed to determine if it is rising above your baseline. As a rule of thumb, a value greater than 0.035 seconds indicates that the selected disk drive's response time is uncommonly slow.
Logical Disk: Disk Bytes/sec	Disk Bytes/sec is the rate bytes are transferred to or from the disk during write or read operations.	Sum this counter's value for each disk drive or disk array attached to the same SCSI/fibre channel and compare it to 80% of the theoretical throughput for SCSI or fibre channel technology in use. If the summation of Disk Bytes/sec is close to this 80% value, it is the SCSI/fibre channel itself that is becoming the disk subsystems bottleneck. Use this data and some basic math to review the complete disk subsystem data path.
Logical Disk: Split IO/sec	Split IO/sec reports the rate that I/Os to the disk were split into multiple I/Os.	A split I/O may result from requesting data in a size that is too large to fit into a single I/O or the fact that the disk is fragmented. If you observe a higher rate than your normal baseline, run the Windows 2000 defragmenter to check if the disk subsystems are excessively fragmented.

Detecting the Obvious Disk Subsystem Bottleneck

Trying to observe an inordinate amount of disk counters at the same time may become confusing. The two most important counters to keep an eye on at a minimum are Logical Disk: Transfers/sec and Average Disk Queue Length. If the workload utilization on a single disk drive rises consistently above 80%, as indicated by the Transfers/sec counter reaching 120 (assuming 150 I/Os per second is the maximum a 10,000rpm Ultra2 disk drive can support on average), disk performance should be investigated. Once this counter moves into this range, it is like a flashing red light indicating more disk problems may be occurring and should be investigated. Note that %Disk Time can be used, but it is not as good an indicator of disk workload as Transfers/sec is. If this high number of Transfers/sec is associated with an Average Disk Queue Length greater than 2, the disk has become a bottleneck. To investigate if the queue length is not just being affected by spikes of heavy disk workload activity, observe the Current Disk Queue Length counter by changing the system sampling period to a finer granularity to glean a better understanding of the workload patterns.

Determining the Disk Queue Length for RAID Devices

The disk queue length is very important when tracking down a disk subsystem bottleneck located on a disk array. When determining the Average Disk Queue Length for a disk array, values greater than 2 for the entire disk array are acceptable. A disk array is composed of multiple disk drives that can support concurrent disk operations. To determine if the disk array's queue length is above the acceptable level of 2 outstanding requests per disk drive, divide the Average Disk Queue Length by the number of disk drives in the array. For example, if you had a 10-disk RAID 0 array and the reported Average Disk Queue Length was 11, the normalized disk queue length would be 11/10—1.1 which, rounded up to the nearest integer, is 2. One outstanding disk queue operation per disk drive is acceptable. However, if the reported Average Disk Queue Length is 29, the normalized disk queue length would be 3 per drive, which is unacceptable. Without knowing exactly what is configured in your server, the values reported by Sysmon are practically useless.

Calculating Disk Workload (I/Os per Second) for RAID Devices

When workloads approach 80% of the capacity that can be supported by the disk subsystem, response time from the disk subsystem begins to slow down dramatically. This is why it becomes important to track the workload utilization when sleuthing out disk subsystem bottlenecks.

Workload utilization is straightforward on a single disk drive. Based on Table 6.5, a single 10,000rpm Ultra2 disk drive can support approximately 150 I/Os per second. Thus an 80% utilization rate is 120 I/Os per second, which the Transfers/sec counter displays. But what about a disk array? When determining the I/Os per second for RAID arrays, Sysmon's Logical Disk Transfers/sec reports on only the logical drive, not each individual disk in the array. To determine the I/Os per second for each drive in the array, use the following guidelines:

- RAID 0 stripe I/Os per second per drive equals
  Disk Transfers/sec / number of drives in the array for this RAID 0 array
- RAID 1 mirror I/Os per second equals
  Disk Reads/sec + (2 × Disk Writes/sec) / number of drives in this RAID 1 array
- RAID 5 stripe with parity I/Os per second per drive equals
  Disk Reads/sec + (4 × Disk Writes/sec) / number of drives in this RAID 5 array
- RAID 10 mirrored disk I/Os per second per drive equals
  Disk Reads/sec + (2 × Disk Writes/sec) / number of disks in the RAID 10 array

Detecting the Not-So-Obvious Slow Disk

Transfers/sec climbing into the 80% and a higher utilization range is a good indication that you should begin an investigation into other areas of disk performance. Even if the Average Disk Queue Length is not greater than 2, the disk subsystem could still be hindering overall system performance because the response time from the disk subsystem can degrade. There can be times when the Transfers/sec peaks very high but the disk queue length is not greater than 2; subsequently, there is no definitive disk bottleneck. Figure 6-24 shows an example in which a 12-disk RAID 5 array is experiencing greater than 80%-and-growing utilization level, but the disk queue has not yet indicated a sustained bottleneck (a sustained value above 24). When this condition occurs, the disk subsystem is working hard and you are obtaining a good return on your disk investment. However, it can also indicate that the performance being provided, although not causing a bottleneck, is becoming increasingly slower. In this example, the application begins to slow down once 1,800 transfers/sec is approached (later this application receives really slow response once the queues begin to form). If you see this type of condition occurring, review the Transfers/sec counter, which indicates the disk I/O-per-second workload that the disk device is experiencing.

As illustrated earlier in this chapter, if the per-disk I/Os per second are in the range of 100–150 transfers/sec and rising in a random environment, review the Average Disk sec/Transfer. This counter will show how long the disk device is taking to service both read and write requests. If this value

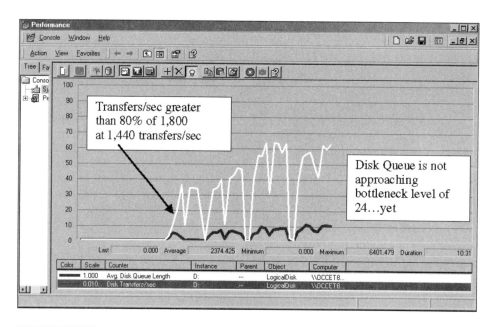

FIGURE 6–24   *High Transfers/sec Slowing the System Down*

steadily rises above your baseline or what you consider acceptable, it is a prelude to a disk bottleneck. As a general rule of thumb, if this value rises above 40ms (0.04 seconds), you should consider some of the tuning methods outlined in the next section. A more aggressive response-time goal would be 0.035 sec. This concept of slow disk response times is also illustrated in the electronic mail solution scenario in chapter 8 in which the disk write times are getting slower. For the case study environment, some of the write-intensive log file activity was relocated from the RAID 5 array to a RAID 1 array to alleviate the situation. By proactively managing a performance slowdown, you can tune around it before it ever becomes an actual bottleneck experienced by your customers. Proactive systems management!

DISK SLOWDOWN: FRAGMENTED DISKS

Have you ever noticed how fast a brand new system runs? One of the reasons for this is the fact that, on new systems, the disk drives are typically formatted and the files are placed onto them in a very contiguous fashion, i.e., not fragmented. How can you determine if your disk subsystem needs to be defragmented to improve performance? You can run a disk defragmentation tool that is included with Windows 2000 found under Start / Programs / Accessories / System Tools / Disk Defragmenter to analyze whether your disk subsystem requires defragmentation and defragment it as needed. Numerous third-party tools provide even more options in the arena of disk defragmentation than the native Windows 2000 defragmentation tools. However, Sysmon now provides some insight into whether or not you should consider defragmenting your disk subsystem—monitor the Logical Disk object's Split IO/sec counter.

Split IO/sec reports the rate that I/Os to the disk were split into multiple I/Os. A split I/O may result from requesting data in a size that is too large to fit into a single I/O or it could result from the disk being fragmented. If you observe a higher rate than your normal baseline, run the Windows 2000 defragmenter to check for excessively fragmented disk subsystems. If you have not developed a baseline for this new counter yet, a good rule of thumb is to run Disk Defragmenter to analyze the state of the disk subsystem when the Split IO/sec value is greater than 1–2. Note that defragmentation is excellent for single-disk and RAID-based disk subsystems.

REMEMBER THE DATA PATH

If the disk drive is not a bottleneck or even experiencing high workload levels, but the disk subsystem feels sluggish from your application perspective, what could be wrong? Even before configuring your system, follow the disk sizing guidelines presented in this chapter, but remember that computer performance is part art as well (there, I slid it into this chapter too). In addition to the Transfers/sec, occasionally sum up the Disk Bytes/sec value of all of the logical disk devices on a particular SCSI chain. Once you have this information in hand, work from the beginning of the I/O data path (the disk drive), and then continue working your way up through the SCSI channel and start doing your math equations.

If the sum of the Disk Bytes/sec is closing in on 80% of the theoretical bandwidth of the SCSI/fibre channel technology in use, the SCSI/fiber bus itself may be slowing down the disk subsystem operations. To solve this, either less work must traverse the SCSI/fibre channel or another SCSI/fibre channel must be added. To lower the workload on the specific disk subsystem in question, you can add physical memory or SCSI/fibre channels to the server. If new SCSI/fibre channels and perhaps disks are added to the server, the workload should be evenly spread across the new hardware. Also, compare the summation values of the Transfers/sec counter of all of the SCSI channel devices feeding the host bus adapter. Is the HBA rated to support such a workload? To remove the bottleneck, you could use an HBA with an increased workload capacity, or you could implement additional HBAs, again distributing the disk I/O workload across the new hardware.

Tuning Strategies for Removing Disk Subsystem Bottlenecks

We have configured and sized the fastest disk subsystem. You should have an understanding of how Windows 2000 uses the disk subsystem and how to detect when disk subsystem bottlenecks are forming. Now that we have all of this wonderful information, how do we make the disk subsystem go faster or, at least, become more efficient? In this section, we will review the strategies surrounding disk subsystem tuning and then get into the actual hands-on tactics.

At first glance, it would appear that tuning a Windows 2000 system to remove a disk subsystem bottleneck is difficult. With all of the options and flexibility available with Windows 2000 systems, this cannot be further from the truth. Now, purchasing more hardware is a valid technique, and we will discuss when it is appropriate to add memory and/or disks, but I do not care for typical responses. The case studies presented in chapter 8 move step-by-step through the strategies and tactics involved with tuning various areas of Windows 2000.

I cannot stress enough how important it is not only to know which operating system knob to tweak, but also to understand why something may need to be changed. Becoming properly armed with an understanding of how Windows 2000 and the system hardware work is actually the first step in tuning the disk subsystem. The following are the primary strategies to consider when tuning around a disk subsystem bottleneck.

- Ensure another system resource is not acting as a bottleneck.
- Evenly distribute the disk workloads.
- Select the appropriate memory management strategy.
- Lower the overhead associated with disk operations.
- Try to improve the efficiency of disk operations.
- Understand the workload characteristics and implement RAID technology accordingly.
- Tune and optimize virtual memory (pagefile).
- Remove potential disk subsystem roadblocks.
- Remove unnecessary workload from the system (applications, services, etc.).
- Control when application jobs are run.
- Update device drivers, system BIOS, and Windows 2000.
- Add additional RAM.
- Use advanced tuning tools–thinking outside of the box: SuperSpeed RAM Disk.

Let's review a variety of practical hands-on tactics that we can use to implement these strategies.

Hands-on Tactics for Tuning around Disk Subsystem Bottlenecks

ENSURE ANOTHER SYSTEM RESOURCE IS NOT ACTING AS A BOTTLENECK

A common occurrence I have encountered when tuning around disk subsystem bottlenecks is the removal of other system bottlenecks or a determination that another resource was the bottleneck. If another system resource is acting as a bottleneck, adding more disks will not significantly improve overall performance (although you will make your hardware vendor happy). Refer to the core tuning methodology that we covered in chapter 2 to ensure that another resource(s) is not the bottleneck before spending time and effort tuning disk resources.

Some bottlenecks appear to be disk related when in fact they are not. For example, in extreme cases, memory shortages disguise themselves as disk subsystem problems. When memory resources become scarce, two actions occur that affect disk subsystem performance. First, the disk(s) where the pagefile resides can quickly become very overworked. If the pagefile is not on its own dedicated disk(s), it may appear that another application is requiring significant disk resources when it is actually a memory issue. Second, when memory resources are scarce, fewer disk I/O operations are completed in the file system cache and/or the application's cache. This again leads to heavy disk activities that could be avoided by properly managing memory resources.

Avoid these conditions by configuring the memory and disk subsystem from both a performance perspective and a capacity perspective.

EVENLY DISTRIBUTE THE DISK WORKLOADS

Review the Sysmon logs regularly to ensure that you have evenly distributed the workload across the entire disk subsystem. If the Logical Disk Average Disk Queue Length or Transfers/sec approaches the thresholds mentioned earlier—2 and 120, respectively, or 80% utilization—consider spreading the data off the affected logical drives to other physical devices that are less in demand. A common source of contention is having all applications loaded and running on the root Windows 2000 disk. The root disk is where WinNT (%SystemRoot%) resides, most commonly the "C: partition." The root disk can quickly become a bottleneck. Note that when redistributing disk workloads, just moving files from one logical partition to another on the same physical disk drive does not help the situation. It actually makes it worse! When balancing the disk workload, ensure it is completed along physical disk drive boundaries.

To distribute the disk subsystem workload, you need to understand where the workload is emanating from. Then you can work with the particular application generating the workload and tune it to place its data or logs in another location. Look at the documentation associated with the applications you are running. The documentation usually provides insight into which files the application uses and where they reside by default.

A tool that is helpful in determining what processes are accessing which disk subsystems on your system is filemon.exe. This tool is freeware and is available at http://www.sysinternals.com. Figure 6-25 is a short output that you might expect from filemon.exe.

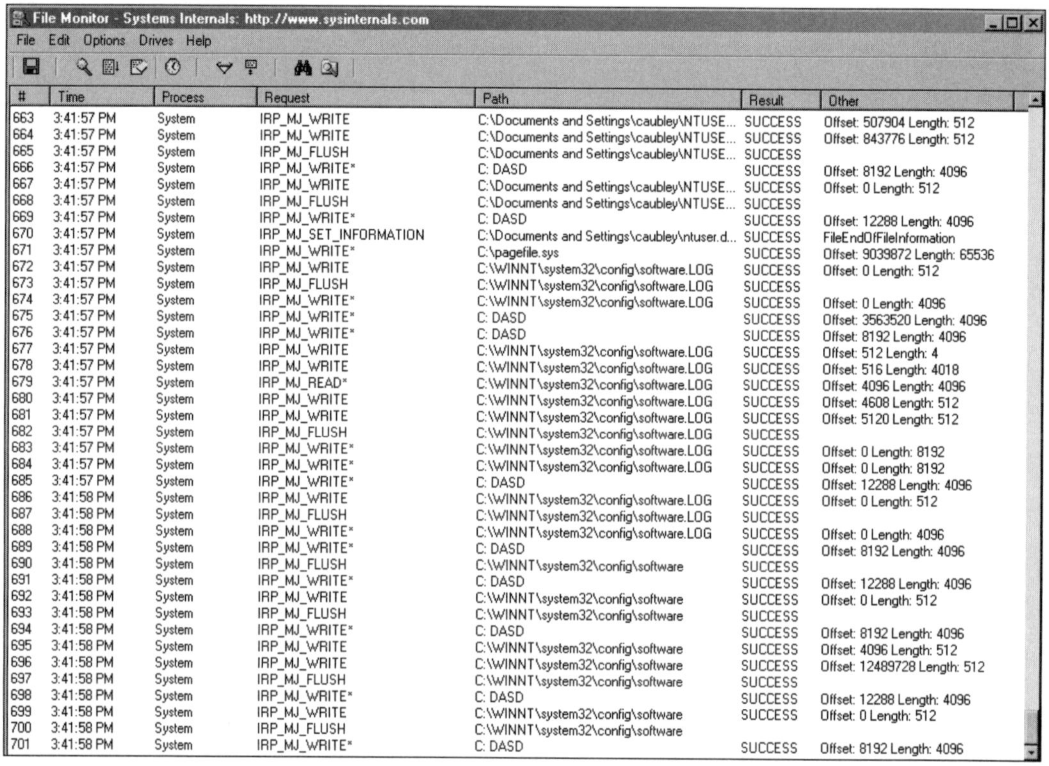

FIGURE 6–25   *Using filmon.exe to Determine Disk Activity and the Guilty Processes*

Another useful tool for determining which processes are using which files on the disk is handle.exe. Handle.exe is a utility that displays information about open handles (files) and dynamic linked libraries (DLLs) for any process in the system and provides a different perspective than filemon.exe Where filemon.exe displays real-time disk access that is helpful in determining the frequency of a process's disk activity, handleex.exe does a good job showing all the files that a specific file is using, as shown in Figure 6-26. These tools are available from http://www.sysinternals.com. Use these tools in conjunction with Sysmon to help you understand where to distribute the disk I/O workload among the entire disk subsystem. These tools are also very helpful for troubleshooting application and operating system issues.

MEMORY MANAGEMENT: TUNE THE WINDOWS 2000 FILE SYSTEM CACHE USAGE

Memory tuning in the disk tuning section? Absolutely! Sufficient and properly tuned memory resources lower the workload on the disk subsystem and improve overall performance. The most common ways to control how Windows 2000 uses available RAM for disk caching purposes (outlined in the

Process	PID	Owner	Priority	Handles
System	8	<unable to open token>	8	47
smss.exe	B4	NT AUTHORITY:SYSTEM	11	50
csrss.exe	D0	NT AUTHORITY:SYSTEM	13	324
winlogon.exe	E8	NT AUTHORITY:SYSTEM	13	388
services.exe	104	NT AUTHORITY:SYSTEM	9	510
lsass.exe	110	NT AUTHORITY:SYSTEM	13	191
svchost.exe	1C8	NT AUTHORITY:SYSTEM	8	210
msdtc.exe	1E4	NT AUTHORITY:SYSTEM	8	154
ati2plab.exe	268	NT AUTHORITY:SYSTEM	8	33
svchost.exe	278	NT AUTHORITY:SYSTEM	8	287
llssrv.exe	288	NT AUTHORITY:SYSTEM	9	97
mstask.exe	2C4	NT AUTHORITY:SYSTEM	8	93
snmp.exe	2EC	NT AUTHORITY:SYSTEM	8	244
termsrv.exe	320	NT AUTHORITY:SYSTEM	10	142

Base	Size	Version	Time	Path
0x1000000	0xA000	5.00.2184.0001	12/7/1999 8:00 AM	C:\WINNT\system32\lsass.exe
0x77F80000	0x79000	5.00.2163.0001	12/7/1999 8:00 AM	C:\WINNT\System32\ntdll.dll
0x77E80000	0xB6000	5.00.2191.0001	12/7/1999 8:00 AM	C:\WINNT\system32\KERNEL32.dll
0x50900000	0x7C000	5.00.2184.0001	3/7/2000 11:06 PM	C:\WINNT\system32\LSASRV.dll
0x78000000	0x46000	6.01.8637.0000	12/7/1999 8:00 AM	C:\WINNT\system32\MSVCRT.DLL
0x76670000	0xE000	5.00.2135.0001	12/7/1999 8:00 AM	C:\WINNT\system32\CRYPTDLL.DLL
0x77DB0000	0x5A000	5.00.2191.0001	12/7/1999 8:00 AM	C:\WINNT\system32\ADVAPI32.DLL
0x77D40000	0x6F000	5.00.2193.0001	12/7/1999 8:00 AM	C:\WINNT\system32\RPCRT4.DLL
0x77BE0000	0xF000	5.00.2154.0001	12/7/1999 8:00 AM	C:\WINNT\system32\SECUR32.DLL
0x77E10000	0x65000	5.00.2180.0001	12/7/1999 8:00 AM	C:\WINNT\system32\USER32.DLL
0x77F40000	0x3C000	5.00.2180.0001	12/7/1999 8:00 AM	C:\WINNT\system32\GDI32.DLL
0x76450000	0x5B000	5.00.2192.0001	12/7/1999 8:00 AM	C:\WINNT\system32\SAMSRV.DLL

lsass.exe pid: 110

FIGURE 6–26   *Using handle.exe to Track Handle (File) and DLL Usage*

section on selecting Windows 2000 memory strategy options in chapter 5) include the following:

1. Maximize data throughput for file sharing.
2. Maximize data throughput for network applications.

Properly selecting Windows 2000 memory strategy will drastically affect your system's disk I/O performance.

Although it depends on your environment, adding RAM will also improve the disk I/O performance. If Windows 2000 is functioning as a file server, you have added more RAM, and you choose to maximize data throughput for file sharing (tuning option 1), ensure the pagefile is twice as large as the size of the new RAM configuration and reboot the system to take advantage of the additional RAM. If you added more RAM and selected option 2, again ensure the pagefile is twice as large as the size of the new RAM configuration. However, just rebooting the server will have a smaller impact on improving disk I/O performance since less of the additional RAM available is for the Windows 2000 file system cache. When option 2 is used, the application's working set is favored, not the file system cache; thus you will also need to tune any applications that can be adjusted internally to take advantage of the additional RAM that is now online. For example, Microsoft

Exchange enables the amount of memory allowed for use to be easily set via the Exchange Optimizer Program. So, if you add more memory to the server, tune the applications accordingly to take full advantage of your investment.

CONTROL ACCESS TO NETWORK-SHARED DISK SUBSYSTEM RESOURCES

It is normal to find disk resources shared to the network under Windows 2000. If a specific popular network disk subsystem resource becomes a bottleneck, but it is not currently possible to tune around the bottleneck, what can you do? One technique is to control the number of users accessing the disk resource concurrently until the bottleneck can be removed. To control the concurrent user access for a specific shared resource, use the following command from the command prompt: c: > net share SharedDiskResource=F:\DirectoryShared /users:40 /remark: "For a limited time only 40 concurrent users can use this resource."

Now that this popular shared-resource access is limited, let's not allow people to tie it up. To control the amount of time a shared resource connection can sit idle before disconnecting the user, use the following command from the command prompt: c:>net config server /autodisconnect:5. The net config server command sets the maximum number of minutes a user session can be inactive before it is disconnected. The default value for this command is 15 minutes. Also, this command is immediate and permanent. To change this value, you will need to rerun the command. For information on the status of a network share, perhaps to determine how many sessions are timed out, run the following command from the command prompt: c:>net statistics server | more.

LOW-LEVEL FORMAT DISK DRIVES BEFORE YOU FORMAT THEM UNDER WINDOWS 2000

When using a SCSI disk drive on a different SCSI HBA, always use the HBA's provided tools to low-level format the disk drive before attempting to create a file system on the drive with Windows 2000. The geometric translation combination in use varies for each HBA and disk combination. When SCSI disk drives are placed onto a new HBA, you want to ensure that the correct translation information is being used. Low-level formatting the disk drive with the tools provided by the HBA vendor confirms that the translation in use is correct. This will give you the proper functionality, reported capacity, and performance you want when using the disk drive with Windows 2000.

ALIGN DISK TRACKS AND SECTORS

Windows has an internal structure called the master boot record (MBR) that limits the maximum default hidden sectors to 63. For this reason, the default starting sector for disks that report more than 63 sectors/tracks is the 64th sector. For disks with 64 or more sectors/tracks, this can cause misalignment when data is transferred to and from the disks. To optimize the transfer of data to and from the disk drives that is due to misaligned disk tracks and sectors by setting the proper starting sectors, diskpar.exe is provided with the Windows 2000 Resource Kit. Diskpar.exe is a command-line tool that finds and modifies the starting sector on a disk to improve disk performance. It is used only with multidisk systems. To get all of the diskpar.exe options, run diskpar.exe -?. Note that, when diskpar.exe is used, all data will be lost on the target disk drive; thus it is best to use the Logical Disk Manager to bring the disk drive off line, run diskpar.exe, then bring the disk drive back on line and format it with the file system of your choice.

Windows File-System-Level Tuning

ALLOCATE ONLY ONE LOGICAL PARTITION PER PHYSICAL DISK DRIVE

One way to isolate disk performance problems and then improve disk drive performance is to format only one partition per physical drive. This technique can lower the amount of head movement (seek) over the disk drive. For example, if you have three disk drives, create only three partitions: C:, D:, and E:.

To illustrate the concept behind this tuning technique, consider a single disk drive formatted with two logical NTFS file systems E: and D: (see Figure 6-27). Suppose application 1 locates data files on E:, and application 2 has data files on D:. When application 1 requires data, the disk head moves to the E: partition to locate the data. For this example, the data is on the outside edge of the platter. If the data for application 2, which is on D:, is on the inside edge of the drive platter, there is a significant amount of head movement or seek time added to access the disk data.

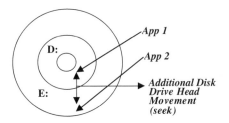

FIGURE 6-27 *Illustration of One Logical Partition per Physical Disk Drive*

With seek time being the costliest portion of a disk operation, it makes sense to attempt to lower it. If only a single NTFS file system is placed on the entire drive, the data has a better chance of being written together instead of being forced to different areas of the disk based on logical partitioning. Seek time has a greater chance of being lowered when the data being read is grouped close together. Lowering the disk drive's seek time significantly improves overall disk drive response time. The concept of seek time was explored in the sections on disk drive technology and SCSI technology in this chapter.

ALLOCATE MULTIPLE PARTITIONS FOR VERY LARGE RAID ARRAYS

In the last section, we recommended that you allocate only one partition per physical disk drive. This holds true for single disk drives and small RAID arrays, but, with the advent of high-density disk drives and RAID technology, you may also want to consider multiple partitions in some circumstances for two reasons. The first is availability. If you have a 10-disk 36GB RAID 5 array, there is 324GB of usable disk drive storage capacity. A single NTFS partition can be used, but, if it becomes corrupt and the *chkdsk* command is needed to be run against the partition, it can take an amazing amount of time to recover.

The NTFS file system is a journaling file system; thus checkpoints are periodically written to the NTFS log located on each NTFS partition. For very large NTFS partitions, contention can build for the NTFS log, causing the overall disk subsystem to run more slowly. This outweighs some of the disk geometry advantages of a single logical partition for RAID arrays. For these reasons, I recommend that, for very large RAID arrays, you configure multiple partitions as needed. In our example, create two 163GB NTFS partitions. This approach has the added benefit of allowing one partition to be backed up while the other partitions are on line.

SELECT THE APPROPRIATE NTFS LOG FILE SIZE

The NTFS file system is a journaling file system; checkpoints are periodically written to the NTFS log located on each NTFS partition. For larger partitions, it is important that this log is large enough to support the file system activity and to ensure that the log file does not become fragmented. For larger NTFS volumes, increase the size of the NTFS log file to 64MB or larger, by using the *chkdsk* command chkdsk drive-letter: /l:65536.

SELECT THE APPROPRIATE ALLOCATION UNIT SIZE

Match the file system ALU to the block size of the application you are using. If SQL Server is using an 8KB block size, when you format a file system on a new disk drive using the Logical Disk Manager, set the ALU to 8KB. Matching the file system block sizes can improve the efficiency of the disk transfers when you use the application. The Logical Disk Manager now supports a full range of ALU sizes. You can also use the format command from the command prompt in exchange for the Disk Administrator tool. An example using the format command from the command line to set up an NTFS file system with a 64KB ALU size format h: /FS: NTFS /A:64K. For all of the format command options, type format /? at the command prompt.

The NTFS file system uses clusters as the fundamental units of disk allocation. A cluster is composed of disk sectors. When using the format command or the Logical Disk Administrator, clusters are referred to as the *allocation unit size*. In the NTFS file system, the default ALU depends on the volume size. Utilizing the format command from the command line to format your NTFS volume, you can specify any ALU shown in Table 6.17. The default cluster sizes for the NTFS file system are shown in Table 6.17.

TABLE 6.17	Automatic Windows 2000 Format Option's Default Allocation Unit Sizes		
Partition Size	**Sectors per ALU (cluster)**	**Default ALU (cluster) Size**	
512MB or less	1	512 bytes	
513MB–1,024MB (1GB)	2	1K	
1,025MB–2,048MB (2GB)	4	2K	
2049MB–4,096MB (4GB)	8	4K	
4,097MB–8,192MB (8GB)	16	8K	
8,193MB–16,384MB (16GB)	32	16K	
16,385MB–32,768MB (32GB)	64	32K	
> 32,768MB	128	64K	

This technique of setting the proper ALU is implemented when tuning the server in chapter 8's solution scenarios. You always have to make trade-offs somewhere when tuning your system. There is some loss of available capacity when using the larger ALUs. Unless you are really low on disk space or value every byte of possible storage, the slightly lower capacity sizes associated with larger ALUs is a nonissue.

Another trade-off when tuning ALU sizes is that the Windows 2000 native defragmentation tool does not work on ALU sizes greater than 4KB.

To determine the size of disk I/O operations, consider reading the friendly vendor manuals or completed research on the operation of the application. Sizes of disk I/O operations can also be determined by using Sysmon and observing the Logical Disk counters: Average Disk Bytes/read and Average Disk Bytes/write.

File System—Related Tuning

File System Selection

Select the appropriate file system to meet the solution requirements. Which file system to choose has traditionally been a heavily debated topic, and I am going to stray away from performance for a moment while we talk about it. Under Windows 2000, there are three file system options: NTFS, FAT32, and FAT. If security is a consideration at all, there is only one choice—NTFS. If FAT/FAT32 file systems are in use, try to limit their use to disk drives or partitions smaller than 500GB. For smaller file systems characterized by many small files, FAT can actually outperform NTFS. FAT file systems are more apt to become fragmented in a shorter period of time and begin to degrade in overall performance for larger file systems. Thus, for all file systems larger than 500GB, use NTFS.

Disabling Short-Name Generation

Disabling short-name generation on an NTFS partition can increase directory performance significantly if a high number of non-8.3 file names are in use (i.e., long file names). This is becoming increasingly common as legacy clients and applications are updated. Windows 2000 must calculate the short 8.3-compliant file name every time a long Windows 2000 file name is used. This increases CPU overhead and causes additional writes to the disk subsystem. To disable short-name generation, use regedit32.exe to set the registry DWORD value of 1 in the following Registry location: HKEY_LOCAL_MACHINE\SYSTEM\CurrentControlSet\Control\Filesystem\NtfsDisable8dot3nameCreation. It is very important to remember that this will cause problems if applications based on legacy 16-bit MS-DOS or MS-Windows are still in use on the Windows 2000 system you tune using this technique.

Disabling Last Access Updates

Another registry tunable that can improve file system performance by lowering file system overhead is located in HKEY_LOCAL_MACHINE\SYSTEM\CurrentControlSet\Control\FileSystemNtfsDisableLastAccessUpdate. Changing the default REG_DWORD value of this key from 0 to 1 will stop Windows 2000 from updating the last access time/date stamp on directories as directory trees are traversed.

Defragmenting NTFS

Like any other file system, NTFS can become fragmented over time on heavily used disks. Windows 2000 does have a native defragmentation tool that is found at: Start / Programs / Accessories / System Tools / Disk Defragmenter. There are also commercial products available to defragment disk drives, which can improve performance of the file system. Current lists of defragmenting utilities are available at http://www.microsoft.com. Some of these disk defragmentation tools market that they not only defragment the file system, but also place files not touched for longer periods of time together on slower areas of the disk drive. Conversely, they group recently used files together on faster or more commonly traveled areas of the disk. These techniques, if successful, will improve disk access time by lowering the time for seek operations and freeing up contiguous areas of disk for Windows 2000's use. If these defragmentation tools are in use on your system, you may not want to disable the last access updates, a tuning technique mentioned above, because it may conflict with the defragmentation tool's operations.

Currently there isn't an industry standard benchmark you can use when reviewing these disk defragmentation tools. The performance gains achieved will vary greatly from one environment to another. Custom server baseline tests, such as the ones mentioned in chapter 2, are helpful in determining the value that these disk defragmentation tools might have in your environment. Your Sysmon baseline is also a helpful tool when evaluating the effectiveness of disk defragmentation. Compare the Sysmon counter Average Disk sec/ Transfer before and after the disks are defragmented under similar workloads (same time of day during similar workload activity, etc.) to help determine if they are providing a beneficial service.

To lessen the impact of fragmentation and to take advantage of the physical characteristics of disk drives without a defragmentation tool, try to keep file systems at a capacity lower than 60–80%. This will allow NTFS to compensate for fragmentation by taking less time to find additional free space when needed.

Avoid Compression

When file system compression is turned on, it taxes all of the system's resources. The CPU is needed to make the calculation; memory is required; also during this period the process is waiting for the disk I/O to complete. Unless absolutely necessary, do not use disk compression.

Avoid Encryption

When file system encryption is turned on, it taxes all of the system's resources. The CPU is needed to make the calculation, memory is required, and the process is waiting for the disk I/O to complete. Unless absolutely necessary, do not use disk encryption. If encryption is needed, consider encrypting at the desktop level and then just saving the files to a server.

Tuning Disk Subsystem SCSI Channel and HBA

Balance PCI Bus Usage

Whenever possible, use the latest adapter technology. Currently, the latest adapter technology is 64-bit PCI I20-enabled adapters. If using a system with a single PCI bus architecture, populate the bus slots closest to the system bus first (Slot 0) with the adapter that is the most active. In some cases this will be the NIC and in some cases this will be the SCSI HBA—it depends on your environment. If your system supports two or more peer PCI buses, balance usage across the 64-bit PCI buses first. In general, place the SCSI/fiber/RAID adapters on a separate bus from the NICs for optimum performance. Refer to chapter 3 for interrupt binding techniques that can aid in the performance of HBAs through binding CPU ownership to specific adapters.

Group Similar Devices on the Same SCSI Channels

To maximize the performance and efficiency of your SCSI channels, group similar external devices on the same SCSI bus. By placing an active tape backup unit on the same SCSI bus as a 10-disk RAID 0 array, the tape backup device can effectively slow down access to the faster disk array. When SCSI commands are sent to request data from the tape backup unit, which is a slower device than a disk drive, the other devices on the SCSI bus must wait until the tape backup device (or other slower device) transfer is complete before transferring the data associated with the other devices.

A good rule of thumb to follow is to place CD-ROMs on their own SCSI channel, place each tape unit on its own SCSI channel, and group disk drives with similar features (size, rpm, throughput) on their own SCSI channels. Also, avoid configuring SCSI devices using different levels of SCSI standards on the same SCSI channel, because they will be limited to running at the speed of the slowest SCSI standard on the particular SCSI channel. For example, operating Fast and Wide SCSI (20MB/sec) and Ultra Fast and Wide SCSI (40MB/sec) on the same SCSI channel limits the SCSI channel to the slower Fast and Wide SCSI speed.

As another example, let's look at the SCSI configuration for a higher end file server that supports an NIC, a large external disk array, and a two-tape robotic backup system. First, place the NIC in the first PCI bus and place the SCSI HBAs in the second PCI bus. The two-channel RAID controllers will use one SCSI channel for each 12-disk external RAID array. The internal disk drives will use the built-in RAID controller on the system's motherboard. The robotic tape backup unit will connect via another HBA that supports three SCSI channels. One SCSI channel is connected to the tape unit's robotic unit that is used for sending commands to the tape backup unit's robot. This is on a separate channel since these commands typically are serial in nature and would slow down any SCSI devices on the same channel. One SCSI channel is then attached to each tape unit.

SCSI Command Queuing

Some drivers for SCSI adapters have registry settings for SCSI command queuing. By increasing this value, you can improve the performance of the attached disk subsystem. When this value is increased, more SCSI commands can be in the disk device queue. This technique is particularly helpful in disk array environments. Due to the multiple disk drive nature of disk arrays, they are capable of coalescing multiple SCSI requests in the most efficient manner to achieve higher levels of performance. Use this technique cautiously, and test your performance before and after editing the registry values. For most large disk array environments (>10 disks), doubling the default value for the driver improves disk performance. Contact the disk adapter vendor for assistance in finding the SCSI command queuing entry in the registry. For example, for Symbios SCSI adapters whose default is 32, the SCSI command queue entry is found in the following location: `HKey_Local_Machine\System\Current-ControlSet\Services\symc8xx\Parameters\Device\NumberOfRequests` (REG_DWORD 32).

Monolithic SCSI Drivers

In an effort to improve SCSI HBA performance, some vendors have implemented what is referred to as monolithic device drivers. These specialized drivers appear to have been born out of necessity to improve Windows 2000 performance for the TPC-C benchmark. Monolithic device drivers incorporate the Windows 2000 SCSI port driver and miniport driver into one large monolithic driver. These monolithic device drivers lower the amount of code required that a disk I/O must traverse. The benefits of these drivers are twofold. First, these drivers tend to improve the disk I/O performance on heavily utilized disk subsystems. Second, they require fewer CPU cycles when implementing the actual disk I/O activity, which is particularly beneficial in a CPU-intensive server environment. Vendors such as Compaq, Dell, and IBM offer the monolithic device drivers for some of the SCSI HBAs that they use. Check the respective server or the HBA vendor's web site or contact them directly for information on how to obtain this technology.

Properly Configure the HBA

The proper setup of the HBA determines the performance level of the SCSI channels connected to it. Because technology moves so fast, even though an HBA may be rated for Ultra Fast and Wide SCSI speeds, this does not guarantee that they are configured for it. As the system boots, or by using the tools provided by the HBA vendor, be sure that you set the SCSI channel speeds to operate at the desired performance level. HBA settings you'll need to doublecheck and enable include SCSI bus speed, tagged command queuing, disconnect, and wide transfers. You have an investment in the technology for your system—make sure you get to use it.

Update HBA Device Drivers and BIOS (Firmware)

This is one of the easiest techniques to implement to improve disk I/O performance. Manufacturers of disk drive adapters are constantly working on removing bugs and improving the performance of their respective disk adapters. Most of the newer drivers are available from the manufacturers' web sites. Even before installing Windows 2000 for the first time, check the web sites to see the latest, best-performing, and most stable disk adapter device driver available. Then continue to check your chosen manufacturer's web site periodically. It is amazing how much you can improve performance through the use of the best in device drivers.

RAID Tuning Considerations

RAID Array Background Services

When Windows 2000 utilizes a disk array, either through software or hardware implementations, the data consistency of the actual array is not checked by the operating system by default. Parity or mirrored operations are completed, but the health of the disk array itself is not checked during regular disk I/O operations. Either through hardware implementation or Windows 2000 background services, vendors commonly implement routines to periodically check the disk array's health. This is an important activity that should occur on a regular basis.

For example, the SMART-2 Array HBAs from Compaq default to checking the disk array's health once every hour. On very busy systems, consider lowering the frequency of these health checks or postponing them to periods of lower workloads. By controlling the frequency of disk array health checks, you control the overhead that would detract from the array performance while ensuring the health of the array. Array-checking techniques differ between vendors, so you'll want to look at the vendor's documentation closely on this one.

Tuning RAID Controller Cache

If there is a built-in cache on the RAID HBA and a battery backup unit, the general rule of thumb is to configure it to ensure that the read-ahead and the write-back caching is turned on. The default setting for most adapter caches is *write-through* caching. Having the write-back cache enabled is particularly helpful in write-intensive environments implemented with RAID 5 disk arrays where there are pauses between periods of heavy disk activity. When your environment is characterized by heavy disk write activity followed by a lull, the write-back cache takes advantage of this workload slowdown to write the cache data to disk.

There are, however, some instances when write-back caching is not helpful. One such instance is log files that are continuously being written to. When data is constantly being written to a disk array, the write-back cache's effectiveness is diminished because it does not get a chance to take advantage of a workload slowdown window in which to flush its cache. For these continuous activity environments, disabling the write-through cache provides a higher level of performance. Many hardware RAID vendors allow you to selectively control how the cache is used on the various arrays under its control. For example, perhaps you have a RAID 1 mirror configured for the application logs and a RAID 5 array configured for a transaction-based database. You can set write-through caching for the RAID 1 mirror and write-back caching for RAID 5 array. Customizing your cache settings to match the workload's characteristics helps to improve the performance of the overall disk subsystem. This technique can be quite effective, but it is application dependent. This technique should always be tested for the specific application and RAID technology in use before fielding.

Setting RAID Stripe Sizes

Ideally, you want the typical system I/O operation size to be the same as the stripe size on the RAID array. We investigated this concept earlier in this chapter in the section on RAID stripes. For now, use this condensed version as a reminder. Depending on the hardware RAID implementation, there are numerous options available for setting up the RAID array stripe size. When you set the array's stripe size, the array will require a new low-level format using the hardware RAID vendor's tools. Stripe size is not the same as ALU, which can be set under Windows 2000 with the format command or Logical Disk Manager. If you implement a software-based RAID array using Windows 2000, stripe size cannot be tuned.

Short of tuning the RAID array stripe size, you should consider at least setting it according to your general disk subsystem workload characteristics. In general, larger stripe sizes provide better performance for large sequential data transfers, while smaller random data transfers benefit from smaller stripe sizes (chunks).

Single-Application Sequential Disk Behavior Dedication

Isolate sequentially accessed data on its own disk subsystem per application (thread) for maximum I/O performance. This maximizes the performance of the disk subsystem since it is supporting only one type of disk workload at a time. By dedicating the disk subsystem to a specific application, less contention is created, ensuring that the disk characteristic you are planning for is occurring without outside interference. For example, if you have three applications that are sequential in nature but share the same portion of the disk subsystem, the sequential behavior would become more random because the three applications might all be requesting the disk heads to move in different directions. You can avoid this by dedicating a single application to a physical portion of the disk subsystem. Common applications that sequentially access data are database log files and the Windows 2000 pagefile.

Hybrid Tuning: Grouping Similar Disk Activities Together

It may not be possible to dedicate a specific application workload to a specific portion of the disk subsystem due to application or cost constraints. When this occurs, attempt to group workloads with similar characteristics together. For example, group all random disk activity on the same set of RAID arrays, group all sequential write behavior applications together, and so on.

Grouping Similar Physical Disk Drives into the Same Array for the Best Capacity and Performance

It is tempting to build a disk array from different makes and models of disk drives. Whatever is lying around the office will do, right? If you place a lower-capacity disk drive into an array with a higher-capacity disk drive, you lower the array's overall capacity. For example, placing a 2GB disk drive into a RAID 0 (stripe) array with four 4GB disk drives will limit the overall array capacity to 5 × 2GB = 10GB, not 4 × 4GB + 2GB = 18GB. This same concept is true for performance of disk arrays. Grouping one older 5,400rpm drive into the same array as 10,000rpm disk drives will lower the overall performance of the array.

Using More Than One RAID Level in Your Solution: Grouping Similar Disk Work Load Characteristics

You can group all of your disks into one large array and let the system's applications have at it. With fast enough hardware in large enough quantities, this tactic actually can provide acceptable performance. Unfortunately, implementing this tactic can become expensive and may not meet other requirements such as the required fault tolerance levels. To properly lay out the disk subsystem, you need to understand the technology you are implementing (hardware and software) and the server disk subsystem's workload characteristics.

Either through reading those famous manuals (RTFM) that come with software products or by using Sysmon and filemon.exe (http://www.sysinternals.com), try to determine the characteristics of the disk I/O activities occurring on your system. Determine which applications exhibit sequential activities, which are random activities, and which are read or write intensive. A little research before you begin provides insight on how the server applications do or do not behave, whichever is the case.

Once fielded, user access patterns influence which areas of the disk subsystem are used more heavily than others. To help in determining which disk resources are under siege, use the Sysmon counters listed in Table 6.18 to determine which disk resources are being used more heavily than others. For an even more granular view of what is going on in your disk subsystem, review the Sysmon counters in Table 6.16 as well.

TABLE 6.18	Detailed Disk Subsystem Sysmon Counters	
Object: Counter	**Definition**	**Rule of Thumb for Bottleneck Detection**
Logical Disk: %Disk Write Time	%Disk Write Time is the percentage of elapsed time that the selected disk drive is busy servicing read requests.	This counter becomes crucial in determining disk I/O characteristics that directly influence how to lay out and size the disk I/O system.
Logical Disk: %Disk Read Time	%Disk read time is the percentage of elapsed time that the selected disk drive is busy servicing read requests.	This counter becomes crucial in determining disk I/O characteristics that directly influence how to lay out and size the disk I/O system.
Logical Disk: Disk Read Bytes/sec; Disk Write Bytes/sec	Disk Read (or Write) Bytes/sec is the rate at which bytes are transferred from (or to) the disk during read (or write) operations	These counters help provide insight on the amount of throughput being used for either read or write operations. This data is helpful in spreading disk subsystem activity across multiple HBAs, SCSI channels, and disk drives.

It is sometimes helpful to draw a logical picture of the system's disk subsystem or to build a table of the disk usage for each resource. With this data, you can then determine how and where to rearrange or add disk subsystem hardware.

Once you have determined the characteristics of your disk activities, group similar activities on the same disk drives or arrays. This is a corollary rule to the rule: *evenly distribute file system activity*. For example, place large log files on a separate disk drive and file system from where you place a general user database. Once the workload characteristics are evenly distributed, group disk activities across the disk subsystems utilizing the various RAID levels based on the performance guidelines provided in the next section. For example, to improve the performance of sequentially write-intensive logs files, place them onto RAID 1, or 0+1 arrays and avoid RAID 5. For a predominantly random environment that is read intensive, RAID 10 and 5 are good selections. The more clearly you understand your environment, the better tuned your Windows 2000 system will be.

Data Placement and RAID Selection

With this disk workload characterization information in hand, you are in an educated position to make decisions on which RAID level—or combination of RAID levels—to implement, where to add disk drives, and perhaps where to take them away. In the electronic mail case study in chapter 8, the disk subsystem workload characteristics for Microsoft Exchange were reviewed very closely. Repeated here is a high-performance and availability example of distributing the disk workload among various RAID levels to meet performance and availability objectives (see Table 6.19).

TABLE 6.19			Optimized Example of a Multi-RAID Implementation of MS Exchange	
Logical Disk Assignment	**SCSI Bus**	**Physical Disk Arrangement**	**Motivation behind Data Placement and RAID Selection**	**Microsoft Exchange File Location**
C:	1	2-disk RAID 1 mirror	Critical resource—if Windows 2000 does not boot, the server is useless. A RAID 1 mirror allows for loss of drive with loss in operation.	Windows 2000 operating system and exchange binaries
E:	1	2-disk RAID 1 mirror	Log data is sequential and write intensive. RAID 1, does not provide the best performance, but it provides much better write performance than RAID 5 and still provides data integrity.	Information store logs
F:	1	2-disk RAID 1 mirror	Same as above	Directory service logs
D:	2	1-disk no RAID, JBOD	Windows 2000 paging activities are sequential in nature, so good write/read performance is required. This drive is not as critical as other data drives, but provides good performance and overall value.	Windows 2000 pagefile
G:	2	2-disk RAID 1 mirror	General read/write database characteristic workload. This is deemed critical for exchange operation. Same motivation as the other RAID 1 implementations above.	Message transfer agent
I:	2	3-disk RAID 5 array	Random read/write database characteristic workload. Provides excellent read/write performance with cost-effective fault tolerance.	Directory service

Logical Disk Assignment	SCSI Bus	Physical Disk Arrangement	Motivation behind Data Placement and RAID Selection	Microsoft Exchange File Location
E:	3 (external array)	10-disk RAID 5 array	Intense random read/write database characteristic workload. Most heavily used disk subsystem in case study environment. RAID 5 composed of a large number of disk drives. Provides excellent random read performance and a sound level of fault tolerance.	Private information store
E:	3 (external array)	3-disk RAID 5 array	Potential intense random read/write database characteristic workload. RAID 5 provides excellent random read performance and a sound level of fault tolerance.	Public information store (if used)

TABLE 6.19 *Optimized Example of a Multi-RAID Implementation of MS Exchange (Continued)*

I/O Memory Lock Tuning

Windows 2000 does a great job at covering a large number of situations. However, it does not always know your environments as well as you do. If you have a large RAID subsystem, you can increase the number of pages the system will read/write simultaneously to the hard disk so that you take full advantage of your disk subsystem investment. To increase the number of pages your system can write/read to the disk subsystem, edit the key HKEY_LOCAL_MACHINE\System\CurrentControlSet\Control\Session Manager\Memory Management\IoPageLockLimit. The REG_DWORD IoPageLock-Limit value to which this key should be set varies from system to system. A value of 0 is the default Windows 2000 entry—this indicates that Windows 2000 will determine what is needed. In general, if you have a high-performance disk subsystem and sufficient RAM in your system, IoPageLockLimit should be set to a value of 1/8 the amount of RAM in the system.

The Most Important Disk Tuning Concept

Disk Capacity Storage and Disk Capacity Performance

This concept is reviewed in depth throughout this chapter because it is so important. However, it is commonly misunderstood, so I'll review the condensed version.

Should you choose three 9GB disk drives in a RAID 5 array, which provides 18GB of usable storage, to meet an 18GB disk requirement, or should you choose six 4GB disk drives in a RAID 5 array, which provides 20GB of usable storage? Both solutions meet the requirement of 18GB of usable disk space storage, but the 3-disk 9GB solution provides a lower level of performance. Which you choose depends on the level of performance required and the economics of your situation.

If economics is a greater concern than disk performance scalability, the three 9GB disk drives meet the requirements. Alternatively, if performance is more important, choose the six 4GB or twelve 2GB disk drive solution. Mileage may vary for every environment, but in general the addition of disk drives (spindles) can greatly improve your disk subsystem's throughput performance and I/Os per second supported. In general, the three 9GB disk drive solution can support 450 I/Os per second and a sustained physical drive sequential read throughput of 6MB/sec. The six 4GB disk drive solution supports 900 I/Os per second and a sustained physical drive sequential read throughput of 12MB/sec. This comparison is based on using the same family (SCSI connection, rpm level, etc.) of disk drives at different capacities.

Disk Storage Capacity Tuning

Is disk storage capacity related to tuning? Yes, we have investigated and determined that the seek time incurs the highest amount of overhead to the disk subsystem. As the space utilization of the disk drive exceeds 50%, any data required past the 50% mark causes the disk drive to seek at least halfway across the disk partition, which is time expensive. In a perfect world without budgets, you should always try to keep your disk drives less than 50% full. This is one of the reasons a new desktop always feels fast—the data is on the faster, outside portion of the disk.

Keeping 50% of a disk drive free of data may not be realistic for all environments. However, target a maximum space usage capacity of 75%. This approach is a compromise for performance and also allows enough room for disk defragmentation tools to operate. If your disk space usage exceeds 75%, most defragmentation tools will not run effectively with less than 25% of available space in which to operate.

Additional Disk Subsystem Hardware—The Last Resort

As with any resource that has become a bottleneck, additional resources can normally be added if all other efforts to improve performance do not meet your requirements or if you just need more disk storage capacity. Always select the fastest components that have a positive life cycle.

For the example, this would involve selecting the fastest available disk drives and disk adapter technology for insertion into the fastest I/O bus available. For example, if there is a need to add three additional disk drives, selecting a PCI-based Ultra2 SCSI Disk Adapter and Ultra2 SCSI disk drives rotating at 15,000rpm would be a good place to start.

Thinking Outside of the Box: Windows 2000 RAM Disk

RAM Disk Technology

Even with the best-performing Windows 2000 solutions, occasions arise in which disk subsystem *hot spots* are created that are difficult to resolve. Hot spots are areas of the disk subsystem from which application(s) consistently request service, resulting in the formation of disk queues, greatly impacting on the application's performance. No matter how well you sized and tuned your Windows 2000 disk subsystem, it is still composed of physical devices that are slow when compared to RAM. There may be times, regardless of how well you have load balanced and tuned your disk subsystem, when hot spots still exist. What can you do about these hot spots? If you had access to the application code, you could optimize the application. If you do not have access to the application source code and the vendor that provided it is not offering much support since you have not spent more than $10 million with it, consider an alternate technique to alleviate hot spot situations—try implementing RAM disks.

RAM disk technology is available in two forms. The first RAM disk form is also referred to as solid-state disk drives. These devices look similar to normal disk drives, but are composed of nonvolatile or battery-backed RAM and appear to Windows 2000 as regular disk drives. These solid-state disks connect to a Windows 2000 system over a SCSI connection, but are much faster than traditional disk drives. The second type of RAM disk is software based and allows you to configure part of Windows 2000's memory subsystem to appear as a disk drive. We will investigate this type here since it provides better performance and is easier to implement.

RAM disks are not native to Windows 2000, so I obtained a RAM disk product from SuperSpeed systems (http://www.eecsys.com) through SunBelt Software (http://www.sunbeltsoftware.com) named SuperSpeed. An evaluation copy of SuperSpeed is available from http://www.SunBelt-Software.com. This software actually provides two RAM disk options. The first option is a traditional RAM disk in which you can allocate some of Windows 2000 main memory to act as a disk drive. The second option allows for a disk-drive-backed RAM disk implementation—in other words, the RAM disk is mirrored to a physical disk drive.

Installing the SuperSpeed product is similar to installing other Windows 2000 applications. To configure the RAM disk, you bring up the SuperSpeed configuration tool and set the RAM disk size as needed and then reboot the server. Server RAM that is designated for the RAM drive is removed from use by Windows 2000 Virtual Memory Manager. For example, if you created a 200MB RAM disk on a server that is configured with 1GB of RAM, only 800MB would be available to normal Windows 2000 RAM operations. Once the server is rebooted, another drive letter—S:—is now available to use as needed (your RAM disk). Files can now be placed into this area either manually or via a start-up script. When applications that use these files are launched, they will operate at much higher performance levels while interacting with the RAM disk subsystem. This is a great way to speed up your disk subsystem, but there is a drawback. If the files are critical, they probably should not be on a RAM disk; however, if you do wish to keep them, you must copy them to a normal disk drive before powering down Windows 2000. As with all tuning, there are trade-offs for improved performance. When power is removed from the server, any files located in the RAM disk area will be lost.

Another option available from SuperSpeed is to provide a normal disk drive to back up RAM disk operations. This option provides higher performance levels by using the normal (non-disk-drive-backed) RAM disk, but then it saves the data written to the RAM disk in an efficient lazy-write mode process. This lazy-write mode of operation periodically saves the data from the RAM disk to a designated Windows 2000 partition (this same lazy-write concept was reviewed earlier in this chapter). The goal of this combination is to provide improved performance through the use of a RAM disk and nonvolatile data storage. Using this technique, data is not lost when Windows 2000 is powered down. When Windows 2000 is booted, the SuperSpeed driver again creates the RAM disk, but then it populates it with the data from the RAM drive backup partition.

Stress Test Environment and Results

So, how much performance improvement might you expect when using RAM disk technology? To address this question, we again employed the Neal Nelson Business Benchmark for Windows 2000. Tests 18, 19, and 26 were selected and executed at a copy level 16 workload. A copy level 16 workload exercises the disk subsystem under a load of 320 simulated users using a combined work file size of 400MB. The system under test was a Compaq 6400R configured with Windows 2000 server, 768MB of RAM, 12 Ultra2 SCSI 10,000 rpm disk drives, and two Pentium 550MHz/1MB cache CPUs.

To accommodate the 400GB benchmark work file, a 512MB RAM disk was created using SuperSpeed. In this configuration, 256MB of RAM was left for normal Windows 2000 operations (768MB of RAM total used in test). With this scenario, we can compare the performance results from the RAM disk tests with the conventional RAID array tests completed earlier in this chapter. Table 6.20 reports the benchmark results.

TABLE 6.20	SuperSpeed RAM Disk Benchmark Results	
Neal Nelson Business Benchmark Workload/Copy Level 16 (400MB Work File, 320 Simulated Users)	**6-Disk RAID 5 (Ultra2 SCSI 10,000rpm disk drives) (MB/ sec)**	**RAM Disk Only (MB/sec)**
Test 18 Sequential 1KB Reads	25.6	53
Test 19 Sequential 1KB Writes	7.1	40
Test 26 Random 4KB Reads	10.85	80

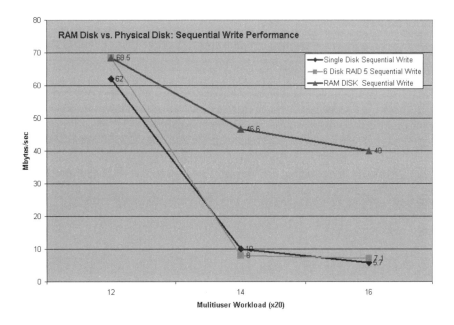

FIGURE 6–28	RAM Disk vs. Physical Disk: Sequential Write Performance

ANALYZING RAM DISK PERFORMANCE RESULTS

Performance improvements provided by the RAM disk are dramatic! Even more important than the specific throughput values reported are the relative performance differences between using the RAM disk and a traditional disk array. For the sequential read-intensive environment, the RAM disk provides over twice the performance of a 6-disk RAID 5 array, an eightfold improvement in the random read environment, and over seven times the performance in a write-intensive environment. With this information, you are now aware of the relative disk subsystem performance that a RAM disk can provide and can use this to your advantage when sizing and tuning your Windows 2000 system for maximum performance. You can make your own decision as to whether the additional cost of the extra RAM for use as a RAM disk is justified by the increase in performance.

Using a RAM disk to improve disk subsystem performance is not a replacement for utilizing sound tuning and sizing techniques for the rest of your disk subsystem. It does, however, provide a strong ally to add to your arsenal of tuning techniques. The benchmark used in this test is a particularly intense multiuser benchmark. The performance you achieve is influenced by the various elements of your specific environment such as user workloads, application in use, CPU performance, type of memory, and memory bandwidth (system bus) of your system.

WHEN TO USE RAM DISKS: OTHER POSSIBILITIES FOR RAM DISK TECHNOLOGY

Now that you are familiar with some of the positive and negative aspects of using a RAM disk product like SuperSpeed, there are numerous areas you might consider when implementing this technology to improve the disk subsystem performance of your Windows 2000 solution. Before determining that you need a RAM disk, you must understand where to place it. Determine this by using the Sysmon tool (bottleneck counters from Table 6.16) to identify which disk subsystem is experiencing hot spots; then use the filemon.exe tool to track down exactly which application and files are being used. Once this information is in hand, we can move into some of the scenarios where you might use RAM disk technology. The most common justification for using a RAM disk is to remove disk subsystem hot spots, but don't let this one example limit your imagination. Other areas where you might employ RAM disk technology are:

- **TEMP directory/file system replacement.** Some applications use the TEMP directory to store frequently accessed but temporary files, thus creating a potential hot spot. Most applications will use the %temp% system variable. If this is the case, you do not have to change the application to use a RAM disk; you can just change where the %temp% variable points. Accomplish this by selecting Start / Settings / Control Panel / System / Advanced / Environment Variables; then select temp and edit the variable to point at the location of the directory that the RAM disk is mounted on.
- **Database enhancements.** If you have a database and enough memory, it is possible to place the entire database on a SuperSpeed partition. Consider how fast your 2GB database will run if it is entirely in RAM. If you don't have a lot of memory, but the index to your data-

base can be separated from the rest of the database, you could place it on a RAM disk mirrored to a disk drive.

- **Web site enhancements.** If your server is hosting a web site, you can improve the access speed of your web pages by placing the web site, or the frequently accessed web pages, on a RAM disk mirrored to a disk drive.

You may think of even more options. The best time to implement these options is based on your environment and requirements.

Summary

When reviewing each link in the disk subsystem data path, remember that it is the weakest link that throttles Windows 2000's overall disk subsystem performance. In this chapter, we closely examined the importance of understanding the entire path that disk subsystem data follows in conjunction with reviewing how Windows 2000 takes advantage of and maximizes the performance of the disk subsystem. With this information, it becomes easier to identify potential bottlenecks that can throttle your system's overall performance and to size new solutions. Building upon this foundation, we provided specific practical examples of how to tune and size the disk subsystem to help you get the maximum performance from Windows 2000's flexible disk subsystem architecture.

Windows 2000 and Network Performance

CHAPTER OBJECTIVES

- Network Subsystem Technology: Following the Data........ *395*
- Network Interface Card........ *397*
- Relative Throughputs of Different Network Technologies........ *397*
- Realistic Network Throughput under Windows 2000........ *398*
- Windows 2000 and GBE Performance........ *402*
- Applications Can Affect Network Performance........ *403*
- Windows 2000 Ethernet Performance Characteristics........ *403*
- Other Network Technologies........ *404*
- Understanding the Network Architecture in Which Your Windows 2000 System Operates........ *405*
- Windows 2000 Server Placement in the Network........ *405*
- How Windows 2000 Takes Advantage of the Network........ *409*
- Windows 2000 TCP/IP Performance Enhancements........ *412*
- Windows 2000 Network Performance and the CPU........ *413*
- It Takes Two to Tango........ *414*
- Network Subsystem and Intelligent I/O (I2O) Technology........ *415*
- Sizing the Windows 2000 Network Subsystem........ *415*
- Detecting Windows 2000 Network Bottlenecks........ *422*
- Beyond Windows 2000 Systems: Tracking Down Internetwork Device Performance Problems........ *429*
- Tuning Strategies for Removing Network Subsystem Bottlenecks........ *431*

If you want to tune or size a Windows 2000 system, it is important to have an understanding of how the system hardware, operating system, and applications actually work. Once you understand how and why these various components of an overall solution are trying to complete their respective tasks, you will be much more knowledgeable about how to tune and size the system resources for maximum performance. Throughout this and each of the other subsystem chapters, descriptions, explanations, and examples are provided to help you understand how the system components interact—understanding their interaction is to understand the big picture. When you are armed with this information, some of the black magic of tuning and sizing will disappear, and you will be able to use more effective tuning and sizing tactics. It is tempting to jump in and start adding this or tuning that. Knowing which "knob to turn" to tune a Windows 2000 system is good; understanding when to "turn a tuning knob" and why it will help is better.

In this chapter, we focus on Windows 2000 and the network subsystem. The network subsystem is the superhighway where end users access your Windows 2000 solutions. When users are working with an application, it's easy for them to complain that the server is slow since it is a physical object that they can easily relate to. It could of course be a slow client, an ill-behaved application, or that nebulous network stuff that is more difficult for users to point their fingers at. Nonetheless, it is the customer's perception that is of the highest importance—if the customer doesn't *perceive* the system to be performing at a high level, then you have a customer who is dissatisfied with your system solution, no matter how well you think it is performing.

When you log onto a Windows 2000 active directory network domain via a Windows 2000 client, you are actually logging onto the network, a network that is backed by Windows 2000 servers and perhaps other servers as well. In this chapter, we focus on network performance from the perspective of Windows 2000. The entire network architecture in place has a large impact on overall network performance of Windows 2000 systems. Because of this fact, the technologies that are implemented to achieve the network architecture will be referenced as needed and used as a frame of reference.

Specifically, the detailed focus of this chapter is on network performance from a Windows 2000 perspective when connected via a local area network (LAN) environment. We will start by reviewing the performance of network technologies that are normally found in Windows 2000 environments and the network architectures used to connect Windows 2000 systems. We then move on to how Windows 2000 utilizes the network. Once we have established a basic understanding of the network subsystem, we then determine when network subsystem bottlenecks are occurring while running Windows 2000. From there, we move into sizing network subsystems strategies and using hands-on tactics to learn how to tune around network subsystem bottlenecks to obtain the maximum performance possible in a networked environment. Windows 2000 supports a much wider array of networking options than Windows NT; thus it adds much more flexibility to your solutions and tuning options. The bottleneck detection techniques along with the sizing and tuning strategies and tactics reviewed in this chapter are not just theory-based; they were developed and fine-tuned from real-world production environments and are also used throughout the rest of this book.

Different network technologies and architectures exhibit different performance characteristics when under load. It is of paramount importance that you understand the performance characteristics of the network technology that is implemented with your Windows 2000 solution so that you can take advantage of the network technology's positive characteristics and understand its potential pitfalls so that bottlenecks are avoided. This important fact is applicable to any networked environment that is either LAN or wide area network (WAN)–based. To illustrate this principle, several common networking technologies are used here as practical examples. Besides Windows 2000 itself, the network technologies concentrated on are Ethernet (10BaseTX, Fast Ethernet 100BaseTX, 1000BaseT/GX), and TCP/IP. The references made to networking hardware devices pertain to getting data to and from the Windows 2000 systems. These references are not intended to be a comprehensive overview of all available internetworking device technology. You can extrapolate from the concepts that are illustrated using these technologies in your own environment. Of course, that might require obtaining a good reference book on the technology you are implementing.

We will again *follow the data* as we have in previous chapters. Here we will be following the general network data path of information through the network and Windows 2000.

Network Subsystem Technology: Following the Data

Few of today's environments are stand-alone. It is extremely important that you ensure a sound network data path from your Windows 2000 system to your customers expecting services or to other systems that interact with yours. Following the data path between your Windows 2000 system clients and the inside of your Windows 2000 Server greatly aids in developing a sound networking and Windows 2000 network subsystem solution. A well-tuned, high-performance Windows 2000 system is not effective if you cannot communicate with it well. The same standard high-volume (SHV) server logical diagram used in earlier chapters will be our reference system architecture. Adding the primary components required in accessing the network subsystem, we arrive at the logical data flow diagram illustrated in Figure 7-1.

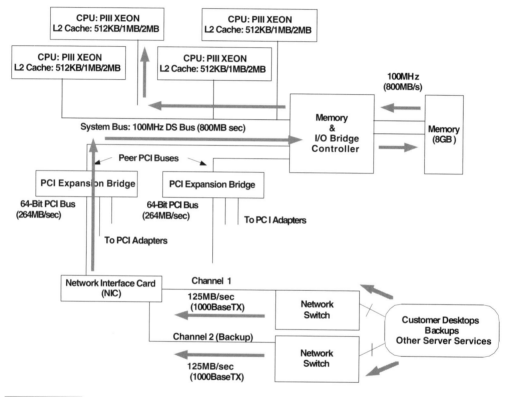

FIGURE 7-1   *Tracking the Data Flow from the Network through Windows*

It is important to understand the different transfer rates of the components of the system and the system's network subsystem. This information helps you to size your system properly and to identify potential bottlenecks that can throttle your system's overall performance. In Figure 7-1, data travels from the customer desktops/other servers via a switched network connection operating at Gigabit Ethernet speeds (1000BaseTX = 125MB/sec = 1,000Mbits/sec). From here the data travels through PCI slot 1 on PCI bus 1 at 264MB/sec to the memory subsystem (800MB/sec) and is then transferred to the CPU at a Pentium III front side system bus speed of 800MB/sec.

Review each link in the data path. It is the weakest link that throttles overall network subsystem performance.

If one component is trying to send more data than the next component can handle (accept), there is a bottleneck. A good analogy involves plumbing: if the primary water pipe carrying water away from your basement is 5 inches in diameter and you have ten 2-inch pipes placing water into the 5-inch pipe, water will be spilling out, your basement will be flooding, and no one will be happy.

By completing a little mathematical word problem, you can avoid bottle-necks even before they begin. For example, placing three Gigabit Ethernet (GBE) network interface cards (NIC) (theoretical aggregate maximum throughput of 3 × 125MB/sec = 375MB/sec) into a single PCI bus can over-whelm a single 64-bit 33MHz PCI bus data link if all of the GBE NIC channels are active. A single 64-bit 33MHz PCI bus can support a theoretical maximum of only 264MB/sec. Jamming 375MB/sec of data into it just does not work very well. If this configuration were actually implemented, you would have created a bottleneck from the start. Placing two of the GBE NIC cards into one PCI bus 0 and the third GBE NIC into PCI bus 1 will help to spread the net-work I/O activities across the 528MB of total aggregate PCI bus throughput and avoid the creation of a bottleneck the first day of service. Of course, you have to run a stress test to baseline this solution before entering it into pro-duction to ensure everything is performing as expected. This will catch any potential bottlenecks before production.

Network Interface Card

The NIC is the adapter that enables the system (via the PCI interface) to inter-face with the physical network; it also handles the electrical signaling. As each network packet arrives, the NIC must request CPU assistance in some manner to properly handle the network requests. NICs now come I2O enabled (I2O technology was reviewed in chapter 6). I2O technology adds new intelligence into the NIC itself, thus off-loading CPU and system bus resource usage.

Relative Throughputs of Different Network Technologies

So what type of physical network will you put in place? Before you make that selection, it is helpful to understand the protocol's behavior, what throughput it can achieve, and the topology needed to support your selection. To provide a basis for network subsystem performance, let's first review what is theoreti-cally possible when networking a Windows 2000 system. Table 7.1 summa-rizes the relative theoretical network throughputs and the basic protocol characteristics of a wide range of network technologies. The standard bits/sec notation is provided as well as the bytes/sec equivalent (1 byte = 8 bits) so that we'll have a common frame of reference in later discussions.

TABLE 7.1	Relative Theoretical Network Throughput and Media Access Characterization

	Throughput (Mbits/sec)	Throughput (MB/sec)	Topology Media Access (protocol characteristics)
LAN Network Technology			
Ethernet (10BaseT)	10	1.25	CSMA/CD
Token Ring (16MB Ring)	16	2	Token Passing
Ethernet (100BaseT)	100	12.5	CSMA/CD
FDDI	100	12.5	Token Passing
Ethernet (Gigabit Ethernet/ 1000BaseTX/FL)	1,000	125	CSMA/CD
WAN Network Technology*			
Dedicated PPP/SLIP	modem (up to 56Kbits/sec)	0.007	Point to Point
PPP ISDN	128Kbits/sec	0.016	Point to Point
T1	1.544Mbits/sec	0.193	Shared
Cable Modems/Systems	0.5–8Mbits/sec	0.06–1	Point to Point
Digital Subscriber Line (DSL)	0.5–8Mbits/sec	0.06–1	Point to Point
T3	45Mbits/sec	5.5	Point to Point
ATM	155Mbits/sec	19.3	Point to Point

* The WAN technology information provided is for reference to illustrate the throughput disparity between common LAN and WAN technologies.

Realistic Network Throughput under Windows 2000

To quantify realistic network throughput is a bold thing to do since every environment is different; thus, network throughput mileage always varies. In general, the most common misapprehension when configuring the network subsystem is a misunderstanding of what the network can actually provide in terms of throughput and of what the load characteristics are of the network protocol in use. Just because one network technology implementation states that a certain level performance can be achieved does not mean that this particular level can actually be achieved when working in Windows 2000–based application environments.

There are two key pieces of information presented in Table 7.1 to consider when configuring the system's physical network subsystem:

1. The theoretical throughputs of all of the various networks are typically referred to in bits/sec, *not* bytes/sec. Mixing up bits/sec and bytes/sec is a common slip, so always keep this in mind when determining the aggregate network requirements of the client.

2. Consider the *topology—media access* method or protocol characteristics—of each type of network technology that you are implementing with Windows 2000. Each network type displays different response time characteristics under higher utilization levels. The amount of work each specific network technology can support is based on its characteristics under load. For example, because of the deterministic nature of *token passing* network technologies such as Token Ring and FDDI, they are capable of supporting much higher network utilization levels before exhibiting slower response times to the end users, when compared to a shared or collision-based technology such as Ethernet. To illustrate an example of a specific network characteristic, we will look more closely at Ethernet.

Ethernet

SHARED CHARACTERISTICS

Ethernet is one of the most popular, lowest-cost, and easiest network technologies to deploy with Windows 2000. Pick up a trade magazine and look for an advertisement for an entry-level Windows 2000 and you will find an Ethernet-based NIC bundled with the package. Ethernet 10BaseT (IEEE 802.3), Fast Ethernet 100BaseT (IEEE 802.3U), and Gigabit Ethernet (1000BaseXX) technologies are based on the Carrier Sense Multiple Access/Collision Detection (CSMA/CD) protocol to carry the actual electrical signals across the physical wire (medium). This is just a fancy way to say that Ethernet is a *shared bus* technology.

In Ethernet environments, all devices on the same network segment (collision domain) have equal access to the entire network segment, and all stations on this network segment are considered as peers (multiple access). Before transmission, a network station is required to listen to the network (carrier sense) to determine if anyone is using the network segment. If no other network station is already sending data over the network segment, then data can be sent over the network. Using this technique, only one station at a time can transmit data over this shared bus network segment. If more than one network station on the same network segment sends data at the same moment in time, there will be a network segment collision. The data sent from both (or all) stations is assumed lost. Each station will detect the collision (collision detection), wait for a random period of time, and then repeat the process to resend the same data.

10BASET ETHERNET PERFORMANCE

When the workload on the network increases, collisions occur or the station must wait for the shared Ethernet network segment to be calm before sending any data. Each time this occurs, it slows down the response time back to the Windows 2000 system application/process that is requesting use of the network or to an end user trying to get to the system on the network.

In an Ethernet environment, when the average network utilization goes above 20%, a Network General Expert Sniffer will generate a network usage alert event that the network is becoming a potential bottleneck. This is a little conservative for me, but it will catch my attention to take a closer look at the network. At which percentage of utilization Ethernet performance degrades depends on your environment and the published reference you use. It is generally accepted that, when Ethernet network utilization rises above the 50–70% range, response times increase dramatically due to the associated network congestion bogging down the shared bus environment.

Some level of overhead is added to every packet of data that is placed onto the network by the protocols in use. When data is sent from Windows 2000 over the network, various protocols such as the physical Ethernet and TCP/IP protocols add a certain amount of overhead to each packet of information that heads out onto the network. An analogy to this overhead is that each protocol places the original data into another envelope: four protocols, four envelopes. This overhead takes up some of the available bandwidth on the network. Sending a smaller piece of information over the network takes up the same amount of protocol overhead as sending a larger piece of data. Thus, sending many smaller pieces of data over the network is less efficient than sending data in larger pieces.

Because of Ethernet's (10BaseTX) loading characteristics and protocol overhead, expecting to get a full 10Mbits/sec (1.25MB/sec) of throughput in conjunction with acceptable user response times is unrealistic. Depending on the characteristics of the network that your Windows 2000 system is a part of, throughput achieved for a multiple-client hub-based Ethernet network falls into the range of 5–7Mbits/sec (0.6–0.8MB/sec).

100BASETX FAST ETHERNET PERFORMANCE

To improve on the performance of 10BaseT Ethernet, 100BaseTX Fast Ethernet was developed. Electrically, Fast Ethernet and Ethernet operate at the same speed; however, Fast Ethernet increases the amount of bandwidth available by a factor of 10. A good way to visualize this is to look at 10BaseT

Ethernet as a 2-lane highway and Fast Ethernet as a 20-lane highway—while cars still operate at the speed limit, in a Fast Ethernet environment many more cars can travel at the same time.

The Fast Ethernet protocol is also based on CSMA/CD. Hence, it exhibits similar network loading characteristics to Ethernet. Depending on the characteristics of the network that your Windows 2000 system is a part of, the realistic throughput that can be achieved for a multiple-client Fast Ethernet network segment ranges from 50 to 70Mbits/sec (6–8MB/sec).

SWITCHED AND FULL-DUPLEX FAST ETHERNET

Networking technology moves just as fast as, if not faster than, the rest of the information technology world. In an effort to improve the performance of the Ethernet protocol, shared media Ethernet has given way to switched and full-duplex Fast Ethernet technologies. As outlined above, Ethernet's original design was based on a shared bus topology that is commonly implemented by using a shared Ethernet hub. With the advent of Ethernet switches, an existing network is dynamically divided as needed into multiple parallel networks. Now, instead of implementing Ethernet with a shared Ethernet hub, an Ethernet switch can be used.

In a switched Ethernet environment, the Ethernet switch is able to allow two or more pairs of network nodes to communicate together at the same time as other network nodes are communicating. Depending on the number of network connections or ports that an Ethernet switch has available, multiple Ethernet connections can occur in parallel on the same Ethernet network segment without affecting the other stations on the network. Consider the Windows 2000 environment in Figure 7-2. In this Ethernet switch-based implementation, data is passed between the Windows 2000 server and client 2. While this occurring, data is being passed between client 1 and client 3 at the same time, or in parallel. Ergo, in an Ethernet switch environment, the switch manages the electrical interfaces that allow simultaneous transmission between multiple nodes, thus eliminating collisions. When two clients want to access the same network station—for example, if client 1 and client 2 wanted to access the Windows 2000 server simultaneously—essentially the traditional Ethernet CSMA/CD still applies once the buffers in the switch are exhausted. When the target destination is not able to keep up with the client's request, the server's NIC sends a signal to switch and subsequently requests that the data rates be slowed.

Under half-duplex communications, data is transmitted in only one direction at a time. Full-duplex Ethernet technology is an enhancement that allows simultaneous two-way transmission between nodes while eliminating collisions. Full-duplex transmission increases performance and efficiency by doubling the theoretical bandwidth of 10BaseT to 20Mbits/sec (200Mbits/sec for 100BaseT).

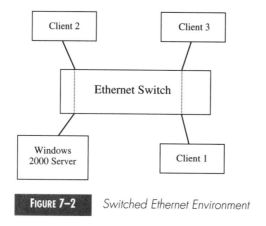

FIGURE 7-2 *Switched Ethernet Environment*

GIGABIT ETHERNET

Gigabit Ethernet (GBE) technology is the next step in improving Ethernet network performance. As the name implies, Gigabit Ethernet operates at a throughput of 1 gigabit (Gbit)/sec (1,000Mbits/sec or 125MB/sec) unless operating in full-duplex mode. Full-duplex mode enables network-attached devices to transmit approximately 1Gbit/sec while simultaneously receiving 1Gbit/sec—2Gbits/sec (2,000Mbits/sec or 250MB/sec) total—and utilizes the same signaling as the other members of the Ethernet-protocol-based family. However, since GBE uses a 4B/5B transmission scheme that consumes approximately 10–20% of all transmission bandwidth for signal clock synchronization, the overall throughput that a single GBE can support is lowered approximately 100MB/sec of data while simultaneously transmitting 100MB/sec of data (200MB/sec total). GBE is not a completely new protocol, just a faster implementation of the Ethernet protocol. Its ease of use has made its adoption rate very high, leading to a high volume of products being manufactured resulting in lower prices. In the near future, look for agreement on the 10Gbit Ethernet standard, which will provide the next stepping-stone in Ethernet-based network performance.

Windows 2000 and GBE Performance

GBE introduces such an increase in performance that many older platforms are not powerful enough to fully drive GBE-based networks. Many legacy systems and some new systems just cannot generate enough throughput to fully utilize GBE technology. For example, if you were going to read all of the data from the disk subsystem of one server and send it to another server across the network for a backup and the target server to be backed up had a 12-disk

RAID 5 array, you would be able to generate approximately 32MB/sec of data across the network (based on data from chapter 6). Since a full-duplex GBE connection can support 250MB/sec, you would need over seven 12-disk RAID 5 arrays to fully drive the theoretical bandwidth of a single GBE channel!

Applications Can Affect Network Performance

Another factor to consider when planning how much network performance a system can support is the application being used and the Windows 2000 TCP/IP network stack itself. Every environment is different. The number of applications interacting with Windows 2000 can influence how quickly data can move across the network.

To illustrate application differences, we ran a small test to move 5GB of data across a switched 100BaseTX network. The two Windows servers and the network involved were dedicated for this test only, so no outside influences were at work. We first copied the files across the network using the native Windows 2000 copy command. Then, after cycling the power on both servers and deleting the copied files, we copied the files across the network using the native Windows 2000 Backup tool (Start / Programs / Accessories / System Tools / Backup). The results? The backup application was five times faster using the *copy* command! We tried this same test using several other backup applications and got similar results. The moral of this example? Applications themselves can limit the performance across the network!

Windows 2000 Ethernet Performance Characteristics

So, how fast can a Windows 2000 system drive a network? Close to the limits of the physical system on which it resides, when properly sized and tuned. To better understand how Windows 2000 performs with different networking technologies, review Table 7.2, which lists the throughput levels achieved from a Windows 2000 server perspective as measured by the server, in a switched network environment using TCP/IP as the network protocol. Various results are reported based on the system configuration, Windows 2000 tuning (TCP/IP stack configuration), and the application in use. Under different conditions, the performance ratings may be different. What is important to recognize here is that Windows 2000 can take full advantage of the technology available today. In this example, Windows 2000 can drive gigabit-speed networks and scale with multiple NICs if Windows 2000 is properly tuned and sized, if the application can support this level of throughput, and if the network architecture is designed to support it.

TABLE 7.2	Windows 2000 Gigabit Ethernet Throughput and Scalability

Testing Team and Test Application Type	Number of NICs	Number of CPUs	NIC Type	Throughput (Mbits/sec)
Microsoft Windows 2000 Performance Tuning White Paper; NetBench Benchmark	1	1	Intel *100BaseTX* Full Duplex	188
Network Computing; Chariot Application http://www.ganymedsefotware.com	1	2	Compaq 64-bit, 33MHz NC6132 Gigabit Ethernet card	662.5
PC Magazine, Windows 2000 Review; NetBench Benchmark http://www.zdnet.com/products/stories/reviews/0,4161,2426063,00.html	1	4	AlteanAceNIC	400
Microsoft Windows 2000 Performance: An Overview; Enterprise configuration; NetBench Benchmark	1	4	Intel GBE NIC	334
Microsoft Windows 2000 Performance: An Overview White Paper; NetBench using NTttcp	1	1	Intel GBE NIC	590
Microsoft Windows 2000 Performance: An Overview White Paper; NTttcp	2	2	Intel GBE NIC	810
Microsoft Windows 2000 Performance: An Overview White Paper; NTttcp	4	4	Intel GBE NIC	1,650
Microsoft Windows 2000 Performance: An Overview White Paper; *Jumbo Frames*	1	1	Intel GBE NIC	800
Windows 2000 Performance: An Overview White Paper; *Jumbo Frames*	2	2	Intel GBE NIC	1,600
Windows 2000 Performance: An Overview White Paper; *Jumbo Frames*	4	4	Intel GBE NIC	3,400
Windows 2000 Performance: An Overview White Paper; *Jumbo Frames*	8	8	Intel GBE NIC	3,800

Other Network Technologies

Beware of the network technology of the week. When new technologies are implemented, they bring new functionality, flexibility, and (sometimes) improved performance to your Windows 2000 solution. As new technologies are brought to market, they need to be supported in the Windows 2000 framework, especially in regard to how they utilize Windows 2000 and how

Windows 2000 communicates to them through device drivers. Maturity of the device drivers and how well they handle the multiuser workloads of a server environment are very important.

Understanding the Network Architecture in Which Your Windows 2000 System Operates

What may appear to be a performance problem blamed on the poor unsuspecting Windows 2000 system could actually be caused by the network hardware and data workload patterns used to implement your network architecture. When implementing switching technology to get data to your Windows 2000 system, keep potential bottlenecks from occurring outside of your system in the network. Look closely at the data flows of the network and the aggregate throughput of the switch being employed. If your environment is such that many of the clients utilize peer-to-peer networking, an Ethernet switch is an excellent choice since it will be able to take advantage of the multiple parallel Ethernet communication paths that a switch provides.

When Is an Ethernet Switch Really Almost a Shared Ethernet Hub

If the network environment is one in which the clients rarely utilize peer-to-peer networking but rely primarily on the Windows 2000 servers or Internet access, be sure to do your data path link math. If you utilize a switch that has ten 100Mbit/sec ports to connect nine clients and one Windows 2000 system, there may be a problem. In a worst-case scenario, each of the clients would be active at the same time, generating a theoretical throughput of 900Mbits/sec. This amount of data driving into an Windows 2000 system that has only a 100Mbit/sec network connection—whether it is switched or not—would create a network bottleneck before the data ever reached the Windows 2000 system. For this specific environment, the benefits of the switch are not truly being realized (although the switch may be helpful), and it is in essence acting like a shared media hub.

Windows 2000 Server Placement in the Network

So, where are the best places to locate Windows 2000 servers in the network? Of course, it depends on your environment. However, when reviewing your environment information, closely track the network usage of your Windows 2000 servers and the data paths between the clients and the servers. Windows

2000 supports several options beyond simply upgrading the NIC to higher speeds. It can be relatively easy to move from a 10Mbit/sec NIC to a 100Mbit/sec NIC, since internetwork hardware devices commonly support these performance levels. Gigabit Ethernet is an excellent choice if the internetwork hardware devices that are available can support it. Consider Figure 7-3, which illustrates a hierarchical network architecture that centralizes the Windows 2000 servers, which is becoming more common. In switch-based networks like the one shown in Figure 7-3, throughput to and availability of Windows 2000 servers are very important as server consolidations become more popular as a way to lower overall total cost of ownership. To increase the network throughput that a Windows 2000 server can support, you can split the network in half. This is accomplished by subnetting the network (which is also referred to as network segmentation) by adding a second network NIC to the Windows 2000 server and the associated second IP address. This adds additional complexity to the Windows 2000 configuration because routing must be configured on the server or a routing engine must be added to the network architecture so that clients can pass data between the two subnets. Also, half of the clients would be

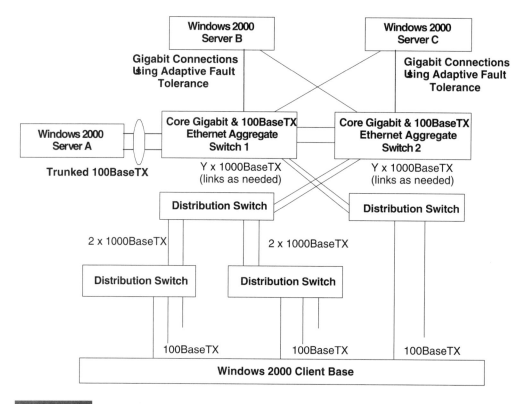

FIGURE 7–3 *Hierarchical Network Architecture Centralizing Windows 2000 Servers*

required to be re-addressed with the new subnet addresses either by manually updating static IP addresses or through Dynamic Host Configuration Protocol (DHCP) scope changes. Another way to improve network throughput on a Windows 2000 server is to use one of the following network trunking technologies:

- **Adaptive Load Balancing (ALB).** Developed by Intel Corporation. ALB supports the teaming of up to four NICs to provide scalable bandwidth up to 400MB/sec or 4GB/sec in a Gigabit Ethernet environment. This is configured using the third-party utility that is included with the NICs and is implemented at the Windows 2000 driver level; thus it is transparent to the Windows 2000 application layer. Since a lion's share of the bandwidth added using this approach is for downloading data to clients, closely track the network characteristics of the server you are upgrading by using Sysmon's Network Interface object's bytes received per sec and bytes sent per sec. This technology is best used when a bulk of your Windows 2000 Server is flowing as bytes sent per sec. Applications that exhibit this type of behavior are web servers, file servers, and video servers. When implementing this technology, all network links from the server must terminate in the same network switch. This approach is depicted in Figure 7-4.

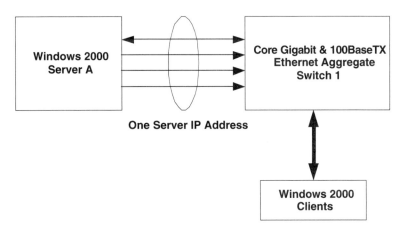

FIGURE 7–4   *Windows 2000 Using Adaptive Load Balancing (ALB)*

- **Link Aggregation.** Link Aggregation supports scalable bandwidth using four NICs (i.e., four Ethernet channels) to provide up to 800Mbps full-duplex throughput in a 100BaseTX environment or up to 8GB/sec in a Gigabit Ethernet environment. Link Aggregation requires support in the NICs and the switch. This approach is illustrated in Figure 7-5.

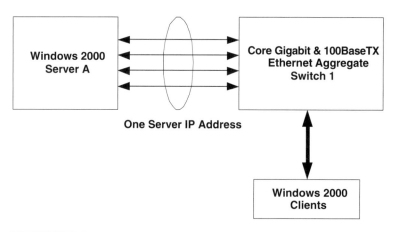

FIGURE 7-5 *Windows 2000 Using Link Aggregation, Fast EtherChannel, and Giga-bit EtherChannel Technologies*

- **Fast EtherChannel (FEC).** Developed by Cisco, FEC supports scalable bandwidth using up to eight NICs (i.e., eight Ethernet channels) to provide 800MB/sec full-duplex throughput. FEC requires support in the NICs and the switch. This approach is also illustrated in Figure 7-5.
- **Gigabit EtherChannel (GEC).** Developed by Cisco, GEC supports scalable bandwidth using up to four NICs (e.g., eight Ethernet channels) to provide 8GB/sec full-duplex throughput. GEC requires support in the NICs and the switch. This approach is also illustrated in Figure 7-5.

When using the Link Aggregation, FEC, and GEC technologies, you must ensure that the NICs and network switches support this technology and that they are both properly configured. The process for configuring all of the NICs and network switches to use these trunking technologies is essentially the same, but we won't give the details here because the syntax is slightly different for each NIC and switch vendor. With these technologies in use, all network links support bidirectional full-duplex traffic—more flexible than ALB. It's less important to fully understand the network characteristics than it is to be able to take advantage of the increased bandwidth. Of course, the trade-off for enjoying this increase in bandwidth is that configuration updates are needed on the network switch.

All of these technologies implement a form of network trunking that creates a virtual circuit between the server and the internetwork device (switch). From the Windows 2000 server's perspective, the multiple trunked NICs appear as one large network connection with only one TCP/IP network address. You must ensure only that the NIC you select supports the technology you are interested in as well as the network switch for the particular technology you implement. From clients' perspective, there is still only one TCP/IP address to interact with, and they do not need to change their TCP/IP addresses. Both Fast Ethernet and Gigabit Ethernet support this same network trunking approach. Sometimes, you do not need a full GBE connection, just another 100Mbits/sec.

From an availability perspective, NICs that support Adaptive Fault Tolerance enable you to team NICs for fault tolerance. Two separate NICs can be configured so that they both connect to the same switch or, more optimally, a redundantly configured switch. One NIC is active while the other is passive. If the active NIC fails, the second NIC becomes active, assuming the same TCP/IP addresses of the failed primary NIC, ensuring continued operations. Since Windows 2000 supports hot swappable PCI adapters, the failed NIC can be swapped out, thus becoming the backup NIC.

How Windows 2000 Takes Advantage of the Network

Windows 2000 Networking Performance Considerations

Many of the factors influencing network subsystem performance of Windows 2000 have already been reviewed throughout this book. Applications, CPU, memory, and disk subsystem performance all influence how well the network subsystem operates and how Windows 2000 takes advantage of the I/O subsystem. Taking a cue from chapter 6, let's continue to follow the data path of network traffic as a client accesses data from a Windows Server. For this example, the client is a Windows 2000 Professional client and the server is based on a Windows 2000 Server (illustrated in Figure 7-6).

Figure 7-6 is a simplification of the logical Windows 2000 architectural data path followed when a Windows 2000 Professional client application/process requests data from a shared resource on a Windows 2000 Server, but it suffices to point out the primary data paths involved around Windows 2000 performance considerations. Once the client process makes the data request, the client's I/O Manager realizes that the requested data is not located on the local disk subsystem and sends the data requests to the network redirector for service. The network redirector must be able to access the remote server's resource using some type of client software. Under Windows 2000 Server or Professional, the client software that handles the client portion of this clieWindows 2000 connection is the workstation service. (Under Windows 2000 Server or Professional, a *service* is an application/process running in the background.) The network redirector in turn sends the request across the network using a network transport. For the example in Figure 7-6, the network transport is TCP/IP, which in turn connects to the physical network (Ethernet in

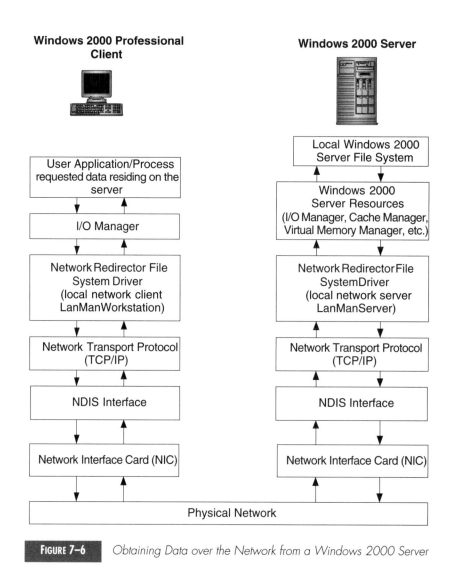

Windows 2000 Professional Client

Windows 2000 Server

FIGURE 7-6 *Obtaining Data over the Network from a Windows 2000 Server*

this example) via the NDIS driver that interfaces with the NIC, which then sends the packets to the target Windows 2000 server.

The networking software component on Windows 2000 checks the first network transport bound to the NIC and then continues through the list of available transports until a match is found or an error is generated. Once the correct network transport is located, it is utilized to get the data to the server's redirector. Under Windows 2000 (or Workstation), the network software component that accepts data from the client-side workstation service is the server service. Locating the server service with Task Manager is not obvious when using Windows 2000 because it operates under the Service Control Manager's services.exe executable. You can observe the LanManServer, LanManWorkstation, and some of the other services that the Service Control Manager (services.exe) is running by executing the tlist command from the support tools directory on the Windows 2000 distribution media. To do this, type tlist.exe – s | find "services.exe". This is the same server service component that enables the Windows 2000 server to share data across the network as well as accept client requests. Back on our data path, the client request for data is then passed to the Windows 2000 I/O Manager which, working with other Windows 2000 components, obtains the data from the disk subsystem attached to the server. The data is then returned to the client making the request using the same data path.

From a performance perspective the physical network technology has already been discussed in detail. But what about the other components of the data path? From the perspective of the client application requesting data from the shared resource—perhaps a word processing file that resides on the server—the client application is not concerned where the file is located; the requesting process considers it as just a file. From Windows 2000's perspective, the I/O Manager takes advantage of the Cache Manager in the same general manner as outlined in chapters 5 and 6. If multiple clients are requesting the same data from the server, this data will quickly be cached in the file system cache on the server. Once the requested data is cached, the response time provided back to the clients is greatly improved because the amount of disk I/O required is lowered. The file system cache is an important factor to consider when sizing the memory subsystem for both disk and network subsystem performance.

This example illustrates the importance of understanding the network data flow and what Windows 2000 does with a request. In some aspects, Windows 2000 handles a request for data on a networked resource the same way it would if the data were requested by a locally running (on the server) application. The same techniques outlined in chapters 5 and 6 for monitoring and tuning memory and disk resources also apply in the networked environments.

New Windows 2000 TCP/IP Services That Affect Performance

There are three new services that have been added to Windows 2000 that can dramatically affect the performance of any Windows 2000 system. Note that many new services have been added to Windows 2000, but these three pop up on the performance radar screen the fastest.

- **Quality-of-service (QoS/RSVP) services.** For applications and network devices that support it, Windows 2000 can now be configured to give priority service to certain applications over others. This helps ensure that mission-critical applications requiring certain network bandwidth and response to work will now be supported natively on

Windows 2000. Multimedia applications and Voice Over IP (VOIP) are examples of applications that benefit from QoS services. Since QoS services can drown out other applications, when planning troubleshooting performance issues, closely review the QoS service configuration if in use.

● **IP Security Encryption Protocol (IPSEC).** Windows 2000 supports the latest TCP/IP security enhancements. IPSEC is a service that enables data encryption at the IP layer. This is transparent to Windows 2000 applications, but it places a significantly heavier workload on the Windows 2000 systems operating in this mode. Some refer to this as virtual private network (VPN) technology. While IPSEC alone is not a complete VPN solution, it is a key part of a standards-based VPN solution. We investigate the performance ramifications of IPSEC traffic on Windows 2000 systems later in this chapter. In short, IPSEC adds significant overhead to any CPU, system bus, or network to calculate and transmit the encrypted data.

● **Multicast operations.** Multicast is a technology that enables more efficient network bandwidth usage. When multicast-aware applications, networks, servers, and client systems are in use, multicast lowers the reliance on network packet broadcasts to reach large numbers of clients at the same time. Multimedia applications are common uses for multicast. This technology can be used to lower overall traffic on your networks. This is another topic that has some thick books associated with it. Refer to the Cisco (http://www.cisco.com) and Nortel (http://www.Nortel.com) network vendor sites for more information on multicast technology.

All of these services consume additional processing in one way or another on Windows 2000 systems, so be sure to proactively manage the performance of all facets of your solution when implementing these new services.

Windows 2000 TCP/IP Performance Enhancements

Windows 2000 has introduced many new features at the TCP/IP driver level to enhance the performance of the network subsystem. These include but are not limited to support for the following new TCP/IP features:

● Protocol stack tuning, including increased default window sizes and new algorithms to compensate for high delay links, increases throughput
● TCP scalable window sizes (supported by RFC 1323)
● Support for jumbo frames
● Selective acknowledgments (SACK)

- TCP fast retransmit
- Round trip time (RTT) and retransmission timeout (RTO) calculation improvements
- Improved performance for management of large numbers of connections
- Numerous hardware task off-load mechanisms (ability to off-load TCP/IP: checksum, segmentation, IPSEC, and fast packet forwarding)

Specific tuning recommendations for many of these new features are outlined in the network tuning section later in this chapter. The support for jumbo frames is of particular interest from a performance perspective. The larger the network packets are, the more information can be passed per packet. This results in increased overall performance due to low overhead incurred transmitting the data (constructing and decomposing packets takes time and resources—if you have less to build, you lower your overhead!). On a GBE network, performance is doubled from 400Mbits/sec to 800Mbits/sec when jumbo frames are used (see Table 7.2 earlier in the chapter). In fact, when vendors run the SpecWeb (http\\www.spec.org) network-based web server performance benchmark, they always use jumbo frames due to the tremendous increase in performance they provide. To use jumbo frames, the Windows 2000 NIC driver on the client, server, and internetwork network devices must support jumbo frames.

Windows 2000 Network Performance and the CPU

Windows 2000 utilizes an NIC to physically attach itself to the network. As network data packets arrive, they are passed through the system's data path into memory where the CPU then decides where to transfer the packets (to another network, the disk subsystem, etc). For this to happen, the NIC must interrupt the system's CPU and request service. This occurs as an interrupt request (IRQ). When a hardware device such as an NIC interrupts the processor, the system's CPU interrupt handler may elect to execute the majority of its work in a deferred procedure call (DPC). This is typical of network device drivers that adhere to the Windows 2000 miniport device driver specification. DPCs run at a lower priority than other IRQs while permitting new interrupts to occur while DPCs are being executed. The system's CPUs are assigned to handle IRQs for a particular network interface during initialization. More powerful CPUs are capable of handling higher numbers of IRQs, which results in fewer DPCs and subsequently higher network load levels and better response time to the end user. This becomes very important with the advent of Gigabit Ethernet–based NICs that generate much higher interrupt levels than their Fast Ethernet cousins.

In multiple-CPU Windows 2000 environments that are characterized by high amounts of network activity, one of the CPUs can become overloaded servicing network-generated IRQs. When a bottleneck occurs in a single CPU in a multiple-CPU-based system, the reason is this: A single CPU is assigned to handle interrupts for a particular NIC at boot time. The other CPUs in the system are not assigned to handle interrupts directly from the specific NIC, but do provide a supporting role servicing DPCs. If the network traffic is intense and multiple CPUs are available, additional NICs can be added to take advantage of the other CPUs in the server. The addition of multiple NICs spreads the network interrupt servicing between CPUs. When Windows 2000 is booted after adding additional NICs, interrupt handling for the different NICs is spread across the system CPUs. In this manner, more network-intensive workloads can be supported.

When to Use Multiple NICs

Whenever a Windows 2000 system is supporting an intensive network workload, the system is a candidate to support multiple CPUs and NICs in network segmenting or NIC trunking roles. Windows 2000 supports multiple NICs attached to the same logical network segment or subnet using the trunking technologies discussed above. A logical network segment is defined as networked computers in the same collision domain, and it is serviced by a network switch. When multiple NICs are used on the same network segment, response time can be improved because the CPU workload is spread across the CPUs in the server; consequently each NIC can be provided with better service.

It Takes Two to Tango

Up to this point, we have reviewed the various links in the data path except one, the client. Windows 2000 supports a plethora of networking protocols and clients running various operating systems. True performance in an interactive user application is measured by the perceived response time that the end user experiences. Many of the concepts investigated in this book can be applied directly to detecting and tuning client computer bottlenecks as well, regardless of the operating system. Obviously it is easier to apply the concepts covered in this book if the client computer is running a version of the Windows 2000 operating system family. However, even if the operating system in use is different, the principles are the same, with the biggest difference being in the tools that are utilized for collection of pertinent data. One suggestion when working with the performance of client systems: closely investigate the application design and the client's video display card. The combination of a well-designed front-end application and a fast video display card greatly influences the user's perceived response time. If working in a secure network environment using IPSEC, use an NIC that off-loads IPSEC encryption; this will also improve the client's response time.

Network Subsystem and Intelligent I/O (I2O) Technology

With the overhead introduced by the network protocols in current use (e.g., the extensive code path that many device drivers must follow and CPU interrupts overhead generated by NIC cards) a new technique to implement Windows 2000 networking is available to address these concerns. The same Intelligent I/O Initiative (I2O) technology reviewed in chapter 6 is applicable for the network subsystem as well.

I2O allows the CPU and system bus overhead traditionally handled by the system's CPUs to be off-loaded to more intelligent I2O-based NICs. I2O-based devices utilize their own CPUs to off-load low-level I/O handling and create a secondary PCI bus to move I/O activity off the primary PCI buses and subsequently the system buses. This hardware technology, in conjunction with the I2O split driver architecture, enables the design of more efficient network device drivers. With less data traversing the system bus and more of the system CPU power available for the applications, Windows 2000 systems drastically improve their overall performance.

When selecting new NIC technology, the rule of thumb is to obtain NICs that take advantage of I2O technology.

Sizing the Windows 2000 Network Subsystem

Over time it is inevitable that Windows 2000 and applications need more and more network bandwidth capacity for performance. The classic design approach for developing network architectures used to be the 80/20 rule, where you tried to keep 80% of your network traffic on local segments close to your clients, while the other 20% would move through servers on your backbone. With the advent of intranets, increased Internet access (from inside your company and from outside companies coming into your secured networks), and centralized server consolidations to lower total cost of ownership, the current trend is to move to a 20/80 rule, where 20% of your network traffic is local and 80% traverses your network backbone or core. This imposes increased challenges on your Windows 2000 systems, as they must support more customers than ever before. Supporting more customers and multiple applications on the same system is the key challenge for sizing the network subsystem for Windows 2000. Fortunately, the combination of a flexible Windows 2000 architecture and advances in network subsystem technology enables increased flexibility in your Windows 2000 solution design.

Sizing the network subsystem is directly related to your business needs, as is sizing other portions of your system. Network subsystem resources can be both a shared and a dedicated resource. A *shared resource* is one that cannot be physically separated (unless using multiple systems), such as a shared file server data area for multiple users. A *dedicated resource* is one that is used for a single process/thread and those process/thread activities only, such as a private network used only for backups. These concepts of shared and dedicated network resources are illustrated in the network subsystem NIC partitioning section of Figure 7-7.

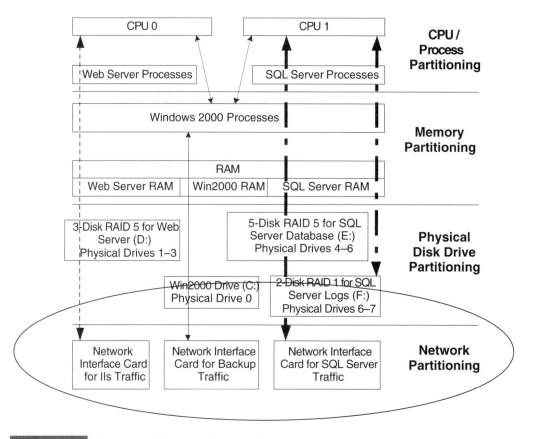

FIGURE 7–7   *Illustration of Network Subsystem Partitions*

Key Facets of Network Subsystem Sizing

Here we focus on sizing the network subsystem, but do not forget the rest of the system! Even when sizing the network subsystem, follow the core sizing methodology from chapter 3 so that the key facets surrounding your solution (such as CPU, Disk, and Memory resources) are taken into consideration.

The best-performing Windows 2000 network subsystem solutions I have encountered

- Are always attached to switched network architecture
- Have network backups placed on their own networks (a second NIC or SAN)
- Use full-duplex Fast Ethernet (100BaseTX) at a minimum
- Do not have the NIC operating at higher than 70% utilization in a sustained manner

Network Subsystem Sizing Methodology: Step by Step

When sizing the network subsystem, consider the following selection factors at a minimum:

1. Cost
2. Fault tolerance level required (availability)
3. Performance capacity needed (throughput and latency)
4. Backup speed
5. The amount of server resources (such as CPU, memory, disks, and network) configured
6. Data path sanity check

These are not the only factors involved when sizing and selecting your network subsystem. However, they do cover the major areas of concern. As with all methodologies presented in this book, use them as a guide, not gospel. If you have more criteria you want to add, go for it and have fun!

Let's look at each of these network subsystem selection factors more closely.

COST

Basic NICs are relatively inexpensive. I2O-enabled NICs or those that support multiple channels on the same card do increase the overall price but are not extravagant. The larger costs to be concerned with are those focused on ensuring that sufficient system resources are configured to drive the NICs you have selected, as well as the cost of making sure that the network architecture into which you are placing your Windows 2000 system does not introduce any bottlenecks before the data even arrives at your Windows 2000 systems.

FAULT TOLERANCE LEVEL REQUIRED (AVAILABILITY)

Choose the appropriate NIC technology that will support the level of availability you require. It is relatively inexpensive to configure two NICs in a fault tolerant fail-over configuration. Many NICs such as the Intel Pro 100–based NICs support this feature. Typically you configure redundant fail-over NICs under Start / Settings / Control Panel / Network and Dial-Up Connections / Local Area Network Connection Properties / Configure Tab / Advanced Tab. For the highest level of fault redundancy in the network subsystem, place each NIC in a different PCI bus and attach them to different network switches.

PERFORMANCE CAPACITY NEEDED (THROUGHPUT AND LATENCY)

The next factor to consider is performance. When determining performance requirements, the challenge is trying to determine how much throughput is needed. This is typically based on three factors.

HOW MUCH PERFORMANCE THE WINDOWS 2000 SYSTEM CAN DELIVER. ● If the application needed by your customers resides completely in memory, the performance capable by a Windows 2000 system over the network can match almost any NIC technology available. However, this is unrealistic. Typically the disk subsystem must be accessed, and it is the throughput obtained from the disk subsystem that drives how much network bandwidth is really needed. Review chapter 6 for information on disk subsystem performance. For example, if your disk subsystem is configured to provide 8MB/sec (64Mbits/sec), a 100BaseTX full-duplex connection will suffice.

HOW MANY CONCURRENT CUSTOMERS WILL BE ACCESSING THE WINDOWS 2000 SYSTEMS. ● When sizing a Windows 2000 network subsystem, you must determine how many concurrent users or clients a single network segment can support. It may sound much more impressive to say that your system can support 500 users than to say that it can support 50 concurrent users. While each client logged into a server does consume some level of server resources, it is the clients who are *concurrently* making requests of the server that are the primary focus when sizing the network subsystem. This is an important distinction. The total number of users impacts the sizing of other server resources such as required user disk space more than it affects sizing of the network subsystem.

A simplified rule of thumb for determining the number of concurrent clients that can be connected per network segment: ascertain the least-acceptable throughput for each concurrent network client; then divide that amount into the selected network throughput. For example, if each client should have no less then 1.5Mbits/sec of available bandwidth and the network supports 100Mbits/sec, the segment could possibly support 66 clients. Unfortunately this simple calculation does not take into account the network media characteristics, but it does provide a starting point for figuring the maximum amount of clients per network segment.

HOW CUSTOMERS WILL BE ACCESSING THE WINDOWS 2000 SYSTEMS. • If your customers are accessing your system over the Internet via a T1 connection to obtain information, a 10BaseTX connection will suffice. Why? A T1 operates at 1.5Mbits/sec, while a 10BaseTX connection operates up to 20Mbits/sec—no reason to throw a GBE NIC into it if you have only one or two T1 connections to the Internet and that is how your customers connect. This exemplifies the importance of understanding the data path that your target customer traverses to connect to your Windows 2000 system.

BACKUP SPEED

Depending on your environment, this may or may not need to move to the top of the sizing list. If you have a business requirement that needs a 4-hour return to service and you have an 8-hour backup window, your network subsystem performance requirements may rise drastically. However, you may need to support customers and run backups at the same time. What can you do? Consider partitioning the network subsystem so that you have a separate network just for backups. When backups must be run, they can operate across a separate NIC channel; this avoids network contention with your production network, which is supporting your customers.

THE AMOUNT OF SYSTEM RESOURCES (SUCH AS CPU, MEMORY, DISKS, AND NETWORK) CONFIGURED

Don't forget about the rest of the system. You will need CPU cycles to drive the network subsystem and other components you require. Commonly overlooked, do not overload the channels that are used to connect your network subsystem NICs to your overall I/O subsystem (PCI buses). Plain and simple, the more NIC channels that are implemented, the more network subsystem performance you will have. This is a true statement up to the point when either the aggregate throughput of the I/O buses is overwhelmed or when there is not enough CPU horsepower to drive the extensive NICs and the application at the same time.

The type and number of network cards required for a server is obviously dependent on the network architecture into which the Windows 2000 system will be deployed. Once the other basic requirements such as throughput and number of network segments are determined, keep in mind that Windows 2000 can support a high number of NICs. You can now get 100BaseT Ethernet cards in single-, dual-, and quad-channel configurations. The largest benefit from the use of higher-density channel NICs is the conservation of PCI slots on the server and easier trunking options to increase your overall network throughput. In real-world testing, a dual Pentium III server easily supports four 100BaseT NIC channels.

DATA PATH SANITY CHECK

Configuring huge data paths that overwhelm the NIC or PCI I/O channel is not desirable. After developing the network subsystem solution, follow the data path from the customers all the way through the internals of your Windows 2000 system. Utilize the performance charts throughout this book to aid in making an initial sanity check that none of the data paths are overloaded before you field the solution.

Use Historical Performance Information Whenever Possible

Historical information is the best place to start when sizing the network subsystem. If you are going to deploy a system in your department to support 200 users running a 50GB file server, find out if other departments have implemented a similar solution. If they have, observe their end users working with their applications to determine if the response times you observe are adequate for your environment. Also, ask to review their performance logs to determine how the disk subsystem is being stressed and how much memory is normally being used, as well as how much, if any, memory paging is occurring, the overall CPUs in use, and how much network bandwidth is needed. Use the information you obtain to size your network subsystem.

Windows 2000's Sysmon tool provides insight into how each process is behaving on your system, which is crucial information when you are trying to determine how much network bandwidth and network-related overhead are required for your new system. If you understand the network subsystem characteristics and behavior of processes running under load, you can extrapolate from this information for your own system. If historical information is not available, consider extrapolating from industry standard benchmarks that might be similar to your environment. You will be seeking the information as though reviewing historical information.

Table 7.3 outlines the key Sysmon counters to review from that similar system when sizing your network subsystem.

INDUSTRY BENCHMARKS ARE YOUR NEXT BEST FRIEND

Studying a combination of historical information and your own stress tests as outlined in chapter 3 is an excellent starting point when initially sizing your network subsystem. But what if you can't find any historical information on systems that resemble yours? With luck, you will be able to find *some* type of background information that might be helpful, even if it doesn't match your requirements exactly. Also try to match this background information against

TABLE 7.3	Sysmon Counters Helpful for Sizing the Network Subsystem

Object: Counter	Definition	Why Use for Sizing the Network Subsystem
Network Interface: Bytes Total/sec	Bytes Total/sec is the rate at which all bytes are sent and received on the selected network interface, including those bytes used as overhead (framing, etc.).	This value informs you directly of the network throughput being used. This information helps to determine if the same or a higher bandwidth configuration is needed to support the projected workload.
Network Interface: Bytes Received/sec and Bytes Sent/sec	Bytes Received/sec is the rate at which bytes are received on the interface, including framing characters. Bytes Sent/sec is the rate at which bytes are sent on the interface, including framing characters.	These values help characterize the system's network usage. Depending on whether the system is sending more data or receiving more directly influences the type of network trunking technology you can consider selecting. These technologies were reviewed earlier in this section to remove network system bottlenecks and improve overall network throughput that a Windows 2000 system can provide.
Redirector: Current Commands	Current Commands counts the number of requests to the Redirector that are currently queued for service.	If this number is much larger than the number of NICs (network channels) installed in the computer, then the network(s) and/or the server(s) being accessed is seriously bottlenecked. This is a good indicator as to whether multiple NIC channels will be needed.
Server: Server Sessions	Server Sessions are the number of sessions currently active in the server. Indicates current activity.	The Server Sessions counters provide a count of the number of active sessions or concurrent users on the server. Review the network %Utilization, Bytes/ sec, and Server Sessions over time. With this information you can conclude how much bandwidth is required to support a specific number of concurrent users. If only 20% of an Ethernet- based network is utilized when supporting 25 users, the current network technology in place has room to grow or plenty of headroom to support potential surges in network traffic. Other applications such as SQL Server provide Sysmon extensions that enable tracking how many users are using that specific application, which assists in extrapolating similar information for sizing your Windows 2000 system.

the various industry benchmarks (chapter 3) available, and then extrapolate from them for your personal environment.

To determine the initial network subsystem requirements for a file server environment, the Ziff Davis NetBench is a relevant industry benchmark. For this file server scenario, consider a system that will be placed into the current network architecture via a 1000BaseT-switch uplink. *PC Magazine*'s NetBench results implied that a file server with two 1000BaseT NICs could support a throughput up to 400MB/sec while servicing 40 intense NetBench concurrent clients. This indicates that each network adapter was able to support approximately only 200MB/sec and 20 concurrent clients. This extrapolation would be a good place to start if the NetBench workload is similar to your own.

Vendor web sites such as Compaq, Microsoft, Dell, IBM, and Intel, as well as other vendors that develop Windows 2000 solutions, are good places to search for industry benchmarks to use in your sizing efforts. One site that gathers multiple benchmark results and posts them together in one place is the IDEAS International site located at http://www.ideasinternational.com/benchmark/bench.html.

Detecting Windows 2000 Network Bottlenecks

Recall from chapter 2 that it is important to consider the entire system performance picture when trying to locate a Windows 2000 system bottleneck. There can be more than one system resource area that is contributing to the throttling of the system's overall performance. Once you have evaluated all of the major system resource areas, focus in on the resource that is farthest to the left in the performance resource chart (PRC) introduced in chapter 2 and repeated here in Figure 7-8 for reference. This strategy will provide the greatest immediate gain to the system's overall performance. For this discussion, all other system resources (except for the network subsystem) have already been investigated and determined not to be the bottleneck impeding the system's performance. Remember to revisit the PRC after tuning around a network bottleneck. Once one system resource is removed as the bottleneck, others may take its place, which will subsequently influence where you focus additional tuning efforts.

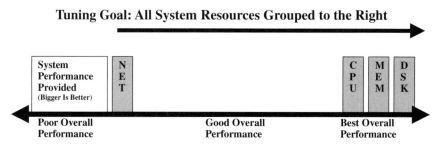

FIGURE 7–8   *Performance Resource Chart Depicting a Network Resource Bottleneck*

Quick Reference: Helpful Tools to Use When Tracking Down Windows 2000 Network Subsystem Details

Throughout this section on bottleneck detection, several different tools are used to track down memory details. Having a tool to complete this mission is nice; having specific examples of how to use specific tools is even better. In this and other chapters, there are some specific examples. For quick reference, I've included a list of tools in Table 7.4 for investigating network use in Windows 2000. Most of the tools functionally overlap each other in some fashion. If you do not find what you are looking for with one tool, try another! Regardless of overlaps, sometimes just being able to investigate and interrogate network resources from a slightly different angle can spark the idea that helps you to find what you are looking for. Note that most tools obtain and present

TABLE 7.4   *Tools to Investigate Network Subsystem Usage*

Tool	Where Do You Find It? (package)	Command Line Image	Key Times to Consider Using This Tool
Sysmon (System Monitor, Alerts, Logging)	Native to Windows 2000	Sysmon MMC (Sysmon)	Long-term trend analysis. Provides very detailed information across the board.
Task Manager	Native to Windows 2000	Taskman.exe	Short-term analysis. Displays the I/O Column Counter to track general I/O usage per process in real time. (Network and disk based)
Ping.exe	Native to Windows 2000	Ping.exe	Provides information on the response time of the network layer by sending generic ICMP echoes. Also immensely helpful in troubleshooting network connectivity problems.
Pathping.exe	Native to Windows 2000	PathPing.exe	Provides the same information as ping.exe and tracert.exe and more, such as detailed information on how each network device in the path is handling packets. If PathPing.exe shows that network devices are dropping packets, those network devices may be running low on CPU and memory resources and are not able to keep up with demand.
Netstat.exe	Native to Windows 2000	netstat.exe	Provides details on routing and which applications are using which ports on your system. Helpful for TCP tuning, determining what is running on your system, and troubleshooting routing problems.

TABLE 7.4	Tools to Investigate Network Subsystem Usage (Continued)		
Tool	**Where Do You Find It? (package)**	**Command Line Image**	**Key Times to Consider Using This Tool**
Nbtstat.exe	Native to Windows 2000	Nbtstat.exe	Advanced debugging of specific applications, especially if using legacy WINS/NetBIOS connections. Is also helpful for tracking down which clients are using your system. From a debugging perspective, the new -RR option enables the refreshing of the WINS database for the system it is run from.
Network Monitor	Native to Windows 2000 (must be installed, though)	Netmon.exe	Network sniffer application that provides detailed information on the packets that are traversing your Windows 2000 system network connections. Helpful in tracking down network problems and determining which clients are connecting to your system.
Netdiag	Windows 2000 Support Tools (found on Windows 2000 media)	Netdiag.exe	If your network connections are not healthy, they will not run fast. Netdiag provides a quick mechanism to check the health of the local systems network configuration.

information slightly differently. Do not be surprised if slightly different results are presented when querying for the same information.

Always Consider the Big Picture

Before looking at Windows 2000–specific network-related counters, let's step back and consider a broader view of the Windows 2000 solution in place. Why? The Sysmon counters that we review below to help in detecting a network bottleneck are not as distinctive as the Sysmon counters covered in previous chapters that are used for detecting other bottlenecks in the server. When you look at disk usage, the data paths involved are internal to the system (clustering is another discussion). For network environments, the data paths outside of your server influence the end user's perception of the server's performance.

> *When tracking down network bottlenecks, you must understand the network architecture that surrounds your Windows 2000 system in order to decide that the network is a bottleneck.*

Stop and read that last sentence a few more times, it is that important. When detecting network bottlenecks, a reverse-detection strategy is prudent. Instead of sleuthing out a network bottleneck directly by looking at Windows 2000's network-related Sysmon counters, first look at the other system resources. Are they acting as bottlenecks? This reverse network bottleneck detection strategy is a process of elimination. If none of the other system resources are responsible for the bottleneck, and if the system's application response times to the end users have seen better days, look closely at the system's network subsystem.

When reviewing the network subsystem to sleuth out Windows 2000 network bottlenecks, you must have a detailed understanding of which network technology is in use and its characteristics. The information provided in Windows 2000 can be so detailed that it can sometimes be deceiving in what it reports at first glance.

EXAMPLE OF BIG-PICTURE NETWORK BOTTLENECK DETECTION: FOLLOW THE NETWORK DATA FLOW

Consider: a Windows 2000 system is connected to a Fast Ethernet network via a network switch that has recently been replaced for service. A few weeks later when the end of the month reports are due, users begin reporting slow response times. Under Sysmon, you observe that the Network Interface object counter Current Bandwidth is reporting that the NIC is operating at 100Mbits/sec (12.5MB/sec); you also observe the Network Interface object counter Bytes/sec is operating at 6.5Mbits/sec (0.813MB/sec).

Your obvious reaction would be that there is plenty of bandwidth available, since less than 6.5% of the network is utilized. Thus, let's look for the bottleneck elsewhere. Employing the reverse-detection strategy, you use the methodologies and techniques outlined throughout this book until you check all the server resources and find them well within acceptable limits. Now what?

If all of the system resources are operating normally and the applications are running normally, follow the data flow out from the client to the server's network connection. In this example, Sysmon's Total Bytes/sec counter data flattens out during each network surge, but at significantly lower levels than the network technology can support. This is indicative of something holding back the network's performance. Even though the Current Bandwidth counter might indicate a 100BaseT connection, the NIC could be in an autosensing mode and be providing false information.

This real-world discovery was made when following the data from the system to its first stop, the new network switch. As the switch was examined, even though it looked like the old network switch, it was mistakenly configured as a 10BaseTX connection. Because of this, the network segment the system was attached to was running at 10Mbits/sec (1.25MB/sec). Now compare this newly acquired knowledge about the network architecture with the Network Interface object's Average Bytes/sec counter that reported 6.5Mbits/sec (0.813 MB/sec). It can now be determined, from the information provided here and the Ethernet characteristics reviewed in the beginning of the chapter, that it was indeed a network bottleneck. The 10Mbit/sec Ethernet-configuration-based network was near its saturation level by trying to operate at an average utilization level of 65%. If you are curious, this problem was removed by reconfiguring the 100BaseTX switch to a set bandwidth of 100Mbits/sec, full duplex, as was the Windows 2000 system.

HOW BAD IS BAD?

In the example above, a 100BaseT switch was accidentally configured as a 10Mbit/sec mode and used by the client systems to access the Windows 2000 system. When the network is the resource throttling the overall perceived Windows 2000 performance, what type of effects might the end users experience? The throughput and response times provided would obviously go down considerably. To find out just how much, the 100BaseT shared Ethernet switch was reconfigured to 10Mbits/sec. No other changes were made. The file server stress test user loads introduced using the Bluecurve stress-testing tool (http://www.blucurve.com) were also identical. Figure 7-9 shows the average response time (ART) experienced before and after the slower configuration was introduced—the lower the ART, the better. Figure 7-10 shows the average network throughput for the same situation, but in this case the higher values are better. It is amazing the effect one slow performance link in the network data patch can make!

Tracking Down Network Bottlenecks with Sysmon Objects and Counters

OK, you know your environment, understand the network technologies in use, and have employed the reverse-detection strategy. What indicators does Windows 2000 itself provide that a network bottleneck may be forming?

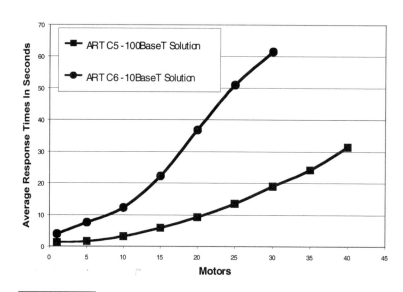

FIGURE 7–9 *Average Network Response Time When Comparing 100BaseT Network vs. 10BaseT Network*

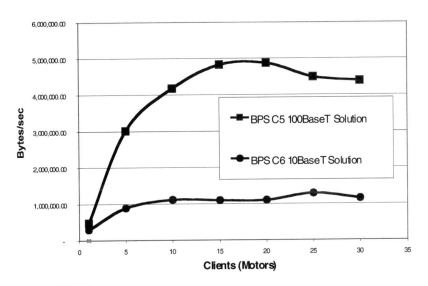

FIGURE 7–10
Average Network Throughput When Comparing 100BaseT Network vs. 10BaseT Network

Listed in Table 7.5 are the primary Sysmon objects and counters to consider when investigating a Windows 2000 network system bottleneck.

When the network subsystem is unable to keep pace with the requested workload (packets/sec), the response time provided by the network subsystem begins to degrade when the network becomes overworked. If the requested workload increases to an even higher level than the network subsystem is capable of servicing, the network I/O requests begin to back up. When I/O requests back up, network queues form, network-level errors begin, and packet retransmissions occur—this only exasperates the bottleneck condition. When network queues form and network errors are encountered, the Windows 2000 or application process requesting the network I/O operation must wait in line for service from the network subsystem, and even more system resources are needed to overcome the network errors and retransmissions.

ADDING NETWORKING-RELATED COUNTERS TO SYSMON

Remember, both the Network Interface and Network Segment objects are not installed under the default Windows 2000 installation. To add these Sysmon objects, follow these steps:

1. Add the SNMP Agent service: Start / Settings /Control Panel / Add/ Remove Programs / Add/Remove Windows Components and select SNMP Service. Adding this service installs the Network Interface Segment object to Sysmon. *Security Alert: When configuring your SNMP agent,*

TABLE 7.5	Core Sysmon Counters for Baselining and Network Bottleneck Detection

Object: Counter	Definition	Rule of Thumb for Bottleneck Detection
Network Interface: Output Queue Length	Output Queue Length is the length of the output packet queue (in packets).	If this value is longer than 3 for sustained periods of time (longer than 15 minutes), the selected network interface instance is becoming a network bottleneck. *Note: This is valid only for single-CPU Windows 2000 systems*
Network Segment: %Network Utilization	Percentage of network bandwidth in use on this network segment.	The network architecture in use determines the acceptable level of % Utilization. For Ethernet-based network segments, if this value is consistently above the 50–70% range, the network segment is becoming a bottleneck and is increasing the response times to everyone using the network.
Network Interface: Bytes Total/sec	Bytes Total/sec is the rate at which all bytes are sent and received on the selected network interface, including those bytes used as overhead (framing, etc.).	This value is directly related to the network architecture in use. If the value of Bytes Total/sec for the network instance is consistently close to the maximum transfer rates of your network and no other system resources are acting as a bottleneck, you have a network bottleneck on the specific NIC channel.
Network Interface: Current Bandwidth	Current Bandwidth is an estimate of the interface's current bandwidth in bits per second.	For interfaces that do not vary in bandwidth or for those where no accurate estimation can be made, this value is the nominal bandwidth reported by Windows 2000. Use this information in conjunction with the Bytes Total/sec counter to determine the network utilization levels. Be careful! This counter states what Windows 2000 thinks the bandwidth is. Sometimes information provided by the NIC is incorrect.
Network Interface: Packets Outbound and Received Errors	Packets Outbound and Received Errors is the number of outbound and received packets that could not be transmitted/ processed because of network errors.	If this value is >1, the selected network interface is experiencing network problems that are causing the network to slow down (the system must spend resources handling the error and retransmit the data) and potentially become a bottleneck. This problem could be emanating from any NIC or network device connected to the network segment.
Redirector: Current Commands	Current Commands counts the number of requests to the Redirector that are currently queued for service.	If this number is much larger than the number of network adapter card channels being utilized in the system, then the network(s) and/or the server(s) being accessed are seriously bottlenecked.
Server: Work Item Shortage	The number of times STATUS_DATA_NOT_ ACCEPTED was returned at receive indication time.	This indicates that Windows 2000 has not allocated sufficient initworkitems or maxworkitems and this is causing network limitations. Consider tuning InitWorkItems or MaxWorkItems in the registry (under HKEY_LOCAL_MACHINE\SYSTEM\CurrentControlSet\ Services\LanmanServer).

TABLE 7.5	Core Sysmon Counters for Baselining and Network Bottleneck Detection (Continued)	
Object: Counter	**Definition**	**Rule of Thumb for Bottleneck Detection**
Server: Pool NonPaged Failures	The number of times allocations from NonPaged pool have failed.	Windows 2000 network operations use paged pool and nonpaged pool memory. If this value is >1 on a regular basis, there is not enough physical memory in the server to support network operations.
Server: Pool Paged Failures	The number of times allocations from paged pool have failed.	Windows 2000 network operations use paged pool and nonpaged pool memory. If this value is >1 on a regular basis, there is not enough physical memory in the server to support network operations.

ensure that the community string at a minimum is not set to PUBLIC and that any network management systems you employed are configured as the only systems that your Windows 2000 system can communicate with via SNMP. For more details on SNMP security settings, visit http:// www.sans.org.

2. Add the Network Tools and Agent: Start / Settings / Control Panel / Add/ Remove Programs / Add/Remove Windows Components and select Network Tools and Agent. This will install the Network Segment object to Sysmon, Network Monitor Agent, and the real-time Network Monitor–based application. After these services are added, you must reboot Windows 2000 before the changes will take effect.

Beyond Windows 2000 Systems: Tracking Down Internetwork Device Performance Problems

With the information provided in this book, you can help prove that the Windows 2000 system is not the bottleneck. But what if the problem is with the network outside of Windows 2000 and is not as obvious as an incorrectly configured network switch? A detailed answer on network troubleshooting is outside the scope of this book's focus on Windows 2000 tuning and sizing. In general, however, continue to follow the data path through the network all the way to the client experiencing the poor response times. The pathping.exe command, which is introduced with Windows 2000, helps to provide insight into how well the network data path is performing. Consider the pathping.exe output in Figure 7-11 which was run from a Windows 2000 client to a target server. Here we see how some of the hops that the client's data must traverse are dropping packets. In Figure 7-11, various routers between our Windows 2000 Professional client and the target system are dropping up to 9% of all packets! Every dropped packet triggers some type of retransmission, which

```
C:\TEMP>pathping www.yahoo.com

Tracing route to www.yahoo.akadns.net [216.32.74.53]
over a maximum of 30 hops:
  0  ice
  1  oao-gw.oao.com
  2  dca1-cpe7-s6.atlas.digex.net
  3  dca1-core13-g5-0.atlas.digex.net
  4  dca1-core9-pos7-0.atlas.digex.net [165.117.48.193]
  5  ord2-core1-pos4-2.atlas.digex.net [165.117.51.246]
  6  ord2-core2-pos7-0.atlas.digex.net [165.117.48.86]
  7  .ibr02-s2-7.okbr01.exodus.net [216.32.132.141]
  8  bbr01-g4-0.okbr01.exodus.net [216.34.183.97]
  9  bbr02-p6-0.jrcy01.exodus.net [216.32.132.110]
 10  bbr01-p5-0.stng01.exodus.net [209.185.9.98]
 11  .dcr03-g10-0.stng01.exodus.net [216.33.96.161]
 12  216.33.98.18
 13  216.35.210.122
 14  www4.dcx.yahoo.com [216.32.74.53]

Computing statistics for 350 seconds...
            Source to Here   This Node/Link
Hop  RTT    Lost/Sent = Pct  Lost/Sent = Pct  Address
  0                                            ice
                              6/ 100 =  6%    |
  1  419ms   7/ 100 =  7%    1/ 100 =  1%     oao-gw.oao.com
                             0/ 100 =  0%     |
  2  411ms   6/ 100 =  6%    0/ 100 =  0%     dca1-cpe7-s6.atlas.digex.net
                             4/ 100 =  4%     |
  3  374ms  14/ 100 = 14%    4/ 100 =  4%     dca1-core13-g5-0.atlas.digex.net
                             0/ 100 =  0%     |
  4  431ms  15/ 100 = 15%    5/ 100 =  5%     dca1-core9-pos7-0.atlas.digex.net [165.117.48.193]
                             0/ 100 =  0%     |
  5  430ms  16/ 100 = 16%    6/ 100 =  6%     ord2-core1-pos4-2.atlas.digex.net [165.117.51.246]
                             0/ 100 =  0%     |
  6  400ms  16/ 100 = 16%    6/ 100 =  6%     ord2-core2-pos7-0.atlas.digex.net [165.117.48.86]
                             0/ 100 =  0%     |
  7  381ms  19/ 100 = 19%    9/ 100 =  9%     ibr02-s2-7.okbr01.exodus.net [216.32.132.141]
                             0/ 100 =  0%     |
  8  412ms  10/ 100 = 10%    0/ 100 =  0%     bbr01-g4-0.okbr01.exodus.net [216.34.183.97]
                             1/ 100 =  1%     |
  9  350ms  19/ 100 = 19%    8/ 100 =  8%     bbr02-p6-0.jrcy01.exodus.net [216.32.132.110]
                             0/ 100 =  0%     |
 10  428ms  20/ 100 = 20%    9/ 100 =  9%     bbr01-p5-0.stng01.exodus.net [209.185.9.98]
                             0/ 100 =  0%     |
 11  468ms  13/ 100 = 13%    2/ 100 =  2%     dcr03-g10-0.stng01.exodus.net [216.33.96.161]
                             0/ 100 =  0%     |
 12  479ms  15/ 100 = 15%    4/ 100 =  4%     216.33.98.18
                             0/ 100 =  0%     |
 13  421ms  16/ 100 = 16%    5/ 100 =  5%     216.35.210.122
                             0/ 100 =  0%     |
 14  443ms  11/ 100 = 11%    0/ 100 =  0%     www4.dcx.yahoo.com [216.32.74.53]

Trace complete.

C:\TEMP>_
```

FIGURE 7–11   *Using the pathping.exe Command to Track Down Network Performance Issues*

slows down overall performance to the Windows 2000 Professional client system. If the Windows 2000 Server and client are both running well, the additional information provided by the pathping.exe command will give you insight into where to investigate.

At the client level, you can apply the same strategies and techniques used throughout this book to sleuth out client and network bottlenecks, although the actual tools you use may be slightly different if the client system is not based on Windows 2000.

These troubleshooting roads actually lead us back to chapter 2's recommendation of creating a prototype of your Windows 2000 solution and developing a baseline of it in a controlled environment before deployment. With a sound baseline to use as a frame of reference, it becomes easier to detect system, network, or applications bottlenecks.

Tuning Strategies for Removing Network Subsystem Bottlenecks

Now that we have told you how to configure and size the fastest network subsystem, as well as how Windows 2000 uses the network subsystem and how you can detect when network subsystem bottlenecks are forming, let's use this information to our advantage. How do we tune the network subsystem to make it go even faster or, at least, become more efficient? In this section, we will review the strategies surrounding network subsystem tuning, and then we'll get into actual hands-on tactics. At first glance, it would appear that tuning a Windows 2000 system to remove a network subsystem bottleneck is a real challenge since there are few obvious actions you can take and that the only remedy is to add additional NICs in a creative fashion. This option of adding hardware is a technique you may wish to explore earlier than you would when tuning the other Windows 2000 subsystems. However, with all of the options and flexibility that are available with Windows 2000 systems, there are always other options that should also be explored. Now, purchasing more hardware is a valid technique and we will discuss when it is appropriate to add NICs. Chapter 8 includes specific solution scenarios that will move step-by-step through the strategies and tactics presented here that involve tuning various applications in a Windows 2000 environment.

I cannot stress enough how critical it is not to simply know which operating system "knob" to tweak; it is also important to understand why something can or may need to be changed. Being properly armed with an understanding of how Windows 2000 and the system hardware works is actually the first step in tuning the disk subsystem. The following are the primary strategies to consider when tuning around a network subsystem bottleneck:

- Ensure that another system resource is not acting as a bottleneck.
- Lower the overhead associated with network operations and improve efficiency.
- Tune the Windows 2000 network subsystem directly.
- Tune the Windows 2000 TCP/IP stack.
- Tune the Windows 2000 administration level.
- Tune the NICs.
- Remove unnecessary Windows 2000 data on the network and control the data flows of needed Windows 2000 traffic
- As a last resort, change the NICs.
- Use Windows 2000 Interrupt Control Manager for advanced tuning.

Now let's review a variety of practical hands-on tactics that we can use to implement these strategies.

Hands-on Tactics for Tuning around Network Subsystem Bottlenecks

ENSURE ANOTHER SYSTEM RESOURCE IS NOT ACTING AS A BOTTLENECK

When tuning around network subsystem bottlenecks, I have often found that it is actually a bottleneck in another system that must be removed. I have also come across another resource acting as a pseudo-bottleneck. If another system resource is acting as a bottleneck, adding more NICs will not significantly improve overall performance. Refer to chapter 2 for ways to ensure that the other resources are not the bottleneck before spending effort tuning network resources. Some pseudo-bottlenecks appear to be network related when they are not. For example, network resource shortages in some cases disguise themselves as disk subsystem and memory problems. When a backup or a large file transfer does not fill the available network bandwidth, the first concern that comes to mind is that the network cannot support the required performance. However, it is commonly the driving system that is the culprit. To fill the available network bandwidth, the system must be able to drive it. For example, you may hear concerns that the network is slowing down nightly backups, when in reality the three-disk server that must be backed up is limited by its lack of an appropriately configured and tuned disk subsystem. The network can be a superhighway connecting your Windows 2000 systems. An analogy might be cars on a highway: If you place a three-cylinder Yugo on the road (a poorly configured Windows 2000 system), you will not be able to go as fast on the highway as you would if you were driving the latest C5 Corvette (a well-configured Windows 2000 system). The highway has not changed (no network change); it's just the engine (Disk and CPUs) that has changed (OK, and a few other items besides the engine). Of course, if you needed a better network, you might upgrade your two-lane highway to an eight-lane highway so that eight Corvettes could drive at the same time at top speed vs. two Corvettes.

LOWER THE OVERHEAD ASSOCIATED WITH THE NETWORK OPERATIONS AND IMPROVE EFFICIENCY

Remove Nonessential Network Protocols/Redirectors. One technique that can help you optimize your Windows 2000's network subsystem performance is to bind only those protocols and redirectors (server components other than Windows 2000 server and workstation services) that your network is actually using to your network adapter. Binding is a technique Windows 2000 utilizes to establish a communications channel between the protocol driver (TCP/IP, IPX, etc.) and the NIC itself. These bindings are set under: Start / Settings / Network and Dial Up Connections / Local Area Connection Properties. Then check which protocols (TCP/IP, NetBEUI, etc.) are currently installed. Also check which redirectors (RIP for NwLink, RPC support for Banyan, etc.) are installed. Removing unnecessary protocols and redirectors lowers the amount of memory that Windows 2000 requires for network I/O (which can then be used for other tasks), ensures that your network is not generating any unnecessary traffic (such as unwanted broadcasts), and lowers the number of bindings that must be searched. For example, if you operate a TCP/IP-based network with Microsoft clients, use only TCP/IP and Microsoft client support.

Network Binding Selection Order. If more than one network protocol or redirector is in use, tune the binding search order by placing the protocol/redirector most commonly used on the top of the bindings list. These bindings are set under: Start / Settings / Network and Dial Up Connections / Local Area Connection Properties. All network calls are routed to the protocol/redirector first on the list, and then Windows 2000 waits for a response before submitting to the next protocol/redirector.

Multiple CPU Advantages. Slow network response can on occasion be attributed to an overworked CPU. Track the Sysmon Processor object's %Processor Time and %Interrupt Time counters. If you see that the CPU is becoming a bottleneck (review chapter 4), then consider a faster CPU or multiple CPUs. Windows 2000 can support multiple CPUs and NICs on the same network segment. By splitting the network into multiple segments or trunking network segments together, you can distribute the network load across the multiple NICs and CPUs. This distributes the interrupts required for servicing the NIC cards across the CPUs and frees up the CPU cycles to work on other tasks besides low-level networking I/O.

Remove Unnecessary Windows 2000 Services. Similar to tuning the other Windows 2000 subsystems, you never want to run a service you do not need because it adds overhead to your system (potentially more network, memory, and CPU resource usage) and may pose a security risk. For example, many folks will enable services such as simple TCP/IP services by default but be unaware of what these services provide. Few Windows 2000–based services or applications require these services, and having them enabled adds overhead to your system. Simple TCP/IP services also poses a potential security risk due to services like character generation. Explaining why character generation is a security risk is behind the scope of this book, but over at http://www.SANS.org, articles are posted on why this and other commonly used configurations introduce increased security risks into your Windows 2000 systems. Know what services and applications are running on your system and why.

A Special Network Tuning Note. Run the Windows 2000 Network Monitor tool on occasion (Start / Programs / Administrative Tools / Network Monitor) and watch what is running around on your network at the packet level. You might be surprised at what you see. You may have thought that you standardized with one protocol or another, but then what are all of these other protocols running around taking up bandwidth on your network?

TUNING THE WINDOWS 2000 NETWORK SUBSYSTEM DIRECTLY

Tuning Multi-Homed Computers. When a multi-homed computer is connected to two different networks using NetBIOS over TCP/IP, there can be a delay connection. This problem occurs when more than one path exists to the destination computer and the redirector selects the less optimal path. This can cause packets sent to a directly connected subnet to be routed internally to the destination, causing a delay.

To avoid this delay, you can edit the registry to force Windows 2000 to have the redirector connect using the first successful call to the destination, thus ignoring the transport binding order when establishing a NetBIOS connection. Use regedit32.exe or your favorite registry editor to add the 'IgnoreBindingOrder' key of data type REG_DWORD with a value of 1 to the registry location `HKEY_LOCAL_MACHINE\System\CurrentControlSet\Services\Rdr\Parameters`. Note that this area of the registry is typically blank except for entries you add.

TUNING A WINDOWS 2000 TCP/IP STACK

The Windows 2000 TCP/IP stack has demonstrated many improvements over that of Windows NT 4 in both real-world and test environments. In general, Windows 2000 autotunes itself very well. However (there is always a however), in some environments—particularly network-intensive environments that have significant memory resources available and that support high numbers of clients—consider these TCP/IP tuning options:

- *Tuning Transmission Control Blocks (TCBs).* Typically, you want your Windows 2000 server to respond to as many connections as your resources will allow, so don't let an ill-tuned TCP stack stand in your way and slow you down—tune it! The TCBs store data for each TCP connection. A control block is attached to the TCB hash table for each active connection. If there are not enough TCBs available when a web request (http) arrives at your server via TCP/IP, there is an added delay while it waits for additional TCBs to be created. By increasing the TCB time wait table size, latency overhead is reduced by allowing more web connections to be serviced in a faster fashion. To adjust this value, add the following registry value: `HKEY_LOCAL_MACHINE\System\CurrentControlSet\Services\Tcpip\Parameters\MaxFreeTcbs=0xFA0`. This example increases the TCB time wait table to 4,000 entries from the default of 1,000.
- *Tuning TCP Hash Table.* Now that overhead time introduced by TCP is lowered for the networked system, you must adjust the corresponding hash table which is where the TCBs are stored. Accomplish this by adding the following registry value `HKEY_LOCAL_MACHINE\System\CurrentControlSet\Services\Tcpip\Parameters\MaxHash`

`TableSize=0x400`. This increases the TCB hash table size from 512 to 1,024, allowing more room for connection information. Note: TCB information is stored in the nonpaged memory pool.

- *Maximum Transmission Unit (MTU) Window Size Tuning (Use Jumbo Packet Sizes Whenever Possible)*. Larger MTU sizes can be dynamically adjusted according to your network adapter. When MTUs are optimized to the largest possible size, fewer packets are required to transfer the data. Thus the system has to do less work to send and receive the data. This lowers the overall overhead on the Windows 2000 system (fewer packets to assemble and disassemble, less interrupts, less CPU cycles, etc.). MTU size can be set to a standard frame of 1.5KB or a jumbo frame of 9KB on Windows 2000. Using jumbo frames for your Windows 2000 servers, clients, and internetworking devices can yield tremendous improvements in overall performance. The trade-off here is that there is a risk of an inefficient use of resources if the application transfers data that is less than 4KB in size. The MTU size is either configured manually on the NIC advanced properties tab or dynamically discovered/determined by the NIC and Windows 2000.

- *TCP Window Size Tuning*. The TCP receive window size specifies the number of bytes that a sender can transmit without receiving an acknowledgment. In general, larger receive windows improve performance over high-delay, high-bandwidth networks. However, if the window size is too large over an unreliable network, this will result in having to repeat an excessive number of transmissions due to timeouts occurring on the network. For the greatest efficiency, the receive window should be an even multiple of the TCP maximum segment size `HKEY_LOCAL_MACHINE\System\Current-ControlSet\Services\Tcpip\Parameters\TcpWindowSize`. This variable is a REG DWORD. Consider increasing this value if your customers connect to your Windows 2000 system via a reliable WAN connection.

Note: It is important to monitor all system resources when tuning, but it is particularly important to monitor memory resource usage when tuning TCP/IP options under Windows 2000, because tuning TCP/IP values in an upward direction will incur more memory usage.

Also note: More specialized TCP tuning is covered in chapter 8's web server solution scenario.

WINDOWS 2000 ADMINISTRATION-LEVEL TUNING

Permanently Cache Media Access Control (MAC) Addresses. A MAC address is a unique address that a manufacturer burns into an NIC, such as a 100BaseT Ethernet card. TCP/IP uses the address resolution protocol (arp) broadcasts over the network to associate an IP address with a physical layer MAC address. To lower the number of broadcasts and time required to obtain MAC addresses, you can permanently (until the next reboot unless a start-up script is used) place the associated MAC/IP address pair into memory. Use the following example command sequence from the command prompt to implement: arp -s 137.111.141.101 01-01-01-12-s3-44. This feature is particularly helpful when accessing a commonly networked system that uses static IP addressing. This is not a suggested technique when the networked system uses dynamic IP addressing.

Controlling Network Users' Timeout Periods. There are only so many resources allocated for network connections, so, if a user strolls away from his desk to enjoy a sunny day, disconnect him. This frees up resources for active uses. The command net config server lists the Windows 2000 current settings. Running the command net config server /AUTODISCONNECT: 10 sets the automatic disconnect time (idle session time) to 10 minutes. This command is run from the Windows 2000 command line and is permanent until it is run again. The registry entry for this value is located at: HKEY_LOCAL_MACHINE\ SYSTEM\CurentControlSet\Services\lanmanServer\Parameters\Users.

Update to the Latest Software Revision Levels. As with other subsystems, always test and upgrade to the latest revisions of patches for Windows 2000 and associated device drivers for your NICs. Do not forget, especially for I2O-enabled NICs, to update the BIOSs that reside on the NIC itself.

Controlling When Network-Intensive Jobs Are Run. Using the many scripting options now available with Windows 2000 and the Windows 2000 scheduler (reviewed in chapter 2), it is possible to control when network-intensive jobs are run. The most common network-intensive applications are backups, antivirus signature file updates, and software distribution jobs. Track closely which jobs are run when, and never take the default time out of the box (this is what others may do, which results in immediate conflict of network resources). Time how long it takes for your various jobs to run, and then space them out accordingly to avoid unneeded network load conflicts.

NETWORK INTERFACE CARD TUNING

Basic NIC Tuning. In some cases, it is possible to tune an NIC itself. Some NICs allow the maximum number of receive lists that the driver allocates for receive frames, which can improve the NIC's performance. For example, the registry entry to add for a Compaq Netelligent 10/100TX NIC is MaxReceives. This key is a REG_DWORD and values are placed into it in hex. The Compaq web site http://www.compaq.com suggested increasing the MaxReceives counters for this NIC to 500 (a hex value of 0 × 1F4). Place this registry value into the following location: HKEY_LOCAL_MACHINE\SYSTEM\CurrentControl-Set\Services\cpqnf3(#)\Parameters.

Some of these tunables can also be set by selecting Start / Settings / Network and Dial Up Connections / Properties of LAN Adapter / Configure NIC / Advanced Tab. These settings can make a big difference. Back up your system before testing and watch memory usage. Some of these settings enable you to increase the buffers for the NIC itself, which is good, but that increased buffer memory must come from somewhere! Refer to Table 7.6 for example settings.

IPSEC and TCP NIC-Based Off-Loading (Highly Recommended). For network-intense environments, the combination of advanced Windows 2000 device drivers and advanced NIC technology enables many of the calculations associated with Windows 2000 networking to be off-loaded to the NIC itself; specifically IPSEC and TCP operations. Two of the TCP operations that can be off-loaded onto NICs are checksums (receive and transmit) and segmentation calculations. For IPSEC-enabled NICs, the calculations required to encrypt the data are off-loaded onto the NIC, which can result in substantially improved network performance and lowered CPU resource utilization! On tests I completed and in various other independent published tests, throughput improvements were commonly in the 10–25% range, with a subsequent reduction in CPU usage of 20–40%. This tuning technique is highly recommended for both Windows 2000–based servers and clients, but, as always, is dependent on your specific environment.

Advanced NIC Tuning. I2O-enabled NICs for GBE and occasional Fast Ethernet are enabled with numerous tuning options. These are typically located under: Start / Settings / Control Panel / Local Area Connection Properties / Configure NIC / Advanced. NIC vendors implement their technology in a slightly different manner. This is where stress testing and proactive management come into play. Table 7.6 lists a generic rule of thumb for a commonly used Compaq and Intel-based GBE.

As noted many times, it is important to monitor all facets of Windows 2000 resource utilization when tuning any Windows 2000 subsystem. Specifically when tuning the network subsystem, track memory usage (available memory, page pool, and nonpaged pool) very closely to ensure a memory bottleneck has not been introduced.

Avoid Automatic NIC Settings. Setting the NIC properly is an area that is commonly taken for granted. Even though there are various standards defining the physical and logical specifications of network communications, some compatibility issues show up when you are not looking. Set your Windows 2000 system's NIC and any other network devices your system may communicate with to the best network speed setting available. For example, if full-duplex 100BaseTX is available and the other network devices support this setting, choose it. Only as a last resort, select autosensing. This does incur more work, but it can be well worth the effort because it guarantees the speed at which your network subsystem is operating.

TABLE 7.6	*Advanced NIC Tuning Settings*

Vendor	Default Value	Recommended Value	Description
Compaq NIC			
CoalesceBuffers	8	64	Number of buffers before an interrupt occurs
ReceiveBuffers	48	512	Number of posted receive buffers on the adapter
Intel Pro 1000 NIC			
NumberOfReceiveBuffers	200	800	Number of posted receive buffers on the adapter
NumberOfCoalesceBuffers	200	512	Number of buffers before an interrupt occurs
NumberOfTransmitDescriptors	448	512	Number of transmit buffer descriptors on the adapter
ReceiveChecksumOffloading	Off	On	Task off-loading onto hardware in receiver path
TransmitChecksumOffloading	On	On	Task off-loading onto hardware in sender path

Tuning Interrupt and Deferred Procedure Calls (DPCs). Each network request received over the network generates an interrupt to the processor requesting service. If you are using an I2O-enabled NIC, the amount of CPU overhead is lowered. Regardless of the NIC technology in use, if the processor does not find the request urgent enough (a high enough interrupt level), it will defer the request. This deferred interrupt request becomes a deferred procedure call. As more and more requests come into the system, the number of interrupts and DPCs increases. When an interrupt is sent to a particular CPU and it gets deferred, additional system overhead is incurred if this DPC is shipped off to another CPU in the system. This can be costly from a performance perspective. To stop this from happening, set the following registry value: `HKEY_LOCAL_MACHINE\System\CurrentControlSet\Services\NDIS\Parameters\ProcessorAffinityMask` to 0. This will force the CPU that handled the interrupt initially to also handle any subsequently associated DPCs that are generated. This tuning can improve the CPU's service of interrupts and DPCs generated by the NICs in multi-CPU configurations.

REMOVE UNNECESSARY WINDOWS 2000 DATA AND CONTROL NEEDED DATA FLOWS ON THE NETWORK

Controlling Network Traffic Patterns. If you can lower the amount of unnecessary network traffic traversing the network, the overall percentage of network utilization is lowered and more bandwidth is available. Controlling all user network traffic flow is unrealistic. You can, however, control some aspects of it. In a Windows 2000 environment, there is a large amount of traffic generated around the network that can be tuned from the perspective of where it emanates from and where it goes.

We have omitted legacy network services such as WINS and the browser services. Our focus is on Windows 2000–based services that generate network traffic: domain name services (DNS) and active directory (AD) services. AD relies on DNS as its primary name service. Now that DNS Internet standards have been updated to support dynamic DNS so that clients can register their network addresses on the fly (similar to WINS), much more care must be taken with your DNS infrastructure. Since DNS is used to find AD domain controllers and other network resources, every client on your network will regularly require DNS services. This is a significantly higher DNS network load than many organizations have experienced, which also makes DNS a very important service. Consider multiple DNS servers to control your DNS network traffic.

Many large books are dedicated to the AD subject. In general, watch your selection of AD sites closely, because they greatly influence your AD network data flows. All Windows 2000 systems inside of an AD site are considered to have a fast network connection (10Mbits/sec or faster). However, network connections between AD sites are typically slower (1.5 Mbit/sec). Between sites, AD will compress its data and limit the amount of AD traffic sent. Again, watch those site selections closely!

SNMP Agent Control. Simple network management protocol agents can be a source of significant performance and security problems for both Windows 2000 systems and the network if not properly configured. Many of today's networks are managed using SNMP technology. If the network management station that is requesting SNMP event information from a Windows 2000 system (or any station on the network, for that matter) is configured incorrectly, overhead is created on Windows 2000 and the network. For example, if a network management station requests event information every 15 seconds instead of every 15 minutes, this causes much more network overhead with very little associated gain. Thus, ensure that you have correctly configured the appropriate level of granularity polling on the network management system that is polling your Windows 2000 systems.

Under Windows 2000, an snmp.exe process consuming large amounts of CPU time via Task Manager or Sysmon can help alert you to this type of incorrect network management configuration. Optimally, the SNMP Agent is very useful and consumes less than 1% of systems resources. To tune around this potential problem, a two-phase approach should be taken. First, work with the network management team to ensure that the SNMP polling periods are set correctly. Second, under Windows 2000, you can view the SNMP Agent setup information under Start / Programs / Administrative Tools / Computer Management / Services and Applications / Services /SNMP Service Properties;

configure this service to accept only SNMP requests from designated network management hosts based on their IP addresses.

NIC CHANGES—THE LAST RESORT

When other network subsystem tuning options do not achieve your goals and all of the networking components in your Window 2000–based solution are running at their optimum levels, making a change at the hardware layer is the next logical step. The following are the key hardware-level changes to consider:

- Select a different networking technology with higher bandwidth.
- Distribute the Windows 2000 network load.

SELECT A DIFFERENT NETWORKING TECHNOLOGY WITH HIGHER BANDWIDTH

Select only stable PCI-based NICs that use the latest technology for your system. Whenever possible, use 64-bit, 66MHz, I2O-enabled NICs that support off-loading network calculations. At a minimum, implement Fast Ethernet technology and consider Gigabit Ethernet technology in the future. There are other network technologies available, but none are as common. If you have a 10BaseTX-based network today, consider upgrading at least to 100BaseTX for your Windows 2000 systems. Review Table 7.7 to see the increased throughput that can be generated by using higher bandwidth NIC. Performance levels achieved always vary based on the workload. But, even with a fairly large deviation, which technology would you choose based on the test results in Table 7.7?

TABLE 7.7	*Real-World Results of Using Higher Bandwidth NICs*
Network Technology (Switched Full-Duplex Ethernet)	**Real-World File Transfer Throughput (Mbits/sec)**
10BaseTX	7
100BaseTX Full Duplex	188
1000baseTX Full Duplex	680

DISTRIBUTE THE WINDOWS 2000 NETWORK LOAD

If upgrading a single NIC's Ethernet channel does not meet your performance requirements, there are always more options! There are two primary techniques for increasing the bandwidth to your Windows 2000 system when a single NIC upgrade is insufficient:

- Network trunking
- Network segmentation

Both are valid approaches, but network trunking is the preferred method for adding network channels to your Windows 2000 system because it scales better and has fewer infrastructure changes. Why increase your own workload if you don't have to?

Network Trunking. Network trunking takes multiple network segments or channels across the same or multiple NICs and has them work together to increase the overall bandwidth to your system. The most common four technologies supported by Windows 2000 are:

- Adaptive load balancing (ALB)
- Link aggregation
- Fast EtherChannel (FEC)
- Gigabit EtherChannel (GEC)

These technologies were investigated in the section on Windows 2000 server placement in the network earlier in this chapter. In summary, these technologies are implemented at the device driver and IP network layer, which enables them to work transparently to your applications. This approach also lowers the overall workload that must be implemented because the Windows 2000 system still uses a single IP address for client connectivity; thus no client changes are required.

Network Segmentation. When a faster network technology and network trunking are not options, consider balancing your network load by distributing the more heavily used network segments between two or more NICs. Even though network segmentation can involve some new cabling (physical) and subnetting (logical addressing), it is a proven technique that can optimize your Windows 2000 system's network I/O.

To accomplish this, a tool generically referred to as a network sniffer becomes helpful in analyzing the network traffic associated with Windows 2000 to determine where on the network your heaviest workloads are emanating from. There are software- and hardware-based sniffers dedicated to this task. Fortunately, Windows 2000 provides a limited-functionality network sniffer that is an excellent addition to the growing native Windows 2000 tool set introduced in Windows NT 4.

The Network Monitor tool is installed under Windows 2000 when the Network Tools and Agent are installed. This procedure is outlined earlier in this chapter. Start the Network Monitor by selecting Start / Programs / Administrative Tools / Network Monitor. Once activated, the Network Monitor tool provides a large amount of data in the default configuration view. Figure 7-12 is a screen shot of the Network Monitor tool. As shown in the figure, Network Monitor can be used to quickly isolate that unruly power user or users. In the Network Monitor screen shot in Figure 7-12, the top network stations are two Windows 2000 servers. Data from each capture can be saved over time to help in developing a network traffic baseline. Once you determine which users are slowing the network down for everyone, connect an additional NIC to your

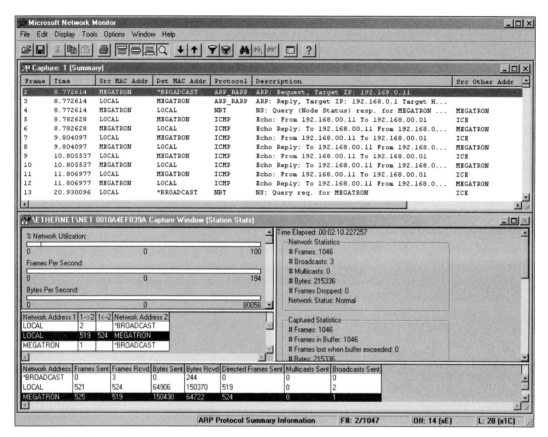

FIGURE 7–12   *Using Network Monitor to Isolate Network-Intensive Clients*

Windows 2000 system and reconfigure your network to support another network segment. This will lower the amount of traffic on the first NIC and allow the interrupts from both NIC workloads to be spread across multiple CPUs (if needed). This will improve the overall response times to the end users. If the network is in need, the bottleneck throttling Windows 2000 performance on the network segment of interest, this performance technique will be quite helpful.

The Network Monitor is not a fully functional network sniffer as can be found in tools dedicated to this function, but it does provide some packet drill-down capabilities. Install and investigate this tool. You may find it a helpful ally to have.

> *Special note: Periodically run Network Monitor. You might be surprised at all of the network traffic and protocols that are running around your network taking up valuable network bandwidth!*

Advanced Tuning: Windows 2000 Interrupt Control Manager

When a Windows 2000 system is configured with more than two CPUs, the Windows 2000 interrupt allocation algorithm is not always optimal for every network environment due to differences in the hardware platforms. The Windows 2000 Resource Kit now provides a tool that enables you to control—i.e., tune—which hardware interrupts from what NICs are serviced by which CPUs. This technology was reviewed in depth in chapter 4. We review it here as it applies to the network subsystem.

If you operate a single NIC on a Windows 2000 system with a single CPU, this approach is not applicable. If your environment has a single NIC in a multiple-CPU environment, you may consider binding all of your NIC-based interrupts to the CPU that is not as heavily used as the other CPUs. In multiple-NIC and multiple-CPU environments, consider limiting NIC interrupt processing to the two least-used CPUs in the system. If all CPUs are equally utilized, then consider dedicating one CPU to each NIC.

To determine the interrupts used by each NIC, use the System Information MMC snap-in via Start / Administrative Tools / Computer Management / System Tools / System Information, or type in the command winmsd.exe from the Windows 2000 command prompt. Once the System Information tool is running, select the Hardware Resources / IRQs folder for a listing of interrupts and the NIC device association.

Configuring Microsoft Interrupt Affinity Filter Control Tool (IntFiltr). To install the IntFiltr, locate the IntFiltr folder in the Windows 2000 Resource Kit, and then complete the following steps:

1. As with any technology you introduce into your environment, be sure to test this tool on a nonproduction system to ensure that it behaves as you envision. Also, make sure you have fully backed up your system and registry.
2. Copy the IntFiltr folder to a folder on your system, and then copy intfiltr.sys to your %SYSTEMROOT%\system32\drivers directory (this is typically c:\system32\drivers).
3. Update your registry to include the changes listed in intfiltr.reg. To make these changes, you can simply run 'regedit intfiltr.reg' and it will automatically update your registry.

Once installed, start IntFiltr by running intfiltr.exe from the command line; upon starting, the GUI shown in Figure 7-13 will appear on screen. The GUI provides a listing of all the devices in the system. Highlight the device whose interrupts you wish to tune and then select Add Filter to turn on interrupt filtering for that device. Now that the filter is activated, select Set Mask and then select the CPU or CPUs to bind the target device's interrupts to. Once the mask is set, the current value will change with the CPU current mask information. This configuration series is depicted in Figure 7-14. From

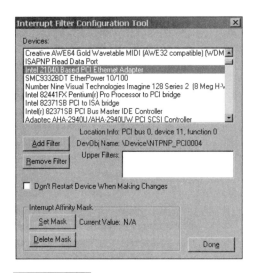

FIGURE 7-13   *Configuring the IntFiltr Interrupt Affinity Tool*

here, you can restart the device on line or reboot the system to activate the filter. To update the filter settings in the future, start IntFiltr.exe and scroll down
to the target device. At this point, you will see the current filter/mask settings
that can be adjusted as needed, based on your proactive performance management.

Summary

This chapter emphasized the importance of understanding all of the Windows
2000 resources covered in this book and the characteristics of the network
technologies in use. Focusing in on a single Sysmon network counter does
not provide much in the way of assistance when trying to tune and size Windows 2000's network subsystem. Several examples were used to illustrate the
importance of understanding the correlation between low-level network characteristics, technology, network architecture in use, and the Windows 2000
systems in place to understand what is actually occurring. Armed with this
knowledge, it becomes much more apparent how to size Windows 2000 network solutions, detect Windows 2000 network bottlenecks, and tune around
network subsystem bottlenecks. Always remember to follow the data paths
from your clients, over the network, and through your Windows 2000 Server
to determine where bottlenecks are occurring and plan around them. When
in doubt about finding a performance issue, just follow the data!

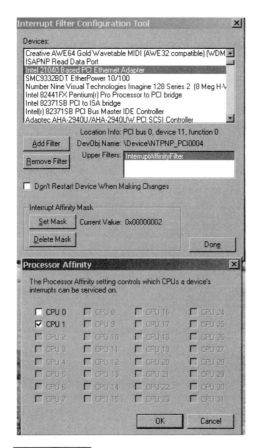

FIGURE 7–14   *Setting the IntFiltr's Filter and Mask to Bind a Device's Interrupt Traffic to a Single CPU*

Putting Theory into Practice: Sizing and Tuning Back Office Solution Scenarios

CHAPTER OBJECTIVES

- Solution Scenario 1: Windows 2000 File Server Consolidation........ *450*
- Scenario 1 Step by Step: Sizing and Tuning a Mid-Range Windows 2000 File Server........ *452*
- General Windows 2000 File Server Sizing Configuration Chart Summary........ *462*
- Windows 2000 File Server Tuning Summary........ *463*
- Solution Scenario 2: Windows 2000 Backup Servers........ *467*
- Scenario 2 Step by Step: Mid-Range Windows 2000 Backup Server........ *474*
- Backup Server Sizing Configuration Chart Summary........ *484*
- Windows 2000 Backup Server Tuning Summary........ *485*
- Solution Scenario 3: Windows 2000 Exchange Servers........ *489*
- Scenario 3 Step by Step: Sizing a Mid-Range (3,000 User) Windows 2000 Exchange Server........ *493*
- Exchange Server Sizing Configuration Chart Summary........ *510*
- Windows 2000 Exchange Server Tuning Summary........ *511*

● Solution Scenario 4: Database Server Implemented with Microsoft SQL 7.0........ *516*

● Scenario 4 Step by Step: Sizing and Tuning Mid-Range Windows 2000 SQL Server........ *521*

● SQL Server Sizing Configuration Chart Summary........ *533*

● Windows 2000 SQL Server Tuning Summary........ *533*

● Solution Scenario 5: World Wide Web Server Implemented with Microsoft IIS 5.0........ *544*

● Scenario 5 Step by Step: Sizing and Tuning a Mid-Range Windows 2000 Web Server........ *549*

● IIS 5.0 Web Server Sizing and Configuration Chart Summary........ *560*

● Windows 2000 IIS 5.0 Web Server Tuning........ *561*

● ASP CPU Optimization........ *574*

● Optimizing IIS for Web Publishing........ *575*

● Thinking Outside of the Box: Xtune........ *579*

● Literally Thinking Outside of the Box: Network Load Balancing........ *580*

● Windows 2000 IIS 5 Web Server Tuning Summary........ *581*

● Web Server Solution Scenario Summary........ *586*

Introduction

*H*ave *you ever wanted specific, practical, hands-on configuration recommendations that include guides for tuning and sizing Windows 2000 systems? Or have you ever wished for a performance checklist that can help you design and tune your new Windows 2000 solution? If so, you are in the right place. This chapter focuses on implementing specific Windows 2000 system solutions in the following application areas:*

● Windows 2000 file servers and server consolidation
● Windows 2000 backup servers
● Messaging servers: Microsoft Exchange server
● Database servers: Microsoft SQL 7.0
● eCommerce: World Wide Web servers using Microsoft IIS 5.0

I worked with experts in all of the above fields to investigate strategies and tactics, perform stress testing (too many hours in the lab), and discuss real-world deployments. Following is the team that provided excellent input: file servers and backups—John Pollen and Arnie Shimo; Microsoft Exchange—Jeff Lane, Mike Gillam, and Rick Patrick; Database Servers—Rob Cochran and Troy Landry; and Web Servers—Dan Matlick and Yemi Famogun. These colleagues are an outstanding mix of senior engineers and architects who develop and manage IT solutions for NASA's ODIN IT Outsourcing project for the Office of Space Flight, OAO Corporation, and MightyView Corporation.

Chapters 2 and 3 introduced tuning and sizing methodologies that serve as a foundation for developing Windows 2000–based solutions. Chapters 4 through 7 investigated tuning and sizing techniques for each of Windows 2000's major resources and provided examples. This chapter integrates the entire system, using the methodologies and techniques of previous chapters to work through various scenarios to implement Windows 2000 systems. These solution scenarios are designed to be realistic (and fun) and are based on feedback from my previous book, *Tuning and Sizing NT Server*, and associated web site: http://www.TuningAndSizing.com (formerly http://www.TuningAndSizingNT.com).

These case studies may or may not fit your environment exactly, which is okay. Why? The goal here is to help provide insight into tuning and sizing of Windows 2000 for maximum performance; to improve your understanding of the methodologies used; and to provide specific configuration recommendations via worksheet templates that you can reference (electronic copies of templates are available at http://www.TuningAndSizingWindows.com). Use these worksheet templates for reference; they may help your design process for Windows 2000 solutions. You may end up not using some areas while adding others that arise from your own experience. These configurations provide a solid starting point when developing a Windows 2000 solution for your unique environment. Remember, tuning and sizing systems is part science and part art; thus, based on knowledge you have acquired or enhanced with the previous chapters, you can take these configurations as a starting point and customize them for your environment.

It does not matter if the Windows 2000 solution you are developing is based on Microsoft Exchange Server, Oracle, Microsoft SQL Server, or a file server. Once you understand the concepts behind the methodology, you can use them to your advantage whenever you tune and size any type of Windows 2000 solution—even as technology changes. Do not get bogged down in the very small details. Even if your solutions are 12MB to the left or right, following a sound methodology will get you to a solution that is in the ball park, which can then be tuned to a very good fit.

For each of the scenarios, a consistent outline approach is followed so that you can quickly get the specific information for each application area.

Solution Scenario 1: Windows 2000 File Server Consolidation

Introduction

This scenario presents the most common services provided with the Windows 2000 platform, file servers. Many people today have older file servers that are ready to be retired. This scenario addresses that challenge.

Application Description

File servers are the most common Windows 2000 application function. A file server does just what the name implies—it acts as a data repository for storing and sharing files.

Application Performance Characterization

The key application that provides Windows 2000 file services is the native Windows 2000 server service. The server service provides RPC support and file, print, and named pipe sharing services.

Configuring the server service itself is completed in three places. Basic operations are controlled under Start / Programs / Administrative Tools / Computer Management / Services and Applications / Services / Server properties. Here you can control what is active on your server and what the system should do if it fails, such as try to restart the process. You also have the option of activating the File and Print sharing capabilities of the server service under Start / Settings / Network and Dial Up Connections / Properties for your LAN connection. You can then activate or disable File and Print Sharing for Microsoft Networks. When you select the properties of File and Print Sharing you access the controls for Windows 2000 memory management, specifically the file system cache. Memory management options are reviewed in chapter 5.

Windows 2000 file servers use the native file system to store files on the disk subsystem. For smaller file servers (< 4 disk drives), performance bottlenecks typically occur in the disk subsystem, memory subsystem, and then the other subsystems. On large file servers (> 5 disk drives), performance bottlenecks typically occur in the network subsystem, memory subsystem, disk subsystems, and then CPU subsystems.

When a client connects (Windows 2000 workstation) to the file server (Windows 2000 server service) over the network, the Windows 2000 file system cache is used heavily because it caches the network file services requests.

Sysmon Objects and Counters: File Server Bottleneck Detection and Sizing

The Sysmon objects and counters outlined in the previous chapters for CPU, memory, disk, and network subsystems are still applicable to Windows 2000 file servers. It is important to understand the big picture when tuning or sizing your system. In addition to the previously reviewed rules of thumb for solving bottlenecks and sizing objects and counters, specific objects and counters for file servers are outlined in Table 8.1.

In addition to the Sysmon counters in Table 8.1, it is helpful to understand which Windows 2000 process is running the server service. Locating the server service with Task Manager (launched when ctrl+alt+delete is depressed and Task Manager is selected) is not as obvious when using Windows 2000, because it operates under the Service Control Manager's services.exe executable. You can observe the LanManServer, LanManWorkstation, and some of the other services that the Service Control Manager (services.exe) is running by executing the tlist command from the support tools directory on the Windows 2000 distribution media (*tlist.exe –s | find "services.exe"*). With this information, you gain insight if other applications are using resources besides those associated with file services. If you are running a system management application, such as Concord's System Edge (http://www.Concord.com) or HP Open View's ManageX (http://www.hp.com), you will want to be alerted if for any reason the server service stops operating. If you do not have these types of system management software packages available, you can configure Windows 2000 to take action. This is accomplished by selecting Start / Programs / Administrative Tools / Component Services / Service / Server services / Recovery Tab; set Windows 2000 to take action on a service that has stopped. Actions include restart the service if it fails or run a file. Since the option to run a file is available, the options available to you with Windows 2000 are limited only by your imagination and scripting abilities.

TABLE 8.1	Sysmon Counters for File Servers	
Object/Counter	**Definition**	**Value to Monitor**
Server: Sessions	The number of sessions currently active in the server. Indicates current server activity.	Influences sizing. Determines concurrent file server users.
Server: Bytes Total/sec Bytes Received/sec Bytes Sent/sec	The number of bytes the server has sent to and received from the network.	Influences tuning and sizing. Provides a good indicator of how much workload is contributed to file server services particularly if other applications are being hosted on the same system. Total Bytes/sec are helpful in sizing the server (network, disk subsystems). Bytes sent/received helps to characterize workload which is used when tuning network and disk subsystems.

TABLE 8.1	Sysmon Counters for File Servers (Continued)	
Object/Counter	**Definition**	**Value to Monitor**
Server: Work Item Shortages	The number of times STATUS_DATA_NOT_ACCEPTED was returned at receive indication time. This occurs when no work item is available or can be allocated to service the incoming request.	Influences tuning. File servers must be healthy to run well. This counter indicates whether the InitWorkItems or MaxWorkItems parameters might need to be adjusted.
System: System Uptime	System Uptime is the elapsed time (in seconds) that the computer has been running since it was last started. This counter displays the difference between the start time and the current time.	Commonly referred to as CYA. File servers have become more important in the enterprise. This counter helps track the availability of your server. If you ever debate whether the physical server was down or a physical network was down, consider tracking this counter. If the network is down and the counter is greater than the detected down time, the network was the problem, not the server. This information can be obtained via SNMP requests also, if the proper security information is available such as the SNMP community string.

Scenario 1 Step by Step: Sizing and Tuning a Mid-Range Windows 2000 File Server

Sizing the Initial File Server Configuration

In chapter 3, the core sizing methodology was presented for sizing your Windows 2000 solution. That methodology is followed here for the development of the initial Windows 2000 server configuration.

1. DEFINE OBJECTIVE(S)

Due to almost constant hardware maintenance failures, multiple small servers have—after five years—reached the end of their usefulness. A new system is needed to share data for a mid-sized company. Since long-term costs—total cost of ownership (TCO)—are a concern, a decision is made to consolidate the current 20 file servers to 2 Windows 2000 file servers. This will meet the company's two objectives: (1) implement a new file server solution and (2) lower TCO by reducing the number of servers that must be managed. Using two Windows 2000 file servers reduces concern about availability, even though a single file server could suffice.

2. UNDERSTAND BUSINESS AND TECHNICAL REQUIREMENTS NEEDED TO MEET YOUR OBJECTIVE(S)

- Which application(s) will meet your functional objective(s)?
  For security, all clients are Windows 2000 Professional or Windows NT. Thus, a desktop that supports international security standards is in place. Core file services provided with Windows 2000 will meet the company's requirements. It is important to understand that the servers will support multiple departments, and each department has its own specific needs.
- What are the availability requirements?
  These are very important servers; they will support the entire company. Backups must be completed every night (after 7:00 P.M. and before 5:00 A.M.) and the system must be restored to service within four hours.
- What are the ramifications if your system is down?
  It is important to keep a high availability Monday through Friday, but planned weekend maintenance is acceptable.
- What are the disk subsystem storage capacity requirements?
  The old system of 20 servers supports 200GB of data. It is estimated that this disk storage capacity will grow to 400GB in the next year.

3. DETERMINE LOADING CHARACTERISTICS

- *Number of total users per server*
  500
- *Number of concurrent users per server*
  60
- *Disk workload characteristics (read/write environment)*
  File server characteristics vary from department to department. Generally a mix of 70% read and 30% write based on a similar office environment.
- *Size of records/transactions*
  400KB documents on average.
- *Transaction rates*
  Based on historical information, the average document size is 400KB. Business customers expect a two-second response time. To determine the throughput needed to provide this response time, follow this basic formula: Number of concurrent users (60) multiplied by the size of average records (0.4MB) divided by response time (2 sec). For

this environment, a server that provides 12MB/sec (96Mbits/sec) is needed to meet the company's requirements. Another view of this is to consider that, in two seconds, 30MB of data must be transferred when 60 of the 500 users are concurrently accessing the file server.

- *Physical location of users (influences communications such as WAN, LAN, dial-up, terminal services, etc.)*
  All users reside on site and are connected via the local LAN.
- *Type of work the user will complete*
  Office automation to support sales activities and some engineering. Heavy on presentations and proposals.

4. DETERMINE PERFORMANCE REQUIREMENTS

Response time is the most important factor for the office. They would love to have their average response time less than two seconds on average.

5. UNDERSTAND FUTURE BUSINESS REQUIREMENTS

This is a public company, so growth is very important. The company expects to expand by at least 20% each year.

6. UNDERSTAND FUTURE SYSTEM ARCHITECTURES

The local team would like to quickly put in a system and run it without replacement for three years. Local support staff is small, which is just unheard of in the IT industry. Everyone always has the right size IT team so that long hours never occur. Rebuilding servers every few months to meet growing demands is undesirable, as is the associated downtime.

7. CONFIGURE THE SYSTEM

Finally, we get to the good stuff. At this point, you can configure the system. Choose the system resources required by your objective, with consideration for steps 1 through 6, and obtain the system. As you configure the system, look at each individual resource to meet the overall system's goals. Software and hardware vendors are good sources of information. They can suggest configurations that will get you started. Reviewing relevant industry benchmarks also can help provide insight into the initial configuration. Industry benchmarks are explored later in this chapter. The following steps are presented to help guide you through the actual system configuration process.

Having some sort of idea on how each system resource works and relates to the overall system performance is helpful when configuring your system. Chapters 4 through 7 reviewed each system resource in greater detail.

7.1 APPLICATION CHARACTERISTICS REVIEW • The application characteristics review was completed at the top of the Windows 2000 file server section.

7.2 REVIEW EACH SYSTEM RESOURCE

Disk I/O Requirements • This is the driving requirement and one where Windows 2000 gives you significant control, especially for file servers. First, we size the disk subsystems; then we can work backward from the disk subsystem configuration to size the rest of the file server. From the business requirements above, we will determine the disk storage and performance requirements.

Availability • Since this is a critical server, all data will reside on hot swappable RAID array–based disk subsystems that use some level of fault tolerance. Hot spare disk drives will also be incorporated into the solution to increase overall availability.

Performance Workload Characteristics • From the requirements above, the workload characteristics are typically read-intensive and will undoubtedly be random in nature. RAID levels 5, 10, and 1 are all valid options.

Performance Throughput and Transfers/sec • In this environment, the basic information provided is not Transactions/sec but throughput. There are two aspects to consider: operational performance and backup performance. Operationally, the file server must support 12MB/sec of continuous throughput based on the business's requirements. Although caching of data will aid in overall performance delivery, it is the disk subsystem that drives the performance of the file server in this random workload environment. Assuming that we use RAID level 5 due to its strong combination of availability, performance characteristics that match the expected workload, and good price/performance, we can use the disk performance data from chapter 6 (Table 6.9, Executive Summary of RAID Performance) to size the disk subsystem. Each 10,000rpm disk drive in a RAID 5 disk array provides approximately 1.11MB/sec of random read performance. Thus, to achieve 12MB/sec of continuous throughput, 11 disk drives are required. Yes, the math works out to 10.8 disk drives, but you always round up to the next integer. If we use 11 18GB disk drives in a single RAID 5 array, we will have only 180GB of available disk storage due to the parity overhead from RAID 5. (Usable disk space in a RAID 5 array = [(capacity of the N disk drives) × $(1/N)$]; thus, a twelfth disk drive is needed so that 198GB of usable storage is available.

Backup performance is reviewed in more detail in the Windows 2000 backup server scenario below. For now, there are two backup performance factors to consider: backup and restore. The current disk storage capacity is planned to start at 100GB and grow to 200GB within the year. Planning for 200GB to be backed up, a 12-disk RAID 5 array provides 32.04MB/sec (115GB/hour) when being read in a sequential fashion (2.67MB/sec per disk drive × 12 disk drives × 60sec/min × 60min/hour), which results in a full backup in less than four hours.

However (there is always a trade-off!), when you wish to restore the disk array, each disk in a RAID 5 array provides only 0.95MB/sec of sequential write performance. Thus, a 12-disk array provides 41GB/hour of restoration throughput (12 disk drives × 0.95MB/sec × 60sec/min × 60min/hour). Based on this data, it will take approximately 4.8 hours to restore the data. This does not meet the business goal of a full restore in four hours. To meet the business goal, three more disk drives must be added to the array to improve the total overall write performance throughput of the raid performance array from 41GB/hour to 51.3GB/hour. This results in a restore time that meets our target of a four-hour restore.

From the above analysis, we take the highest number of disk drives that meets our goals. Thus, 15 disk drives are needed to meet our business performance requirements.

Storage Capacity • Each file server must support 100GB today and 200GB by the end of the year. For maximum performance and to have the capability to run disk defragmentation tools, we do not want the disk drives' used capacity to exceed 60–80%. Cost is a concern to this company, so they plan on 74% used disk space. Factoring this tuning tactic into our total disk capacity needed, we will require 270GB of available disk space. The 270GB of disk capacity spread across 15 disk drives indicates each drive must support 18GB. Factoring in RAID 5 overhead, a sixteenth disk drive is needed to account for the parity overhead so that a full 270GB is actually available for use.

Reality Check • Industry benchmarks are always good for reference. Here we used internally run benchmarks on Windows 2000 disk subsystems for many of the measurements, calculations, and estimates for sizing. For file servers in general, the Ziff Davis NetBench benchmark is relevant. Keep in mind that real-world environments tend to cache activities slightly more than a well-designed benchmark. The NetBench benchmark results reviewed in chapter 3 were obtained from a Windows 2000 file server configured with a two-CPU Pentium III 650MHz Server, 1GB of RAM, 1 Gigabit Ethernet NIC, and a 14-disk RAID 5 array. This configuration resulted in providing 225Mbits/sec (28MB/sec) of throughput. This higher performance was achieved—with one less disk drive than is used in our scenario—because many of the operations were cached in the Windows 2000 file system cache. Our approach is slightly more conservative. Although the two examples are not an exact match, the comparison helps us to ensure that our current disk subsystem sizing is in the ball park and provides an excellent starting point to build our system.

Other Disk Requirements • Are there any other applications that require disk space? For our file server example, we still need to place Windows 2000 somewhere. Chapter 5 showed that you never want to place the operating system and pagefile on a RAID 5 array, for both operating system and performance reasons. Due to the availability requirements, the operating system will be placed on its own RAID 1 mirror composed of two 9GB disk drives configured with one partition. The pagefile will be placed on this same RAID 1 Mirror in an effort to lower costs (vs. placing the pagefile on its own dedicated high-speed drive). As long as we do not page on a regular basis (something you never want to do!), this configuration will suffice but may need to be modified later.

Based on all of the above disk information, Table 8.2 outlines the overall disk subsystem requirements.

TABLE 8.2   *File Server Disk Subsystem Solution*

Application	Minimum Disk Storage Needed	Logical Partition	Recommended Configuration (All 10,000rpm, Ultra2 SCSI Disk Drives)
Windows 2000 operation system requirement	<500MB	C:	2 9GB Disk Drives in RAID 1 Array (9GB usable/3.15GB filled)
Pagefile	2GB	C:	
System management agent	5MB	C:	
Antivirus application	20MB	C:	
Security application (server-based firewall and IDS)	30MB	C:	
Data store 1	100GB	H:	9 18GB Disk Drives in a RAID 5 Array (162GB usable/100GB filled—61% used)
Data store 1	100GB	I:	9 18GB Disk Drives in a RAID 5 Array (162GB usable/100GB filled—61% used)

Note: More disk drives are used here than planned, 9 vs. 8. Why is that? The container that holds the RAID array will hold only 12 disk drives at a time. Thus, two containers were needed. This forced us to use two RAID 5 arrays, one for each container, and, of course, that introduced more overhead for parity. This drove the need for additional disk drives in the solution.

CPU Requirements • The primary application to support is the server service that provides file services. The CPU's workload consists of supporting network operations, disk operations, and the associated logging and security checking of customers' rights. From historical information, the 20 Pentium 133MHz CPU-based servers (single CPU) that provided these file services ran at 70% usage on average. Twenty Pentium 133MHz CPUs running at 70% works out to 14 Penitium 133MHz CPUs running at 100%. Using the CPU consolidation chart from chapter 4, these 14 Pentium 133MHz CPUs equates to the CPU power of approximately two Pentium III class CPUs. What? An eight to one ratio? Yes, this is a good place to start. As always, there are other factors that affect overall performance and these are discussed at length in earlier chapters. For this small configuration, however, we are reviewing only the CPU subsystem. Refer back to chapter 4 for a detailed discussion on CPU performance.

Industry standard benchmarks are also helpful when sizing systems. For a network-intensive file server environment, the Ziff Davis benchmark is a relative benchmark. Our solution needs to drive 96Mbits/sec (12MB/sec) during regular operations. From the benchmark information provided in chapter 3, a Windows 2000 file server with two Pentium III CPUs drove over 250Mbits/sec of overall throughput. Thus, a single Pentium III CPU should suffice. However, during backup operations, we will need to drive an even higher rate of disk and network operations to support just over 250Mbits/sec of throughput, similar to the Ziff Davis results. Based on this information, two Pentium III CPUs will be required, even though the bulk of the processing power will not be needed during normal operating hours. It is the backup and restore-to-service operations that drive the computing power of this specific file server solution.

Memory Requirements • Sizing RAM is an additive process. Our first step in sizing memory resources is to outline all applications that will use any memory resources.

TABLE 8.3	*Windows 2000 File Server Memory Sizing*
Application	**Memory Usage (Working Set)**
Windows 2000 operation system requirement	128MB
Windows 2000 file system cache (max for configurations less than 1GB in size)	432MB
Overhead for antivirus software running on server	10MB
Overhead for system management software running on server	8MB
Overhead for intrusion detection software	12MB
Memory needed per user connection	Included in file system cache overhead
Total Estimated Memory Usage	*592MB*

From historical data, each of the 20 former servers contained 128MB/sec of RAM. Since sizing RAM is an additive process, our analysis of the system's memory usage indicates that 1GB of RAM is needed in the new server. If we again review the Ziff Davis benchmark results, 1GB of memory was configured in the system.

Great data, but what amount of memory should be configured? Although memory usage is an additive process, there are some shared memory resources. Each of the 20 servers used in the earlier historical extrapolation had 64MB of memory used by the operating system, leaving approximately 640MB. In our memory sizing chart above—and what we have learned from our Windows 2000 memory usage investigation—adding any more than 592MB would not help this file server configuration. (Remember that Windows 2000 limits its file system cache usage to 432MB when less than 1GB of RAM is in the server.) Thus, from this information and the fact that server hardware supports memory in 512MB blocks, 512MB should handle the workload. Through proactive performance management, more RAM can be added as needed, but for now let's save a few dollars and not overconfigure the server.

Network I/O Requirements • This file server solution is projected to support the delivery of 96Mbits/sec in a local area network. The current LAN is planned to receive a switched Gigabit Ethernet in two years. For now, a full duplex 100BaseTX Ethernet-based connection should easily support the current bandwidth requirements. From chapter 7 we see that Windows 2000 can support 188Mbits/sec using a 100BaseTX full duplex Ethernet-based switched connection. Thus, we do have some room to grow until the Gigabit Ethernet network upgrade. Since this is an estimate of network usage, two Network Interface Cards (NIC) will be obtained that support Adaptive Load Balancing (ALB) so that two 100BaseTX channels can be teamed/trunked together if the need arises.

Leveraging two NICs also enables us to meet our customers' concerns over availability. Besides the increase in available bandwidth, NICs that support ALB also support fail-over operations. If one NIC fails, the second NIC will handle all the network traffic. One company that provides NICs with these features is Intel Corporation (http://www.intel.com). If even higher levels of availability were required, the next step would be to consider clustering technologies.

7.3 SYSTEM ARCHITECTURE RELATIONSHIP CHECK • This is a final, common-sense check of a server. Since the business requirements mandate keeping this new file server for at least three years, leading-edge server technology will be obtained. Not cutting edge, as that technology tends to demand a premium price. From all of the sizing information above, we now have the following configuration: a one- to two-CPU-capable server, two Pentium III 800MHz CPUs, each with 256KB of full-speed (ATC) Level 2 cache, a 133MHz System Bus, 512MB of RAM, a single 64-bit 33MHz PCI I/O bus, a single hardware-based RAID controller, two disk drives for the operating system, 20 disk drives for the internal and external RAID array, and two 100BaseTX NICs. This configuration also meets our architecture checklist from chapter 4, which recommends a minimum of 256MB of RAM per Pentium III CPU.

An example server that would support this configuration is the Compaq DL-380 and standard Compaq external RAID array. Unfortunately, the external

RAID array only supports 12 disk drives per array. Due to this, two external SCSI RAID array units are obtained and the disk drives split between the two. Nine disk drives in one RAID 5 array, and nine disk drives in the second RAID 5 array. Why is another disk drive needed? Since one contiguous RAID array cannot be used, the second array must have an additional disk drive to support the disk capacity lost to RAID 5 overhead. Remember, if you have nine disks in a RAID 5 array, you lose the capacity of one disk drive to the parity information. All disk drives are active; you just lose the capacity of a single drive. In our example, 18GB (one disk drive) of logical data is lost to parity overhead per RAID 5 array, but 125GB is available for customer usage in each array.

Looking at the data path from the RAID arrays through the NICs, this file server configuration has no bottlenecks in place before we deploy. Potentially the CPU resources may be underpowered, but since we will proactively manage this file server, any shortcomings will be quickly detected and removed.

7.4 FUTURE BUSINESS AND SYSTEM ARCHITECTURES CHECK REVIEW ● This server has room to grow as needed—CPUs can be upgraded, disks can be dynamically added to the external disk arrays, RAM can be expanded to 4GB, and the NICs can be upgraded to Gigabit Ethernet.

7.5 INITIAL HARDWARE CONFIGURATION AND TUNING ● In this step, the initial configuration of the server hardware begins to take shape based on steps 7.1 and 7.2. See the Sizing and Tuning File Servers section below.

TABLE 8.4   *Windows 2000 File Server Hardware Configuration Data*

Mid-Range File Server Hardware Configuration
Compaq DL-380 (Why select the DL-380? We needed a solid system to use for a real-world reference.)

CPU Configuration	CPUs Used in Solution	CPU Family	Level 2 Cache Size	Speed of CPU	Available CPU Slots
	2	Intel Pentium III	256KB	733–1GHz	2 of 2 used
RAM Configuration	*Amount of RAM Used in Solution*	*System Bus Speed*	*Type of RAM*		*RAM Expansion*
	512MB	133MHz	ECC SDRAM		4GB
I/O Subsystem Configuration	*Number and Type of Adapters*	*Number of PCI I/O Buses*	*Placement of PCI Cards*		*Speed of PCI Bus*
	2 Single Channel Full Duplex 100BaseTX	1	Second to top slot on PCI bus 0		64-bit 33MHz
	I2O Enabled Ultra2 SCSI 2 Channel RAID Adapter		Top slot on PCI bus 0		

TABLE 8.4	*Windows 2000 File Server Hardware Configuration Data (Continued)*

Mid-Range File Server Hardware Configuration
Compaq DL-380 (Why select the DL-380? We needed a solid system to use for a real-world reference.)

Disk Subsystem Configuration	*Partition/ Mount Point*	*Files Located on partition*	*Placement of PCI Cards*	*Type of RAID Adapter*	*SCSI Channel*	*RAID Level*	*# Of 10K RPM UF Drives*
	C:	Windows 2000 installation, pagefile	N/A	Built-in RAID Adapter Compaq	1 of 1	1	2
	F:	Data Set 1	First Slot on PCI Bus	2-Channel External UF SCSI	1 of 2	5	9
	G:	Data Set 2	Same as adapter in row above	Same as adapter row above	2 of 2	5	9

7.6 INITIAL SOFTWARE CONFIGURATION AND TUNING • In this step, the initial software configuration of the server configuration begins to take shape based on steps 7.1 and 7.2. See the Tuning File Servers section below.

7.7 INITIAL GENERAL TUNING • See the Tuning File Servers section below.

8. STRESS TEST AND VALIDATE THE SERVER CONFIGURATION

For this scenario, historical information and industry standard benchmarks were relied upon to develop the file server configuration. File server behaviors are well known across the industry. Due to time constraints, a full stress test validation is not feasible.

9. PROACTIVELY FOLLOW THE CORE TUNING METHODOLOGY DURING STRESS AND VALIDATION TESTING

Not applicable as no stress tests were run.

10. DEPLOY THE SYSTEM INTO PRODUCTION

This was a real scenario and the file server system was deployed successfully. Expecting something else?

11. PROACTIVELY FOLLOW THE TUNING METHODOLOGY AFTER THE SYSTEM IS DEPLOYED

Environments do change. The information gathered following the core tuning methodology is helpful for staying one step ahead of user demand (see chapter 2). We can use that information to identify current load demands and solve potential system bottlenecks. This information is also useful when you are developing and sizing future system solutions and when you are adding additional capacity to your current system(s). If you have not quantifiably determined where and how to add additional capacity to your system, you are in great risk of wasting your initial investment.

General Windows 2000 File Server Sizing Configuration Chart Summary

Even though every environment is different, the following file server configuration chart provides excellent sizing guidelines for your initial server configurations. Follow the sizing template above, customize it to your environment and then proactively manage your Windows 2000 file server to an optimal fit!

TABLE 8.5   *Specific Configurations for Sizing File Servers*

Concurrent File Server Users (400KB average record size, 2-second response time)	System Bus Speed	Number of PCI I/O Buses	Pentium III 800MHz Class CPU	RAM	Number of UltraFast 10K rpm SCSI-3 Disk Drives (for data) in a RAID 5 array	Network Interface Card (NIC)
Small Scale <= 200 Users < 30 Concurrent	133MHz	1	1 (256KB Level 2 Cache)	256MB	5	100BaseTX
Mid-Level Scale <= 500 Users, <= 60 Concurrent (Scenario 1)	133MHz	1	1-2 (256KB Level 2 Cache)	512MB	11	100BaseTX Full Duplex
Enterprise Scale <= 1,000 Users, <= 110 Concurrent	100MHz	2	2-4 (512HB Level 2 Cache)	1-2GB	20	1-2 100BaseTX Full Duplex NICs (channels) teamed/ trunked together or Gigabit Ethernet
Extreme Scale <= 2,000 Users, <= 220 Concurrent	100MHz	2	4-8 (1-2MB Level 2 Cache)	2GB	40	2-3 100BaseTX Full Duplex NICs (channels) teamed/ trunked together or Gigabit Ethernet

Note: It is important to understand that, as we scale each system, a balanced approach is taken between all server resources so that no artificial bottlenecks are created before the file server is even deployed.

Windows 2000 File Server Tuning Summary

File Server—Specific Application Tuning

From an application perspective, the primary control of how well Windows 2000 file server services run is based on:

- Server hardware configuration optimized for your environment's workloads
- Windows 2000 memory management configuration, as it affects the behavior of the file system cache which file services relies on heavily
- Windows 2000 I/O subsystem optimization for delivery of file services

File server functions are handled natively to Windows 2000. Because of this, all tuning recommendations provided below are for general Windows 2000 file server tuning. As always, follow the core tuning methodology (chapter 2) when tuning your servers. However, the tuning recommendations provide a solid baseline to start with before your stress tests are run, baselines are developed, and your solution is deployed.

For the hands-on specifics of why, when, and how these tuning recommendations work and steps to implement them, refer back to the tuning sections in the previous chapters. Here, select information is provided to give you a jump-start into an optimized Windows 2000 solution.

SERVER HARDWARE TUNING

The server configuration section above reviewed specific recommendations for the file server configuration. However, every server and workstation implement the architecture and BIOS settings slightly differently; thus this section is more of a general reminder of what you should check at the hardware level. Refer to earlier chapters for specific information on each subsystem area that requires close attention, such as placement of I/O adapters, location of adapters on the PCI bus, and RAM configuration. Also, remember to update the BIOS and Windows 2000 drivers on all server hardware, which includes motherboards and the associated adapters. Once the BIOS levels and drivers are updated, go into their perspective setup and ensure that they are set correctly. For example, is the CPU set to run at its maximum speed? Are you sure you received the correct hardware? Did you get the 900MHz instead of the 1GHz CPU? Are all disk drives the 15,000rpm version you ordered instead of 7,200? I've observed many instances when a Windows 2000 system did not meet expectations because a vendor sent the wrong hardware, the BIOS setting was incorrect, or a driver was not up-to-date.

WINDOWS 2000 FILE SERVER SPECIFIC APPLICATION TUNING

- Check the Windows 2000 memory management strategy. File servers rely heavily on the file system cache. By default, the Windows 2000 file system cache is set to maximize data throughput for file sharing. However, check this setting anyway at Start / Programs / Settings / Network and Dial Up Connections / Properties of your LAN adapter / File and Print Sharing for Microsoft Networks.
- Set application response to favor background processes (Start / Settings / Control Panel / System / Advanced / Performance Options / Set Background Services).
- Set the pagefile size to twice the amount of RAM in your server. Use a fixed size.
- Never place the pagefile on a RAID 5 array.
- If your system must page (which should be avoided), consider multiple pagefiles on physically separate disk drives, which are all configured to the exact same size and are on the same speed disks.

WINDOWS 2000 CPU SUBSYSTEM RESOURCE TUNING

Key CPU-related tuning you should consider:
- Off-load CPU operations to I2O enabled I/O adapters.
- Do not implement compression or encryption.
- If encryption is in use, additional resources (CPU, memory, disk) will need to be added depending upon workload patterns.
- If multiple CPUs are in use with Multiple NICs, consider using the Microsoft Interrupt-Affinity Filter Control Tool (IntFiltr; see chapter 4) to ensure interrupts are properly distributed among NICs and CPUs. (For step-by-step details on this, review chapter 7.)
- Do not use the server as your personal workstation (bad for your customers' response time).
- Do not use a 3GL or other fancy screen saver.
- Check all services running on your server. Operate only those you need and stop all others.
- Avoid running other applications on your file server.
- Run only those file services needed to provide file server services and manage the server.

WINDOWS 2000 MEMORY SUBSYSTEM RESOURCE TUNING

Key memory-related tuning you should consider:

- Check all services running on your server. Only operate those you need and stop all others.
- Force Windows 2000 to keep the Windows 2000 executive (kernel) from paging any of its executive system drivers to disk and ensure that they are available immediately if needed.
- Do not use a 3GL or other fancy screen saver.
- Do not use exotic wallpaper; it wastes memory resources.
- Ensure the pagefile is set to twice the size of physical RAM in your server to ensure physical memory can be committed to action.

WINDOWS 2000 DISK SUBSYSTEM RESOURCE TUNING

Key disk subsystem–related tuning you should consider:

- Defragment your disk subsystem on a regular basis; this will result in significant performance improvements!
- Perform a fresh, low-level format on all disk drives at the lowest level using the disk or RAID adapter in your system.
- Freshly format all disk drives with NTFS when installing Windows 2000.
- When formatting the disk drive with NTFS, select the ALU size that best matches your disk workload characteristics. For scenario 1, the recommended ALU is 64KB, as the workload is based on large file size. (Note: You must use a third-party defragmentation tool if the ALU is larger than 8KB.)
- If large NTFS partitions or volumes are in use, increase the size of the volume logs.
- Turn on write-back caching and read-ahead caching on hardware RAID adapters.
- Use only I2O enabled RAID adapters and those with their own CPUs.
- Keep storage capacity on the disk subsystem under 60–80% so that the fastest portion of the disk drive is used and so that there is room on the disk drives to perform defragmentation.
- Evenly distribute disk workload across the physical disk drives in the server.
- Defragment your disk subsystem on a regular basis; this will result in significant performance improvements!
- If DOS file names are not required (i.e., legacy DOS-based desktops are not in use), disable short name (8.3) file generation. (Note: To disable short name generation, use regedit32.exe to set the registry DWORD value of 1 in the following Registry location: `HKEY_LOCAL_MACHINE\SYSTEM\CurentControlSet\Control\Filesystem\`

NtfsDisable8dot3nameCreation. For more information on this technique, see chapter 6.

- Disable last access updates. HKEY_LOCAL_MACHINE\SYSTEM\CurrentControlSet\Control\FileSystemNtfsDisableLastAccessUpdate. Changing the default REG_DWORD value of this key from 0 to 1 will stop Windows 2000 from updating the last access time/date stamp on directories as directory trees are traversed.
- Understand the characteristics of all RAID levels and leverage different RAID levels as needed in the same file server solution.
- Use one Windows 2000 partition per physical disk device/array.
- Check all services running on your server. Operate only those you need and stop all others.
- Did I mention to defragment your disk subsystem on a regular basis; this will result in significant performance improvements!

WINDOWS 2000 NETWORK SUBSYSTEM RESOURCE TUNING

Key network subsystem related tuning you should consider:

- Teaming/trunking multiple NICs (Ethernet channels) together as needed to add network bandwidth to your Windows 2000 server seamlessly to your customers.
- Balance network activity across NICs if you cannot use NIC teaming/trunking technologies.
- If possible, use jumbo packets on your network.
- Remove all unnecessary protocols and Redirectors.
- Standardize on one network protocol: TCP/IP.
- If more than one network protocol is in use, set binding order such that the most commonly used protocol is first on the list.
- Tune the NIC driver to off-load IPSEC security operations and TCP operations on the NIC itself instead of the main system CPUs.
- Tune the NIC driver to increase its send and receive buffers.
- Use only I2O-enabled NICs.
- Use the fastest I/O bus enabled NIC possible (64-bit, 66MHz Peer PCI buses).
- Tune the Windows TCP/IP stack to your environment (TCP Hash Table, MTU Window Size). (Review the IIS 5.0 Solution Scenario for details on how to accomplish this.)
- Do not use autodetect for your NIC. Set it to the best performance level the internetwork devices will support. For example, 100BaseTX full duplex.

THIRD-PARTY TOOLS FOR TUNING WINDOWS 2000 FILE SERVERS

Key network subsystem–related tuning you should consider:

- Obtain a third-party disk defragmentation tool that provides enhanced defragmentation features such as scheduling and support of multiple NTFS ALU sizes. For example, Norton Speed Disk http://www.Norton.com.

Solution Scenario 2: Windows 2000 Backup Servers

Introduction

Backup servers are not very glamorous until, of course, you need to have a critical file or system restored. Keeping enterprise data backed up and having the capability to reliably restore data as needed is one of the most important aspects of any Windows 2000 administrator's job description. In this scenario, we review backup servers from a generic technology approach and how Windows 2000 can be optimized to improve the performance of your backup servers. Windows 2000 provides an improved native backup application and there are numerous vendors that also provide backup applications, such as Legato, Veritas, Retrospect, IBM ADSM, HP Omniback, and others. Specific applications are not investigated here, but a general approach to backup tuning and sizing is taken that can be applied to any backup application environment. The focus here is performance, of course. But for backup and disaster planning, there is more to consider than just performance. For more information on backup software and technology, and strategies of when and how to back up your systems, refer to the tape vendors' web sites such as Quantum (http://www.Quantum.com) or application vendors such as Legato (http://www.Legato.com) and look for their many white papers on these subjects. For a good overview of Windows NT (applicable to Windows 2000 also) backups and strategies, review *Windows NT Backup & Restore* by Jody Leber published by the folks over at O'Reilly.

Application Description

Windows 2000 servers, acting as backup servers, are very similar to file servers except that they have a very specific mission—backing up and restoring data—and require special-purpose hardware and storage management software.

Application Performance Characterization

Backup application performance characterization can be investigated from three perspectives: at the hardware system technology level, Windows 2000 level, and from a backup application level. Here the major focus is on the first two areas. Why? Once these areas are tuned and sized for maximum performance, the backup application is then free to be configured to its maximum potential. Many backup application vendors focus heavily on ensuring that the hardware technology and Windows 2000 solution are optimized first and then will consider addressing questions with their technology. The following methodology helps you focus immediately on optimizing the backup application.

When characterizing the performance of backup servers, it is critical to follow the data all the way from every system you want to back up to the backup media in which the data will be stored. The weakest link will determine how fast your data is backed up and restored.

Typically there are two approaches to providing backups: locally attached backup devices and backup devices provided by a server across the network. If you must have the fastest possible backups, attach the backup media directly to the server you are backing up. Since locally attached backup media are also needed even when backups are completed across the network, our focus will be on backing up systems from across the network to a central backup server. This network approach is typically much more cost effective, thus its popularity. This statement is based on experience. Initially, centralized backup servers tend to be slightly more expensive than a locally attached backup, but over the long term, costs of labor to support the distributed environment tend to be significantly more. The network-based backup solution is illustrated in Figure 8-1.

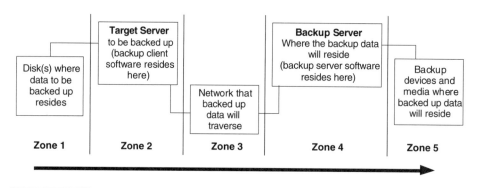

FIGURE 8-1   *Following the Backup Data from Beginning to End*

If you understand the performance characteristics of each zone that your backup data traverses, I guarantee that you will meet your expectations! Remember that when following the data through these zones, it is the slowest zone that will become a bottleneck and slow the overall backup throughput.

From here, let's review each zone and how it relates to backups.

ZONE 1. DISKS WHERE DATA TO BE BACKED UP RESIDE

Zone 1 is your starting point. If your application is taken off-line for backups (no customer interacting with the system), the backup software will sequentially read the data from your disk arrays. It is very important that the disk subsystem not be fragmented, as this will slow down the backup client software's performance. If your disk subsystem can only deliver 2MB/sec (7.2GB/hour) of throughput, that is all you will ever achieve even if you have a Gigabit Ethernet–based network and 30 DLT 8000 tape units. Internal disk subsystem data paths were investigated in depth in chapter 6, and an example of sizing and tuning the disk subsystem taking backups into account was covered in detail in Scenario 1 above. Note that backing up from disk subsystems is typically faster than restoring. Review carefully the characteristics of the disk subsystem technology in use. Also, the density or number of files that must be backed up influences disk performance.

ZONE 2. THE TARGET SERVER TO BE BACKED UP

The target server to be backed up must have enough horsepower to read the data from the disk subsystem and transfer it onto the network, Zone 2. The backup application agent lives here and will transfer the backup data from the target server to the backup server application across the network.

ZONE 3. THE NETWORK MEDIUM

The network that the backed up data will traverse is your superhighway to the backup server and is commonly the limiting factor for backup performance. Network technology was investigated in depth in chapter 7; however, just as a refresher, Table 8.6 is a condensed version of one that appeared in chapter 7. Table 8.6 provides a quick frame of reference of the throughput that key network technologies can achieve in a Windows 2000 environment.

TABLE 8.6   *Zone 3: Backup Data Traversing Different Windows 2000 Network Technologies*

Network Technology	Throughput Megabits/sec	Throughput MB/sec	Throughput per Hour
Ethernet (10BaseT)	10	1.25	4.5GB/hour
Ethernet (100BaseT)	100	12.5	45.0GB/hour
FDDI	100	12.5	45.0GB/hour Note: Shared token technology—not a switched solution
Ethernet (Gigabit Ethernet/ 1000BaseTX/FL)	1000	125.0	450.0GB/hour
T1 (WAN)	1.544	0.193	695.0MB/hour

The information in Table 8.6 is based on theoretical throughputs; thus, the throughputs that you achieve will be slightly less due to protocol and application level overhead. Note that full duplex network technologies provide only a slight benefit to backup throughput over the network. This is due to the fact that a majority of the data flow is one way: to the backup server (for backups) or from the backup server (for restores).

Just because your backup server and target server to be backed up both have a 100BaseTX NIC, that does not guarantee that there is a full 100Mbits/sec link between the two. This is when having a strong understanding of your environment—specifically the network architecture—comes into the picture. Review the complete data path between your backup server and target servers and closely review the network workloads so that your network is not the bottleneck in your backup solution. Remember, you may have many clients to backup!

On some networks, Zone 3 can become so congested that it interferes with other production work. When this occurs, consider an alternate nonproduction network to be used exclusively for backups. Server Area Networks (SAN) technology is a leading approach to resolving these types of issues and enables backups to occur during business hours provided the backup application software supports backing up live data. SAN technology uses fibre channel technology to build a second network just for server-to-server traffic. This has obvious network benefits but also leverages I2O technology to off-load much of the backup workload from the systems themselves. SAN technology was reviewed in chapter 6. This technology is quickly maturing, but it is not always cost effective for all environments. If your budget allows you to implement a full-blown, SAN-based implementation, I highly recommend it. If you are on a tighter budget, consider the following SAN-like approach.

When your production network is either not fast enough or overwhelmed with production data, consider configuring a second Local Area Network (LAN) between your backup server and the systems that must be backed up. This helps you overcome limitations in the current network, reap SAN-like benefits, and avoid impairing production networks. From a Windows 2000 perspective, each system now is connected to two network subnets. Once configured, the new network configuration looks logically like Figure 8-2.

ZONE 4. WINDOWS 2000 BACKUP SERVER

The backup server must have enough horsepower to receive the data from the network, run the backup server software, and drive the backup system. Watch CPU, memory, SCSI throughput, and network performance closely. The backup server is where the backup application resides which communicates and coordinates backup operations with the backup agents residing on the servers targeted for backup.

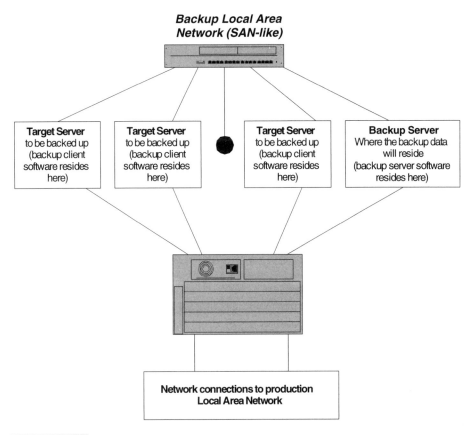

**Backup Local Area
Network (SAN-like)**

Target Server	Target Server	Target Server	Backup Server
to be backed up (backup client software resides here)	to be backed up (backup client software resides here)	to be backed up (backup client software resides here)	Where the backup data will reside (backup server software resides here)

**Network connections to production
Local Area Network**

FIGURE 8–2   *Windows 2000 Dedicated Backup LAN*

ZONE 5. BACKUP DEVICES

The backup server must place its backup data somewhere. There are numerous approaches to storing backup data—from fibre channel SAN-connected backup devices to SCSI-based backup devices. Since SCSI-based backup devices are more common, the focus here is on tape devices that support SCSI interfaces. Of course, the moment this is stated, someone reading this says, "This is not what I use." Perhaps not, but the concepts are just as important as the specific details!

So, how fast can backup devices operate? If tuned and sized well, with all zones optimized, they are very fast. Table 8.7 compares several different tape backup technologies. These are theoretical values; thus mileage will vary based on what is being backed up, SCSI protocol overhead, and your backup schedules.

TABLE 8.7	*Zone 5: Backup Device Capacity and Sustained Data Rates*

Backup Device Technology	Data Capacity per Tape Uncompressed/ Compressed GB	Throughput Uncompressed/ Compressed* MB/sec	Throughput Uncompressed/ Compressed GB/hour
Digital Linear Tape (DLT) 8000	40/80	6/12 (Estimated)	21.6/43.2 (Estimated)
Digital Linear Tape (DLT) 7000	35/70*	5/10	18/36
Digital Linear Tape (DLT) 4000	20/40	1.5/3	5.4/10.8
Digital Linear Tape (DLT) 2000	15/30	1.25/2.5	4.5/9
8mm, Exabyte 8900 Mammoth	20/40	3/6	10.8/21.6
4mm DDS 3	12/24	0.8/1.6	2.8/4.6

*Compression is based on a 2:1 ratio. How much compression is achievable greatly varies based on the type of data that is being compressed.

ZONE X. BACKUP APPLICATIONS

What is Zone X? It is not in Figure 8-1. Every backup application performs differently. Also, every backup application works differently, backing up specific applications (SQL, Exchange, file, etc.). Some excel at how user friendly they are or the number of operating systems and applications they can back up. My recommendation is that, once you have sized and tuned Zones 1 through 5, consider benchmarking several different backup applications in your specific environment and select the one that works best for you. In some environments, two different backup applications are needed to meet your goals.

Real-World Backup Performance

Every environment is different, but if you can find one similar to yours, the historical information is very helpful in sizing your solution or investigating why your backups are not running as well they should. Following are several real-world backup performance statistics shared with me by friends in the industry. Also included for reference are the corresponding theoretical throughput that each zone can achieve (obtained from tables throughout this book and shared here for your viewing pleasure so you do not have to hunt around for this information). Once the theoretical information is obtained for each zone, the lowest throughput is selected as the limiting factor for all zones that compose the backup solution.

Depending on your environment, mileage will vary from the values shown in Table 8.8. But using these backup zone matrices with theoretical and some real-world examples can aid in sizing and optimizing your Windows 2000 backup solution.

TABLE 8.8	Real-World Backup Rates

Example 1: Exchange Server Backup

Zone 1 Actual (Disk Subsystem)	Zone 2 Actual (Target Server)	Zone 3 Actual (LAN)	Zone 4 Actual (Backup Server)	Zone 5 Actual (Tape Backup Device[s])	Actual Backup/ Restore Rates GB/ hour
Exchange Server 5.5 Information Store housed on an 8-disk RAID 5 array	Dual Pentium III 550MHz XEON CPUs, 1GB RAM, 100BaseTX NIC	100BaseTX Dedicated Switched Network	Dual Pentium III 450MHz XEON CPUs, 512MB RAM, 100BaseTX NIC	Single DLT 7000 Tape Backup Device Connected to the backup server via its own dedicated Ultra2 SCSI channel	Backup: 30GB/ hour Restore: 18GB/ hour

Zone 1 Theoretical	Zone 2 Theoretical	Zone 3 Theoretical	Zone 4 Theoretical	Zone 5 Theoretical	Theoretical Backup/Restore Rate GB/hour (based on slowest zone)
Backup: 76GB/ hour Restore: 27.3GB/ hour (limiting factor)	Assume not a limiting factor	45GB/hour	Assume not a limiting factor	36GB/hour (limiting factor)	Backups: 31.9GB/ hour Restore: 27.3GB/ hour

Example 2: File Server Backup

Zone 1 Actual (Disk Subsystem)	Zone 2 Actual (Target Server)	Zone 3 Actual (LAN)	Zone 4 Actual (Backup Server)	Zone 5 Actual (Tape Backup Device[s])	Actual Backup/ Restore Rate GB/ hour
Windows NT 4 EE 360GB of data housed on two 10-disk RAID 5 arrays	Dual Pentium III 550MHz XEON CPUs, 2GB RAM, 1000BaseTX NIC	1000BaseTX Dedicated Switched Network	Dual Pentium III 450MHz XEON CPUs, 512MB RAM, 1000BaseTX NIC	Two DLT 7000 Tape Backup Devices Each Connected to the Backup Server via its own dedicated Ultra2 SCSI channel	Backup: 45GB/ hour Restore: 40GB/ hour

Zone 1 Theoretical	Zone 2 Theoretical	Zone 3 Theoretical	Zone 4 Theoretical	Zone 5 Theoretical	Theoretical Backup/Restore Rate GB/hour
Backup: 192GB/ hour Restore: 68.4GB/ hour	Assume not a limiting factor	450GB/hour	Assume not a limiting factor	72GB/hour (limiting factor)	Backups: 72GB/ hour Restore: 68.4GB/ hour

Sysmon Objects and Counters: Backup Server Bottleneck Detection and Sizing

The Sysmon objects and counters outlined in the previous chapters for CPU, memory, disk, and network subsystems are still applicable to Windows 2000 backup servers as it is important to understand the big picture when tuning or sizing backup solutions. In addition to the previously reviewed rules of thumb for bottleneck and sizing objects and counters, it is recommended that you become familiar with the ping.exe, tracert.exe, and pathping.exe commands. Since the network plays such an important part in a network-based backup server solution, consider running these tools on a regular basis to track your backup performance and alert you to any potential problems. Operation of these Windows 2000 tools was outlined in Chapter 7. Many advanced third-party network tools are available to track the performance of your network. Two vendors that provide these tools are Concord (http://www.Concord.com) and Visual Networks (http://www.VisualNetworks.com).

It is helpful to understand the behavior of the backup application processes running on your backup server for ongoing, proactive tuning and sizing. If you do not know which background service is your backup application, use the tlist.exe command run from the command line to determine which processes are associated with the backup application. The backup application can then be monitored using Task Manager and Sysmon, as outlined in chapter 2.

Scenario 2 Step by Step: Mid-Range Windows 2000 Backup Server

Sizing the Initial Backup Server Configuration

In chapter 3, the core sizing methodology was presented for sizing your Windows 2000 solution. That methodology is followed here for the development of the initial Windows 2000 Server configuration.

1. DEFINE OBJECTIVE(S)

Develop a network-based backup server solution to support current file servers and potentially additional systems over time. Above, we developed two file servers for Acme Rockets. Well, Acme Rockets merged with Ajax systems to form Ajax Rockets. This merger resulted in both companies consolidating into the same office building, adding four file servers to the two servers that we configured in the file server scenario above. Luckily for us these new file servers were configured identically to our original two; they must have read the same book.

We now have six file servers that each support 100GB of on-line storage. With this increased capacity, each file server's storage capacity is planned to expand to 200GB of data by the end of two years. This data will need to be backed up on a regular basis to mitigate the risk of losing valuable company data.

2. UNDERSTAND BUSINESS AND TECHNICAL REQUIREMENTS NEEDED TO MEET YOUR OBJECTIVE(S)

- Which application(s) will meet your functional objective(s)?
  Legato is selected as the backup server application for our solution since the new company already licensed it.
- What are the availability requirements?
  These are important servers that will be backed up, as they will support the entire company.
  Backups must be completed nightly (after 8:00 P.M. and before 6:00 A.M., about eight hours) and the system must be restored to service within four hours, if cost effective. If it is not cost effective to restore the servers in this time period, up to an eight-hour restore to service is acceptable.
  The backup server itself is considered important, but if it fails, it is sufficient to have it back in service the next business day.
- What are the ramifications if your system is down?
  It is important to keep a high availability Monday through Friday, but planned weekend maintenance is acceptable.
- What are the disk subsystem storage capacity requirements?
  Disk storage capacity that the backup server must support internally: the Windows 2000 operating system, the backup application, and the backup index database that tracks the backups on the backup devices tape media.

3. DETERMINE LOADING CHARACTERISTICS

- *Number of total users per server*
  For our examples, a user here is a target server that must be backed up. There are six servers to be backed up.
- *Number of concurrent users per server*
  All six servers will need to be backed up incrementally each evening, with a full backup every weekend. So our concurrency is six.

- *Disk workload characteristics (read/write environment)*
  For the target servers that must be backed up, backups are primarily sequential and read intensive while restore operations are the inverse, sequential and write intensive. Because of this, we must factor in the different performance characteristics of the target server's disk subsystems for both the backup and restore operations.

  For the backup server itself, many backup applications keep a local database to index the backup tapes so that the application can find what it is searching for on the tape backups. These backup application database files are very important and must be backed up as well as reside on a fast disk subsystem that includes fault tolerance. Unless running a restoration process, these operations are typically write intensive.

- *Size of records/transactions*
  The backup application will use the largest block size that the Windows 2000 backup and target servers will support. Throughput is important in backup server environments. How fast can files be read or written to the target servers and the backup server? Fast enough so they can meet your business goals.

- *Physical location of users (Influences communications such as WAN, LAN, dial-up, terminal services, etc.)*
  All servers reside on site and are connected via the local switched Ethernet 100BaseTX LAN. After closely reviewing the current network architecture, the file servers are on different subnets (i.e., a routing device separates them). The plan is to place the backup server in the same network switch as one of the file servers.

- *Type of work the user will complete*
  Backup system operations.

4. DETERMINE PERFORMANCE REQUIREMENTS

From a performance perspective, throughput is the most important factor for a backup solution. The goal is to run backup operations during each evening and be able to restore the backup data within four hours, if cost effective. Based on current business requirements' worst-case scenarios, 600GB of aggregated data from across the target servers must be backed up in 12 hours and restored in 4 hours. For backups, this translates to 50GB per hour and 150GB per hour for restores! Quite speedy.

5. UNDERSTAND FUTURE BUSINESS REQUIREMENTS

As this is a public company, growth is very important and the company does expect to expand by at least 20% each year.

6. UNDERSTAND FUTURE SYSTEM ARCHITECTURES

The local team would like to put a system in quickly and would like it to run without replacement for three years. Local support staff is still small, which is just unheard of in the IT industry.

Since no one wants to change tapes, an automated tape library will attach to the backup server. Overall, 600GB of data must be backed up. If we assume a compression ratio of 2:1, then each DLT 7000 tape can store 70GB and nine tapes are required for a full backup. Due to Ajax Rockets' backup policy, one set is always kept off site, and four weeks of full backups must be kept. This would result in a scenario where 45 DLT 7000 tape cartridges are required, with the automated tape supporting at least 36 tape cartridges (one set is always kept off site). If the compression ratios are found to be less than 2:1 during testing, a larger tape library will be required.

7. CONFIGURE THE SYSTEM

Finally, to the good stuff. At this point, you can configure the backup server. Choose the system resources required in meeting your objective, with consideration for steps 1 through 6, and obtain the system. As you configure the system, look at each individual resource to meet the overall system configuration. Software and hardware vendors are good sources of information. They can suggest configurations that will get you started. Reviewing relevant industry benchmarks also can help provide insight into the initial configuration. The following steps are presented to help guide you through the actual system configuration process.

Having some sort of idea of how each system resource works and relates to the overall system performance is helpful when configuring your system. Chapters 4 through 7 review the overall system architecture of each system resource in greater detail.

7.1 APPLICATION CHARACTERISTICS REVIEW • The general backup application characteristics and backup technology review was completed at the top of the Windows 2000 Backup Server section.

7.2 REVIEW EACH SYSTEM RESOURCE (FOR THE BACKUP SERVER)

Backup Devices • Note: New addition to the basic sizing methodology due to the unique requirements of a backup server.

Backup Device Selection • How can you determine how many backup devices are needed? Consider both the performance of your backup devices and the capacity of the backup media you will need. First we will look at the performance requirements, as faster backup devices typically have corresponding higher density backup media capacity, which lowers the number of tape cartridges that are needed.

Based on current business requirements' worst-case scenarios, 600GB must be backed up in 12 hours and restored in 4 hours. For backups, this translates to 50GB per hour and 150GB per hour for restores. If a compression ratio of 2:1 is assumed—and considering that the DLT 7000 supports 36GB/hour of throughput—five to six DLT tape backup units would be required to meet our business needs. DLT units are not inexpensive. After a discussion of costs with the local business management team, it was decided that a restore-to-service in six hours would be acceptable. This lowers our throughput restoration requirement to 100GB/hour, which can be met by four DLT 7000s (144GB/hour).

SCSI Configuration • The DLT 7000 tape backup units and the automated robotic library are both Ultra2 SCSI-based. Each backup device should have its own SCSI channel for optimum performance. Why? Each DLT 7000 operates at approximately 10MB/sec or 36GB/hour; however, don't be fooled into thinking you can just chain these together to fill the 80MB/sec bandwidth available from an Ultra2 SCSI channel. Tape units are physical devices. Every time a tape unit must be stopped or started, its overall performance is lowered. Keeping a continuous stream of data fed into the tape unit is critical. When multiple tape units share the same SCSI channel, there is a high degree of probability that SCSI commands destined for one tape unit may slow the operation of other tape units on the same SCSI channel. This same concept is applicable to the control signals that are sent to the robotic arm of the tape library that automatically changes tapes in and out of the DLT drives. Optimally, each DLT 7000 and the tape library's robotic arm have their own SCSI channel. In a worst-case scenario, configure two DLT 7000 tape units on the same Ultra2 SCSI channel, but always have a dedicated SCSI channel for the robotic arm!

Disk I/O Requirements • The primary disk requirements for the backup server are that it support Windows 2000 (operating system and pagefile) and the backup server application (application installation and location for the backup metadatabase).

Availability • Since this is an important server, all data will reside on hot swappable RAID array-based disk subsystems that use some level of fault tolerance.

Performance Workload Characteristics • Intense disk activity is not expected, but fast response to the disk subsystem that houses the backup application's tracking database is expected.

Performance Throughput and Transfers/sec • A significant disk subsystem performance for the backup server itself is not required. The backup devices are another story, however, and are reviewed above.

Storage Capacity • Storage requirements tend to grow over time for the backup application's database. The rate of growth varies from vendor to vendor. For our scenario, we expect it will not grow past 4GB. A pair of 9GB 10,000rpm disk drives in a RAID Level 1 mirror will meet our capacity and fault tolerance requirements.

Other Disk Requirements • Are there any other applications that require disk space? For our Backup Server example, we still need to place Windows 2000 and the backup application binary executables somewhere. From previous discussions, it was shown that you never want to place the operating system and pagefile on a RAID 5 array for both operating system and performance reasons. Due to the availability requirements, the operating system and backup application will be placed on the same RAID 1 Mirror comprising two 9GB disk drives configured with one Windows 2000 logical partition. The pagefile will be placed on this same RAID 1 Mirror in an effort to lower costs (vs. placing the pagefile on its own dedicated high-speed drive, which is preferred).

CPU Requirements • The primary application to support is the backup application service. CPU workload involves supporting the backup application and network operations and driving the backup devices, some disk operations, and the associated logging and security checking of customers' rights. This is very similar to the Windows 2000 File Server scenario, but instead of driving the disk subsystem, the CPUs are driving intense network activities and backup device operations (in this case, 4 DLT 7000s).

After searching for an industry standard benchmark for backup performance and coming up empty, a combination of vendor white papers, lab testing, and historical information was used to assist in sizing the CPU requirements for backup servers. Compaq (http://www.compaq.com) and Quantum (http://www.quantum.com) both have various white papers on backup server performance. When I checked, these performance results were based on older Pentium Pro technology, but are still applicable. Perhaps updates will arrive shortly. For the interim, recall from chapter 3 that two Pentium Pro CPUs provide roughly the same performance as a single Pentium III CPU. My own historical information and testing demonstrate that two Pentium III 450MHz CPUs easily drove two DLT 7000 tape units with less than 35% of total CPU usage. From these white papers, historical information, and lab tests completed on backups, a single Pentium III–class CPU can drive two DLT 7000 tape units. Since our solution requires four DLT 7000 units and a Gigabit Ethernet card, two CPUs should suffice.

Memory Requirements • Sizing RAM is an additive process. Our first step in sizing memory resources is to outline all applications that will use any memory resources.

TABLE 8.9	*Sizing CPU Resources for Backup Servers*	
Application		**CPU Usage (Estimate)**
Windows 2000 operation system requirement		10%
Network Operations		30%
Overhead for system management software running on server		1%
Overhead for intrusion detection software		1%
Backup Server Application and driving the four DLT 7000 units		70%
CPU needed per target backup server connection		Included in backup server overhead
Total Estimated CPU Usage		***111% (2 CPUs)***

So what amount of memory should be configured? Memory usage is an additive process and it is used here primarily to cache backup requests in memory until the requests are placed into one of the four tape backup units. From Table 8.10 and from what we have learned from our Windows 2000 memory usage investigations, adding more than 590MB is unlikely to help this backup server configuration, because Windows 2000 limits its file system cache usage to 432MB when less than 1GB of RAM is in the server. From this information and the fact that the physical server hardware supports memory in 512MB DIMM sets, 512MB should handle the workload. Through proactive performance management, more RAM can be added as needed, but for now, let's save a few dollars and not overconfigure the server.

TABLE 8.10	*Backup Server Memory Sizing Matrix*	
Application		**Memory Usage (Working Set)**
Windows 2000 operating system requirement		128MB
Windows 2000 File System cache (max for configurations less than 1GB in size)		432MB
Overhead for system management software running on server		8MB
Overhead for intrusion detection software		12MB
Backup Server application		10MB
Memory needed per target Backup Server connection		Included in file system cache overhead
Total Estimated Memory Usage		***590MB***

Network I/O Requirements • During the most intense portion of the backup solution, the backup server will need to support 75GB/hour (600GB/8 hours to backup) of sustained throughput that the six file servers will be providing. A 100baseTX network can only support 45GB/hour, so a single 100BaseTX NIC is out. We could trunk multiple 100BaseTX cards, but the current network switch environment does not support that technology. Based on this, the backup server is configured with a 1000BaseTX NIC, which will support 450GB/hour. Some room to grow! This takes care of the network connection into the backup server, but what about the path between the target backup servers and the backup server?

To determine this, trace the network path between each targeted backup and the backup server. If there are any conflicts where multiple target servers must share the same 100BaseTX switch, our backup rate will slow and we will not meet our business requirement backup and restore times. For this environment, three servers are on one 100BaseTX switch, four servers on another 100BaseTX where the backup server also resides. Since there is only a single 100BaseTX link between the two switches, this creates a network bottleneck for our backups. To resolve this situation, a second network switch with 12 100BaseTX ports and two Gigabit Ethernet connections is needed to form a second network (pseudo-SAN) that will be dedicated for backups. This backup server LAN will connect all target servers directly with the backup server via 100BaseTX connections and 1000BaseTX connection to the backup server. It will also use private addressing (10.x.x.x) to ensure this LAN does not affect other portions of Ajax Rocket's IT architecture.

7.3 SYSTEM ARCHITECTURE RELATIONSHIP CHECK • This is a final, common-sense check of the Windows 2000 Server configuration. Since the business requirements require keeping this new backup server for at least three years, leading-edge server technology will be obtained. Not cutting edge, as that technology tends to demand a premium price.

From all of the sizing information above, we now have the following configuration: a one- to two-CPU-capable server, two Pentium III 800MHz CPUs with 512KB of full speed (ATC) Level 2 cache, a 133MHz System Bus, 512MB of RAM, a single 64-bit 33MHz PCI I/O bus, a single hardware-based RAID controller, two disk drives for the operating system, two disk drives for the backup index metadatabase, two quad Ultra2 SCSI adapters, four DLT 7000 tape units, one 36-tape unit robotic library, and one Gigabit Ethernet NIC.

There is a potential problem with this configuration in the I/O subsystem. A single 64-bit 32MHz PCI bus can only support 266MB/sec of throughput. The Gigabit Ethernet Card can drive 125MB/sec, and having four 80MB/sec SCSI channels active (about 144MB/sec) will potentially overwhelm the single PCI bus (269MB/sec). For the backup server, a dual peer PCI server is needed to increase overall I/O throughput. Moving up to a higher power server moves us up to a platform that will support up to four CPUs.

An example server that would support this configuration is the Compaq ML-580. Compaq ML-580 has two peer PCI buses and supports up to four CPUs if it is ever needed.

Backup Zone Checking: Final Sanity Check for Backup Server Sizing

To determine the performance of the backup solution needed to meet your business goals and to ensure you did not miss an important consideration (that is why empty templates are posted on http://www.TuningAndSizingNT.com), review the backup zone approach outline above and repeated here. After reviewing the throughput that each zone can provide, ensure the slowest zone will not stop you from achieving your goals.

TABLE 8.11	*Scenario 2 Windows 2000 Backup Server Sizing Zones Analysis*

Scenario 2: Sizing a Windows 2000 Backup Server

Zone 1 Actual (disk subsystem)	Zone 2 Actual (target server)	Zone 3 Actual (LAN)	Zone 4 Actual (backup server)	Zone 5 Actual (tape backup device[s])	Theoretical backup/restore rates GB/hour
Target file server to be backed up File system to be backed up resides on two 9-disk RAID 5 disk arrays.	Dual Pentium III 550MHz XEON CPUs, 512MB RAM, 100BaseTX NIC*	100BaseTX NIC* for each target server 1000BaseTX* NIC for backup server	Dual Pentium III 550MHz XEON CPUs, 512MB RAM, 1000BaseTX NIC*, 2 Quad SCSI adapters	Four DLT 7000 tape backup devices (36GB/hour each; 144GB/hour total) Connected to the backup server via its own dedicated Ultra2 SCSI channels (80MB/sec per channel)	
Backup: 6 servers (1038GB/hour) (173GB/hour per server)	Proactively tuned not to be a bottleneck	270GB/hour (45GB/hour per server)	450GB/hour	Backup: 144GB/hour (Limiting factor)	Backup: 144GB/hour
Restore: 6 servers (361GB/hour) (61GB/hour per server) Number of Servers: 6 (limiting factor)				Restore: 144GB/hour	Restore: 144GB/hour

*Note: For backup/restore operations, the NIC is primarily operating in half duplex mode.

7.4 FUTURE BUSINESS AND SYSTEM ARCHITECTURES CHECK REVIEW • This server has room to grow—two more CPUs can be added, disks can be dynamically added to the external disk arrays, RAM can be expanded to 4GB, additional DLT units can be added to the three unused SCSI channels, and the NICs can be upgraded to trunked Gigabit Ethernet.

7.5 INITIAL HARDWARE CONFIGURATION AND TUNING • In this step, the initial configuration of the server hardware begins to take shape based on steps 7.1 and 7.2. See the Sizing and Tuning File Servers section below as needed.

TABLE 8.12	*Backup Server Hardware Configuration Data*

Windows 2000 Backup Server Hardware Configuration
Compaq DL-580 (Why select the DL-580? We needed a solid system to use for a real-world reference.)

CPU Configuration	*CPUs Used in Solution*	*CPU Family*	*Level 2 Cache Size*	*Speed of CPU*	*Available CPU Slots*		
	2	Intel Pentium III	512KB	700MHz	2 of 4 available		
RAM Configuration	*Amount of RAM Used in Solution*	*System Bus Speed*	*Type of RAM*	*RAM Expansion*			
	512MB	100MHz	ECC SDRAM	8GB			
I/O Subsystem Configuration	*Number and Type of IO Card*	*Number of PCI I/O Buses*	*Placement of PCI Cards*		*Speed of PCI Bus*		
	2 Four-Channel Ultra2 SCSI Adapters	2	Both SCSI cards are placed into PCI bus 0, in the two top slots.		Two (2) 64-bit 33MHz		
	1 Single-Channel Full Duplex 1000BaseTX	2	The 1000BaseTX NIC is placed in the first slot of PCI bus1.				
Disk Subsystem Configuration	*Partition/ Mount Point*	*Files Located There*	*Type of RAID Adapter*	*SCSI Channel*	*RAID Level*	*# Of 10K RPM Ultra2 Disk Drives*	
	C:	Windows 2000 installation, pagefile	Built in RAID Adapter Compaq	1 of 2	1	2	
	G:	Backup Application index database	Built in RAID Adapter Compaq	1 of 2	1	2	

7.6 INITIAL SOFTWARE CONFIGURATION AND TUNING • In this step, the initial software configuration of the server configuration begins to take shape based on steps 7.1 and 7.2. See the Tuning Backup Servers section below.

7.7 INITIAL GENERAL TUNING • See the Tuning Backup Servers section below.

8. STRESS TEST AND VALIDATE THE SERVER CONFIGURATION

For this scenario, historical information, lab tests, and vendor white papers were relied upon to develop the backup server configuration. The backup servers were moved into production and tested over the weekend. Business goals were met.

9. PROACTIVELY FOLLOW THE CORE TUNING METHODOLOGY DURING STRESS AND VALIDATION TESTING

This approach was followed and a baseline was developed.

10. DEPLOY THE SYSTEM INTO PRODUCTION

This was a real scenario, and the backup server system was deployed successfully. Expecting something else?

11. PROACTIVELY FOLLOW THE TUNING METHODOLOGY AFTER THE SYSTEM IS DEPLOYED

Environments do change. The information gathered following the core tuning methodology is helpful for staying one step in front of user demand by identifying current load demands and potential system bottlenecks. This information is also helpful when developing and sizing future system solutions and when adding additional capacity to your current system(s). If you have not determined where and how to add additional capacity to your system, you are in great risk of wasting your time.

Backup Server Sizing Configuration Chart Summary

Even though every environment is different, the following backup server configuration chart provides sound sizing guidelines on which to base your initial server configurations. Follow the sizing template above to custom fit the solution to your environment and then proactively manage your Windows 2000 backup server to an optimal fit!

Note: It is important to understand that as we scale each system, a balanced approach is taken between all server resources so that no artificial bottlenecks are created before the backup server is even deployed.

TABLE 8.13	*Specific Configurations for Sizing Backup Servers*				
Backup Server Size based on tape units supported	**System Bus Speed**	**Number of PCI I/O Buses**	**Pentium III 800MHz Class CPU**	**RAM**	**Network Interface Card (NIC)**
Small Scale 1–2 DLT 7000	133MHz	1	1 (256KB Level 2 Cache)	256MB	100BaseTX
Mid-Level Scale 2–4 DLT 7000	100MHz	2	1–2 (512KB Level 2 Cache)	512MB	100BaseTX Full Duplex
Enterprise Scale 4–8	100MHz	2	2–4 (1MB Level 2 Cache)	1–2GB	1–2 100BaseTX Full Duplex NICs (channels) teamed/trunked together or Gigabit Ethernet

Windows 2000 Backup Server Tuning Summary

Backup Server–Specific Application Tuning

In general, apply the previous tuning recommendations for file servers directly to backup servers. Where there is either an important distinction from a tuning and/or configuration perspective, they are noted below. Here, tuning is reviewed from the perspective of Windows 2000 and the hardware platform, since there are so many different backup programs available today. Most backup applications work with the same concepts, but it is paramount that you understand the backup application itself and its agents, if they are in use. If not properly configured, the backup application itself can introduce a bottleneck. Many backup applications have various degrees of parallelism and have numerous settings that directly affect performance. Know your backup application! Search vendor web sites and ask your sales representative for white papers on performance and their application for optimum settings.

> *For the hands-on specifics of why, when, and how these tuning recommendations work and steps to implement them, refer back to the subsequent tuning sections in the previous chapters. Here, select examples are provided to give you a jump-start into an optimized Windows 2000 backup solution!*

BACKUP SERVER HARDWARE TUNING

The previous file server hardware tuning scenario above is directly applicable. In addition to the information in that section, consider the following specific recommendations for backup servers.

- Dedicate a SCSI channel for each tape backup unit.
- Dedicate a SCSI channel to control the tape library's robotic arm, if one is in use.
- Use the highest speed SCSI channel possible (see chapter 5 for SCSI technology discussions and investigations).
- Ensure the latest SCSI and tape unit drivers are in use and locally tested before introduction into production, of course!
- Use Storage Area Network (SAN) technology if possible.
- Use a second backup LAN if needed.

BACKUP APPLICATION TUNING

- Configure the application correctly!
- Use client compression if available (assuming sufficient CPU resources on target server to be backed up are available).
- Review running multiple backup jobs/streams at the same time if your servers and clients support it. This improves overall throughput to the backup devices. Stopping and starting the tape backup unit slows its overall performance. Keep the tape units fed.
- Overcommit the number of backup streams per tape backup device by at least 20%. This will help keep the backup application's buffers full, which ensures a continuous stream of data is presented to the tape backup device. Continuous data flows to the tape backup device help it to run at its optimal speed. Remember, every time a tape backup device must stop and wait for data, even for a moment, overall throughput provided is reduced dramatically.
- Closely watch the backup application's local backup index database it uses to track where backups are kept on the backup media. This database may need its own RAID 1 or RAID 10 array under intense workloads.

WINDOWS 2000 CPU SUBSYSTEM RESOURCE TUNING

Key CPU-related tuning you should consider:

- Set application response to favor background processes (Start / Settings / Control Panel / System / Advanced / Performance Options / Set Background Services).
- Off-load I/O-intensive CPU operations to I2O-enabled I/O adapters.
- Since multiple CPUs are in use with multiple NIC and SCSI adapters, consider using the Microsoft Interrupt-Affinity Filter Control Tool

(IntFiltr; see chapter 4) to ensure interrupts are properly distributed between NICs and CPUs.

- Log off the server to ensure security and ensure no CPU cycles are wasted on your login session.
- If you do not log off, do not use a 3GL or any other fancy screen savers because they consume significant CPU resources.
- Check all services running on your server. Operate only those you need and stop all others.
- Avoid running another CPU-intensive application on your backup server.

WINDOWS 2000 MEMORY SUBSYSTEM RESOURCE TUNING

Key memory-related tuning you should consider:
- Check the Windows 2000 memory management strategy. Backup servers rely heavily on the file system cache. By default, the Windows 2000 file system cache is optimized for Maximize Data Throughput for file sharing. However, check this setting anyway at Start / Programs / Settings / Network and Dial Up Connections / Properties of your LAN adapter / File and Print Sharing for Microsoft Networks.
- Check all services running on your server. Operate only those you need and stop all others. Every running service consumes precious memory resources.
- Set the pagefile size to twice the amount of RAM in your server and to a fixed size.
- Never place the pagefile on a RAID 5 array.
- If your system must page (which should be avoided), consider multiple pagefiles on physically separate disk drives which are all configured to the exact same size.
- Force Windows 2000 to keep the Windows 2000 executive (kernel) from paging any of its executive system drivers to disk and ensure that they are immediately available if needed (see chapter 5).
- Do not use a 3GL or other fancy screen saver.
- Do not use exotic wallpaper; it wastes memory resources.

WINDOWS 2000 DISK SUBSYSTEM RESOURCE TUNING

Key disk subsystem–related tuning you should consider:
- Bigger block sizes are best when trying to increase the throughput to tape backup devices. Increase the native transfer size for the SCSI buses connecting to the tape devices. The registry entry is specified on a per-bus basis, and the REG_DWORD value within HKEY_LOCAL_MACHINE is: System\CurrentControlSet\Services\ DriverName\ Parameters\Devicen\MaximumSGList. The DriverName is the name of the miniport driver, such as AIC78XX, and n in Devicen is the bus number

assigned at initialization. If a value is present in this subkey at device initialization, the SCSI port driver uses MaximumSGList as the initial maximum for scatter/gather list elements. The miniport can lower this value. The maximum value for this key is 255. What this means is that the miniport must support the higher value, and if it does you will be able to do transfers of up to 1020KB.

- Defragment your disk subsystem on a regular basis; this will result in significant performance improvements!
- Perform a fresh, low-level format on all disk drives at the lowest level using the disk or RAID adapter you are using.
- Freshly format all disk drives with NTFS when installing Windows 2000.
- When formatting the disk drive with NTFS (target servers and the backup server itself), select the ALU size that best matches your disk workload characteristics. For scenario 1, the recommended ALU is 64KB, as the workload is based on large file size.
- Turn on write-back caching and read-ahead caching on hardware RAID adapters.
- Use only I2O-enabled RAID adapters and those with their own CPUs.
- Keep storage capacity on the disk subsystem under 60–80% so that the fastest portion of the disk drive is used and so that there is room on the disk drives to perform defragmentation.
- Defragment your disk subsystem on a regular basis; this will result in significant performance improvements!
- Use one Windows 2000 partition per physical disk device/array.
- Check all services running on your server. Operate only those you need and stop all others.

WINDOWS 2000 NETWORK SUBSYSTEM RESOURCE TUNING

Key network subsystem–related tuning you should consider:

- Teaming/trunking multiple NICs (Ethernet channels) together as needed to add network bandwidth to your Windows 2000 server.
- Balance network activity across NICs if you cannot use NIC teaming/trunking technologies.
- If possible, use jumbo packets on your network, especially for dedicated backup networks.
- Remove all unnecessary protocols and Redirectors.
- Standardize on one network protocol: TCP/IP.
- If more than one network protocol is in use, set binding order such that the most commonly used protocol is first on the list.
- Tune the NIC driver to off-load IPSEC security operations and TCP operations on the NIC itself instead of the main system CPUs.
- Tune the NIC driver to increase its send and receive buffers.

- Use only I2O-enabled NICs.
- Use the fastest I/O bus-enabled NIC possible (64-bit, 66MHz PCI slot).
- Tune the Windows TCP/IP stack to your environment (TCP Hash Table, MTU Window Size). (Review the IIS 5.0 Solution Scenario for details on how to accomplish this.)
- Do not use autodetect for your NIC. Set it to the best performance level the internetwork devices will support. For example: 100BaseTX Full Duplex.

Solution Scenario 3: Windows 2000 Exchange Servers

Introduction

Messaging servers have become the heart of many traditional and eBusinesses alike. As one of today's most commonly used applications, many have come to rely on it like they do the telephone. People expect messaging systems to always be available and to run fast.

Application Description

Microsoft Exchange is a scalable and robust messaging platform that has rapidly matured over the past several years. From a performance perspective, instead of thinking of this application as a mail and collaborative computing platform, consider it an advanced database system with a messaging application residing on top of it.

Application Performance Characterization

When we understand how an application operates, we can then correlate its operations with the performance concepts we have learned from the earlier chapters. The whole world is not quite "point and click" yet. There are several performance areas of an Exchange platform to consider at the most basic level. First, Exchange provides directory structure and directory information; e.g., e-mail address information for the people in your Exchange sites. This involves looking directory information up in Exchange itself (if in a Windows NT environment) or looking up addresses via Active Directory if you are in a Windows 2000 environment. Directory information is stored in the directory services (DS) database, which typically exhibits random performance characteristics.

Two more basic functions that Exchange provides are storage and delivery of e-mail. When e-mail arrives at the Exchange server, it is placed into buffers in memory. Then it is placed into the transaction log (EDB.log), committed to the exchange message store by placing it into the Private Information Store's buffers, and finally into the Private Information Store's database. These steps are very important to remember, as they illustrate the importance of tuning and sizing memory and disk resources. We will need to configure enough memory to support all of the caching Exchange will need, a fast disk subsystem optimized for the sequential and write-intensive log files, and one to support the information store which is very random in nature and supports a good split of read and write operations. If you are using public folders (Public Information Store), consider it another database to manage with workload characteristics similar to that of the private information store.

It is highly recommended that the Exchange log files and information store databases be kept on different disk subsystems for improved performance and reliability.

Of course, you will want a fast, low-latency network for your customers to access the Exchange server and enough CPU horsepower to drive the overall solution.

The final performance consideration is the transfer of the e-mail messages either internally, for addresses inside the Exchange site, or externally, to the Internet via the Exchange Internet Mail connector. These messages are first placed into the delivery or send transactions logs to track their status.

Table 8.14 shows a summary of Exchange's key components.

TABLE 8.14	*Exchange Database Component Descriptions*

Exchange Database Components	**Exchange Database Component Descriptions and Characterizations**
Private Information Store	This component is a database, which maintains all messages in users' mailboxes, enforces storage limits, and delivers messages to users on the same server. Disk workload is characterized as random in nature.
Public Information Store	This component is a database that maintains information stored in public folders and replicates public folders as required. Disk workload is characterized as random in nature.
Information Store Logs	This component records all information store transactions. Disk workload is characterized as sequential and write intensive in nature.
Directory Service Logs	This component records all directory store transactions. Disk workload is characterized as sequential and write intensive in nature.
Directory Service	This component maintains information about an organization's recipients, servers, and messaging infrastructure. It is an implementation of the directory services standard that is roughly defined by the ISO X.500 specification except the entire directory is automatically replicated to all servers in the organization instead of portions being distributed among the servers as in X.500. The Directory Service is used by the other three core components to map addresses and route messages. Disk workload is characterized as random in nature.

TABLE 8.14	Exchange Database Component Descriptions (Continued)

Exchange Database Components	Exchange Database Component Descriptions and Characterizations
Message Transfer Agent	This component is responsible for moving messages between Information Stores, connectors, and third-party gateways. It is the service that performs the actual routing, submission and delivery of messages. Disk workload characterized as random in nature.

Sysmon Objects and Counters: Exchange Server Health, Bottleneck Detection, Tuning, and Sizing

The Sysmon objects and counters outlined in the previous chapters for CPU, memory, disk, and network subsystems are still applicable to Windows 2000 Exchange servers as it is important to understand the big picture when tuning or sizing messaging solutions. If one server resource becomes a bottleneck (i.e., queues begin to form in the CPU or disk subsystem), response time to the end user begins to suffer and message queues in the Exchange Server application begin to grow.

In addition to the previously reviewed rules of thumb for bottleneck and sizing objects and counters, it is recommended that you become familiar with the following Sysmon objects and counters that are added to Sysmon when Exchange is installed. These objects and counters—shown in Table 8.15—are helpful in determining the health of your Exchange server application and for tuning and sizing.

TABLE 8.15	Sleuthing Out Microsoft Exchange Specific Health, Tuning, and Sizing Information

Object: Counter	Definition	Value to Monitor
MSExchangeMTA: Work Queue Length	How many items are waiting for processing at the message transfer agent (MTA).	Health indicator and bottleneck detection The work queue length should be less than 1% of the users the Exchange server supports. It should also not grow over time. If it is > 1%, or growing for a significant amount of time, either a bottleneck is forming or another subsystem or external system is running slow or is not available.
MSExchange IS Private: Send Queue Size (also public if used)	The send queue size provides insight into how many requests to send messages are currently queued for delivery.	Health indicator and bottleneck detection The average send queue length should be less than 1% of the users the Exchange server supports. It should also not grow over time. If it is > 1%, or growing for a significant amount of time, either a bottleneck is forming or another subsystem is running slow. In the most optimally configured servers, this value is close to zero even under heavy loads!

Object: Counter	Definition	Value to Monitor
MSExchange IS Private:Average Time for Delivery	How long it takes for the IS to deliver a message.	Health indicator and bottleneck detection Baseline this value for your environment to determine what is acceptable. Once you baseline this value, if it begins to consistently grow to higher levels, a bottleneck is forming. Note, this counter collects information in the format of tens of milliseconds; hence a counter of 100 corresponds to 1 second.
MSExchange: IMC Internet Mail Connector in queues outbound	The send queue size provides insight into how many requests to send messages are currently queued.	Health indicator and bottleneck detection The average send queue length should be less than 1% of the users the Exchange server supports. It also should not grow over time. If it does, numerous problems could exist such as Domain Name Service (DNS) problems, issues with your Internet network connection, or a remote mail system that is down.
MSExchange Database Information Store (IS) and Directory Store (DS): Cache % Hit & Database Session hit ratio	This counter displays the percentage of message information that was found in the IS cache in memory that fulfilled the request vs. going to IS database on the physical disk subsystem.	Influences tuning and sizing The higher these values are, the better. The more you can cache in memory, the faster your Exchange server will be while lowering the workload on the disk subsystem housing the Information Store and Directory Store (DS). If you do not have a high hit rate (>90%), consider adding additional RAM and rerunning the Exchange Optimizer to improve the situation.
MSExchangeIS: Active User Count	How many users have done something in the last 10 minutes.	Influences sizing and tuning This counter comes closest to indicating the concurrent user rate on your Exchange server.
MSExchangeIS: User Count	How many users have logged on since the service has been restarted.	Influences sizing and tuning This counter takes some close tracking. Since it is a cumulative number, if your goal is to review usage over a week, the IS must be stopped and restarted at the start time (not realistic) or you must write down the start value and review it later in the week.
MSExchange IS Private: Messages Submitted/min and Messages Recipients/min	How many messages per minute are being sent and received.	Influences sizing and tuning This information is a good indicator of how much workload your Exchange server is experiencing. This can be helpful information for load balancing customers across multiple exchange servers in your site.

Microsoft provides a number of statistics through Sysmon for monitoring the performance of Exchange servers, but Sysmon counters do not provide every aspect of detailed instrumentation data. Critical data are also available in the Exchange Tracking Logs and the Windows 2000 Event Logs.

Scenario 3 Step by Step: Sizing a Mid-Range (3,000 User) Windows 2000 Exchange Server

Sizing the Initial Exchange Server Configuration

In chapter 3, the core sizing methodology was presented for sizing your Windows 2000 solution. That methodology is followed here for the development of the initial Windows 2000 Exchange server configuration.

1. DEFINE OBJECTIVE(S)

Ajax Rockets has decided to collapse the two different mail systems they have into one unified messaging system based on Microsoft Exchange. Next to payroll and their customer engineering application, e-mail is the most important application that they run and must be always available and very responsive.

2. UNDERSTAND BUSINESS AND TECHNICAL REQUIREMENTS NEEDED TO MEET YOUR OBJECTIVE(S)

- Which application(s) will meet your functional objective(s)?
  Microsoft Exchange 5.5 will be the messaging platform. However, it is also important to consider that Exchange 2000 will be considered once Windows 2000 Active Directory is in place.
- What are the availability requirements?
  These are critical servers, as they will support the entire company. The goal is to have a highly available solution. This is a high-profile, business-critical application. Backups must be completed nightly (after 9:00 P.M. and before 5:00 A.M., about eight hours) and the system must be restorable to service within four hours.
- What are the ramifications if your system is down?
  Similar to a denial of service attack, downtime will slow down many work projects and it is considered unacceptable.
- What are the disk subsystem storage capacity requirements?
  Currently there are 3,000 e-mail customers at Ajax Rockets who use approximately 20GB of storage in their mail server. This works out to approximately 7MB per user. The current plan is to have each customer keep all mail local on his or her desktop/laptop and use the mail server as a post office using Microsoft Outlook clients (with the

proper security patches installed). This approach will lower the size of the Information Store and consequently lower disk storage requirements. However, a 7MB mailbox on the server could be used up in just a few large attachments. 16GB used to be the largest Information Store Exchange could handle, but with better server technology, an updated Exchange 5.5, service packs, and better procedures, larger sized Information Stores are realistic. Ajax Rocket's goal is to provide each customer with 50MB of storage, which results in 150GB of required overall storage. Some customers will require much less than this, while others will require much more. Overall, this is a good starting point to meet their business needs.

Looking at the big picture, all disk storage requirements are outlined in Table 8.16.

TABLE 8.16 *Exchange Server Disk Storage Sizing Matrix*

Application	Disk Storage Capacity Needed
Windows 2000 operation system requirement	<500Mbytes
page file	2GB
Exchange server application	<600Mbytes
System management agent	5Mbytes
Antivirus application	20Mbytes
Security application (server-based firewall and IDS)	30Mbytes
Information store (private)	150GB
Information store logs	3GB (1Mbyte per user × 3000 users)
Information store (public)	Not used in this solution
Message transfer agent and directory services (DS) databases	2.4GB (0.8MB per user × 3,000 users)
Directory services (DS) logs	6GB (2MB per user × 3000 users)

3. DETERMINE LOADING CHARACTERISTICS

● *Number of total users per server*
There will be 3,000 total customers. Due to availability concerns surrounding this project, having all of your eggs (e-mail customers) in one basket is not desirable. The 3,000 customers will be split across two servers, which results in 1,500 users per server. Now, in the

highly unlikely event one server were to fail, we only have half of the customers yelling and screaming!

- *Number of concurrent users per server*

  We expect all customers to use these servers each day, but from historical information we expect a 20% (on Friday night) to 100% (on Monday morning) concurrency rate, depending on the day of the week and if a large project is due.

- *Disk workload characteristics (read/write environment)*

  Understanding disk workload characteristics is paramount in an Exchange server environment and reviewed in detail in the above Application Performance Characterization section.

- *Size of records/transactions*

  Mail messages are expected to average approximately 2KB when no attachments are used and 400KB when attachments are used. We will investigate this closer during the stress test.

- *Physical location of users (Influences communications such as WAN, LAN, dial-up, terminal services, etc.)*

  All servers reside on site and are connected via the local switched Ethernet 100BaseTX LAN.

- *Type of work the user will perform*

  E-mail system operations, of course! Office automation and rocket scientist activities.

4. DETERMINE PERFORMANCE REQUIREMENTS

From a performance perspective, response time to the customer is the most important factor for a messaging solution. Ajax Rocket's business goal is to always have subsecond response time when interacting with the mail system. The second most important performance requirement is backup operations during each evening and being able to restore service within four hours. Of particular importance is the Information Store that houses recently received messages. Based on current business requirements, a worst-case scenario is that 75GB (per server) must be backed up in eight hours and restored in four hours. For backups, this translates to 9GB per hour for backups and 18GB per hour for restores. No problem, now that we mastered backup solutions from the previous scenario! Of course, this assumes that Exchange is offline during the restoration process. If Exchange is kept online, it generally takes twice as long to complete a restore.

5. UNDERSTAND FUTURE BUSINESS REQUIREMENTS

As this is a public company, growth is very important and the company does expect to expand by at least 30% each year, which is higher than the original 20% projection. This indicates that, in year two, there will be 3,900 customers to support and in year four there will be 6,240.

6. UNDERSTAND FUTURE SYSTEM ARCHITECTURES

The local team would like to put a system in quickly and would like it to be run without replacement for three years. Local support staff is still small, which is just unheard of in the IT industry. Additionally, Microsoft will continue to release new versions of Exchange and mail attachments are expected to continue to grow in size. Because of these facts, a truly leading-edge solution will need to be deployed.

7. CONFIGURE THE SYSTEM

Finally, to the good stuff. At this point, you can configure the Windows 2000 Exchange server. Choose the system resources required to meet your objective, with consideration for steps 1 through 6, and obtain the system. As you configure the system, look at each individual resource to meet the overall system configuration. Software and hardware vendors are good sources of information. They can suggest configurations that will get you started. Reviewing relevant industry benchmarks also can help provide insight into the initial configuration. Industry benchmarks are explored in depth in chapter 3. The following steps are presented to help guide you through the actual system configuration process.

Having some sort of idea of how each system resource works and relates to the overall system performance is helpful when configuring your system. Chapters 4 through 7 review the overall system architecture and each system resource in greater detail.

7.1 APPLICATION CHARACTERISTICS REVIEW • The general Exchange application characteristic description and backup technology review was completed at the top of the Windows 2000 Exchange Server scenario section.

7.2 REVIEW EACH SYSTEM RESOURCE FOR THE WINDOWS 2000 EXCHANGE SERVER

Disk I/O Requirements • The disk subsystem drives the sizing of the rest of the Exchange solution. Why? The restore-to-service and response time requirements, and the database characteristics of Exchange, require a very well planned out disk subsystem. Sizing and tuning the disk subsystem will result in a highly available and high-performing solution. From the business requirements above, we will determine the disk storage and performance requirements.

Availability • Since this is a critical server, all data will reside on hot swappable RAID array–based disk subsystems that utilize some level of fault tolerance. Hot spare disk drives will also be incorporated into the solution to increase overall availability.

The database characteristics of Exchange require the physical separation of the log files and the databases they support for maximum performance and availability.

This is a critical requirement. If the database and log files were on the same RAID array and the array failed, you would lose all data entered since the last backup. If the databases (Information Store) and the logs (Information Store logs) are on separate RAID arrays, you can recover! If the IS database fails, you can restore the database from the backup system and then replay the logs (which would not have been affected since they were on another physical RAID set), and all transactions up to the point of the failure can be recovered. Any new messages that were sent to the Exchange server while it was temporarily off line would be queued at the sender's mail systems (until the retry intervals expire) and would be resent when your Exchange server was back on line.

Performance Workload Characteristics • From the workload characteristics of a general Exchange server above, we will use multiple fault-tolerant RAID levels to meet the performance requirements.

Performance: Throughput and Transfers/sec • In chapter 6 we saw that it is desirable to group applications with similar disk workload characteristics together on the same physical disk subsystem for maximum performance. Taking this approach with our current Exchange Server environment, each of the major databases (random read/write) and logs (sequential write) will be grouped together on the same physical disk subsystem. This also aids in sizing the overall disk subsystem.

In this environment we have two performance requirements: response time to the end user and throughput needed for backup operations. The largest portion of the disk subsystem requirement centers on the Information Store, so to begin we will focus our efforts there. Then we'll look at the Information Store logs. If the transactions/sec occurring on the disk subsystem become too slow or a disk queue begins to form, it will affect end user response time. To determine the transfers/sec required to support subsecond response time for a user, we can review industry standard benchmarks, sizing tools from vendors (Compaq & Dell provide these on their web sites), and historical information.

The most common industry benchmark for Exchange environments is LoadSim, which is a free benchmarking tool from Microsoft. LoadSim's operations were reviewed in detail in chapter 2. Recall that LoadSim can be installed on several clients (server class systems, really) to emulate an e-mail-based workload directed at a target Exchange server under test. Based on industry benchmark information collected from several vendor web sites (Microsoft, Compaq, Dell, etc.), my own tests, and those completed by my associates Jeff Lane, John Polen, and Dan Matlick, we determined that the following extrapolation characterizes the workload an Exchange Server would need to support to obtain a subsecond response time: 0.2 to 0.4 transactions/sec per concurrent user. Thus for our environment, 1500 users would require an Information Store that supported between 300 and 600 transactions/sec to meet our response-time requirements. Because the Information Store must be placed on a fault-tolerant array, a RAID 5 array will be used. If we assume a cache hit ratio of 65%, the transactions/sec that need to be supported range from 75 to 150. From chapter 6 (Table 6.5), we found that on average each disk in a RAID 5 array experiencing a random read/write workload could support approximately 100 transfers/sec. Completing the math (150 transfers/sec / 100 transfers/sec/disk), we will need at least 2 disks to support the Information Store. Because we will store this data on a RAID 5 volume, however, we will need to calculate the write performance overhead incurred with RAID 5 arrays. From historical information at Ajax Rockets, we determine that there is a 60% read–40% write split of transactions. So the transfers/sec that must be supported are

[150 disk read transfers/sec × 0.6] + [4 × (150 disk write transfers/sec × 0.4) × 1.25 utilization factor]/100 transfers/sec/disk]

which works out to approximately 4.2 disk drives, which you always round up to the next nearest integer: 5. Now the utilization factor of 1.25, or 125%, is added in to ensure disk operations can be sustained at an 80% utilization rate. Each disk drive can support a random read/write workload of 100 transfers/sec, but the best response time is provided if the disk drives run at 80% of their maximum workload rate. For more detailed information on these disk concepts, review chapter 6.

Based on current business requirements worst-case scenarios, 75GB must be backed up in eight hours and restored in four hours. For backups, this translates to 9GB per hour and 18GB per hour for restores! Again referring to chapter 6 (Table 6.9), each disk in a RAID 5 array experiencing a random read workload can support 1.11MB/sec of throughput and 0.95MB/sec for sequential write environments. To meet the backup requirements, 3 disk drives are needed to achieve 9GB/hour (2.5MB/sec / 1.11MB/sec/drive = 2.25 drives, rounded up to 3 drives). To meet the restore requirements, 6 disk drives are needed to provide 18GB/hour of restoration performance (5MB/sec / 0.95MB/sec/drive = 5.2 drives rounded up to 6 drives). Here we used random disk workload characterizations for backups (Exchange is still online) and sequential write workload characterizations since restores are complete on an idle system (Exchange is offline).

To meet our response time and throughput performance requirements, we take the greater number of disk drives that were calculated in the above two steps. Thus, 6 disk drives are required to meet our projected performance requirements for the Exchange Information Store. For more detail on overall backup performance, review the backup server scenario above.

The Information Store logs play a very important part in overall Exchange Server availability and performance. From these same extrapolations, we find that to support subsecond response times, the Information Store logs will need to support 0.03 to 0.05 transactions/sec per concurrent user. Thus for our environment, 1500 users would require an Information Store log that supported between 45 and 75 transactions/sec to meet our response time requirements. If we assume a 50% cache hit ratio for the Information Store logs, this transaction rate lowers to 23 to 38 transactions/sec. Since we will want a fault-tolerant, low-latency environment for this sequential write-intensive environment, a RAID 1 or RAID 10 array would best meet our needs. A RAID 1 array would be desirable due to cost considerations. In chapter 6 we determined that in a sequential write-intensive workload, a single disk could support between 150 and 200 transfers/sec. Being conservative (all those safety features on Rockets!), Ajax Rockets prefers to us the 150 transfers/sec estimate for single-disk write-intensive sequential workloads (Table 6.9). However, since we are using a RAID 1 configuration, the actual number of I/Os we will need to support is

$$[0 \text{ disk reads/sec} + (2 \times 38 \text{ disk writes/sec}) \times 1.25 \text{ utilization factor}] / 150 \text{ transfers/disk}$$

which works out to approximately 0.6 disks. We round up to 1, but obviously 2 disks are required in a RAID 1 array. Thus a 2-disk RAID 1 array per database log will meet our projected needs. In future, if this workload begins to increase, we will consider using either a RAID 10 array or multiple transaction logs for each database log set.

Also note that we assume a high cache hit rate on the Information Store, which is the result of a well-tuned Exchange application and memory subsystem. A high Information Store cache hit ratio lowers the workload on the disk subsystem.

For the other Exchange databases and logs, we will determine the storage capacity requirements and follow the tuning recommendations above.

Storage Capacity • Even when focusing on disk storage capacity, continue to think performance. For Exchange Servers, it is not desirable to have the disk drive used storage capacity exceed 50–60%. There are several reasons for this. The first reason revolves around maintenance and recovery. If one of the major Exchange databases—such as the Information Store—becomes corrupt, a significant amount of free disk space is needed to run the recovery tools. The second reason revolves around performance. The fastest portion of the disk subsystem is the outer edge of the physical disk. If you keep the disk subsystem at less than 60% filled, it will just run faster! Disk defragmentation tools typically require at least 20% disk free space to operate, and 30%–40% to run optimally. The final reason involves the advent of self-replicating viruses that can quickly fill an Information Store; having additional disk space provides an increased buffer that gives the administrator more time to react before a store or log fills and the Exchange server becomes unstable.

Based on all of the above disk information, Table 8.17 outlines the overall disk subsystem requirements.

TABLE 8.17	Exchange Server Disk Subsystem Solution (Server 1 of 2)

Application	Minimum Disk Storage Needed	Logical Partition	Recommended Configuration (All 10,000rpm, Ultra2 SCSI Disk Drives)
Windows 2000 operating system requirement	<500Mbytes	C:	2 9GB disk drives in RAID 1 array (9GB usable/3.15GB filled)
Pagefile	2GB	C:	
Exchange server application	<600MB	C:	
System management agent	5MB	C:	
Antivirus application	20MB	C:	
Security application (server-based firewall and IDS)	30MB	C:	
Information Store (private)	75GB	H:	8 18GB disk drives in a RAID 5 Array (126GB usable/75 GB filled)
Information Store logs and DSA logs	3GB (1MB per user × 3,000 users) DSA—6GB (2MB per user × 3,000 users)	I:	2 18GB disk drives in RAID 1 array (18GB usable/9GB filled)
Information Store (public)	Not Used	N/A	N/A
MTA database and DS directory	MTA—2.4GB (0.8MB per user × 3,000 users) DS—2.4GB (0.8MB per user × 3,000 users)	J:	3 9GB disk drives in RAID 5 array (18GB usable/4.8GB filled)

CPU Requirements • The primary application to support from a CPU perspective is Exchange server application operations and the antivirus application. CPU workload involves supporting the messaging services, underlying message databases (stores), driving the disk subsystem, and network operations. Antivirus workloads can be significant, as we will learn later during the stress tests.

Searching for an industry standard benchmark for similar Exchange environments resulted in locating a published LoadSim Benchmark from Compaq. In this benchmark "Microsoft Exchange Server 5.5 on Compaq 1850R" found on the Compaq web site (http://www.compaq.com), a Compaq 1850R server supported 8,000 simultaneous medium workload LoadSim users with subsecond response times. The Compaq 1850R server was configured with Windows NT 4 (sorry, not enough Windows 2000 results in yet, but still relevant), two Pentium III 400MHz/512KB cache CPUs, 1GB of memory, two disk drives in a RAID 1 mirror for the logs, a single disk drive for the page file, a single disk drive for the operating system, and a 10-disk RAID 0 array for the Information Store. On the positive side, even while supporting this workload, 25% of each CPU was still available. This would indicate that two 400MHz Pentium III CPUs would meet our CPU requirements. Note that this older Pentium III CPU technology did not use full-speed Level 2 cache even though it was 512KB in size. Newer, full-speed Level 2 (256KB) CPU cache—although smaller—provides equivalent and sometimes better performance in one- to two-CPU servers. Review chapter 4 for detailed information on CPU technology comparisons.

On the negative side, the Compaq 1850R was a benchmark special; that is, it was configured for speed only, not operations. Using a non–fault tolerant RAID 0 disk subsystem is not relevant to a production environment. It does provide insight into how many CPU cycles are needed to drive this size of disk array, but it does not provide enough performance workload insight for our Exchange server solution. Based on this, we will be completing a stress test of our total solution.

The sizing estimate in Table 8.18 does not provide much room for growth or surges in workload. Fortunately, our initial solution sizing recommendation will be to operate with dual 733MHz CPUs and faster system bus (133MHz vs. 100MHz). From a CPU-only perspective, a 733MHz CPU provides approximately 37% more performance per CPU than the older 400MHz CPU (see chapter 4).

TABLE 8.18   *Initial Exchange Server CPU Sizing*

Application	CPU Usage (Estimate) Based on Two Pentium III 400MHz CPUs
Windows 2000 and Exchange, Network operations	70% usage per CPU, CPU Queue of 2 (From Compaq LoadSim Benchmark)
Overhead for system management software running on server	1% (estimated)
Overhead for intrusion detection software	1% (estimated)
Overhead for antivirus software	10% (estimated)
Total Estimated CPU Usage	***82% per CPU***

Memory Requirements • Sizing RAM is an additive process. Our first step in sizing memory resources is to outline all applications that will use any memory resources. Microsoft Exchange manages its own cache and memory resources and does not rely heavily on the Windows 2000 dynamic file system cache. The amount of memory that Microsoft Exchange uses for caching operations is tunable using the Exchange Performance Optimizer application. It would be wonderful if all applications provided the ability to control their memory usage. The Compaq 1850R LoadSim results indicate that 1GB of RAM would meet the memory requirements for our solution. Table 8.19 is a breakdown of where the memory resources are being focused.

| **TABLE 8.19** | *Exchange Server Memory Sizing Matrix* |

Application	Memory Usage (Working Set)
Windows 2000 operation system requirement	128MB
Windows 2000 File System Cache	64MB
Overhead for system management software running on server	8MB
Overhead for intrusion detection software	12MB
Backup server application	10MB
Exchange server application and cache	802MB
Total Estimated Memory Usage	***1024MB***

Through proactive performance management, more RAM can be added as needed. The Exchange environment is one area where the old adage—more memory is better—is very true (true, that is, when the memory is tuned; see below). We will gain more insight once the stress test is run, but this estimate provides us a good starting point.

Network I/O Requirements • There are two network I/O requirements to consider—customer access to the services that Microsoft Exchange server provides and the bandwidth needed for backups and restores. The network (LAN) rarely hinders typical Exchange server environments, so for this configuration we will assume that Ajax Rocket's standard network policy of using 100BaseTX NICs in a switched network setting should suffice. Typically, it will be the backup and restore operations that drive the network requirements for this environment.

During the most intense portion of the backup process, the backup server will need to support 18.75GB/hour (75GB/4 hours to back up each server) of sustained throughput. A 100baseTX network can support 45GB/hour, so a single 100BaseTX NIC will provide the needed bandwidth. This takes care of the network connection into the Exchange server, but what about the network paths between the target Exchange servers that will be backed up and the backup server? As always, we will check the network data path for potential bottlenecks—follow the data! Refer to the backup server scenario above and chapter 7 for more discussion on that investigation.

7.3 SYSTEM ARCHITECTURE RELATIONSHIP CHECK • This is a final, common-sense check of the Windows 2000 Exchange server configuration. Since the business requirements call for keeping this new Exchange server for at least three years, leading-edge server technology will be obtained. Not cutting edge, as that technology tends to demand a premium price.

From all of the sizing information above, we now have the following configuration: a one- to two-CPU capable server, two Pentium III 733MHz CPUs with 256KB each of full-speed (ATC) Level 2 cache, a 133MHz system bus, 1024MB of RAM, a single 64-bit 33MHz PCI I/O bus (266MB/sec), one fibre channel adapter (100MB/sec), one 12-disk fibre channel RAID array system, one internal hardware–based RAID controller, two disk drives for the operating system, two disk drives for the log files, eight disk drives for the Information Store, and two 100BaseTX Ethernet NICs. This server configuration is balanced and there is nothing notable in the way of data path bottlenecks. One side note, notice that fibre channel is used versus SCSI for increased scalability and improved cable management.

There is one potential concern. First, only a single, fast Ethernet connection is planned for. From a network availability perspective, some of the folks at Ajax Rockets have encountered failed NIC cards in the past. With the mail server being such a critical item, they have elected to obtain two NICs and use adaptive fault tolerance. This is surprisingly easy to configure on NICs that support this feature and is found under the NICs' advanced tab.

7.4 FUTURE BUSINESS AND SYSTEM ARCHITECTURES CHECK REVIEW • This server has room to grow in the disk and network areas but is limited in the CPU area. If the workload stays the same but more disk storage capacity is needed, that can easily be added to the external arrays. From a performance perspective, if the workload increases, some additions can be made but eventually another two-CPU class server would be required. We could go with a four-CPU class server, but this would significantly increase the cost of the current solution.

7.5 INITIAL HARDWARE CONFIGURATION AND TUNING • Table 8.20 shows the initial configuration of the server hardware, based on steps 7.1 and 7.2. See the Sizing and Tuning Exchange Servers section below.

Note: The Public Information Store is not used for this solution. If it were actively used, it would not be recommended to be located on the same disk array as the Private Information Store.

TABLE 8.20	*Exchange Server Hardware Configuration Details*

Windows 2000 Exchange Server Hardware Configuration Server Selected:
Compaq ML-380 (Why select the ML-380? We needed a solid system to use for a real-world reference.)

CPU Configuration	*CPUs Used in Solution*	*CPU Family*	*Level 2 Cache Size*	*Speed of CPU*	*Available CPU Slots*
	2	Intel Pentium III	256KB	733MHz	2 of 2 Used
RAM Configuration	*Amount of RAM Used in Solution*	*System Bus Speed*	*Type of RAM*	*RAM Expansion*	
	1024MB	133MHz	ECC SDRAM	4GB	

TABLE 8.20	*Exchange Server Hardware Configuration Details (Continued)*

Windows 2000 Exchange Server Hardware Configuration Server Selected:
Compaq ML-380 (Why select the ML-380? We needed a solid system to use for a real-world reference.)

I/O Subsystem Configuration	*Number and Type of I/O Card*	*Number of PCI I/O Buses*	*Placement of PCI Cards*	*Speed of PCI Bus*
	1 Compaq Fibre Channel Adapter	1	Fibre Channel Card is placed into PCI bus 0, in the top slots	One (1) 64-bit 33MHz
	2 Single Channel Full Duplex 100BaseTX		The two 100BaseTX NICs in the next two slots in PCI bus 0.	

Disk Subsystem Configuration	*Partition/ Mount Point*	*Files Located There*	*Type of RAID Adapter*	*SCSI Channel*	*RAID Level*	*# of 10K RPM Ultra2 Disk Drives*
	C:	Windows 2000 installation, Exchange Application, pagefile, System Management Software, Exchange Antivirus Software	Built-in RAID Adapter Compaq	1 of 1	1	2 9GB Disk Drives
	H:	Private Information Store	Fibre Channel Attached RAID Unit	1 of 1	5	8 18GB Disk Drives
	I:	Private Information Store Logs and DSA Logs	Fibre Channel Attached RAID Unit	1 of 1	1	2 18GB Disk Drives
	J:	MTA and Directory Services (DSA)	Internal RAID Array	1 of 1	5	3 9GB Disk Drives

7.6 INITIAL SOFTWARE CONFIGURATION AND TUNING ● In this step, the initial software configuration of the server configuration begins to take shape based on step 7.1 and 7.2. See the Tuning Exchange Servers section below.

7.7 INITIAL GENERAL TUNING ● See the Tuning Exchange Servers section below. These recommendations were followed before the stress test was run in step 8.

8. STRESS TEST AND VALIDATE THE SERVER CONFIGURATION

Congratulations! We now have a solid configuration that will run Microsoft Exchange and should support the required number of users and provide sub-second performance. The key word here is "should." We have a solidly sized and tuned solution, which provides a great starting point for moving into production and proactive management. But, since this is such an important application to Ajax Rocket's business, it was relatively easy to convince management that a stress test should be run to validate the solution.

To ensure that this configuration will support our objective, we will stress test the server before it enters production. We also wanted to see how well the Exchange server would react under the heavier workloads that we expect to experience as the company eventually grows to approximately 5,000 customers, which would mean that each server will need to eventually support 2,500 customers. One last concern—created by the recent waves of viruses being distributed through e-mail—was to see how our solution would react under load while running antivirus software directly on the Exchange server. This antivirus approach was taken because we could not rely on our customers not to turn off the antivirus software at their desktops. To accomplish this stress test, we used the Microsoft stress-testing tool LoadSim.

LoadSim is a tool used for simulating a client user load on an Exchange server. Its purpose is to enable a single Windows 2000 machine—called a LoadSim client—to simulate multiple Microsoft Exchange client users from a single Windows 2000 server. The operation of the LoadSim users is governed by a LoadSim profile. This profile controls factors such as how long a LoadSim "day" is; how many e-mail messages are sent in a day's time; how many times existing e-mail is open and read; whether to use distribution lists; whether to use public folders; etc. LoadSim emulates actual Microsoft Exchange/Outlook clients. Although customer profiles are configurable, the Heavy LoadSim Canonical Profile is a very close fit to the information obtained from Ajax Rockets in historical data. Table 8.21 outlines the various LoadSim Canonical Profiles.

TABLE 8.21	LoadSim Canonical Profile			
LoadSim User Attribute	**Attribute Detail**	**Light**	**Medium**	**Heavy**
TEST DURATION	Length of a day (hours)	8	8	8
READING MAIL	New mail (times/day)	12	12	12
	Existing mail (times/day)	5	15	20
AFTER READING MAIL	% of reply	5%	7%	15%
	% of reply All	3%	5%	7%
	% of forward	5%	7%	7%
	% of move	20%	20%	20%
	% of copy	0%	0%	0%
	% of delete	40%	40%	40%
	% of do nothing	27%	21%	11%
DISTRIBUTION LISTS	Minimum size	2	2	2
	Maximum size	20	20	20
	Average size	10	10	10

TABLE 8.21	LoadSim Canonical Profile (Continued)			
LoadSim User Attribute	**Attribute Detail**	**Light**	**Medium**	**Heavy**
	Distribution lists per site	30	30	30
	Cover 100% of users (no overlap)	Yes	Yes	Yes
ATTACHMENTS	% to run/load mail attachment (if one exists)	25%	25%	25%
INBOX SIZE	Inbox size limit (# messages)	20	125	250
SENDING MAIL	New mail (times/day)	2	4	6
	Save a copy in Sent Mail Folder?	Yes	Yes	Yes
	Number of random recipients	3	3	3
	% of time to add a Distribution List	30%	30%	30%
	Message priority	Normal	Normal	Normal
	Delivery receipt?	No	No	No
	Read receipt?	No	No	No
NEW MAIL MESSAGE CONTENT Text-only, no attachment	1K body (ups1K.msg)	Weight 90	Weight 60	Weight 50
	2K body (ups2K.msg)	0	16	10
	4K body (ups4K.msg)	0	4	5
NEW MAIL MESSAGE CONTENT 1K mail body, with attachment	10K attachment (ups10Kat.msg)	10	5	10
	Embedded bitmap object (upsBMobj.msg)	0	2	5
	Word attachment (upsWDatt.msg)	0	2	5
	Excel attachment (upsXLatt.msg)	0	4	5
	Embedded Excel object (upsXLobj.msg)	0	2	10
SCHEDULE+ CHANGES	Changes per day	1	5	10
	Update free/busy information?	No	No	No
	Average schedule file size	22K	22K	22K
PUBLIC FOLDERS	Folder activity	None	None	None
CALCULATED DAILY LOAD (based on these defaults)	TOTAL MAIL RECEIVED PER DAY	22.94	66.30	118.89
CALCULATED DAILY LOAD (based on these defaults)	TOTAL MAIL SENT PER DAY	4.70	14.18	30.67
	Mail sent as new mail	2.00	4.00	6.00
	Mail sent as a reply	1.05	3.76	13.03
	Mail sent as a reply to all	0.60	2.67	5.82
	Mail sent as a forward	1.05	3.76	5.82
CALCULATED DAILY LOAD	AVG. # RECIPIENTS FOR EACH MESSAGE	4.88	4.68	3.88

STRESS TEST CONFIGURATION • To generate the load on the Exchange server, five client systems were configured on the same 100BaseTX switched network as the Exchange server. The stress test configuration is shown in Figure 8-3.

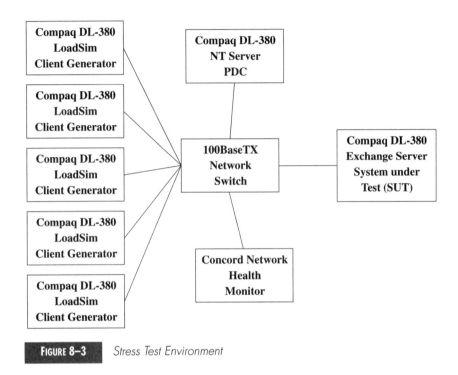

FIGURE 8–3   *Stress Test Environment*

The performance of the LoadSim client generators and Ethernet-based network was monitored at all times to ensure that they were not a source of any bottlenecks during the stress test. This step is critical during stress testing to ensure that the stress is correctly being placed on the system under test (SUT). Each client was configured with two disk drives, two Pentium III CPUs, 1024MB of RAM, and a 100BaseTX full duplex NIC. The Concord Network Health management system was used to ensure that there were not any significant numbers of network errors and that the network capacity was not exceeded.

STRESS TEST RESULTS • Once the stress test environment was in place, Exchange server configuration 1 was stress tested at the 1,000- and 2,500-user level with and without the antivirus software running (Table 8.22). Performance logging mode was enabled during all of the tests. The following are the LoadSim results. *Lower LoadSim scores indicate better Exchange server performance as perceived by the end user!*

TABLE 8.22	LoadSim Results for Exchange Server under Test Configuration 1

Number of Heavy LoadSim Users	Antivirus Software Running	95th Percentile Response Time Score (seconds)
1,000	No	0.115
1,000	Yes	0.138
2,500	No	0.152
2,500	Yes	0.161

The LoadSim Score represents a weighted average of the 95th percentile Exchange client response time (in milliseconds) for the various Exchange tasks defined in Table 8.21. The READ task is the task weighted highest, accounting for over half of the score.

9. PROACTIVELY FOLLOW THE CORE TUNING METHODOLOGY DURING STRESS AND VALIDATION TESTING

ANALYZING THE RESULTS: KEY OBSERVATIONS • This Exchange server under test configuration will indeed support 2,500 heavy LoadSim users while running the antivirus software, meeting Ajax Rocket's short- and long-term business objectives. We have now validated the initial configuration solution. Always thinking about a well-tuned solution, the performance logs were analyzed. The biggest surprise was the amount of processing power required. When the 2,500-user test was run without the antivirus, approximately 20% of each CPU was in use during the stress test. However, when the antivirus software was running and checking every message for viruses, CPU processing requirements jumped up to 60% per CPU! Forty percent more processing per CPU, 80% total overhead! This is quite a bit. Every antivirus package does work differently, but as we have learned from this test series, be very careful when planning new Exchange servers or adding antivirus software to current Exchange servers.

This is where proactive performance management comes into play and the importance of following the core tuning methodology (chapter 2) is stressed. If your current Exchange servers are running close to capacity, adding antivirus software and a slight increase in workload may cause harm to your Exchange servers! Always test! And stress test! Something may work functionally (installing it in a lab), but under load it is entirely different.

Reviewing the other server resources: all but 38MB of RAM was used during the test due to the way Exchange was tuned (we will be slightly more conservative before we enter production) and there was not a significant network load. The cache hit rate for the Information Store was in the range of 93–99%, which is very good and a significant factor in providing subsecond response time.

The disk subsystem performance data was interesting enough to share more detail on, and it's shown in Table 8.23.

TABLE 8.23	Disk Subsystem Performance Data			
	OS/Page/App	**DSA & MTA**	**Logs**	**Information Store (IS)**
Object: LogicalDisk	**C:**	**J:**	**I:**	**H:**
% Disk Read Time	1.059	0.004	0.019	100
% Disk Write Time	32.68	0.002	7.679	100
Avg. Disk Bytes/Read	6,066.119	4,096	3,924.9	4,127.417
Avg. Disk Bytes/Transfer	6,470.954	4,096	2,178.7	4,367.2
Avg. Disk Bytes/Write	6,515.883	4,096	2,178.3	4,737.6
Avg. Disk Queue Length	0.337	0	0.077	3.292
Avg. Disk sec/Read	0.005	0.002	0.011	0.011
Avg. Disk sec/Transfer	0.016	0.003	0.001	0.014
Avg. Disk sec/Write	0.018	0.006	0.001	0.019
Disk Bytes/sec	132,528.891	85.065	157,772.469	1,003,611.125
Disk Transfers/sec	20.481	0.021	72.416	229.807

Reviewing the disk subsystem performance, we see that the workload was well spread out across the disk subsystem. Response time was good for the disk subsystem housing all subsystems, particularly the log files with an average of 0.001 seconds. We also gain some tuning insight into how to set the Allocation Unit (ALU) size of the various disk subsystems. All of the disk subsystems associated with Exchange should be set to an ALU size of 4KB (except for the Information Store, which should be set to an ALU size of 8KB), while the operating system disk subsystem should be set to 8KB for optimal performance. ALU size is set when formatting a disk drive or RAID array at the Windows 2000 disk administrator. Details on setting the ALU size are reviewed in chapter 6. This test also validates some of our sizing estimates, such as the Information Store disk subsystem configuration. Disk Transfers/sec average 229, with occasional spikes into the 400 range, which the eight-disk subsystem can support by noting the fast disk sec/Transfer response time and an average disk queue of only three (a queue greater than 16 would not have been acceptable).

10. DEPLOY THE SYSTEM INTO PRODUCTION

This was a real scenario, and the Exchange servers were deployed successfully. Expecting something else? Well, everything doesn't always work, but you reap the benefits of "best practices" as we share with you what worked and note some of the potential pitfalls along the way.

11. PROACTIVELY FOLLOW THE TUNING METHODOLOGY AFTER THE SYSTEM IS DEPLOYED

Environments do change. The information gathered following the core tuning methodology is helpful for staying one step in front of user demand by identifying current load demands and potential system bottlenecks. This information is also useful when developing and sizing future system solutions and when adding additional capacity to your current system(s). If you have not determined where and how to add additional capacity to your system, you are at great risk of wasting your time.

Exchange Server Sizing Configuration Chart Summary

Even though every environment is different, the Exchange server configuration shown in Table 8.24 provides sound sizing guidelines on which to base your initial server configurations. Follow the sizing template to customize the configuration to your environment and then proactively manage your Windows 2000 file server to an optimal fit!

| **TABLE 8.24** | *Specific Configurations for Sizing Exchange Servers* |

Concurrent Exchange Users	Pentium III Class CPU	RAM (MB)	Number of Ultra2 SCSI 10K RPM Disk Drives	Network Interface Card
<= 1000	1	512	7	100BaseTX
<= 2,500	1-2	1024	15	100BaseTX
<= 5,000	2-4	2GB	20+	(1-2) 100BaseTX or 1000BaseTX

It is possible to configure larger Exchange servers, and numerous vendors have achieved benchmark results in the 20,000 plus range. Even though it is possible to support more than 5,000 customers on a single server, very few will consider a single server due to the risks associated with a possible failure. Only you know the threshold of customers you are willing to accept on a single system!

Note: It is important to understand that as we scale each system, a balanced approach is taken between all server resources so that artificial bottlenecks are not created before the Exchange server is even deployed.

Windows 2000 Exchange Server Tuning Summary

Exchange Server Specific Application Tuning

The characteristics for Exchange's operation were reviewed at the beginning of this section. The two major areas in which Exchange must be tuned are in the memory and disk subsystems. Fortunately, Exchange provides a friendly and helpful tool—the Exchange Performance Optimizer—for most of the actual Exchange tuning. It is important to fully understand what your Exchange server will be running and the physical configuration of your server before running this tool! You will need this information to effectively leverage it to your advantage.

From a general tuning perspective, the first screen that shows up when running the Exchange Optimizer covers CPU and memory tuning of Exchange parameters (these parameters live in the registry and are adjusted after the Optimizer is complete). The first screen to review closely is shown in Figure 8-4.

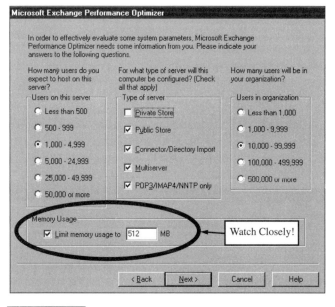

FIGURE 8–4   *The First Key Screen of the Exchange Optimizer*

Select options that are indicative to your environment. One key parameter that is commonly overlooked is the memory usage parameter. If you take the default, you are stating that "Exchange is the only application running on my server, take ALL the memory." This is very important. If you are running another application on the server, such as a SQL database (not recommended), antivirus software, or even general management software, take the memory usage into account.

Earlier, when sizing the Exchange solution, we outlined memory for our system in Table 8.19. From this table, we estimated 802MB would be used for Exchange and the rest of the 1GB of total memory was for Windows 2000, the file system cache, and other management applications. If over time you observe memory not being used and your Exchange database cache hit ratio decreasing, rerun the optimizer and tune appropriately.

For the disk subsystem that we focused on so closely, the optimizer provides assistance in this area, too. Even though the optimizer tests the subsystem to determine which disks/arrays are the fastest and which are the largest, understand your disk subsystem design and place your key files where we planned. The optimizer is even nice enough to move the files for you. Figure 8-5 is a screen shot of the optimizer and disk subsystem tuning.

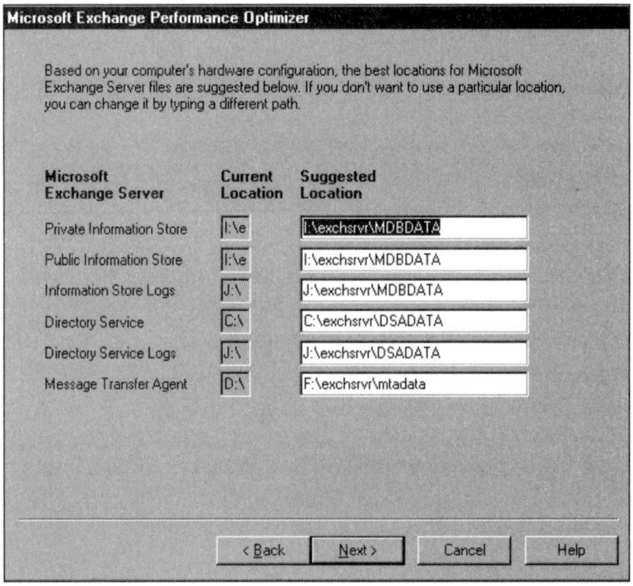

Microsoft Exchange Performance Optimizer

Based on your computer's hardware configuration, the best locations for Microsoft Exchange Server files are suggested below. If you don't want to use a particular location, you can change it by typing a different path.

Microsoft Exchange Server	Current Location	Suggested Location
Private Information Store	I:\e	I:\exchsrvr\MDBDATA
Public Information Store	I:\e	I:\exchsrvr\MDBDATA
Information Store Logs	J:\	J:\exchsrvr\MDBDATA
Directory Service	C:\	C:\exchsrvr\DSADATA
Directory Service Logs	J:\	J:\exchsrvr\DSADATA
Message Transfer Agent	D:\	F:\exchsrvr\mtadata

< Back   Next >   Cancel   Help

FIGURE 8-5   *The Exchange Optimizer and Tuning the Disk Subsystem*

Always rerun the optimizer any time server hardware components have been added or removed to ensure that the tuning settings take advantage of the resources available. The Optimizer does not take into consideration other applications that may reside on the server; thus manual intervention for those environments are required.

For additional hands-on specifics on why, when, and how these tuning recommendations work in detail and steps to implement them, refer back to the subsequent tuning sections of the previous chapters. Here select reformations are provided to give you a jump-start into an optimized Windows 2000 solution!

EXCHANGE SERVER HARDWARE TUNING

- Update the BIOS and Windows 2000 drivers on all server hardware (includes motherboards and the associated adapters).
- Ensure that the BIOS is configured for maximum performance.
- Ensure that the BIOS performance settings match the hardware you have installed.
- Ensure that you received the correct hardware.

EXCHANGE SERVER APPLICATION TUNING

- Configure the application correctly!
- Test and install the latest service packs for Exchange and Windows 2000.
- Configure each Exchange component in the best RAID array for its workload characteristics.
- Do not place the logs and stores on the same disk array.
- Run the Exchange Performance Optimizer after any server hardware or software changes.
- Review the Exchange Server Specific Application Tuning section above.

WINDOWS 2000 CPU SUBSYSTEM RESOURCE TUNING

Key disk CPU subsystem-related tuning you should consider:

- Set the application response optimization to background services (Control Panel / System / Advanced / Performance Options).
- With Microsoft Exchange V5.5, CPU utilization can be a bottleneck. On high-end systems (those with a large number of users), it may be necessary to add to the number of threads used by the STORE process that impact various queues in Exchange server in order to obtain the maximum amount of CPU utilization from the system. To accomplish this, edit the following registry key and add approximately 50% as a starting point: `HKEY_LOCAL_MACHINE\System\CurrentControlSet\Services\MSExchangeIS\ParameterSystem\Maxthreads` (Public and Private). If you run the Exchange Performance Optimizer in verbose mode, Perfwiz –v, you can see the current setting if the optimizer has changed this. Use this setting with caution. If CPU queues begin to form, throttle this value back. If you have plenty of CPU resources,

try increasing this value until you find the best value for your unique environment.

- Off-load CPU operations to I2O-enabled I/O adapters.
- Since multiple CPUs are in use with multiple NIC and SCSI adapters, consider using the Microsoft Interrupt-Affinity Filter Control Tool (IntFiltr; see chapter 4) to ensure interrupts are properly distributed between NICs and CPUs.
- Log off the server to ensure security and ensure no CPU cycles are wasted on your login session.
- If you do not log off, do not use a 3GL or other fancy screen savers, as they consume significant CPU resources.
- Check all services running on your server. Operate only those you need and stop all others.
- Avoid running another CPU-intensive applications on your Exchange server.

WINDOWS 2000 MEMORY SUBSYSTEM RESOURCE TUNING

Key memory-related tuning you should consider:

- Add the Heaps 8, Reg_dword parameter to `HKEY_LOCAL_MACHINE\System\CurrentControlSet\Services\MSExchangeIS\Parameter-System` to improve overall memory performance.
- Check the Windows 2000 memory management strategy. Exchange servers manage their own cache and do NOT rely on the file system cache. Ensure the Windows 2000 file system cache is set to optimize for Maximize Data Throughput for Network Applications. This tunable is set at Start / Programs / Settings / Network and Dial Up Connections / Properties of your LAN adapter / File and Print Sharing for Microsoft Networks.
- Check all services running on your server. Operate only those you need and stop all others.
- Set the pagefile size to twice the amount of RAM in your sever and to a fixed size.
- Never place the pagefile on a RAID 5 array.
- If your system must page (which should be avoided), consider multiple pagefiles on physically separate disk drives that are all configured to the exact same size and are housed on the same speed disk drives.
- Force Windows 2000 to keep the Windows 2000 executive (kernel) from paging any of its executive system drivers to disk and ensure that they are immediately available if needed (chapter 5).
- Do not use a 3GL or other fancy screen saver.
- Do not use exotic wallpaper; it wastes memory resources.

WINDOWS 2000 DISK SUBSYSTEM RESOURCE TUNING

Key disk subsystem–related tuning you should consider:
- Perform a fresh, low-level format on all disk drives at the lowest level using the disk or RAID adapter you are using.
- Freshly format all disk drives with NTFS when installing Windows 2000.
- When formatting the disk drive with NTFS, select the ALU size that best matches your disk workload characteristics. For Exchange servers, the recommended ALU is 4KB for all file systems except for the Information Store (IS). For the operating system and IS, use an 8KB ALU size.
- Match the stripe size of the low level RAID format with the ALU size used (see chapter 6 for details).
- Since we are using large NTFS volumes, increase the size of the NTFS log file size to 64MB, by using the *chkdsk* command: chkdsk drive-letter: /l:65536.
- Turn on write-back caching and read-ahead caching on hardware RAID adapters (ensure your RAID adapters have battery backed cache and are on the Microsoft certified hardware list).
- Use only I2O-enabled RAID adapters and those with their own CPUs.
- Keep the disk subsystem storage capacity usage under 50–60%, so that the fast portion of the disk drive is used, so that there is room on the disk drives to perform defragmentation, and operate exchange database recovery tools.
- Defragment your disk subsystem on a regular basis; this will result in significant performance improvements!
- Use one Windows 2000 partition per physical disk device/array.
- Group similar disk activities on the same physical disk subsystem and do not separate them via logical partitions on the same physical disk drive/array.
- Use more than one RAID level in your Exchange solution!
- Add disk drives as needed to keep the sec/transfers low and average queue size less than twice the number of disk drives in the disk array.
- Check all services running on your server. Operate only those you need and stop all others.

WINDOWS 2000 NETWORK SUBSYSTEM RESOURCE TUNING

Key network subsystem–related tuning you should consider:
- Teaming/trunking multiple NICs (Ethernet channels) together as needed to add network bandwidth and availability to your Exchange server (seamlessly to your customers), as shown in chapter 7.
- Remove all unnecessary protocols and Redirectors.
- Standardize on one network protocol: TCP/IP.

- If more than one network protocol is in use, set binding order such that the most commonly used protocol is first on the list.
- Tune the NIC driver to off-load IPSEC security operations and TCP operations on the NIC itself instead of the main system CPUs.
- Tune the NIC driver to increase its send and receive buffers.
- Use only I2O-enabled NICs.
- Use the fastest I/O bus enabled NIC possible (64-bit, 66MHz PCI slot)
- Tune the Windows TCP/IP stack to your environment (TCP Hash Table, MTU Window Size). See chapter 7 for the details on this or the web server scenario in this chapter for step-by-step details on how to implement.
- Do not use autodetect for your NIC. Set it to the speed that is the best performance level the internetwork devices will support. For example: 100BaseTX full duplex.

THIRD-PARTY TOOLS FOR TUNING WINDOWS 2000 EXCHANGE SERVERS

There are key third-party tools you should consider for enhancing the performance of your Exchange environment.

- Obtain a third-party disk defragmentation tool that provides enhanced defragmentation features such as scheduling and support of multiple NTFS ALU sizes. Recommended vendor to consider: Norton Speed Disk http://www.Norton.com.
- For heavily loaded Exchange servers, consider running a Windows 2000 scheduler and kernel subsystem enhancer. One such product is Autopilot from SunBelt software. Autopilot analyzes performance data to assist the operating system in making scheduling decisions. In my LoadSim performance testing, adding Autopilot to an Exchange server under load improved response times to the end user from 10–40%. Autopilot is available at: http://www.SunBeltSoftware.com.

Solution Scenario 4: Database Server Implemented with Microsoft SQL 7.0

Introduction

If you want to truly optimize a database server, hire a database application expert. The database applications that reside on any database engine can be very complex. A well-designed and indexed database and an application with efficient queries are key to an outstanding database solution. However, even with well-tuned queries and applications, you need a sound and optimized server for your application and database.

In this scenario, we focus on sizing and tuning the core database server to provide a jump-start for an optimal database solution. Microsoft SQL Server 7, the Windows 2000 operating system, and associated server hardware are covered in this scenario. Databases are becoming more and more important for their scalability, which can be used in delivering dynamic web content, improving web site maintenance, and rendering of complex eCommerce solutions.

Application Description

Microsoft SQL 7 provides a dramatic improvement from earlier database generations through its ease of use and scalability. Some of its new features include the ability to grow databases and the ability to dynamically set memory cache sizes. From a performance perspective, think of a database as an intense transaction engine. When transactions are completed quickly, the overall database server runs faster. To achieve fast transaction response from a system level, we will need a disk subsystem that provides low latency responses to transaction requests and to cache as many transactions in memory as possible. Why is low latency important? Depending on the database design, while a database is working to complete a transaction, certain tables, rows, or columns may be locked for exclusive use. If you have a high volume of concurrent transactions that need access to the same data, the entire system slows down. Think low latency! You may not have a true bottleneck, but slow transactions can affect every facet of a database server, particularly the response time to the customer.

Application Performance Characterization

When we understand how an application operates, we can then correlate its operations with the performance concepts we have learned throughout the earlier chapters. Two of the more basic functions that SQL Server 7 provides are storage of data in a relational database and placement and retrieval of that data. When data first arrives to an SQL Server database, it is placed into database buffers for the transaction logs in memory; then it is placed into the appropriate log (transaction log); then it is committed to the appropriate database (placed into a database buffer in memory and then and finally to the database itself). These steps are very important to remember, because they illustrate the importance of tuning and sizing memory and disk resources. We will need to configure enough memory to support all of the caching that will be needed to meet our performance requirements, a fast log disk subsystem that is optimized for sequential and write-intensive workloads, and a good split of read and write operations to support the databases which are typically random in nature.

It is highly recommended to keep the SQL Server log files and information store databases on different disk subsystems for improved performance and reliability.

Of course, you will want a fast, low-latency network for your customers to access the SQL Server and enough CPU horsepower to drive the overall solution.

Table 8.25 is a summary of the key components of a SQL Server database server.

TABLE 8.25	*SQL Server Database Component Descriptions*
SQL Server Components	**SQL Server Component Descriptions and Characterizations**
SQL Server binaries	Executable programs. These are typically not a disk performance issue and can be installed in the root partition of the operating system, which is typically the C: partition.
Database transaction log(s)	The database transaction log files are used to recover from data loss and it is very important to fully protect these files with a fault-tolerant RAID array. *The transaction log for each database should be isolated on its own physical array device for optimum performance.* This is very important since during heavy update activities, most of the insert/update transactions of online transaction processing applications use the log device. *It is common to find that the physical I/O performance of the log file will limit the overall throughput of the database.* Disk workload is characterized as sequentially write intensive. RAID 1 and RAID 10 are recommended.
Master database	SQL Server files, which include the master database, are typically installed in the same location as the initial installation. The server files require little in the way of disk storage but must be protected from loss. Disk workload is characterized as light. RAID 1 and RAID 10 are recommended for fault tolerance.
Database	This is where the actual data for the database is stored. Typically this supports a bulk of the workload. Due to the typically random nature of databases, it is recommended that it reside on its own physical disk array. If other components must be added to the same physical array, select another component with similar workload characteristics, such as another database to share space and workload with. Disk workload is characterized as combinations of read- and write-intensive random workload. RAID 5, and RAID 10 are recommended.
TempDb	This is a very important area to understand for overall SQL Server performance. The TempDb database is where intermediate result sets are stored for *all* SQL server queries that require them. In addition to temporary tables and stored procedures created "by design," TempDb also stores intermediates generated during Data Markup/Manipulation Language (DML) queries. As a result, database applications executing DML queries against large tables can consume a great deal of space (albeit temporary) in TempDb. The size of an intermediate ("work table") can be, and often is, as large as the Cartesian product of the involved tables. The number of columns in a Cartesian product table is the sum of the number of columns in the individual tables, but the number of rows is the *product* of the

TABLE 8.25	SQL Server Database Component Descriptions (Continued)

SQL Server Components	SQL Server Component Descriptions and Characterizations
TempDb (continued)	number of rows in each individual table. Care should be taken in determining TempDb size allocations, as a simple join between two simple 1,000-row tables with 5 columns each can result in a work table with 10 columns and 1,000,000 rows! TempDb is a holding space only, which means that if TempDb is lost, current transactions and queries may be affected, but no committed database changes will be lost. SQL Server will automatically recreatesTempDb every time SQL Server is started.
	If you believe that TempDb will be used a significant amount (applications with high levels of reporting, for instance), move it away from the root partition onto a separate physical disk array. Additionally, size TempDb initially so that it does not need to grow frequently, and when it does, it grows by a substantial amount; frequently growing a database is perhaps the most expensive of all routine SQL Server functions.
	Disk workload is characterized as combinations of read- and write-intensive random workload. RAID 5, and RAID 10 are recommended.

Sysmon Objects and Counters: Exchange Server Health, Bottleneck Detection, Tuning, and Sizing

The Sysmon objects and counters outlined in the previous chapters for CPU, memory, disk, and network subsystems are still applicable to Windows 2000 SQL Server. These objects and counters should be kept in mind when tuning or sizing database solutions because it is important to understand the big picture. If one server resource becomes a bottleneck (queues begin to form in the CPU or disk subsystem), response time to the end user begins to suffer.

In addition to the previously reviewed rules of thumb for Sysmon objects and counters to track, it is recommended that you become familiar with the Sysmon objects and counters that are added to Sysmon when SQL is installed (Table 8.26). These objects and counters are helpful in determining the health of your SQL Server application and for tuning and sizing.

TABLE 8.26	Sleuthing Out SQL Server–Specific Health, Tuning, and Sizing Information

Object: Area: Counter	Definition	Value to Monitor
SQLServer: General Statistics: Logins/ sec and User Connections	How many people are directly logging into and out of SQL Server. Number of user connections	Sizing and tuning Since each user connection consumes some resources (memory, CPU, disk, network), the number of interactive users with the database is important for sizing the solution. This does not take into account ODBC connections from web servers that might be using a single login for the ODBC connections.

TABLE 8.26	*Sleuthing Out SQL Server–Specific Health, Tuning, and Sizing Information (Continued)*

Object: Area: Counter	Definition	Value to Monitor
SQLServer: Database Object: Active transactions and Transactions/ sec	Number of active transactions for the database Number of transactions started for the database per second.	Sizing and tuning These counters provide insight into the number of transactions that the specific database instance is supporting. Excellent information to determine disk and memory subsystem configurations.
SQLServer: Buffer Manager buffer Cache Hit Ratio	Percentage of pages found in the buffer cache without having to read from disk. The ratio is the total number of cache hits divided by the total number of cache lookups since SQL Server was started.	Tuning and sizing The higher this value is, the better. The more you can cache in memory, the faster your SQL Server solution will be while lowering the workload on the disk subsystem housing the database. If you do not have a high hit rate (>90%), consider adding additional RAM and tuning SQL Server's memory usage.
SQLServer: Buffer Manager Page Reads/sec	Number of physical database page reads that are issued per second. This statistic displays the total number of physical page reads across all databases.	Sizing and tuning This counter helps to determine how well your database is designed from a performance perspective. If this value is high and the buffer cache manager hit ratio is low, consider a larger data cache (more memory), improved index, optimized queries, and database designs. (Hire a good DBA!)
SQLServer: Buffer Manager: Page Writes/sec	Number of database page writes that are issued per second. Page writes are expensive.	Tuning and sizing Reducing page-write activity is important for optimal tuning. One way to do this is to ensure that you do not run out of free buffers in the free buffer pool. If you do, page writes will occur while waiting for an unused cache buffer to flush.
SQLServer: Buffer Manager: Free Buffers	How many buffers are available (used in caching data written to disk)	Tuning and sizing If SQL Server runs out of free buffers, response time will suffer. Each buffer is approximately 8KB in size. If the amount of buffer spaces consistently runs close to or lower than 5MB, SQL Server is running short on memory. Consider adding and/or tuning memory usage.

Microsoft provides a number of statistics through Sysmon for monitoring the performance of SQL Servers, but Sysmon counters do not provide every aspect of detailed instrumentation data. Critical data is also available in the Windows 2000 Event Logs.

Scenario 4 Step by Step: Sizing and Tuning Mid-Range Windows 2000 SQL Server

Sizing the Initial SQL Server Configuration

Chapter 3 presented the core sizing methodology for sizing your Windows 2000 solution. That methodology is followed here for the development of the initial Windows 2000 SQL Server configuration.

1. DEFINE OBJECTIVE(S)

Now that they are one company, Ajax Rockets has decided merge their eCommerce systems into one single system using a single database solution. They are moving in this direction to sell their current products and prepare for the holiday season. They are expecting an enormous ordering storm for their new personal hovercraft product.

2. UNDERSTAND BUSINESS AND TECHNICAL REQUIREMENTS NEEDED TO MEET YOUR OBJECTIVE(S)

- Which application(s) will meet your functional objective(s)?
  Ajax Rockets currently has an online eCommerce site for both their customers (B2C) and business partners (B2B). However, with the advent of the merger, they plan to move off of their current, proprietary, internally developed database solutions to Microsoft SQL Server 7 and Internet Information Server (IIS) version 5 for their web server front end (see the web server scenario in the next solution scenario).
- What are the availability requirements?
  These are critical servers, as they will support eCommerce. The goal is to have a highly available solution. Ajax Rockets hopes this is a revenue-generating solution. The system must be immediately back on line if there is a failure. A four-hour restore to service is not acceptable.
- What are the ramifications if your system is down?
  A large loss of revenue will occur!
- What are the disk subsystem storage capacity requirements?
  Good historical information is available form Ajax Rocket's current database solutions that they are collapsing. Overall, they expect to have two 30GB databases online. One database will contain a set of product information that is updated on a regular basis and online transactions, and the other database contains an enormous amount of personal information obtained from customer web browsers and questionnaires. This database is queried by the customer relationship management system (CRM) upon every order to determine if there is something else they should recommend with that order.

Looking at the big picture, all disk storage requirements are outlined in Table 8.27.

TABLE 8.27	*SQL Server Disk Storage Sizing Matrix*
Application	**Disk Storage Capacity Needed**
Windows 2000 operation system requirement	<500MB
Pagefile	2GB
TempDb	<150MB
SQL Server application (including 14.25MB for master, model, and msdb databases)	<600MB
System Management Agent	5MB
Security Application (server-based firewall and IDS)	30MB
Database 1 and 2	60GB
Logs 1 and 2	6GB

3. DETERMINE LOADING CHARACTERISTICS

- *Number of total users per server*
  Every day they expect to complete 100,000 customer visits, placing orders or requesting information.
- *Number of concurrent users per server*
  Concurrent users are important in a database system, but what they are doing is even more important. From historical and marketing projections, it is estimated that databases will experience approximately 6,000 disk subsystem level Transactions/sec and the log files will experience 600 disk subsystem level Transactions/sec. These underlying disk transactions support approximately 300 total online customer transactions per second. Popular products! Review chapter 1 for information on how to use Windows 2000's Sysmon tool to collect the Transfers/sec information.
- *Disk workload characteristics (read/write environment)*
  Understanding disk workload characteristics is paramount in an SQL Server environment. From historical information collected through proactive management practices, it is determined that a fast log disk subsystem—that is sequential and write intensive—is needed to support the databases. The SQL Server databases are typically random in nature and support a good split of read and write operations.
- *Size of records/transactions*
  Upon closer analysis of the historical information, we found that:
  SQL Server: primary database—random workload, typical transfer is 8KB with a mix of 60% reads and 40% writes.

SQL Server: log files—sequential workload, typical transfer is 64KB, close to 100% write intensive.

Windows 2000 core operating system: random workload, read intensive.

Windows 2000 pagefile: sequential workload, mix between read and write activities, used only when under extreme workloads.

- *Physical location of users (Influences communications such as WAN, LAN, dial-up, terminal services, etc.)*

  Customers will reside both internally on the LAN and on the Internet. However, customers from the Internet will be attaching to a separate web server farm, which will then connect to the database server via the LAN.

- *Type of work the user will complete*

  Customers will be placing orders and Ajax Rockets associates will only be completing scheduled maintenance activities on the database server.

4. DETERMINE PERFORMANCE REQUIREMENTS

From a performance perspective, response time to the database queries and eventually to the end user is the most important factor for an interactive on-line transaction processing database solution (vs. some sort of large-scale batch processing or data warehousing system). Ajax Rocket's business goal is to always have at least one-second response time when interacting with the database system.

5. UNDERSTAND FUTURE BUSINESS REQUIREMENTS

Because this is a public company, growth is very important and the company does expect to expand by at least 30% each year. However positive the marketing department is in their projections, everyone is taking a wait-and-see attitude before building additional capacity into the current solution.

6. UNDERSTAND FUTURE SYSTEM ARCHITECTURES

The local team would like to put a system in quickly and would like it to be run without replacement for three years. Local support staff is still small, which is just unheard of in the IT industry. Additionally, new versions of SQL Server will continue to be released and workloads are expected to grow, so a truly leading-edge solution will need to be deployed.

7. CONFIGURE THE SYSTEM

Finally, to the good stuff. At this point, you can configure the Windows 2000 SQL Server. Choose the system resources required to meet your objective, with consideration for steps 1 through 6, and obtain the system. As you configure the system, look at each individual resource's involvement in meeting the overall system configuration. Software and hardware vendors are good sources of information. They can suggest configurations that will get you started. Reviewing relevant industry benchmarks also can help provide insight into the initial configuration. Industry benchmarks are explored in depth chapter 3. The following steps are presented to help guide you through the actual system configuration process.

Having some sort of idea on how each system resource works and relates to overall system performance is helpful when configuring your system. Chapters 4 through 7 review the overall system architecture and each system resource in greater detail.

7.1 APPLICATION CHARACTERISTICS REVIEW ● The general SQL Server application characteristics review was completed at the top of the SQL Server scenario section.

7.2 REVIEW EACH SYSTEM RESOURCE FOR THE WINDOWS 2000 SQL SERVER ●

Disk I/O Requirements ● The disk subsystem and memory subsystem drive much of the sizing of the SQL Server solution. Why? The response time requirements and the database characteristics of the SQL Server require a very well planned and designed disk and memory subsystem to achieve the overall business requirements. Sizing and tuning the disk subsystem will result in a highly available, high-performing solution. From the business requirements above, we will determine the disk performance and storage requirements.

Disk Subsystem Availability ● Since this is a critical server, all data will reside on hot swappable RAID array–based disk subsystems that use some level of fault tolerance. Hot spare disk drives also will be incorporated into the solution to increase overall availability.

> *The database characteristics of the SQL Server require the physical separation of the log files and the databases they support for maximum performance and availability.*

This is a critical requirement. If the database and log files were on the same RAID array and the array failed, you would lose all data since the last backup. If the databases and the logs are on separate RAID arrays, you can recover! If the database fails, you can restore the database from the backup system, then replay the logs (which were not affected since they were on another physical RAID set), and all transactions up to the point of the failure can be recovered.

Disk Performance Workload Characteristics ● From the workload characteristics of a general SQL Server (outlined above), we will use multiple fault-tolerant RAID levels to meet the performance requirements.

Disk Performance: Transfers/sec ● Based on what we learned in chapter 6, it is desirable to group applications with similar disk workload characteristics together on the same physical disk subsystem for maximum performance. Taking this approach with our current SQL Server environment, each of the two major databases (random read/write) and two sets of logs (sequential write) will be placed on its own physical disk subsystem. This also aids in sizing the overall disk subsystem.

In this environment, we have one key performance requirements: response time to the end user. The largest portion of the disk subsystem requirements centers on the two databases, so we will first focus our efforts there. If the transactions/sec occurring on the disk subsystem become too slow, or a disk queue begins to form, it will affect end user response time. To determine the Transfers/sec required to support at least one-second response time for a user, we can make some estimates using historical information.

Each database must be able to support 3000 disk-level Transactions/sec. If 90% of the transactions were cached, this would leave 10% of the transactions (300 Transactions/sec) that would need to be supported by the disk subsystem that supports the database. To meet this performance requirement, the fact that the workload is read/write random in nature, and the need for fault tolerance, a RAID 5 array will be used for each database. Each disk in a RAID 5 array can support approximately 100 I/Os/sec in a random read/write environment, thus three disk drives could support the projected workload. However, remember that you must also calculate the write operations overhead for a RAID 5 array. So the Transfers/sec that must really be supported are [300 disk read transfers/sec × 0.6] + [4 × (300 disk write transfers/sec × 0.4)] × [1.25 utilization factor/100 transfers/sec/disk] which works out to approximately 8.2 disk drives. Rounding up to the next nearest integer gives a total of nine disk drives. Here the utilization factor of 1.25, or 125% is added in to ensure disk operations can be sustained at an 80% utilization rate. Each disk drive can support a random read/write workload of 100 transfers/sec, but the best response time is provided if they run at 80% of their maximum workload rate. For more detailed information on these disk concepts, review chapter 6.

The log file transaction rate was measured to be 600 Transactions/sec with a 60% cache hit ratio (i.e., 60% of disk transactions are cached, thus 40% will be missed and go straight to the disk arrays), which is split across two physical log files. This results in 120 I/O's/sec that each log file will need to support ([600 transactions/sec × 0.4]/2). Since fault tolerance is required, we will not place the log file on the same array as the database, which subsequently improves performance by not having a sequential log file workload intermingled with the random database workload. Having two separate arrays improves the mean time between failures for each array.

To support the log files, a RAID 1 array would be desirable due to cost considerations. From chapter 6, we determined that in a sequential write-intensive workload, a single disk could support between 150–200 Transfers/sec. Being conservative (all those safety features on rockets), Ajax Rockets prefers to use the 150 Transfers/sec estimate for single disk write-intensive sequential workloads. Because of this, the actual number of I/Os we will need to support is [(0 disk reads/sec) + (2 × 120 disk writes/sec) × (1.25 utilization factor/150 transfers/disk)] which works out to approximately 1.2 disks, which we round up to the next integer. Thus, a two-disk RAID 1 array per database log will meet our projected needs. If this workload begins to increase, we will consider using a RAID 10 array in the future or using multiple transactions logs for each database log set.

For our Windows 2000 workload, we have observed historically fewer than 100 I/Os/sec. Thus, the operating system and database application will reside on their own two-disk RAID 1 array. We do not anticipate heavy paging, but just in case a single disk drive is dedicated to support the pagefile.

Disk Backup and Restore Performance ● From a backup and restore perspective, Ajax Rockets cannot afford to wait four hours for a restore. If this system is down, revenue is lost. Instead of a traditional approach to backups, they have decided to replicate the entire server to an off-site facility for a near real-time server backup using a third-party replication software package. Traditional backup methods are used to back up the hot spare server, so eventually a tape backup is created. Using this strategy, Ajax needs only to redirect their web farm to point to the hot spare database server in case of a failure. For a detailed discussion of disk subsystem backups and restores, review the file, Exchange, and backup scenarios.

Disk Storage Capacity ● Even when focusing on disk storage capacity, continue to think performance. For SQL Servers, it is not desirable to have the used disk storage capacity exceed 50–60%. There are several reasons for this. The first reason revolves around maintenance and recovery. If one of the major databases becomes corrupt, a significant amount of free disk space is needed to run the recovery tools.

The second reason revolves around performance. The fastest portion of the disk subsystem is the outer edge of the physical disk. If you keep the disk subsystem at less than 60% filled, it will just run faster! Disk defragmentation tools typically require at least 20% disk free space to operate in and 30%–40% to run optimally. Finally, we hope that there will be an amazing holiday season rush on Ajax's new product line, particularly an exciting new book on how to make Rockets go faster; that will result in strong sales which will require the database to grow larger than originally predicted. Having additional disk space provides a buffer that gives the administrator more time to react before a disk array fills (SQL Server 7 has the ability to automatically grow the database as needed).

Based on all of the above disk information, Table 8.28 outlines the overall disk subsystem solution.

CPU Requirements ● The primary application to support from a CPU perspective is SQL Server application operations. CPU workload involves supporting all of the database and application calculations, driving the disk subsystem, and network operations.

From a historical perspective, each of the older servers used four Pentium Pro 200MHz/1MB cache Intel CPUs running at 75% utilization. From the CPU analysis in chapter 4, the six Pentium Pro CPUs equate to approximately

| TABLE 8.28 | SQL Server Disk Subsystem Solution |

Application	Minimum Disk Storage Needed	Logical Partition	Recommended Configuration (All 10,000rpm, Ultra2 SCSI Disk Drives)
Windows 2000 operation system requirement	<500MB	C:	2 4GB disk drives in RAID 1 array (9GB usable/1.55GB filled)
Security application (server-based firewall and IDS)	30MB	C:	
SQL Server TempDb	150MB	C:	
SQL Server application	<600MB	C:	
System Management Agent	5MB	C:	
Antivirus application	20MB	C:	
Pagefile	2GB	P:	1 9GB disk drive (2GB used, 7GB available)
Database 1	30GB	E:	9 9GB disk drives in a RAID 5 array (72GB usable/30GB filled)
Database Log 1	3GB	F:	2 9GB disk drives in RAID 1 array (9GB usable/3GB filled)
Database 2	30GB	G:	9 9GB disk drives in a RAID 5 array (72GB usable/30GB filled)
Database Log 2	3GB	H:	2 9GB disk drives in RAID 1 array (9GB usable/3GB filled)

three Pentium III CPUs (two Pentium Pro CPUs provide approximately the same CPU processing power as one Pentium III CPU). From this analysis, three CPUs would handle our projected workload. What about a second opinion?

Searching for an industry standard benchmark similar to our online transaction processing (OLTP) eCommerce environment, a Compaq-published TPC-C benchmark was found. The TPC-C benchmark simulates an OLTP environment which defines throughput as how many new-order transactions per minute a server can support while keeping the response times for these transactions less than five seconds (for more information and examples on TPC-C and other benchmarks, review chapter 3). The TPC-C benchmark obtained from the Compaq web site was based on the following configuration: Compaq 6400R, four 550MHz Pentium III CPUs with 2MB Level 2 caches, 4GB of RAM, 100BaseTX NIC, five SCSI disk array controllers, and 240 disk drives. The TPC-C rating for this benchmark was 25,663 customer transactions per minute or 427 customer transactions per second. Obviously the underlying disk and memory subsystem is larger than our environment, but the CPU horsepower to support this level of transaction is applicable.

Table 8.29 shows an expected breakout of CPU usage based on the historical information available.

TABLE 8.29	*Initial SQL Server CPU Sizing*
Application	**CPU Usage (Estimate) Based on four Pentium III 700MHz CPUs with 2MB Level 2 Cache**
Windows 2000 and SQL Server, network operations	55% usage per CPU, CPU Queue of two (estimated)
Overhead for system management software running on server	1% (estimated)
Overhead for intrusion detection software	1% (estimated)
Overhead for replication software	10% (estimated)
Total Estimated CPU Usage	***62% per CPU***

Based on our historical information, industry standard benchmark, and a projected holiday season rush, a four-CPU server will be used for our solution. This provides a good starting point. In this eCommerce environment, it is prudent to design in more capacity, since any surges in workload must be supportable. If not, customers may go elsewhere. Also, since this is a four CPU server and an SQL Server application, larger level 2 caches are used to help improve scalability.

Memory Requirements • Sizing RAM is an additive process. Our first step in sizing memory resources is to outline all applications that will use any memory resources. Microsoft SQL Server manages its own cache and memory resources and does not rely heavily on the Windows 2000 dynamic file system cache. The amount of memory that Microsoft SQL Server uses for caching operations is tunable using the SQL Server Enterprise Manager application. It would be wonderful if all applications provided the ability to control their memory usage. From historical information, each of the legacy database servers used approximately 800MB of memory for caching each (1600MB total).

One of our design goals is to cache 90% or more of the transactions, so enough memory must be configured and tuned for SQL Server's operations. Table 8.30 provides an estimate of total memory required based on the provided information.

Through proactive performance management, more RAM can be added as needed or be removed if it is not. Databases love memory! Rarely is adding too much RAM a bad thing.

Network I/O Requirements • There are two network I/O requirements to consider—customers' access to the services that Microsoft SQL Server provides and the bandwidth needed for replicating the data to the hot spare off-site SQL Server. The network rarely hinders typical SQL Server environments, so for this configuration we will assume that Ajax Rocket's standard network policy of using 100BaseTX NICs in a switched network setting should suffice. Typically, it will be the backup operations that drive the network require-

TABLE 8.30	*SQL Server Memory Sizing Matrix*	
Application		**Memory Usage (Working Set)**
Windows 2000 operating system requirement		128MB
Windows 2000 file system cache (max for configurations less than 1GB in size)		64MB
Overhead for system management software running on server		8MB
Overhead for intrusion detection software		12MB
Replication application		20MB
SQL Server executables and cache		1024MB
Each concurrent connection to SQL Server (0.125MB × 300 customers)		38MB
Total Estimated Memory Usage		***1.5GB***

ments for this environment. But since in this environment each individual change is replicated across the network in near real time, the bandwidth needed is not as great; the total volume of data is spread over a much longer period of time. The replication is an asynchronous operation, which really means that the live database server does not have to wait for its replication partner to commit the transaction before continuing.

Two 100BaseTX channels in a fault-tolerant configuration should handle both the customer and replication traffic. If more bandwidth is needed, we can trunk them together for increased bandwidth and add another card if needed. The greatest potential network bottleneck is not between the web server and database server, but the web server farm and the customers!

7.3 SYSTEM ARCHITECTURE RELATIONSHIP CHECK • This is a final, common-sense check of the Windows 2000 SQL Server configuration. Since the business requirements require keeping this new SQL Server for at least three years, leading-edge server technology will be obtained. Not cutting edge, as that technology tends to demand a premium price.

From all of the sizing information above, we now have the following configuration: a one- to four-CPU capable server, three Pentium III 700MHz CPU with 1MB each of full-speed (ATC) Level 2 cache, a 100MHz system bus, 1.5GB of RAM, two 64-bit 33MHz PCI I/O bus (2×266MB/sec), one fibre channel RAID array container, one internal hardware–based RAID controller, two disk drives for the operating system, four disk drives for the log files, 16 disk drives for the databases, and two 100BaseTX Ethernet NICs (adaptive fault tolerance). This server configuration is balanced and there is nothing notable in the way of data path bottlenecks. One side note: notice that fibre channel is used vs. SCSI for increased scalability and improved/easier cable management.

Alternate Sizing Approach: Sizing Tools • What about another second opinion? Based on lab tests, industry standard benchmarks like TPC-C, and engineering experience, the folks at Compaq and Dell have developed software-based server sizing tools. You can find these tools by searching their web sites for "sizing tools." For this configuration, Compaq Sizer 3.01 for SQL Server 7 was run with the configuration parameters from this scenario. The result? See for yourself in Figure 8-6.

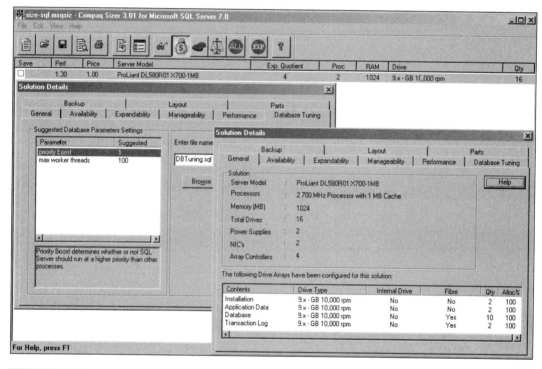

FIGURE 8–6   *Compaq Sizing Tool Example*

No tool will match your environment perfectly, but when setting the initial parameters it was possible to request a database server that supported 270 Transactions/sec of disk transactions with a one-second response time to the customers. Compaq recommended a Dl-580 server with two Pentium III 700MHz/1MB Intel CPUs with 1GB of RAM, 16 disk drives, and a 100BaseTX NIC. The number of disk drives and amount of memory were similar, but the sizing tool was much more aggressive with CPU power stating only two CPUs would be needed. But they did place those two CPUs in a server that could support four, thus providing room to grow. Although the methodologies and extrapolations are slightly different, as a second option the sizing tool provides good insight into the fact that we are in the same ballpark. Overall, I have found these tools to be very useful.

Even if you use the automated sizing tools as your primary tool, the sizing information obtained by following the core sizing methodology presented in these scenarios is still needed to properly use the sizing tools. Now you also have some general insight into how the sizing tools work. These sizing tools are helpful because they put all of the parts and pieces needed to order and build the suggested solution.

7.4 FUTURE BUSINESS AND SYSTEM ARCHITECTURES CHECK REVIEW • This   server has room to grow in all areas.

7.5 INITIAL HARDWARE CONFIGURATION AND TUNING • In this step, the initial configuration of the server hardware begins to take shape based on steps 7.1 and 7.2 (Table 8.31). See the Sizing and Tuning SQL Servers section below as needed.

7.6 INITIAL SOFTWARE CONFIGURATION AND TUNING • In this step, the initial software configuration of the server configuration begins to take shape based on steps 7.1 and 7.2. See the section on tuning file servers below.

7.7 INITIAL GENERAL TUNING • See the Tuning SQL Server section below.

8. STRESS TEST AND VALIDATE THE SERVER CONFIGURATION

Due to time-to-market pressures, Ajax Rockets has decided to move this system directly into production once its final quality and security checks are complete. This is not recommended, but they do plan to proactively manage the server performance.

TABLE 8.31	*SQL Server Hardware Configuration Data*

Windows 2000 SQL Server Hardware Configuration Server Selected:
Compaq DL-580 (Why select the DL-580? We needed a solid system to use for a real-world reference.)

CPU Configuration	*CPUs Used in Solution*	*CPU Family*	*Level 2 Cache Size*	*Speed of CPU*	*Available CPU Slots*
	3	Intel Pentium III	2MB	700MHz	3 used, 1 available

RAM Configuration	*Amount of RAM Used in Solution*	*System Bus Speed*	*Type of RAM*	*RAM Expansion*
	1.5GB	100MHz	ECC SDRAM	8GB

I/O Card Configuration	*Number and Type of I/O Card*	*Number of PCI I/O Buses*	*Placement of PCI Cards*	*Speed of PCI Bus*
	1 Compaq Fibre Channel Adapter	2	Fibre Channel Card is placed into PCI bus 0, in the top slot—slot 0	Two (2) 64-bit 33MHz Peer PCI Buses
	2 Single Channel Full Duplex 100BaseTX		The two 100BaseTX NICs are placed into PCI bus 1, in the top two slots	

TABLE 8.31   *SQL Server Hardware Configuration Data (Continued)*

Windows 2000 SQL Server Hardware Configuration Server Selected:
Compaq DL-580 (Why select the DL-580? We needed a solid system to use for a real-world reference.)

Disk Subsystem Configuration	Partition/ Mount Point	Files Located There	Type of RAID Adapter	SCSI Channel	RAID Level	# of 10K RPM Ultra2 Disk Drives
	C:	Windows 2000 installation, SQL Server application, pagefile, system management software, IDS software	Built-in RAID adapter Compaq	1 of 1	1	2 9GB disk drives
	H:	Database 1	Fibre Channel Attached RAID Unit (1 of 2)	1 of 1	5	9 9GB disk drives
	J:	Logs 1	Fibre Channel Attached RAID Unit (1 of 2)	1 of 1	1	2 9GB disk drives
	K:	Database 2	Fibre Channel Attached RAID Unit (2 of 2)	1 of 1	5	9 9GB disk drives
	L:	Logs 1	Fibre Channel Attached RAID Unit (2 of 2)	1 of 1	1	2 9GB disk drives
	P:	pagefile	Built-in RAID adapter Compaq	1 of 1	None JBOD	1 9GB disk drives

9. PROACTIVELY FOLLOW THE CORE TUNING METHODOLOGY DURING STRESS AND VALIDATION TESTING

Analyzing the results: Not applicable as no stress test was completed.

10. DEPLOY THE SYSTEM INTO PRODUCTION

This was a real scenario and the SQL Servers were deployed successfully. Expecting something else? Well, not everything always works, but you reap the benefits of "best practices," as we share with you what worked and note some of the potential pitfalls along the way.

11. PROACTIVELY FOLLOW THE TUNING METHODOLOGY AFTER THE SYSTEM IS DEPLOYED

Environments do change. The information gathered following the core tuning methodology is helpful for staying one step in front of user demand by identifying current load demands and potential system bottlenecks. Also, use this information when developing and sizing future system solutions and when adding additional capacity to your current system(s). If you have not quantifiably determined where and how to add additional capacity to your system, you are at great risk of wasting your time.

SQL Server Sizing Configuration Chart Summary

Even though every environment is different, the SQL Server configuration chart in Table 8.32 provides sound sizing guidelines on which to base your initial server configuration. Follow the sizing template above to customize to your environment and then proactively manage your Windows 2000 SQL Server to an optimal fit!

| **TABLE 8.32** | Specific Configurations for Sizing SQL Servers |

Database Server Based on disk transaction rates and 90% cache hit ratio	Pentium III Class CPU	RAM (MB)	Number of Ultra2 SCSI 10K rpm Disk Drives	Network Interface Card
<= 1,000	1–2	512MB	7	100BaseTX
<= 3,000	2–4	1–2GB	16	100BaseTX
<= 6,000	4–8	2–8GB	32+	(1–2) 100BaseTX or 1000BaseTX

When very large SQL Server database solutions are developed, it is common to see automated off-site replication and local hot spare solutions, as well as shared disk subsystem–based clusters.

Note: It is important to understand that, as we scale each system, a balanced approach is taken between all server resources so that no artificial bottlenecks are created before the SQL Server is even deployed.

Windows 2000 SQL Server Tuning Summary

SQL Server–Specific Application Tuning

The basic operational characteristics for SQL Server's operation were reviewed at the beginning of this section. If you are interested in learning more details on the internal architecture of SQL Server, there are several good books such as such as *Inside SQL Server 7* published by Microsoft. We look at the high-level holistic system approach of tuning SQL Server. The three major areas in which SQL Server must be tuned are in the memory, CPU, and disk subsystem areas. Fortunately, SQL Server provides a friendly and helpful tool, the SQL Server Enterprise Manager Optimizer for most of the actual SQL tuning. Even with a GUI, you still must know what all of the options provide, match them against what operations your SQL Server will be running and the physical configuration of your server before even running this tool!

SQL Server CPU Tuning

From a CPU perspective, you can increase the amount of work that SQL Server can complete by using the SQL Server fibers feature. As reviewed in chapter 4, when a context switch occurs and one thread is moved off of the CPU and another gets its turn, there is a significant amount of performance overhead associated with this operation. The Windows 2000 kernel's scheduler in privileged mode handles thread level context operations. If threads from the same process are switched on and off of the CPU, there is less overhead than if threads from another process switch positions on the CPU.

Based on the concept of lowering of overhead and increasing the number of CPU cycles available for productive work, SQL Server implements fibers that are components of threads from the same process. When fibers are switched, it is handled in user mode (vs. the kernel or privileged mode) by SQL Server, which results in lower overhead than a thread-level context switch. When you implement fibers, you are now relying on the SQL Server algorithms for scheduling much of your workload vs. the Windows 2000 scheduler.

Activate fibers if you observe context switches higher than your baseline or if you have a heavy workload on your CPUs and want to try out how well the SQL Server scheduler does at relieving some of the overall CPU overhead associated with context switches. In general, implementing fibers lowers CPU overhead so that more productive work can be completed by the SQL Server application. The number of worker threads/fibers is set by default to 255. You can activate the use of fibers and tune the number of fibers by running SQL Server's Enterprise Manager, selecting properties for your server, and then selecting the processor tab. Try the default fiber setting first; it is a good starting point for small- to mid-range database servers. Increase this value on servers that support large customer databases. Watch Sysmon's Processor: Process queue counter closely when working with threads. If you observe threads beginning to queue, you may have overconfigured the number of thread/ fibers your system can sustain. If this occurs, it is time to tune in the other direction. Activating fibers is shown in Figure 8-7.

SQL Server provides a mechanism that enables the use of CPU affinity, which was also reviewed in chapter 4. This is an advanced tuning technique, so use with caution and ensure you fully understand your environment before

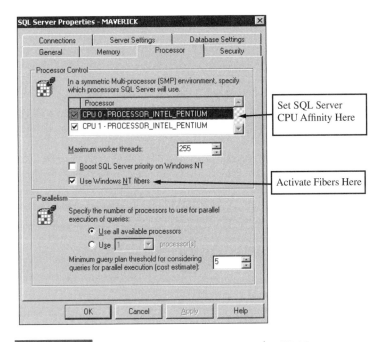

FIGURE 8-7   *SQL Server Enterprise Manager for CPU Tuning*

implementing. Using SQL Server's Enterprise Manager interface in conjunction with Microsoft Interrupt-Affinity Filter Control Tool (IntFiltr; see chapter 4), you have significant amount of control over processor usage. The biggest advantage you can gain by controlling processor usage is maximizing cache coherency (how well and often SQL Server finds data or instructions in Level 2 cache) and lowering overall system overhead (the more Level 2 cache hits, the less data traverses the system bus). If you do apply affinity tuning, consider using the boost SQL Server priority tuning option on the SQL Enterprise Manager, so that SQL Server has a higher CPU scheduling priority than other processes! In essence, you are giving the designated CPUs to SQL Server and not other processes.

For example, if you had a three-CPU server where each CPU had a 1MB second level cache and a very busy database server, consider limiting SQL Server to using only two of the CPUs. This is accomplished by using the SQL Server Enterprise Manager and checking which CPUs you wish to allow SQL Server to run on. Then, using the Microsoft Interrupt-Affinity Filter Control Tool (IntFiltr), tie those busy NIC and disk adapter workloads to a specific CPU not used by SQL Server. In this example, you force the SQL Server to limit itself to two CPUs, which increases the chances that a Level 2 CPU cache hit will occur. Why is this? There are no hardware process interrupts trying to chase your SQL Server threads and fibers off of the CPU they are using!

Extra for experts! If you want to maximize CPU performance for SQL Server by removing every last bit of possible overhead, you can start SQL Server from the command line with the –x option and disable SQL Servers recording of CPU time and cache hit ratio. The command to start SQL Server from the Windows 2000 console is: SQLServer –d C:\path of master database –e c:\path of error log –l c:\path of master database log file. I suggest using this option only if you are truly running out of CPU resources or you are in a benchmark competition.

SQL SERVER MEMORY TUNING

SQL Server dynamically adds and removes memory as needed based on the memory available to it. Like other applications, if left in its default state, SQL Server assumes it is the only application running on the server and takes all the memory available! Dedicating a server to the function of a database server is highly recommended.

If you did take the SQL Server defaults during installation and have another application hungry for memory resources running on the same server, a contention will be created, the server will run low on memory, the system will page, and everything will run slow!

Part of how SQL Server dynamically controls its memory usage is that it periodically queries the server it resides on to determine the amount of free physical memory available. SQL Server then grows or shrinks its dynamic caches to keep free physical memory at least at 5MB (+/− 200KB). If there is less than 5MB free, SQL Server releases memory to Windows 2000. If there is more than 5MB of physical memory, SQL Server recommits memory to the dynamic buffer cache. SQL Server adds memory to the buffer cache only when its workload requires more memory; a server at rest does not grow its buffer cache unless there is a memory leak.

Through the SQL Server Enterprise Manager, you can control how SQL Server uses its memory resources. Select options that are indicative of your environment. Earlier, when sizing the SQL Server database solution, we created Table 8.30 that outlined memory for our system. From this table, we estimated 1024MB would be used for SQL Server while the other 512MB of memory was for Windows 2000, the file system cache, and other management applications. Based on this information, you can set the slide bars to a maximum value of 1GB, which will then allow SQL Server to dynamically grow to 1GB as needed, but still leaves 512MB available for the other applications. If you know that there is a minimum memory setting that SQL Server appears to run well with, use the Minimum slide bar and set a memory value that will be set aside for SQL Server from the start of the server and will not be available to any other processes. The SQL Server Enterprise Manager's memory configuration view is shown in Figure 8-8.

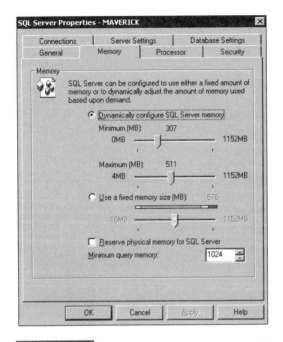

FIGURE 8-8   *SQL Server Enterprise Manager for Memory Tuning*

These settings can be also be configured from the command line. Why review the command line technique for tuning the SQL Server? Some of the advanced tuning options outlined below are not available via the Enterprise Manager MMC snap-in. To access the tunable areas via the command line, start a command prompt session and type in "ISQL -S*serveralias* -U*user_id* [-P*password*] [-d*database_name*]." This will bring up the ISQL command prompt. Note, if you leave out the -P parameter, isql will prompt you for a password and mask it. If you leave out the -d parameter, your *isql* session will start in your default database (master for the sa login). Once logged in, the *isql* prompt looks like this (case sensitive!).

```
1>
2>
```

From here you can run the sp_configure command to tune your server as shown below:

```
----------------------------------------------------------------------
C:\> isql –SSERVER_NAME -Usa
Password: XXXXXXXX
1>              sp_configure 'min server memory', 100
2> go
```

```
Configuration option changed. Run the RECONFIGURE statement to install.
1> sp_configure 'max server memory', 307
2> go
Configuration option changed. Run the RECONFIGURE statement to install.
1> reconfigure with override
2> go
1> quit
```

If your server is running with the allow updates server configuration option set to No(0), you will need to substitute "reconfigure with override" for "reconfigure" when changing any server configuration option.

If you are interested in reviewing all of the SQL Server internal options, run the "sp_configure" command with no arguments from the ISQL command prompt. If you wish to see the advanced options, run the following command sequence:

```
1>sp_configure 'show advanced options', 1
2>go
1>sp_configure
```

Revisit any settings you make in your environment whenever there are any configuration changes either in software or hardware. For example, if you just added another 512MB of memory and had previously limited SQL Server to 1GB, you will now have to tune the maximum memory size so that SQL Server and ultimately your customers can take advantage of it.

If over time you observe memory not being used in your server, adjust the SQL Server memory settings to use what you paid for!

SQL Server Disk Subsystem Tuning

We have focused heavily on the disk subsystem. Once SQL Server's dynamic cache must be flushed or is defeated due to a heavy workload, the disk subsystem must respond. The most important facet of disk subsystem tuning for SQL Server is placing the different databases and logs on disk subsystems that are designed to support the expected workload. When the database log file is first created, you can control on which disk subsystems the log file is placed. If you are working on very large log systems, you can use multiple different disk arrays. This is done by creating more than one transaction log per database and placing each one on its own RAID 1 array. SQL Server will then distribute the logging workload among logs in a sequential (not striped) fashion.

This same concept applies to the database as well. It is possible when creating your database to create file groups that enable you to have one database represented by multiple files, where each file can then be placed on its own disk array for maximum performance. For these steps, I will refer you to that database expert that we started this section with.

A great feature of SQL Server is that it can grow automatically as needed by your databases! The bad news is that it can grow automatically as needed by your databases! If you know or can estimate how large your database or logs will grow, create them at that size. If your database server is under heavy stress and the database must grow dynamically, it places extra stress on the server when it is not wanted and the initial internal structures are not as optimal as they could be. On the positive side, it is great that the database can be easily extended manually or extended as needed so no transactions are lost to a filled predetermined database size.

To avoid data loss, never turn off the option for your databases to grow automatically in case you have an unplanned surge of workload that your initial database sizing did not compensate for. However, ensure that when your database *does* grow, it grows by a significant amount. This will keep the number of very expensive expansions to a minimum until you can resize your databases based on the new workloads. One of the worst performance-killing mistakes that can be made is a large (e.g., 30GB) database set to expand 1MB at a time (the default if using size expansion as opposed to percentage expansion). Always use percentage expansion, and always grow your database by at least 10% at a time.

SQL Server uses the max async I/O parameter to control the maximum number of asynchronous I/O requests that can be submitted to a single SQL Server file. This option also limits the number of concurrent reads on the file. The default value is 32, which specifies 32 reads and 32 writes, which can be outstanding at any one time on a file (255 is the maximum value). The default value is very good for servers that do not use RAID or use low-end or older RAID adapters. However, if you have newer (post-1999) high-powered I2O-enabled RAID controller and more than four disk drives in your array, consider increasing the value of the max async I/O parameter. This will allow SQL Server to generate more asynchronous I/O write requests so that the disk subsystem can be used to its full potential. Your starting value should be at least three times the number of disks in your array. For our scenario, 18 disks are in the RAID array; thus the max async I/O value would be increased to 54 to start (2 × 9 disk RAID 5 arrays × 3 async I/O). Watch the Sysmon object logical disk's current and average disk queues closely when leveraging this tuning technique. At no time should there be more than two outstanding I/O requests per disk in the disk arrays for an extended period of time. If you are not experiencing any disk queues, consider increasing the max async I/O parameter. If you begin to form queues, consider other disk subsystem tuning or add additional disk drives to lower the outstanding queued request levels. This option is configured from the command line using the sp_configure command (no GUI for this one).

For additional hands-on specifics on why, when, and how the following tuning recommendations work in detail and for the steps to implement them, refer back to the subsequent tuning sections of the previous chapters.

Here select recommendations are provided to give you a jump-start and a checklist for an optimized Windows 2000 SQL Server solution!

SQL SERVER HARDWARE TUNING

- Update the BIOS and Windows 2000 drivers on all server hardware (includes motherboards and the associated adapters).
- Ensure BIOS is configured for maximum performance.
- Ensure BIOS performance settings match the hardware you have installed.
- Ensure you received the correct hardware.
- Ensure the latest drivers and BIOS are tested and in use.
- Follow the guidelines in the configuration above for placement of I/O adapters.

SQL SERVER APPLICATION TUNING

Key SQL Server–related tuning you should consider:

- Place all log files on their own physical RAID 1 or RAID 10 array (failure to do so will slow your system).
- If additional log file performance is needed, implement the transaction log across multiple files each residing on its own RAID 1 or RAID 10 array.
- Place database(s) on their own physical RAID 5 or RAID 10 array.
- Watch for TempDb usage on the C: drive; it may need to be moved if it is heavily used.
- If additional database file performance is needed, implement file groups and spread the database across multiple RAID 5 or RAID 10 arrays.
- Configure for, but avoid the need for, automatic database or log file growth. Plan for the database size and precreate!
- Configure your system to use SQL fibers if context switches are higher than your baseline and you have an overworked CPU system.
- Test and install the latest service packs for SQL Server and Windows 2000.
- Consider a RAM disk for temporary database space if it is determined to be a bottleneck (see chapter 6).
- Apply affinity to isolate SQL Server to select CPUs as needed (see above).
- Review the SQL Server Specific Application Tuning section above.

WINDOWS 2000 CPU SUBSYSTEM RESOURCE TUNING

Key CPU subsystem–related tuning you should consider:

- Set the application response optimization to background services (Control Panel / System / Advanced / Performance Options).

- Off-load CPU operations to I2O-enabled I/O adapters.
- Since multiple CPUs are in use with multiple NIC and Fibre Channel adapters, consider using the Microsoft Interrupt-Affinity Filter Control Tool (IntFiltr; see chapter 4) to ensure interrupts are properly distributed among NICs and CPUs (strategy and step-by-step tactics are reviewed in chapter 4).
- Log off the server to ensure security and ensure no CPU cycles are wasted on your login session.
- If you do not log off, do not use a 3GL or other fancy screen savers as they consume significant CPU resources.
- Check all services running on your server. Operate only those you need and stop all others. (Although environment dependent, a dedicated SQL Server can operate with very few services: Workstation, Server, Event Log, Microsoft SQLServer, and the TCP/IP protocol.)
- Avoid running another CPU-intensive application on your SQL Server.

WINDOWS 2000 MEMORY SUBSYSTEM RESOURCE TUNING

Key memory-related tuning you should consider:
- Check the Windows 2000 memory management strategy. SQL Servers do not rely on the File System Cache. By default, the Windows 2000 File System Cache is set to optimize for Maximize Data Throughput for file sharing. Check this setting and ensure it is set for Maximize Data Throughput for Network Application by selecting: Start / Programs / Settings / Network and Dial Up Connections / Properties of your LAN adapter / Maximize Data Throughput for Network Applications.
- Check all services running on your server. Operate only those you need and stop all others. Each erroneous service wastes precious RAM!
- Set the pagefile size to twice the amount of RAM in your sever and to a fixed size.
- Avoid paging whenever possible. It is bad enough that the 10% (or less, we hope) of buffer cache requests will miss and result in disk hits by SQL Server. When coupled with O/S-level pagefile hits, the results can be disastrous. It is better to cap the amount of memory SQL Server can allocate using the max server memory server configuration option (to eliminate paging) than to allocate memory to SQL Server in an amount that will cause paging. Paging is much easier to control than buffer cache hits!
- Never place the pagefile on a RAID 5 array.
- If your system must page (which should be avoided), consider multiple pagefiles on physically separate disk drives that are all configured to the exact same size.
- Force Windows 2000 to keep the Windows 2000 executive (kernel) from paging any of its executive system drivers to disk and ensure that they are immediately available if needed.

- Do not use a 3GL or other fancy screen savers.
- Do not use exotic wallpaper; it wastes memory resources.

WINDOWS 2000 DISK SUBSYSTEM RESOURCE TUNING

Key disk subsystem–related tuning you should consider:
- Defragment your disk subsystem on a regular basis; this will result in significant performance improvements!
- Perform a fresh, low-level format on all disk drives at the lowest level using the disk or RAID adapter you are using.
- Freshly format all disk drives with NTFS when installing Windows 2000.
- When formatting the disk drive with NTFS, select the ALU size that best matches your disk workload characteristics. For this scenario, the recommended ALU is 8KB for all file systems except the transaction logs. Use 64KB for them.
- Match the stripe size of the low-level RAID format with the ALU size used (see chapter 6 for details) which is 8KB for SQL Server databases and 64KB for transaction logs.
- Since we are using large NTFS volumes, increase the size of the NTFS log file size to 64MB, by using the *chkdsk* command: chkdsk drive-letter: /l:65536.
- Turn on write-back caching and read-ahead caching on hardware RAID adapters.
- Use only I2O-enabled RAID adapters and those with their own CPUs.
- Keep storage capacity on the disk subsystem under 50–60% so that the fast portion of the disk drive is used and so that there is room on the disk drives to perform defragmentation and operate SQL database recovery tools.
- Defragment your disk subsystem on a regular basis; this will result in significant performance improvements!
- Use one Windows 2000 partition per physical disk device/array.
- Group similar disk activities on the same physical disk subsystem and do not separate them via logical partitions on the same physical disk drive/array.
- Use more than one RAID level in your SQL Server solution!
- Add disk drives as needed to keep the disk latency low (sec/transfers) and average queue size less than twice the number of disk drives in the disk array.
- Check all services running on your server. Operate only those you need and stop all others.

WINDOWS 2000 NETWORK SUBSYSTEM RESOURCE TUNING

Key network subsystem–related tuning you should consider:

- Team/trunking multiple NICs (Ethernet channels) together as needed to add network bandwidth and availability to your SQL server (seamlessly to your customers).
- Remove all unnecessary protocols and Redirectors.
- Standardize on one network protocol: TCP/IP.
- Configure SQL Server for only the required protocol support. Avoid, whenever possible, support for unused protocols (IPX, Vines, or anything other than named pipes and TCP/IP). Which network protocols SQL Server uses is completed during the SQL Server installation.
- If more than one network protocol is in use, set binding order such that the most commonly used protocol is first on the list.
- Tune the NIC driver to off-load IPSEC security operations and TCP operations on the NIC itself instead of the main system CPUs.
- Tune the NIC driver to increase its send and receive buffers.
- Use only I2O-enabled NICs.
- Use the fastest I/O bus-enabled NIC possible (64-bit, 66MHz PCI slot).
- Tune the Windows TCP/IP stack to your environment (TCP Hash Table, MTU Window Size). See chapter 7 and the web server scenario for more details.

THIRD-PARTY TOOLS FOR TUNING WINDOWS 2000 SQL SERVERS

Key third-party tools to consider for enhancing the performance of your SQL environment:

- Obtain a third-party disk defragmentation tool that provides enhanced defragmentation features such as scheduling and support of multiple NTFS ALU sizes. Recommended vendor to consider: Norton Speed Disk http://www.Norton.com.
- For heavily loaded SQL Servers, consider running a Windows 2000 scheduler and kernel subsystem enhancers. One such product is Autopilot from SunBelt software. Autopilot analyzes performance data to assist the operating system in making scheduling decisions. Autopilot is available at: http://www.SunBeltSoftware.com.
- If after analyzing your system, you find that SQL Server's tempDb is being used heavily or another area of the disk subsystem is used heavily such as c:\temp, consider implementing a RAM disk. RAM disks create a file system in memory, so from the application's perspective, it just sees a disk drive "r:" and runs much faster than a physical disk drive.

  This technology was investigated in chapter 6 and the resulting tests looked fantastic, with performance improvements greater than 200%. RAM disks are not native to Windows 2000. The RAM disk tested was a product from Super Speed Systems (http://www.eecsys.com) obtained through SunBelt Software (http://www.sunbeltsoftware.com).

Solution Scenario 5: World Wide Web Server Implemented with Microsoft IIS 5.0

Introduction

Web servers are the front-line warriors of the Internet, providing everything from information portals to robust eCommerce sites to a new generation of application services. With higher reliance on web servers, their performance has become increasingly important; in fact, from end users' perspective, web server performance is paramount. A web site that makes a customer wait for more than a few seconds has just lost that customer! Even worse than that, whenever your web site is running slow, the customer's perception of your company's reputation sags too!

In this scenario, the focus is on sizing and tuning web servers. Here, I do not harp on such obvious information as it is better to use compiled web applications native for your web server software engine (such as ASP or ISAPI for IIS, NAPI for Netscape, etc.) versus using a scripting language (such as Perl under CGI). Advising folks what language to use for their web applications is not new information and, besides that, everyone has their own development skill sets and may not be in a big hurry to change. Here the focus is on what you can do to tune your web server at the system level, which encompasses areas such as Windows 2000's use of server resources (CPU, network, disk, memory) and Microsoft Internet Information Services 5.0's software engine itself.

Application Description

Microsoft IIS 5 is a scalable and robust web (httpd) platform that has matured over the past several years. From a performance perspective, consider it an advanced communication system that delivers static and dynamically generated content.

Application Performance Characterization

When we understand how an application operates and the workload it is expected to support, we can then correlate its operations with the performance concepts we have learned throughout the earlier chapters. The whole world is not quite point and click yet. The primary services provided by IIS are web and ftp services that reside in the Inetinfo.exe process. Understanding this process is important for overall optimization of your IIS 5.0 web server. The Inetinfo.exe process not only includes these key services, but internally also handles a shared thread pool, object cache, and logging services. This is one very important process and it will be the focus of much of our IIS specific tuning.

People are creative. Web servers have now morphed into online file services, front end GUIs for back-end applications, as well as a secure portal into a company's Intranet or for collecting private information over the Internet such as credit card information. Heck, you can even run terminal services through a web browser (no terminal service client required!). Because of this, it becomes just as important to really understand the workload that IIS must complete because that affects sizing and tuning. The most common bottlenecks for IIS 5.0 are, in order, network, CPU, memory, and the disk subsystem.

Table 8.33 shows a summary of the key components of IIS 5 and those it relies on from Windows 2000.

TABLE 8.33	*IIS Component Descriptions*
IIS 5.0 Components	**IIS 5.0 Component Descriptions and Characterizations**
Inetinfo.exe	This is the primary IIS 5.0 process that drives web, ftp, and SMTP services. It also includes the shared thread pool, cache, and logging services. Special performance note: *never* let memory get so low that parts of this process are paged out! If this occurs, your web server will run very slowly.
Windows 2000 File System Cache	IIS 5 uses the Windows 2000 dynamic file system cache to cache web pages and files that are requested from the web server or pushed to it. Performance note: Review chapter 5 to ensure you understand the detailed performance characteristics of the file system cache so you can take the best possible advantage of it. IIS 5 relies heavily on the file system cache.
IIS 5.0 Logs	IIS 5 supports one memory mapped log file for each web site it supports that has logging enabled. These files are part of the working set of the InetInfo.exe process and are mapped in 64KB chunks. Performance note: Besides using memory from the Inetinfo.exe process itself, it also uses memory resources from the Windows 2000 file system cache when data is written to the log files residing on disk subsystem.
IIS Object Cache	Contrary to popular opinion, general files are not cached in the object cache which resides inside of the working set of Inetinfo.exe. Objects such as file handles, file directory information listings, and other objects that are used frequently and are expensive to retrieve get stored in the object cache. Performance note: Configure and tune sufficient memory such that the object cache provides > 90% hit rate.
ASP Template and Scripting Engine Caches	Active server pages (ASP) have their own support structure inside of IIS, customized to ASP environments. These two cache structures work hand in hand. The IIS template cache holds pointers to script engines while the script engine cache holds precompiled scripts of ASPs that are ready to run. As more cache hits that are achieved in these two caches, the more CPU overhead is decreased, as fewer pages will be required to be dynamically generated. Performance note: Since these caches do support ASP's dynamic page generation nature, it is a challenge to ensure that they are effective.

TABLE 8.33	*IIS Component Descriptions (Continued)*
IIS 5.0 Components	**IIS 5.0 Component Descriptions and Characterizations**
Shared Pooled Thread Resources	This component resides inside of Inetinfo.exe and provides the worker bee threads that actually execute the applications and services that reside inside of InetInfo.exe. These threads are stored in the nonpaged pool of memory resources. Performance note: Track nonpaged memory usage; you may need to tune what Windows 2000 makes available (chapter 5). Also, track the number of threads as they can be optimized to your environment (later in this chapter).
Http Connection Data Structures	This component is responsible for tracking active connections. Each connection consumes a small amount of system resources (CPU and Memory). This component is also part of the Inetinfo.exe working set. Performance note: Were you already reminded to never let Windows 2000 page portions of Inetinfo.exe page to disk?

Unleash Your Web Server's True Power!

You might be surprised just how much web power is available via a two-CPU-based Windows 2000 IIS 5.0 web server. No single industry benchmark is perfect, but for a frame of reference, let's review a published web performance result based on the SPECweb99 industry standard benchmark. This benchmark measures the throughput of simultaneous web connections that the web server can support. A quick check of the http://www.spec.org web site found a Compaq DL-360 with two 800MHz Pentium III CPUs supporting 1,020 concurrent customers. For this example above, the amount of data delivered when 1,020 customers are all simultaneously pulling data at the benchmark minimum allowable throughput level of 320,000 bits/sec translates into 326Mbits/sec. If you were serving this data over the Internet, you would require seven T3 (45Mbits/sec each) lines to the Internet.

At this performance level, the Compaq DL-360 server provided 2,831 operations (hits)/sec. This works out to roughly 10,191,600 web operations per hour! Even with multiple operations required to provide a single web page, this is enough power to handle some serious web sites. Most sites will rarely require this level of performance, but it is nice to know what an optimized Windows 2000 web solution running on some basic server iron can provide.

By the end of this scenario, you should be able to unleash the power of your web server, but how large a network connection will you need for your customers? Consider the common network connectivity options shown in Table 8.34 when thinking about where your web server bottleneck may be occurring. Note that we do not take network protocol overhead into account in this example, just a relative comparison of how many 10KB web pages each medium can support.

| TABLE 8.34 | Relative Theoretical Network Throughput and Media Access Characterization |

LAN Network Technology	Throughput Megabits/sec	Throughput MB/sec	Number of 10KB Web Pages that Media Can Simultaneously Download
Ethernet (100BaseT)	100	12.5	1,250
Ethernet (Gigabit Ethernet/ 1000BaseTX/FL)	1,000	125	12,500
WAN Network Technology	**Throughput Megabits/sec**	**Throughput MB/sec**	**Number of 10KB Web Pages That Media Can Download**
Dedicated PPP/SLIP	Modem (up to 56Kbit/s)	0.007	0.7
T1	1.544	0.193	19.3
Digital Subscriber Line (DSL)	7	0.875	87.5
T3	45	5.5	550

Sysmon Objects and Counters: IIS 5.0 Server Health, Bottleneck Detection, Tuning, and Sizing

The Sysmon objects and counters outlined in the previous chapters for CPU, memory, disk, and network subsystems are still applicable to Windows 2000 web servers as it is important to understand the big picture when tuning or sizing web server solutions. If one server resource becomes a bottleneck (queues begin to form in the CPU or disk subsystem), response time to the end user begins to suffer.

In addition to the previously reviewed rules of thumb for bottleneck and sizing objects and counters, it is recommended that you become familiar with the Sysmon objects and counters that are added to Sysmon when IIS 5.0 is installed (Table 3.35). These objects and counters are helpful in determining the health of your IIS 5 server application and for tuning and sizing.

Microsoft provides a number of statistics through Sysmon for monitoring the performance of IIS 5 servers, but Sysmon counters do not provide every aspect of detailed instrumentation data. Critical data is also available in the IIS Tracking Logs and the Windows 2000 Event Logs.

TABLE 8.35	*Sleuthing Out Microsoft IIS Specific Health, Tuning, and Sizing Information*

Object: Counter	**Definition**	**Value to Monitor**
Web Service: Total Not Found Errors	Total Not Found Errors is the number of requests that couldn't be satisfied by the server because the requested document could not be found. These are generally reported as an HTTP 404 error code to the client. The count is the total since service startup.	Health indicator and bottleneck detection Why waste resources looking for pages that are not there? This counter is a good indicator of questionable web site maintenance (cleaning up of old links).
Process: Inetinfo.exe All parameters	Obtain and track information on the InetInfo.exe process to determine its overall performance health.	Health indicator and bottleneck detection Tracking all of the Inetinfo.exe counters provides insight into the health and performance of your web server.
Active Server Pages: Errors/sec	The numbers of errors per second, including connection errors, compile errors, and run-time errors.	Health indicator Why waste resources looking for pages that are not there? This counter is a good indicator of how well the ASPs are written. If this number is greater than 0, something is wrong with the test scripts, server configuration, or scripts in ASPs
Active Server Pages: Requests Queued	The number of requests waiting for service from the queue.	Bottleneck detection If you are running ASPs on your web site, track this value. If the ASP queue grows at all, customer requests are failing and they will receive server busy errors in their browsers (if a customer message was not defined). To resolve this condition, ensure that CPU cycles are available, then increase the IIS queue. This is reviewed later in this scenario.
Internet Information Services Global: Cache Hits %	Instantaneous value of how well the IIS object cache is doing.	Tuning and sizing If this value is < 90% and you have additional memory resources available, increase its available cache size through the registry. (See IIS 5.0 tuning section.)
Internet Information Services Global: Cache Flushed	How often the cache is emptied due to time-out or because object changed.	Tuning and sizing If objects are moving through the object cache too swiftly, consider upping the time to live values in the registry.

TABLE 8.35	Sleuthing Out Microsoft IIS Specific Health, Tuning, and Sizing Information (Continued)	
Object: Counter	**Definition**	**Value to Monitor**
Internet Information Services Global: File Cache Hits % and Cache: Data Map Hits %	How well the Windows 2000 file system cache is performing for IIS related tasks.	Tuning and sizing Is the percentage of data maps in the file system cache that could be resolved without having to retrieve a page from the disk, because the page was already in physical memory. The higher this percentage, the better performance the customer will receive.
Web Service: Total Connection Attempts	Total Connection Attempts is the number of connections that have been attempted using the Web service (counted since service startup). This counter is for all web servers hosted on this server.	Influences tuning and sizing This information is helpful in sizing the overall solution.
Web Service: Maximum Connections	Maximum Connections is the maximum number of simultaneous connections established with the web service.	Health of IIS If the Web Services: Total connection attempts is much greater than the maximum connections, then there may be a performance or configuration problem that is stopping customers from connecting to the web site.
Web Service: Current Connection	Current Connections is the current number of connections established with the web service.	Influences sizing and tuning How much simultaneous activity is your web site experiencing. Excellent for tuning and sizing.

Scenario 5 Step by Step: Sizing and Tuning a Mid-Range Windows 2000 Web Server

Sizing the Initial Web Server Configuration

In chapter 3, the core sizing methodology was presented for sizing your Windows 2000 solution. That methodology is followed here for the development of the initial Windows 2000 web server configuration.

1. DEFINE OBJECTIVE(S)

Before the merger of the two companies, both companies ran into regular problems with their web and eCommerce presence regularly being overwhelmed. Now that the merger is complete, Ajax Rockets has decided that its Internet presence is too important to continually run into performance issues. The web server will primarily be the front end for eCommerce operations. It will also be used to host internal documents accessible by internal associates only. Although the technical team recommended separate systems for intranet and eCommerce web solutions, they were overruled by management. Go figure. The technical team will still provide an outstanding solution.

2. UNDERSTAND BUSINESS AND TECHNICAL REQUIREMENTS NEEDED TO MEET YOUR OBJECTIVE(S)

- Which application(s) will meet your functional objective(s)?
  Microsoft IIS 5.0 will be the web server engine.
- What are the availability requirements?
  These are critical servers, as they will support the entire company for eCommerce and intranet activities. The goal is to have a highly available solution. This is a high-profile, business-critical application. No downtime is considered acceptable.
- What are the ramifications if your system is down?
  If the system does not provide service, loss of revenue and loss of associate productivity will occur.
- What are the disk subsystem storage capacity requirements?
  There are approximately 1GB of web server application space required and 10GB of various marketing material required. This web server will front end the eCommerce database and intranet document database repository.

Looking at the big picture, all disk storage requirements are outlined in Table 8.36.

TABLE 8.36   *IIS 5.0 Server Disk Storage Sizing Matrix*

Application	Disk Storage Capacity Needed
Windows 2000 operation system requirement and IIS 5	<500MB
Pagefile	2GB
Web server application	3GB
System management agent	5MB
Security application (server-based firewall and IDS)	30MB
Web Content eCommerce and Intranet	10GB

3. DETERMINE LOADING CHARACTERISTICS

- *Number of total users per server*
  Marketing's best estimate is that 240 customers/sec will visit and interact with the web site. This works out to 14,400 hits/minute or 864,000

hits per hour in a worst-case—or best-case—scenario, depending on how you look at it. On average, the customer visitation rate is expected to be much lower. However, for a critical eCommerce solution, Ajax Rockets has decided to design a solution for a worst-case scenario to handle the holiday rush.

Also, due to availability requirements, they intend to spread the web workload across two IIS 5 servers using Network Load Balancing (NLB), which is included in the Windows 2000 Advanced Server. Using this technology, a shared-nothing cluster is created that will respond to the same IP or web site address in a load balanced manner. Thus, the workload will be split between the two servers. For more information on NLB, check out the following web site: http://www.microsoft.com/TechNet/win2000/nlbovw.asp

- *Number of concurrent users per server*
  240. See discussion under total users.
- *Disk workload characteristics (read/write environment)*
  The goal is to cache as much as possible in memory to improve overall performance. Except for logging, all data are considered random in nature with most of the requests being read intensive, as all write-intensive information is stored in the back-end databases.
- *Size of average records/transactions*
  Average size of each web page is 20KB.
- *Physical location of users (Influences communications such as WAN, LAN, dial-up, terminal services, etc.)*
  All servers reside on site and are connected internally via the local switched Ethernet 100BaseTX LAN for Internet access. Currently, two redundant T3 lines are in place.
- *Type of work the user will complete*
  This web site is part of the overall eCommerce and intranet solution for Ajax Rockets. Primary work that will be completed includes eCommerce transactions centered on sales and marketing information, an Intranet Knowledge management services, and search engine services for the web site.

4. DETERMINE PERFORMANCE REQUIREMENTS

From a performance perspective, response time to the customer is the most important factor for a web server solution. Ajax Rocket's business goal is to provide all web responses to customers within three seconds. The second most important performance requirement is backup operations during each evening and being able to restore the backup data within four hours. For this environment, using Windows 2000 NLB, only one of the servers must be backed up, since all data is replicated to each of the web servers (using a third-party tool named Double Take, available at http://www.SunBeltSoftware.com) to ensure each web server provides the same consistent data to customers. Data such as ASP updates are placed onto the primary web server and Double Take replicates this data to the other servers in the cluster over the network.

Based on current business requirements worst-case scenarios, 13GB must be backed up in eight hours and restored in four hours. If a failure occurs, Ajax Rockets relies on the other web servers in the cluster to provide web services while the down server is restored. To restore this amount of data in four hours (which is more disk intensive than backing up the data), the disk and network subsystem will need to support a restoration rate of 3.25GB/hour, which works out to 0.9MB/sec. This is relatively easy to accommodate. Follow the approach outlined in the backup server scenario in this chapter to meet the backup goals.

5. UNDERSTAND FUTURE BUSINESS REQUIREMENTS

Ajax Rockets is an optimistic company and expects that orders will grow by at least 30% per year. To accommodate this, they could build larger servers or add additional web servers to the NLB Cluster, which supports up to 32 servers in a shared-nothing cluster. Ajax Rockets has decided to take the cluster approach to scale their solution. As needed, they plan to add identical servers to meet the projected demand. This concept is referred to as Redundant Array of Inexpensive Servers (RAIS).

6. UNDERSTAND FUTURE SYSTEM ARCHITECTURES

By taking and adopting the RAIS strategy, Ajax Rockets is looking to implement cutting-edge but smaller servers to meet its web services needs.

7. CONFIGURE THE SYSTEM

Finally, to the good stuff. At this point, you can configure the Windows 2000 IIS 5 server. Choose the system resources required in meeting your objective, with consideration for steps 1 through 6, and obtain the system. As you configure the system, look at each individual resource to meet the overall system configuration. Software and hardware vendors are good sources of information and can suggest configurations that will get you started. Reviewing relevant industry benchmarks also can help provide insight into the initial configuration. Industry benchmarks are explored in depth in chapter 3. The following steps are presented to help guide you through the actual system configuration process.

Having some sort of idea on how each system resource works and relates to the overall system performance is helpful when configuring your system. Chapters 4 through 7 review the overall system architecture of each system resource in greater detail.

7.1 APPLICATION CHARACTERISTICS REVIEW • The general IIS 5 application characteristics and backup technology review was completed at the top of the web server scenario section.

7.2 REVIEW EACH SYSTEM RESOURCE FOR THE WINDOWS 2000 WEB SERVER

Disk I/O Requirements • The disk subsystem houses much of the information provided via the web server while the back-end databases provide the dynamic content data. The goal is to cache much of the data needed for web transactions, but at 10GB of potential data, we will need an optimized disk subsystem for low latency, as this is an interactive solution. From the business requirements above, we will determine the disk storage and performance requirements.

Availability • Even though clustering is used in this solution, all data will reside on hot swappable RAID array–based disk subsystems that use some level of fault tolerance. Transactional data is kept on the back-end database servers.

Performance Workload Characteristics • From the workload characteristics of a general IIS server above, we will need to support only two RAID levels to meet the performance requirements: the random nature of the eCommerce and intranet data and the sequential write-intensive data from the IIS logs.

Performance: Throughput and Transfers/sec • Based on what we learned about tuning disk subsystems in chapter 6, it is desirable to group applications with similar disk workload characteristics together on the same physical disk subsystem for maximum performance. Taking this approach with our current web server environment, the eCommerce and intranet data will be grouped together on the same physical disk subsystem while the write-intensive log file data will be placed on a separate disk subsystem.

In this environment, we have two performance requirements—response time and throughput to the end user and throughput needed for backup operations. If the transactions/sec occurring on the disk subsystem becomes too high and disk queues begin to form, it will affect end-user response time. To determine the transfers/sec required to support three-second response time for a user, we can review industry standard benchmarks and historical information.

The most common industry benchmark for web server environments is SpecWeb99. SpecWeb99 results are available at http://www.spec.org. However, for this environment, historical information is more helpful.

Backup performance was discussed in the backup scenario and is not a very large workload component in this scenario, so we will not cover it here. In a worst-case scenario—assuming that the file system cache that supports IIS 5 is not effective—the disk subsystem will need to simultaneously support 240 eCommerce customers, each requesting 20KB documents, and 20 internal associates, each requesting 20 400KB documents. This would require that the disk subsystem provide 4.8MB for eCommerce requests in three seconds (1.6MB per second) and 8MB for intranet operations in three seconds (2.6MB/sec) of overall throughput. If each disk transaction provided 32KB of data, this indicates that we need to support 50 transactions/sec for eCommerce applications and 81 transactions/sec for intranet operations. Since this environment is random in nature, read intensive, and fault tolerance is required, a RAID 5 array would be perfect. If we placed the eCommerce and intranet data on the same array, we will need to support 131 transfers/sec and 4.12 MB/sec of throughput. From chapter 6, we found that each disk drive in a RAID 5 array can support approximately 1.11MB/sec of throughput and 100 transfers/sec. Reviewing the worst case of what we need to support, two disks would provide the transactions/sec [131 disk read transfers/sec] + [4 × (0 disk write transfers/sec)] × [1.25 utilization factor/100 transfers/sec/disk] needed, but we will need four disk drives to support the throughput requirements (4.12MB/sec / 1.11MB/sec per drive).

To meet our response time and throughput performance requirements, we take the greater number of disk drives that were calculated in the above steps. Thus, four disk drives are required (the higher number between the response time and throughput time calculations above) to meet our projected performance requirements. For more details on disk subsystem performance, review chapter 6.

Storage Capacity • Even when focusing on disk storage capacity, continue to think performance. The fastest portion of the disk subsystem is the outer edge of the physical disk. If you keep the disk subsystem at less than 60% filled, it will just run faster! Disk defragmentation tools typically require at least 20% disk free space to operate and 30–40% to run optimally. Based on all of the above disk information, Table 8.37 outlines the overall disk subsystem requirements.

TABLE 8.37	Web Server Disk Subsystem Solution (Server 1 of 2)		
Application	**Minimum Disk Storage Needed**	**Logical Partition**	**Recommended Configuration (All 10,000rpm, Ultra2 SCSI Disk Drives)**
Windows 2000 operation system and IIS requirements	<500MB	C:	2 9GB disk drives in RAID 1 array
System management agent	5MB	C:	
Antivirus application	20MB	C:	
Security application (server-based firewall and IDS)	30MB	C:	
Web applications	3GB	C:	

| TABLE 8.37 | Web Server Disk Subsystem Solution (Server 1 of 2) (Continued) |

Application	Minimum Disk Storage Needed	Logical Partition	Recommended Configuration (All 10,000rpm, Ultra2 SCSI Disk Drives)
Pagefile and IIS log file (historical data on who visited the web site and their patterns)	Pagefile: 2GB IIS Logs: ~2GB	L:	2 9GB disk drives in RAID 1 array (9GB usable/4GB filled)
eCommerce and intranet data	10GB	H:	4 9GB disk drives in a RAID 5 array (27GB usable/10GB filled)

CPU Requirements • The primary operations to support from a CPU perspective are the IIS web server, the static and dynamic web application operations, delivering content over the network, and security related operations associated with Secure Socket Layer encryption (SSL). SSL operations introduce a CPU overhead of three to six times more than non-SSL operations. SSL operations will be used in this site, but are leveraged only when absolutely necessary. From a CPU perspective, the initial creation of an SSL session is the most expensive portion of the SSL operation. Later we will look into tuning techniques of how to lessen the effect that SSL has on our site.

Table 8.38 shows historical information for two current web servers that are online.

| TABLE 8.38 | Initial Web Server CPU Sizing |

Application	CPU Usage (Estimate) Based on One Pentium III 800MHz CPU	Total CPU Usage
Windows 2000 and General operations		10%
Overhead for system management software		1% (estimated)
Overhead for intrusion detection software		1% (estimated)
Per eCommerce user connection CPU requirements	0.4% of CPU resource/user × 240 users	96%
Per intranet user connection CPU requirements	0.8% of CPU resources/user × 20 users	16%
Search engine requirements		6%
Total Estimated CPU Usage		*130% Total CPU usage or 65% per CPU if 2 CPUs are used*

For a general reality check we should ask: Can two CPUs provide this level of web server workload? To answer that question, we obtained a SpecWeb99 benchmark from http://www.spec.org to see how much performance two CPUs in an intense web server environment could provide. The benchmark was configured using a Compaq DL-360 with two Pentium III 800MHz CPUs. This benchmark configuration was able to sustain 2,831 operations (hits)/sec. This level of performance is higher than our currently projected workload.

With the above information, two 800MHz/256K Pentium III CPUs will be configured. We are estimating that only 63% of each CPU will be used during peak hours, which provides room to grow. However, since Ajax Rockets is concerned with performance availability, there will be two servers configured identically with Windows 2000 NLB software, which will balance the workload between the two servers. This should provide more than adequate performance support for the projected workload in a worst-case scenario.

Memory Requirements • Sizing RAM is an additive process. Our first step in sizing memory resources is to outline all applications that will use any memory resources. Microsoft IIS manages only some of its own cache and memory requirements and relies heavily on the Windows 2000 dynamic file system cache.

The amount of memory that IIS 5 uses for caching operations is tunable by editing the IIS management GUI in conjunction with direct registry tuning. Table 8.39 shows a breakdown of where the memory resources are being focused. This information is based on historical data and our own targets.

Through proactive performance management, more RAM can be added (or removed) as needed. Web server environments love properly tuned RAM! This estimate is based on historical information collected (memory working set was monitored on the two precious web servers) and insight into how Windows 2000 takes advantage of memory resources. It provides us a good place to start. For a more detailed discussion of Windows 2000 and memory resources, refer to chapter 5.

TABLE 8.39	*Web Server Memory Sizing Matrix*
Application	**Memory Usage (Working Set)**
Windows 2000 operating system requirement	128MB
Windows 2000 file system cache (maximum for configurations less than 1GB in size)	432MB (This is the maximum amount of memory that Windows 2000 will commit to the file system cache when less than 1GB of memory is configured)
Overhead for system management software running on server	8MB

TABLE 8.39	Web Server Memory Sizing Matrix (Continued)	
Application	**Memory Usage (Working Set)**
Overhead for intrusion detection software	12MB
Backup server application	10MB
Memory used for each user concurrent user connection (300 × ~20KB)	6MB
IIS 5 (program code, object cache, template cache, script engine cache, HTTP structures, pooled threads, etc.)	428MB
Total Estimated Memory Usage	*1024MB*

Network I/O Requirements • This is the critical component in the web server solution and where most web servers run into problems. How much bandwidth is required? Let's review Ajax Rocket's expected workload for the web server. Note that for network calculations, we convert to Megabits per second, as that is the common notation used with networking technologies.

First, we have the eCommerce requirement to simultaneously support 240 customers each requesting a 20KB document with a three-second response time, which works out to 12.8Mbits/sec (1.6MB/sec) in a worst-case scenario; remember, this is before web and network overhead. If we add a 20% overhead ratio, we will need 15.36Mbits/sec of bandwidth. For our simultaneous intranet customers, each requesting a 400KB document, we require 20.8Mbits/sec (2.6MB/sec). Adding 20% network and web server overhead, this works out to 24.96Mbits/sec. From a backup and restore perspective, less than 7.2Mbits/sec (0.9MB/sec) is needed. With this information, we compose the network bandwidth summary chart shown in Table 8.40.

TABLE 8.40	Web Server Network Sizing	
Service	**Network Throughput Required Internally**	**Network Throughput Required to Internet**
eCommerce Operations	N/A	15.36Mbits/sec
Intranet Operations	24.96Mbits/sec	8.32Mbits/sec
Backup Operations	7.2Mbits/sec	N/A

Sizing network bandwidth is not all science; there is some art involved. It is also important to know your environment well. A partial T3 connection to the Internet would meet the immediate eCommerce requirements, and a single 100BaseTX NIC (100Mbits/sec) would meet the network requirements of the web server itself. However, one third of the company is still located at another location and the network connection between them is based on a

Virtual Private Network (VPN) connection that uses the Internet. Thus, at a minimum, the network bandwidth required to support both the eCommerce and intranet applications is estimated to be 24Mbits/sec.

7.3 SYSTEM ARCHITECTURE RELATIONSHIP CHECK ● This is a final, common-sense check of the Windows 2000 web server configuration. Since the business requirements require keeping this new web server for at least three years, leading-edge server technology will be obtained. Not cutting edge, as that technology tends to demand a premium price.

From all of the sizing information above, we now have the following configuration: a one- to two-CPU capable server, two Pentium III 800MHz CPUs with 256KB each of full-speed (ATC) Level 2 cache, a 133MHz system bus, 1024MB of RAM, a single 64-bit 33MHz PCI I/O bus (266MB/sec), one internal hardware based RAID controller, two disk drives for the operating system and log files, four disk drives for the static web content, and one 100BaseTX Ethernet NIC. This server configuration is balanced and there is nothing notable in the way of data path bottlenecks.

There is one problem with this solution and a potential concern. First, only a single fast Ethernet connection is planned for. From a network availability perspective, some of the folks at Ajax Rockets have encountered failed NICs in the past. With the web server being such an important item, they have elected to obtain two NICs and use Adaptive Fault Tolerance. This is surprisingly easy to configure on NICs that support this feature and is found under the NIC's advanced tab.

7.4 FUTURE BUSINESS AND SYSTEM ARCHITECTURES CHECK REVIEW ● This server has room to grow in the disk and network areas but is limited in the CPU area. If the workload stays the same but more disk storage capacity is needed, that can easily be added to the external arrays. From a performance perspective, if the workload does increase additional servers can be added to the Windows 2000 Network Load Balanced cluster to meet the increased demands.

7.5 INITIAL HARDWARE CONFIGURATION AND TUNING ● In this step, the initial configuration of the server hardware begins to take shape based on steps 7.1 and 7.2 (Table 8.41). See the Sizing and Tuning Web Servers section below as needed.

TABLE 8.41	*IIS 5.0 Web Server Hardware Configuration Specifications*

Windows 2000 Web Server Hardware Configuration
Compaq ML-370 (Why select the ML-370? We needed a solid system to use for a real-world reference.)

CPU Configuration	CPUs Used in Solution	CPU Family	Level 2 Cache Size	Speed of CPU	Available CPU Slots
	2	Intel Pentium III	256KB	800MHz	2 of 2 used

TABLE 8.41	*IIS 5.0 Web Server Hardware Configuration Specifications (Continued)*

Windows 2000 Web Server Hardware Configuration
Compaq ML-370 (Why select the ML-370? We needed a solid system to use for a real-world reference.)

RAM Configuration	*Amount of RAM Used in Solution*	*System Bus Speed*	*Type of RAM*	*RAM Expansion*
	1024MB	133MHz	ECC SDRAM	4GB

NIC Card Configuration	*Number and Type of I/O Card*	*Number of PCI I/O Buses*	*Placement of PCI Cards*	*Speed of PCI Bus*
	1 Internal RAID Adapter	2	Not applicable. Built into motherboard.	One (1) 64-bit 33MHz; one 32-bit 33MHz
	2 Single Channel Full Duplex 100Base TX		The two 100BaseTX NICs are placed into the first two available PCI slots 0 and 1 in the 64-bit PCI bus.	

Disk Subsystem Configuration	*Partition/ Mount Point*	*Files Located There*	*Type of RAID Adapter*	*SCSI Channel*	*RAID Level*	*# of 10K rpm Ultra2 SCSI Disk Drives*
	C:	Windows 2000 installation, IIS application and logs, system management software, intrusion detection software	Built-in RAID adapter Compaq	1 of 1	1	2 9GB disk drives
	L:	IIS logs and page file	Built-in RAID adapter Compaq	1 of 1	1	2 9GB disk drives
	H:	eCommerce and Intranet Data	2 Channel Ultra2 SCSI	1 of 2	5	4 9GB disk Drives

7.6 INITIAL SOFTWARE CONFIGURATION AND TUNING • In this step, the initial software configuration of the server configuration begins to take shape based on steps 7.1 and 7.2. See the Tuning Web Servers section below.

7.7 INITIAL GENERAL TUNING • See the Tuning Web Servers section below.

8. STRESS TEST AND VALIDATE THE SERVER CONFIGURATION

Although not recommended, Ajax Rockets has decided that they do not have the time to stress test their solution, due to time to market pressures. However, Ajax Rockets feels strongly that with the current design and through proactive management, they can quickly scale the solution as needed to meet their needs.

9. PROACTIVELY FOLLOW THE CORE TUNING METHODOLOGY DURING STRESS AND VALIDATION TESTING ANALYZING THE RESULTS: KEY OBSERVATIONS

Not applicable since no stress testing was completed.

10. DEPLOY THE SYSTEM INTO PRODUCTION

A very similar scenario to this was deployed successfully after some Internet connectivity problems were resolved.

11. PROACTIVELY FOLLOW THE TUNING METHODOLOGY AFTER THE SYSTEM IS DEPLOYED

Environments do change. The information gathered following the core tuning methodology is helpful for staying one step in front of user demand by identifying current load demands and potential system bottlenecks. Also, use this information when developing and sizing future system solutions and when adding additional capacity to your current system(s). If you have not quantifiably determined where and how to add additional capacity to your system, you are in great risk of wasting your time.

IIS 5.0 Web Server Sizing and Configuration Chart Summary

Even though every environment is different, the IIS 5 web server configuration chart (Table 8.42) provides sound sizing guidelines on which to base your initial server configurations. Follow the sizing template above to customize to your environment and then proactively manage your Windows 2000 Web Server to an optimal fit!

| **TABLE 8.42** | *Specific Configurations for Sizing Web Servers* |

Concurrent **Web Users** (Hits/sec – 10KB page)	**Pentium III Class CPUs**	**RAM**	**Number of Ultra2 SCSI 10K rpm Disk Drives**	**Network Interface Card**
<= 100 (8,640,000 hits/day)	1	512MB	4	100BaseTX
<= 250 (20,736,000 hits/day)	1–2	1024MB–2GB	7	100BaseTX
<= 500 (43,200,000 hits/day)	2–4	2–4GB	14	(1–2) 100BaseTX or 1000BaseTX

Wow, more than 8 million hits per day! These numbers can be deceiving if you look fast. Few eCommerce solutions or basic web sites have their workload well balanced throughout the day. Reality is sink or swim! You may have an enormous storm of 7 million hits in one hour, and only a few hundred the rest of the day; that works out to 7.2 million per day. Interesting, isn't it? The real challenge for eCommerce environment is to plan for and be able to stay alive during the peak, or worst-case, workload scenarios!

Windows 2000 IIS 5.0 Web Server Tuning

IIS 5.0 Web Server Specific Application Tuning

The basic characteristics for IIS 5.0 web server operations were reviewed at the beginning of this section. Here we look at the high-level holistic system level approach of tuning an IIS 5.0 web server. Before we jump into the hands-on tactics, let's cover some web optimization strategies first. Remember that to get the most out of your web server it is important to understand what type of content is really being provided. Follow the guidelines presented in the sizing section of this scenario so that you can be sure of starting with a sound, properly sized platform. This is important, since each content type taxes your web server resources in a slightly different manner.

When tuning your IIS 5.0 web server, remember to follow the core Tuning Methodology Review in chapter 2.

From a holistic system perspective, the primary parts of our Windows 2000 IIS 5.0 web server tuning strategy are:
- Size the disk subsystem layout for low latency (completed in the earlier sizing section).
- Size the CPU, memory, and network subsystems for the workload so that you can meet the business requirements (completed in the earlier sizing section).
- Optimize the Windows 2000 network subsystem for web-based workloads.
- Tune the web server software engine to use all available server resources (CPU, memory, network, disk, etc.).
- Optimize Windows 2000 subsystems.

So, how can you accomplish these strategies? Read on. We will now review the step-by-step tactics that you can quickly employ to maximize your web server's performance.

> ***Caution 1: There are numerous tuning options outlined below that require editing the Windows 2000 registry and the IIS metabase. Ensure that you properly back up the registry and metabase and understand how to recover them. Test your backups before tuning any registry entries or metabase entries.***

Caution 2: Many of the tuning options presented increase either the CPU or memory resource usage. Ensure that you have followed the tuning methodology from chapter 2 and have a solid baseline of the performance of your web server before beginning any tuning. With this information and continued proactive management of your web server, you can then quantitatively determine if your efforts are successful. At a minimum you should track the following key system monitor objects and counters throughout the web server tuning process so that you do not overwhelm your server (Object: Counter): Processor: %Processor Time, Process: All Counters for Inetinfo.exe process, System: Processor Queue Length, Server: Pooled & NonPooled Memory: System Cache Resident Bytes, Memory: Available Mbytes, and Memory: Pages/sec. Also consider running the customer perspective scripts from chapter 2 that measure the http response time of your web server over the network.

Strategy: Optimize the Windows 2000 Network Subsystem for Web-Based Workloads

OPTIMIZING WINDOWS 2000 TCP SUBSYSTEM FOR WEB SERVER APPLICATIONS

Assume that our sizing for the network above, in conjunction with proactive tuning, is successful and we have no physical network bottlenecks between us and our customers. So, now that the superhighway leading to your web server is not a bottleneck, consider optimizing the Windows 2000 TCP stack for web server operations. You will want your IIS 5 web server to respond to as many connections as your resources will allow, so don't let an ill-tuned TCP stack stand in your way and slow you down—tune it!

Before we begin optimizing the TCP stack, remember that, as with all tuning, track all other system resources so that you ensure your tuning operations result in no adverse effects. Specifically when tuning TCP parameters, monitor the nonpaged and paged pool resources closely with Sysmon, since increasing these TCP parameter settings increases the amount of pooled resources that are used.

The transmission control blocks store data for each TCP connection. A control block is attached to the TCB hash table for each active connection. If there are not enough control blocks available when a web request (http) arrives at your server via TCP/IP, there is added delay while it waits for additional control blocks to be created. By increasing the TCB timewait table size, latency overhead is reduced by allowing more web connections to be serviced in a faster fashion. To adjust this operation, add the following registry value: `HKEY_LOCAL_MACHINE\System\CurrentControlSet\Services\Tcpip\Parameters\MaxFreeTcbs=0x9c4`.

This example increases the TCB timewait table to 40,000 entries from the default of 2,000.

Now that overhead time introduced by TCP is lowered for the web server, you must adjust the corresponding hash table, which is where the TCBs are stored. Accomplish this by adding the following registry value `HKEY_LOCAL_MACHINE\System\CurrentControlSet\Services\Tcpip\Parameters\MaxHashTableSize=0x2000`.

This increases the TCB hash table size from a default of 512 to 8,192, allowing more room for connection information.

In addition to increasing the size of the TCP hash table, we want also to improve the efficiency of how TCBs are located by increasing the number of TCB table partitions available; that helps to mitigate search contention. To accomplish this, add the following registry value: `HKEY_LOCAL_MACHINE\System\CurrentControlSet\Services\Tcpip\Parameters\NumTcbTablePartitions` to 8 from its default value of 4. Note, this value must be a power of 2 and is typically optimized when you have between two to four times the number of CPUs in your server.

When one user stops communicating with the web server, perhaps moving off to another web site (which you hope does not belong to a competitor), the original web server keeps the TCP socket pair in an open state for a default time of 240 seconds. However, on very busy web sites, this behavior may use all of the available ports before they are freed. You can adjust this behavior by adding the registry value: `HKEY_LOCAL_MACHINE\System\CurrentControlSet\Services\Tcpip\Parameters\TcpTimedWaitDelay=0x3c`, sets TIME_WAIT parameter to 60 seconds.

This is a non-RFC 1122 value, but should be acceptable for most large web sites. What if all of the TCP ports are being used? Add more. The default maximum port range is 1024 to 50,000. You can expand this range by adding the key `HKEY_LOCAL_MACHINE\System\CurrentControlSet\Services\Tcpip\Parameters\MaxUserPort` to 0xfffe. This would set the maximum open ports to 65,534.

If you can lower the amount of overhead associated with each web transaction, more data can be passed in every network exchange, thus improving the effective bandwidth throughput (web pages load faster). Windows 2000 has improved its TCP stack performance, but you can further enhance its performance by tuning the TCP window size, which is the amount of data received at one time on a TCP connection. Windows 2000 does dynamically tune this value and supports TCP windows scaling as needed; however, by default, the TCP window size is only 8KB. It is desirable to increase this value for 10BaseTX or greater performing networks to 17,520 by adding the following registry key: `HKEY_LOCAL_MACHINE\System\CurrentControlSet\Services\Tcpip\Parameters\TcpWindowSize`. To improve performance on high delay but reliable networks (such as satellite links or long-haul, intercontinent fiber runs), consider increasing the TCP WindowSize to 64KB. When a value of this size is used, Windows 2000 negotiates the windows size using the TCP three-way handshake to find an optimal size. Having a larger TCP window enables more data to be sent before an acknowledgment is needed, again improving the effective bandwidth of the media in use.

It is important to note that TCB information is stored in the nonpaged memory pool. If the web server is experiencing memory bottlenecks and more memory cannot be allotted to the server, lower the above values shown in this section.

TUNING NIC USAGE FOR IMPROVED WEB SERVER RESPONSE TIME

Another way you can improve your web server response time is by optimizing the NIC and CPU relationship for web server workloads. Each web request received over the network generates an interrupt to the processor requesting service. If the processor does not find the request urgent enough (a high enough interrupt level), it will defer the request. This deferred interrupt request becomes a Deferred Procedure Call (DPC). As more and more requests come into the web server, the number of interrupts and DPCs increase. When an interrupt is sent to a particular CPU and it gets deferred, additional server overhead is incurred if this DPC is shipped off to another CPU in the server. This is Windows 2000's default behavior and can be costly from a performance perspective in high load situations. To stop this from happening, set the following registry value: `HKEY_LOCAL_MACHINE\System\CurrentControlSet\Services\NDIS\Parameters\ProcessorAffinityMask` to 0.

This forces the CPU that handled the interrupt to also handle any associated DPCs. This also ensures that the network interface card or cards are not associated with a specific CPU. This improves the CPU's servicing of interrupts and DPCs generated by the network interface card(s).

TUNING WINDOWS 2000 AND IIS 5.0 TO KEEP INETINFO.EXE WHERE YOU WANT IT: IN RAM

Regardless of whether you're providing an Internet- (WAN) or intranet- (LAN) based solution, networks introduce enough latency to slow down web requests to your users, so avoid adding any more in your web server solution. Accessing memory is tremendously faster than going to the disk drive to get what your web server might need. It's the difference between running 50 yards (memory access) to your refrigerator for your favorite cold beverage compared with running a 25-mile marathon (disk drive access) for the same item. Which would you prefer? With this in mind, there are several tuning activities we can complete to improve the chances that what we want is found in RAM.

IIS is a multithreaded application that runs as a single process instance, referred to as Inetinfo.exe under Windows 2000. Included in this process, IIS provides an object cache, which is a cache of objects associated with Active Server Pages (ASP), web services (http), FTP, and SMTP services. The object cache is part of IIS's working set; i.e., the area in physical RAM that Inetinfo.exe occupies. So our goal is to keep Inetinfo's working set, and consequently as much of its frequently used objects in RAM as possible. Unfortunately, there are a few other activities occurring on your web server that may want memory space too. Every web connection provided by your web server takes up some RAM, and if the request references data residing on the web server's file system, then Windows 2000's file system is called into action.

HOW TO TUNE THE WINDOWS 2000 FILE SYSTEM CACHE FOR IIS 5

So what can one do to keep this important process in memory? It depends on how much memory you have in your server. If you have planned for the Windows 2000 file system cache to grow to its maximum size (432MB if you have 1GB of memory, 960MB if you have 2GB of memory), then select the "Maximize Data throughput for file sharing" Windows 2000 memory management strategy. How to implement this setting was covered in chapter 5, but as a reminder you can set the File System Cache strategy by right-clicking My Network Places, then selecting properties for your local area connection, then properties for File and Print Sharing for Microsoft Networks.

For example, in this web server solution scenario, 1GB of RAM was configured. Using this tactic, Windows 2000 will allow the file system cache to grow to its full size of 432MB, leaving the rest for other applications, specifically IIS 5.0, that will be tuned to leverage the available memory resources. This is where the information from sizing the memory subsystem reviewed above becomes invaluable, as you must know what is running on your web server and how much memory is taken before tuning the file system cache or IIS directly.

If, however, you are running a web server with less than 1GB of memory and plan to let the file system cache grow as needed and contend with other processes for memory resources, set the Windows 2000 memory strategy to "Maximize data throughput for network applications." Using this tactic, the file system cache will most likely not grow to its maximum size, as the working set of other applications will take priority over file system cache requests. This is a good approach to use if you do not have enough memory resources configured and your web server has other applications residing on it.

If you ever observe the working set of Inetinfo.exe get smaller, other applications' working sets get larger, the pages/sec increasing, and the pagefile growing (using the System Monitor—Sysmon), it is time to tune the system and possibly add more memory. When this situation occurs, parts of Inetinfo.exe are most likely being paged to disk and your web server will begin to run slowly. You can observe the working set of any processes under Sysmon's Process Object, select the process to track, and watch its working set counter.

OPTIMIZING IIS LARGE FILE, FILE CACHE USAGE

We have optimized the Windows 2000 memory subsystem, but what about IIS interaction with the file system cache? By default, IIS does not like to cache files that are larger than MaxCachedFileSize. If you have a web site that is working with larger files (greater than the default value of 256KB) and you do not find the file system cache effective, you will want to increase the size of files IIS will cache. This is accomplished by editing the following registry entry: `HKEY_LOCAL_MACHINE\System\CurrentControlSet\Services\Inet-Info\Parameters\MaxCachedFileSize`. This will ensure IIS will cache the files that may be indicative of your larger, file-based web server environment.

OPTIMIZING IIS GENERAL FILE CACHE USAGE

How much of Windows 2000 file system cache will Inetinfo.exe use? By default, 50% of available memory. You can adjust this higher for dedicated web servers or lower it for servers that host multiple applications. Adjust this behavior by adding the MemCacheSize (MB) REG_DWORD to `HKEY_LOCAL_MACHINE\System\CurrentControlSet\Services\InetInfo\Parameters\MaxCachedFileSize`. If for some reason the file system cache is not working well at all, ensure that `HKEY_LOCAL_MACHINE\System\Current-ControlSet\Services\InetInfo\Parameters\MaxCachedFileSize\Disable-MemoryCache` is set to 0. If it is set to 1, IIS's use of the file system cache will be disabled. You can observe the effectiveness of the file system cache from IIS's perspective by reviewing the Sysmon object Internet Information Systems Global File Cache Hits % counter.

Strategy: Tune the Web Server Software Engine to Use All Available Server Resources

IIS 5.0 has its own application-specific tunable areas. Our primary goal in tuning IIS is to ensure that it takes advantage of all available resources and does not limit performance from a web server engine perspective. For the IIS 5 application itself, we look at how we can tune it to optimally leverage each resource in the server. IIS 5 tuning is not relegated to the IIS snap in GUI interfaces found in the Microsoft Management Console (MMC) and registry (accessed with regedt32.exe and regedit.exe tools) settings alone. IIS 5 also includes a metabase of configuration information that is leveraged for its operations and optimization also. The IIS metabase can be accessed from the command line using the adsutil.vbs administrative utility that is located in the c:\Inetpub\AdminScripts directory structure. There is also a metabase editor named MetaEdit 2.1 that can be downloaded from Microsoft that is located at: http://support.microsoft.com/support/kb/articles/Q232/0/68.ASP?LN=EN-US&SD=gn&FR=0. This is a helpful tool for backing up your metabase and reviewing all of the different metabase entries and associated values.

GENERAL IIS 5 TUNING

Now that you have a handle on how Windows 2000's memory operations can be tuned for IIS 5 environments, the easiest memory tuning setting for IIS 5 itself is found under the IIS MMC snap-in by taking the following steps: Start / Programs / Administrative Tools / Computer Management / Services and Applications / Right Click and Select Properties for Internet Information Services (not a specific web site, the top level IIS bar / Performance tab).

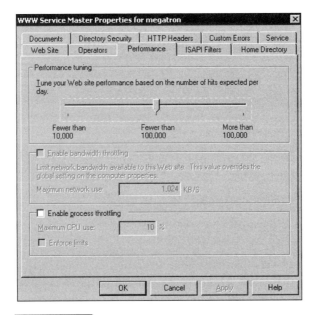

FIGURE 8–9   *IIS 5 General Performance Property Settings*

The settings in Figure 8-9 can have a significant impact on IIS 5.0 performance. The slider is used to set the expected number of hits in a day—fewer than 10,000, fewer than 100,000, or more than 100,000. The setting directly affects how much memory is set aside for connections. If you have enough memory resources, adjust it to its maximum value. If you begin to run low on memory resources, add more RAM or scale back its resource usage. This GUI-based tuning option is helpful and nice for the normal Windows administrator and will work well for most sites. If you are interested in more advanced topics, continue on!

So, now that you have all of this general web server tuning knowledge, let's look deeper into some additional specific IIS 5.0 optimization settings.

TUNING THE INETINFO.EXE OBJECT CACHES

The object cache resides inside of the Inetinfo.exe process and is used to store objects such as file handles, file directory information listings, and other frequently used objects that are expensive to retrieve. We can tune the size of Inetinfo.exe's object cache larger as needed so that we achieve a greater than 90% hit ratio.

The default value of the IIS object cache is 10% of memory, but you can set it to any value you want. If you have a large number of static web pages (which many people are beginning to use again, since serving them induces less overhead on your server), perhaps 320MB worth, you will want to set the IIS object cache to be larger. With a larger cache, you create more room in cache to support other services that reside in Inetinfo.exe, too. For example, perhaps we planned to provide 100MB of memory for the object cache. We adjust the object cache size by adding following the registry entry: `HKEY_LOCAL_MACHINE\System\CurrentControlSet\Services\InetInfo\Parameters\MemoryCacheSize=0x 5F5E100`.

Note that this value was added as a REG_DWORD using hexadecimal notation.

To determine if the IIS cache is large enough to be effective, check the Perfmon Counter Internet Information Services Global: Cache Hits %. How effective the cache is depends on the workload being placed on the web server. Typically, if the cache hit rate percentage is less than 90%, then the IIS object cache size should be increased. Remember, before increasing the IIS object cache size, ensure that there is sufficient available memory. You may encounter a greater challenge when trying to improve the cache hit rates for web environments that generate high amounts of dynamic web page content, unless they are generating the same dynamic content over and over. There are third-party tools we mention later in this scenario that focus on caching dynamic content when they are based on Active Server Pages.

If you run a large web site that serves many files, you can improve the performance of delivering these files by keeping their associated file handles with these files in the object cache. You can control how many cached file handle objects IIS 5 keeps in memory for file-related web service by adjusting (you may need to add this registry key) the OpenFileInCache registry entry located at: `HKEY_LOCAL_MACHINE\System\CurrentControlSet\Services\InetInfo\Parameters\OpenFileInCache`. Interactively increase this value 20% until you meet your objective. For a static environment or one in which the dynamic generated pages are low, this is a good tactic. As always, closely watch memory resource usage when implementing.

Any cache is more effective if, when the request is placed, the relevant data is already in the cache. Based on your web server customers' habits, you can tune the IIS 5 object cache to keep related web page information in its cache for longer periods of time. Note the converse of this can also happen, in which case you will want to increase the rate in which the IIS object cache is flushed by lowering the ObjectCacheTTL value. To accomplish this, edit the following registry entry: `HKEY_LOCAL_MACHINE\System\CurrentControlSet\Services\InetInfo\Parameters\ObjectCacheTTL=xFFFFFFF`. This example keeps the IIS open descriptors active forever. Once information is in the cache, it stays until more information is needed and the old information is flushed out.

Track your successes with this tuning technique by monitoring Sysmon's Internet Information Services Global object's File Cache Hits %. & File Cache Flushes counters. If the rate of cache flushes is a high value and is associated with a high value of cache misses and page faults (Memory: Page Faults/sec), the cache may be flushing too quickly. When the cache is flushed too quickly, repeated requests for the same data do not result in a cache hit when it should. If this occurs, increase the ObjectCacheTTL (if you have not already set it to no time-out), MemoryCacheSize, and OpenFileInCache even more.

Tune Your Web Application to Use Available CPU Resources

CONTROLLING WHERE WEB SERVER APPLICATIONS (PROCESSES) EXECUTE

One of the most important CPU-related tuning you can complete is determining where your web applications run. Whenever possible, develop and implement your web applications with applications native to IIS; e.g., ASP and ISAPI as they are the most efficient in the IIS 5 environment.

As we investigated in chapter 4, less overhead is introduced into a system when context switches occur from within the same process, vs. two threads changing context, each from a different process. IIS 5 has three modes of web application process operations, which are shown in Table 8.43.

| **TABLE 8.43** | *IIS 5 Application Process Operations Run Time Options* |

Application Protection Level	Availability	Performance Level	Description
Low	Highest Risk	Highest	Web application processes are run in the same process as web services (Inetinfo).
Medium	Medium Risk	Medium	Web application processes are run in an isolated pooled process in which other web applications are also run.
High	Lowest Risk	Lowest	Web application processes are each run in isolated process separate from other processes.

By default IIS 5.0 runs web applications in an out-of-process state (Medium Application Protection level) so they cannot directly interfere with IIS operations and possibly crash IIS. This approach improves the likelihood that a poorly written web application does not adversely affect the Inetinfo.exe process and subsequently IIS 5. However, this approach provides a lower level of performance, since context switch overhead is much higher for each web application since it involves a complete thread change from different processes. The default approach also consumes more memory. For maximum performance, run your well-written and tested web applications in the IIS process (Low Application Protection Level). Of course, there is always a trade-off: if your well-written web application panics while running in Application Protection Level Low, it will most likely cause IIS 5 to stop serving web pages!

You can tune which application protection level your web site runs on your web server either through the MMC IIS snap-in under the Home Directory Tab (shown in Figure 8-10) or via the command line using the IIS metabase which is accessed using the adsutil.vbs administrative utility located in the c:\Inetpub\AdminScripts directory structure or Metaedit GUI-based metabase editor.

> *It is important to note that, when making any changes to the IIS 5 metabase, those changes can be reflected across the entire web server or for a specific web site instance (you may host multiple web sites on one physical IIS 5 Web Server) that you are tuning! This is when the ability to manipulate the IIS 5 metabase really begins to shine. If you wanted to change the performance configuration of 200 web sites that your web server is hosting, do you really want to manually click through 200 screens? By using the command option with tools such as adsutil.vbs, you can change all 200 web sites, correctly, with one point and click! Once you have written and tested your script, of course.*

TURN OFF DEBUGGING OVERHEAD FROM PRODUCTION SERVERS

Just in case your developers used some of the debugging features in IIS, you can ensure they are turned off and not adding CPU overhead (i.e., constricting IIS to a single threaded mode of operation) by setting the IIS 5 metabase variable disablesocketpooling to true. To set this variable, run the adsutil.vbs (Active Directory Services Interfaces ADSI) utility in the following manner:

C:\inetpub\adminscripts\cscript.exe adsutil.vbs set w3svc/ X/AppAllowDebugging False

The value of X corresponds to the web site on your web server on which you are turning debugging off. You will need to run this command for each web site—0, 1, 2, etc.—where you wish to turn debugging off.

Another debugging feature you can ensure is not running on your production web server is to set AspAllowSessionState to FALSE. When this is changed, commands must explicitly override this setting in pages that need to make use of the session object.

C:\inetpub\adminscripts\cscript.exe adsutil.vbs set w3svc/ AspAllowSessionState false

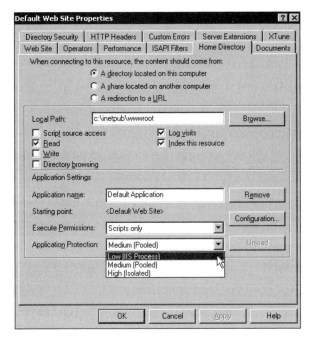

FIGURE 8–10 *Tuning the Application Protection (Performance Level) of an IIS Web Site (Note: These settings are implemented on a per web site basis, not web server basis. Here we edit the default web site)*

TUNING THE IIS QUEUE SIZE

CPU resources are not so inexpensive that you want them to sit around idle, so let's ensure they are put to good use. Under heavy web workloads, keeping IIS 5.0 properly fed with data is important. First determine if you have additional CPU capacity available by monitoring Sysmon's Processor object's %Processor Time counter and the System object's Processor Queue Length for the CPUs in your web server. Not all workloads are distributed well across all processors, so watch each processor's usage closely. If your processor usage looks relatively well distributed, and only 30% of processor resources are being used, consider increasing the workload that IIS will accept. To increase the workload IIS will accept, add the following registry value: `HKEY_LOCAL_MACHINE\System\CurrentControlSet\Services\Inet-Info\Parameters\ListenBacklog=0x1E`. This increases the maximum active connections that are held in the IIS queue from the default of 25, to 300 (150 per CPU to start). Whenever this queue length limit is reached, IIS will reject any new connections until the queue length shortens. Tune this queue length lower if a system bottleneck begins to occur and subsequently increase this value if web requests are being rejected and you have the CPU resources to support more workload. Setting the ListenBackLog value high when you do not have the CPU resources available to support the increased workload will cause longer waiting periods for your web server's end users. This is sometimes worse than no response at all!

Based on this same concept, you can increase the number of IIS threads that are used to respond to web requests by adding the following registry entry: `HKEY_LOCAL_MACHINE\System\CurrentControlSet\Services\Inet-Info\Parameters\MaxPoolThreads=20`. This registry entry specifies maximum network request threads per processor. The default is 10. Here we increased the value to 20, or 10 per CPU. Use extreme caution when tuning IIS; with all of these CPU specific options more is not always better. You must always ensure that you have sufficient processor resources, as it is possible to increase these values to high and actually lower your server's overall performance. If Inetinfo threads—which can be observed under Perfmon's processor object processor usage counter—are overworking your CPUs, lower the MaxPoolThreads and ListenBackLog values. Related to the MaxPoolThreads is the PoolThreadLimit, which relates to the number of threads that can be created in IIS. This variable is a hard limit and should always be greater than or equal to MaxPoolThreads.

Tuning IIS 5 for Common Gateway Interface (CGI) Operations

What can you optimize under IIS 5 if you are running CGI scripts? By default, IIS5 sets the maximum number of threads for CGI operations to four. Thus, only four CGI applications can run simultaneously. If your web server has the CPU resources to support additional workload (e.g., processor usage is low and there are no processor queues) increase the MaxPoolThreads value by 50%. MaxPoolThreads parameter specifies the number of pool threads to create per processor. Each pool thread watches for a network request and processes it. The MaxPoolThreads count does not include threads that are consumed by ISAPI applications. The MaxPoolThreads is located at `HKEY_LOCAL_MACHINE\System\CurrentControlSet\Services\InetInfo\Parameters\MaxPoolThreads`.

LOWERING OVERHEAD ASSOCIATED WITH SSL OPERATIONS

The initial creation of the SSL connection for a customer is very expensive in terms of CPU cycles. To help mitigate this you could turn SSL (this is not realistic for security reasons) off or try to lower how often the initial SSL connection must be created. This can be accomplished by lengthening SSL session time-out period. In this manner, if someone starts a SSL session, but works on something else for a short time, then continues to work with the SSL encrypted session, it still will be active and no new connection will be required. This is more art than science, as you must estimate how long you expect your customer to need the SSL session. You can control the SSL session time-out period by editing the `HKEY_LOCAL_MACHINE\System\Current-ControlSet\Services\InetInfo\Parameters\ServerCacheTime` registry entry.

OPTIMIZING ACTIVE SERVER PAGE OPERATIONS

If you operate your web site using Active Server Pages (ASP), which is quite common, there are several ASP-related metabase settings that can have a significant impact on the performance and queuing of your web server, based on your environment and workload. This is almost like tuning inside of tuning. We tuned Windows 2000 to run IIS 5 well, then we optimized IIS 5 web server operations, then we looked into tuning how ASPs interact with IIS 5 and the rest of the system.

The following outlines the different parameters for ASP tuning grouped by functions and when they should be used. All of the parameters below are IIS 5 metabase parameters and are tuned using the adsutil.vbs utility or the metaedit metabase tuning tool. The standard syntax for implementing these parameters is:

C:\inetpub\adminscripts\cscript.exe adsutil.vbs set w3svc/ X/PARAMETER value, where X is the integer representing the web site you are tuning.

ASP Caching

Each process that hosts an ASP will have its own ASP template and script engine caches. By default, that is just one process because ASP applications run at Application Protection Level medium, but could be more depending on how your system is tuned. When an ASP gets a request for a page, it checks the ASP template cache first. If there's an instance of that page cached there, the request is forwarded to the script engine cache. If the requested page is not in the template cache, it is compiled into a template and forwarded to the ASP script engine cache. This avoids the cost of reparsing the template into byte code. If there is no script engine associated with the page, ASP takes the precompiled template from the ASP template cache, creates a new script engine and has it compile the template into byte code, and then executes it. The following three metabase parameters influence the ASP cache operations.

- The AspScriptEngineCacheMax parameter determines the maximum number of script engines to cache in memory. A hit in the script engine cache means that you can avoid recompiling the template into byte code. If you have a significant number of unique pages being generated, increasing this value should improve overall performance and lower CPU operations. The default value is 50. Increase at 100% increments and test for your specific environment.
- The AspScriptFileCacheSize parameter specifies the number of precompiled script files to store in the ASP template cache. If 0, no script

files will be cached. If –1, all script files requested will be cached. The default value is 256. Increase at 100% increments and test for your specific environment.

● The AspBufferingOn parameter default behavior allows all output from an application to be collected in the buffer before the buffer is flushed to the client browser. If this property is set to FALSE, output from ASP scripts will be written to the client browser as it becomes available. Ensure this property is set to true on all production web servers.

ASP CPU Optimization

Increasing Workload That IIS 5 Will Accept

IIS 5.0 dynamically changes the number of threads it operates in response to changing workloads if the AspThreadGateEnabled parameter is set to true. The maximum number of threads that IIS will allow per ASP process is AspProcessorThreadMax multiplied by the number of processors on your server. When dynamic tuning is activated, IIS performs thread gating which dynamically controls the number of concurrently executing threads in response to varying load conditions. When processor utilization drops below 50%—which could indicate that threads are blocked and waiting for an external database server to return the results of a query—IIS 5.0 increases the number of active threads so that other requests can be serviced in a timely manner. When processor utilization exceeds 80%, indicating a heavier load, IIS 5.0 deactivates threads to reduce the amount of context switching. Both lower and upper limits can be set: AspThreadGateLoadLow defaults to 50%, while AspThreadGateLoadHigh defaults to 80%. Try it. Set AspThreadGateEnabled parameter to true. For many environments it works well.

If your web server is under a heavy workload and accepts too much work, then many people get slow responses. If your web server accepts less work, some people get great responses while others get none. This simple example of providing web services illustrates the need to know your environment. If you have significant resources available, you should consider increasing the AspRequestQueueMax variable another 20% to enable more concurrent ASP requests to be serviced. AspRequestQueueMax specifies the maximum number of concurrent ASP requests that are permitted into the queue.

Dropping Distracted Customers: Managing ASP Connections

Would you want to service a request if a customer was distracted and discounted from your web server? Probably not. There is no reason to waste limited server resources. If a request has been in the queue longer than the queue connection test time, the web server checks to see that the client is still connected before beginning execution. You can adjust the queue connection time by tuning the AspQueueConnectionTestTime parameter. Again, you must know your environment. If your web server typically generates web pages that take a long time to download, this parameter should be raised. If the opposite is true, consider lowing the value. Based on this same concept of connection time, consider disconnecting inactive customers if they are inactive. This is accomplished by tuning the ConnectionTimeout parameter that is 15 minutes by default.

Optimizing IIS for Web Publishing

If you support customers who run the Microsoft Front Page web-publishing application, you can optimize operations for those important customers, too. Don't forget that as you tune the web server for web publishing customers, you will be taking memory resources that IIS uses for delivering those published pages! Whenever possible, do not allow multiple direct publication of web content to highly loaded web servers. Instead, use a staging web server for development and then use other techniques—such as one-way replication software—to move data from the staging web server to the production web server. An added value of this staging server approach is that you can optimize the staging server for its mission and optimize the production web server for its associated mission.

IIS 5 provides a friendly interface to access the key tunables to optimize web publishing that are installed when you install server extensions. Access this GUI by selecting Start / Programs / Administrative Tools / Computer Management / Services and Applications. Right-click and select Properties for Internet Information Services (not a specific web site, the top-level IIS bar), then select the Server Extensions Table. Once you follow these steps, Figure 8-11 is presented.

From this interface, you can select the number of web pages that your web site supports. In general, select a range of pages that matches your environment and you are off like a herd of turtles! This typically works, but you will want to understand how the standard settings really map to the IIS 5 metabase if you want to truly optimize your web server publishing services.

If you would like to customize your tuning even more than the standard settings provide, or learn which IIS 5 metabase values are changed, select the upper settings box shown in Figure 8-11. This will provide a detailed performance screen shown in Figure 8-12.

The following is a description of what each IIS 5 metabase tunable does to support web publishing and how the standard settings preset options map to the custom IIS metadata variables. These definitions and variable settings

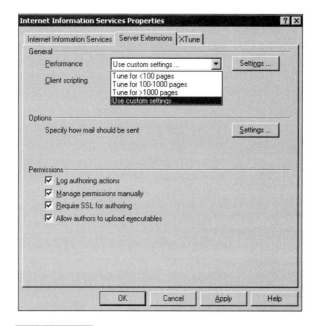

FIGURE 8–11   *Tuning IIS to Support Web Publishing Customers*

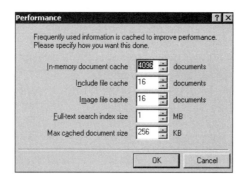

FIGURE 8–12   *Custom Tuning IIS to Support Web Publishing Customers*

are based on information obtained from the Microsoft Q article found at:
http://support.microsoft.com/support/kb/articles/q201/8/03.asp.

In-Memory Document Cache (IIS 5 Metabase Value: CacheMaxDocMeta)

CacheMaxDocMeta represents the maximum number of documents (property information, such as link maps and Web parameters) that can be held in the cache. For example, if you specify 4,096 documents, when the 4,097th document is read, then the cache clears itself and only includes the 4,097th document. The cache will then increase in size as documents are read and clear itself again after the 4,096th limit is reached again. If you have the available memory, it is better to have these settings slightly larger than is projected in case your estimates are incorrect. A complete cache flush will slow down other web publishers working with your web server.

When you use the preset options, you set the values shown in Table 8.44.

TABLE 8.44	*Preset Values for CacheMaxDocMeta*
Preset	**CacheMaxDocMeta**
Tune for less than 100 pages	Predefined for 4,096 (documents)
Tune for 1 to 1,000 pages	Predefined for 4,096 (documents)
Tune for greater than 1,000 pages	Predefined for 16,384 (documents)

Include File Cache (IIS 5 Metabase Value: CacheMaxInclude)

CacheMaxInclude represents the number of files that you want to keep available in memory for inclusion in other files. For example, there might be header, footer, and copyright files that you want to include in some or all of a web site's web pages. The predefined setting is set for 16. Consider increasing if you have more than 16 files that are used in the development of other web pages.

TABLE 8.45	*Preset Values for CacheMaxInclude*
Preset	**CacheMaxInclude**
Tune for less than 100 pages	Predefined for 16 (documents)
Tune for 1 to 1,000 pages	Predefined for 16 (documents)
Tune for greater than 1,000 pages	Predefined for 16 (documents)

Image File Cache (IIS 5 Metabase Value: CacheMaxImage)

CacheMaxImage is the number of image files in memory that the FrontPage Server Extensions can use to create layered pictures in web pages. For example, one file may consist of a background, another of a Navigation button. The server extensions can compose a picture by adding the background to a web page and then overlaying the Navigation button image. The picture can be composed faster if the component files are in a cache. Adjust to match your development environment.

TABLE 8.46	*Preset Values for CacheMaxImage*
Preset	**CacheMaxImage is set to**
Tune for less than 100 pages	Predefined for 16 (documents)
Tune for 1 to 1,000 pages	Predefined for 16 (documents)
Tune for greater than 1,000 pages	Predefined for 16 (documents)

Full-Text Search Index Size (IIS 5 Metabase Value: TextMemory)

TextMemory is the maximum amount of disk space that can be allotted for storing a full-text search index. When this amount is reached, no other pages on the web site can be indexed (unless you increase this number). If you have large web sites, increase this value (start with 10MB) as full-text indexes can improve overall performance as long as they do not grow too large.

TABLE 8.47	*Preset Values for TextMemory*
Preset	**TextMemory is set to**
Tune for less than 100 pages	Predefined for 1 MB
Tune for 1 to 1,000 pages	Predefined for 2 MB
Tune for greater than 1,000 pages	Predefined for 4 MB

Max Cached Document Size (IIS 5 Metabase Value: CacheMaxIncludeSize)

CacheMaxIncludeSize is the maximum size of a document that can be stored in memory. This size limit applies to include files, image files, and other files that may be stored in a cache. Adjust to match your development environment. If you work with 100KB documents, this is a great setting. If you work with 300KB files, tune!

TABLE 8.48	*Preset Values for CacheMaxIncludeSize*
Preset	**CacheMaxIncludeSize**
Tune for less than 100 pages	Predefined for 256K Windows NT and UNIX, 32K Windows 95/98
Tune for 1 to 1,000 pages	Predefined for 256K Windows NT and UNIX, 32K Windows 95/98
Tune for greater than 1,000 pages	Predefined for 256K Windows NT and UNIX, 32K Windows 95/98

Thinking Outside of the Box: Xtune

There are a lot of potential tunables in this section, both in the registry and in the IIS 5 metabase. Web servers are a dynamic environment and fill many roles. Is there a tool to track all of these tunables and make life simpler? Yes, there is one that covers many of the most important tunables. Xtune from Post Point Software (http://www.PostPointSoft.com) provides a very friendly and free tool for observing many of the registry and IIS metabase tunable parameters reviewed in the IIS 5 tuning section and even provides some recommendations. Screen shots of this tool are shown in Figures 8-13 and 8-14.

Windows 2000 does a good job of setting these tunables for general environments, but tools like Xtune make life a little easier when working in more diverse, performance-challenged environments. Remember, every environment is different. Knowing your environment, workload, server design, web server applications, and how and why Windows 2000 and IIS operate as they do provides you a distinct advantage in improving your web server's performance. Always test your ideas for your specific environment to determine what is best for you.

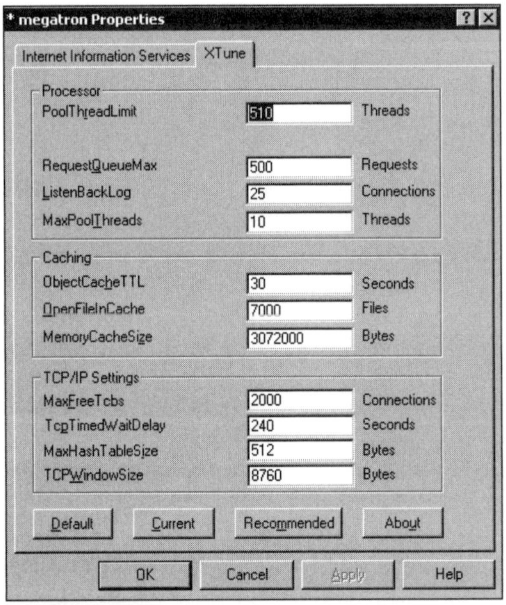

FIGURE 8–13   *Automating Some of the Key Windows 2000 Registry IIS 5.0 Web Server Tuning Options (Note: These are global web server settings that affect the entire web server. These tuning changes are not completed on a web site-by-web site basis.)*

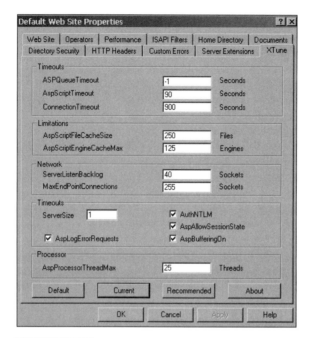

FIGURE 8–14 *Xtune Automating Some of the Key IIS 5.0 Metabase Server Tuning Options (Note: These settings are implemented on a per web site basis, not web server basis)*

Literally Thinking Outside of the Box: Network Load Balancing

What can you do if you have a perfectly sized and tuned Windows 2000 web server and you still need more performance? You could purchase a larger web server or you could implement Network Load Balancing (NLB). NLB is a new technology included in Windows 2000 Advanced Server that enables the implementation of an active-active, shared-nothing web cluster server solution that supports up to 32 nodes. Active-active refers to the fact that all nodes in the cluster provide web services; no node sits idle. Shared-nothing cluster refers to the fact that no servers directly share their disk subsystems to another. NLB is a software-based solution and works by installing on each web server a virtual NIC that load balances the workload across all web servers configured into the virtual web server. One IP address is advertised to the Internet. When the web server request arrives, it is sent to a web server in your cluster based on your configuration settings. Here we do not go into each step needed to install NLB, but Windows 2000 Help provides easy to follow directions. NLB is installed as a network driver under Start / Settings / Network and Dial-Up Connections / Local Area Connection / Properties. This approach provides a method of scaling your web server solution to meet your performance needs by just adding additional servers that provide a single managed interface to your customers. Note one odd occurrence in NLB environments. If your server is reachable over the network—e.g., you can ping.exe the server—NLB will forward requests to it even if your web application has stopped serving web pages! Although a rare occurrence, it is something you should be aware of. Custom solutions to this challenge are available, but I have yet to see any official third-party products for this special case.

All of the tuning techniques and sizing techniques discussed are directly applicable to NLB environments. The first challenge in NLB environments is to ensure that the web content stays identical on each web server in the cluster. To accomplish this, you can either manually copy files as needed or use software replication over the local area network, ensuring that when one web server is updated, the other web servers in the cluster are automatically updated too. The second challenge is ensuring that no back-end servers that the front-end web server cluster relies on for processing activities such as database services create a bottleneck.

Windows 2000 IIS 5 Web Server Tuning Summary

For the hands-on specifics of why, when, and how these tuning recommendations work in detail and steps to implement them, refer back to the subsequent tuning sections of this section and the previous chapters. Here select information is provided to give you a jump-start into an optimized Windows 2000 IIS 5 web server solution!

IIS WEB SERVER HARDWARE TUNING

- Update the BIOS and Windows 2000 drivers on all server hardware (includes motherboards and the associated adapters.)
- Ensure BIOS is configured for maximum performance.
- Ensure BIOS performance settings match the hardware you have installed.
- Ensure you received the correct hardware.

WEB SERVER APPLICATION TUNING

- Use native application development environment for IIS 5 such as ISAPI and ASP.
- Use static and thin (low KB) web pages whenever possible.

- Limit the use of SSL for when it is absolutely necessary.
- Tune Windows 2000 TCP/IP Stack to match your web workload.
- Tune IIS 5 operational behavior to maximize use of CPU resources and lower overhead.
- Tune IIS 5 operational behavior to maximize use of memory resources to improve caching.
- Ensure the IIS 5.0 Web Server process Inetinfo.exe so it is never paged to disk.
- Configure your web site applications to run in the same process as Inetinfo.exe by setting the Application Protection level to low (ensure these are stable applications).
- Consider Network Load Balancing to scale your web site as needed.
- Follow the tuning and sizing methodologies from chapters 2 and 3.
- Review the Web Server Specific Application Tuning section above for details on these steps.

WINDOWS 2000 CPU SUBSYSTEM RESOURCE TUNING

Key disk subsystem–related tuning you should consider:

- Set the application response optimization to background services (Control Panel / System / Advanced / Performance Options).
- Off-load CPU operations to I2O-enabled I/O adapters.
- If Secure Socket Layer (SSL) encryption is in use, consider obtaining an I/O card that off-loads all SSL calculations from the main CPUs or plan for the additional CPU overhead by monitoring your server closely.
- Since multiple CPUs are in use with Multiple NIC and SCSI adapters, consider using the Microsoft Interrupt-Affinity Filter Control Tool (IntFiltr; see chapter 4) to ensure interrupts are properly distributed between NICs and CPUs.
- Do not use a 3GL or other fancy screen saver.
- Check all services running on your server. Operate only those you need and stop all others.
- Avoid running another CPU-intensive application, such as a database, on your web server.

WINDOWS 2000 MEMORY SUBSYSTEM RESOURCE TUNING

Key memory-related tuning you should consider:

- Check the Windows 2000 memory management strategy. IIS Web Server relies heavily on the File System Cache. If you have over 1GB of RAM in your IIS web server, use the system cache setting Maximize Data Throughput for file sharing. With 1GB of memory in the server, Windows 2000 will commit 432MB for the system cache. The remaining memory can then be used by IIS. However, if you have less than

1GB of memory in your IIS Web server, configure Windows 2000 system cache algorithm to Maximize Data Throughput for network applications. These options are selected under: Start / Programs / Settings / Network and Dial-Up Connections / Properties of your LAN adapter / File and Print Sharing for Microsoft Networks.

- Check all services running on your server. Operate only those you need and stop all others.
- Ensure the pagefile is set to twice the size of physical RAM in your server to ensure physical memory can be committed to action.
- Set the pagefile size to twice the amount of RAM in your server and to a fixed size.
- Never place the pagefile on a RAID 5 array.
- If your system must page, consider multiple pagefiles on physically separate disk drives which are all configured to the exact same size.
- Force Windows 2000 to keep the Windows 2000 executive (kernel) from paging any of its executive system drivers to disk and ensure that they are immediately available if needed.
- Do not use a 3GL or other fancy screen saver.
- Do not use exotic wallpaper on the server console; it wastes memory resources.

WINDOWS 2000 DISK SUBSYSTEM RESOURCE TUNING

Key disk subsystem–related tuning you should consider:

- When formatting the disk drive with NTFS, select the ALU size that best matches your disk workload characteristics. For this scenario, use an 8KB ALU size for all disk subsystems.
- Match the stripe size of the low-level RAID format with the ALU size used (see chapter 6 for details).
- Since we are using large NTFS volumes, increase the size of the NTFS log file size to 64MB, by using the *chkdsk* command: chkdsk driveletter: /l:65536.
- Turn on write-back caching and read-ahead caching on hardware RAID adapters.
- Use only I2O-enabled RAID adapters and those with their own CPUs.
- Keep storage capacity on the disk subsystem under 60–80% so that the fastest portion of the disk drive is used and so that there is room on the disk drives to perform defragmentation.
- Defragment your disk subsystem on a regular basis; this will result in significant performance improvements!
- Evenly distribute disk workload across the physical disk drives in the server.
- If DOS file names are not required (i.e., legacy DOS-based desktops are not in use), disable short name (8.3) file generation. Note: To disable short name generation, use regedt32.exe to set the reg-

istry DWORD value of 1 in the following Registry location: HKEY_LOCAL_MACHINE\SYSTEM\CurrentControlSet\Control\File-system\NtfsDisable8dot3nameCreation. More information on this technique in chapter 6.

- Disable last access updates. `HKEY_LOCAL_MACHINE\SYSTEM\Current-ControlSet\Control\FileSystemNtfsDisableLastAccessUpdate`. Changing the default REG_DWORD value of this key from 0 to 1 will stop Windows 2000 from updating the last access time/date stamp on directories as directory trees are traversed.
- Understand the characteristics of all RAID levels and leverage different RAID levels as needed in the same web server solution.
- Use more than one RAID level in your IIS solution!
- Group similar disk activities on the same physical disk subsystem and do not separate them via logical partitions on the same physical disk drive/array.
- Use one Windows 2000 partition per physical disk device/array.
- Group similar disk activities on the same physical disk subsystem and do not separate them via logical partitions on the same physical disk drive/array.
- Add disk drives as needed to keep the sec/transfers low and average queue size less than twice the number of disk drives in the disk array.
- Check all services running on your server. Operate only those you need and stop all others.

WINDOWS 2000 NETWORK SUBSYSTEM RESOURCE TUNING

Key network subsystem–related tuning you should consider:

- If SSL sessions are in use, expect more bandwidth to be needed due to the encryption overhead. More of the data stream is taken up with encryption data; thus either a larger network connection is needed or more time to deliver the encrypted data. Expect at least a 10% increase.
- Team/trunk multiple NICs (Ethernet channels) together as needed to add network bandwidth and availability to your IIS Web Server (seamlessly to your customers).
- Remove all unnecessary protocols and Redirectors.
- Standardize on one network protocol: TCP/IP.
- If more than one network protocol is in use, set binding order such that the most commonly used protocol is first on the list.
- Tune the NIC driver to off-load IPSEC security operations and TCP operations on the NIC itself instead of the main system CPUs.
- Tune the NIC driver to increase its send and receive buffers.
- Use only I2O-Enabled NICs.

- Use the fastest I/O bus-enabled NIC possible (64-bit, 66MHz PCI slot).
- Tune the Windows TCP/IP stack to your environment (TCP Hash Table, MTU Window Size) as per the guidance above for IIS network tuning.
- Do not use autodetect for your NIC. Set it to the best performance level the internetwork devices will support. For example: 100BaseTX full duplex.

THIRD-PARTY TOOLS FOR TUNING WINDOWS 2000 IIS WEB SERVERS

Key third-party tools to consider for enhancing the performance of your SQL environment:

- Obtain a third-party disk defragmentation tool that provides enhanced defragmentation features such as scheduling and support of multiple NTFS ALU sizes. Recommended vendor to consider: Norton Speed Disk http://www.Norton.com.
- If, after analyzing your system, you find that specific web server files are being used heavily or another area of the disk subsystem is used heavily such as c:\temp, consider implementing a RAM disk. RAM disks create a file system in memory, so from the application's perspective, it just sees a logical disk drive, such as "r:" to interact with, so no application changes are needed. When applications interact with the RAM disk, they run a lot faster than they do on a physical disk drive. The trade-off for this performance boost is the risk of data loss, so do not use this technology for critical data. This technology was investigated in chapter 6 and the resulting tests looked fantastic—performance improvements greater than 200%. RAM disks are not native to Windows 2000. The RAM disk tested was a product from Super Speed Systems (http://www.eecsys.com) obtained through SunBelt Software (http://www.sunbeltsoftware.com).
- To assist in tuning the many registry settings associated with IIS, use the free Xtune utility software tool from http://www.postpointsoft.com. This tool provides a GUI front end to the most common (not all) and beneficial registry tuning options for IIS and also provides recommended settings based on your environment. A very helpful and easy tool to use.
- To improve cache-hit ratios of ASPs, consider using the Xcache product. This product works to improve the caching of ASP-based web requests. When effective, this product lowers the number of back-end database queries and local ASP processing load. Xcache is available for download at http://wwww.postpointsoft.com. From my testing, this product looked promising.

Web Server Solution Scenario Summary

In this scenario, we focused on sizing and tuning of your Windows 2000–based web server from a system perspective to improve overall performance. It is important both to understand the type of web content you are providing and to closely monitor your web server resources. Armed with this information and knowing what tuning options are available, you are empowered to make informed decisions for maximizing the performance of your web server. Windows 2000 Server provides a very capable web server platform; now you can truly take advantage of its capabilities!

Summary

In this chapter, the tuning and sizing methodologies and strategies discussed in chapters 2 and 3 are applied to develop real-world solutions with specific step-by-step, hands-on recommendations and guidelines. Using sound and repeatable methodologies when developing your solution will give you more confidence that the solution will meet your requirements. These case studies used the various tuning and sizing concepts presented in chapters 4–7 in conjunction with new, application-specific optimizations to develop the overall solutions. It becomes much easier to intelligently size and tune Windows 2000 and back office solutions when you have an understanding of what, how, and why operations are occurring in the system from both a software application and hardware perspective. These solution scenarios provide you with a template to size and tune your own solutions but, as always, remember that they are guides! Your environment and experiences are unique, so customize as needed. These solution scenarios get you into the game. From there it is up to you!

INDEX

▼ A

access time, 293, 294, 296
Active Server Pages (ASP)
  caching, 573–74
  CPU optimization, 574–75
    dropping distracting
      customers, 574–75
    increasing workload, 574
  optimizing operations, 573
adaptive load balancing (ALB), 37,
  407
advanced customer perspective
  pulse tests: web services, 81–82
Advanced Transfer Cache (ATC), 176
Advanced Windowing Extensions
  (AWEs), 246
affinity, 191
  using sound tuning
    methodology, 227–29
AIM benchmark vendor, 148
ALB. See adaptive load balancing
  (ALB)
Allocation Unit Size, selecting
  appropriate, 24
applications
  backup tuning, 486
  determining those running
    under Windows 2000, 5–6
  effect of, on network
    performance, 403
  file server-specific, tuning, 463
  maximizing data throughput for
    network, 17–18
  server CPUs in driving, 170–71
  tuning web, to use available
    CPU resources, 569–72
architecture review for CPU system,
  175–76

ASP. See Active Server Pages (ASP)
ATC. See Advanced Transfer Cache
  (ATC)
auditing
  security, 40–41, 219
  in zeroing in on resource usage,
    116
autonegotiation, 308
average latency, 294
average seek time, 294
AWEs. See Advanced Windowing
  Extensions (AWEs)

▼ B

backup application tuning, 486
backup server hardware tuning, 486
baselines. See also historical
  baselines; performance baselines
  importance of, for bottleneck
    detection, 205
Basic Input/Output System (BIOS),
  16
  updating, 380
benchmarks, 147
  extrapolating
    in memory sizing, 268
    server guidelines and, 268
  fitting of sizing methodology,
    148–55
  industry standard, 147–48,
    420–22
  NetBench, 158–60
  SPECweb99, 155–58
  TPC, 148–55
Binary Circular Logging, 110–11
binding search order, tuning, 33

BMC's Patrol, 96
bridged peripheral component interface
approach, 316–17

▼ C

cache. *See also* file system cache
advanced transfer, 176
image file, 577–78
in-memory document, 576–77
Cache counter, 254
caching
Active Server Pages, 573–74
of Media Access Control (MAC)
addresses, 33–34
read requests, 345–46
write requests, 346–47
write-through, 380
capacity sizing, 131–72
benchmarks in, 147–60
fit of, in sizing methodology, 148–55
industry standards, 147–48
NetBench, 158–60
SPECweb99, 155–58
TPC, 148–55
commercially available tools for, 171
goals of, 132
memory in, 168–69
methodology, 133–36
benchmarks in, 148–55
configuring system, 141–44
defining objectives, 136–37
determining loading characteristics,
138–39
determining performance
requirements, 139–40
displaying system into production,
146
fit of historical baselines into, 160–66
proactively following core tuning
during stress and validation
testing, 146

proactively following tuning after
system is deployed, 146–47
stress test and validating server
configuration, 144–46
understanding business and
technical requirements needed to
meet objectives, 137–38
understanding future business
requirements, 140
understanding future system
architectures, 140–41
reality of, 132–33
server architecture relationships in, 166–
68
server CPUs in driving applications, 170–
71
server I/O relationships in, 169–70
CA's Unicenter, 96
central processing units (CPUs), 174–75
advanced tuning
helping Windows 2000 control
application (process/thread)
affinity, 226–27
helping Windows 2000 control
process priorities, 225–26
architecture review, 175–76
comparing architectures, 176
configuring Microsoft InterruptAffinity
filter control tool (IntFiltr), 229–30
detecting and tuning around Windows
2000 bottlenecks, 11, 14–15, 193–207
adding CPUs, 202–3
applying artful privileged and user
mode tuning, 202–3
importance of baselines in, 205
interrupt-driven bottlenecks, 203–7
in multiple-server system, 196
%User and %Privileged Time, 197–98
privileged mode and user mode
processor usage, 198–201
processor queue length, 196–97
resource usage analysis with Sysmon,
205
in single-server system, 195

tools in tracking down Windows 2000 memory details, 193–94
distributing power to peripherals to improve I/O scalability, 319–20
HBA and, 313–14
memory sizing relationships and, 210–14
Pentium III, 176–86
  changes in technology, 181
  comparing performance, 181–83
  level 2 cache sizes, 179–81
  planning around bottlenecks, 179
  selection of, 183
  upgrading, 183–86
Pentium III XEON, 176–86
  changes in technology, 181
  comparing performance, 181–83
  level 2 cache sizes, 179–81
  selection of, 183
  upgrading, 183–86
resource usage, 186–94
  affinity, 191
  determining which process is associated with which application, 188–89
  processes, threads, jobs (new), and context switching, 186
  scheduler and priority levels, 190–91
  single unit environment and, 186–87
  symmetric multiprocessing, 186
  viewing processes and threads running under, 188
sizing, 47–48
  subsystems, 208–9
sound affinity methodology in, 227–29
subsystem resource tuning, 464, 486–87, 513–14, 540–41, 582
tuning resources, 37–38
tuning strategies for removing bottlenecks, 214–25
  hands-on tactics for, 214–25
tuning web application to use available resources, 569–72
Windows 2000 network performance and, 413–14

chart mode, 4, 100–101
Common Gateway Interface (CGI) operations, tuning IIS.5 for, 572–73
compression, 40
  avoiding, 25, 377
Concord NetHealth, 96
concurrency rate, 139
context switch, 186
core sizing methodology, 179, 183–84, 208, 212
core tuning methodology, 461
CPUs. *See* central processing units (CPUs)
CPWMM scripts, customizing, 83–96
CreateFil.exe, 123
CustomerBaseLineCheck2.pl, 68
CustomerPerspectiveFileServicesModule.bat, 68
customer perspective file services pulse testing, enhancing, 76–81
customer perspective pulse test, file services, 72–74
customer perspective scripts, scheduling, with Windows 2000, 74–76
customer perspective system performance and trend analysis, 94–96
CustomerPerspectiveWebMonitoringModuleScript.pl script (CPWMM), 114
customer perspective web service pulse test, tactical steps needed for implementing, 82–83
CustomerPulseTest2.bat, 68
CustomerWebMonitoringModuleScript.pl, 68

D

data, logging with Sysmon, 4
data flow
  in disk subsystem technology, 291–93
  in improving I/O bus scalability, 318–19
  in network bottleneck detection, 425–26
  in network subsystem technology, 305–97

data placement, and Redundant Array of Inexpensive Disks (RAID) selection, 384

data throughput, maximizing
    for file sharing, 17
    for network applications, 17–18, 259

dedicated resource, 349, 416

Deferred Procedure Call (DPC), 229, 438
    rate counter for, 229

device drivers, updating, 287

diminishing returns, law of, 58

disk array scaling, investigating with Sysmon, 344

disk bottlenecks, detecting, 11–12

disk capacity performance, 20–21, 385–86

disk drives
    determining number of per SCSI bus, 46
    low-level formatting of, 23
    operations terminology, 294
    selection, 297–98
    technology, 293–97

Diskperf, 5

disk platter rotation (rpm), 295

disk queue length, determining, for Redundant Array of Inexpensive Disks (RAID) devices, 364

disk resources, tuning, 20–23

disk storage capacity, 20–21, 385–86
    tuning, 21, 386

disk subsystems
    availability, 45
    bottlenecks in, 11–12
        detecting, 361–75
        hands-on tactics for tuning around, 368–73
        tuning strategies for removing, 367–68
    hardware, 29
    performance, 43–45, 289–391
        behavior characteristics, 300–301
        data flow in, 291–93
        disk capacity storage and disk capacity performance, 385–86
        disk drive selection, 297–98
        disk drive technology, 293–97

disk storage capacity tuning, 386

fibre channel technology, 310–12

file system, related tuning, 375–77

hardware, 386–87

HBAs, 312–14

I/O bus technology and selection, 315–20

physical view versus Windows 2000 view, 299–300

Redundant Array of Inexpensive Disks, 321–23
    disk mirroring, 323–24
    disk striping with parity, 324–44
    tuning, 380–85

SCSI technology, 307–9
    implementing, 308–9

system bus, 320–21

throughput, 302–3

tuning SCSI channel and HBA, 377–80

Windows 2000 device drivers, 347–49

Windows 2000 use of, 345–47

workload, 303–7

resource tuning, 465–66, 487–88, 515, 542, 583–84

SCSI channel and host bus adapter tuning, 25–27

sizing, 43–45, 351–55, 356–61
    amount of resources configured, 354, 359–60
    backup speed, 353–54, 359
    cost, 351, 357
    data path sanity check, 355, 360
    fault tolerance level required (availability), 351–52, 357
    performance capacity needed (throughput, latency, I/O per second), 352–53, 357–59
    storage capacity, 45, 354, 360
    Windows 2000's requirements, 354, 360

disk transaction workload, 303–7
disk workload
    calculating, for Redundant Array of
        Inexpensive Disks (RAID) devices,
        364–65
    grouping similar characteristics, 28
DLLs. *See* Dynamic Link Libraries (DLLs)
Domain Name Server (DNS) server log file,
    126
double-data rate (DDR), 237
DPC. *See* Deferred Procedure Call (DPC)
DRAM future, 236
Dual Independent Bus (DIB) architecture,
    176
Dual Inline Memory Modules (DIMM), 235
    effective use of, 236
    performance alert, 236
Dynamic Link Libraries (DLLs), 121

E

encryption, 219
    avoiding, 25, 377
EPIC. *See* Explicitly Parallel Instruction
    Computing (EPIC)
Error Checking and Correcting based RAM,
    235
Ethernet, 399–400
    gigabit, 402
    100BaseTX fast performance, 400–401
    performance characteristics, 403–4
    shared characteristics, 399–400
    switched and full-duplex fast, 401
    10BaseT performance, 400
Ethernet switch, 405
Event.pl, 68
Explicitly Parallel Instruction Computing
    (EPIC), 240
Extended Data Out (EDO) DRAM technology,
    236
extrapolating benchmarks, in memory sizing,
    268

F

Fast EtherChannel (FEC), 37, 408
fast page mode RAM, 236–38
fault tolerance, 418
FEC. *See* Fast EtherChannel (FEC)
fibre channel technology, 310–12
file servers
    bottleneck detection and sizing, 451–52
    hardware tuning, 463–64
    third-party tools for tuning, 466–67
file server-specific application tuning, 463
file sharing, maximize data throughput for,
    17, 258–59
file system
    even distribution of activity in, 22
    related tuning, 375–77
file system cache
    effect of adding Random Access Memory
        (RAM) for, 252–53
    investigating behavior, 249–52
    optimizing IIS general usage, 566
    in read-intensive disk I/O environment,
        248
    sizing of, 248–49
    tuning, for IIS.5, 565
Filmon.exe, 124
freeware performance management tools, 123
    Filmon.exe, 124
    Handle.exe, 125
    Regmon.exe, 124
Full-text search index size, 578

G

general system hardware tuning, 16
Gigabit EtherChannel (GEC), 37, 408
Gigabit Ethernet (GBE)
    performance, 402–3
    technology, 402
Goals, setting, for tuning Windows 2000-
    based systems, 54–55

H

HAL. *See* Hardware Abstract Layer (HAL)
Handle.exe, 125
Hardware Abstract Layer (HAL), 224
hardware-based Redundant Array of
    Inexpensive Disks (RAID), 328–29
        benefits of, 329
        tuning flexibility when utilizing solutions,
        329–30
HBAs, 312–14
        CPU power and, 313–14
        proper configuration of, 379
        updating device drivers, 380
Hennessy, John, 175
Hewlett Packard's OpenView ManageX,
    96
historical baselines
        fitting of, into sizing methodology, 160–
        61
        using, 161–66
historical performance
        information, 355–56, 420
        in memory sizing, 264
horizontal scaling, 208
hybrid environments, 301
hybrid tuning, 28, 382

I

I2O technology, benefit of, 319–20
IBM's Tivoli, 96
Image file cache, 577–78
Include file cache, 577
industry standard benchmarks, 147–48, 420–
    22
inetinfo.exe
        tuning object caches, 568–69
        tuning Windows 2000 and IIS 5.0 and,
        564–65
In-memory document cache, 576–77

Input/Output (I/O) bus scalability
        distributing CPU power to peripherals to
        improve, 319–20
        following data to improve, 318–19
Input/Output (I/O) bus technology and
    selection, 315–20
Input/Output (I/O) memory lock tuning,
    385
Input/Output (I/O) operations per second,
    303–7
Intel Itanium (IA-64 Merced) processors, 98,
    181
intelligent I/O technology, network
    subsystem and, 415
Intel Pentium III, 98
Intel Pentium III XEON, 98
interleaving, 239
InternalDiskTest2.bat, 68
internal system resource usage and
    performance executive summary, 15
Internet Protocol Security (IPSec), 219
Internetwork device performance problems,
    429–30
interrupt-driven CPU bottlenecks, 203–5
Interrupt Handler, 41
IntFiltr, 229–30, 443–44
IP Security Encryption Protocol (IPSEC),
    412

J

job object, 186
just bunch of disks (JBOD), 328

K

kernel paging activities, 283
key performance metrics, in detecting system
    bottlenecks, 7–9
Kill.exe, 121–22

▼ L

last access updates, disabling, 24
Layer 2 Tunneling Protocol (L2TP), 218–19
link aggregation, 37, 407
Logical Disk Average Disk Queues, 22
Logical Disk Manager, 24
Logical Disk object counter activation, 5, 100
log mode
    starting, 4
    Sysmon counter, 109–10

▼ M

Max cached document size, 578
maximizing data throughput
    for file sharing, 258–59, 260
    for network applications, 17–18, 259
Maximum Transmission Unit (MTU) Window
    Size Tuning, 435
Mean Time Between Failures (MTBF), 322–23
memory
    configuration of, 267–68
    CPU and sizing relationships, 210–14
    identifying and removing leaks in, 286
    implementing server, 51–52
    pool problems in, 273–75
    proper sizing in, 168–69
    removing potential road blocks, 281–83
    sizing requirements, 50–51
    sizing subsystem, 262–64
    standard physical, 240
    virtual, 241–43
        optimizing, 18–19, 278
        pagefile size in limiting, 244
memory bottlenecks
    detecting, 9, 10–11, 269–70
    diagnosing, 271–75
    hands-on tactics for tuning around, 276–81
    tuning strategies for removing, 275–76

memory counter relationships, 271, 273
memory-intensive jobs, scheduling during
    off-peak hours, 19, 286–87
memory management strategies
    comparing, 259–62
    controlling, 276–78
memory performance, 233–88
    hardware, 234–35
        DIMM server memory, 235–36
        DRAM future, 236
        fast page mode RAM, 236–38
        RAM, 238, 239
        SIMM server memory, 235–36
memory resources
    removing unnecessary personal
        attributes that use, 20
    tuning, 16–20
    Windows 2000 use of, 239–46
memory strategies, 256–58
    maximizing data throughput for file
        sharing, 258–59
memory subsystem resource tuning, 465, 487,
    514, 541–42, 582–83
Microsoft IIS 5.0. *See also* World Wide Web
    server implemented with Microsoft IIS 5.0
        optimizing, for web publishing, 575–78
        tuning, for Common Gateway Interface
        (CGI) operations, 572–73
Microsoft InterruptAffinity Filter Control Tool
    (IntFiltr), 228–29
        configuring, 229–30, 443–44
MmAvailablePages, 270
MmMinimumFreePages, 270
monolithic SCSI drivers, 349, 379
MTBFs. *See* Mean Time Between Failures
    (MTBF)
multicast operations, 412
multiple logical partitions, for very large RAID
    arrays, 23
multiple Network Interface Cards (NICs),
    414
multiple pagefiles, configuring, 281

▼ N

NCR Teradata, 137
Nelson, Neal, and Associates, 148
    Business Benchmark (NNBBM)
        Simulated Database Test, 259
Nelson Business Benchmark Suite, 249
NetBench, 158–60
NetIQ, 96
network
    controlling timeout periods of users, 34
    interface object counter activation, 4–5,
        99
    load balancing in, 580–81
    lowering overhead associated with
        operations in, and improving
        efficiency, 32–33
    maximizing data throughput for
        applications, 17–18, 259
    sizing I/O subsystems in, 48
    Windows 2000 server placement in, 405–
        8
network architecture, 405
network bottlenecks
    detecting, 11, 12–13, 422–29
    tracking with Sysmon objects and
        counters, 426–27
networking-related counters, adding to
    Sysmon, 427, 429
Network Interface Cards (NICs), 213, 219,
    313, 397
    avoiding automatic settings, 35
    changes, 35–36
    multiple, 414
    server selections, 49–50
    tuning, 34–36, 436–38
        usage for improved web server
            response time, 564
network load balancing, 580–81
network performance, 394–445, 409–11
    CPU and, 413–14
    data flow in, 395–97
    detecting Windows 2000 bottlenecks in,
        11, 12–13, 422–29

    effect of applications on, 403
network segmentation, 37, 441–42
network segment object counter activation, 5,
    99–100
network selection, 48–49
network subsystem
    controlling access to resources, 22
    intelligent I/O technology and, 415
    key facets of sizing in, 417
    optimizing, for web-based workloads,
        562–64
    resource tuning, 466, 515–16, 542–43,
        584–85
    sizing, 415–22
        methodology in, 417–20
    tuning strategies for removing
        bottlenecks in, 431–44
network subsystem bottlenecks, tuning
    strategies for removing, 431–44
network technologies, relative throughputs of
    different, 397–98
network throughput, realistic, under
    Windows 2000, 398–402
network trunking, 36–37, 441
next-generation PCI I/O bus, 320
next-generation system bus, 321
NTFilemon, 273
NT file system (NTFS)
    defragmenting, 24–25, 276–77
    disabling short name generation on
        partitions, 24
    selecting appropriate log file size, 23
NTFS. *See* NT file system (NTFS)
Ntimer.exe, 123
number clients, per shared network segment,
    49

▼ O

off-load CPU-intensive operations
    Redundant Array of Inexpensive Disks
        (RAID) calculations, 218

security (IPSEC) calculations, 218–19
    TCP CHECKSUM off-loading to NIC, 218
100BaseTX fast Ethernet performance, 400–401
optimizing Microsoft IIS for web publishing, 575–78
    full-text search index size, 578
    imaging file cache, 577–78
    including file cache, 577
    in-memory document cache, 576–77
    max cached document size, 578
Optmod.pl, 68
Oracle, 137

P

pagefiles, 243–44
    configuring
        for maximum performance, 278–80
        multiple, 281
    implementing multiple, 18
    optimizing, 281–82
    sizing, 269, 280–81
    tuning, 278
Patterson, David, 175
PCI-X, 320
Pentium III Central Processing Units (CPUs), 176–86
    comparing performance, 181–83
    level 2 cache sizes, 179–81
    planning around bottlenecks, 179
    selection of, 183
    upgrading, 183–86
Pentium III XEON-based SHV design, 175
Pentium III XEON Central Processing Units (CPUs), 176–86
    changes in technology, 181
    comparing performance, 181–83
    level 2 cache sizes, 179–81
    planning around bottlenecks, 179
    selection of, 183
    upgrading, 183–86

performance baselines, 65
    advanced customer perspective pulse tests: web services, 81–82
    commercial tools for, through stress testing, 67
    customer perspective, through pulse testing, 71–74
    enhancing customer perspective file services pulse testing, 76–81
    freely available tools through stress testing, 67–68
    internal and customer perspective, 66–67
    internal server perspective through pulse testing, 69–71
    performance scripting tools, 68
    pre- and postproduction measurements, 65–66
    scheduling customer perspective scripts with Windows 2000, 74–76
    scripting tools, 68
    steps to implement perspective web service pulse test, 82–83
performance capacity, 418–19
performance counters, collection of, 4–5
performance engineering, 58
performance management
    freeware tools for, 123–25
    statistics gathering and logging, 96
    third-party tools, 96–100
    Windows 2000 Resource Kit, 122–23
performance monitor
    activating essential counters, 99–100
    versus Task Manager, 97
    understanding effects of, 98–99
performance monitor console, 97–98
performance-related tools, from Windows 2000, 120–22
performance scripting tools, 68
performance statistics, 3–4
Peripheral Component Interface (PCI)-based Ultra2 SCSI Disk Adapter, 29
Peripheral Component Interface (PCI) bridge, 316–17

Peripheral Component Interface (PCI) bus
approach, peer, 317–18
Peripheral Component Interface (PCI) bus
usage, 25
Peripheral Component Interface (PCI) I/O
bus architecture, 316–18
Permanently Cache Media Access Control
(MAC) Addresses, 435–36
personal attributes, removing unnecessary,
that use memory resources, 20
Physical Address Extension (PAE X86), 178,
245–46
physical disk drives
allocation of one logical drive per, 23
grouping similar, 28
physical disk view versus Windows 2000
view, 299–300
plug-and-play PCI, 313
Poll.pl, 68
Pool Paged Resident Bytes, 254
privileged mode and user mode processor
usage, 198–201
Ptree.exe, 123
pulse testing
customer perspective baseline
development through, 71–74
enhancing customer perspective file
services, 76–81
internal server perspective baseline
development through, 69–71
web service, 81–83

▾ Q

Quality of service (QoS/RSVP) services, 411–
12

▾ R

RAID. *See* Redundant Array of Inexpensive
Disks (RAID)

RAIS. *See* Redundant Array of Inexpensive
Servers (RAIS)
Rambus DRAM (RDRAM), 237
Random Access Memory (RAM)
configuring enough, when sizing CPUs,
209
effect of adding for file system cache,
252–53
interleaving, 239
need for additional, 20
performance, 238
performance and, 234–35
purchasing additional, 287–88
Random Access Memory (RAM) disks
analyzing performance, 389–90
technology, 387–88
using, 390–91
random disk read operations throughput, and
response time analysis, 335
random read/write environments, 301
read-intensive disk I/O environment, file
system cache in, 248
Redundant Array of Inexpensive Disks
(RAID), 5, 29–32, 321–23
background services, 27, 380
calculating disk workload, 364–65
combining stripes and mirroring, 326–28
determining disk queue length for, 364
disk mirroring, 323–24
disk striping with parity, 324–44
hardware-based, 328–30
implementing, with Windows 2000, 328–
29
multiple logical partitions for very large
arrays, 23
O-disk striping, 321–23
optimizing stripes, 338–41
performance under Windows 2000, 330–
32
scaling, 341–44
selection and data placement, 384
setting stripe sizes, 381
tuning, 27–28, 380–85

Redundant Array of Inexpensive Servers
(RAIS), 146, 209
registry size limit, maximum, 283
Regmon.exe, 124
resource partitioning and server
consolidation, 211–13
resource usage, using auditing to zero in on,
116
response time, 139
analysis of
random disk read operations
throughput and, 335
sequential disk read operations
throughput and, 333–35
rotational latency, 293, 294, 296

▾ S

SC.exe, 123
SCSI bus
determining number of disk drives per,
46
determining throughput, under Windows
2000, 309–10
implementation, 46
SCSI bus technology, 307–9
implementing, 308–9
practical perspective of, 307–8
SCSI channels, grouping similar devices on
same, 25–26, 378
SCSI command queuing, 26–27, 378–79
SCSI drivers, monolithic, 379
sector, 294
security auditing, 40–41, 219
seek time, 293, 294, 296
sequential disk read operations throughput,
and response time analysis, 333–35
sequential read/write environments, 300–301
sequential write analysis and observations,
333
server architecture relationships, effect of, on
system configurations, 166–68

server CPUs, in driving applications, 170–71
server hardware tuning, 463–64
server I/O relationships, 169–70
server memory, implementing, 51–52
Server Memory Assessment Engine, 50
server network interface card selections, 49–
50
server services, delivery of, to clients,
55–57
services management, 284
shared network segment, number clients per,
49
shared resource, 349, 416
short name generation, disabling, on NTFS
partition, 24
Simple Network Management Protocol
(SNMP), 4–5
agent control, 439–40
single-application sequential disk behavior
dedication, 27–28, 381–82
Single Inline Memory Modules (SIMM), 235
sizing and tuning mid-range Windows 2000
SQL server, 521–43
sizing initial SQL server configuration,
521–33
SQL server CPU tuning, 534–38
SQL server disk subsystem tuning
SQL server application tuning, 540
SQL server hardware tuning, 540
third-party tools for tuning Windows
2000 SQL servers, 543
Windows 2000 CPU subsystem
resource tuning, 540–41
Windows 2000 disk subsystem
resource tuning, 542
Windows 2000 memory subsystem
resource tuning, 541–42
Windows 2000 network subsystem
resource tuning, 542–43
SQL server sizing configuration chart, 533
SQL server-specific application tuning,
533–34
SPECweb99 (formerly SPECweb96), 155–58
split seek, 323

SQL servers, 137
    application tuning, 533–34, 540
    CPU tuning, 534–36
    disk subsystem tuning, 538–40
    hardware tuning, 540
    memory tuning, 536–38
        subsystem resource, 541–42
    third-party tools for tuning Windows
        2000, 543
Standard High Volume (SHV) system
    motherboards, 175–76
    design of, 235
Standard Performance Evaluation
    Corporation (SPEC), 148
standard physical memory, 240
stress testing
    commercial tools for baseline
        development through, 67
    environment and results, 388
    freely available tools for baseline
        development through, 67–68
    validation of server configuration and,
        144–46, 461, 484, 504–8, 531
stripe size optimization shortcut, 341
switched and full-duplex fast Ethernet, 401
symmetric multiprocessing, 187
synchronous DRAM (SDRAM), 236–37
Synclink DRAM (SLDRAM), 237–38
Sysmon, 97–98, 100
    alerts, 112–16
    chart mode, 100–101
    collecting data with, 4, 110–12
    counters, 254
        adding networking-related, 427, 429
        backup server bottleneck detection
            and sizing, 474–75
        exchange server health, bottleneck
            detection, tuning, and sizing, 491–
            93, 518–20
        keying, to monitor, 101–9
        log mode, 109–10
        Microsoft IIS 5.0 server health,
            bottleneck detection, tuning, and
            sizing, 547–49

        tracking down network bottlenecks
            with, 426–27
    CPU resource usage analysis with, 205
    in investigating disk array scaling, 344
    Logging Scheduler, 110–11
    objects
        backup server bottleneck detection
            and sizing, 474–75
        exchange server health, bottleneck
            detection, tuning, and sizing, 491–
            93, 519–20
        Microsoft IIS 5.0 server health,
            bottleneck detection, tuning, and
            sizing, 547–49
        tracking down network bottlenecks
            with, 426–27
    starting, 3–4
system Basic Input/Output System (BIOS),
    updating, 287
system bus, 320–21
System Code Resident Bytes, 254
system configurations, effect of server
    architecture relationships on, 166–68
System Driver Resident Bytes, 254
system interrupt setting strategy, 313

T

Task Manager, 117–20, 189
    versus performance monitor, 97
10BaseT Ethernet performance, 400
third-party tools
    for tuning Windows 2000 file servers,
        466–67, 516
    for tuning Windows 2000 SQL servers,
        543
    for tuning Windows 2000 web servers,
        585
thrashing, 38, 215, 254–56
throughput, 139
Tlist.exe, 121
track, 294

tradeoffs, law of, 58

Transaction Processing Council (TPC), 148

transfer rate, 294

Transmission Control Blocks (TCBs), tuning, 434

Transport Control Protocol (TCP), window size tuning, 435

Transport Control Protocol (TCP) hash table, tuning, 434–35

tuning, 54–130, 63–65

  achieving nirvanic state, 60–62

  affinity methodology in, 227–29

  architecture, 55–58

  customizing the CPWMM scripts, 83–96

  disk subsystem SCSI channel and HBA, 377–80

  flexibility in, when utilizing hardware-based Redundant Array of Inexpensive Disks (RAID) solutions, 329–30

  focusing efforts, 62–63

  hands-on tactics for memory bottlenecks, 276–81

  in helping Windows 2000 to control applications, 226–27

  in helping Windows 2000 to control process priorities, 225–26

  methodology, 59–60, 461, 462, 484, 532–33

    conceptual walkthrough of core, 64–65

  performance baselines, 65

    advanced customer perspective pulse tests: web services, 81–82

    commercial tools for, through stress testing, 67

    customer perspective through pulse testing, 71–74

    enhancing customer perspective file services pulse testing, 76–81

    freely available tools through stress testing, 67–68

    internal and customer perspective, 66–67

    internal server perspective through pulse testing, 69–71

    performance scripting tools, 68

    pre- and postproduction measurements, 65–66

    scheduling customer perspective scripts with Windows 2000, 74–76

    steps to implement perspective web service pulse test, 82–83

performance management

  freeware tools, 123–25

  resource kit tools, 122–23

  statistics gathering and logging, 96

  third-party tools, 96–100

performance-related tools, 120–22

practical guidelines, 58–59

Redundant Array of Inexpensive Disks (RAID) controller cache, 27, 380–81

removing CPU bottlenecks, 214–25

removing disk subsystem bottlenecks, 367–68

removing memory bottlenecks, 275–76

removing network subsystem bottlenecks, 431–44

setting goals for, 54–55

Sysmon operations, 100

  alerts, 112–16

  chart mode, 100–101

  collecting data, 110–12

  counter log mode, 109–10

  keying counters to monitor, 101–9

tips in implementing, 15–16

using auditing to zero in on resource usage, 116

Windows 2000 interrupt control manager in, 443–44

Windows 2000 system checkup, 125–27

Windows Task Manager, 117–20

▼ U

Ultra2 SCSI Disk Drive, 29

upgrading to faster CPUs, 220

V

very large Redundant Array of Inexpensive
Disks (RAID) arrays, multiple logical
partitions for, 23
virtual memory, 241–43
optimizing, 18–19, 278
pagefile size in limiting, 244
Virtual Private Network (VPN) technology,
218–19

W

walkthrough, conceptual, of core tuning
methodology, 64–65
web applications, tuning, to use available
CPU resources, 569–72
web-based workloads, optimizing Windows
2000 network subsystem for, 562–64
web publishing, optimizing Microsoft IIS for,
575–78
web server software engine, tuning, to use all
available server resources, 566–69
Windows 2000
administration-level tuning, 33–34
advanced tuning to help control process
priorities, 226–27
applications running under, 5–6
backup servers for, 467–89
application description, 467
application performance
characterization, 467–72
backup server sizing configuration
chart, 484–85
backup server-specific application
tuning, 485–89
real-world backup performance,
472–74
sizing initial backup server
configuration, 474–84
Sysmon objects and counters, 474–75
checkup, 125–26

event viewers, 126
information, 127
comparing memory management
strategies, 259–62
controlling CPU quantum allotment, 38–
41
controlling kernel paging activities, 19–
20
CPU resource usage and, 186–94
affinity, 191
determining which process is
associated with which application,
188–89
processes, threads, new jobs, and
context switching, 186
scheduler and priority levels, 190–91
and single unit environment, 186–87
symmetric multiprocessing, 187
viewing processes and threads
running under, 188
detecting bottlenecks, 6–7, 9–15, 269–70,
422–29
determining SCSI bus throughput under,
309–10
device drivers, 347–49
diagnosing memory bottleneck, 271–75
distributing network load, 36–37
exchange servers, 489–516
application description, 489
application performance
characterization, 489–91
mid-range, 493–510
sizing initial exchange server
configuration, 493–510
sizing configuration chart, 510
specific application tuning, 511–16
Sysmon objects and counters, 491–49
file server, sizing and tuning, 452–62
file server consolidation, 450–67
application description, 450
application performance
characterization, 450
file server-specific application
tuning, 463–67

sizing initial file server configuration, 452–63

Sysmon objects and counters, 451–52

file system cache, 21, 246

application level control of cache manager operations, 247–48

effect of adding more RAM for, 252–53

implementation of, 246–47

investigating behavior, 249–52

memory strategies, 256–58

in read-intensive disk I/O environment, 248

sizing of, 248–49

Sysmon counters, 254

thrashing, 254–56

file-system-level tuning, 23–25

GBE performance and, 402–3

hands-on tactics for tuning around memory bottlenecks, 276–81

helpful tools to use when tracking down memory details, 270–71

implementations based on, 52

implementing RAID with, 328–29

kernel, 98

key performance metrics to observe in detecting system bottlenecks, 7–9

maximizing data throughput

for file sharing, 258–59

for network applications, 259

memory management, 240–41

memory resources use by, 239–46

networking performance, 409–11

pagefile, 243–44

size of, and virtual memory, 244

performance tools, 97–100, 120–22

RAID performance under, 330–32

RAM disk, 387–91

realistic network throughput under, 398–402

removing unnecessary services, 33

resource kit performance management tools, 122–23

CreateFil.exe, 123

Ntimer.exe, 123

Ptree.exe, 123

SC.exe, 123

WPerf.exe, 123

scheduler and priority levels, 190–91

scheduling customer perspective scripts with, 74–76

server placement in network, 405–8

service packs, 41–42, 223–24

setting goals for tuning systems based on, 54–55

single CPU environment and, 186–87

sizing disk I/O subsystem, 349–61

sizing memory subsystem, 262–64

benchmark extrapolations and server guidelines, 268

configuration considerations, 267–68

determining starting point, 267

historical performance information in, 264

sizing pagefile, 269

step by step, 264, 266–67

sizing network subsystem, 415–22

sizing rules of thumb for, 42–43

SQL server

sizing and tuning mid-range, 521–43

sizing configuration chart, 533

tuning, 533–43

system checkup, 125–26

system observations, general, 6–7

TCP/IP performance enhancements, 412–13

TCP/IP services and performance, 41–412

tools in tracking down memory details, 193–94

tools to investigate subsystem usage, 7–9

transfer rate, 295

tuning network subsystem of, 32

tuning resources, 16–32

tuning strategies for removing memory bottlenecks, 275–76

Windows 2000 (continued)
  understanding environment equals
    performance, 262
  updating, 287
  use of disk subsystem by, 345–47
  viewing processes and threads running
    under, 188
  virtual memory, 241–43
  web server
    Microsoft IIS 5.0 tuning, 561–74, 581–
      85
    sizing and configuration chart, 560
    sizing and tuning mid-range, 241–43,
      549–60
Windows file-system-level tuning, 373–75
Windows Network Load Balancing (WNLB),
  208
workload, removing unnecessary, 284–87
World Wide Web server implemented with
  Microsoft IIS 5.0, 544–86
  application description, 544
  application performance
    characterization, 544–46
  Microsoft IIS 5.0 web server sizing and
    configuration chart, 560–61
  sizing mid-range web server
    configuration, 549–60
  Sysmon objects and counters, 547–51
  unleashing power of, 546–47

Windows 2000 Microsoft IIS 5.0 web
  server tuning, 561–74, 581–85
  ASP caching, 573–74
  optimizing Windows 2000 network
    subsystem for web-based
    workloads, 562–67
  tuning IIS 5 for common gateway
    interface (CGI) operations, 572–73
  tuning web application to use
    available CPU resources, 569–72
  tuning web server software engine to
    use all available server resources,
    566–69
WPerf.exe, 123
write-through caching, 380

▼ X

Xtune, 579

▼ Z

Ziff-Davis, 148
  benchmark operation, 158–59
  server bench performance, 180

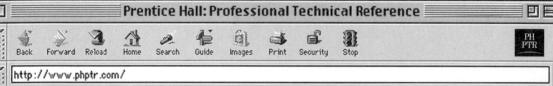